DR CAROLYNE LARRINGTON lives and works in Oxford where she is Supernumerary Fellow in Medieval English at St John's College. She has written several articles on Old Norse mythological poetry, and is the author of *A Store of Common Sense* (OUP), a study of Old English and Norse wisdom literature.

'A most useful contribution to the field.' BARBARA C. SPROUL, author of *Primal Myths: Creating the World*

'This book marks a significant contribution to Myth Studies in two ways: It reflects the materials with a consciousness of gender and with an acute awareness of multiple cultures. Refreshingly devoid of jargon, this scholarly work is written simply, in language as accessible to the beginning student as to the expert without condescending to either ... This presentation of mythological materials emphasizing the importance of women, goddesses, and female principles is bound to attract the interest of many readers put off by older, male-centred approaches to our collective heritage of human wisdom.' KATHRYN ALLEN RABUZZI, author of *The Sacred and the Feminine* and *Motherself: A Mythic Analysis of Motherhood*

'In this important volume, a group of highly qualified women scholars succeed in reclaiming, firmly but gently, Joseph Campbell's third function of mythology: "To validate, support and imprint the norms of a given specific moral order" (in this case the dominant canons of the patriarchal approach). Thus they render a service not only to feminist scholars, but poets, novelists, filmmakers and artists who draw creative nourishment from the inexhaustible (and now increasingly clarified) wellsprings of mythology.' STEPHEN and ROBIN LARSEN, authors of *A Fire in the Mind*, the authorized biography of Joseph Campbell.

THE FEMINIST COMPANION TO
MYTHOLOGY

Edited by

CAROLYNE LARRINGTON

Pandora

An Imprint of HarperCollins*Publishers*

Pandora Press
An Imprint of HarperCollins*Publishers*
77–85 Fulham Palace Road
Hammersmith, London W6 8JB

Published by Pandora Press 1992
1 3 5 7 9 10 8 6 4 2

A CIP record for this book
is available from the British Library

ISBN 0 04 440850 1

Typeset by Harper Phototypesetters Limited
Northampton, England
Printed in Great Britain by
Mackays of Chatham, Kent

CONTENTS

ACKNOWLEDGEMENTS

As Editor, I would like to register my gratitude firstly to the contributors to the *Companion*, for kindly agreeing to write for the book, and then for producing their contributions with remarkable promptness. I would also like to thank those who were involved with the project at various stages, but who sadly were unable to contribute a section themselves: Mary Lefkowitz, Marj Evasco and Julia Leslie, and to register the continuing support and interest of Shirley Ardener, Julia Leslie and members of the Centre for Cross-Cultural Research on Women at Queen Elizabeth House, Oxford.

For my own contribution, I would wish to thank Robin Lane Fox and Ian Kershaw for suggesting references and reading, Ursula Dronke for her guidance in Old Icelandic matters over the years, and Matthew Driscoll, Ragnheiður Mósesdóttir, Guðrún Nordal and Peter Robinson for discussion and intelligent criticism. John Davis is to be thanked for general encouragement and for taking photographs, and I am also grateful to Alice Sheppard for offering herself as a 'naïve reader' of the final version.

Thanks are due also to all those who suggested contributors for the *Companion*, too numerous to list, to the Sisters of the Cherwell Centre where a one-day workshop on the book was held in the summer of 1990, to Judith Pallot for continued liaison between Oxford and Moscow, to Catriona Kelly for kindly translating Julia Vytkovskaya's contribution, and to all at Pandora Press, especially to Debbie Licorish, and, above all, to Philippa Brewster whose good humour, expertise and flexibility has been invaluable. Ginny Iliff has been a skilled, patient and friendly editor, who has done so much to keep the book on course. Finally, warm and grateful thanks to Louise Hudd and Sian Williams for their heroic endeavours in the indexing of this book.

CAROLYNE LARRINGTON

Introduction

ABOUT THIS BOOK

When, in his 1955 'Statement' of his views on poetry,[1] Philip Larkin asserted his refusal to use the 'common myth-kitty' in creating his poems, he was probably reacting against those poets who laced their work with Classical allusion (a literary practice rooted in class-bound Victorian ideals of High Culture) or, following Robert Graves,[2] retreated from contemporary reality into imagined or ancient worlds – two opposing conceptions of myth as High Culture[3] or childish escapism which remain influential today. Larkin himself may have refused to broach the 'myth-kitty', but his image is none the less telling, evoking mythology as a fruitful, communal resource: a fund of stories, images and characters into which poets and myth-makers have dipped.

Myth furnishes us with more than a repertoire of literary plots and themes however. Mythology, the study of myth, introduces us to new ways of looking at social structures, so that we can examine constants and variables in the organization of human society, in particular – the express aim of this book – women's roles across different cultures and historical periods. For westerners, our interpretation of our mythological heritage conditions the way in which we think about ourselves. Myth has been appropriated by politicians, psychiatrists and artists, among others, to tell us what we are and where we have come from. Thus Germanic mythology is hijacked by Nazi ideologues, as I show in the Scandinavian section below; Greek myth becomes the pattern upon which Freudian psychiatrists base their interpretation of human behaviour; painters, composers, sculptors and writers, deliberately or unconsciously, imitate the mythical patterns of the past.

Within the study of mythology, female figures have too often been viewed reductively, purely in terms of their sexual function and thus confined in a catch-all category labelled fertility. In her account of Sumerian myth, Iris Furlong exemplifies how previous scholarship has misrepresented female figures in the *Epic of Gilgamesh* precisely through anachronistic sexual stereotyping. Women need to know the myths which have determined both how we see ourselves and how society regards us.

Feminist anthropologists and literary historians in recent years have discovered new evidence about how women have been perceived; they have illuminated mythical patterns and re-examined historical traditions from a feminist perspective, in discussion mainly limited to academic journals and books, and often in languages other than English. This book is a wholly new collection of essays, by experts writing from first-hand knowledge of the languages and texts with which they deal, designed to bring the new insights to the non-specialist reader and the scholar of adjacent disciplines.

The mythologies explored range widely across space and time; some cultures have long been extinct, while other myths are products of traditional societies still surviving today. Only a limited number of mythologies could be included in the space available. One regrettable absence is any myths from Africa; likewise, from the rich variety of American myth, only three mythologies could be treated. It is the hope of the editor and contributors that this volume may be only the first in a series of books analysing women's myths on a regional basis; plans are already in train for an East Asian collection centred on the Philippines.

Different types of myth need to be elucidated by appropriate strategies, for a unitary approach will flatten those differences which the student of myth aims to highlight. Unlike Mr Casaubon in George Eliot's *Middlemarch*, the *Companion* is not striving for the grand Victorian overview, 'the Key to all Mythologies'; rather, structuralist and non-structuralist, historical, narratological and anthropological approaches are variously employed where they prove valuable. At one stage, I evolved a model on which to structure each contribution, but the very fact that my classificatory system was – inescapably – generated by my own understanding of Scandinavian myth, meant that this attempt to impose a rigid order on non Indo-European myth from outside was doomed to failure. Thus each contributor has been given leeway to develop her section as seems most appropriate to her topic and interests: Veronica Seton-Williams explores the freedom and autonomy given to queens ruling in ancient Egypt, testing whether the sexual equality depicted in the myths has a historical reflex; Elizabeth Diab investigates in detail the Hawaiian myth of Pele, a goddess considered of marginal importance in traditional analyses, but central to the lives of those islanders who live near her volcano; Barbara Smith relates the Greek myths most familiar to western readers to women's ritual practice, showing one way in which the meanings of myth for women, in the culture which originated them, may be recovered.

Although the thematic organization of the index will assist the reader in tracing parallels in mythologies widely separated in space and time, the intention in this book has been to demonstrate difference, variety and uniqueness among the women who appear in its narratives. In this, the *Companion* stands in contra-distinction to much recent work on the 'Goddess' which frequently blurs important differences, generalizing, often inaccurately, about the goddesses of different cultures, in order to assimilate them to a single supreme figure, often Eurocentrically conceived. In her section, Juliette Wood shows how peculiarly prone Celtic goddesses have been to this kind of misrepresentation, while Emily Kearns clarifies the problematic issue of Goddess versus goddesses in Hindu myth.

Nor can we ignore the historical circumstances which gave rise to myths, and the plurality of meanings which myths have had at successive stages of their existence. In the last section of this book, Rosemary Ellen Guiley traces the history of *Wicca*, a Goddess religion which has grown up since the Second World War, showing how it employs mythological figures and narratives; Jane Caputi relates how US feminists have taken over revitalizing mythological symbols from both European cultures and Native American and African sources in their struggle to resist the male, technocratic system; and, bringing us full circle to Larkin's 'myth-kitty', Diane Purkiss elucidates the raids which twentieth-century women poets have made on the mythic domain, showing the difficulties involved in trying to bring the meanings of mythological figures under the poet's control.

ABOUT MYTHOLOGY

The *Companion*'s working definition of a mythology is that it comprises a collection of stories belonging to a single cultural group — often though not always synonymous with a language group — which frequently feature both anthropomorphic or theriomorphic divine figures, such as the Native American Spider Woman (see Marta Weigle's contribution, p. 346), heroes or animals. Often there is a sense that the narrative has a subtextual meaning — perspicuous to, if not explicitly expressed by, the culture which formed it. There is a tendency to think of this meaning as 'the real meaning' of the myth; however, most of the myths outlined in this book are at the centre of a web of meanings, drawn out of the body of the myth by different interpreters for different purposes. So Birgitte Sonne gives an account of how Eskimos reinterpreted the important myth of Sea Woman for political purposes during their struggle with Denmark for Home Rule; Margaret Orbell writes of Māori women making their own interpretations of their heritage, previously the domain of European scholars; while Penny Harvey, demonstrating the Inka reshaping of indigenous origin myths for imperial purposes, warns that our own understanding of gender relations is so deeply inscribed in western discourses of gender and patriarchy, that we are likely to face problems when we approach myths of non-western peoples, unless we make allowance for the different conditions under which narratives are produced, and the many ways in which they can be understood.

Historically, westerners have tended to envisage mythology as pre-eminently Greek mythology, assessing the 'mythologicalness' of a myth system by its likeness to the Greek complex. But the way in which we westerners employ Greek mythology at a conscious level, as a 'myth-kitty' to be utilized or ignored at will, may be wholly unlike the relationships which other mythologies bear to their originating cultures. Isobel White and Helen Payne's discussions of Australian Aboriginal mythology amply demonstrate the complexity of the attitudes towards mythic story and its necessary relationship to the whole perceived world, characteristic of Australian myth-systems.

Many of the contributions address legend and folk-tale, in addition to 'myth proper'. The distinction between myth and folk-tale can never be hard and fast, for while many myths incorporate folk-tale motifs, so many stories are simple narratives which happen to have a god as a protagonist. For the purpose of the *Companion*, folk-tales are to be regarded part of a broad continuum between myth proper, heroic legend and the fairy-tale. J.S. Kirk's distinction is a useful one:

> Myths often have some serious underlying purpose beyond that of telling a story. Folktales, on the other hand, tend to reflect simple social situations; they play on ordinary fears and desires as well as on men's appreciations of neat and ingenious solutions; and they introduce fantastic subjects more to widen the range of adventure and acumen than through any imaginative or introspective urge.[4]
>
> (KIRK, 1970, 41)

Given the impossibility of formulating a unitary theory of myth embracing all cultures and all manifestations of story-telling, flexibility of definition is vital. Hence Tao Tao Liu includes legends about human women in her account of Chinese myth, while Julia Vytkovskaya's investigation uses folk-ritual to demonstrate the persistence of Slav mythological ideas long after the establishment of Christianity.

Questions of transmission must also be addressed, for myths about women are not necessarily women's myths. Susanna Rostas shows, for example, how in the myth of Xochiquetzal, symbolic of the Aztec connection between flowers and the feminine, Christian thinking about women and sin has contaminated the myth with notions about virginity, impurity and punishment. Historically women have been disbarred from the means to fix their myths in literary form, to give them a distinctively female perspective, although some oral cultures have story-telling castes in which women are prominent and their roles positively valued. While authoritative and monolithic readings of women in many Indo-European texts have been established by generations of male scribes and interpreters, the *Companion* argues that meanings and emphases can change, and can be reclaimed and reinterpreted over time; moreover, the 'original' meaning of a myth is simply one among many. Among living religions, Emily Kearns contrasts the waning popularity of the Hindu goddess Radha during this century, with the emergence since Independence of a new goddess, *Santoshi Mata* (Mother Contentment), while Athalya Brenner demonstrates that even the monolithic masculine figure of the Old Testament *Yhwh* has female consorts, long suppressed by tradition.

The *Companion* is able to bring to light only a small proportion of the resources of the 'myth-kitty', myths neglected, overlooked or subjected to inflexible and misogynist interpretation. Yet the work of rediscovery, rehabilitation and reinterpretation of myth is going on in the readings and writings of women all over the world, as Marj Evasco writes in her poem 'Caravan of the Waterbearers':

> When we seize the watersource
> our ranks will complete the circle
> we used to mark around our tents,
> making homes, villages, temples,

schools, our healing places.
And we will bear witness
for our daughters and sons,
telling them true stories
of the caravan.[5]

Notes

1 P. Larkin, *Poets of the 1950s*, D.J. Enright (ed.) (published in Japan in 1956), reprinted in (1983), *Required Writing: Miscellaneous Pieces 1955–82* (London: Faber) p. 79.

2 See Diane Purkiss' contribution to this volume, p. 441.

3 See Alicia Ostriker (1981, reprinted 1986), 'The Thieves of Language: Women Poets and Revisionist Mythmaking' in E. Showalter (ed.), *The New Feminist Criticism: Essays on Women, Literature and Theory* (London: Virago), pp. 314–38.

4 J.S. Kirk (1970), *Myth: Its Meaning and Function in Ancient and Other Cultures* (Cambridge: Cambridge University Press).

5 'Caravan of the Waterbearers' in Marjorie E. Pernia (1987), *Dreamweavers: Selected Poems 1976–1986* (Manila, Philippines: Editorial and Media Resources Corporation). Reproduced with the author's permission.

PART 1

The Near East

IRIS FURLONG

The Mythology of the Ancient Near East

INTRODUCTION

The mythology of ancient Mesopotamia has become known to the modern world only in comparatively recent times. This has followed discoveries of clay tablets at archaeological sites all over the Middle East, and the eventual decipherment of the cuneiform script inscribed upon them, which was accomplished by the middle of the last century. The hymns, songs and literary compositions preserved on these clay tablets have revealed a system of cosmological belief that was formulated in the pre-literate period by the peoples of Sumer and which survived, with adaptations and modifications, for well over two thousand years.

The ancient land of Sumer corresponded with the flat alluvial plain of the lower Tigris and Euphrates rivers, today within the territory of southern Iraq. It was there that some time towards the end of the fourth millennium BC, the population which had been more or less evenly distributed in small settlements and villages, successfully practising irrigation agriculture, began to coalesce into larger, more widely-separated units, leaving stretches of unoccupied steppe-land between. Whatever the forces may have been which triggered off this change in the human settlement pattern, the outcome was the first experiment in urban civilization, observable in the archaeological record by the presence of monumental temples incorporating extensive public and administrative premises.

With the emergence of cities came the invention of writing, using a stylus to incise signs on the surface of a prepared clay tablet which could then be fired to the consistency of brick or pottery. At first, writing seems to have been employed primarily for keeping records connected with the management of the temple estates and enterprises. Gradually, with the development of the cuneiform script, writing came to be employed for other purposes, including recording what we might today describe as the promulgation of law and the composition of literary works. What language the first city-dwellers spoke, we have no means of knowing, as the earliest documents are in a pictographic script which may be 'read' in any language. This gives no clue as to the grammar and phonetics of the language they were originally 'written' in. All that can be said is that the earliest written language which can be identified is Sumerian.

The ancient Sumerians acknowledged their common cultural tradition and referred to themselves collectively as 'the black-headed people'. However, each city was a separate entity, run as an independent city state, and rivalry between cities was such that it could lead to open warfare. In due course, the city states of Sumer became rich and prosperous from their trade and commercial enterprises. But, situated on the flat alluvial plain, they were always vulnerable to attack from outsiders: from the mountains in the east in present-day Iran, or down-river from the north and north-west, the area of modern Syria and Turkey. Ancient Mesopotamian history is a long succession of invasions, but the invaders who came to conquer stayed. Each took over the Sumerian cultural tradition in turn and adapted it to their own needs and purposes.

By the beginning of the second millennium BC, Sumerian had given way to Semitic Akkadian as the spoken language. It was, however, preserved as the language of the educated scribes working in the temple or the palace. That is why cuneiform texts, from which we derive our knowledge of the ancient mythology of the Near East, are written in both the Sumerian and Akkadian languages.

The Sumerians were polytheists and visualized a cosmos run and maintained on corporate lines by a large number of divine beings. Natural phenomena, such as the sky, fresh water, the sun, the moon and the planets, were each in the charge of a deity whose responsibility it was to see that they conformed with the laws decreed for them. Cultural traits and technology were also under divine supervision. There were deities in charge of implements like the pickaxe and the brick mould; processes such as beer-making; and professional skills such as writing and accounting – these last two being in the care of goddesses.

These divinities were visualized by the Sumerians as differing little from human beings, except in that they were immortal, and the divine world as being organized along much the same lines as a Sumerian city state. The divine population met in assembly to consider all matters of major importance. At this divine assembly, issues were debated and decisions arrived at by general agreement and all deities were bound by policy decisions taken in assembly. There was a recognizable hierarchy within the pantheon, the senior and most powerful deities acting as chief advocates and executants of the assembly, with one of their number acting as supreme head.

Senior members of the original Sumerian pantheon were all patron deities of individual cities, regarded in some way as being the city's owner. This being so, it follows that events which took place in the cities here on earth were most likely to have been reflected in the activities of the city-owning deities in the supernatural world. Major political changes consequent upon a military coup or an invasion of the land would result in a comparable shake-up in the power structure of the pantheon (*see The Creation Epic*, p. 5).

This connection between Sumero-Akkadian mythology as it has survived in literary form and contemporary politico-military history has been widely recognized and discussed. In the Sumero-Akkadian myths related here, however, particular attention has been given to the role played by goddesses in the stories.

At different periods of ancient Mesopotamian history different deities were regarded as head of the pantheon: Enlil and An both filled this role for the Sumerians; while Marduk, the Babylonian national god, and Ashur, chief god of the Assyrians, each in turn headed the pantheons in later times. A recently translated Sumerian text dating to the late third/early second millennium BC, describes how, on An's command, Inanna was given his crown and sceptre and seated upon the throne of majesty from which she rendered judgement in all the lands. This suggests that at this time, at one centre in Sumer at least, Inanna was regarded as the head of the pantheon, but corroborative evidence that this was indeed so has not yet come to light.

THE CREATION EPIC

This long epic poem, written in the Akkadian language, was recited or enacted as a drama on the fourth day of the cultic celebrations of the Babylonian New Year. It was recorded as a literary text on seven clay tablets, each with 140 to 170 lines, making a total of well over one thousand lines in all. Individual tablets or fragments of tablets containing parts of the poem have been recovered from a number of ancient sites in Babylonia and Assyria, and between them, the Epic can now be restored almost in its entirety.

All the copies of the Epic which have come to light so far were made in the first millennium BC. There is, however, little doubt that the poem was composed earlier, some time during the second millennium BC. The mythological content of the poem is much older still, since it refers to rivalries and conflicts between deities, many of whom have Sumerian names and were city-gods and members of the early Sumerian pantheon.

The main purpose of the original composition was to explain the elevation of Marduk, the national god of the Babylonians, to his position at the head of the pantheon and to present him as the creator of all things. Assyrian versions of the Epic differ from the original in one significant detail in that they substitute the name of the god Ashur, the national god of the Assyrians, for that of Marduk and give him a different but equally ancient and venerable ancestry. The outline of the story given here follows the Babylonian version in which Marduk features as the creator god.

Before heaven and earth came into existence, there was, according to the opening lines of the poem, nothing but water: fresh water personified by the god Apsu; salt, oceanic water personified by the goddess Tiamat. Commingling their waters together, these two primordial beings engendered all the gods, Apsu being described as their begetter, Tiamat as she who bore them. The exact number of divinities brought into being is not stated, but there were many of them and they seem to have been visualized as a population living inside Tiamat's belly.

In a brief introductory passage, six deities are mentioned by name. First to come forth were a divine pair named Lahmu and Lahamu, about whom little is known from other sources. (The Assyrian version of the Epic takes advantage of this fact to make this pair the parents of their national god, Ashur.) The first couple were followed by a second pair, Anshar and Kishar, about whom, again, not much is known, although their names include the Sumerian words for sky (*an*) and earth (*ki*). Then Anu is named as Anshar's first-born, and Ea as Anu's son. Both Anu and Ea are described as rivalling their fathers in strength and power. Marduk is not mentioned here but he is introduced later in the poem as Ea's son.

The first incident to occur in the primordial womb was that a band of young gods started, for no given reason, a rowdy disturbance. Their riotous behaviour annoyed Tiamat but upset Apsu much more. He complained that he could neither rest by day nor sleep by night because of the noise they were making. Finally, reaching the end of his patience, he went to Tiamat and declared that he was going to get rid of the lot of them. Tiamat was shocked and horrified, and strongly opposed any proposal to annihilate the trouble-makers, arguing in their defence that they were young and should be treated with tolerance. But Apsu's vizier (prime minister), Mummu, was not prepared to accept Tiamat's decision on the matter, and he urged Apsu to go ahead with his plan of destruction. This support appealed to Apsu greatly. He clapped Mummu on the shoulder and the two sat down to work out a plan of action.

When news reached the rebellious young gods that Apsu and Mummu were plotting to destroy them, they were very frightened and became quiet. Then Ea came forward with a plan to save them. He cast a spell over Apsu and Mummu which sent them both to sleep. When they were asleep and at his mercy, Ea took the crown from Apsu's head and placed it on his own, thereby effectively transferring the old god's authority to himself. He took Mummu prisoner and then killed Apsu. Over Apsu, Ea built himself a dwelling, declaring that this and all other cult shrines built for him in the future should be called Apsu. It is a historical fact that Ea's main cult centre at the ancient city of Eridu and cultic installations dedicated to him in other sacred precincts elsewhere were traditionally referred to as *Apsu*.

A period of tranquillity followed, during which Ea lived in the Apsu with his wife, Damkina, and Marduk, their son, was born. This interlude of calm was brought to an end by Anu. He conjured up four whirlwinds which he caused to blow through Tiamat's belly, making life for the gods who dwelt therein thoroughly uncomfortable. No motivation for Anu's onslaught against Tiamat is offered in the poem which merely states the fact with laconic brevity (Tab. I, ll.105–8). The effect of Anu's tempests on the divine population was, however, to rally support for Tiamat. A delegation of Tiamat supporters went to plead with the great goddess in person. She was their mother but, they argued, she couldn't love them any more since she had done nothing either to avenge Apsu's death, to rescue Mummu from captivity or to stop Anu's whirlwinds.

The petitioners' argument galvanized Tiamat into action and she declared war. This was greeted with great excitement and enthusiasm and many gods rallied to her side. She set up a council of war and created seven (or eleven?) venomous monsters, all of terrifying appearance, to augment her troops. From the ranks of senior gods, she elected Kingu as her commander-in-chief, ratifying the appointment by declaring before the assembly that she had chosen him as her consort and conferring on him full authority to act on her behalf.

The divine population was now quite clearly split into two opposing factions, Tiamat and her supporters on one side, and on the other the anti-Tiamat faction, presumably comprising, or at least including, the original band of young rebel gods, with Anshar, Anu and Ea as their leaders.

Ea was the first to hear that Tiamat was preparing for war and he told Anshar. Anshar was alarmed by the news and suggested to Ea that he should use his magic powers to overcome Kingu in the same way he had previously overcome Apsu. There is a break in the tablet here and the next few lines of the poem are missing, so Ea's response is unknown. However, he must have had some convincing reason why this couldn't be done because, when the text resumes, Anshar has decided to adopt a diplomatic approach.

Anu was sent off with instructions to talk to Tiamat and calm her down. This mission failed because Anu was too frightened to face her and he came back saying that the goddess had the power to slay any god with a single look. Morale amongst the rebel gods plummeted and they became convinced that they could not survive a battle with Tiamat and escape with their lives. Their only possible salvation, declared Anshar, lay with the young hero god, Marduk.

Ea sent for Marduk and told him to present himself before Anshar, offering some good fatherly advice as to how he should comport himself at the interview. In the event, when he saw him, Anshar was mightily impressed with the young Marduk and was ready to accept that it wasn't a male but a female enemy who had to be dealt with (Tab. II, ll.109–10). He, Marduk, would lay Tiamat low, so that Anshar could stand on her neck in triumph. Marduk then set out his terms. As a reward for his services to the gods, Marduk demanded that he should be elevated to a position of supreme authority over all of them.

Anshar could not agree to a deal of this kind without the consent of his supporters, so he sent his vizier, Gaga, to invite them all to a banquet. This was an outstanding success. Filled with good food and primed with a lot of intoxicating liquor, the gods, in high spirits, elected Marduk as their king and hailed him as their champion and avenger.

Marduk then assembled his weapons for the coming confrontation with Tiamat. These included a bow and arrow, a mace, seven whirlwinds and a net, a gift from Anu. Accompanied by a whole host of helpers, Marduk reconnoitred the inside of Tiamat. The confusion between the visualization of Tiamat as a deity in female human form and as the all-enveloping territory, both at the same time, is nowhere more evident than in this part of the Epic.

When the two protagonists came face to face, the confrontation between the old goddess and the young god was too dazzling for Marduk's supporters to see what was happening. The two started by hurling accusations at each other. Tiamat's taunt is obscurely worded, but she seems to have charged Marduk with getting above himself. Marduk, for his part, accused Tiamat with setting herself up too haughtily;

stirring up trouble so that sons turned against their fathers (i.e. causing civil war); no longer loving her own offspring; and raising Kingu to the same high rank as Anu. He then issued his challenge to single combat, which enraged Tiamat. A fearful struggle ensued, until Tiamat opened her mouth with the intention of devouring Marduk. This was a mistake as it gave Marduk the chance to employ the whirlwinds which he drove into Tiamat's belly until it became obscenely distended. He then fired an arrow into Tiamat which tore her insides, split her heart and killed her.

Marduk's mopping-up operations consisted of taking all the dead goddess's supporters prisoner, turning into stone statues the seven or eleven monsters she had created to augment her troops and stripping Kingu of all his powers, which, it was alleged, Tiamat had had no right to confer upon him in the first place.

After receiving acknowledgement of his victory from his fellow gods, Marduk considered Tiamat's body with the idea of creating the universe. He split Tiamat's carcass in two, like a bi-valved shellfish. The top half he set up to form the sky, setting barriers and guards to stop her waters escaping. He ordered the moon to number the days of the week and the months of the year by its phases, and put Shamash, the sun god, in charge of the daytime. He then created the earth, using parts of Tiamat's body to form the geographical features that would have been most familiar to the ancient Mesopotamians: streams flowing from her two eyes formed the Tigris and Euphrates rivers, the mountains were piled over her head and the foothills were formed from her 'udder'.

Marduk then proposed that the city of Babylon should be founded to serve as overnight accommodation for the gods, either on their way up from the Apsu or on their way down from heaven. The gods agreed to the plan and volunteered to work on building the city. But Marduk had a better idea. Why not make creatures of flesh and bone to do all the hard work, so that the gods could take it easy? This suggestion was further elaborated by Ea who said that these flesh-and-bone creatures should be created out of the blood of one of the rebel gods and this would be a fitting punishment for Kingu. It was, he argued, Kingu and not Tiamat who was the guilty party because he had incited the old goddess to rebellion. This highly dubious case against Kingu was put to the divine assembly, and, at the same time, it was pointed out that if Kingu were condemned to death and his body used to create a human taskforce, it would be very much in the gods' interest. They brought in a verdict of 'guilty'. Kingu was slain and the human race was created out of his blood.

When the job of building Babylon with all its magnificent temples and sacred edifices was completed, the gods held a great celebratory banquet. In festive spirits, they hailed Marduk as sovereign without rival, and sang his praises at great length. The last sixty-odd lines of Tablet VI and the whole of the seventh and last tablet are devoted to a catalogue of Marduk's fifty names, each signifying one of the multiple aspects of his supreme authority over all things, human and divine.

When the plot is stripped of all its convoluted detail, the story told in the Akkadian *Creation Epic* is basically about a rebellion in the divine world against the primordial mother goddess, Tiamat. In the beginning, Tiamat is portrayed in a position of authority over all the divine population, including her consort. It is noticeable that she is presented as having a monstrous aspect to her character, giving birth to dragons and vipers, only after she has declared her intentions to take retaliatory action against the young rebel gods: before that point in the narrative, she appears as a compassionate and tolerant ruler, commanding the love and loyalty of her subjects. When a faction of the gods rose in revolt against her, others flocked to her side in support of her cause. The prospect of a new, alternative power-structure under the rebel gods was not, it would seem, welcomed by all, and there were many who were prepared to fight for the status quo. Hence Marduk's accusation that she had caused civil war.

The Akkadian Epic clearly makes use of traditional Sumerian stories, since so many of the characters who take an active part in the anti-Tiamat revolt are Sumerian gods. Which of the Sumerian gods had been the first to challenge the authority of the old goddess cannot be determined. A case can be made for it having been any one of the three great gods of the Sumerian pantheon in the third millennium BC: An, Enki (referred to in the Epic by their Akkadian names of Anu and Ea) or Enlil, who appears only as a shadowy figure in the Epic. Enlil was the Sumerian god of the atmosphere and as such, after the creation of the universe out of the two halves of Tiamat's body, he would have occupied the space between heaven and earth and held them apart. It is probable that the author of the Akkadian poem drew on a number of original Sumerian sources, each featuring a different god in the role of rebel, hero and creator god, all of which were amalgamated in the poem as we know it.

What can be said, however, is that, on the basis of the evidence of the Babylonian and Assyrian version of *The Creation Epic*, Sumerians, Babylonians and Assyrians alike visualized the pre-creative state as originally comprising a divine population living under the matriarchal rule of the primordial goddess, Tiamat.

THE GILGAMESH EPIC

The Gilgamesh Epic was composed and written in the Akkadian language between 1800 and 1600 BC. It could be seen to be a best-seller of the ancient world, since the story it tells maintained its popular appeal for at least one and a half thousand years. Over the centuries, it was copied and reworked, some passages being shortened, other elaborated with the inclusion of additional material. It was translated into Hittite and Hurrian, and fragments of variants of the original, differing widely in date, have turned up at places all over the Middle East – in northern, southern and central Iraq, Palestine, Turkey and even Armenia.

The hero of the Epic was one of the early kings of Uruk, named in the Sumerian King List as the fifth ruler of the city after the flood. Although there is as yet no contemporary evidence to prove it, it is generally assumed that he was an historical personage. Tales had been told about the exploits of several of the early kings of Uruk and Kish, but, such was his charisma, Gilgamesh inspired more legends than others. *The Gilgamesh Epic* draws freely on this rich fund of traditional Sumerian stories but, in the selective editing and in the development of the story line, the

Akkadian poem is widely regarded as an original literary masterpiece. The brief outline of the plot given here does not do justice to the poetic insight into the human dilemma expressed in some passages of the work.

A substantial part of a late variant of the Epic was preserved on tablets dating to the seventh century BC found at Nineveh. This version of the Epic, which is referred to as the *Standard Version*, was written on twelve tablets, of which Tablets I to XI contain the Epic proper. Tablet XII consists of an Akkadian translation of the last part of a Sumerian story known from elsewhere. The significance of this addendum and the differences between this later version and the original Old Babylonian composition are discussed later (*see* p. 15).

The Gilgamesh Epic opens with a eulogy to the hero's wisdom, experience and achievements. He is described as being two-thirds god and one-third human and is credited with building the city walls of Uruk. Archaeological evidence is not at variance with this tradition since the foundations of the massive defence walls at Uruk can be dated to the period when Gilgamesh is presumed to have lived, that is, sometime in the second quarter of the third millennium BC.

However, his energetic style of leadership made Gilgamesh unpopular with the citizens of Uruk because it meant that all the young men, commoners and nobles alike, had to leave their families to fight in his campaigns. The citizens were so concerned about the situation that they appealed to the god Anu for help. Anu considered their predicament and then called upon the goddess Aruru to create Enkidu, who would be the equal of Gilgamesh in every way, and by contending with him would leave the city in peace.

Enkidu was set down not in Uruk but in the steppe-lands some way distant from the city. He was a strange and wild man. Dressed roughly and with his hair long, Enkidu lived with the gazelles and other wild animals of the steppe, drinking with them at the water holes. He was the terror of the local huntsmen, tearing up their traps and destroying the snares set to catch game.

News of the arrival of this strange man of the steppe was brought to Gilgamesh by one of the huntsmen, who went into the city to complain about him, appeal for help and suggest a plan for his capture. While the huntsmen had failed to capture Enkidu, they suggested that one of the women from the temple might have more success. Gilgamesh agreed to the plan and the huntsman returned to the steppe accompanied by a *harimtu*. (The term *harimtu* is usually translated, on sound lexicographic evidence, as 'prostitute', 'harlot' or 'courtesan': all words which today have pejorative connotations inappropriate to the period of the original composition of the Epic, when sex and the fertility principle were accorded a value in religious practice that is difficult or impossible for us to assess nowadays. The title *harimtu* therefore has been retained here.)

On her arrival in the steppe, the *harimtu* went to the watering-place where Enkidu was accustomed to come to drink. When, after she had waited there for two days, Enkidu finally arrived, the *harimtu* made overt sexual advances to him to which his response was immediate and without reserve; for the next six days and seven nights they made love. After this initial experience with a civilized woman, Enkidu found to his dismay that he had lost his touch with the wild animals. Now, when he approached the watering hole, the wild creatures fled from him. He had, however, gained in wisdom and understanding. In this newly acquired state of self-awareness, he went back to the *harimtu* and asked for her advice. What she had to say was, in effect, that Enkidu was wasting his time in the steppe; that he ought to go to the city where she could introduce him to Gilgamesh; but that first he must learn how to behave in the society which he would meet at the king's court. Enkidu accepted both her advice and her offer to coach him in the social graces.

The *harimtu* may have taken Enkidu to be a stray member of one of the nomadic tribes who at that time wandered the desert with their herds of animals. The ancient Mesopotamians considered these people their cultural inferiors because they did not grow grain, eat bread or live in houses. As related in the Epic, the *harimtu* led Enkidu 'like a child' to a shepherd's dwelling to eat in company there. When food and drink were placed before him, Enkidu at first stared with amazement. But, encouraged by the *harimtu*, who explained that this was how things are done in polite society, Enkidu ate the food and drank seven jugs of beer, which made him elated and fully prepared to go with her to Uruk. This episode is described at length in the original Old Babylonian version of the Epic. The *Standard Version*, dating to some thousand years later, is much shorter and differs from the original in certain detail. The significances of these differences in the earlier and later versions and discussed later (*see* p. 15).

In Uruk, Gilgamesh had been given forewarning that he was to meet a rival through a dream which was interpreted for him by his mother, Ninsun. But he was not prepared for what was to come. A bridal chamber and nuptial bed had been prepared for one Ishara. (As this is one of the names by which Ishtar, the Akkadian goddess of love, was known, this may be a reference to the Sacred Marriage ritual, *see* pp. 19–20.) Gilgamesh was on his way to the bridal chamber when Enkidu arrived, stood in the doorway and barred his entry. Gilgamesh was enraged and the two of them started to fight. They fought so furiously, they shattered the doorposts and shook the walls. But as his anger subsided, Gilgamesh lost his taste for the fight and Enkidu, on his part, made conciliatory overtures. The outcome was a reconciliation and the two swore friendship to one another.

Gilgamesh had learned of a terrible monster called Humbaba (or Huwawa in some variants of the text) who lived in the far-off cedar forest. He proposed to Enkidu that they should team up and go to kill Humbaba. This proposal dismayed Enkidu who told Gilgamesh that the great god Enlil had appointed Humbaba as guardian of the forest to be a terror to all mortals. Enkidu's caution was echoed by the elders of the city but Gilgamesh overrode them too and issued orders to the armourers to prepare the necessary weapons. When all preparations were finally completed and Gilgamesh had prevailed upon his mother, Ninsun, to give her blessing to the enterprise, he and Enkidu, armed with swords and axes, left Uruk for the land of the cedar forests.

When, after six days and nights Gilgamesh and Enkidu reached their destination and began to fell the cedars, Humbaba came raging out of the forest to discover who was destroying his trees. In the ensuing fight, Humbaba would have got the better of them but for the intervention of the sun god, Shamash. Humbaba yielded and begged for mercy. But on Enkidu's advice, he was despatched with a sword-thrust in the neck. The two heroes returned to Uruk in triumph, oblivious of the wheels of destiny they had set in motion.

The return of Gilgamesh to Uruk was that of a conquering hero. Discarding his travel-worn clothes, he bathed, dressed his hair and put on his ceremonial robes and royal regalia. Thus arrayed, he presented so magnificent a spectacle of manhood that Ishtar, the goddess of love, fell in love with him. 'Come, Gilgamesh,' she wooed him, 'Be my husband and I will be your wife.' As added inducements, she offered him a chariot of lapis lazuli fitted with golden wheels, the promise of adulation from kings, princes and lords, a bountiful increase in his flocks of sheep and goats and draught-oxen of unequalled strength.

Gilgamesh's response to these fulsome overtures was vituperative, detailed and lengthy. He started by asserting that the goddess was too expensive in her tastes for there to be any benefit to him if he married her. He then progressed to personal abuse, accusing Ishtar of being, amongst other things, like a back door which does not keep out the wind, a leaky water-skin which drenches the person who carries it and a shoe which pinches the wearer's foot. He went on to accuse the goddess of infidelity, and regaled her with a whole list of her past lovers and adoring husbands, and the awful fates she had wished upon them. Amongst these he specifically mentions Dumuzi, for whose death she had ordained an annual festival of lamentation, year after year (*see* below, p. 21).

In fury at this rebuff, Ishtar rushed off to the great god Anu to protest. Now, Ishtar was not only the goddess of love, she had close connections with the realms of the dead, too. Ishtar used this darker side of her character to take revenge on Gilgamesh. She threatened Anu that if he didn't send a bull to kill Gilgamesh, she would smash down the door of the underworld and let out all the dead. After only a short demur and a little bargaining, Anu agreed to do as she wished.

Gilgamesh and Enkidu responded to this latest challenge from the gods with characteristic bravura. When they heard of the ravages the bull of heaven was making among the populace, felling hundreds of people at a single snort, they went out to get him. Together they overcame the bull and he was killed with a sword-thrust between neck and horns. To further the insults to Ishtar, Enkidu tore off the bull's right leg and threw it down in front of her saying that if he could only get his hands on her, he would tie her up in the bull's entrails as well. While Ishtar gathered the *harimtu* and other members of the female priesthood together to mourn the death of the bull, Gilgamesh strode around the streets of Uruk bragging about his prowess.

But this time the two heroes had gone too far, even for their champion Shamash, the sun god. There was a furious debate among the gods, and it was decided that one of them must die. In spite of Shamash's pleas, it was decreed that Enkidu should pay the price for both of them.

Enkidu was not struck down dramatically. Indeed, that was part of Enkidu's complaint about his fate. If he had fallen in battle, he would have been blessed. As it was, he wasted away in pain and suffering, lying on a couch, tended by the grieving Gilgamesh. When Enkidu finally died, Gilgamesh refused to believe that his friend was dead and not asleep until finally the body began to putrefy. Distraught with grief, and overwhelmed by the implications of mortality for himself and all mankind, he fled the city and wandered into the wild lands.

In his despair, Gilgamesh decided that the only person who would know about death and life was Utnapishtim, the hero of the flood story. After the flood had subsided, the gods had conferred immortality upon Utnapishtim and his wife, and sent them to live in a far-distant land beyond the sea of death. Even with the knowledge that no mortal had ever before undertaken the hazardous journey to this far-off land, Gilgamesh set out, determined to get there.

Following directions given to him by the scorpion people, the guardians of the gates of the rising and setting sun, Gilgamesh struggled along the route and arrived at last on the shores of a deep sea. There he found Siduri, usually and quite inaccurately called 'the ale-wife', or the even more derogatory 'bar-maid'. Siduri was neither: she was a *sābītu*, one of the professional women holding something akin to consular status, who managed the staging-posts and as such, played a vital entrepreneurial role in the workings of the vast network of early Sumerian international trade. It is no coincidence that she should be stationed there, at the edge of the world, ready to provide banking facilities, an information service or any other help that might be required by the long-distance trading merchants. Gilgamesh poured out his troubles to Siduri and asked how he could find Utnapishtim. She explained that Utnapishtim lived on the other side of the waters of death and the only chance of reaching him was to be ferried across by Utnapishtim's boatman, Urshanabi. If he was not able to contact Urshanabi, then he should turn back and go home, Siduri advised. This was probably the kind of local information and advice a *sābītu* was habitually handing out to passing merchant travellers.

Gilgamesh succeeded in attracting Urshanabi's attention and getting the offer of a lift in his boat. Scrupulously following the boatman's instructions about not allowing a single drop of the water of death to touch his hands, which involved using a new punt-pole – one hundred and twenty in all – for every thrust, Gilgamesh finally arrived in the presence of Utnapishtim. Once more he poured out his grief over the death of his friend and the ultimate fate of all mankind, but Utnapishtim had little comfort for him. Only the gods allot life and death, he said, and that was not something they revealed to mortals.

To illustrate his point, Utnapishtim told Gilgamesh the story of the flood. His account is along much the same lines as the Biblical analogue, for Utnapishtim is the prototype for Noah. There are a few minor differences between the two accounts but the most significant difference of all lies in the identities of the deities involved. In the Biblical story, the Lord sent the flood, warned Noah of the impending disaster and, after it was all over, said that the rainbow would serve as a reminder of the promise not to send another deluge. In Utnapishtim's version, it was the god Enlil who was chiefly responsible for the gods' decision to send the flood; the god Ea who warned Utnapishtim and advised him to build a boat; and Ishtar who suffered the fit of divine remorse and vowed that her blue lapis lazuli necklace would be a reminder to her never again to agree to inflict such a disaster on the human race.

That, concluded Utnapishtim at the end of the tale, was how it came about that he and his wife were granted immortality. For Gilgamesh it must be otherwise. If he could stay awake for a week, then, perhaps he might stand a chance. But far from being able to keep awake for a week, Gilgamesh fell asleep for seven days. Utnapishtim's wife baked bread daily and placed a fresh loaf beside him each day. When Gilgamesh woke up, and tried to deny that he had been asleep that long, there were the seven loaves in progressive stages of staleness and mouldiness as evidence against him. Totally demoralized, Gilgamesh left for home.

But Gilgamesh had aroused the compassion of Utnapishtim's wife. At her suggestion, Utnapishtim called Gilgamesh back and told him that he would reveal one of the secrets of the gods. There was a plant which grew at the bottom of the sea. The plant could not impart immortality since that was the prerogative of the gods, but it did have the power to rejuvenate anyone who ate it. Equipping himself with the traditional pearl-diver's gear, Gilgamesh dived to the sea-bed and returned with the plant. With great triumph, he displayed the plant to Urshanabi, declaring that its name was 'The Old Man becomes a Young Man' and that he would take it back with him to Uruk and eat it there.

The return journey was long and hard and Gilgamesh became dusty and travel-worn. Passing a pool, he was tempted by the cool water to stop and bathe. But while he was bathing, a serpent, attracted by the sweet smell of the wondrous plant, came up and took it, casting its skin as it slithered back into the water. This might be an ætiological tale explaining why snakes shed their skin, but for Gilgamesh it was the final ironic twist of fate. The Epic ends, as it began, with praise for the city of Uruk, making the point that the only immortality to which human beings can aspire lies in their achievements during their lifetime.

The Gilgamesh Epic has been studied and commented upon extensively since its rediscovery in modern times. Two particularly intriguing aspects of the Epic are noted here. Firstly, there is the marked antagonism between Gilgamesh, King of Uruk, and Ishtar, who as the Sumerian Inanna, was the city's goddess. Secondly, there are veiled allusions to the Sacred Marriage ritual, all of which appear to be of a derisive or derogatory nature.

The initial face-to-face encounter between Gilgamesh and Enkidu, as it is related in the Epic, contains an oblique reference to the Sacred Marriage ceremony. When Enkidu first arrived in Uruk, Gilgamesh was on his way to the nuptial chamber which had been prepared for Ishhara. Now, Ishhara was one of the names by which the goddess Ishtar was known, and although the author does not expressly say so, Gilgamesh must have been on his way to perform the Sacred Marriage. Consequently, when Enkidu stood in the doorway and barred his entry, he was, in terms of royal ritual, challenging Gilgamesh's right to the throne. But then it could be argued that, by the same token, Enkidu had an equal claim to kingship, since the author has already described him, in a parody of the Sacred Marriage, coupling at great length out on the steppe with a priestess from Uruk whose title *harimtu* was sometimes applied to the goddess Ishtar herself.

The quarrel between Gilgamesh and Ishtar as related in the *Standard Version* of the Epic may have been an elaboration of the theme added to the Old Babylonian original by another author some 200 or 300 years later. In this episode, when Ishtar proposed to Gilgamesh, the further inducements she offered him included an increase in his livestock and the homage of foreign potentates, which were precisely those with which the goddess endowed her chosen royal spouse at the Sacred Marriage ceremony. Gilgamesh's extensive and vituperative rebuttal of her proposal thus constitutes a detailed and learned argument against the principles involved in the Sacred Marriage rite — that the prosperity of a king's reign was dependent upon the favours of the goddess of fertility, Ishtar herself. That Ishtar was responsible for consigning Dumuzi to the netherworld, rather than ensuring his prosperity, is specifically mentioned. (*See* p. 18.)

The Sacred Marriage was essentially a Sumerian royal ceremony. It was celebrated by successive kings of the Sumerian cities of Ur and Isin up to the time of the rise to power of the Amorites and the establishment of the Old Babylonian empire under Hammurabi. The author of the original *Gilgamesh Epic* was clearly working under the aegis of one of the newly founded centres of Amorite power, since the work is in the Akkadian and not in the Sumerian language. It is notoriously difficult to identify humour in an ancient or alien culture, but it is possible that in all those episodes where indirect reference to the Sacred Marriage appears, the author — or authors — intended something in the nature of a political lampoon aimed at an outmoded and discredited concept of kingship.

Certainly, the antagonism between Gilgamesh and the goddess of love as portrayed in the Akkadian Epic, is totally at variance with the relations shown in one Sumerian myth known as *Gilgamesh, Enkidu and the Underworld*. Here, Gilgamesh is portrayed as being on warm terms of 'brotherhood' with the goddess, so that when she called on both of them for assistance, both Gilgamesh and Enkidu responded gallantly. She rewarded Gilgamesh with two precious objects which were lost when they dropped down into the underworld. Gilgamesh tried to retrieve them but failed; then Enkidu made a brave descent to the netherworld to recover them in person. On his return, Gilgamesh questioned him about what he had seen there.

The royal Assyrian scribe at Nineveh who copied *The Gilgamesh Epic* in the seventh century BC was obviously familiar with this old Sumerian story. He added an Akkadian translation of the last part of it as a finale to the Epic in Tablet XII. The first part of the Sumerian tale where Gilgamesh and Enkidu are described as being on cordial terms with the goddess is omitted however.

A further difference between the Old Babylonian original and the *Standard Version* of the Epic dating to some thousand years later, can be seen in the relative treatment of the episode which might be called the education of Enkidu by the *harimtu* (see p. 10). The account given in the later version is much shorter than in the original, and the image of the *harimtu* leading Enkidu by the hand 'like a child' has been changed, as if the portrayal of the *harimtu* in the role of educator was now no longer an acceptable one.

Sufficient textual evidence survives to demonstrate that in the Late Sumerian and Old Babylonian periods, there were women of culture and education among the ranks of the female priestly establishments. Many surviving hymns, songs, ballads and poems, some of considerable poetic merit, are attributed to individual priestesses or are attributable, on stylistic grounds, to female poets. After so long a lapse of time, authorship of these literary works cannot, of course, be authenticated. However, we do have irrefutable evidence from the archives of the *nadītu* priestesses recovered from Sippar, that at least some members of the female priesthood there were literate and educated, and worked as female scribes within their community. There is, therefore, nothing inherently improbable in supposing that the *harimtu* who prepared Enkidu for his introduction to Gilgamesh's court at Uruk, thus bringing about the divine decree that the two men should meet, was herself not only a sexually attractive woman, but also a cultured and educated person, well qualified to take on the role of tutor.

INANNA AND DUMUZI

Myths about Inanna, the Sumerian goddess of fertility, and a mortal man named Dumuzi, go back to pre-literate times and in their origins they are complex and obscure. Festivals in honour of Inanna were being held at Uruk as early as around 3000 BC, as we learn from a contemporary document discovered there, written in an early pictographic script. Symbols for 'festival', 'star', 'Inanna' and 'to set' are enclosed within a square thus forming a 'sentence' which can plausibly be read as: 'Festival on the day on which the star of Inanna sets.' In historic times, Venus was Inanna's star, so, in the Near East, the association of the goddess of love with the planet Venus goes back at least 5,000 years. We can see how the goddess was visualized by the Sumerians from the portrait of her on the great cultic vase found at Uruk, the famous Warka Vase, also dated to around 3000 BC (*see* figs 1 and 2).

Dumuzi, the mortal who figures in the myth as the goddess's lover and husband, is assumed to have been one of the early Sumerian city kings, although later historical tradition is divided as to which city he was associated with. According to the Sumerian King List, the city of Badtibira claimed a Dumuzi, the shepherd, as one of their ancient kings who reigned there before the flood; and Uruk preserved the tradition that a Dumuzi, a fisherman, who originally came from Eridu or Kuara, ruled as King of Uruk after the flood, one generation before Gilgamesh.

Versions of the Inanna and Dumuzi myth in current circulation in the first quarter of the second millennium BC have been preserved in two compositions, both written in Sumerian and both dated to about 1765 BC. The stories told in these two works, briefly outlined here, complement each other. The first, known today as 'Inanna's Descent to the Netherworld', tells the story from the goddess's point of view; the second, known as 'Dumuzi's Dream', relates events from Dumuzi's standpoint.

Fig. 1 Full-length view of the cultic vase found at Uruk. The cultic vase, dated c. 3000 BC, was found in the precincts of the Temple of Eanna at Uruk. The vase is about a metre tall and made of alabaster. The scene, depicted in relief, shows a procession of animals and offering-bearers, headed by 'the man in the net kilt', usually referred to as the king. The king, whose figure is largely destroyed, is followed by his sash-bearer and preceded by an offering-bearer (*see* detail, fig. 2). *Hirmer Verlag München*

Fig. 2 Detail of the top register of the vase, showing the female figure who stands waiting to receive the procession. The two reed bundles behind her identify her as Inanna or a priestess assuming the role of the goddess at the ceremony. The vase was broken and repaired in antiquity with a riveted inset of plain stone. *Hirmer Verlag München*

'Inanna's Descent to the Netherworld' opens with the statement that the goddess decided to abandon heaven and all her temples on earth and descend to the underworld. No reason is given for her decision. After arraying herself in the ceremonial robes and royal regalia of a ruler, Inanna gave instructions to her vizier, Ninshubur, that, if she failed to return, he was to go to the great god Enlil and ask for his help in rescuing her from death in the underworld. Should Enlil refuse to offer assistance, he was then to go to her father, the moon god, Nanna, with the same request. If Nanna was unwilling to help, then Ninshubur was to approach Enki, the god of wisdom and sweet water.

Inanna arrived at the gates of the underworld and proceeded to behave in a peremptory and aggressive manner. She demanded that the gatekeeper let her in, saying that he was to inform the queen, her elder sister Ereshkigal, that she had come to witness the funeral rites of Ereshkigal's lately slain husband, the lord Gugalanna. The mythological implications of Inanna's statement are as yet unknown but this is the one and only reason stated in the myth for Inanna's decision to venture into the underworld.

Ereshkigal gave orders to the gatekeeper that Inanna be permitted to enter but she was to be informed that she must comply with the accustomed rules of the underworld. Accordingly, at each of the seven gates to the underworld, in spite of her outrage and protestations, Inanna was stripped of her robes and adornments, one by one, starting with the crown and royal regalia, then her jewels and robes, and finally, her body garment. When she arrived in Ereshkigal's presence she was naked. The seven dread judges of the underworld fixed her with their eye of death. She died and her corpse was hung upon a stake.

After three days and three nights and no sign of her return, Ninshubur went to Enlil as he had been instructed. Just as Inanna had foreseen, Enlil was not prepared to go into action on her behalf, and neither was Nanna, the moon god. Enki, however, was sympathetic. He fashioned two sexless creatures and gave them the 'water of life' and the 'food of life' with instructions that they were to revive Inanna by sprinkling her corpse sixty times with each. This they did and Inanna was restored to life.

Inanna returned to earth accompanied by a host of demons from the netherworld. The function of this ghostly throng is not explicitly stated in the narrative but from what subsequently took place, it seems that they were to carry off whomever Inanna condemned to the realms of the dead. The goddess and her ghostly retinue made first for Ninshubur, whom they found mourning in sackcloth and dust. Immediately upon her appearance, he threw himself at Inanna's feet. The demons were eager to carry him off but Inanna protected him on the grounds that he had helped her escape death and he had gone into mourning for her.

Inanna and her demonic horde then moved on to Umma, where they found the tutelary god of that city also in sackcloth and dust, mourning for the goddess. The demons wanted to seize him too but the god threw himself at Inanna's feet in an acceptable expression of self-abasement; she defended him too. The same thing happened at Badtibira and the goddess and her followers finally came to Kullab, a district of some special cultic significance within the city of Uruk. There they found the king, Dumuzi. Far from displaying any signs of mourning, he was seated high on his kingly throne, dressed in royal robes and, furthermore, he made no sign of self-abasement or humility when Inanna arrived at his court. This time, Inanna made no effort to intervene and turned him over to the demons. Dumuzi was very frightened and beseeched the sun god, Utu, for help. The tablet on which this work is written is broken and the end of the story is missing. But Dumuzi's attempts to avoid the fate decreed for him by Inanna were doomed to failure, as the other contemporary work, known as 'Dumuzi's Dream', makes clear.

'Dumuzi's Dream' is a poetic composition which, according to the colophon, was intended to be sung as a lament for Dumuzi. We don't know how Sumerian music sounded but from the pictures of musicians playing percussion, wind and stringed instruments, it would perhaps be reasonable to imagine something after the style of traditional vocal music still popular in the Middle East today. The song starts with a refrain describing Dumuzi as a young man wandering out into the plain in a state of great apprehension and mental distress. Exhausted, he fell asleep and had a dream which he called on his sister, Geshtinanna, to interpret for him. She had only bad news: the dream was not favourable. It foretold that Dumuzi would be seized by demons and would die, and she would be left to mourn for him. In a bid to escape his fate, Dumuzi asked Geshtinanna to keep watch for the demons who were after him and in the meantime he would go into hiding.

In their search for Dumuzi, the demons came upon Geshtinanna. They offered her bribes of a river of water and a field of grain to reveal his hiding place, but she refused and they went off saying, 'Who has ever heard of a sister betraying her brother?' They then met a friend of Dumuzi and offered him the same bribes to tell them where Dumuzi was to be found. The friend took the bribes but procrastinated somewhat by saying that he was hidden somewhere, in the short grass, in the long grass or in the ditches of Arali, but he didn't know exactly where. But this was enough information for the demons and they finally caught up with Dumuzi in the ditches of Arali.

Before the break comes at the end of 'Inanna's Descent to the Netherworld', Dumuzi, in his great terror of being seized by the demons, appealed to Utu the sun god for help. His appeal to Utu is preserved at length in 'Dumuzi's Dream'. He called upon Utu as his brother-in-law, reminding him that he, Dumuzi, was the husband of Utu's sister, Inanna, the one who had brought the wedding gifts to the goddess at Uruk, the one who had kissed the goddess's sacred lips and danced on the holy knees. Utu responded to this appeal by changing Dumuzi's hands and feet into those of a gazelle and he was thus able to escape. Once more Dumuzi was captured by the demons and again escaped to take refuge in Geshtinanna's sheepfold. But this time, the demons had him cornered, and, entering the sheep fold one by one, they set fire to the stalls and overturned the milk churns. When the last demon entered the sheep fold, Dumuzi was dead.

INANNA, DUMUZI AND THE SACRED MARRIAGE RITUAL

The myth related in 'Inanna's Descent to the Netherworld' makes clear the fact that Inanna, the Sumerian goddess of fertility, was responsible for consigning Dumuzi, the king of Uruk, to the realms of the dead. It is equally evident from 'Dumuzi's Dream' that Dumuzi had foreknowledge of what his fate was to be. The Inanna and Dumuzi legend may therefore draw on some memory from pre-historic times when the king was sacrificed either annually or periodically for some purpose connected with ensuring vegetal, animal or human fertility in the community which he served. Whether or not some such ancient practice lies at the heart of the myth cannot be demonstrated, but by the historic period, when records become available, the Inanna and Dumuzi myth is found to be inextricably interrelated with a contemporary concept of kingship, expressed in the cultic ritual known as the Sacred Marriage.

The theological assumptions behind the Sacred Marriage ritual were threefold. Firstly, the ruler was regarded as responsible for the agricultural prosperity of the territories under his control. Secondly, there was the belief that all sexual reproduction on earth, vegetal, animal and human, was dependent on the sex act performed by the goddess of fertility. Thirdly, that the roles of the fertility goddess and her chosen spouse could be played by human surrogates in a ritualized and liturgical enactment of the divine coupling.

Some form of ritual marriage between the king and a priestess of the rank of *nu gig* may have been performed in Sumer before the middle of the third millennium BC, if the evidence of an inscription on a royal seal from Ur can be interpreted correctly. The seal itself has never come to light but among the debris overlying the royal tombs at Ur there was a clay impression of a seal belonging to Mesanepada. Mesanepada was, according to the Sumerian King List, the first king to reign at Ur after the flood. Mesopotamian archaeologists of today date his reign to some time around the middle of the third millennium BC. The inscription on the seal reads, 'Mesanepada, husband of the *nu gig*.' This suggests that some form of ritual marriage involving the king and a priestess of the rank of *nu gig* was known in Ur at this time.

The first documentary evidence for the Sacred Marriage appears at the end of the second millennium BC. It was celebrated as a royal ritual by successive kings of the Sumerian cities of Ur and Isin well into the twentieth century BC. At the ceremony, the king identified himself with Dumuzi, the husband of Inanna, and a priestess from Uruk of the rank of *lukur*-priestess acted as surrogate for the goddess. Some idea of how spectacular a piece of cultic theatre the Sacred Marriage ceremony may have been is conveyed by a composition written in the Sumerian language, known today as 'Inanna, Dumuzi and the Prosperity of the Palace', which is a kind of script for an allegorical masque. It has speaking parts for Inanna, the goddess Ninlil and a chorus, and was almost certainly performed with musical accompaniment.

Inanna's speeches in 'Prosperity in the Palace', and the responses spoken by the chorus, contain explicit references to the sex act and sexual organs which can be translated today only by using medical terminology or bawdy language, and are enriched by a wealth of poetic euphemism and innuendo which Sumerian erotic poetry is so skilled at handling and is all but completely lost in modern translation. In this literary style, Inanna anticipates the coming pleasure of the sex act with the king as Dumuzi and promises to guard his palace and well-stocked storehouses. The principles implicit in the Sacred Marriage rite are reiterated in a concluding speech by the goddess Ninlil, Inanna's mother. She pledges Inanna's continuing love for the king whereby he will be ensured a long, successful and prosperous reign.

THE CULT OF TAMMUZ

By the first millennium BC, the original Inanna and Dumuzi mythology of the Sumerians had split into two separate and differing traditions. In the heartlands of the Assyrian and the Babylonian empires, the goddess, under the name of Ishtar, retained her power over fertility. This is explicitly stated in 'The Descent of Ishtar to the Netherworld', an Akkadian variant of the original Sumerian myth, composed at the end of the second millennium BC. Here it says that when Ishtar went down to the underworld, all sexual conception ceased – the bull did not mount the cow, the ass no longer covered the jenny and men did not impregnate women.

In the west, however, in Syria, Palestine and the countries along the Mediterranean seaboard, the fecundity factor was, in mythological terms, transferred from the female to the male principle. How far this reversal in the roles of the goddess and her lover was due to the influence of invaders from the north who arrived and settled in the area in substantial numbers around the beginning of the second millennium BC, it is impossible to say. Certainly, newcomers, some speaking Hittite, one of the Indo-European group of languages, made a greater cultural impact in the west than they did in Assyria and Babylonia. But whatever the reason, the cult of Tammuz – a local variant of the name Dumuzi – as it was practised in Palestine, the Lebanon and the cities of Phoenicia, was one of a dying and resurrecting god, associated with the regrowth of vegetation in spring after the dearth of winter.

The myth of Tammuz is familiar to us from the Greek legend of Adonis. The Greeks, as maritime traders, would have encountered the cult as it was celebrated at the Phoenician port of Byblos and elsewhere in the Levant where Tammuz was addressed by the cult adherents as 'Adon', a Semitic word meaning 'lord'. The story tells of a youth so beautiful that the goddess of love, known by the name of Astarte, fell in love with him. When he was killed by a boar in the mountains of Lebanon, Astarte was so distraught with grief that the gods took pity on her and allowed Tammuz to return to earth for part of the year. The annual death of Tammuz was lamented with mournful flute music and wailing; although in the Akkadian myth, 'The Descent of Ishtar to the Netherworld', there is reference to wailing men and women, the cult had a particular appeal for women. In the Bible, Ezekiel reported that he had observed women wailing for Tammuz at the north door of the Temple in Jerusalem (Ezekiel 8.14). The Tammuz cult maintained its popular appeal in the Middle East for a very long time: an annual 'Festival of Weeping Women' in honour of Tammuz was still being held at Harran as late as the tenth century AD.

References and Further Reading

For English translations of the original Sumerian and Akkadian myths:

Heidel, A. (1951), *The Babylonian Genesis* (Chicago: University of Chicago Press)

Kovacs, M.G. (1989), *The Epic of Gilgamesh* (California: Stanford University Press)

Kramer, S.N. (1963), *The Sumerians: Their History, Culture and Character* (Chicago; University of Chicago Press)

Pritchard, J.B. (ed.) (1955), *Ancient Near Eastern Texts Relating to the Old Testament* (Princeton: Princeton University Press)

Pritchard, J.B. (ed.) (1969), *The Ancient Near East: Supplementary Texts and Pictures* (Princeton: Princeton University Press)

HISTORICAL BACKGROUND:

Bottéro, J., Cassin, E. and Vercoutter, J. (eds) (1967), *The Near East: The Early Civilizations* (London: Weidenfeld and Nicolson)

Saggs, H.W.F. (1984), *The Might that was Assyria* (London: Sidgwick and Jackson)

For a study of the nadītu *priestesses of the Old Babylonian period:*

Jeyes, U. (1983), 'The *Naditu* Women of Sippar' in A. Cameron and A. Kurht (eds), *Images of Women in Antiquity* (London and Sydney: Croom Helm), pp.260–72

M.V. SETON-WILLIAMS

Egypt:
Myth and the Reality

SECTION I

If one defines feminism as the advocacy of the claims of women to political, economic and social equality with men as *Chambers Dictionary* does, then, in ancient Egypt, all these aims had already been achieved.

Goddesses play an important part in Egyptian mythology. The primeval goddesses, the mother figures that go back to the prehistoric beginnings of Egypt, were female. They always had their own separate temples. Egyptian goddesses were creator deities, and were protectors of the king in the form of cobras, vultures or lionesses; they also had a human, female aspect. Not only did nearly all the goddesses have temples, they also had separate shrines in the main temples. There were female priestesses in the goddesses' temples, and in those of the male deities there were female choirs, such as the 'Chantresses of Amun'.

Men and women were treated equally before the law. Property was vested in the women of the family and the descent was through the female line: up to the end of the Middle Kingdom (c. 1786 BC) men and women's names appear to have been interchangeable. As property means power, there was no need to claim an independence that they already possessed. It was not until the Ptolemaic period, after Alexander's entry into Egypt in the fourth century BC, that Greek law was introduced and women began to have an inferior position.

The beginning of Egyptian history is marked by an important dynastic marriage, between an early king, the Horus Aha, and Neith-Hotep, a Delta princess, probably from Sais, who was the royal heiress of Lower Egypt. This marriage marked the union of Upper and Lower Egypt and took place about 3100 BC. It was the beginning of Egyptian greatness and the commencement of her long history as the oldest unified country in the world. There were several Egyptian queens who ruled alone, usually at either the beginning or at the end of a dynasty. Queens were also the link between one dynasty and another, as the kingdom, like private property, descended through the female line (*see* Section V, p. 37).

The first queen who seems to have ruled alone, in her own right, was the Great

Royal Heiress Mer-Neith, who became king in the First Dynasty, c. 2800 BC, probably after the death of her husband. She had two tombs, one at Saqqara and the other at Abydos, both every bit as splendid as those of the kings. According to Manetho (*Aegyptiaca*, 1956, p. 37) it was declared that women could legitimately rule over Egypt. Diodorus Siculus mentions five queens of Egypt who ruled independently but does not name them.

The last independent queen of Egypt was Cleopatra VII Philopater who reigned from 51–30 BC when Egypt was annexed by Rome. If one regards her not as the languorous mistress of Caesar and Mark Anthony but as an ambitious woman who wished to restore Egypt to her former greatness, who manipulated her Roman lovers, both generals, to this end, her misfortune was that Octavian was a better general than Anthony. Thus she lost Egypt, her son and her life. One could adapt the saying that the Scots used after Culloden to fit Egypt, 'the throne of Egypt came with a lass and went with a lass'.

The Myths

When dealing with the myths and legends of a country as old as Egypt one is bound to have problems. A choice must be made among the legends as they cannot all be included, and many are incomplete and known only from references in other myths as the complete texts have never been found.

Egypt was considered as having been created from the Watery Waste of Nun, who was also a god, a form of Chaos from which all things came. The main and continuous preoccupation of the daily temple services was to prevent ordered Egyptian society ever slipping back into the abyss of Chaos. Not only might order and the rule of law be destroyed, by which the Egyptians set great store, but the natural order was not regarded as stable and its various elements were only kept in position by constant prayer and ritual. It was for this purpose that Tutankhamun was buried, as were several of his predecessors, with four wooden supports to hold up the sky. There was an annual service held in all the main temples to ensure that the sky remained in position and this practice continued right up to the beginning of the Roman period.

The goddess who was in charge of law, order and a balanced way of life was Ma'at, through whose power the kings governed. She is shown with the feather of Truth, an ostrich plume, upon her head and was always depicted in human form. She was the goddess representing Cosmic Harmony and her worship dates back at least to the Old Kingdom and probably to the beginnings of Egyptian history. Ma'at was worshipped throughout the country in all the main temples, although she only had a small shrine within the Temenos wall of Montu's temple, south of Karnak. The kings called themselves 'beloved of Ma'at' and a kneeling figure of the goddess was always a favourite offering.

Originally, the two major deities of Egypt were both female. These were Nekhbet, the vulture goddess of Upper Egypt, and Wadjet, the cobra goddess of Lower Egypt. They were the protectors of the kings and, as such, of the realm – a position recognized by the second of the king's five titles, the 'Nebty' name, 'He of the Two Ladies', which indicated his especial position regarding the two primeval deities who were the principal goddesses at the dawn of Egyptian history. Sometimes both goddesses, but always the cobra, are represented on the brow of the king as the royal *uraeus*.

These two unlikely creatures, the vulture and the serpent, were chosen by the ancient Egyptians because they were thought to be self-producing and therefore divine. The temples of the goddesses were both situated in twin cities, in Upper Egypt at Nekheb with Neken close to it on the other side of the river, and in Lower Egypt at Dep with Pe, the city of Horus, in very close proximity. Both cities were near to the borders of Egypt – Nekheb close to the southern frontier, before it moved to Syene (modern Aswan), and Dep on the edge of the marshes stretching to the Mediterranean.

The city of Nekheb stood at the entrance of a long valley, winding down to the Red Sea, which had been inhabited since early times and bore on its rock faces prehistoric drawings and early inscriptions. Here, in the Wadi Hillal, were set the vulture rocks in which the great birds nested and lived. A scatter of temples, both rock-cut and free standing, testifies to the site's popularity from prehistoric times. The Egyptian queens established early their affinity with Nekhbet, the vulture goddess, by adopting the Vulture head-dress as the royal prerogative. The temple of Nekheb was eventually destroyed in the Persian period, sometime before 332 BC, and as religion and nationalism went hand in hand at this time, this had a devastating effect upon Egypt.

The northern city of Dep was built originally on low islands in marshes. One of these was the floating island of Chemis where Horus was placed for safety, under the care of the cobra goddess, while his mother Isis pursued her long search for the body of her husband, Osiris, murdered by his brother Seth at a feast ordered in his honour (*see* below, p. 32). As the swamps receded a massive limestone temple was built to the goddess Wadjet by the Saites (664–525 BC) and later rebuilt by the Ptolemies after the earlier structure was destroyed by the Persians.

The Creation Myths

The unification of Egypt, the setting up of a centralized government in 3100 BC and rule by a single king, replaced the dual southern and northern capitals; thus the scheme of Egyptian religion changed. The two primeval goddesses were replaced by groups of deities established in the various cities. The earliest, and most authoritative, was that of Heliopolis, ancient On, now a suburb of Cairo. This centred on the worship of nine deities, the *Ennead*, led by Atum, an ancient sun god, who was said to have been self-created from the watery waste of Nun (Chaos), where all things began. Atum then created Shu, god of the air, and Tefnut, goddess of moisture. They in their turn made Geb, the earth god, and Nut, the sky goddess. The children of Geb and Nut were Osiris, a fertility god and later King of the Dead, and his sister-wife Isis, Mistress of Magic, Seth and his sister-wife Nephthys, one of the goddesses of the dead, and Horus the Elder, often shown in man's form with the mask of a hawk. These deities were worshipped throughout Egypt and always shown in human form.

THE CREATION ACCORDING TO HELIOPOLIS

This creation, according to tradition, is one of the earliest extant, dating back to the VIth Dynasty (c. 2345–2181 BC). It was found in the *Pyramid Texts* in the pyramids of the last two kings of the dynasty, Merenre and Pepi II, and there are other later versions in the thirteenth century BC:

> O Atum-Khephrer, thou wast on high on the (primeval) hill; thou didst rise as the *Ben bird* of the *Ben stone* in the *Ben house* in Heliopolis; thou didst spit out that which was Shu, thou didst splatter out that which was Tefnut; thou didst put thy arms about them as the arms of a *Ka*; for thy *ka* was in them.

The text goes on to give the names of the Heliopolitan Ennead:

> O you great Ennead which is in On [Heliopolis] namely Atum, Shu, Tefnut, Geb, Nut Osiris, Isis, Seth and Nephthys, O you children of Atum extend his heart to his child [Pepi II] in your name of *The Nine Bows*.
>
> (*ANET*, P. 4)

The Theology of Memphis

When the First Dynasty was established, with its capital at Memphis, just south of Cairo, it was felt necessary to justify the emergence of the city and its claim to importance. It was therefore suggested that the temple of Ptah, in Memphis, was the 'Balance of the Two Lands' (Upper and Lower Egypt). It was also claimed that Ptah took precedence over the other creator gods and that he, like Atum, was the primeval being first created. The following text was found on the Shabaka Stone (now in the British Museum, no. 797), dating to c. 700 BC. It is obviously a copy of a much earlier text perhaps going back some two thousand years. It reads in part:

> It happened, that the *reed and papyrus* were set at the great double door of the house of Ptah. This means that Horus and Seth, who were reconciled and united so that they associated, and their quarrelling ceased in the place which they reached, being joined in the House of Ptah 'The Balance of the Two Lands' in which Upper and Lower Egypt have been weighed . . .
>
> The Gods who came into being as Ptah.
> Ptah who is upon the great Throne . . .
> Ptah-Nun the father who begot Atum;
> Ptah-Nunet the mother who bore Atum;
> Ptah the Great, that is the heart and tongue of the Ennead;
> (Ptah) who gave birth to the gods; . . .
>
> (*ANET*, P. 3)

All the cult centres claimed that they were the first to be formed, and all of them had different creation legends. When Thebes became the capital of Egypt, it claimed the Ennead came into being there. Many of the hymns found at Thebes claim Amun as the creator god; they are mainly XIXth Dynasty in date:

The first who came into being in earliest times was Amun, who came into being at the beginning, so that his mysterious nature is unknown. No god came into being before him, there was no other god with him, so that he might tell his form. He had no mother, after whom his name might have been made. He had no father who had begotten him and who might have said

'This is I . . . The divine being who came into existence by himself.'

(ANET, P. 368)

The same position was claimed for the Aton, in the hymn to the Aton, in the tomb chapel of Aye at el-Armana (de Garis Davies, 1903–8, VI, p. 34).

In addition to those mentioned, each of the cities had its own pantheon. These usually consisted of a triad: a male god, his wife, and a child, usually male. These gods and goddesses had originally been independent, but were grouped together for convenience. One exception to this were the deities of the First Cataract, where Khnum, the ram-headed creator god, was supreme. He was assisted by two goddesses, Satet and Anuket, who represented aspects of the Nile in flood, and were hence regarded as fertility goddesses. Khnum was said to fashion mankind on his potter's wheel.

Another version of the triad was the Ogdoad of Khemenu, a town in central Egypt, where eight deities were worshipped. The town was known as the 'City of the Eight', and these were the primeval gods of Chaos. They were Nun and Nunet representing the primeval abyss; Heh and Hauket, infinity; Kek and Kauket, darkness; and finally Amun and Amunet representing the unknown gods. They also served to mark the male and female principles in the cosmic system, as in the 'Creation According to Hermopolis'.

Hermopolis was the second of the great schools of religious thought in Egypt after Heliopolis. The eight gods of the city were associated with Thoth (the Egyptian Djhuti, identified by the Greeks with Hermes); he was a moon god and the reckoner of time, depicted in human form with an ibis mask, and was also the scribe of the gods. Here as at Edfu, life was said to have started on the primeval hill, where Re took his stand, and the world began. The creation at Hermopolis was not such a coherent story as that of Heliopolis, and there must have been disputes between the two religious centres, about which we know nothing, but gradually the priests of Heliopolis gained the mastery, and the services carried out in the temples throughout Egypt were based upon the Heliopolitan order.

SECTION II

The Goddesses

SEKHMET

In the triads the goddesses often lead a completely independent life, as at Memphis. Sekhmet, the consort of Ptah, was thought to have been a daughter of Re, the sun god. Many stories are told of her: how she guarded the boat of the sun god as it passed through the twelve zones of the afterworld. The best known is that of the 'Destruction of Mankind'.

When Re became displeased with mankind who had ceased to worship him and provide the necessary offerings, he ordered Sekhmet, in her lion form, to destroy them. But after many had been killed, Re took pity on the humans and ordered Sekhmet to stop the killing. However, she refused, and after consulting the Council of the gods, Re decided to have quantities of beer brewed, which he coloured with red dye from a fruit (*kakadi*, which grew near Aswan). This was done and the red beer spread out over the fields as though it were blood. Sekhmet, rising heavy with sleep after her long, previous day's work, mistook the beer for blood, drank it and became incapable of doing further damage. This story is sometimes attributed to Hathor but seems far more in keeping with Sekhmet who represented the fierce rays of the sun at midday.

NEITH

Other goddesses were even more independent and had their own temples, like Neith at Sais and Hathor at Dendera. Neith was the national goddess of Lower Egypt, a great huntress whose symbol was a crossed bow and arrows. She was worshipped right from the beginning of Egyptian history and her temple, apparently constructed of reeds with her symbol on a pole in the courtyard, is the earliest picture of a religious building that we have in Egypt. Neith's temple in Sais in the Western Delta, is now totally destroyed. She always had an entirely separate existence of her own and was never paired with any male god.

Many of the early queens had their names compounded with that of Neith, such as Neith-Hotep already mentioned, whose name means 'an offering to Neith'. The early queens' names were written in a *serekh* like the kings and their tombs were just as imposing as the kings'. Neith-Hotep's tomb was at Naqada in Upper Egypt and was even larger and more important than her husband's, the Horus Aha. The worship of Neith played a major role at Esna where she appears as a creator goddess who formed all things.

The Creation According to Neith

This must be the Saite theology from the town of Sais, but owing to the destruction of that city, it is unlikely that the local version will ever be found. The text comes from Esna and was written in the second century BC, copying a much earlier text.

Fig. 3 The Ennead of Heliopolis

Again, it is like the theology of Memphis, basically a creation by thought.

The Father of Fathers, the Mother of Mothers was a divine being who was formed in the beginning. She found herself in the watery waste of Nun, she formed herself when the world was still in shadow and when there was

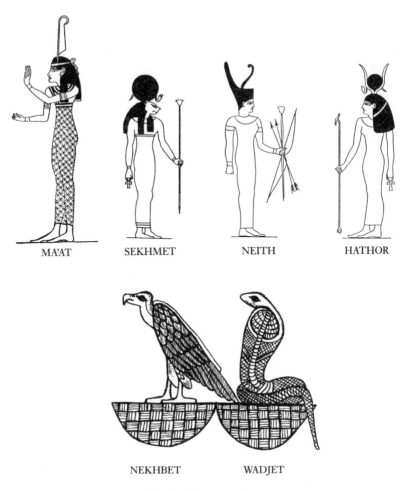

MA'AT   SEKHMET   NEITH   HATHOR

NEKHBET   WADJET

Fig. 4 Various Goddesses

no earth on which to rest, when no plant grew. She first appeared as a divine cow but changed to a Lates-fish [Nile perch] as being more suitable to the watery environment and went on her way.

First she created light, from her eyes, then she said this place where I am, it shall become for me a platform of earth supported upon the primeval waters upon which I may rest. And it was so. And this was Esna and also Sais. Neith took flight from here to the house of the gods which was at Buto/Dep, the house of the goddess Wadjet. So far everything that she thought had been realized straight away and she meditated on what was to happen next. And the next to emerge was the land of Egypt and this was born in gladness. She then created the thirty gods by pronouncing their names . . .

The name of these gods was Khemenu from the city of the eight. Then

the divine cow [Neith] called in a loud voice to all that she had created
and they came with open arms and smiles on their faces but Re, who could
not see her, wept and men sprang from the tears in his eyes. And the gods
rested in their shrines and guarded Re in his place, his cabin on the solar
boat. While at the same time as Re was born, Apopi, was created, a serpent
120 cubits long, for good must always be balance by evil, and Apopi was
the core of the revolt against Re.

(SAUNERON, 1962, PP. 253–65)

The birth of Re marked the beginning of the civil year.

HATHOR

Another powerful goddess was Hathor, 'the Golden One'. She was the 'Lady of
Dendera' where she has a temple that survives to this day, although she was
worshipped throughout Egypt. She was a sky and a cow goddess. One suspects that
she had early origins as her horns in the early representations are often those of an
antelope, as opposed to being bovine. She acted as nurse to the king and when the
Greeks arrived, she was identified with Aphrodite with whom in fact she had little
resemblance, being more like the Near Eastern mother goddesses. Officially, she was
paired off with Horus but he had a separate temple at Edfu. Their child was either
little Horus or Ihy, the god of music, at Edfu or Dendera respectively.

Hathor had many aspects, one as a goddess of the dead, particularly in Western
Thebes where she is shown as a cow emerging from the hillside above the tombs.
Mainly, however, she is represented as a woman with cow horns on her head and
a golden disc between the horns. Ritual music was important in her worship and
the sistrum, a sort of rattle made of metal, was her symbol. This is still used within
the Christian Church in Ethiopia to ward off evil spirits. Hathor was the most popular
of the afterworld deities and is portrayed in all the royal tombs. She has another
aspect representing the fates who can foretell a child's future at its birth. There were
seven forms of these Hathors known by special names, such as 'You from the Land
of Silence'.

Hathor was also a strong fertility figure. Even today Egyptians who are barren
come from miles away to her temple to jump over certain figures such as Bes,
protector of children, and to pass their hands over figures of the goddess Hathor
and Horus carved in the crypts.

ISIS

Isis, the wife of Osiris and mother of young Horus, is probably the most important
of Egyptian goddesses. She is known as the Mistress of Magic and Speaker of Spells.
This is made very clear in the story of 'How Isis obtained the Secret Name of Re',
when she caused the god to be bitten by a scorpion who had been fashioned by her
from earth and the god's spittle. As the scorpion was made of the divine essence
of the god, no remedies against its poison could prevail and Re suffered agonies until
finally he was forced to reveal his secret name to Isis, who thus obtained power over
him.

Isis appears as the perfect wife and mother, and when her husband was murdered by his brother, Seth, who was jealous of his good works, she hunted for his dead body. This involved her in a long journey throughout the length and breadth of Egypt, asking the children if they had seen Osiris's coffin, as she knew that children would notice such things. Her search took her to Byblos, on the coast of Phoenicia. There, the coffin had been washed ashore, and a tamarisk tree, realizing the coffin contained a god, wrapped its trunk around it to protect him.

As Osiris was a fertility god, the tree grew to a gigantic size, and was noticed by the king of Byblos, who ordered it to be cut down and placed in the hall of his palace to support the roof. Isis, still searching, disguised herself as a middle-aged woman, and became nursemaid to the ailing prince of Byblos. Thus she found the tamarisk pillar containing the coffin of Osiris. Her efforts to cure the child were frustrated by the queen, so Isis returned to her true form and the king and queen, in alarm, offered her anything she wanted. She asked for the pillar and so was able to take back the coffin to Egypt. On her return she placed the coffin under a bush while she went to see her son, the young Horus, whom she had left in the care of the goddess Wadjet. Seth, out hunting by moonlight, came upon the coffin and recognizing it, opened it and tore the body of Osiris into sixteen pieces, and scattered them throughout the land, saying, 'I have done the impossible, I have destroyed a god.' Isis had to begin her search all over again, and every time she found a piece of the body she built a shrine over it. Meanwhile, the young Horus was bitten by a scorpion, sent by Seth, and only survived with the help of Thoth, the god of wisdom, scribes and the moon.

Isis played an important part in ensuring that her son, Horus, received his rightful inheritance. Seth and Horus had many battles over which one should succeed to the throne of Egypt after the death of Osiris. The battles were known as 'The Contendings of Horus and Seth' (Seton-Williams, 1988). Their quarrel was put before a court, consisting of the nine gods of Heliopolis, presided over by Re-Harakhte, who favoured Seth. The god Thoth was scribe of the court, and he favoured Horus.

The nine gods could not decide one way or the other, and were always swayed by the last witness they heard. According to a papyrus (Chester Beatty papyrus No. I), the case had already been going on for over eighty years, with Isis intervening when necessary, when eventually Seth refused to plead if Isis were present. Re-Harakhte arranged to hold the court on an island in the middle of the Nile, and instructed the ferryman not to allow Isis to cross over. In order to be present in court, Isis disguised herself as an old woman and bribed the ferryman with bread and a gold ring, saying she was taking flour to her son who was herding cattle on the island. Once across, and determined to eliminate Seth from the contest, she turned herself into a beautiful young woman. Seth, on seeing her, immediately fell in love. Isis told him she was the widow of a cattle herder and wanted his help as a foreigner was trying to deprive her son of the cattle he had inherited from his father. Seth said that this was wrong and that a son should have his father's inheritance. Thereupon, Isis said Seth had condemned himself out of his own mouth. Even so, the court was still undecided, and the case was finally settled by Osiris, threatening to send his dog-headed messengers of death from the afterworld to destroy the nine gods. Thus Horus was given the throne of Egypt, and Seth wept when he found he was defeated.

As the mother of Horus, Isis became the symbolic Mother of the Egyptian King, who was known as the living Horus. Her worship and that of the child Horus posed the biggest obstacle to the advancement of Christianity because of her murdered husband and the belief in his resurrection, and the appeal of the small boy. She had shrines all over Egypt; in Roman times her worship spread to Europe, and she had a temple near London Bridge. Isis's worship was not suppressed until the fourth century AD when her temple at Philae was destroyed and her priests murdered.

BASTET

Bastet, the cat goddess, was an important goddess in the late period, that is the last thousand years BC. Her shrine was at Bubastis, in the Eastern Delta. Originally a lion goddess, of whom there were several in Egypt, by the sixth century BC she had become entirely feline, and it is to her that the many bronze cats seen in museums are dedicated.

LION GODDESSES

There were many lion goddesses in various parts of Egypt. Tefnut is shown in this form, as is Sekhmet. These cults were established when lions freely roamed in the Egyptian hills and deserts. Sekhmet was a lion goddess associated with Middle Egypt, hunting in the Western Desert; she is mentioned in the *Pyramid Texts*, and was worshipped at Beni Hasan. She is referred to as 'the night huntress with the sharp claws'. Mekhit, another lion goddess, was paired with Onuris, a hunter and a warrior god. Nafdet was a panther goddess who was particularly effective against snakes and scorpions.

Mut, the consort of Amun at Thebes, where she replaces his original wife Amunet, was both a lioness and a warrior goddess. She had her own temple in Ishru, a suburb of Thebes, and is often shown as a woman with a lion mask; otherwise she appears as a woman, wearing the queen's vulture head-dress and a brightly-coloured linen garment, and carrying the lily sceptre of the South.

SNAKE GODDESSES

There were many other female deities in Egypt, so many in fact that it would be impossible to list them all. For instance, in addition to Wadjet (*see* above, Section I, p. 24), there were many other snake deities. One of these was Meretseger, cobra goddess of the peak overlooking the Valley of the Kings. Her name meant 'she who loves silence', and she was particularly worshipped by the workmen in the village at Deir el-Medina, who were engaged on building the royal tombs. She was thought to afflict those who displeased her with blindness or some other misfortune, and many pleas for her clemency are found in inscriptions of the XIXth and XXth Dynasties. Her popularity waned with the XXIth Dynasty when the royal burial ground at Thebes fell into disuse.

Another snake goddess was Renenutet, a protector of the king and of the harvest. Her worship first appears in the Pyramid Age, where as the king's protector she doubles with Wadjet and protects the king on his way to the sky. She is popular as a harvest goddess in the XVIIIth Dynasty, where she appears often in officials' tombs on the West Bank at Thebes, as in the case of Kah'emhet (Tomb Chapel No. 57), royal scribe and overseer of the Granaries of Upper and Lower Egypt at the time of Amenhotep III. Here the goddess is shown suckling the king as a child. Later she is also connected with human destiny. In the Ptolemaic Period, Renenutet becomes absorbed by a goddess called Thermouthis, and is finally assimilated with Isis. She is frequently shown as a woman with a cobra on her head. One of her many tasks was to ensure the constant fertility of the Egyptian soil; the king is often shown offering her the first fruits of the harvest.

Towards the end of the Pharaonic period, with the move towards monotheism, the goddesses tended to merge one into another. Thus Isis and Hathor became one, and all the other female divinities became different aspects of the one divine female — the perfect wife, protector and intercessor!

SECTION III

Goddesses of Childbirth

There were two classes of popular deities, those dealing with birth and those dealing with death. The goddesses of childbirth were particularly esteemed and much worshipped by the common people. Meskhenet was one of these; her symbol was a tile, representing the bricks on which women in Ancient Egypt squatted to give birth. She is shown as a woman with two loops over a vertical stroke, thought to be the bicornate uterus of a heifer, on her head. She ensures the safe delivery of the child by acting as a sacred midwife, and she also has a say in the destiny of the child. Like Hathor, she is sometimes found (as at Esna) in a plural form, assisting Khnum with the destiny and protection of children. She also has a role in the Hall of Judgement when the dead person's heart is weighed on the scales against the feather of Ma'at (truth).

Another goddess of childbirth is Taweret, the hippopotamus goddess, also a protectress. She was in fact a composite figure with the head of a hippopotamus, the legs and arms of a lion, the tail of a crocodile and drooping human breasts. She was a great favourite with the Egyptian peasants, and a large number of amulets have been found showing her important protective role; these faience amulets were in great demand for pregnant women. Vases were moulded in her shape and filled with milk which poured out through her nipples, thus giving the milk a magic property. A very old deity, Taweret appears first in the Old Kingdom, but she was equally popular in the later periods, right up to Roman times. She also had a cosmic aspect, as her name 'Mistress of the Horizon' indicates, and in this form she is represented on the astronomical ceiling of the burial chamber in the tomb of Seti I (1318–1304 BC).

Accompanying Meskhenet and Taweret was Bes, also a protector of children. Usually shown as a dwarf in a plumed crown, either naked or wearing a short kilt or a panther skin, he not only looked after ordinary women in childbirth, but his role extended to the royal family, and he appears on the foot-board of Tutankhamun's bed. At the end of Egyptian history, his worship spread through much of the Roman Empire and he was shown dressed as a Roman legionary.

All these deities, and Isis, appear in the Westcar Papyrus, dating to the XIIth Dynasty, when the wife of the priest of Re is assisted by the divinities during the birth of her male triplets, the future kings of the Vth Dynasty. For their help, the divine assistants were paid in grain which was left in the priest's storeroom; the divinities buried their musical instruments in the sacks of grain and these played of their own accord, thus drawing attention to the divine intervention at the birth. A servant girl, who was going to report these marvels to the king, fortuitously fell into a canal where she was eaten by a crocodile, thus saving the children from being killed by the king, fearing that their birth threatened the succession of his own children. This is an early reference to divine parenthood.

The placenta was, and still is, highly regarded in Egypt. The king's placenta was one of the royal standards, carried in a leather bag on a pole, and shown on temple walls during the royal processions.

Goddesses of the Afterworld

The goddesses concerned with death and burial were equally important. There were four, Isis, Nephthys, Neith and Serkhet. They looked after the jars that contained the viscera after the embalming, which were in the immediate care of the four sons of Horus. The great goddess Nut also helped with the dead. Although primarily a sky goddess, already mentioned in the Heliopolitan creation legend, she had another role: she prevented the forces of chaos from breaking out through the sky, and so engulfing the world. In some myths she swallowed the sun god Re in his boat at sunset and he passed through her body to re-emerge at dawn. In her funerary aspect, she sometimes appears as a divine cow, spangled with stars, the night sky or as a woman represented on the lid of the coffin of the deceased to protect them. Generally, in this form she is a protective goddess: in the Inner Shrine of Tutankhamun, she is shown thus, and is also very popular on coffins of later dynasties. To Tutankhamun she says:

My son Osiris, King, Lord of the Lands, Neb-Keperu-Re, thou art happy, thou art strong, thou art victorious, there happens to be no evil to thy limbs, thou livest eternally.

(PIANKOFF, 1955, P. 142)

SECTION IV

Ancient Egyptian Stories

In ancient Egyptian stories, we move out of the realm of pure myth and closer to reality. There are, however, still traces of magic: the gods constantly intervene − not always on the right side − but there is a greater tendency towards normality. In the tale of 'The Two Brothers', for instance, from XIXth Dynasty, the beautiful woman created by the gods to keep one of the brothers, Bata, company appeared to be an Egyptian version of the Greek Pandora, and it seems that the Egyptian gods were no more capable than the Greek gods of making a beautiful woman with a soul and a conscience. She disobeyed Bata by bathing in the river, and enticing Hapi, the Nile god, and later, after Bata's death, she continually tried to destroy his soul. No wonder she died a 'sharp death', as foretold by the Seven Hathors at her creation.

The 'Scorpions of Isis' (really a spell for expelling scorpion bites) tells how Isis neutralized the bites of her seven scorpions after they had attacked the child of a woman at Per-Swi who had refused food and shelter to the goddess. This is meant to show the power of Isis.

In 'The Princess of Bekhten', the princess plays a rather passive part, in that she is only possessed by an evil spirit, and its expulsion is the reason for the tale. It is probably from the Ptolemaic period, and the stele on which it was written was found in the temple of Khonsu, at Thebes − although it may not have originated there.

Perhaps the most extraordinary of Egyptian tales is that of 'Helen in Egypt', told by Herodotus, in Book II. Here, Paris is said to have been blown by adverse winds to the Canopic mouth of the Nile, on his way back to Troy with Helen. Helen, who appears already to have become disenchanted with Paris, takes refuge in the temple of Aphrodite (the 'Strange Hathor'), and the Egyptian gods send a *ka*, the double of Helen, to Troy instead. This story is well known to modern Greek poets, such as George Seferis who alludes to it in his poem 'Helen'.

Many years later, when Menelaus was returning from Troy, after the fall of the city, he was also blown off course and became wrecked in Egypt. He took refuge in one of the temples and there learnt that Helen was lodged nearby in the temple of the 'Strange Hathor'. He met her and together they made a plan for escape. The old king of Egypt, who had befriended Helen, had died, and his successor wished to marry her because she was reputed to be the most beautiful woman in the world. She had always refused him, on the grounds that she did not know whether her husband was alive. So she arranged that Menelaus should pretend to bring news of his own death at Troy and that she, Helen, would agree to marry the king.

First certain funeral rites for the dead would have to be carried out, for which she must have wine for offerings, a bull for sacrifice, and a ship to take her and Menelaus beyond Egyptian territorial waters, to the open sea, where the offerings could take place. All this the king agreed to do, and a ship was made ready for Helen and Menelaus with a Greek crew. After embarking they sailed out of sight of land, threw overboard the Egyptian officials and sailed for Greece. This is a tale in which

Helen is undoubtedly the heroine (Seton-Williams, 1988, pp. 100–2).

The story, however, in which a woman comes out by far the best is that of 'The Doomed Prince'. The prince married a Syrian princess. This woman was very determined and original. First she refused to obey her father when he wished to marry her off to another prince instead of the Egyptian prince of her choice. Then one night on the journey back to Egypt she killed a serpent, who was one of her husband's fates, when it came into the tent to bite him. Once they arrived in Egypt she saved the prince from a crocodile, his second fate, through her knowledge of simples. However, finally she and the prince were killed by robbers on their way to Thebes, and their resting place was betrayed by their dog's bark. The moral of this story is that you cannot escape your fate, especially if it is foretold by the Seven Hathors, as was the case here (Seton-Williams, 1988, pp. 70–3).

In many of the Egyptian stories, the woman seems to take a more reasonable view than the man, and is more aware of the dangers that may ensue if a certain course is pursued. The story of 'Satni-Khamose and the Mummies' is one of these. Ptolemaic in date, there are several versions written on papyri to be found in the Cairo Museum. Satni-Khamose was looking for the Book of Thoth which was supposed to contain all the wisdom in the world. He was told that the book was in the tomb of Nefer-ka-Ptah, in the cemetery at Saqqara. When he arrived there, Ahura, who is the wife of Nefer-ka-Ptah, described to Satni-Khamose all the misfortunes that had befallen her husband and herself while the book had been in their possession. Unfortunately, he took no notice, with the result that he underwent equally unfortunate experiences, which could have been avoided had he followed her advice (Seton-Williams, 1988, pp. 82–8).

SECTION V

Reality: The History

The position of women in Ancient Egypt was in many ways unique. They enjoyed a peculiar position in that all landed property descended through the female line, from mother to daughter. The entail in the female line seems to have been fairly strictly adhered to, particularly in the case of the royal family. The practical result of this was that the husband enjoyed the property as long as his wife was alive, but on her death, her daughter and her daughter's husband came into possession. To avoid this loss of power on the death of the main royal heiress, the king then married anyone else who could be considered the next royal heiress, in order to assure his own position. This was done irrespective of the age of the royal heiress, and is why sometimes kings married their own daughters, as in the case of Ramesses II. The royal pattern does not seem to have mirrored the general behaviour of the freemen of Egypt. The king had one principal wife, the Great Royal Heiress, who would have royal ancestors on both the mother's and father's side, and in addition, secondary wives and concubines.

The position of these women was very clearly defined. Whereas the principal queen wore the vulture head-dress and so sometimes the *uraeus*, the secondary queens wore a gazelle insignia attached to a golden circlet on their heads. Sometimes these were single gazelle heads, at other times they were double; one even had four heads. As Cyril Aldred has pointed out (Aldred, 1971, pp. 204–6), the term 'gazelle' signified, at Ugrarit in northern Syria, young princes or princesses; these symbols may have been introduced first in foreign jewellery, brought in by minor foreign wives. Some crowns had stags rather than gazelles; stags were not indigenous to Egypt but were listed among the Syrian tribute in the XVIIIth Dynasty lists. It is interesting to note that queens in the Old Kingdom do not seem to have had an especial head-dress or worn a crown: this is noticeable in the tomb of Meres-Ankh at Giza. It was not until the Middle Kingdom that royal insignia seems to have come in – for example, the princess Sit-Hathor-Yunet's jewellery was found at Lahun and she wore a gold circlet with a *uraeus* insignia.

Not only did the descent pass through the female line but women had the right to inherit the throne if there was no male heir. This was laid down in the IInd Dynasty by the third king, but it was only confirming an already existing custom: in the Ist Dynasty, one woman at least, Mer-Neith, ruled as king. It seems that the line of succession to the throne established from the Ist Dynasty was transmitted through the principal queen, who was usually called 'She Who Unites the Two Realms'. The pattern of descent through the female line and the linking of the different dynasties, through the royal heiress, is first clearly distinguishable in the IIIrd Dynasty, where Queen Nyma'athap was the wife of Khasekhemwy, last king of the IInd Dynasty, and the mother of Netjerykhet Djoser, second king of the IIIrd Dynasty. Queen Nyma'athap was obviously highly regarded and her cult at Saqqara was carried on for some time after her death.

It is not known exactly why the Egyptian rulers were divided into dynasties. This was so in ancient times, as stated in Manetho, a priest who wrote an account of Egyptian history. The linking figure between the dynasties seems to have been the royal heiress, who carried the blood royal from one dynasty to another. However, our information for the early dynasties is very scanty, and it is only in the XVIIIth Dynasty that many of the queen's titles are explained. No attempt was made by the ancient Egyptians to explain changes of dynasty. Queen Kentkawes serves as a link between Dynasties IV and V. She seems to have been a daughter of Menkhare. Shepseskaf, last king of the IVth Dynasty, who only reigned about four years, died in 2494 BC. He had no heir and his funerary rites were performed for him by his wife, Queen Bunefer, according to the inscriptions found in her tomb. Kentkawes seems to have taken office after Shepseskaf: her titles read 'King of Upper and Lower Egypt'. She may have held this position briefly and married Userkaf, first king of the Vth Dynasty. She was buried in an extraordinary building near the causeway of Mekhaure, sometimes called the Unfinished Pyramid, at Giza – it is really a sarcophagus-shaped construction, rather than a pyramid.

There is not another case of a queen ruling alone until the XIIth Dynasty, when the last ruler of the dynasty was Sobkkare Sobknefru, who reigned for three years from 1789–1786 BC. She was the sister of Amenenhat IV, and presumably came to the throne as there was no male heir. In the Labyrinth at Hawara, her name occurs almost as often as that of her father, according to Petrie (Petrie, 1911). She was undoubtedly the royal heiress and her titles leave no doubt that she was ruling Egypt. Thus she was called 'The Horus beloved of Re', 'The Living Beloved of Sobek', 'The Royal Daughter', 'The Lady of the Two Lands', 'The Established One who Rises as the Golden Horus' (one of the five titles of the king) and 'The King of the South and North'. Little is known of her reign beside her building works in the Faiyum.

From the Middle Kingdom the queens assumed the title 'Divine Wife' which was included in the preamble to their names and implied the rank of chief high-priestess of Amun.

At no period in Egyptian history were women more prominent than in the XVIIIth Dynasty. It was during this period that the queen's royal titles seem to have been finally established. The royal heiress and hereditary queen bore as her natural right all the royal titles of the Royal Daughter, the Royal Sister, the Great Royal Wife, the Lady of the Two Lands, and the Hereditary Princess. They also bore the title 'Divine Wife' which was changed early in the XVIIIth Dynasty to 'God's Wife of Amun'. The title 'Mistress or Lady of the Two Lands' was not originally a royal title, as it was used in the XIth and XIIth Dynasties for some of the wives of *nomearchs*, but in this case they were daughters of a 'Ha' prince and may have been royal princesses, though this is uncertain. This title was found in Tomb Chapel No. 2, that of Amenenhat, the *nomearch* of the Oryx Nome whose wife Hotep was a priestess of Hathor and of Pacht.

In the beginning of the XVIIIth Dynasty, sometimes called the New Kingdom, three royal queens played particular parts. These were Tetisheri, Ahotpe and Ahmose-Nefertiry. It was these three women that set the tone for the XVIIIth Dynasty and doubtless influenced the ambitions and behaviour of Hatshepsut (*see* below). Tetisheri appears not to have been of royal parentage, but as the wife of Seqenenre Tao I and the mother of Seqenenre II and of his wife Ahotpe, she is regarded as the foundress of the XVIIIth Dynasty and was especially honoured as such in the founding years of this conquering line. She had a long life, surviving her husband, her son and one of her grandsons, Kamose. She died full of honours in the reign of her other grandson Amosis. A stele found in her chapel at Abydos explains how he, Amosis, wished to honour her by erecting, in addition to her tomb and cenotaph, a pyramid and chapel at Abydos equipped with land and staff. She also had a memorial at Memphis, the northern capital.

Another remarkable woman was the mother of Amosis, Ahotpe, who seems to have taken over from Tetisheri as the principal Egyptian queen before the advent of Ahmose-Nefertiry. She was buried with great care by Amosis and it is possible that at one time she may have ruled as co-regent with him. In this situation, she seems to have succeeded in putting down a rebellion at least once and played a part in guarding Egypt's frontiers.

The last of these great queens was Ahmose-Nefertiry. She was the Great Royal Heiress and of royal blood on both sides. She seems to have been the daughter of Kamose and a half-sister of Amosis whom she married. Her name is found frequently inscribed on the Egyptian frontiers of Nubia and Sinai. In one of the Karnak inscriptions she is referred to with her husband, Amosis, and her son, Ahmose-Ankh, making a presentation to Amun-Re. On this stele Ahmose-Nefertiry is shown as the same size as the king, a sure sign of her importance. She is styled on contemporary monuments as 'royal daughter, royal sister, royal mother, divine wife of Amun, Mistress of the Two Lands, Great Ruler joined to the "Beautiful White Crown" ', which probably means that she was the heiress of the South Land. On the death of her husband in 1546 BC, Ahmose-Nefertiry seems to have ruled jointly with her son Amenhotep I and shared with him a mortuary temple. Her coffin was found at Deir el-Bahri but unfortunately her mummy was never scientifically examined. She became a cult figure for the workmen in the royal necropolis and as such was worshipped at Deir el-Medina. She is shown in many of the tomb chapels along with the gods and goddesses of the dead, like Osiris and Hathor.

Amenhotep I married Aahotepe II, Ahmose-Nefertiry's daughter and hence the Royal Heiress, and Aahmes, who was also the Great Royal Heiress, was their daughter. She in turn married Tuthmosis I who was not in the direct line of succession, so owed his accession to his wife's position. Tuthmosis had a daughter, Hatshepsut, by Aahmes and a son, Tuthmosis II, by his second wife, Mut-Nefert. It is not clear who Mut-Nefert's mother was — probably she was one of the secondary wives of Amenhotep I and not of royal blood. Tuthmosis II and Hatshepsut were married but he died after about six years. He always seems to have been sickly — so much so that Tuthmosis I decided to associate Hatshepsut with himself in a co-regency and to make her his heir. He held a coronation ceremony for her before he died, according to inscriptions at Deir el-Bahri and Karnak.

In some cases, where there was doubt about the legitimacy of a ruler or where the mother was not the royal heiress, attempts to overcome the problem were made by claiming that the father was really Amun who had 'come' to the queen disguised as her husband. Hatshepsut made this claim in her temple of Deir el-Bahri where Amun is shown visiting her mother Aahmes. Both are seated on a couch supported in the air by two goddesses so that the meeting would be between heaven and earth. This was not the only time divine parentage was claimed by a ruler; it happened also in the case of Amenhotep III whose mother was Queen Mutemua, a Mitannian princess, and again by Nectanebo of the XXth Dynasty.

Tuthmosis I died about six months after Hatshepsut's co-regency/coronation ceremony. Throughout the reign of her husband Tuthmosis II, she seems to have been the dominant force and bore all the formal titles of a princess and queen. Tuthmosis I had left a second son who was to become Tuthmosis III but he was a minor — his mother Queen Esi (or Isis) was a non-royal wife and therefore he did not have as much claim to the throne as Hatshepsut. On the death of Tuthmosis II, Tuthmosis III was proclaimed king with Hatshepsut acting as regent. However, in the second year of Tuthmosis III's reign, the god Amun is said to have confronted Hatshepsut in public when she was visiting his temple of Ipetisut at Thebes and he proclaimed her King of the Two Lands and had her crowned in the chapel of Ma'at at Karnak. This act is recorded on an unpublished stele of the queen found at Karnak.

Tuthmosis III was married off to Hatshepsut's surviving daughter Meryt-Re; her eldest dauther had died in around 1493 BC. Hatshepsut took the titles: Female Horus Wosretkau; the King of Upper and Lower Egypt Makare Hatshepsut; the Daughter of Re; and Khnum-et-Amun Hatshepsut. Although in a later monument Hatshepsut is formally called king, the term queen was still often used of her.

As pointed out by Redford, many historians state that Hatshepsut's reign was a peaceful one (Redford, 1967, p. 57), but in 1957 Habachi published a text from the island of Sehel which provides evidence of a campaign of Hatshepsut's in Nubia, described by one Tiy who accompanied her on the campaign:

> I followed the good god, the king of Upper and Lower Egypt Makare [Hatshepsut], may she live, when he overthrew the Nubian bowmen, and when their chiefs were brought to him as living captives . . .
>
> (HABACHI, 1957 PP. 99ff)

This implies that Hatshepsut was present at the bringing of the captive chiefs of Nubia so she must have been at the battle, as the spoils of war were always divided at once. Habachi thought that there was a war in the south early in the reign of Hatshepsut and that the queen was present at the battle. Redford points out that there is a scene at the Deir el-Bahri temple of the Nubian god Dedwan, leading captive Nubians to the queen (Naville, 1908, VI, pl. 152). There is also an inscription on the Lower Colonnade at Deir el-Bahri referring to Hatshepsut's Nubian campaign and comparing it to that of her father. The occasion of her campaign was a Nubian plot which may have involved an attack upon one of the Egyptian frontier fortresses.

There is less evidence to support her carrying out an Asiatic campaign, although some does exist. In one of her texts, mutilated by Tuthmosis III at Deir el-Bahri, it is said that her arrow is shot among the Northerners (Syrians) (Naville, 1908, VI, pl. 167), and in another inscription it says, 'You shall seize the chiefs of Retenu by force . . . and you shall take captive men by thousands for work on your temple lands' (Urk, p. 248).

This evidence shows clearly that Hatshepsut did fight at least two campaigns, one in the north and another in the south, and that in both cases she personally led the army and was present in the field. Yet the general view of Hatshepsut's reign is that she occupied herself with peaceful pursuits, such as her expedition to Punt in search of incense and sandalwood, and the building of her temple masterpiece at Deir el-Bahri. This is largely the result of the anti-Hatshepsut views held by American Egyptologists – the most notable of whom were Wilson and Hayes (Wilson, 1951, pp. 174ff). Hayes definitely states, 'in the absence of any military activity Hatshepsut's expedition to Punt and the quarrying and transport of her two pairs of Karnak obelisks stand out among the major achievements of her reign' (Hayes, 1973, p. 19).

Hatshepsut's building enterprises were not her only contributions to architecture. She developed, for the first time, a school of royal sculpture, she moved two obelisks, ninety-seven-and-a-half feet high, from Aswan to Karnak, she reopened the Sinai turquoise mines, and rebuilt the temple at Serabit el-Khadim in Sinai and the Speos of Artemis at Beni Hasan, as well as her own temple. Hatshepsut reigned for twenty-one years and during this time her famous architect, Senenmut, acted not only in this capacity but as steward of the land and tutor to her children. He was probably leader of the powerful clique of officials who helped to keep the queen in position. Senenmut died before the queen; in fact there is no mention of him after year sixteen of her reign and after the queen's death his two tombs were despoiled. The queen died apparently on the twentieth day of the sixth month in the twenty-second year of her reign. There is no evidence that she was murdered or that her passing was anything but peaceful.

At first Tuthmosis III does not appear to have defaced her monuments; it was only later in his reign that this took place. Tuthmosis built his second mortuary temple behind that of Hatshepsut at Deir el-Bahri and robbed her mortuary temple of much of its stone to use in his structure. Redford puts this down to expediency rather than the king's hatred for his predecessor. Hatshepsut seems to have left Tuthmosis a free hand in his military career and this was what really interested him. Redford regards Hatshepsut's reign as a strong-minded woman's attempt to impose a matriarchal system upon the choice of rulers in the XVIIIth Dynasty but that she was thwarted in this idea by the premature death of her daughters and the lack of other strong-willed female candidates.

There were, however, several remarkable women who were queens towards the end of the XVIIIth Dynasty. The first was Queen Tiy who married Amenhotep III, either just before he ascended the throne or soon after. She had a very powerful personality and influenced Amenhotep in many ways as she was not only his wife but also his close advisor. She was not of royal blood but was the daughter of Yuya, an Egyptian priest of Min, at Panopolis. His wife, Tuyu, was one of the royal nurses and Mistress of the Robes, as well as being a Chantress of Amun.

They had a tomb in the Valley of the Kings (No. 46), an unusual privilege for commoners. There seems no doubt of the strong influence Tiy had on her husband: she is shown closely associated with the king on his monuments, and on his scarabs. A temple was built for her at Sedeinga, and she acted as regent for her son during his minority. That she was known to be the power behind the throne is shown by letters addressed to her by Tushratta, the king of Mitanni. She was buried with her husband, Amenhotep, in the Western Valley at Thebes but her body was removed and turned up in the tomb of Amenhotep II (No. 35), among a cache of unidentified mummies.

In his attempt to legitimize his rule, Amenhotep also claimed that his mother, Mutamua, was united with Amun in the guise of Tuthmosis IV. These scenes were shown both in the temple at Luxor and in one of the temples he erected at the shrine of Mut in Ashur, a suburb of Karnak. In order to strengthen his position he married Sit-Amun, who is often stated to be his daughter by Queen Tiy, but was more probably his half-sister, daughter of Tuthmosis IV and Queen Iaret, who was the Great Royal Heiress. There is no doubt that she married Amenhotep and was called the Great Royal Wife, which indicated her status. She may have died young, as the only pictures we have of her are as a child.

The parentage of Queen Nefertiti, wife of Amenhotep IV/Akhenaton, is uncertain. It has been suggested that she belonged to the family of Queen Tiy, but this seems unlikely as her physiognomy appears entirely different, as is her bone structure. The chances are that she is another royal heiress, as she assumes very independent attitudes on the scenes in the temple reliefs from Karnak, early in Akhenaten's co-regency with his father. Here Nefertiti is shown, in the majority of the scenes, serving alone in the temple without her husband. In some cases, her name appears with two cartouches as though she were a king when she was making offerings. The king is seldom present which is most unusual. In certain cases, she is shown in the king's role, slaying the *Nine Bows* of Egypt.

In these scenes on the temple walls, she wears a variety of head-dresses – the disc with horns topped by feathers is probably the most common – but she always has the *uraeus* on her forehead. The arrangement of the royal name and divine name on the tablets indicates the deity served and who was the royal celebrant. As a result of the study made by Redford (Redford, 1976, p. 82), he decided that the majority of the buildings constructed at Karnak by Akhenaten were for the queen to carry out various cult practices. Nefertiti's titles include 'Mistress of Upper and Lower Egypt', 'Great King's Wife' and 'His Beloved Lady of the Two Lands', but nowhere is she referred to as the 'Great Royal Heiress'.

At Akhetaten (el-Amarna), Nefertiti also appears in an unusual role; she has a royal barge with her head represented on the prow and stern. This evidence came from Hermopolis (el-Ashmunein) and must be from late in Akhenaten's seventeen-year reign. The queen is also shown occasionally in a masculine role as a sphinx trampling the enemies of Egypt, or as a victorious ruler smiting the enemy – a role usually reserved for the king. Personally I cannot subscribe to the theory recently put forward that Nefertiti and Semenkhare, Tutankhamun's elder brother, were one and the same person.

Tutankhamun, the last legitimate king of the XVIIIth Dynasty, married young his cousin, Ankhesen-Paaten, later called Ankhesenamun, the daughter of Akhenaten and Nefertiti. After the death of Tutankhamun, Ankhesenamun wrote to Shuppililiumas, the Hittite king, requesting him to send one of his sons to Egypt as her husband was dead and she could not bear to marry a commoner. A Hittite prince was sent, but he was murdered soon after crossing the Egyptian frontier. Ankhesenamun was then married off to 'the divine father Ay', brother of Queen Tiy, then an old man, old enough to be Ankhesenamun's father. He only reigned two to three years and was succeeded by General Horemheb whose chief wife was a Queen Tiy, as shown in his tomb in the Western Valley at Thebes, but he also seems to have married Nezem-Mut, probably a sister of Nefertiti, through whom he claimed the right to the throne. As he was the last king of the XVIIIth Dynasty, it will be seen that right up to the end of the dynasty the ruling queens played an important part in the succession to the throne.

Unusually, there appears to have been no linking queen as the royal heiress, joining and legalizing the position of the XIXth Dynasty. There may have been a link through Tua'a, the wife of Seti I, to whom her son, Ramesses II, was devoted, and who seems to have been regarded, in some way, as the ancestress of the dynasty. Tua'a was particularly important for the first twenty or so years of Ramesses's reign. She exchanged letters with the Hittite royal family, and when she died she was buried in a splendid tomb in the Valley of the Queens.

Ramesses II married one of his younger sisters, Henmire, who may have been regarded as the Royal Heiress, but his principal wife, for the early years of his reign, was Nefertari. She is shown often with the king, and a temple in her honour, and that of Hathor, was erected at Abu Simbel in Nubia, near the temple of Ramesses. She seems to have died about the time Ramesses consecrated the temples at Abu Simbel, for Ramesses is shown accompanied by his eldest daughter, Princess Meryet-Amun. After the death of Nefertari, the place of principal queen appears to have been taken by Queen Istnofert, but she too was dead by year thirty-four of Ramesses's reign, and her position was taken by Princess, now Queen, Bint-Anath, who was her daughter, with Queen Meryet-Amun occupying second place. Although Nefertari had a son he did not live to ascend the throne owing to Ramesses's long life, and the succession passed to a son of Istnofert, Merneptah.

The next queen of note is Tausert, who seems to have been the Royal Heiress, and claimed to rule jointly with her father, Seti II, as had Hatshepsut. On his death, she reigned, in association with her younger brother, Siptah, for about eight years. Her tomb and temple were both unfinished, suggesting perhaps that she came to a violent end.

The most remarkable office for royal princesses was that of Divine Votresses of Amun. In 1085 BC, during the XXIst Dynasty, the throne passed from the last of the Ramesside princes to the High Priest of Amun, in the person of Herihor, the High Priestesses became the Divine Votresses and assumed both temporal and spiritual power at Thebes. Here the succession passed not from mother to daughter but from aunt to niece – the aunt adopting the niece in each case. This sequence ran unbroken from 870 BC until 525 BC, when it was ended by the Persian invasion; and during the period the Votresses reigned almost unchecked at Thebes. A shrine to several of them stands in the forecourt of Ramesses III's temple on the West Bank at Thebes.

However, the last of the Egyptian queens, Cleopatra VII Philopater was undoubtedly one of the greatest and it is perhaps fitting that the history of independent Egypt as such should end with a queen – Egypt became incorporated into the Roman Empire in 30 BC. It is very difficult to achieve a true picture of Cleopatra. There are no portraits, though she was said to be beautiful. Much of our information comes from Plutarch and he did not take a favourable view of her. She was an extremely able and ambitious woman; she was well-educated, the only Ptolemy who knew and wrote Egyptian. It is unlikely that Cleopatra loved either Caesar or Anthony but she needed an able general to fulfil her ambitions for a return to Egypt's greatness. She came to the throne at about the age of 17 or 18 and took as co-ruler her younger brother, Ptolemy. The two did not get on and shortly afterwards the boy drowned in Lake Mareotis, at the time when Caesar defeated the army of Achillas who was aspiring to make Ptolemy the sole ruler of Egypt.

Cleopatra never married Caesar. He was already married to Calpurnia and Roman law only allowed one wife. Cleopatra was his mistress and bore him a son whom she called Ptolemy Caesar, but who is remembered as Caesarion. After this she went to Rome to try and persuade Caesar to carry out her plans for a greater Egypt. She failed in this, and was still in Rome with her other brother, also Ptolemy, when Caesar was murdered. Soon after she returned to Egypt and her second brother died or was killed in Alexandria. She found the finances of Egypt in a poor state, but like all the Ptolemies, she was a good administrator and in a short time she had reorganized the country and got it on a sound economic basis. Meanwhile, she nominated her son Caesarion to rule jointly with her but as he was an infant this meant in effect that she had sole rulership.

In the meantime the Roman world was split; the Triumvirate led by Octavian (later Augustus) defeated and killed the main conspirators who had murdered Caesar at Philippi in northern Greece. Octavian and Anthony proceeded to divide the Roman Empire between them – the eastern part fell to Anthony. Cleopatra failed to congratulate Anthony on his victory, although she had supported him against Cassius by sending two legions to Syria to assist his governor, Dolabella. Anthony therefore summoned Cleopatra to Tarsus, and in 41 BC she met him there. She captivated him as she had Caesar and in 37 BC they married in Antioch. Unfortunately, Anthony, though a brilliant general, was lazy and pleasure-loving, and life in Alexandria suited him far more than life in the field. Cleopatra wanted the return of territory in Syria which had belonged to Egypt at the time of the Egyptian Empire.

While Cleopatra was inspecting her newly acquired land in Jordan, given to her by Anthony, he was losing his Parthian campaign, which he had arranged in too much of a hurry. His shattered army was, to a certain extent, restored by Cleopatra, who met the army on its return. Additional supplies and troops were brought to Athens by Octavia, Octavian's sister, whom Anthony had married on his previous visit to Rome. Anthony was thus a bigamist, and his marriage to Cleopatra was invalid. Whether this was known to Octavia we do not know, but Anthony ordered her back to Italy, thus severing his ties with Rome. His behaviour caused a breach with Octavian, who declared war on Cleopatra, in an effort to separate her from Anthony. This failed but eventually led to the disastrous battle of Actium, where Cleopatra, who had insisted on accompanying Anthony, withdrew the Egyptian ships after the first skirmish, leaving Anthony's forces outnumbered and Octavian victorious.

After Actium, Anthony and Cleopatra fled to Egypt and offered up no further resistance. In 30 BC when Octavian arrived in Alexandria, Anthony committed suicide, followed by Cleopatra. After their deaths, Egypt was annexed as an Imperial Province of the Roman Empire. Thus independent Egyptian history ended with Cleopatra's life.

Acknowledgements
I would like to thank Angela Godfrey and Carey Miller for their drawings of Egyptian goddesses.

References and Further Reading

Aldred, C. (1971), *The Jewels of the Pharaohs* (London: Thames and Hudson)

Backman, A.M. (1921), 'The Position of Women in the Egyptian Hierarchy' in *Journal of Egyptian Archaeology*, VII, p. 8ff

Erman, A. (1927), *The Literature of the Ancient Egyptians* (London: Methuen)

de Garis Davies, N. (1903–8), *The Rock Tombs of el-Amarna*, Archaeological Survey of Egypt, 13–18 (London: Egypt Exploration Fund)

Hart, G. (1986), *A Dictionary of Egyptian Gods and Goddesses* (London: Routledge and Kegan Paul)

Hayes, W.C. (1973), *Cambridge Ancient History* (Cambridge: Cambridge University Press)

Hornung, E. (1903), *Conceptions of God in Ancient Egypt* (London: Routledge and Kegan Paul)

Kaster, J. (1960), *The Literature and Mythology of Ancient Egypt* (Harmondsworth: Penguin)

Lefebvre, G. (1949), *Romans et Contes Egyptiens de l'Epoque Pharaonique* (Paris: Librairie d'Amerique et d'Orient Adrien-Maisonneuvre)

Lichteim, M. (1973–80), *Ancient Egyptian Literature*, 3 vols, (Berkeley: University of California Press)

Lurker, M. (1980), *The Gods and Symbols of Ancient Egypt* (London: Thames and Hudson)

Manetho (1956), *Aegyptiaca*, Loeb edition (London: Heinemann)

Maspero, G. (1915), *Popular Stories of Ancient Egypt* (London: G.P. Putman and Sons)

Naville, E. (1908), *The Temple of Deir el Bahari*, 6 vols (London: Egypt Exploration Fund)

Petrie, W.M.F. (1915), *Egyptian Tales*, 2 vols (London: Methuen)

Piankoff, A. (1955), *The Shrines of Tutankhamun* (New York: Bollingen Press)

Pritchard, J. (1950), *Ancient Near Eastern Texts* (Princeton: Princeton University Press)

Redford, D.B. (1967), *History and Chronology of the Eighteenth Dynasty* (Toronto: Toronto University Press)

—— (1976), *The Akhenaten Temple Project* (London: Aris and Phillips)

Rundle Clark, R.J. (1959), *Myth and Symbol in Ancient Egypt* (London: Thames and Hudson)

Sauneron, S. (1962), *Les Fêtes Religieuses d'Esna aux derniers Siècles du Paganisme* (Cairo: Publications de l'institut française d'archèologie orientale d'Esna 5)

Seton-Williams, M.V. (1988), *Egyptian Legends and Stories* (London: Rubicon Press)

Wilson, J. (1951), *The Burden of Egypt* (Chicago: Chicago University Press)

Glossary

Afterworld: There were various views of the afterworld. The earliest required the provision of food and drink in the desert tombs in order to enable the dead to regain life. In the Old Kingdom, the Osirian view was imposed on earlier beliefs: this envisaged an afterworld divided into compartments, rather like the Nomes of Egypt, and a judgement of the dead person, overlooked by Osiris, in either the sixth or seventh division. If the soul passed the test, it ended up in the Fields of Yalu, which seems to be an improved version of this world. In the version according to Re, the deceased accompanied Re on his nightly journey in his boat through the afterworld, and Re became the Judge of the Dead, instead of Osiris.

Ben-bird: A bird which in the Fifth Dynasty was associated with the *Ben House* or House of the Sun, at Heliopolis. The Egyptians thought this was the grey heron (*ardea cinera*), which had a long straight beak and a head with a double crest. It was worshipped at Heliopolis, where it was seen alighting in the willows and skimming over the water. It was associated with the emergence of the world from Chaos. When it reappeared each year, flying over the river, it was regarded as a fortunate sign. The Greeks equated the Egyptian heron to the phoenix, a fabulous Arabian bird, worshipped in Egypt and said to live for hundreds of years. It finally burned itself to death and rose again from the ashes of the fire.

Ben House: The Temple of the Sun at Heliopolis.

Ben Stone: An early obelisk connected with sun worship.

Ha prince: One of the titles of a *nomearch*.

Ihy: God of Music, particularly connected with the sistrum, shown as a naked boy.

Ka: The double of a human being, born when it is born and dying with the human. It is to the ka that all offerings are made. Represented by two raised human arms. Also an aspect of the soul.

Kakadi: A red fruit, which is infused like tea into a hot drink or served iced.

Kepherer: A form of the Sun God, shown as a dung beetle pushing the sun over the horizon at sunrise. He is the God of the Dawn.

Nine bows: The traditional enemies of Egypt, i.e. the Libyans, the Syrians and the Nubians. Shown usually as captives in threes with their arms bound behind them. They were depicted on the bases of statues or on footstools – anywhere the king might place his feet upon them.

Nome: Greek word, meaning a district. Introduced under the Ptolemies to define the provinces or Sepats. It has been retained by Egyptologists to mean districts. There were thirty-eight or thirty-nine districts in the Old Kingdom.

Nomearch: Governor of a nome. Originally it meant 'He who digs the canals'.

Primeval mound: The mound that first appeared when the Nile flood waters went down. Sometimes referred to as a hillock or as a sandy island.

Reed and Papyrus: The titulary plants of Upper and Lower Egypt.

Serekh: Rectangular frame, probably representing the facade of the palace, on which the Horus Name, the first of the king's five titles, was written.

Uraeus: The cobra worn on the king's crown or head-dress, representing the female serpent guarding the king. A Latinized form of the Egyptian term *uralos*.

ATHALYA BRENNER

The Hebrew God and
His Female Complements

THE GENDER OF THE HEBREW GOD

At the dawn of religion, so Merlin Stone writes, God was a woman (Stone, 1976, p. 17). Not so the Hebrew god, though. The Hebrew god's gender, from the very beginning as documented in the Hebrew Bible (known as the Old Testament), was always male/masculine (M).

It would be a mistake to attribute this gender definition of the Hebrew divine being to the restrictive usage of the Hebrew language alone. Indeed, Hebrew has no grammatical neuter (N) class, no equivalent of the English 'it'. Thus every animate as well as inanimate entity, abstract concept or concrete phenomenon, has to be grammatically gendered as either M or F (female/feminine). The linguistic practice of relating to the divine through M terminology seems like a matter of choice and world view. Yhwh[1] is not simply a male. This is at first difficult to comprehend, given his lack of physical characteristics beyond metaphor, a lack reinforced by the severe — albeit sometimes transgressed — command not to supply him with plastic representation (cf. the first commandment, Exodus 20.2–4). He is a male nevertheless, and a specific kind of male at that. He is rational and intellectual; hence he creates the cosmos and its contents by speech acts, that is, through language (Genesis 1.1–2.4a). At least according to the mainstream of the biblical canon, he is omniscient, omnipotent, immanent. The question of his morality and justice, the so-called 'theodicy', is not easily settled (Crenshaw, 1983): sometimes, as in the Book of Job or Ecclesiastes, his moral constitution seems questionable. He undoubtedly has his dark side, as well as a graceful and loving side (Exodus 20.5–6, 34.6–7; Jonah 4.2). But, first and foremost, he is a paternal figure.

God is primarily depicted as a (single) M parent, cast and stereotyped from the outset as the Great Father. In the Garden of Eden narrative (Genesis 2.4b–3.24) he is a father who exiles his rebellious children, Adam and Eve, from the original homestead after they have eaten from the forbidden tree of knowledge. He makes explicit his fear that, if not expelled, they will resemble him in divinity (3.22), that is, knowledge and unlimited life. Throughout the Eden story he maintains an

Fig. 5 Lucas Cranach, *The Garden of Eden* (1530). The Hebrew God as father. God is clearly depicted as an authoritative if benevolent patriarch, royally dressed in purple, wagging a warning finger at his naked children, the man and the woman. *Courtesy of Kunsthistorisches Museum, Vienna*

authoritative if benevolent stance: his commands are precisely that – inexplicable but to be obeyed. All humanity but particularly the Hebrews (Amos 9.7; Hosea 11.2) and later King David and his dynasty are his 'sons'.

Humankind, M and F together, is created in god's image (Genesis 1.26–8).[2] Does that actually mean that the Hebrew god embodies both M and F principles, and that he is genderless or bi-gendered? We shall see that this is perhaps intended in places, but infrequently so. At any rate, humankind's destiny is immediately set at the time of its inception: to control the world, much the same as males are to control females (Genesis 3.16), and as fathers their inferiors (women, minors, slaves – everyone). The model for this societal image is obvious. A patriarch in the pre-monarchical biblical period was like a god – his was the right to judge and even condemn to death (see the Tamar and Judah story, Genesis 38). In short, thus man creates his god in his father's image through the statement that god created man in his divine image.

From a psychological perspective, god-as-father corresponds to Freud's analysis of the beginning of religion in the eventual deification of ancestral (M, mainly) spirits, and to Rudolf Otto's attribution of religious sentiments primarily to horror/fear of the holy. The identification of the Father idea with intellect, rational behaviour, justice and control – considered self-evident by orthodox religious and theological systems, and also twentieth century M psychology and psychotherapy – seems to inform the biblical texts too.

A sociological perspective should be considered also. Literature is often reflexive of social attitudes, mores and norms. It is not far-fetched to expect the social realities of the patriarchal order to be reflected in the design of the biblical construction known as the Hebrew god. *Contra* the revisionist feminists who attempt to salvage the Hebrew god for their faith, Christian and Jewish alike (and cf., for instance, Trible, 1973), it should be said emphatically that the Hebrew god was never a woman, was never even fully metaphorized as a woman (but *see* below, p. 59). Nor was he ever, on the whole, a womanly male. Therefore, it is difficult to relate to him – a common feminist practice – as S/HE.

To what extent does the assigning of an M gender to a communal god illustrate the social inferiority of women in that same community? This is a separate issue which, strictly speaking, lies outside the scope of the present discussion. We shall, however, briefly return to it later.

Yhwh is the Supreme (Single) Father, but That Does Not Conceal a Lack

A legitimate way of looking at the M parent-child relationship between Yhwh and his children is to pronounce it a failure in myth as well as in history (Clines, 1990).

In the origin myth (Genesis 1–11), the relationship deteriorates rapidly and steadily. The woman initiates the eating of the fruit, hence the human couple is made to depart from the Garden. The first murder, a fratricide, soon follows the birth of Cain and Hebel (Genesis 4). A brief erotic encounter between the sons of god (who are they anyhow?) and the daughters of man (6) threatens to bring together heaven and earth, earlier drawn asunder by god himself (1). Humanity's morals become so evil that god decides to destroy his children by a flood (6–8). And what happens to the family chosen to survive? No sooner is Noah saved than he starts a vine culture and gets drunk; and two of his sons either show disrespect by looking at his nakedness or, as some of the Jewish sages interpret this passage in their commentaries, castrate him (9). Then humanity attempts to consolidate by building a city and tower, so as to stay together and speak one language. This, once more, is a threat to the divine plan. God frustrates it (11) and scatters his children further afield.

God now concentrates on Abraham's family (12 onwards), calling to him to leave his homestead and go to a new, divinely appointed land: this, of course, is a replay in reverse of the expulsion from the original Garden. But does the new beginning, so promising since Abraham obeys without hesitation, signify an end to the chain of disappointments? Not so. Soon after entry to the land, Abraham has to leave it because of a famine. His wife is in danger of being violated by a foreign king (12; and cf. the two other versions of the story, 20 and 26). He has no son to inherit the divine promises liberally bestowed upon him. When he has two sons, Yitzhak and Yishmael, Sarah makes him send the firstborn away (21). Jacob steals the inheritance rights from his older brother, Esau, and has to leave the land for many years (25 onwards). Later Joseph is sold to Egypt (37 onwards) and the brothers follow him there. Through strife, trickery and dishonesty, the promised land again is evacuated by its presumed inheritors for many years.

After a prolonged sojourn in Egypt, Yhwh sends Moses to deliver the Hebrews back to their land. He saves them from bondage by inflicting plagues upon the Egyptians and parting the Sea of Reeds for them (Exodus 1–15). He reveals himself at Sinai and gives them the Ten Commandments and the Law, formalized as a political treaty binding both sides to one another (19-24). He protects, feeds and guides his children, the Children of Israel. What does Yhwh get in return? Crises. Complaints. A golden calf (32). Rebellions. Incidents of fear, lack of trust and disobedience recur throughout the Books of Numbers and Deuteronomy too. The necessary corrective measure yet again is, as in the case of the Primeval flood, extinction. The people are sentenced to roam the desert for a formulaic period of forty years. The desert generation has to die before a new beginning is embarked upon (once more!).

The remaining Books of the historiography of Israel and Judah until the destruction of the First Temple and Jerusalem in 586 BCE* (Joshua, Judges, Samuel and Kings) are informed by the same vision of failure and disappointment. The Israelites keep turning away from their god, to whom they are supposedly bound orthogenetically as well as by a legal covenant. He tries to save them from the consequences of their own folly by sending intermediaries – judges, leaders, prophets, kings – but to no avail. Finally, and against his will, he has to punish them by taking away both political organization and territory. They have to go into exile.

The second historiographical cycle (the Books of Chronicles, Ezra and Nehemiah) takes us through the Restoration of Jerusalem and the Temple into the fifth century BCE. In it, as well as in contemporary prophetic works (Isaiah 40–66, for instance), the exile is understood as a period of re-education for the erring Children and the tone is, in general, more optimistic. Nonetheless, is the rehabilitation programme considered wholly successful? Only partially so, as the various transgressions of the Law reported in Ezra and Nehemiah show. The Book of Daniel, the last and latest chapters of which refer to the very last years before the Hasmonaean revolt against the Hellenizing Syrian king, Antiochus Epiphanes (at the beginning of the second century BCE), ends with a message similar to its predecessors. Only a few, the chosen ones, will survive the forthcoming political and religious tribulations. Thus the biblical history concludes with a message of hope but, once more, hope underlined by human anxiety of divine disappointment.

It thus seems that that M parent-and-child model which informs the origin myth continues to operate in history. This, by and large, is the societal model operative in the Bible as a literary paradigm. While individual passages or stories may advance

---

*BCE = Before Common Era = BC; CE = Common Era = AD. This usage does not privilege the birth of Christ over other events in world history (*Editor's note*).

a different message, the overall framing ideology is conditioned by the pressing need to exonerate Yhwh of his apparent periodic abandonments of his Children. Rather than destroy the father image (as sons do, either metaphorically and symbolically or figuratively, in many pagan myths), biblical writers and editors opted for an ethos of human responsibility: the sons are blamed for their own bad fortunes, while the fatherhead's theodicy remains intact.

In Lacan's terms, the psychological and cultural construct 'Father' is perceived by his children as the supreme phallic symbol. It is easier, perhaps, to plead recurrent instances of collective non-integrity than to demolish an ideal. However, three observations seem to be in order at this point:

a) It is difficult if not impossible, within the process of education and socialization, to draw a demarcation line between the failure of a child and that of the parent, or their respective burdens of mutual responsibility. The process is one of mutuality, as is its outcome.

b) One cannot help but wonder whether the singularity of the divine parent, and the insistence on his M (justice and morality as prerequisites for love, in so many instances) attributes in his dealings with his children, is not at least one of the reasons for the continuous mutual failure of both partners throughout myth and history.

c) Other solutions in the Hebrew Bible present the Hebrew god in alternative images than that of an ultimately fair Father with errant sons. Broadly speaking, these images fall into two main categories. The first supplies Yhwh with types of F consorts; the second supplies him with F attributes. It remains to be seen to what extent each of these categories is successful in removing the blame from Yhwh. Both categories, though, illustrate an admission of the problematics involved in the divine lack of an overt F element, and also the need to fill this lack.

Human Sexuality and Divine Sexuality: Matters of Fertility and F Principles
It is well established that the Israelites were familiar with various cults practised in the land that eventually became theirs. Moreover and dialectically, they assimilated elements of those cults into their own. The Book of Deuteronomy and the related editorial framework of the Books of Kings make it abundantly clear, through their heated and frequent polemics, that the fertility aspects of the so-called 'Canaanite' rites were too attractive for the Israelites and Judahites to ignore. During one period at least (that of Jezebel and Athaliah in the first half of the ninth century BCE; and see 1 Kings 17 to 2 Kings 10), the cult of Baal and his female consort — called Asherah — became the official state cult in the Northern as well as Southern Kingdoms, alongside that of Yhwh. As late as the beginning of the sixth century BCE, just before the destruction of Jerusalem, a passage in the Book of Jeremiah (7.17–18) asks and answers:

> Do you not see what they are doing in the cities of Judah and in the streets
> of Jerusalem? The children gather wood, the fathers kindle fire, and the

women knead dough, to make cakes for the queen of heaven; and they pour drink offerings to other gods, to make me angry.

In other words, Jeremiah (or whoever wrote in his name) is able to relate the worship of the queen of heaven as an eyewitness. He knows that the cult is a widely practised family cult, in which the women are dominant (see also Jeremiah 44.15–30) and which is considered one of the reasons for Yhwh's wrath. As Carroll says:

> An idyllic picture of egalitarian religion with a strong emphasis on the family worshipping together! The cakes have impressed on them the image of the queen of heaven, the mother goddess of the ancient world [as Jeremiah 44.19 tells us], or they may be cakes in the shape of a star ...
>
> (CARROLL, 1986, PP. 212–13; SEE ALSO PP. 734–43)

Who is this 'queen of heaven'? Carroll rightly maintains that her precise name – the Babylonian Ishtar, the Canaanite Anat or Astarte, the Egyptian Isis – is less than important. All the names point to the same cultural manifestation of a great mother goddess. Significantly, the people claim that her worship is a condition for peace and economic prosperity (44.16–19). Jeremiah, of course, is indignant: Yhwh's anger is provoked by this cult. In his view, that of a bitter unmarried messenger of god, the goddess cult ultimately helped bring about the destruction of temple, city and land.

A few points are worth noting here. It appears that as late as the sixth century BCE the cult of the mother goddess was popular even in Jerusalem, the supposed stronghold of Yhwh's exclusive worship. Therefore, although it constitutes an unwanted 'subculture' for the biblical author of the passage, it should not automatically be labelled as such by the modern reader. Furthermore, it seems that this cult flourished – and significantly, as a family cult – in times of political and economic stress. In such times, people, especially women, turned back from the official cult of the divine Hebrew Father to the divine Mother in the quest for maternal love and assistance. It follows that the accusations voiced by the literary 'Jeremiah' have a sound basis in the reality of his day. The Father's disappointment, so it seems, is mirrored by the disappointment of his 'daughters'. Ironically, the information concerning this muted (minority?) view of the 'daughters' is preserved by the (patriarchal) Yhwh opposition.

The narrators of the Hebrew Bible, who were mostly males narrating for M consumption, often accuse women of turning to pagan religious practices. And when the women are of foreign descent the accusation becomes stereotypic. Such an approach is a useful ideological device, since it makes women the chief culprits in the drama of divine disappointment. For instance, the religious influence of Solomon's many foreign wives is cited as a factor justifying the division of the United Israelite Kingdom immediately upon Solomon's death (1 Kings 11.1–13). Almost half a millennium later, in the age of Ezra and Nehemiah (mid-fifth century BCE), foreign wives and mothers are divorced for their cultural and religious influence on the newly reorganized Jewish community. In other words the usual societal, political and economic rationale for exogamy/endogamy (see Levi-Strauss, 1963, and his overview of his positions, 1983, pp. 39–97; in English translation) becomes secondary to the ideology of the Father, which must be safeguarded against F religiosity and devotion to alternative cults.

It appears that the cult of the great goddess was celebrated all over the ancient Near East. Its hallmarks were the dominance of the F divine element, symbolized by the earth. The female deity stood for both fertility and sexuality: she was lover and mother combined, but did not enact the inferior role of a daughter. Her M consort, on the other hand, started his career by being her son, lover and husband rolled into one. He died periodically, sometimes because of her wrath, while she reigned eternal. Later on (who knows when?) the tables were turned: the M consort became the chief fertility/sexuality symbol through his recurring resurrection, perhaps an imitation of the seasonal fertility cycle; and the goddess became his demoted consort (Neumann, 1955).

It is important to realize that, whatever the internal gender dominance might be, so-called pagan pantheons from the third millennium bce onwards were organized in F/M couples. Imitative fertility rites of the *hieros gamos* (sacred marriage) type – a dramatically enacted 'marriage' of a priestess and a priest, a king and the goddess's priestess, a commoner and a priestess, a F commoner and a M priest (*see* Iris Furlong's contribution to this volume) – were an integral part of Mediterranean culture and known as such to the Hebrews, who finally defined themselves as Israelites and Judahites. Sexual intercourse undertaken under the auspices of a religious sanctuary, designed at least in part as 'white' magic to encourage fertility in the biological and human cosmos, could not fail to be attractive. The prophets, from Hosea (mid-eighth century bce) onwards, acknowledge this attraction indignantly enough. They demote the practice to no more than prostitution, fornication and adultery. However, surprisingly, they put the pagan reality which surrounded them and which, by their own testimony, was practised by their compatriots, to a fresh literary use. They incorporated it into their own metaphorical/symbolical world, thus supplying Yhwh with his lack: the missing F consort.

God the Husband: Love, Marriage and Covenant in the Prophetic Books

The beginning (chapters 1–3) of the Book of Hosea is the earliest passage to contain the new metaphor. The relationship between Yhwh and his people, formalized in the Torah (Pentateuch) in terms of a binding covenant, is metaphorized in terms of a marriage situation. God is depicted as a steadfast, supportive, responsible and loving husband. The Israelites are his adulterous, promiscuous, childish wife. There is no doubt that the scenario is a takeoff of fertility rites: the 'woman's illicit "lovers"' – in the plural! – are named *ba'alim* after Baal, the Canaanite male god of storm and rain (= the fertilizer of the earth); the prophet himself illustrates the marriage principle by taking 'a woman of harlotry', that is, a woman who has participated in those rites, for a wife (1); and women are accused of participating in that cult freely, with the knowledge of their male kin (4.13).

In Chapters 2 and 3 we learn how a change can be effected. The woman-nation is clearly in need of re-education. First, a divorce by the divine husband (in the Hebrew Bible only the husband can initiate a divorce, or legally accuse a wife of adultery); then, a period of isolation and training. Then, and only then, will the woman-nation be worthy again of the divine husband's honourable intentions and he will remarry her.

The same metaphor is employed in the Book of Jeremiah, which refers to a period over a hundred years later. The roles have not changed. On the contrary: they have become further polarized through the exaggerated imaging of the 'wife'. The woman-nation (Judah, in fact, since the Northern Kingdom was destroyed by the Assyrians in 722 BCE), once more in danger of being divorced (3), is even likened to a she-ass on heat (2). Ezekiel, some time later, engages in a synthesis. Yhwh is both foster father and husband to the woman-Jerusalem; she, once grown, is no more than a common whore who commits religious and political adultery (16). The description, as well as that of the twin-sisters Jerusalem and Samaria in chapter 23, is extremely pornographic (van Dijk, forthcoming).

Only after the destruction of Jerusalem and the exile do we get different versions of the same metaphor. Now, after the punishment has been carried out, Yhwh promises to reinstate his 'wife' as mother and spouse in his/her land (Isaiah 49.14–23, 50.1–3 and 17–23, 54, 62.4–5, 66.7–13; within the context of Isaiah 49–66 the image of god-as-father is as frequent as that of god-as-husband).

What can be gleaned from the continuing literary life of the divine husband/human spouse convention? The attribution of (metaphorical) matrimony to Yhwh was probably facilitated not only by his exclusivity but also by his pronounced maleness (which implies a lack and a need for an F complement). The tendency to preserve Yhwh's divine reputation of justice and fairness operates here as in the divine father metaphor. And last but not least, the convention reflects societies in which an androcentric ethos, world view and vision are the norms. The negative F imagery consistently applied to the 'erring' people becomes progressively more extravagant until, with Ezekiel, it achieves vulgar misogynistic proportions. It is designed to humble, to intimidate. It reflects the reality of gender relations in an M world in which F sexuality is the Other, fatally attractive to males and because of that degraded and deemed in need of M control (Setel, 1985).

The Theological Quest for a Female Consort: The Song of Songs

Within the Hebrew Bible, the Song of Songs is unique. It is an anthology of secular (non-matrimonial) love lyrics, erotic and outspoken. Although the poetic material incorporated in it is varied and has no plot (in spite of many readers' attempts to find one) it has a well-organized structure (Exum, 1973) which is probably due – like other features of the Book – to the editor's or editors' efforts. One of the outstanding features of the collection is the predominance of the F voice(s) in it. Most of the lyrics assume the form of monologues and dialogues, and most of these are spoken by an F 'I'. Furthermore, those F voices compare favourably with their M counterparts. They are direct, outspoken, loving, loyal, steadfast, imaginative, enterprising. The M lovers are weak by comparison. No jealousy, no treachery, no accusations are admitted into the lovers' garden. There is no mention of a 'father's house' or a father figure, as against fairly frequent references to a 'mother's house' and mothers. The imagery employed by the M voices in regard to the F love objects is strong, positive, beautiful. In short, egalitarian mutuality and gender equality – with a bias in favour of the F partners – underlie the literary picture.

There may be many reasons for this unusual picture of gender roles in love and sexuality. The most feasible explanation is the attribution of the Song of Songs, as a literary collection, to F authorship or editorship (Brenner, 1989). This is probably less far-fetched that it seems at first, since love poetry is culturally tolerated for women even in patriarchal societies. What is most relevant to our agenda here, though, is not the biblical Song of Songs *per se* but, rather, the theological-allegorical exegesis attached to it by the orthodox Jewish and then Christian establishments from ancient times on.

Post-biblical Jewish interpretation coped with the uniquely secular nature of the Song of Songs and its apparent incompatibility with the rest of the Hebrew canon by promoting its allegorical interpretation as the only legitimate one. In the allegory, first hinted at in a text of the first century CE, the M lover is once more the Hebrew God and the F lover his nation. In contradistinction to the previous love stories and disappointments, this allegorized 'story' is a happy affair in which mood, traditional role and outcome are inverted. The nation-woman now actively and loyally seeks her master; other partners are out of the question. This allegory was taken over by the Christian Church as well: here the partners are Jesus and the church/community (the Christological approach) or Mary and the community (the Mariological approach). Such traditional interpretations of the Book, claiming to decipher its original meaning through the negation of its profane erotic meaning, persist until today.

The religious and theological merits of such an allegorical interpretation are evident. To begin with, it chastises an unusual text and truly canonizes it. It also supplies god, finally, with a worthy loving partner. Its therapeutic value almost cancels out the harsh harangues of the (earlier) Hebrew prophets.

In passing, I would like to note that modern feminist critics share this ancient notion of the therapeutic import of the Song of Songs. Thus, for instance, Trible (1978) reads it as a counterfoil to the Garden of Eden story, a rectification of the gender relations and social F inferiority condoned there. But that, strictly speaking, is outside the scope of our discussion.

Yhwh and His Consort: Contemporaneous Extra-biblical Evidence

At the beginning of the twentieth century, documents written on papyrus in Aramaic[3] were found at Elephantine, a settlement on the small island in the Nile opposite Aswan. The documents discovered – legal, literary, religious – disclosed the existence of an organized colony of Jewish soldiers who populated the site from the beginning of the Persian rule in Egypt (525 BCE) until the beginning of the Common Era. The Jewish settlers had a local temple, were conscious of their religious identity and their priests attempted to correspond with the Jerusalem priests on religious and cultic matters (Cowley, 1923; Kraeling, 1953).

Whom did the Jews of Elephantine worship? The Hebrew god, of course, whom they called Yhw (a shorter form of Yhwh). And alongside him, in the same temple, two goddesses: Asham (probably the Ashmat of Samaria named in Amos 8.14) of Beth'el (a chief city in the northern Israelite kingdom); and Anat (a well-known Semitic goddess of love and war) of Beth'el.

Scholars have found it relatively easy to affirm that Yhw of Elephantine is Yhwh of the Hebrew Bible even though he had two(!) divine consorts. They regarded the religious practice of the place as Jewish, albeit non-normative, and excused it on various grounds. The first excuse cites populist culture:

> The Elephantine Jews brought with them to Egypt the popular religion combatted by the early prophets and by Jeremiah shortly before the destruction of the First Temple. It is true that this religion placed the God of Judah, Yahu . . . in the centre of the faith and worship . . .
>
> (SCHALIT, 1972, P. 608)

Other scholars cite geographical distance and lack of communication with the prescriptive, normative Judaism of Second Temple Jerusalem, and/or assimilation to the foreign (pagan) environment. However, more recent archaeological finds in the land of Israel itself invalidate such apologies.

A Hebrew inscription on a broken storage jar, found in Kuntillet 'Ajrud in north-eastern Sinai and dated from the beginning of the eighth century BCE, has three primitive figures: a standing male figure in the foreground; a female figure just behind him; and a seated musician in the background. The Hebrew inscription above the drawing reads: 'I bless you by Yhwh of Samaria and his Asherah' (Dever, 1984; King, 1989). Furthermore, a tomb inscription from el-Qom in Judea, dated to the eighth century BCE too, concludes with the words: 'to Yhwh and his Asherah' (Margalit, 1989, 1990 and further references there).

Asherah, like Anat, is a well-documented goddess of the north-west Semitic pantheon. We remember that, according to the Bible itself, in the ninth century BCE Asherah was officially worshipped in Israel; her cult was matronized by Jezebel who, supposedly, imported it from her native Phoenician homeland. Other traces in the Bible either angrily acknowledge her worship as goddess (2 Kings 14.13, for instance, where another royal lady is involved), or else demote her from goddess to a sacred tree or pole set up near an altar (2 Kings 13.6, 17.16; Deuteronomy 16.21 and more). The apparent need for the hostile and widely distributed polemics against her worship constitutes evidence for its continued popularity. Linguistically, Margalit claims (1989), 'Asherah' signifies '[she] who walks behind', displaying a prototypic if divine attitude that befits a wife (and is reflected in the Kuntillet 'Ajrud drawing). Thus both the partially suppressed and distorted biblical evidence and the archaeological evidence combine to suggest one conclusion. The cult of a goddess,

Fig. 6 The drawing and inscription from Kuntillet 'Ajrud, c. 800 BCE. The Hewbrew god as husband. The crowned figure to the right and partially behind the one in the foreground appears to be that of a female consort: the arms of the two are locked, spouse-like; and the F figure is smaller. The inscription identifies them as Yhwh and his Asherah. *Courtesy of Institute of Archaeology, Tel Aviv University*

considered the spouse of Yhwh, was celebrated throughout the First Temple era in the land; and beyond this period and the land by the Jewish settlement in Elephantine.

Readers and critics of the Hebrew Bible tend to balk at the idea that Yhwh, the traces of canonical testimony notwithstanding, in fact had a divine consort in biblical times and well into the Second Temple era. They explain away the husband-wife imagery as 'mere metaphor', as if metaphors are 'no more than cool reason' (Lakoff and Turner, 1989). But this is not so. The prophets' polemic appears to have been based on first-hand knowledge of the religious practice prevalent in their day. As hard as they and others fought to promote pure (M) monotheism, popular F cult continued to flourish. And in that cult, the unnatural deficiency of the Father god was supplemented by coupling him with a borrowed goddess figure. The archaeological finds bear the most valuable witness to this phenomenon since, unlike the biblical texts, they are not tendentious.

Finally, scholarly attempts to dismiss a consort status for Asherah in the Kuntillet 'Ajrud and el-Qom inscriptions, which are motivated by the same purist ideology to be found in the Bible itself, have been conclusively repudiated by Margalit (1990) and others. The need for an F complement was felt, the gap filled. Traditionalist protestations can no more obliterate Yhwh's divine consort from the history of biblical religion, even if the Bible itself promotes her rejection with tell-tale vehemence. R. Patai's much criticized book, *The Hebrew Goddess*, should therefore be revalued in the light of recent discoveries.

There are perhaps other traces in the Hebrew Bible for a divine F consort.[4] At this point, however, we shall turn to ancient biblical exegesis of another kind.

Beyond the Hebrew Bible: The Female Principles of the Shekinah and the Sabbath
Jewish mysticism does of course relate to the Hebrew Bible as to a canon and base text. Since Jewish mystical texts date from the first century CE on, they constitute another type of testimony for ancient Bible interpretation. And lest we think that mysticism is esoteric only, one should remember that esoteric it may be, but it is theosophical too. And, at any rate, it has pervaded Jewish life and customs more and more over the ages.

The language of Jewish mysticism is erotic language. The mystic's attempts to come closer to divine phenomena through the *Sefirot* ('stages') are depicted in sexual terminology (as well as in language of light/darkness, letters and numbers). It is therefore not too startling to find, among the imaginative literature of the *Qabbalah* (mysticism), some fresh treatments of Yhwh's F complements. These hark back to biblical notions which are further developed, and with a twist. We shall name two such cases by way of illustrating this point.

According to the Bible, the immanence (Hebrew *kabod*) of god 'dwells' (Hebrew *shakan*) in certain parts of the world and among his people. Post-biblical Judaism developed the concept of 'immanence' and that of god's *Shekinah*, his 'dwelling', alongside it. In the *Qabbalah*, the *Shekinah* is the F element of the *Sefirot*, the first of ten such 'stages'. The mystic's ultimate purpose is to recover god's oneness through the reunification of his M and F elements – the oneness that was damaged by Israel's sins and other factors.

Another divine spouse is the sabbath. In sixteenth-century Safed, a great Qabbalic centre, the sabbath was hailed as 'The Queen' (one of the Hebrew god's appellations would translate as 'The king of the Royal Kings'!). The custom of reciting the Song of Songs for the sabbath became more and more widespread. Another poem cited for it was the biblical passage praising 'the woman (actually, wife) of valour' (Proverbs 31.10–22). In time, the view of the sabbath's matrimonial status spread beyond mystical circles.

YHWH AS MOTHER

God the father is the norm in the Hebrew Bible. An additional partial list of passages referring to his paternal attributes includes the following: Deuteronomy 32.6, 2 Samuel 7.14, Isaiah 63.16 and 64.7, Jeremiah 3.4, 19 and 31.8, Malachi 1.6, Psalms 103.13 and three occurrences in Chronicles (Gruber, 1983, 1985). Nevertheless, in some instances he is likened to a woman and, specifically, woman-as-mother. The F images attributed to Yhwh are infrequent but distributed throughout the Hebrew Bible. They occur in the Torah (Numbers 11.12: see Trible, 1973, p. 32; and against her interpretation, Gruber 1985, p. 77), the psalms (Psalms 123.2), in the prophets (Hosea 11: see Schuengel-Straumann, 1986), but mainly in Isaiah 40–66 (Gruber).

Those chapters in the Book of Isaiah are, by scholarly consent, poems written and delivered not earlier than in the second part of the sixth century BCE, from the time of the return from the Babylonian exile.[5] In passages such as 42.13–14, 45.9–10, 49.14–15 and 66.13, Yhwh is compared to a mother and a woman in labour (Trible, Gruber). Gruber rightly states that, within these same poetic collections, the image of god-as-father features too (in 42.13, 63.16, 64.7). And he explains the sudden proliferation of positive F imagery applied to god in addition to the more traditional M imagery thus:

> Perhaps . . . the anonymous prophet understood that . . . his successors such as Jeremiah and Ezekiel had intimated that in the religion of Israel maleness is a positive value with which divinity chooses to identify itself, while femaleness is a negative value with which divinity refuses to identify itself. Perhaps, as a result of this realization our prophet deliberately made use of both masculine and feminine similes for God.
>
> (GRUBER, 1983, P. 358)

Perhaps. But, on the whole, the literary situation remains unambiguous. References to the motherhood of god, even if they are more frequent in Isaiah 40–66 than elsewhere in the Hebrew Bible, are still rare. Although their existence cannot be denied, on the other hand, it should not be overstated nor magnified out of proportion. Accrediting Yhwh with motherhood is yet another stratagem for filling the lack we have spoken about.

A more traditional formulation of the problematics involved in a one-gender representation of the divine is offered by Gruber. He concludes his discussion of the motherhood of god with the following statement:

> . . . a religion that seeks to convey the Teaching of God who is above and beyond both sexes cannot succeed to do so in a manner which implies that a positive-divine value is attached only to one of the two sexes.
>
> (GRUBER, 1983, P. 359)

A PERSONAL POSTSCRIPT

I readily admit that my reading of the Hebrew Bible is motivated by what I am: Jewish, Israeli, middle class, an academic, a female, a mother, non-religious, politically minded – in that or any other order. My emotional and intellectual sensibilities are the prisms through which I perceive and critique. And, from my perspective, gender issues in the Hebrew Bible can hardly be redeemed for feminists. Small consolations can indeed be gleaned from one specific text or another. But, on the whole, the Good Book is a predominantly M document which reflects a deeply-rooted conviction in regard to woman's Otherness and inferiority. Its M god is made to pretend most of the time and against odds that he does not really need

F company or F properties. Paradoxically, the fight itself is testimony to its futility. In spite of this small victory, the post-reading sensation I experience focuses on the bitter taste in my mouth. This is my heritage, I cannot shake it off. And it hurts.

Notes

1 There is an ancient Jewish ban on pronouncing the deity's name. Instead, in the Hebrew Bible, one is instructed always to use the appellative Adonai, approximately translated 'the Lord'. Since the exact pronunciation of Yhwh is debatable, I have here transcribed the consonants of the name without adding the vowel signs.

2 I use a lower case g for god, as I do not want to give the deity a privileged spelling.

3 Aramaic is a Semitic language akin to Hebrew. During the Persian era (mid-sixth century BCE and until the conquest of the Empire by Alexander the Great in 332 BCE) it was the international language of Jewish learning in Palestine and elsewhere, thus supplanting Hebrew.

4 In the first collection of the Book of Proverbs, 1–9, a personified figure of 'woman wisdom' appears again and again. She is often described in erotic terms, as the right 'consort' for a human male. In chapter 8 she is depicted as Yhwh's daughter; in chapter 9, as a woman with her own household. Many scholars have noted that, in both cases, the 'woman wisdom' cuts a goddess figure. Hence, they ask whether these descriptions of her do not point to her status as Yhwh's divine consort. I think that the main source for this goddess description (Proverbs 9) is too isolated to draw any firm conclusion from. The imagery appears to be derived from a human rather than divine context. And see Camp, 1985, pp.23–147.

5 Most scholars go even further, and consider chapters 49–55 and 56–66 respectively as separate literary and chronological units.

References and Further Reading

Brenner, A. (1989), *The Song of Songs*, Old Testament Guides series (Sheffield: Sheffield Academic Press)

Camp, C.V. (1985), *Wisdom and the Feminine in the Book of Proverbs* (Sheffield: Almond Press)

Carroll, R.P. (1986), *Jeremiah, A Commentary*, Old Testament Library (London: SCM Press)

Clines, D.J.A. (1990), *What Does Eve do to Help and Other Readerly Questions to the Old Testament* (Sheffield: Sheffield Academic Press), pp. 49–66, 85–105

Cowley, A. (1923), *Aramaic Papyri of the Fifth Century BC* (Oxford: Oxford University Press)

Crenshaw, J.L. (1983), *Theodicy in the Old Testament* (London: SPCK Press)

Dever, W.G. (1984), 'Asherah, Consort of Yahweh? New Evidence from Kuntillet 'Ajrud' in *Bulletin of the American Schools of Oriental Research*, 255, pp. 385–408

van Dijk, F. (forthcoming), 'The Metaphorization of Woman in Prophetic Speech: An Analysis of Ezekiel 23' in *Vetus Testamentum*, 42

Exum, J.C. (1973), 'A Literary and Structural Analysis of the Song of Songs' in *Zeitschrift für die alttestamentliche Wissenschaft*, 85, pp. 47–79

Gruber, M.I. (1983), 'The Motherhood of God in Second Isaiah' in *Revue Biblique*, 90, pp. 351–9

—— (1985), 'Female Imagery Relating to God in Second Isaiah' in *Beer Sheva*, 2, pp. 75–84 (in Hebrew)

King, P.J. (1989), 'The Great Eighth Century' in *Bible Review*, 5/4, pp. 23–33, 44

Kraeling, E.G. (1953), *The Brooklyn Museum Aramaic Papyri: New Documents of the Fifth Century from the Jewish Colony at Elephantine* (New Haven: Yale University Press)

Lakoff, G. and Turner, M. (1989), *More than Cool Reason: A Field Guide to Poetic Metaphor* (Chicago and London: University of Chicago Press)

Levi-Strauss, C. (1963), *The Savage Mind* (Chicago: University of Chicago Press) (English translation published 1966)

—— (1985), *The View from Afar* (New York: Basic Books) (original French version published 1983)

Margalit, B. (1989), 'Some Observations on the Inscription and Drawing from Khirbet el-Qom' in *Vetus Testamentum*, 39, pp. 371–8

—— (1990), 'The Meaning and Significance of Asherah' in *Vetus Testamentum*, 40, pp. 264–97

Meyers, C. (1988), *Discovering Eve* (Oxford and New York: Oxford University Press)

Neumann, E. (1955), *The Great Mother* (New York: Pantheon)

Patai R. (1967), *The Hebrew Goddess* (New York: Ktav)

Schalit, A. (1972), 'Elephantine' in *Encyclopaedia Judaica* (Jerusalem: Keter), vol. 6, pp. 604–10

Schuengel-Straumann, H. (1986), 'Gott als Mutter in Hosea 11' in *Tübinger Theologische Quartalschrift*, 166, pp. 119–34

Setel, T.D. (1985), 'Prophets and Pornography: Female Sexual Imagery in Hosea' in L.M. Russell (ed.), *Feminist Interpretations of the Bible* (Oxford: Blackwell), pp. 86–95

Stone, M. (1977), *The Paradise Papers* (London: Virago)

Trible, P. (1973), 'Depatriarchalizing in Biblical Interpretation' in *Journal of the American Academy of Religion*, 41, pp. 30–48

—— (1978), *God and the Rhetoric of Sexuality* (Philadelphia: Fortress Press)

PART 2

European

BARBARA SMITH

Greece

SECTION I:
COSMOGONY, THEOGONY AND PANTHEON

Cosmogony and Theogony

There is more than one Creation Myth in ancient Greek mythology, perhaps reflecting the syncretic nature of ancient Greek religious thought. The generally accepted version is found in the Theogony (Birth of the Gods) of the Boiotian poet, Hesiod, which itself was an attempt to rationalize the various mythic strains.

In the beginning there was Chaos (Void), then Earth (Gaia) and Heaven (Ouranos) separated. Ouranos lay with Gaia and fathered numerous children upon her. However, fearing that they would eventually usurp him, Ouranos refused to allow Gaia to give birth to her children, though he continued to lie with her and impregnate her, till she was so full that her body was groaning. In the end, Gaia gave her son, Kronos (Time), a sickle made of adamantine, which he used to cut off the offending genitals, thus freeing himself and all the other gods contained in Gaia's womb. Kronos then took Ouranos' severed genitals and flung them into the sea; drops of Ouranos' blood fell to earth, from which sprang the Furies, and from the genitals themselves was born Aphrodite, goddess of sexual love.

Kronos then took as wife his sister, Rhea, and fathered numerous children upon her. However, as each child was born Kronos would swallow them whole, fearing that they would usurp him as he had usurped his father. Rhea hid her son, Zeus, and gave Kronos a stone to swallow instead. Then she gave Zeus an emetic to administer to Kronos, forcing him to vomit up all his children. Kronos was then banished and Zeus assumed overall control, taking his sister, Hera, as wife.

Instead of being a tyrant, like his father and grandfather before him, Zeus apportioned 'shares' (*Moirai*) to each god and goddess. To his brothers, Poseidon and Hades, for example, he gave dominion over the sea and the underworld respectively, reserving the sky for himself; between them they would govern the earth. However, the Titans were not satisfied with their shares and rebelled against Zeus and the Olympians, as they were called after their home on Mount Olympos, in a battle known as the *Gigantomachy*, the Battle of the Gods and Giants, which the Olympians finally won. This overall process was known as the establishment of Zeus' *dike*, Justice, imposing order upon previous disorder, which was to end retributive justice and find a place in the cosmos for every god, human and living creature.

The Pantheon

The ancient Greeks were polytheistic and had a pantheon that was referred to as the Twelve Gods, who mainly resided on Mount Olympos; however, there were also a great many other minor deities and deities whose home was not Olympos. Those connected with the earth, rather than the sky, were called chthonic, meaning literally 'of the earth'.

THE GODS

Zeus

Called 'the father of gods and men', Zeus was married to his sister, Hera. It is thought that his name was cognate with the Indo-European sky god *Daos*, and that he was originally a mountaintop/weather god, associated with the weather in general and specifically with thunder and lightning – the thunderbolt being his main weapon. His usual sacrificial offering was a bull. Zeus was represented as a bearded, heavy-set patriarchal figure, usually throwing his thunderbolt. His Roman equivalent was Jupiter.

Poseidon

Poseidon was Zeus' brother and god of the sea and rivers. He was called 'the Earthshaker' since he was also associated with earthquakes and tidal waves. Poseidon's main sacrificial victim was also a bull, but there is extensive evidence of a horse cult dedicated to him. His iconography depicts him as similar to Zeus, except his symbol of authority was a three-pronged trident. His Roman equivalent was Neptune.

Hades

Hades was also Zeus' brother and lord of the underworld. The main myth concerning him is his abduction of Persephone, daughter of Demeter and Zeus. His Roman equivalent was Pluto.

Ares

Ares was the god of war and son of Zeus and Hera. Mortals and immortals alike feared and disliked Ares because he was so belligerent. His Roman equivalent was Mars.

Hephaistos

The divine craftsman and smith, Hephaistos was god of the volcano and anything to do with fire. He was the parthenogenetic son of Hera who, disgusted at Zeus' innumerable infidelities and paternities, decided to bear a child without male help, hence Hephaistos' usual epithet *Amphigu(n)eis*, 'with women all around or on both sides', which is always translated as 'the Limping God'. This refers to the occasion of his birth: Hera was so disgusted by the ugly child she had borne, that she flung him out of Olympos. Hephaistos fell for a very long time, eventually landing on the island of Lemnos with such force that he was lamed. His Roman equivalent was Vulcan.

Apollo

Apollo was the son of Zeus and the mortal Leto. He was god of the sun, an archer god whose arrows could bring 'plague' to humans, though he was not a god of the hunt; he was the main god of prophecy. His oracular shrine at Delphi was the most famous in the ancient world. Apollo was the divine musician, leader of the Muses, and immortal lyre-player. He was generally depicted as the epitome of youthful good looks. His usual sacrificial victim was a male kid or lamb. His Roman equivalent was known by the same name.

Dionysos

Dionysos was the son of Zeus and the mortal Semele. He was god of the vine/wine and also the god of drama. His followers were satyrs (half men, half goats) and *Mainads*, and bacchant women, named after one of his epithets Bacchus (Shout), by which name he was known to the Romans. Uniquely, Dionysos was the only immortal who had the capability of dying in order to be reborn, and was probably a vegetation or 'year' spirit in origin; he could also be seen as a god of paradox. Dionysos was usually depicted as effeminate, bisexual or homosexual, and also quite strangely was felt to be the only non-Greek god in the pantheon, thus a great many of his myths concern his attempts to establish his worship in Greece. His iconography shows a beautiful young man, bearded but not patriarchal. His symbol was the *thyrsos*, a fennel-stalk (a springy wand called a *narthex*), wreathed with ivy, and topped by a pine-cone. He is also associated with thunder through his prodigious birth (*see* below, p. 77).

Hermes

Hermes was the son of Zeus and Maia. He was the divine messenger, and also the Guide (*Psychopompos*) who would lead the souls of the reluctant dead down to the underworld. He was patron of all travellers and merchants, and of the *gymnasion*. His Roman equivalent was Mercury, and his symbols were a traveller's wide-brimmed hat, a pair of winged sandals, and a caduceus, a wand intertwined by two copulating snakes.

THE GODDESSES

Where the gods seem fairly straightforward in their spheres of influence and iconography, the goddesses are less easily differentiated. In myth, for example, there have been obvious attempts to rationalize their domains, as given below; but in ritual, the domains and biosocial roles seem to become confused.

Hera

Hera was the daughter of Rhea and Kronos, and sister-wife of Zeus. Her name is the feminine form of *hero*, and means simply 'lady', though it could also be derived from *hora*, meaning 'season'. She was amorously pursued by Zeus, whose advances she repudiated. However, Zeus turned himself into a cuckoo and nestled in her bosom, thereby seducing her. Hera's Roman equivalent was Juno.

Artemis

A 'maiden' goddess (*parthenos*), Artemis' name is thought to derive from *artamos*, meaning 'butcher' or 'slaughterer'. She was the daughter of Leto and Zeus, and the twin sister of Apollo. Some sources make her slightly older, acting as midwife to Apollo's birth, to explain why Artemis, as a virgin, was called upon by women in childbirth. She is the nature goddess, goddess of the hunt, meadows, forests and fields and the countryside generally, thus she is called Artemis *Agrotera* – 'Of the Countryside'. Many wild or semi-wild animals were both sacred and sacrificed to her, such as the bear, the deer and the goat. Her Roman equivalent was Diana.

Athena

Another maiden goddess, whose proper reference in Athens was *Parthenos Athenaia*, the Maid of Athens, often shortened to The *Parthenos*. Athena was the daughter of Zeus and Metis (Counsel), a Titaness. Zeus, forewarned by the Fates that any son Metis might have would try to overthrow him, swallowed her whole while she was pregnant with Athena. When the baby came to term, Zeus was walking along the shores of Lake Triton, and he experienced an excruciating headache. Hephaistos split his head with an axe and from the crevasse sprang Athena, fully formed and fully armed, with a tremendous shout. Her Roman equivalent was Minerva.

Athena was goddess of justice, wisdom and warfare, and was a very masculinized figure. She was a fearless warrior in the *Gigantomachy*, killing the giant Enkelados, and a ruthless dispenser of justice, turning Medusa into an ugly hag for an involuntary sexual indiscretion (*see* p. 71). However, Athena as *Ergane*, workerwoman, was also patroness of spinning and weaving, and contributed to the making of the *parthenos* Pandora. A minor myth concerning her tells of a young maiden called Arachne, a renowned spinner, who boasted that she was more skillful than the goddess herself. For her insolence, Athena turned Arachne into a spider.

Aphrodite

Aphrodite was the goddess of sexual love, allegedly born from the sea-tossed genitals of the castrated Ouranos. The island of Cyprus also claimed to be her birthplace (hence she is sometimes referred to as the Cyprian), as did the island of Paphos.

For Romanists, Aphrodite was the only Olympian goddess to have lain with a mortal, Anchises, by whom she had the Trojan hero, Aineas. He was one of the few survivors of the Trojan War, renowned for carrying his aged father on his back out of the burning city, and it was of Aineas's subsequent adventures and founding of the city of Rome that the Roman poet Virgil wrote in his *Aeneid*, an epic poem deliberately modelled on Homer's *Odyssey*. It meant, however, that Venus, as the Romans called her, founded the city of Rome and hence its empire, it was from her that the Roman emperors laid claim to a divine ancestry, a fact attested to by the Caesars' veneration of Venus as *Genetrix*, Founding Mother.

SECTION II: THE MYTHS

Maidens

THE ABDUCTION OF KORE-PERSEPHONE

Hades conceived a passion for Persephone, daughter of Demeter and Zeus, but knowing that Demeter would not consent to the union, he appealed to Zeus for his intervention. However, even Zeus did not have the power to persuade Demeter, so he commanded Gaia to send up a beautiful narcissus, with a hundred blossoms and an intoxicating scent. This was to be a trick (*dolon*) to ensnare the Maid (*Kore*) and thus provide a bride for Hades.

One day, Kore-Persephone was playing in the meadows with the young daughters (*korai*) of Okeanos. She was so engrossed with picking flowers that she did not notice she had strayed from the others, and alone she came upon Gaia's unusual flower. Fascinated, Persephone reached out both hands and grasped the stem. Suddenly the ground beneath her opened up and from the chasm there emerged the awesome figure of Hades, driving a magnificent golden chariot drawn by two fiery black horses. He swept the screaming girl up onto his chariot and bore her away to his kingdom.

Demeter heard Persephone's screams and rushed to where she'd been playing, but the chasm had already been covered over again. For nine days and nights, Demeter roamed all of Greece seeking her daughter or news of her whereabouts. Eventually, Hekate told her that she had heard Persephone's scream, and the sun god, Helios, said that he had witnessed the abduction. In all, Demeter wandered for a whole year, during which time she turned her back on the Olympians and neglected her duties as Earth Mother: the land grew barren, animals and human beings alike lost interest in reproduction, and slowly the earth was dying. In addition, mortals forewent their sacrificial duties to the gods.

At length, Zeus sent Iris, goddess of the rainbow, to the cave where Demeter was hiding to persuade her to reappear. Demeter, however, was unmoved. Then Zeus sent the Messenger Hermes down to the underworld to negotiate with Hades for Persephone's release. Reluctantly Hades agreed, but before Persephone left his domain, as a trick (*dolon*), he persuaded her to eat several pomegranate pips. Persephone and Demeter were eventually reunited, but since Persephone had eaten the food of the dead, she was obliged to return to the underworld for one third of the year.

KALLISTO AND THE BEAR

Kallisto was a companion of the goddess Artemis, who required perfect chastity from her followers. However, Zeus transformed himself into a likeness of Artemis, seduced the maiden and got her pregnant. Artemis noticed this and changed Kallisto into a bear, calling up her pack of hounds. In the nick of time, Zeus prevented Kallisto from being torn to pieces by placing her among the stars where she became the constellation known as The Bear. Others say, though, that it was Zeus who turned her into a bear, and the jealous Hera who induced Artemis to pursue her. Kallisto eventually gave birth to Arkas (*Bear*).

ATALANTA

The father of Atalanta had wanted a son so when Atalanta was born he had her exposed. However, Atalanta was found and nurtured by a she-bear. When Atalanta had grown, she sought out her parents and was accepted by them, but her father wanted her married off, something that did not fit Atalanta's way of life, for she was used to the ways of the forest and to fending for herself. However, she agreed on condition that she could challenge each of her suitors to a foot race: if she won, the man would be put to death; if he won, she would marry him. Several young men chanced their leg, so to speak, but none could outrun the swift-footed Atalanta, till one, Hippomenes, a favourite of Aphrodite, took the goddess's advice and borrowed the three apples of the Hesperides. Aphrodite advised Hippomenes to drop an apple each time Atalanta gained on him, she would then stop to pick them up, allowing him to overtake her and win the race.

FOR THE GREATER GOOD: THE SACRIFICE OF IPHIGENEIA

One day, Agamemnon, King of Mykenai, was out hunting in the sacred grove of Artemis. With his bow and arrow he shot and killed a magnificent stag and arrogantly proclaimed himself a better hunter than even Artemis herself. The goddess grew angry and in order to appease her, Agamemnon had to promise her the first 'fruit' of his harvest, thinking he could get away with a simple vegetable thank-offering. Unfortunately for him, his first 'fruit' turned out to be his daughter, Iphigeneia.

Agamemnon was reminded of his promise when he was leader of the Greek troops assembled at Aulis in preparation for the famous Trojan War. Unfavourable winds prevented the Greeks from disembarking, which Kalkhas, a prophet of Apollo, interpreted as caused by Artemis's continuing anger. Under the pretext of marriage to the Greek hero Akhilleus, Agamemnon sent for his daughter. Instead of a bride's dress and veil, however, Iphigeneia was wrapped in a saffron-dyed winding-sheet — the 'clothes' of the dead — and placed on the sacrificial altar where her throat was slit by Agamemnon himself. According to the variant given by the tragedian Euripides, however, at the last minute Artemis relented, substituted a hind for Iphigeneia, and transported the girl to Tauris where she became High Priestess of the goddess identified by the locals with Artemis. Her duties included sacrificing any shipwrecked sailors, especially Greeks. Now the former sacrificial victim had become the instrument of sacrifice herself. Euripides played on this idea and made her brother, Orestes, an intended but unrecognized victim who at the last moment makes his identity plain. Orestes rescued Iphigeneia and took her back to Halai in Greece along with a wooden image sacred to Artemis.

THE LEAP OF AGLAUROS

Aglauros was one of the daughters of Erechtheus, a legendary king of Athens. When the city was threatened with war by a neighbouring city, an oracle said that if a maiden voluntarily sacrificed herself Athens would be saved. Aglauros therefore threw herself from the Akropolis cliff and the Athenians were victorious in their battle. A similar idea can also be found in the myth concerning the daughter of Embaros. Once again, an oracle demanded the sacrifice of a maiden in order to protect the city of Athens. At last, a man named Embaros offered to sacrifice his own daughter in exchange for a priesthood. He led her into the sanctuary of Artemis, but at the last minute substituted a female goat, whom he dressed in his daughter's clothes.

BEAUTY AND THE BEAST: MEDUSA

Medusa was a Libyan princess, daughter of the marine deities Phorkos and Keto. When her father died, she became Queen (the meaning of her name), and she would go hunting and led her people in battle. The most famous occasion was when a man named Perseus led an army against her from the Peloponnese. Medusa was treacherously murdered at night, and Perseus was so taken by her beauty that he cut off her head so that he might show it in Greece. He brought it back to Argos and buried it in the marketplace so that it would give protection to the city.

Another variant tells how Medusa had once been a most beautiful woman. But the god Poseidon pursued her and violated her in a temple of Athena. The goddess was so enraged that she turned Medusa into an ugly hag, whose gaze could turn men to stone.

A third variant tells that Akrisios, King of Argos, had been forewarned by an oracle that any grandson he might have would eventually kill him. For this reason, he locked his *parthenos* daughter, Danaë, in an underground brazen chamber. However, Zeus turned himself into a shower of gold which landed in her 'lap' and impregnated her. When Akrisios found out that Danaë had given birth to a son, Perseus, he locked them both in a coffer and cast it adrift at sea. Eventually the coffer reached the island of Seriphos where a poor fisherman by the name of Diktys rescued them and brought Perseus up as his own son. Diktys's brother, King Polydektes, conceived a passion for Danaë and wished to marry her, deciding to get rid of Perseus at the same time. So he contrived a trick whereby Perseus volunteered to bring back the head of the Gorgon Medusa in exchange for his mother's freedom.

With the assistance of Athena and Hermes, Perseus killed and decapitated the Gorgon and from her dead body sprang the warrior Chrysaor and the magic flying-horse Pegasos. On his way home, Perseus spied a naked maiden (*parthenos*) tied to a rock in the sea. Overcome by her beauty, he made enquiries and was told that she was Andromeda, daughter of Queen Kassiopeia of Ethiopia. The informant went

Fig. 7 Perseus decapitating Medusa. Olpe by the Amasis Painter, from Vulci. *Courtesy of the Trustees of the British Museum, London*

on that Kassiopeia, herself a beauty, had boasted that she was even more beautiful than the Nereids, who had been so enraged at her arrogance that they had pleaded with Poseidon to send a sea-monster to plague the Ethiopians. Upon consulting an oracle, the people had been told to sacrifice Andromeda to appease the sea. Perseus declared that not only would he kill the monster, but he would also take Andromeda's hand in marriage, and duly cut off the monster's head.

He returned to the island of Seriphos, where he rescued his mother by showing Medusa's head to Polydektes and his court. Then he reached Argos where he accidentally killed Akrisios, just as the oracle had foretold. After this, Perseus gave Medusa's head to Athena, who wore it on the breast of her *aigis* or robe.

PALLAS

One of Athena's many cult titles was Pallas. During the *Gigantomachy*, Athena killed a *gorgo*, generally named Enkelados or Pallas, and according to Apollonius Rhodius, this Pallas, a winged, goatish giant, was Athena's father who had attempted to violate her. After the battle, Athena flayed off the monster's skin which became her *aigis*.

Apollodorus claimed that Pallas was in fact a girlish playmate of the young Athena, whom the goddess accidentally killed while they were engaged in friendly combat with shield and spear. Pallas went to strike the goddess but Zeus interposed the aigis (which he also wore). Pallas was 'paralysed' by the sight of it and Athena's retaliatory blow killed her. In remorse, Athena made a wooden image (*xoanon*) of Pallas, placed the *aigis* across its breast, set it next to an image of Zeus and paid honour to it. Athena then placed Pallas's name before her own as a further token of her remorse.

THE DAUGHTERS OF KEKROPS

One day, the goddess Athena wished to take part in a battle and since she had no armour of her own, she was advised to ask Hephaistos to make her a set. Meanwhile, as a trick, Poseidon told Hephaistos that Athena was approaching his smithy in a state of high excitement, expecting Hephaistos to make passionate love to her. When Athena duly arrived Hephaistos was himself sexually agitated and attempted to violate the goddess. She repelled him but not before Hephaistos had ejaculated on her thigh. Athena wiped the semen off with a woollen fillet and in disgust threw it on the earth (Gaia), where it took seed and became the monstrous child, Erichthonios, who had a snake's tail for feet. Gaia protested that she did not want to nurture such an ugly child, so Athena took him back and he nestled in her bosom. Later she placed him in a basket and gave him to the daughters of Kekrops for safekeeping, warning them never to look inside the basket.

Kekrops was a legendary king of Athens, said to have originally come from Egypt, and his name is often given as Kerkops, meaning 'snake face'. His daughters were Aglauros, Pandrosos and Herse. One day they were returning from their duties on the Akropolis when the god Hermes approached them and tried to bribe Aglauros into letting him have sexual access to Herse. Aglauros took his bribe and then reneged on the deal; Hermes turned her into a pillar and violated Herse anyway. Some time later, Pandrosos and her mother Agraulos could no longer resist the temptation, and looked inside the basket. They were so horrified by what they saw that they leapt to their deaths from the Akropolis cliff.

THE MAKING OF A WOMAN: PANDORA

There was a golden time at the beginning of Zeus' reign when there were no women and men were still allowed to sit at the table of the gods and share a meal with them. But one day, a Titan called Prometheus (Foresight) decided to play a trick (*dolon*) upon Zeus. When the time came to divide up the ox into portions (*Moirai*) of meat for each god and each man, Prometheus took all the edible bits and wrapped them up inside the horrible-looking ox's stomach (*gaster*). Then he took all the inedible bits and wrapped them up in white fat, which was considered a delicacy. He then asked Zeus to take his pick.

As the father of gods and men, Zeus was of course omniscient but decided to feign ignorance and so chose the inedible portion wrapped in the enticing white fat. Then upon 'discovering' the trick, as if for the first time, he flew into a violent rage and threatened to punish men by removing eternal fire from them. Prometheus felt sorry for mankind, so he crept up to Mount Olympos, stole a seed (*sperma*) of Zeus' eternal flame, hid it in a fennel-stalk and then gave it to men. Again, Zeus was wise to the deception (*dolon*) beforehand, but only after fire had been stolen did he once again fly into a violent rage.

Prometheus was chained to a rock and every day an eagle, the bird manifestation of Zeus, would come and eat his liver. But each night, because Prometheus was an immortal, the liver would grow back again, thus he was in perpetual torment. However, Prometheus had another trick up his sleeve: Zeus had been warned by an oracle that a mortal son of his would eventually be stronger than him and would overthrow him – Prometheus knew the identity of this man and bargained with Zeus to release him. Eventually, Zeus realized he had little option but to relent and so allowed the hero Herakles, his son by Alkmene, to shoot the eagle with his bow. Thus the oracle had foretold the truth – Herakles *had* overthrown Zeus, but Zeus in the form of an eagle.

Prometheus returned to earth and warned his brother, Epimetheus (Hindsight), never to accept any gift from Zeus because it would be a trick (*dolon*). But Zeus commanded Hephaistos to take a handful of earth (Gaia), mix it with water and thus make an image of a woman. Then the other gods bestowed various attributes upon the maiden (*parthenos*), and she was named Pandora, Gift of all the Gods. When Epimetheus saw Pandora, he was so taken by her enticing beauty that he forgot his brother's warning and took her inside his house. Pandora had a jar (*pithos*) and when she opened it all the troubles (*Keres*) of the world flew out: strife (*eris*), disease, old age and so on. In her fright, Pandora shut the jar again, thus trapping Hope inside. However, she was persuaded to release Hope, who then flew about the world undoing the work of the troublesome sprites.

Wives

THE DEVOTED WIFE: PENELOPE

The epitome of the good and faithful wife was Penelope, married to the Greek hero Odysseus of Ithaka, by whom she had a son, Telemachos. When Odysseus left for the Trojan War, Telemachos was still a baby, and Odysseus's father, Laertes, was by now an old man, so it fell to Penelope to maintain Odysseus's palace and servants – this was no mean feat because he had a large estate that required a great deal of maintenance. At the end of the war, which lasted ten years, Odysseus was caught by unfavourable winds and spent another ten years trying to get home. In that time, a whole host of suitors besieged Penelope, believing Odysseus was irredeemably lost and hoping to marry her and so take over Odysseus's estate. Penelope, however, never lost faith and loyally awaited her husband's return; but the suitors continued to press Penelope. In exasperation, she declared that she would make her choice of them when she had finished the tapestry she was weaving. But this was a clever ruse, for by night she unpicked what she had woven by day, and thus held the suitors at bay for quite some time. Of course, eventually someone uncovered the trick, but in the nick of time Odysseus returned, killed all the suitors, and they lived happily ever after. Sorry.

THE BAD WIFE

'Bad' women always seem to me to be far more interesting than the 'goody two shoes' type, and ancient Greek myths offer a veritable cornucopia of examples, many of which I offer here for your delectation. Myth might have been intended as a didactic exercise in what not to do, but the range of misbehaviour on show must have been sorely tempting for the average Greek woman, and a source of 'good' ideas. And although these myths perhaps demonstrate men's poor opinion of women, they can also be read as a catalogue of highly possible nightmares disturbing an otherwise peaceful male-supremacist sleep. As the Chinese proverb has it: a man should take care not to anger a woman, for he has to sleep sometime – and with his eyes closed!

Helen and the Trojan Whore

On one of his many sexual escapades, Zeus turned his attention to a young woman named Leda. Transforming himself into a beautiful swan, Zeus swooped down on her, bore her away on his back and violated her. At the same time though, Leda was already pregnant by her husband, Tyndareos, and ended up giving birth to two sets of twins: one mortal set of Klytaimestra and Kastor, and one immortal set, born from a swan's egg, of Helen and Pollux. Helen turned into the most beautiful woman in the whole of Greece and soon many men came courting her. Tyndareos set a test for them, but in the end Helen chose her own man, Menelaos. His brother, Agamemnon, married Helen's sister, Klytaimestra.

Meanwhile, a heavenly marriage was taking place, between the mortal Peleus and the marine goddess, Thetis. All the gods and goddesses gathered on Mount Olympos to celebrate the wedding except one, Eris (Strife or Discord), who for obvious reasons had not been invited. As ever, though, Strife turned up invited or not and she threw down a Golden Apple inscribed with the words, 'to the fairest', *kallisto*. The goddesses set to arguing over who should have the apple, especially Hera, Athena and Aphrodite. They appealed to Zeus for arbitration, but Zeus knew better than to tangle with them, since his decision was bound to offend two of the three.

Instead he chose a poor mortal, Alexandros, the adopted son of a lowly shepherd. Each of the goddesses tried to bribe the young man with gifts according to her attributes: Hera promised him that he would rule the world, Athena promised him wisdom and success in battle, but sly Aphrodite, realizing his inexperience, undid her girdle and promised him the most beautiful woman in the world. Without hesitation, Alexandros chose Aphrodite and laid claim to Spartan Helen, already married to Menelaos.

Far from being the son of a lowly shepherd, Alexandros was in fact the youngest son of King Priam and Queen Hekabe of Troy, and his name was really Paris. As a baby he had been left for dead in the mountains because while Hekabe was carrying him it had been foretold that the next-born son of Troy would bring about the city's destruction. Paris returned to Troy and was acknowledged by Priam, against the prophetess Kassandra's advice; then he went to Sparta and, while a guest of Menelaos, he seduced Helen and abducted her to Troy. It was for this rapine that the Greeks pursued war against Troy, and the oracle was fulfilled when the city was razed to the ground.

At the end of the war some say that, despite his anger at her infidelity, Menelaos took one look at the face that had launched a thousand ships, fell in love with her all over again and returned her to Sparta. Others say that Helen never went to Troy at all, that she had been spirited away, like her niece Iphigeneia, to Egypt and that what Paris had taken to Troy was a *daidalon*, merely an 'image' of Helen (*see* Egypt: Myth and the Reality, page 36).

Nor was Helen's sister, Klytaimestra, anything like a good wife. During her husband's absence in Troy, Klytaimestra had taken a lover, Aigisthos, and together they plotted the downfall of Agamemnon upon his return, both having separate reasons. Klytaimestra's main motivation was to avenge the death of Iphigeneia, a crime for which Agamemnon had to be punished for the spilling of kin blood was an offence against the gods. However, only male relatives were allowed to carry out such vendettas. Meanwhile, Klytaimestra sent their young son, Orestes, away so that he might not grow up to avenge his father, and incarcerated her other daughter, Elektra, so that she might not marry and produce a similarly avenging heir. When Agamemnon returned in triumph from Troy, with Kassandra as his captured concubine, Klytaimestra lured them both into the palace, butchered Agamemnon while he was in his bath and dispatched Kassandra.

Elektra brooded and became an embittered woman, still a *parthenos*, but now most unlikely to get married. She harboured an ill-disguised hatred for her mother, a loathing for her aunt, Helen, whose sexual appetite precipitated this situation – for Elektra, along with most others, believed that Helen had gone to Troy willingly – and a passionate yearning for the return of her brother so that together they might wreak a terrible revenge for their father's murder. Orestes indeed returned and by deceit gained entrance to the palace where he butchered his mother and her paramour, in a grisly duplication of Agamemnon's death.

In ancient Greece, matricide was the most repugnant of crimes, worse than mere homicide or incest. The punishment was to be hounded to death and madness by the Furies, goddesses of retributive justice who specifically avenged the murders of mothers. Various endings are then given to this tale. In one, Orestes was given a magic bow and arrow by the archer god Apollo with which to despatch the Furies. In another, Orestes was first pursued to Delphi, where Apollo purified him, and then to Athens where he was put on trial at the homicide court known as the *Areopagos*, and acquitted with the help of Athena and Apollo. In a third variant, however, Orestes was ordered to bring back to Halai a sacred image of Artemis from the Black Sea town of Tauris and institute the worship of Artemis *Tauropolos*, Bull-Slayer.

Pasiphaë and the Minotaur

Minos, King of Crete and son of Europa and Zeus, once boasted that he was so blessed that the gods would answer his every prayer. So he dedicated an altar to the sea-god Poseidon and then prayed that a white bull might emerge from the sea, which he intended to offer as sacrifice to Poseidon. Sure enough, the god sent up the creature but Minos was so taken by its beauty that he kept it in his own herd and sacrificed another inferior animal in its place. Poseidon was so offended by this affront that he caused Minos's wife, Pasiphaë, to fall in love with the bull. Pasiphaë confided her unnatural passion to Daidalos, the master craftsman, and he constructed a wooden cow which Pasiphaë might climb inside and allow the bull to mount her. In due course, Pasiphaë gave birth to a monstrous child, with a human body but a bull's head, called the Minotaur. Minos eventually discovered Pasiphaë's terrible secret and commanded Daidalos to build a labyrinth in which to hide their shame.

At this time the city of Athens was not so powerful and was obliged to pay a tribute to Minos every year. Henceforth, Minos decreed that the tribute should be seven youths and seven maidens (*parthenoi*), who were led to the entrance of the labyrinth and never seen again. One year, an Athenian youth named Theseus volunteered to be part of the tribute, swearing that he would bring an end to Minos's tyranny. Theseus set sail for Crete and inveigled his way into Minos's palace at Knossos. Luckily for Theseus, he caught the eye of Ariadne, one of Pasiphaë's daughters by Minos, who promised to help him if he would marry her and take her away. Theseus saw his chance and agreed, despite preferring Ariadne's sister, Phaidra. Ariadne gave Theseus a ball of twine for him to unravel as he went through the labyrinth maze so that he might find his way out again. All went according to plan: Theseus killed the Minotaur, rescued the tribute, and he and Ariadne made good their escape, along with Phaidra. On the way back to Athens, whether by design or accident, Ariadne was left on the island of Naxos, but the god Dionysos took pity on her and married her himself.

Semele and the Horned Child

Semele was the daughter of King Kadmos of Thebes and upon her Zeus fathered the god Dionysos. However, when Semele was six months pregnant, the jealous Hera appeared to her, disguised as an elderly neighbour. She teased and taunted the young woman, suggesting that the father of her child was not all he claimed to be. In the end, Hera persuaded Semele to demand that Zeus reveal himself to her. Zeus reluctantly agreed, and Semele was blasted, because Zeus' earthly manifestation was the thunderbolt. However, Hermes appeared in time to save the infant, rescuing him from Semele's still smouldering body and sewing him up in Zeus' thigh. When the time came, Zeus himself gave birth to the 'horned' child, and named him Dionysos.

Plataia and the Daidalon

After yet another argument with Zeus, Hera took herself off to Euboia. Zeus consulted with Alalcomeneos, who advised him to make Hera jealous. So Zeus took a plank of wood, dressed it in a bride's veil, and let it be known that he intended marrying Plataia, daughter of the river god Asopos, and placed the image in his ox-cart. Hearing the news, Hera rushed back in a rage, bringing the Plataian women with her, tore the veil from the 'bride' and then burst out laughing when she realized Zeus' trick. They were reconciled, but Hera still insisted that the *daidalon* be destroyed.

Mothers

Note that, like the Christian myth of Mary and Joseph, the ancient Greeks felt that paternity of both gods and heroes was not to be trusted to mortal males. Although this suggests that mortal females were considered important in their role of *genetrix* (a biological mother), at the same time it also says that the role of *genetor* was more significant than *genetrix*.

MOTHERS OF GODS

Leto was the daughter of the Titans Coeus and Phoebe; Zeus turned himself and Leto into quails and fathered Apollo and Artemis upon her. However, Hera was jealous and so sent the serpent Python to pursue Leto all over the earth. At length, Leto came to Ortygia where she gave birth to Artemis; then, crossing the straits to the island of Delos, and with the help of Artemis as midwife, Leto gave birth to Apollo, between an olive-tree and a date-palm.

MOTHERS AS FOUNDERS OF RACES

Europa was the young sister of Kadmos, founder of Thebes. She was playing in the fields one day when a beautiful white bull strolled along and joined her father's herd. Europa was completely enchanted by this creature, which was as gentle as a lamb and allowed her to put flowers into its mouth and a garland of flowers around its horns. Eventually Europa was bold enough to climb upon its back, when suddenly the bull snorted and bore the screaming girl off into the sea, frantically clinging to its horns. The white bull turned out to be Zeus in disguise, who had fallen in love with the girl. He carried her on his back as far as the island of Crete, where he turned himself into an eagle and raped her. Europa subsequently bore Zeus three sons, one of whom was Minos, later King of Crete and husband of Pasiphaë. It was after the maiden Europa that the race of Europeans was named.

The Monstrous Regiment: Mothers and Their Children

DEMETER AT ELEUSIS

Whilst searching for news of the whereabouts of her daughter, Demeter, now in disguise, stopped to rest at a well called Kallikhoros — Of The Fair Dances — where she was approached by the daughters (*parthenoi*) of Keleos, King of Eleusis. They took pity on her, brought her inside their home and she became the nurse to Metaneira's infant son, Demöophon. By day she would take care of the boy but by night she would place Demöophon in the hearth fire in order to burn away his mortal parts, since she wished to make him immortal.

One night, though, Metaneira discovered her and, not understanding what the old woman was doing and in ignorance of her true identity, she wrested the boy from Demeter. The goddess thereupon assumed her normal shape and warned that thereafter the sons of Eleusis would forever wage war against one another. She then commanded Keleos to build her a temple, with an altar underneath, and to follow the rites that she would teach him.

JOKASTA AND THE SPHINX

Jokasta was Queen of Thebes and an oracle forbade her to have any children, warning her that if she and her husband Laios ignored the words of the gods they would have a son who would kill his father and marry his mother. Even so, they decided to thwart the oracle, but when a son was born they took fright and left the baby exposed on Mount Kithairon with his ankles pinioned so that he might not crawl away to safety. However, unknown to Jokasta, her baby was rescued.

Years went by and then the gods grew angry with Thebes and so sent the Sphinx to plague them. The Sphinx was half-woman and half-dog, and sat on the Theban *akropolis*, at the mouth of a bottomless pit, spouting an apparently meaningless riddle. In vain, every man tried to solve the riddle, and as each failed he was either eaten by the Sphinx or thrown into the pit. Eventually, a limping man named Oidipous (Swollen Foot) came to Thebes from Korinth and managed to rid the city of the Sphinx by solving her riddle. Since Laios had long since disappeared, the Thebans wanted to show their gratitude by making Oidipous their king by marriage to Jokasta. In all they had four children. However, when a second plague befell the city, it was discovered that Oidipous was Jokasta's long-lost son, who had killed Laios at a crossroads, not knowing who he was. In remorse, Jokasta hanged herself and Oidipous was exiled.

THE BACCHAE

Kadmos and Harmonia, daughter of the war god, Ares, had four daughters: Semele, Ino, Autonoë and Agauë. Agauë married Echion and had a son named Pentheus. Semele, however, was courted by Zeus and from her womb was taken the god, Dionysos. After Semele's death and Dionysos's birth, Hera transferred her jealousy to the infant boy: in order to protect him, Zeus disguised him as a kid, then as a girl, but Hera saw through all these ruses and eventually sent Dionysos raving mad and thus he travelled throughout the rest of the world.

After his world tour, Dionysos returned to Thebes in order to establish his godhead. He discovered, however, that in his absence his aunts had repudiated his mother, saying that in reality she had had sex with a mortal but said that it was Zeus to hide her shame, and claiming that it was for this that Zeus had blasted her with his thunderbolt. To punish the city of Thebes, Dionysos sent all the women mad and drove them out of the city onto Mount Kithairon.

Pentheus, who by now was King of Thebes, had been away on business and returned to find the city in uproar and all the women gadding about. Pentheus was deeply suspicious of women outside male control and instantly suspected them of giving themselves to lascivious men on the mountain, despite eye-witness accounts to the contrary. Furthermore, he, too, did not recognize Dionysos as a god, even when the god appeared to him in person and tried to persuade him. As Dionysos worked his magic upon Pentheus, the king began to reveal his true self, expressing a wish to actually see these women and their carryings-on for himself. Dionysos now had him under full control and succeeded in dressing Pentheus as a *bacchant* woman (as the female followers of Dionysos were called), to lead him through the streets of Thebes to be mocked by the male inhabitants. He took him up to the mountains, placed him atop the tallest pine (a tree associated with the god), and then with a tremendous shout, like a clap of thunder, Dionysos alerted the women to Pentheus' presence.

Previously, whenever men had tried to disturb the *bacchant* women, they had suddenly become frenzied, rushing down from the mountains and destroying villages and tearing cattle to pieces. Now they turned their attention to Pentheus, ripping down the pine tree and eventually tearing him limb from limb. Finally, only Pentheus's head was left in tact; this they impaled on a *thyrsos* and his own mother, Agaue, led the procession bringing what remained of Pentheus back to Thebes, like a hunting trophy. Indeed, in their madness, the women believed they had caught and killed a wild animal, either a bull calf or a lion cub.

The city of Argos also had a myth about a 'monstrous regiment', this one concerning the daughters of Proitos. They too refused to join the worship of Dionysos (though some say it was Hera they offended) and for their insult they were sent mad, believing they had been turned into cows, for their skin became white and blotchy. They roamed the hills in a wild frenzy, where they behaved in a most unseemly fashion and murdered all of their children. Eventually, two brothers, Melampous and Bios, offered to catch and cure the women. Having cured them by dousing them in water, Melampous and Bios married two of the sisters; the third, however, committed suicide before the madness could be treated.

PHAIDRA

After he had killed the Minotaur, Theseus returned to a hero's welcome in Athens, with his new bride; but he then had to spend a year in exile in the nearby town of Troizen for a crime he had committed previously. He and Phaidra produced two young sons, but their troubles were not yet over, for Theseus already had a grown son, Hippolytos, the result of Theseus's rape of the Amazon Queen, Hippolyta. This caused a certain amount of dynastic friction and, because of Theseus's disgraceful treatment of his mother, Hippolytos showed his disapproval of the marriage-bed by devoting his chastity to the virgin goddess, Artemis, and by refusing to honour Aphrodite in worship.

Aphrodite was understandably furious at this affront and swore her revenge on Hippolytos, using Phaidra as her innocent pawn. While Theseus was away on business, Aphrodite cast a spell on Phaidra and caused her to fall in love with her stepson. Tormented with love pangs, feelings of guilt and betrayal, and remembering the sexual history of the distaff side of her family, Phaidra was eventually driven to confess her love to Hippolytos himself. The rather sanctimoniously chaste young man was doubly horrified at her protestations and brutally repudiated Phaidra. In remorse, and with no little spite on her part, Phaidra hanged herself, leaving an incriminating letter for Theseus in which she accused Hippolytos of attempted rape.

Now it was Theseus's turn to be horrified with Hippolytos. He banished Hippolytos from his sight, calling upon his holy father, Poseidon, to grant him revenge on Hippolytos. As the young man drove his chariot along the coast road, an enormous bull emerged from the sea, having been sent by Poseidon. The bull was so huge, snorting terribly, that Hippolytos's horses took fright and ran amok, pulling Hippolytos and his chariot to pieces.

THE AMAZONS

Probably the most famous band of 'man-eaters' in antiquity were the Amazons, a mythical race of superwomen who were said to come either from Libya or Scythia (in the Russian steppes). They were nomadic horsewomen/warriors, and it was said of them that they detested men so much that when they wanted to conceive they would kidnap likely men, impregnate themselves and then kill the poor victim – rather like black widow spiders. It was also claimed that they would kill any resultant male children; and that Amazons would cut off one of their breasts (hence their name) in order to facilitate firing a bow. To contradict this, however, in vase paintings and statuary, Amazons are always depicted with the full mammary complement, and the archer goddess, Artemis, also does not seem to have found either breast surplus to requirements.

There are several myths featuring the Amazons, but they mainly concern their battles with – and, of course, defeats by – various Greek heroes. Herakles, for example, had to bring back the girdle of the Amazon queen, Hippolyta, as one of his twelve Labours; Theseus fought with and raped Hippolyta, and fathered Hippolytos upon her; the hero Akhilleus killed Penthesilea, though he at least grieved over her dead body. Even the god Dionysos, not renowned as a warrior and usually depicted as quite effeminate, fought a battle with the Amazons and of course got the better of them.

Magical Women: Medeia

Perhaps a little surprisingly, there are few witches or otherwise magically endowed women in ancient Greek myth, the most famous being Medeia. It could well be, though, that ordinary ancient Greek women were felt to be sufficiently bewitching and powerful already not to require the assistance of any arcane or supernatural powers.

Medeia was the daughter of Aietes, King of Colchis on the Black Sea and himself the son of Helios, one of the sun gods. One day, a Greek named Jason came to the city in a ship called the Argosy, accompanied by the Argonauts, in search of the

Fig. 8 The enchantress Medeia rejuvenates 'Aison' by boiling him in a cauldron with magic herbs. Attic Red Figure hydria by the Copenhagen Painter.
Courtesy of the Trustees of the British Museum, London

Golden Fleece. Like Perseus and the head of Medusa, the Golden Fleece was a magical symbol, which conferred sovereignty upon the holder. Unfortunately for Jason, the fleece was kept in a cave, guarded by a fierce, fire-breathing dragon, because of course King Aietes had no intention of letting it out of his control. Jason and Aietes set to haggling till Aietes finally announced he would let Jason have the fleece if he ploughed a large field using two bronze bulls, sowed it with dragon's teeth and then fought the warriors who subsequently sprang from the seed.

Medeia was an enchantress and a priestess of Hekate; Jason was the favourite of Hera, who persuaded Aphrodite to make Medeia fall madly in love with him so that she would use her magic to help him. This she did in the form of a magic ointment which made Jason and his armour immune to fire. He then yoked the bulls, ploughed the field and sowed the dragon's teeth, and when the warriors sprang up he despatched them by the simple method of throwing a stone in their midst which caused them to fight each other.

King Aietes suspected that Jason's 'luck' was somehow due to supernatural help from Medeia, and so he plotted against the Argonauts. But Medeia found out, led the Argonauts out of the city by a secret route and then guided Jason to the dragon's cave. With the aid of Medeia's magic ointment, Jason soon made light work of the dragon, and stole the fleece. Medeia, now a traitor, was forced to accompany him.

Aietes discovered them and sent his son Apsyrtos in pursuit. But Medeia killed him, cut him up into pieces and scattered them along the road so that their pursuers would be delayed when they stopped to pick them up. In gratitude, Jason promised to take Medeia back with him to Greece.

The man who had sent Jason on his quests was Pelias of Iolkos, and Medeia decided to avenge Jason by exercising a little deception. Since by now he was a very old man, Medeia persuaded his daughters that she could rejuvenate him by boiling him in a cauldron with magic herbs. To demonstrate the power of her magic, first she rejuvenated Jason's aged father, Aison, and then she transformed a ram into a male lamb – using her 'boil-in-a-bag' method. The daughters were convinced and eager to perform the same magic on their father; sly Medeia, however, neglected to give them the magic herbs and Pelias was boiled alive. His son, Akastos, was not amused and drove Jason and Medeia out of the country.

Eventually they came to the Greek city of Korinth, where Jason and Medeia lived together for several years. But the problem for Medeia was that she was mad with love for Jason, while he felt nothing but gratitude for her, despite fathering two sons on her. He not only kept Medeia outside the city, but he also became betrothed to Glauke, daughter of the Korinthian King Kreon, because more than anything Jason wished to found a dynasty and provide a heritage for his two sons. Thus, after all she had done and everything she had given up for him, Medeia was abandoned by Jason. This was too much, and Medeia exacted a terrible revenge. Taking another magic ointment, she smeared it on the bridal robe and tiara of Glauke which caused her to burn to death, and also killed Kreon, who had tried to rescue her. Then Medeia made her escape on a winged chariot – perhaps the Chariot of the Sun, since Helios was her grandfather – taking the bodies of her infant sons with her, for in her fury she had killed them to thwart Jason's dynastic ambitions.

SECTION III: LESSER FEMALE FIGURES

ALKYONE

Alkyone was the daughter of Aeolus, guardian of the winds. She and her husband, Ceyx, arrogantly compared themselves to Hera and Zeus. For their boastfulness, Zeus let loose a thunderstorm which capsized a boat in which Ceyx was sailing. His ghost then appeared to Alkyone who, distraught at this visitation, leapt off a cliff into the sea. Zeus then turned Alkyone into a kingfisher and Ceyx into a gannet.

ANTIGONE

She was the daughter of Oidipous and Jokasta. When her brothers, Polyneikes and Eteokles, killed each other after disputing the throne of Thebes, Antigone performed a burial of Polyneikes, against her uncle's decree — for Polyneikes had raised an army against the city in order to claim the throne. The uncle, Kreon, walled Antigone up in a cave and left her for dead; however, Teiresias, seer of Apollo, persuaded Kreon to release her, too late, for Antigone had already hanged herself.

CHARITES

The Charites were goddesses who personified charm, grace and beauty, with an obvious connection to Aphrodite, and therefore with creation and procreation. Myrtle and roses were their special flowers. They were the daughters of Zeus.

CHIMAIRA

A female monster — lioness, serpent and goat — who was eventually killed by the hero Bellerophon.

DAPHNE

A mountain nymph and priestess of Demeter, Daphne was pursued by Apollo. The god attempted to rape her but at the last moment Daphne called upon Demeter for help. The goddess left a laurel tree in Daphne's place and spirited the maiden away to Crete, where she became known as Pasiphaë.

EURYDIKE

A wood nymph and wife of Orpheus, the famous musician. Eurydike was pursued by Aristaeus and accidentally trod on a serpent, whose bite killed her. Orpheus was allowed to retrieve Eurydike from the underworld on condition that he did not look back. However, his faith failed him and Eurydike was forced to return to the land of the dead.

FURIES

Goddesses of retributive justice, the Furies would pursue wrongdoers, especially matricides. They came into being when Kronos castrated Ouranos, being formed from drops of Ouranos's blood which germinated in the earth. They figure in the myth of Orestes's matricide of Klytaimestra, after which they change their ways and become known as the Eumenides, the Kindly Ones. The Eumenides had a sacred grove just outside the city of Athens.

HARPIES

The Harpies were the daughters of Thaumas and Elektra, daughter of Okeanos, a marine deity; they were devious winged spirits who would carry off things or people, such as the daughters of Pandareos.

HEKATE

Hekate is sometimes confused with Artemis and Selene (the moon goddess), whose attributes she shares. Interestingly, her typical sacrificial offering was fish. She was associated with the ghost world and could be invoked to bring good luck in dangerous circumstances, such as at crossroads, where she would be given 'Hekate's Supper', a rite of purification mainly composed of dog's flesh.

HORAI

The Seasons; as the name implies they were goddesses of the seasons who make flowers and plants grow. Their names were Thallo, Karpo and Auxo.

KARYA

Karya was a maiden who was loved and pursued by the god Dionysos. Karya died suddenly at the village of Karyai in Lakonia and Dionysos transformed her into a walnut-tree. The female followers of Karya, the *Karyatids*, became female statues used as architectural columns to support a temple's superstructure, the most famous example being the *Erechtheon*, part of the Athenian Parthenon complex.

KASSANDRA

She was the daughter of Priam and Hekabe of Troy, and sister of Helenos. Apollo, god of prophecy, took a shine to Kassandra and promised her the power of prophecy if she would consent to lie with him. Kassandra agreed and received the gift, but then changed her mind and thus remained a virgin. To punish her, Apollo spat in her mouth, saying that henceforth no mortal would believe her prophecies even though she told the truth.

LAMIA/EMPOUSAI

Lamia was the daughter of Libya and Belos. Hera destroyed her children because of her liaison with Zeus, whereupon Lamia became savage with grief and stole the children of other mothers — a nursery 'bogeywoman', if you like. In some sources, Lamia joined the *Empousai*, or singular *Empousa*, another bogeywoman, who would ensnare young men and then eat them while they slept after making love — in other words, vampires.

MAINADS

Literally 'mad women', they were followers of the god Dionysos, also called *bacchant* women.

MOIRAI

The Three Fates, who were spinners of the lots of both mortals and immortals alike. Their name means 'portions' or 'shares', thus the kind of life allotted to each individual. Although Zeus was the 'father of gods and men' even he had to bow to the power of the Fates.

MUSES

The daughters of Zeus and Mnemosune (Memory), the Muses lived on Mount Helikon. They were the fount of all knowledge, and poets would invoke them at the beginning of each declamation, thus 'proving' that the poet sang the truth. The number of Muses varied from three to nine; originally the triad together held the various powers, but by the Roman period each of the nine was attributed separate spheres of influence in the arts. *Mouseia* were sacred places where birds sang – thought to be manifestations of the gods – and later philosophers, such as Plato and Aristotle, called their Schools 'museums'.

NEMESIS

One of the daughters of Eris (Strife), Nemesis was the main goddess of retributive justice when a mortal had committed *hubris*, meaning overweening pride or some other offence of pride against the gods.

NIOBE

Niobe had so many children that she claimed to be a better mother even than Leto, who had borne the divine twins, Artemis and Apollo. The two deities took their bows and arrows and shot every single one of Niobe's children to preserve the reputation of their mother and to teach Niobe some humility.

NYMPHS

Minor deities, more like spirits or *daimons*, the Nymphs were associated with a location or aspects of nature, and all were daughters of Zeus. The *Alseides*, *Napaiai*, *Dryads* were nymphs of forests and groves, and the Dryads were originally spirits of oak trees (whence their name) but came to be tree nymphs in general. The *Hamadryads* were the true tree nymphs, who were believed to die when their tree did. The *Orestiads* were mountain nymphs; the *Leimoniads* were meadow nymphs; the *Naiads*, *Potameids*, *Creneids*, *Hydriads* and *Nereids* were water nymphs of various kinds. The word *numphe* actually means young, unmarried woman, but implied she was ready for sexual activity, and associated her with the realm of Aphrodite, goddess of sexual love.

PHOEBE

Phoebe was the daughter of heaven and earth (Gaia) and mother of Leto, thus grandmother of Artemis and Apollo, from whom the god takes his epithet *phoibos*. She was a moon deity, like Selene.

SIRENS

The Sirens were woman-headed birds with an irresistible song who lived on an island near the clashing rocks, Skylla and Charybdis. Their songs would enchant sailors so that they would lose control of their boats and be dashed to pieces on the rocks.

SECTION IV: WOMEN, MYTH AND RITUAL

In ancient Greece there were various terms used to describe females, reflecting their age, social and marital status, and reproductive condition.

A young girl, *kore*, would begin life in the household (*oikos*) of her father, attached to his hearth (*hestia*, also the name of the hearth goddess). At around the age of 14, her periods would start, at which point she would be referred to as a *parthenos*, 'unmarried maiden'. She would be betrothed and married off as quickly as possible after this transition; meantime, however, there would be an unavoidable time lapse between the biological event of menarche and the social event of marriage. The 'marriage' ceremony consisted of a torchlit procession at night, where the *parthenos* would be led by her father and mother to the home of her future husband, and ritually transferred from her father's hearth to her husband's.

A married woman was generally referred to as a *gune*, which strictly speaking meant 'woman'. There was another term for 'wife', *damar*, but this does not seem to have been used very often. The most important event in a woman's life was felt to be the birth of her first child, especially if this was a boy, at which point she would achieve the status of mother, *meter*.

So the classification of females, unlike that of males, was, firstly, based on biology – their sexuality and fertility – and the various statuses seem to have been determined by a flow of blood: menarche, defloration and parturition. Secondly, women were classified according to the hearth with which they were associated, in other words, in terms of a social kinship relation to men. The ancient Greek male mind seems to have found the flow of female blood problematic, especially the first flow (menarche), and thus they circumscribed women who bled by a variety of pollution rules and taboos contained in heavily-coded mythology or 'straightforward' medical treatise, such as the famous *Peri Parthenon*, a fifth or fourth century BC text of the Hippocratic corpus, usually translated as 'On the Diseases of Young Girls' or 'On the Diseases of Virgins'. However, it is almost wholly concerned with the male regulation of female menstrual blood, itself viewed as a pathological condition the best cure for which was sexual intercourse followed by pregnancy.

It seems to me that ancient Greek men viewed the *parthenos* herself as an ambivalent sociopathological condition to be 'cured', representing the transitional stage between, firstly, unmarried girl (*kore*) and married woman (*gune*), secondly between virgin (*kore*) and mother (*meter*), so that, thirdly, the *parthenos* articulated the physical and conceptual space between father's household/hearth and that of the husband. In other words, the *parthenos* was in between male-identified statuses.

If we analyse ancient Greek myths about women according to these biosocial groups, we find that by far the majority is about *parthenoi*, reflecting the extreme sexual anxiety of ancient Greek men and crystallizing their ambivalence towards women out of male control. In all of these myths, the *parthenos* is either transformed or destroyed, the point being that *parthenos* had a temporal limitation and a finite social usefulness in its own right. The social objective was that every *parthenos* should eventually be transformed into a *gune/meter*.

It is all very well to list the great number of ancient Greek myths about women and pontificate grandly on what they appear to say about the position of women in ancient Greek society, but how accessible were these myths to the vast majority of women? Indeed, to what extent were women responsible for their formulation and transmission? Unfortunately, any answers we might arrive at can at best only be speculative and reconstructive, but that doesn't mean we shouldn't try.

Could women read and write? Well, on the basis of Phaidra's incriminating note to Theseus, we can only hazard that perhaps some aristocratic women were literate. Were there any books to read? Socrates, in his famous trial, refers to the works of certain philosophers being available in the *Agora* for a drachma apiece, but that price put 'books' beyond the reach of most of the lower classes, male and female alike. Myths from Homeric epic formed the plots of ancient Greek tragic drama, but we do not know for sure whether women were allowed to attend the theatre, and female roles were taken by male actors so perhaps we had better discount that source also. There were other opportunities to hear *rhapsodes* declaim the works of Homer, for example, but again we are not told whether women were allowed to attend, let alone participate, despite the existence of female poets.

The problem is really that most of these opportunities were linked to ritual, and my feeling (for which there is no space here to elaborate) is that such occasions were denied to women on the basis that they were men-only initiation rites. However, there were women-only rituals, which I will come to shortly.

Even at the height of the Classical period in the fifth century BC, Athens at least was still largely an oral-based culture. Certain things, such as laws and ritual calendars, were codified and displayed publicly in monumental inscription form, but almost everything else was transmitted orally — or at least non-literately. Even in schools, attended only by boys, the lessons would be by word of mouth.

In Euripides' *Ion*, the Chorus of Athenian women have accompanied Creusa to Delphi and this is clearly their first trip. They go sightseeing like naïve tourists, pointing out the places of interest and then describe the pedimental sculptures of Apollo's temple, listing the myths articulated therein, and wonder if these are the same stories and characters they are told about at weaving time. Here we have one occasion when women could band together in order to spin and weave, at which time they could tell each other stories. Weaving could be a domestic occupation, on the lines of a cottage industry, but it could also have a ritual significance and provide an occasion for women to be given formal instruction in myth. Unfortunately, however, textiles do not generally survive the ravages of time, and even where they do the dyes used to decorate them have usually faded.

Another non-literary source of myth was pottery, an artefact that does survive, and from the seventh century BC onwards Greek pottery was covered in scenes from myth. Most of this pottery had a ritual purpose and the scenes depicted would have related to the kind of ritual in which they were being used. And it is here, in the relationship of myth to ritual, that women would have found their greatest access to myth. Each of the myths I have selected is either an *aition* – a myth 'explaining' the origins of a particular ritual – or can be indirectly related to a myth that is aetiological. Although women were not generally known as potters, they were the sole providers of textiles, thus if myth was used to decorate textiles employed in ritual they almost certainly discussed them in a formal context, and were therefore responsible for their formulation and transmission.

The purpose of this concluding section is to relate myths about women to the female ritual cycle, and examine the importance of women's role in the religious life of ancient Greece. The majority of examples come from Athens since this city provides the greatest cohesive evidence.

In antiquity, the myth of Kore-Persephone was used as the *aition* for a women-only ritual called the *Thesmophoria*, dedicated to the 'Two Goddesses', generally identified as Demeter and Persephone. It was celebrated in the autumn month of *Pyanepsion* (equivalent to October/November), was thought to be connected to sowing and included a thank-offering to Demeter. The festival was spread over three days, and not only were men excluded but they were not allowed to speak of it and were thought to have been confined to the home for its duration. Women would camp out on the Akropolis hill and, on the first day (called *Kathodos*, Descent, or *Anodos*, Ascent), the Bailers, women who had fasted for three days, would draw up from pits the remains of pigs which had been sacrificed there previously. These remains would be mixed with seeds and used as 'sympathetic magic' to ensure a good crop. This scattering would take place on the third day called *Kalligeneia* (Fair-born, Fair-birth or Birth of the Fair One). On the middle day, *Nesteia*, the women would sit on the ground, fast, and tell each other riddles, supposedly re-enacting Demeter's grief at the loss of Persephone. Our sources also mention a mysterious ritual called the *Chalcidian Pursuit*, for which we have no details.

Many cultures have a myth in which the earth goddess, or goddess of reproduction, hides for part of the year – an obvious explanation for agricultural seasons. However, in the Greek myth two goddesses disappear, and only Demeter is the earth goddess proper. So what are we to make of Persephone's disappearance? The clue is in the pomegranate, a fruit which gives a blood-red juice and which is always associated with Persephone and the underworld. My interpretation is that this myth describes Persephone's arrival at the menarche, symbolized by the pomegranate, and her disappearance articulates the confinement connected with menstrual taboos. She cannot possibly be connected with agricultural 'seasons' since the narcissus, which effects her disappearance, is a spring flower.

Anthropologists generally differentiate between initiation and puberty rituals on the basis that the first is in response to some social impetus and initiates a group, whereas the second is performed on an individual in response to a biological change – in this case Persephone's first menses. This puberty rite sees the transformation of Persephone from a 'bloodless' *kore* into what we might call a 'bride of Death', in other words she becomes a *parthenos*. The narcissus might at a stretch have phallic connotations; more likely, though, is that it was a species of crocus, and it was from crocus petals that the ancient Greeks took saffron, used to dye the robes of young girls who were considered symbolically dead. Additionally, it is thought to derive its name from *narkhe*, meaning 'number', whence 'narcotic'. It seems to imply that Persephone's disappearance and confinement were linked to some narcotic-induced long sleep, perhaps as in a hibernation. In the human biological calendar, this 'winter' could be seen as the non-reproductive period, literally when a woman was menstruating.

The long sleep of hibernation leads us to consider some myths and rituals involving bears, animals which hibernate and which many cultures mythologize as the nearest animal equivalent to humans. Also, the hibernation is seen as a symbolic death, which spring – and the flowers of spring – brings to an end. In Aristophanes' *Lysistrata*, we hear of *arkteuein*, *aletris*, *arrephoros* and *kanephoros*, four ritual roles performed by young girls, which seem to form the basis of a female ritual cycle. We have little information on the *aletris*, 'Corn-Grinder', perhaps an unevidenced link to Kore-Persephone and Demeter, and the *kanephoros* played only a minor role in several rituals.

At the Attic festival of the *Brauronia*, little Athenian girls, aged between 5 and 11, dressed in special saffron-dyed robes and performed a dance to Artemis called *arkteuein*, literally 'to act the bear'. The aetiological explanation for this was that one day a bear, sacred to Artemis, had wandered into the goddess's sanctuary. A little girl teased the bear till it tore out one of her eyes (i.e. she bled), for which her brothers killed the animal. At this, the goddess sent a plague on Athens, which an oracle said could only be removed if henceforth Athenian girls 'acted the bear' in atonement.

Kallisto's name means 'Fairest' and could provide a link with the final day of the *Thesmophoria*, in that *Kalligeneia* could mean 'Birth from Kallisto'. Thus perhaps these Athenian girls are little bears (*Arkas*), who are 'born' after the *Kalligeneia*. Remember, though, that these girls are transformed as a group, so they do not necessarily have to have reached the menarche, even though our sources say that the age limits were very strict. In that case, we should view 'acting the bear' as equivalent to being a 'bride of Death', transforming the *korai* into *parthenoi* in response to a social rather than biological impetus.

The pursuit of Atalanta by Hippomenes, leading to marriage, could find its ritual equivalent in the *Chalcidian Pursuit* of the *Thesmophoria*, but this can only be speculative. However, we know that ritual pursuits of females by males often led to marriage. In this myth, Atalanta is first associated with Artemis through the mountain exposure, the she-bear and her ability to hunt. Her 'downfall' is brought about by Aphrodite, whose intervention transforms her from a virgin into a bride.

In the myths of Iphigeneia, Aglauros and the unnamed daughter of Embaros, we have certain common elements. It is a time just before war has broken out, interpreted as the wrath of Artemis. To appease the goddess, a father 'sacrifices' his daughter, who apparently goes willingly to her death. In two of them, the daughter is substituted by an animal sacred to the goddess; in another two, the daughter herself becomes 'sacred', as High Priestess. However, if we compare Kore-Persephone with Iphigeneia, we have a father who gives his daughter as a 'bride of Death' on behalf of his brother's marital status: Zeus gives Persephone to Hades as his bride; Agamemnon pretends to marry Iphigeneia to Akhilleus but sacrifices her so that ultimately his brother Menelaos might regain his wife, Helen.

Additionally, in 'dedicating' his daughter to Hades, Zeus has symbolically united sky (Zeus), earth (Demeter) and the underworld (Hades) through the instrument of Persephone. In the same way, the body of Iphigeneia, as an unviolated virgin, symbolically comes to stand for the 'integrity' of the Greek community in a time of war (when 'community' might otherwise be wrecked). The female 'body physical' is therefore a metaphor for the (male) 'body politic': if Iphigeneia remains intact till her death, then so will the community she represents; if the authority figure of that community (Zeus/Agamemnon), exercising the supreme power of a patriarch, controls the means and moment of that death, then he can also control the destiny of his community. The wish to retain or restore community integrity must surely be the thinking behind such war-linked virgin sacrifices. It also sets up an opposition between female (biological) interests and male (social/political) interests, where virgin's blood is spilt in a controlled ritual context in order to prevent the uncontrolled and indiscriminate flow of male blood in war. Integrity reduces to order versus disorder, control versus chaos, male versus female.

In the case of Iphigeneia, other substitutions and transformations have also taken place. The stag which Agamemnon originally killed becomes a hind (male for female) when he sacrifices Iphigeneia. Secondly, Iphigeneia's 'marriage' to Akhilleus becomes a death; in myth, Akhilleus was closely associated with the god Apollo, twin brother of Artemis, with whom Iphigeneia is associated, and in a variant of the myth given by Euripides, Iphigeneia narrowly misses sacrificing her own brother, Orestes. Thus we have a male/female/brother/sister doublet, where the 'Artemis' half is apparently killed by a male. This is again echoed in the numerous conflicts between Zeus and Hera who, though husband and wife, are also brother and sister.

We have evidence of a ritual to Artemis *Agrotera*, Of the Outside World, which was performed prior to battle. *Ephebes*, uninitiated young men undergoing their military training, would sacrifice a goat and then swear an oath of allegiance in the Sanctuary of Aglauros, whose myth 'explained' the ritual. They would then hang the goatskin (and head presumably) on an oak stake (the oak was associated with Zeus) in the battlefield. If they were victorious, they would then hang captured arms – helmet, shield and spear – on this 'trophy'. Together, the goatskin (*aigis*) and arms formed the symbols of Athena in her aspect as *Nike*, Victorious. In other words, success in war seems to have transformed Artemis (*Agrotera*) into Athena (*Nike*), the huntress (killer of animals) into the warrior (killer of humans), the goddess of the countryside into the goddess of the city, and 'nature' into 'culture'.

The historiographer Herodotos mentions an annual festival amongst the Libyan Machlyes in honour of Athena, at which the girls divided themselves into two groups and fought each other with stones and sticks. If any girl, during the course of the battle, was fatally injured, they said it was proof that she was not a maiden (*pseudoparthenos*, a 'false maiden'). In the myths of Medusa, Pallas, the Kekropides and the *Gigantomachy*, we again have battle situations resulting in the death of a single opponent. At first sight, these victims are not all *parthenoi*, unless we understand *gorgo* as generally meaning 'monster' or 'monstrous situation'. We have already seen how the *parthenos* was regarded as a pathological condition in females, requiring the spilling of her blood (menarche, defloration, parturition), in which case perhaps we can understand the *parthenos* – or some aspect of *parthenos* – as itself being the *gorgo*. We might view war as a *gorgo* too.

Medusa was an unmarried mother, as was Athena with regard to Erichthonios: an unmarried mother was an ambivalent figure, for the idea transgressed 'normal' category boundaries. Medusa was a warrior queen, representing her community, Athena was the goddess of war and tutelary deity of Athens. Medusa tried to defend her community against invasion by Perseus; Athena helped defend the Olympians against the Giants. In terms of the sexual division of labour, war was supposedly a masculine pursuit, thus both Medusa and Athena are ambivalent. Perseus kills a *gorgo*, just as the *ephebes* sacrifice a goat, and Athena kills Pallas/Enkelados. The Libyan girls enact a mock battle, as do Pallas and Athena, the end result of which merely confirms that the one who dies is not a *parthenos* precisely because *The Parthenos* is Athena. In other words, in all these battles the fact that Athena is the *Parthenos Athenaia* is reconfirmed, making this a ritual of renewal where both killer and victim are opposing aspects of Athena. The ritual of renewal therefore sets up and then destroys ambiguity in order to reconfirm the status quo.

The myth of the Kekropides is quoted as *aition* for a ritual called the *Arrephoria*; unfortunately we do not know for sure in which month it took place and to which festival it was attached, though it has been linked with the *Thesmophoria*. The name of the ritual comes from the *Arrephoroi*, four young girls, aged between 5 and 11, who were in the service of Athena, and they were called the Bearers or 'carriers of the secret things'. However, in lexicons this name is variously given as *Ersephoria* or *Hersephoria*, possibly linking it to one of the daughters' names – all three have something to do with 'dew', which could be a euphemism for 'semen'. We hear of the participation of the *Arrephoroi* in three rituals, the *Chalkeia*, the *Panathenaia* and the *Arrephoria* itself.

Every year, all the girls and women of Athens would contribute towards the making and presenting of a new *peplos*, a short woollen robe, to the cult statue (*xoanon*) of Athena *Polias*, Of the City, which was housed in the Parthenon on the Akropolis. There would be hundreds of cows sacrificed in her honour, and the meat would be distributed to the entire community. This occurred at a festival called the *Panathenaia*, which took place in the first month of the Attic year, *Hekatombaia*, a name which recalls the 'hundreds of victims'. As such it was obviously a ritual of renewal. However, the *peplos* itself was commenced some nine months previously, with obvious reproductive symbolism, at a festival called the *Chalkeia* in *Pyanepsion*, the same month as the *Thesmophoria*.

The *Chalkeia* was a festival of workermen and women, dedicated to Hephaistos and Athena, the 'parents' of the gorgo Erichthonios. The priestess of Athena and two of the *Arrephoroi* would set up a loom on the Akropolis on which the *Ergastinai*, young women in the service of Athena *Ergane*, Workerwoman, would weave the *peplos*. The robe would be woven in bright colours — blue and yellow (the colour of symbolic death) — and traditionally incorporated some scene from the *Gigantomachy*, notably Athena's killing of the gorgo.

This same scene was also depicted in one of the pediments of the Parthenon. Thus the robe presented to Athena's cult statue wore the face of the *gorgo* on its breast, just as Athena wore Medusa's face on her robe, and the image, *xoanon*, of Pallas bore the robe of Athena. We also saw in the Kekropides myth how Erichthonios hid in Athena's bosom, another 'face' on the breast of the goddess, who is a child indirectly born of her but also born of Hephaistos (Fire) and Gaia (Earth). Finally, a fragment of a lost Sophocles play refers to this festival as being dedicated to Athena *Gorgopis*, Grim-eyed or Gorgon-faced, highlighting the crucial point of the ritual — to celebrate the 'killing' of the *gorgo*. Where the *ephebes* kill their *gorgo* as a goat sacrifice, the maidens kill theirs by somehow re-enacting — or re-presenting — Athena's victory, and just as after the victorious battle the *ephebes* become 'blooded' warriors, so the maidens after their re-enactment become 'bloodied' women, no longer either *korai* or *parthenoi*.

Finally, at the *Arrephoria*, whenever this took place, the young girls carried out their final duty to Athena. According to the geographer Pausanias, they had to perform certain ceremonies during the night. They carried on their heads what Athena's priestess gave them to carry, and neither she who gave it nor they who carried it knew what it was she had given them. In the city, not far from Aphrodite-in-the-Garden, was an enclosed space with a natural entrance to an underground descent; this is where the virgin girls went down. They left down there what they were carrying, and took another thing and brought it back covered up. They were then sent away, and other virgin girls were brought to the *akropolis* instead of them.

This is a good example of an excluded male pretending to have authoritative information of women-only rituals. However, excavations have revealed a secret descent into the bowels of the Athenian *akropolis*, and a shrine containing 'cakes' in the shape of pudenda and phalloi — obviously one or both of these things were contained in Athena's basket, and 'snake face' Erichthonios must have been a face with a phallic tail. A case might be made for the Gorgon's face and the concept of 'Bearded Aphrodite' as stylized female genitalia fringed with pubic hair. Freud certainly saw the Gorgon as a 'vagina dentata', but then he would!

That there is a Descent and Ascent links this ritual to Kore-Persephone and the *Thesmophoria*, so the *Arrephoria* also involved a symbolic death and rebirth, hence the discharge from Athena's service. The 'Bride of Death' has herself been killed because she is now ready for marriage to life, hence the involvement of Aphrodite. This completes the ritual cycle of the *parthenos*, for she is now ready to be transformed into a *gune*, 'woman' and 'wife'.

The most obvious theme of Pandora's myth is knowledge — who has it, how much they have, how they use it — and I don't think any of the males come out of it very well. Knowledge is clearly power and in this myth it is misused by males in order

Fig. 9 Restored model of the colossal cult statue of Athena, housed in the Parthenon and showing the goddess's traditional symbols: spear, tufted helmet, shield and *aigis*, or goatskin mantle (with the head of Medusa on her breast). Pausanias says that the original chryselephantine (gold and ivory) statue also depicted the birth of Pandora along one side of the plinth. *Courtesy of the Royal Ontario Museum, Toronto*

to gain power over each other. With Zeus and Prometheus having fought out their cosmic power struggle, the poor 'innocent' victim is Epimetheus, representing mankind.

Although the myth of Prometheus figures in several ancient sources, only Hesiod mentions Pandora. He gives us two versions: in the *Works and Days* and the *Theogony* which, as far as Pandora's role in man's fall from grace is concerned, are fairly consistent. In both cases, Hesiod is bemoaning the loss of the Golden Age of Kronos before the stuff of life (*bios*) had been hidden from men, thus necessitating a life of toil and hardship. He uses mythology to explain his personal situation with regard to his brother, Perses, who, he feels, has unjustly made off with the larger portion of their father's estate. Hesiod's vitriol at Pandora might give the impression of a hen-pecked husband, but in fact he was more a general misanthropist than misogynist since everyone seems to have annoyed him.

Despite this solitary mention, the myth of Pandora is important for two reasons. Firstly, it is the only myth that explains why women came into being. Like the Judaeo-Christian myth of Eve, the currency of man's fall is women's wish for knowledge, but where Eve's inquisitiveness is in direct disobedience of god's commandment not to eat of the Tree which becomes the instrument of that fall, Pandora herself is the punishment for Prometheus's disobedience, and her presence on earth is the everlasting reminder to men of the unbridgeable gap between mortal and immortal.

The notion of a deceptive gift (*dolon*) has been pounced upon with glee by the French scholar Jean-Pierre Vernant, who has produced a quite dazzling structural analysis of this myth in *Myth, Structure and Society* (1982). He analyses the original Greek and finds a linguistic structural framework, especially through use of the words *gaster*, which means 'stomach' but with the connotation of 'womb', and *dolon*. He pulls out and elaborates upon Hesiod's metaphoric link between, on the one hand, the ugly-looking ox stomach in which the goodies were hidden and the tasty-looking white fat in which the nasties were hidden and, on the other, Pandora who, like white fat, is also a delicacy and a luxury, but who hides ugliness because she, and the subsequent race of women, is a 'hungry belly' devouring men's energies.

The apportioning of the ox is Hesiod's explanation for the origins of sacrifice as a form of gastronomic communication between men and the gods, and for the apparently disrespectful fact that the worse portion, i.e. the inedible parts, is donated to the gods. The loss of eternal fire loses men their immortal status and further reduces them to the level of animals. It places them in a precarious balance, hovering like a Sword of Damocles over their own descent into bestiality if the need for toil is ignored. Just as the *sperma* of fire is hungry and must be buried in the hearth and nurtured, so Pandora is a 'hungry belly', like the earth itself, which must be 'fed' with men's seed and laboured over if food and offspring are to be produced and reproduced. This is the kind of Strife (Eris) that Hesiod approves of as absolutely necessary for life – in contrast to the unapproved-of Strife that Pandora's *pithos* holds in the form of *Keres*, Sprites, which initiates wars, brings about illness and disease and old age. So Pandora comes to personify man's ambiguous structural position between divinity and bestiality, the fact that the stuff of life must now be laboured for rather than arriving at without effort, and the fact that in order to persist through time – since he is no longer immortal and a constant – man must constantly reconstitute himself through reproduction and ritual. Pandora is therefore a beautiful evil, a *kalos kakon*, for without her man cannot reproduce himself.

Following on from this, the second reason that this myth is important is that it tells us how woman was made, the various attributes bestowed upon her by the gods from which womankind is thereafter reconstituted. In a ritual context, therefore, it gives us a kind of recipe of acquisition by which a young girl is transformed from *parthenos* into *gune*.

Much is made of the supposedly ironic derivation of Pandora's name, that such a bane of man's existence might be called a gift of all the gods, even if that gift is a deceit. However, it is untrue that all the gods bestowed gifts, since only Hephaistos, Athena, Hermes and, to a lesser extent, Aphrodite are involved, with slight additions from the *Korai*, the *Charites* and Peitho (Seduction or Persuasion):

1. Hephaistos formed her of earth (*gaia*); or he mixed earth and water and gave the image a voice and human strength; or he moulded her of clay;
2. Athena *Glaukopis* gave her a girdle, clothed her and covered her head with the 'finely-wrought' *(polydaidala)* veil; Pallas Athena put a garland of flowers on her head and a crown of gold made by Hephaistos; Athena taught her needlework and weaving (*Ergane*);
3. Golden Aphrodite gave her grace (*charin*) and cruel longing; the *Charites* and Peitho put gold necklaces on her; the rich-haired *Horai* gave her a crown of flowers;
4. Hermes the Guide, also called Killer of Argos, put in her the wiles of a bitch and a deceitful nature;
5. Finally Zeus named her Pandora.

In both versions, the starting point is that Hephaistos, the god of craftsmen, moulds the initial image out of earth and water. Although the usual word for potter's clay, *kelos*, is not used, I think we are still intended to see Pandora as being fashioned in much the same way a pot would be. Thus it is no surprise that, unlike the *Kekropides/Arrephoroi* who are given a basket (*kiste*), Pandora is presented with a *pithos*, an extremely large jar used to store olive oil (Athena's gift to the Athenians), wine (Dionysos) or corn (Demeter). Hephaistos's involvement together with Athena's epithets of *Glaukopis* and Pallas, and the learning of *Ergane*, surely suggest some ritual practice at the *Chalkeia*, and the bestowing of a robe and veil suggest the *Panathenaia*.

The crown of flowers (*anthes*) and Pandora's opening of the pithos point to the *Anthesteria*, a Festival of Flowers held in spring which seems to have been a mixture of wine festival and rite of passage for 3-year-old children passing out of infancy. The festival was dedicated to Dionysos, god of wine, and the first day was called *Pithoigia*, the Opening of the Jars, when the new vintage would be broached. But metaphorically it could also refer to Pandora opening her own 'jar', i.e. being ready for marriage. The lexicographer Hesychius notes that in Rhodes a young maiden 'ripe for marriage' was referred to as *anthesteriades*. Also at the *Anthesteria*, a sacred marriage, *hieros gamos*, took place between the priest of Dionysos and the *Basilinna*,

Queen, who was married to the *archon basileus* (chief king), one of the magistrates who organized the festival. Remember that Medusa's name meant Queen, and that Hera's name was also an honorific title. This *hieros gamos* was said to re-enact the marriage of Dionysos to Ariadne after she had been abandoned on the island of Naxos by Theseus.

The divine archetype of 'wife', *gune*, was Hera, protectress of the social institution of marriage through her sacred marriage to her brother Zeus. Although this was an incestuous union, as wife of 'the father of gods and men', it placed Hera on an equal footing with him. In antiquity, Hera had two main cult centres, between Argos and Lerna, and on the island of Samos, where her temple was probably the oldest in Greece. Just as at Athens Athena was known as the *Parthenos Athenaia*, the Maid of Athens, so at Argos Hera was called *Here Argeia*, the Lady/Heroine of Argos, suggesting that here also there was a biosocial role in myth and ritual.

The commentator Plutarch, himself a Boiotian, recounts the myth of Plataia as *aition* for a strange fire ritual that took place in his country. There was a league of cities, under the direction of the city of Plataia, which would construct *daidala* by performing a sacrifice in a certain sacred grove. They would leave out pieces of the cooked meat and wait until they attracted a flock of ravens. Whichever bird first partook of the meat would be watched very carefully to see which tree it would land in first, this being the one they would cut down for the *daidalon* plank. Then every sixtieth year, all the *daidala* would be gathered together on Mount Kithairon, there would be animal sacrifices — a bull for Zeus and a cow for Hera — and everything would be consumed in a holocaust.

Hera also used her wrath to protect — or at least vindicate — the idea of faithful marriage, and as such she necessarily comes into conflict with Aphrodite, whose power was no respecter of the lines drawn by ties of social kinship. The significance of this cosmic conflict is often understated in the context of the Trojan War. As we saw in the myth of Atalanta, when Atalanta stoops to pick up the apples of the Hesperides strewn by Hippomenes, she is in effect accepting his proposal of marriage. Similarly, the myth of the Golden Apple of Discord, thrown down at the wedding celebrations of Peleus and Thetis, is not really concerned with a divine beauty competition as much as Zeus — or his mortal deputy, Paris — renewing his vows and remarrying Kallisto, 'the Fairest', which in his case should have been Hera.

Instead, Paris elects that Aphrodite should claim the apple — almost a cosmic *non sequitur* since Aphrodite is not directly concerned with marriage — and the loosening of her girdle, usually the ritual act of a new bride on her wedding night, is instead literally the action of a 'loose' woman. Paris has had the choice of 'marrying' Hera, Aphrodite or Athena, but he rejects chastity and faithful marriage (Athena and Hera, respectively) in favour of the unrestrained, marriage-wrecking sexuality that Aphrodite represents. Thus we find both Hera and Athena united in their hatred of the Trojans — whom Paris represents — and in their support for the Greeks: where the latter are sober and restrained, the Trojans are lustful and unrestrained *barbaroi*. In this context, Athena represents chastity and sexual continence as a whole, rather than just unviolated virginity, and she is therefore associated with Hera. The Trojan

War, as a cosmic struggle between the powers of Aphrodite and Hera/Athena, boils down to the conflict between biological sexual impulses – here seen as anathema to civilization precisely because there are no lines or limits – and the social conventions imposed by ties of marriage.

Towards the end of the war, according to Homer's *Iliad*, the prime Trojan hero, Hektor, orders the women of Troy to make an offering to Athena as protectress of their city. They are to sacrifice twelve heifers – heifers or cows were the usual sacrifice to Athena, as well as to Hera – and to dedicate to her the best robe in the royal storehouse. This surely forms the basis of the Athenian *Panathenaia* which as we saw was a ritual renewing the concept of the city's integrity by preventing the loosening of internal lines (faithful marriage) and the breaching of external boundaries (war).

In the case of Troy, however, Athena chooses to ignore their entreaty – she is, after all, on the side of the Greeks. The end result is that Troy is invaded by the Wooden Horse, a 'trick', like the *daidalon*, bearing Greek soldiers hidden inside. The city is subsequently set ablaze and razed to the ground, becoming a holocaust of *hekatombs*, 'hundreds of victims', exactly like the all-consuming fire ritual to Hera and Zeus at the Boiotian *Daidala*. Note also that it was a man named Daidalos who constructed Pasiphaë's wooden cow. The usual Homeric epithet for Hera was *Boopis*, usually translated as 'cow-eyed' or, more accurately here, 'cow-faced', suggesting that the wooden plank referred to as *daidalon* was hung with a cow mask to represent Hera/Pasiphaë: just as Hera hid in Euboia and Pasiphaë hid in the cow, so the real Helen 'hid' in Egypt. We might therefore view this fire ritual as a way of ensuring that the substitute *daidalon* is the object that burns rather than the entity it represents, the *hieros gamos* of Zeus and Hera, and the integrity of the city.

This fire ritual can then be connected to the myth of Semele, herself consumed by Zeus' lightning fire via the agency of Hera, where Semele and Plataia symbolically express the same idea – all the more so because both Thebes and Plataia were in Boiotia. Semele's son by Zeus, Dionysos, returned to Thebes in order to establish his worship and 'vindicate' his mother. The city's refusal to recognize Dionysos as a god provoked him into sending the Theban women 'raving' on Mount Kithairon, an idea which the men of Thebes, represented by its authoritarian King Pentheus, found anathema to their notion of order and civilization. The end result was the tearing apart of Pentheus, that is, the destruction of civilization, and by extension the future of Thebes represented by its children.

In the same way, although in the Pasiphaë myth we hear no more of her after her mating with the bull, suggesting that somehow she is destroyed, a child is born of this union, albeit a monstrous one. In which case, we must view Dionysos and the Minotaur as both symbolically representing the same idea: Minotaur's name reminds us of his bullish nature, he is a man with a bull's head just as Pasiphaë was a woman with a cow's head; one of Dionysos' manifestations was the bull; Pentheus's mother refers to him as a bull calf. Thus the mother/son destruction myths of Dionysos/Pentheus articulate the removal of the bullish in male youths on their way to becoming fully socialized adult males, a transformation that is in part effected by women.

The final myth of Medeia incorporates the majority of the ideas already discussed. She was a *parthenos* who, under the influence of Aphrodite, falls in love with Jason. Her 'abduction' from Colchis is a symbolic death, and provokes various battle situations: with the Sown Men, with the dragon (*gorgo*), and between Jason and Medeia's father. Medeia, whose name like Medusa also meant Queen, herself participates in 'battle' by destroying her brother, Apsyrtos (again, a brother/sister antagonism): she tears him to pieces and strews them along the route to delay her pursuers, a mirror image of Hippomenes delaying Atalanta. Medeia considers herself to be the wife, *gune*, of Jason and has two sons by him, becoming a *meter* but remaining a *parthenos*, 'unmarried'. However, Jason proposes to marry Glauke – whose name links her to Athena *Glaukopis* – which provokes Medeia's jealousy.

Medeia is the granddaughter of Helios, the sun god, and her jealousy is literally fiery. She smears Glauke's bridal dress and tiara with an ointment which causes Glauke to burst into flames, just as Hera's jealousy causes Plataia to be burned and Semele to be consumed by Zeus' thunderbolt. Remember also that Pandora was man's punishment for Prometheus's theft of fire. Finally, Medeia kills her two sons and bears them off in the Chariot of the Sun; this part of the myth is used to explain a ritual to Hera *Akraia*, Of the Heights, at Korinth, where a group of youths and maidens were consecrated to Hera and thereby initiated. This reminds us of the Athenian tribute sent to be 'consumed' by the bull-man Minotaur and rescued by Theseus. The myth of Pasiphaë concerns bulls and cows, just as the Daidala ritual saw a bull sacrificed for Zeus and a cow for Hera, which restores the integrity of their marriage. We also saw how the Trojan entreaty to Athena, as the protectress of their Height (*akropolis*), failed and resulted in the holocaust of the city, and how these fire rituals were all part of a massive ritual of renewal – both the last and first rites of a ritual year – for the city and for that city's tutelary deity.

In myth, fire also endows humans with immortality: Thetis tried to make her son, Akhilleus, immortal by dipping him in fire, but hung onto his heel which made this his only vulnerable part; the hero Herakles, at the end of his Labours, immolated himself on a funeral pyre, after which he was 'adopted' by Hera, who passed him 'through her skirt'. He assumes her name and is accepted on Mount Olympos, the home of the gods. The example I gave, though, concerns Demeter at Eleusis and brings us back to our starting myth, emphasizing the cyclical nature of the ritual round. The myth of Demeter at Eleusis was quoted as *aition* for the most famous and well-attended festival in the ancient world, the Eleusinian Mysteries. Whole books have been written about the nature of these mysteries, but suffice it to say that they were concerned with hierarchies of initiation through revelation, whereby initiates came closer and closer to immortality on earth.

To some extent, ancient Greek married men were right to have reservations about women, because a 'biological' bond to the hearth of their fathers must have severely tested the loyalty of their wives. In aristocratic and wealthy families especially, marriages were based on political and economic alliances rather than love, and men's sexual use of concubines, *hetairai* (high-class courtesans) and young boys, plus an apparent preference for male company, did little to enhance the degree of marital affection. If tomb dedications are anything to go by, however, this was not the case with poor, lower-class marriages and some of the inscriptions from husbands to their wives are quite touching. It must be remembered that the vast majority of myths concern noble families, and are predominantly concerned with the founding of dynasties, rather than with romantic love.

In conclusion, connecting myth to ritual in this way shows how important a role women played not only in women-only rituals but also in the mixed rituals, and therefore how important women were for the production and reproduction of society outside a purely biological context. To equate women with nature might be seen as a devaluation, but only if that society also devalues nature itself. Ancient Greek society harboured the contradiction of both fearing and admiring the power of nature, and therefore women, to destroy civilization and to give birth to it. The power was ambiguous, and whether devalued as a monster or fêted as a supernatural power, the ancient Greeks knew it was never to be ignored or underrated.

References and Further Reading

The best place to read ancient Greek myths is in the original Greek sources, such as the writers I have named in the text (e.g. Pausanias, Apollodoros, Herodotos, Homer and the tragedians Sophocles, Aiskhylos and Euripides) and the Roman poets, Ovid and Virgil. Many good and inexpensive translations exist of the major writers (for example, the Penguin editions). For anyone with a smattering of Greek or better, then the Loeb hardback library – with Greek text and translation opposite – is very good if slightly more expensive, though sometimes the English translations seem almost as archaic as the original Greek!

Probably the best place to start, though, is the perennial *Greek Myths* by Robert Graves, published in two volumes. Graves has collected together the many versions and variants of the majority of ancient Greek myths and related them to Celtic, Semitic and other geographically adjacent mythologies. However, one should be very wary of his notes, which tend towards a Bachofen/Engels style of analysis: that there was originally an earth-based matriarchy which was overthrown by a sky-god patriarchal system. Also, the *Oxford Classical Dictionary* is another good source.

I have included some modern theoretical texts which examine modes of thought and analytical methodologies for those who wish to investigate the 'meaning' of myth. For those who don't, bear in mind that the persistence of ancient myths in modern culture really indicates that meaning is not fixed within one culture or one epoch. As long as the 'facts' are not bent, myths can mean whatever you want them to mean. Their beauty is in their currency.

GREEK

Apollodoros, *The Library*
Herodotos, *The Histories*
Hesiod, *The Works and Days*
——, *Theogony*
Homer, *Iliad*
——, *Odyssey*
Ovid, *Metamorphoses*
Pausanias, *Guide to Greece*
Virgil, *Aeneid*

MODERN

Bernal, M. (1987), *Black Athena* (London: Vintage). Rather dense and specialist, but worthwhile if you can plough through it. Bernal examines racist attitudes among the ancient Greeks, who sought to bury their African and Semitic roots, and also the way in which subsequent modern scholarship has wrapped up this racism inside its own for Victorian imperialist ends.

Burkert, W. (1985), *Greek Religion* (Oxford: Blackwell)

——, (1983), *Homo Necans: The Anthropology of Ancient Greek Sacrificial Ritual and Myth* (Berkeley: University of California Press). The first is an excellent overview of ancient Greek religious thought and gives more detail of the various deities; the second attempts to link myth to ritual in a structural way.

Cameron, A. and Kuhrt, A. (eds) (1983), *Images of Women in Antiquity* (London: Croom Helm). A collection of excellent essays by feminist scholars, examining various aspects of women's life.

Douglas, M. (1966), *Purity and Danger: An Analysis of the Concepts of Pollution and Taboo* (London: Ark Paperbacks). An anthropological text, not directly concerned with the ancient Greeks, but very useful for analysing the reasons why certain groups of people are stigmatized in myth and ritual. Her basic notion is that in structured societies, the body politic (male) uses the body physical (female) as a 'theatre' upon which to enact social dramas.

Dowden, K. (1989), *Death and the Maiden* (London: Routledge). An important text concerning the initiation of girls.

Harrison, J. (1962), *Prolegomena to the Study of Ancient Greek Religion* (London: Merlin Press). Harrison describes in enormous detail the various myths and rituals that concerned women.

Hastrup, K. (1978), 'The Semantics of Biology: Virginity' in S. Ardener (ed.), *Defining Females: The Nature of Women in Society* (London: Croom Helm). A useful look at not only the meaning of (women's) biology, but also how that meaning is itself a cultural construct, and what difference sexual difference makes.

Lefkowitz, M.R. (1986), *Women in Greek Myth* (London: Duckworth)

Lefkowitz, M.R. and Fant, M.B. (1982), *Women's Life in Greece and Rome* (London: Duckworth). An excellent – if not the best – source book on women.

Napier, A.D. (1986), 'Perseus and the Gorgon Head' in *Masks, Transformations and Paradox* (Berlekley: University of California Press). For an interesting examination of the role of Medusa.

Rose, H.J. (1964), *A Handbook of Greek Mythology* (London: Methuen)

Vernant, J.-P. (1982), 'The Myth of Prometheus in Hesiod' in *Myth and Society in Ancient Greece* (London: Methuen). For a structural analysis of the Pandora myth.

JULIA VYTKOVSKAYA

Slav Mythology

(*Note*: Square brackets represent translator's additions.)

At some time in the first millennium [AD] the Urslavs ceased to be a unified group. As they dispersed, a process of differentiation into West, South and East Slavs was initiated. The Old Russian cities of Kiev and Novgorod became established as settlement centres of the Eastern Slavs; these cities still exist today.

A similar process affected the mythology of the Urslav tribes; there was a development of individual local mythologies; these did, however, preserve some traits common to all the Slavic mythologies. Urslav mythology itself has Indo-European roots, as can be observed in the similarity of certain narrative elements, most particularly in a number of archetypal structures.

No Urslav mythological texts have been preserved. The main sources of information on East Slavonic mythology are the *Poucheniya* [ecclesiastical condemnations of paganism], the *Russian Chronicles* and linguistic and archaeological data, as well as ethnographical materials and folkloric texts such as *bylinas* [folk epics], various traditions and legends, folk tales, proverbs and sayings.

Paganism was the sole belief system in Russia until the end of the tenth century. In 980 Prince Vladimir raised a pantheon to the Old Russian pagan gods on a hill at Kiev. Seven wooden idols were erected, one to each of the chief deities of the Russian pantheon. Six of them – those to Perun, Stribog, Dazhbog, Svarog, Khors and Mokosh – stood on the hill's summit, the seventh (to Veles) at its base.

Perun, the thunder god, was the chief amongst the gods of the Eastern Slavs. He was represented as a man in his prime, with a beard and whiskers. The beard was in fact his identifying attribute. His weapons were stones, arrows and axes. Perun was associated with the oak tree and with oak groves, and also with hills; here idols to him would be placed.

The next most important god after Perun was the 'cattle' god Veles (or Volos). Veles and Perun were perceived as opposites, even in a topographical sense. Perun's idol was on a hill-top, up above, but that of Veles stood down below. Perun was the god of princely retinues, Veles represented the rest of Russian society. These deities are linked by their place in thunder myth: the thunder god Perun, who dwells in the heavens, campaigns against his snake-like enemy, who lives on the earth below.

The cause of their strife is Veles' theft of cattle or human beings from Perun, or (in some variants) Veles' theft of his wife. The embattled Veles takes refuge under a tree or rock or transforms himself into a man, a horse or a cow. Whilst duelling with Veles, Perun splits rocks and trees in two and flings down arrows. Perun's victory is signalled by the rain and the fruitfulness it brings.

Stribog is the god of wind, Dazhbog of the sun, Svarog of the sky; Khors is also linked with the sun. The sole female figure in the Old Russian pantheon is Mokosh; she was connected with typically female occupations, such as spinning.

The links between the gods and their hierarchy were laid down as follows: Perun and Veles were paired, and Stribog, Dazhbog and Svarog formed a further group; Mokosh was on the periphery. Sometimes another god was included in the pantheon: Semargla or Semiglava [The Seven-Headed]. His functions are unclear, but most often he is mentioned in connection with the sacred number 7 and personifies the seven-member Old Russian pantheon.

Mokosh is, therefore, the only Old Russian goddess to have a place in the pantheon alongside Perun and the others. In the list of pagan gods given in the *Russian Primary Chronicle*, Mokosh is the last god named, Perun the first. Mokosh also has a special place in later lists of pagan gods. She was a woman with a large head and long arms, who would sit spinning in an *izba* [dwelling hut] at night. Tradition forbade leaving tow around at night 'lest Mokosh spin it away'. She represents the thunder god's wife, or his female counterpart, in Eastern Slavic myth; she is close in type to the Greek Fates – spinning the threads of a man's life. Mokosh was preserved in Ukrainian folk memory as late as the mid-nineteenth century.

As well as the seven gods above, the Eastern Slavs honoured a great many other divinities of various levels of significance. The next level is formed by the gods linked with work cycles and seasonal rituals, and the gods representing the unity of small social collectives. Their functions have a high degree of abstraction, which allows one to suppose that they personify the most basic oppositions: *Rod* [Birth/Ancestry], *Chur* [Taboo], *Pravda/Krivda* [Right/Left/Wrong], *Smert* [Death], *Sud* [Judgement], etc.

Finally, there is the level of spirits, animals and different unindividualized aspects of the unclean: these are linked with every dimension of mythological space, stretching from the home to the forest. They include the *leshii* [male wood spirit], *domovoi* [male house spirit], *kikimora* [female house spirit], *vodyanoi* and *rusalka*, [male and female water spirits], *vil*, *mara* and *likhoradka*.

The central image which the Slavs used to link all the mythological relations just enumerated was that of the world-tree. This was usually a birch, an oak, an aspen or an apple-tree. Similarities with the mythological perceptions of other nationalities can be seen here. In the Urslav consciousness, the world was described according to dualistic contrasts, or binary oppositions. These determined the spatial, temporal, social and all other elements of their world-view. The dualistic principle of what was beneficial or not beneficial to the collective – the community or tribe – was expressed in mythology. The central binary oppositions were as follows:

Life—death. This is personified in the images *Rod* [Birth/Ancestry], a male god, and *Morena/Mara* [Death], a female god; cf. water of life/water of death.

Even—uneven. Even numbers are beneficial and linked with the masculine principle; the even days of the week are dedicated to male gods. Uneven numbers are maleficent: they are linked with the feminine principle. So Thursday [the fourth day] is linked with Perun and Friday [the fifth] with Mokosh.

Right—left. This binary opposition is central to divination and to the celebration of rituals, as well as to the reading of omens, and is reflected in the personifications of Right, who dwells in the sky, and Left/Wrong, who dwells on the earth. In Old Russian rituals women stand to the left of men.

Male—female. This is linked with the Right/Left opposition above; it is manifest in wedding and burial rituals, where the woman's place is on the left of the man. Of great importance is the differentiation of male and female figures according to function, significance and number. The female figures are few in number and generally linked with what is negative. Also characteristic is the repetition of one and the same symbol in two different hypostases, that is, male and female forms. So *Div* [a sea monster] has the female counterparts, the *divas*; *Rod* has the female counterparts, the *rozhanitsas*, etc. The female role in these binary oppositions is especially stressed where magic or sorcery are concerned.

Above—below. i.e. the opposition of sky and earth, ritually reflected in the siting of places sacred to Perun on hill-tops, to Veles in valleys.

Sky—earth. This is reflected in man's ties to earth, the gods' links to the heavens. The opening up of the soil is celebrated as a festival in spring. The earth is also linked with a chain of female figures, the sky is personified as a man. Many rituals, especially agrarian or work rituals, employ the motif of the earth's fertilization as the fertilization of a woman. *Mat' syra-zemlya* [Mother Damp Earth] is the fixed epithet of the highest female divinity.

South—north. This opposition is fundamental to the regulation of ritual behaviour.

Dry land—sea. This binary opposition is also linked with the male/female polarization. The sea has a special significance as the location of large numbers of female figures, most of them negative: it is the abode of death and sicknesses. In spells sicknesses are banished to the sea. The personification of the sea is the sea god and his twelve daughters, the *likhoradkas* [fevers]. Later a further binary opposition, that of Dry and Wet, overlaid this first. The later expressions of these deities have two hypostases, e.g. Ilya [the Prophet Elijah] Dry and Ilya Wet, Nikola [St Nicholas] Dry and Nikola Wet, etc.

Fire—damp. These elements are in conflict.

Day—night. The mythological figures here are the *nochnitsas* [night women] and the *Zors* [dawn spirits].

Spring—winter. Spring is of greater importance here, and is linked with mythical personifications of fertility, such as Yarila, Kostroma and Morena, and also with such rituals as the burial of winter and the opening up of spring, as well as with various vegetable and zoomorphic symbols.

Sun–moon. Personified in the mythological motif of the nuptials of Sun and Moon. The symbol of the sun is a wheel.

White–black. White is positive and black negative. White and black magic, light and dark, etc.

Near–far. This opposition defines spatial structure both horizontally and in temporal terms. In Russian folklore there is often a contrast between home (the near) and the 'twenty-seventh kingdom', that which is strange, far distant.

Home–forest. This opposition embraces the whole of mythological space.

Youth–age. This emphasizes the superiority of maturity to senility.

Sacred–profane.

It is evident from this brief description of the basic mythological figures and structures that feminine images are fewer in number than the masculine, and that the feminine principle in binary oppositions is always represented as damp, dark, bad and non-beneficial to the collective. The feminine principle is seen as more closely associated with pagan rites, the earth, magic and sorcery, and as exercising a direct influence on the surrounding elements. This is why the number of feminine divinities increases sharply as we go down the hierarchy.

As worshippers of nature's elemental forces, the Urslavs tried to express symbolically in their religious ceremonies what was happening in the heavens, or else what they wanted to see happening there. The mythical perceptions linked with song, music and dance gave such ceremonies a sacred significance, and made their presence essential in pagan festivals and rituals. The Slavs' rumbustious festivals were accompanied by dressing-up, drunkenness and songs. They were staged in order to honour the happy return of the spring rains, which drove away the demon of winter, and in order to summon the thunder god in time of drought. Round-dances were an important part of pagan festivals. These were a combination of song and dramatic spectacle; they began to be performed in the spring, when the nuptials of sky and earth took place, calling humans, too, to union. It was this ideal of love and the marriage that followed it which was the central motif developed in pagan dance performances.

In pagan Russia, various types of wedding ritual were customary: amongst steppe-dwellers, the bride was brought to the home of her bridegroom; whilst amongst forest-dwellers an older form of wedding-rite – abduction – was still practised. Polygamy was widespread. Men might have up to seven wives. Marriage was perceived as the permanent union of a man and a woman with obligations incumbent on both sides, but precedence in the union was given to the male partner. The simplicity of ethics and custom inherent in the Slavic conception of entry into the marriage bond is very evident in pagan rites and ritual games.

Only eight years after Prince Vladimir had put up the pantheon, in 988, the Prince accepted baptism; Christianity became the official religion of Old Russia and the hill-top idols were cast down. Pagan belief, its accompanying rituals and traditions were now forbidden by both state (secular) and ecclesiastical (spiritual) authorities.

It might have been supposed that the arrival of Christianity would have put an end to the existence of Slavonic mythology in its Eastern Slavonic form. But the established archetypes of consciousness were in fact preserved for a very considerable length of time in the popular tradition, determining people's way of life and the rituals which they practised. The most important Christian mythological figures were identified with pagan gods. So Perun became associated in the mythological consciousness with Ilya [the Prophet Elijah], as the god of thunder and lightning, Veles with Saint Vlasy [Blaxos], Yarila with St Yury [George], etc.

The lesser mythological figures were more of a fixture in popular consciousness; around these developed the quixotic and complex combinations which make up the system known as *dvoeverie* [belief ambivalence]. This 'belief ambivalence' originated in the years after Christianization and is preserved to this day. The demonology survived more or less intact: belief in *leshiis, domovois, vodyanois* and *rusalkas* persisted. Christian rituals, especially those which had links with agriculture, that is those which were directly connected with the life of the collective, incorporated pagan dances and sacrifices. It is likely, in fact, that only the most educated part of the population became Christianized. The broad masses long remained attached to the earlier, pagan world-view, which gradually underwent adaptations under the new influence of Christian teaching. Enthusiasts for propriety were incensed by this 'belief ambivalence'. Secular and spiritual authorities fought especially furiously against it after the liberation of the Rus from the Tatar-Mongol invasion. But the names of the pagan gods remained preserved in folk memory even in the eighteenth century, and in the nineteenth festivals were still celebrated in many villages which included pagan rites. So, instead of visiting church people would dance and play ritual games; fasts were poorly observed.

The adoption of Christianity also affected those myths relating to the most important female figures. St Paraskeva/Pyatnitsa is a direct continuation of the Old Russian goddess Mokosh. The Christian and pagan cults were fused, and Paraskeva/Pyatnitsa became a women's saint. She was the patron saint of many women's crafts central to the economic life of Old Russia. Flax began to be broken on 28 October — that is, on St Paraskeva's day. Right up to the nineteenth century it was believed that one should not spin on Fridays [Pyatnitsa = Friday], nor break flax, bath children or wash clothes. Fasts were obligatory, and work prohibited. The chief role of this women's saint was probably to give women a break from heavy domestic work. A similar motif can be observed in another feminine mythological image, that of Sereda or Sreda [Wednesday]. She, like Paraskeva, is connected with the feminine principle of uneven numbers. She aided in weaving and bleaching cloth, punishing those who worked on Wednesdays.

The rite which involved a procession around the villages with 'Pyatnitsa' [Friday], a woman with hair let loose and covered in needle pricks, was still observed in the nineteenth century. The needle marks were there as a reminder that only impious women worked on Fridays. Paraskeva/Pyanitsa represents the mother/protector in women's archetypal consciousness; prayers were offered to her to keep order in the home. She had power over health, harvests and stock fertility.

Paraskeva could punish those who ignored her prohibitions by causing illness. She was identified with water, a female symbol amongst the Eastern Slavs. Here, for example, is a common motif in Russian tales: Baba-Yaga, the negative female image [the famous witch who lives in a hut on chickens' legs], gives the heroine a task – often to spin something. The heroine tries to flee, but her path is blocked by a river. She has to persuade it to help, and it agrees. In popular speech Pyatnitsa is often known as *Matushka* [Little Mother]. On the feast of the *Pokrov* [the Protection of the Virgin, a major Russian Orthodox holy day, celebrated on 1 October], girls who are eager to marry appeal to her: 'Matushka, Pyatnitsa/ Paraskeva, cover me quickly!' [The Russian phrase incorporates a sound pun on Paraskeva, Pokrov and *pokryt* – to cover in a sexual sense.]

The image of Paraskeva was much closer to earthly women than that of the pagan Mokosh. If Mokosh was 'responsible' for events which affected the well-being of a whole tribe or community, Paraskeva is much more closely linked with the individual family and home; every woman turns to her with her problems.

More and more female images of the lower gods appear – whilst honouring the higher Christian gods, the people did not forget to communicate, in their everyday lives, with the ordinary gods and goddesses who personified things which happened all the time in their world. The sky maidens – or sky women, as they are in Russian – are connected with many myths of later origin. In summer they rise up out of wells and fly to the clouds, carrying the water which will refresh the soil and help the harvests. When a child is bathed, people chant, 'Water off the goose's back flows/From you that which is bad goes!' or 'Water down should fly/You to on high!'

At the beginning of winter, when the first hail or snow falls, people in villages made snow-women – snow and hail are sent by the very same sky women. When these women came down to earth, they were known as water-women or *rusalkas*. *Rusalkas* were always young and long-haired. Grown-up *rusalkas* were unhappy drowned women, who were condemned to be water-women for ever. Only witches could dare to bathe with *rusalkas*, and anyone who heard their song will fall in the water and drown. When the sky-women coupled with the thunder god (during May and June), it was customary to organize *rusalka* festivals. Ritual games were accompanied by songs, dancing, mumming and sexual intercourse. Christianity forbade these festivals as 'blasphemous' and 'devilish', but they continued up to the twentieth century. In *rusalka* week girls would throw wreaths into the water, praying that they be sent rich bridegrooms.

The personification of unclean forces emerged as a female figure, the goddess of death, winter and night – Morena or Morana. According to Russian tradition, she has no family ties – that is, she has no links with those institutions which supported and furthered a sense of morality amongst the masses. She wanders eternally amidst the snows. The goddess of love was now Lada [Harmony]. Her image was a fusion of beliefs about the cloud-maidens and about the bright sun-maidens. She was the goddess not only of love, but of youth, beauty and fertility. Sometimes she is represented as the all-giving mother:

O, mother, Lada, mother!
Call the spring . . .

The goddess Zarya [Dawn] was courageous, warlike and fully armed. She came out in the morning and brought the sun with her, driving away the gloom and fogs of night with his bright rays. Prayers for protection were addressed to Zarya: 'Defend me, o maiden, with your veil from the enemy, from arquebus and arrow . . .' She was invoked to protect against death in battle.

Rites of 'spring's funeral' are still preserved amongst the people. In Eastern Slavic mythology, Kostroma was the personification of spring and fertility, a young woman wrapped in a white sheet and holding an oak bough, who walks to the accompaniment of round-dancing. At Kostroma's ritual burial her straw-filled image is burnt or torn apart to ritual weeping and laughter. But Kostroma would soon rise again. The ritual ensures fertility, and marks the transition to the spring cycle.

The most important East Slavonic wedding myth before Christianization was that of the marriage of Earth and Sky. According to mythological beliefs, the periodic celebration of this marriage was marked by such natural phenomena as rain and lightning; its fruit was not the universe as a whole, but the annually regenerated gifts of corn, fruits, etc. Such beliefs are incorporated in the rituals of sexual life. Marriage was seen to have a beneficial effect on young people's fertility, and so myths pertaining to the work cycle nearly always employ the motif of copulation in rituals dedicated to fertility enhancement. The connection of paganism and polygamy meant that marriage was perceived by the Eastern Slavs as an essential manifestation of the surrounding natural forces.

The Christian view of marriage as 'sacrament' did not impinge on popular consciousness for a long time. Entry into the married state was considered something natural, inevitable; so, too, the production of large numbers of children, which would ensure the numerical viability and prosperity of the tribal community.

After Christianization, special statutes were laid down (in the codes of Vladimir and Yaroslav), which put power over marriage into the hands of the church. But ordinary people went on living as before, without the presence of clergy. Weddings went on being celebrated in the pagan manner: people would 'dance and make money', make sacrifices, get drunk. Marriage would be celebrated at an early age — often at 12 or 13. For Slav pagans, the aspect of Christian marriage which was hardest to understand was monogamy. Men went on having as many wives as they could feed. Hence the ecclesiastical authorities were forced to allow up to three successive marriages. Every year the church increased its pressure. In the seventeenth century 'depravity' (cohabitation outside the bonds of church wedlock) was punishable by forcible banishment to a monastery. But Christianity's teaching that women had functions outside the bearing of children and eroticism did not take hold amongst the masses. All the same, it must be observed that both 'belief ambiguity' and the presence of a large heathen population in the Rus (a situation which arose because of Mongol/Tatar domination) led, it was thought, to a decline in morals amongst the population. Right up to the eighteenth century, bestiality and sodomy were widely practised in most sectors of Russian society.

The Englishman Giles Fletcher, who visited Russia in 1588, and published his account, *Of the Russe Common-Wealth*, in 1591, writes as follows:

> And yet it may be doubted whither is the greater, the cruelty or intemperancy that is used in that country. I will not speak of it, because it is so foul and not to be named. The whole country overfloweth with all sin of that kind. And no marvel, as having no law to restrain whoredoms, adulteries, and like uncleanness of life.

The sixteenth-century *Domostroi* [a manual of domestic management whose best-known variant was compiled by the archpriest Silvester] can be interpreted as an attempt to right matters. It is an account, by a man of that time for his contemporaries, of what was considered to be the ideal life of a virtuous man: 'The lord and master maintains his wife, children and servants in lawfulness, harmony and in the fear of the Lord.' This lord and master in fact ran everything in the household; he was responsible both for behaviour and for domestic economy. Everything and everyone was under his control. It can be seen that the Slavs continue to place men at the summit of all life — whether that of the family or of the community. Man is the head of the family; women, like children or servants, are of little account.

This emphasis on the man as head of the house is evident in mythological images too. The figure of the *domovoi* [house spirit] illustrates this: he was responsible for running the home and for peace and order within it. Sacrifices were made to him and he was used as a bogey to scare children. This cult is still preserved in some places in Russia.

All the central moments of the marriage rite — the betrothal, the *devichnik* [bride's party to say farewell to her girl friends on the night before the wedding], the events of the wedding day itself — are accompanied by laments from the bride. The bride begs that she should not be given in marriage and expresses terror as she anticipates her life in her new home, where heavy work and indifference or contempt await her. Whilst she sings mournful songs, the rest of the wedding party sing joyful ones.

If one looks closely at the wedding rites, it is clear that marriage as such is not the woman's only aim. She needs a husband for the sake of fertility. The image of herself as bearer of life is a persistent structural element in her consciousness. In Russian folk-tales the bridegroom is subject to many trials, all of which are designed to prove his sexual prowess. But on the other hand, the bride fears marriage and 'going to a strange house'; she fears her mother-in-law. Such fears are reflected in the conflict of step-mother and step-daughter, or heroine and Baba-Yaga, so often depicted in Russian folk-tales.

The theme of incest — an incestuous marriage — can be interpreted, in its most archaic form, as the mythological personification of the interaction of central binary oppositions — of polarities.

One of the myths in which the motif of an incestuous brother-sister marriage is present is the myth relating to the summer solstice. This festival was celebrated

Fig. 10 Baba-Yaga goes off to fight against the crocodile. A 'loubki' woodcut from the 1760s. The woodcut probably satirizes Peter the First (known as the 'Crocodile') and his wife, Catherine the First. *The Saltyknow-Chtchedrine Public Library, Leningrad.*

on the eve of the feast day of Ivan Kupala (24–25 June). Ivan Kupala is the popular name for John the Baptist, and this name was also given to a straw stuffed doll or dummy 'drowned' in water as part of the festival. All the festival participants would jump over the bonfire, leaping as high as possible to help the harvest. The festival was also accompanied by erotic dances and by copulation; its purpose was to ensure fertility. In the myths relating to Kupala, fire and water were characterized as brother and sister. The basis of the myth is an incestuous brother-sister marriage; the most important symbol in the ritual was accordingly the Ivan and Marya plant [heart's ease]. It has bi-coloured, blue and yellow petals; one colour represents the brother, the other the sister. In one variant of the myth, the brother makes to kill his seductress sister, who then asks him to plant flowers on her grave.

In folk-tales the disruption of marital and familial norms by such actions as incest or marriage to brides whose origins are too remote (in spatial terms) leads to various social effects, rather than to the cosmic effects characteristic of myth. If the theme of marriage is peripheral to myth, and familial relations are sometimes depicted as a means to attain economic ends, in folk-tales the means and ends are reversed, so to speak. So, in folk-tales all the trials of the hero are in essence merely a progress to marriage or to incest. Often the incest narrative is linked with disruption or breach of a taboo. In Russian folk-tales incest motifs differ according to the degree of relationship (whether parents and children, or brothers and sisters are involved). It is revealing that the female participant is most often the activator of this norm disruption: a mother seduces her son in the hope of a reward, a sister her brother, a daughter her father, etc. The male participant, on the other hand, is punished as soon as he discovers his sin; the punishment is often death.

Motifs to do with the disruption of marital norms also surface in tales with such plots as that of the totem-wife who casts off her animal guise: the frog-princess and swan-princess, etc. Another such motif is that of abduction by a dragon (i.e. a 'strange' bridegroom from far away) of a woman about to be married, so that he can have her as his concubine; she is then saved by her bridegroom's miraculous actions, signifying a return to the normal forms of marriage.

In some Russian tales the Tsar and father prepares tests which suitors must overcome in order to marry his daughter. But these tests are prepared by him so that only he may complete them: the princess, his daughter, can be happy only with her father.

The idea of birth was linked by the Eastern Slavs with fertility in general and the life-giving powers of the earth in particular. After Christianization, the concept of separate physical and spiritual birth in ordinary mortals developed, and with it the idea of God's participation in the latter. A child's life is 'God-given', his or her soul is 'inspired by God'. Birth is intimately connected with the things that symbolize fertility: water and the rite of bringing rain, in which women call on the sky deity to copulate; beliefs that rainwater aids the barren, etc.

The pagan Slavs believed in goddesses who were present at childbirth and were responsible for assigning fate and good fortune; their name, *rozhanitsas* [the birthresses/ancestresses], indicated their function. The *rozhanitsas* cult is close in type to that of the Greek Fates. A party called the *rodiny* [birth party] was held when women gave birth; meals of grain were cooked and handed round to the guests. A second dish was prepared for the *rozhanitsas*. The honour paid them goes back to archaic ancestor cult, and especially the cult of women forebears. With the coming of Christianity the *rozhanitsas* began to be considered demonic. But belief in them did not disappear: the birth party was renamed the *krestiny* [christening party], but the custom of gathering guests and cooking a meal of grain continued.

What was the origin of the *rozhanitsas* cult? The consciousness that descendants depend on their ancestors is universal to humanity. The inheritance of physical and moral qualities has never been questioned. This is why the ancestor cult is so common: ancestors are honoured as the protectors of the tribe, on whom the fate of their descendants depends. *Rod* [Birth/Ancestry], a male deity, represents the male organs of the tribe and hence is placed in control of the *rozhanitsas*, the mothers of new generations. In tribal or communal marriage the link of a new-born child with its mother is more evident [than its link with its father]. And so Rod and the *rozhanitsas* become the centre of ancestor cult: they have the significance of life-givers and protectors, i.e. they stand for the grandfather and grandmothers; this is a reference to the polygamy which was practised by the Eastern Slavs.

Belief in Luck and Good Fortune is still widespread. The rite of placing the child under divine protection (the christening) has persisted. Fatalism, that is the conviction that a higher power, fate, exists, is part of the psychological make-up of the Russian people; this conviction is present in representatives of almost all strata of Russian society. In some places the pagan cult of the *rozhanitsas*, on whom depend the beginning and the end of a man's life, is fused in popular consciousness with the Christian cult of ancestors' souls; the *rozhanitsas* are identified with stars. In folk-songs one may find formulae of the following type, for example: 'A star falls from the sky/The bright candle gutters/Our young prince cannot stay'.

At one time in Russia – as in many other places – people believed that it was possible to conceive without male participation. The woman was considered solely responsible for continuing the tribe. And although nowadays the mechanics of childbirth are known to even the most backward, belief in the possibility of non-sexual reproduction continues. It is manifest in sorcery, superstitions, and so on. Russian folk-tales are rich in examples of miraculous births. For example, it is possible to conceive by eating a fruit or berry: 'I was walking in the forest and I swallowed a pea.' To this day women will eat peas or yeast in order to become pregnant. This is, evidently, connected with the capacity of such things to swell up: 'The pea swelled up, the tsaritsa felt bad, the pea grows bigger and bigger, the tsaritsa feels heavier and thicker.'

Pregnancy could be brought on by a spell or incantation – by the power of words. A drink of water could bring it on: 'She sees a stream flowing. She drinks her fill, and feels herself with child. Later she gives birth to a son.' To this day women drink water and bathe in it to encourage fertility.

One more miraculous birth motif was the belief that no completely new individuals are ever born. All new arrivals are reincarnations of the dead – most especially one of their ancestors. This reincarnation motif frequently recurs in Russian folk-tales. It is also linked with the fire cult; hence the stove or hearth becomes the place where dead ancestors live. And so the heroes of Russian tales are often born from out of a stove: 'Old woman, go and bury a radish, we'll eat it. We ate one radish, put the other in the stove . . . someone in the stove cried "Hot!" and we found a real live baby boy in there.' The stove is also the place where the youngest son, the hero, is always to be found in folk-tales. Russian *bogatyrs* [the heroes of folk epics] lie on the stove by the hour. Names, too, often reveal a link with the stove: Ivan Zapechny [Johnnie from Behind the Stove], Iskr Zapechny [Sparks from Behind the Stove] and so on.

Yet another such birth motif is that of birth from a fish. As a totem animal, a fish has links with the world of the dead; at the same time, it is possessed of an astonishing fertility. It plays the role of the paternal, rather than maternal, principle, i.e. it has a phallic character. In Russian tales, incantations of the following type are common: 'As commands the pike, as I should like'; 'Have pity on me, madam fish'. Prolonged childlessness is often treated by eating a piece of fish.

In all these rituals, the direct influence of nature's fertility on man can be seen, and likewise the belief that man is subject to her effects on the pattern of sympathetic magic.

The motif of rape is more or less absent in Eastern Slavonic mythology. In very ancient times, rain-bearing clouds were personified as chaste maidens who were fleeing the thunder god; the sound of thunder meant that he was pursuing, capturing and then deflowering them, causing the fruitful rain to fall. The act of sexual possession of women without their consent was a frequent occurrence in real life. Given a background of polygamous marriages and the total subordination of women in an economic sense, rape was, indeed, the norm. The rituals appropriate to different aspects of women's lives were on the whole structured in such a way that the man chose the woman, 'the bride is chosen by her future husband'; the bride simply 'divines whom fate has in mind for her'. Women were always sexually passive: they fled from men or hid from them. Active women were mocked.

In Eastern Slavic mythology there is likewise a paucity of motifs directly linked to women's initiation. But if one analyses linguistic data, as well as the texts of certain rituals, structures come to light which are semantically connected with the physiological changes that come about during a woman's life. To this day, in fact, a large number of names or terms for girls survive in some places; these differ according to sexual maturity and physiological state. Up to the 1950s, a custom persisted according to which married women covered their heads, and only girls might go bareheaded.

Only certain categories of girls were allowed to participate in those rituals concerned with seasonal changes in which erotic elements played an important part (for example, those of Kupala and Maslenitsa [Shrovetide]). Participation depended on sexual maturity, but it was unthinkable that a married woman should take part. It follows that there was a strict distinction in popular consciousness between erotic motifs and motifs of marital and familial life. The round dance was an essential part of such rituals. Only girls who had reached a given age might lead a round dance. In some rituals, the custom was for girls to run off when the round dance was finished; a young man who caught a girl might have sexual relations with her on the spot and become her husband.

The *bylinas* (folk-epics) are a significant category of Russian folklore. In them, women are always presented as sly and demonic; they represent evil of some kind, and the hero does battle with them. (See, for example, *Polyk*; *Luka Danilovich*; *Ivan Golinovich*; *Dobrynya and Marinka*, etc.) But if the folk-epics show how the female negative principle brings ill on the tribe or settlement, the folk-tales devote more attention to everyday life and family relationships. When the tasks in a folk-tale are accomplished, this brings prosperity to an individual hero. And so the semantics of the folk tale can be interpreted only if one goes back to its mythological sources. That said, there is a whole layer of Russian folk-tales which require no special semantic study so far as their representation of relations within the family is concerned, i.e. of marriage, birth, incest, rape and so on. The narratives in these tales are almost devoid of [true] folk-tale attributes.

In 1855–64 the great Russian ethnographer and folk-tale collector Alexander Afanasiev published a [three-volume] collection called *Russian Folk Tales* [which remains the canonical collection of such tales, the Russian equivalent of the *Märchen* of the Brothers Grimm]. A fourth volume of the tales, prepared for publication in 1859, was banned by the censors. It appeared only some years later in Geneva [and was not published in Russia until 1914]. This collection, *Secret* [i.e. Obscene] *Tales*, contains tales of everyday life; the narratives deal with the sexual life of the people, there are motifs of marital life, incest, sexual deception. Certain expressions are used in the tales which might be termed 'uncensored', that is, unprintable, though in fact they are such as are in common use amongst the people. In all the tales, women represent the negative principle: woman, and the images which she personifies, are morally dirty, deceiving and promiscuous. Afanasiev considered these tales as essential a part of Russian folklore, as the other tales in his edition.

In the twentieth century the role of women has changed. Inevitably, the 1917 revolution which brought the Bolsheviks to power has been a major influence. Informed by Marxist writings on the family, Russian communism promised the rapid and complete liberation of the female sex. In the immediate aftermath of the revolution, comprehensive legislation was introduced which improved the status of women and Party members like Alexandra Kollontai campaigned for alternatives to the traditional family to form the basis of the relationship between the sexes. But the Bolshevik revolution was a male event and women's needs ultimately were subordinated to the 'class struggle' and the more pragmatic needs of a state undergoing rapid economic development. The result has been that whilst lip service has been paid to women's rights, in reality the stress has been on women's duties to the state.

The first and clearest duty of women to the state as defined in the early years of Soviet rule was as a worker. In the political iconography of the 1920s and 1930s women were shown engaged alongside men in 'socialist production'. N. Kagout's poster illustrating the slogan 'By the force of arms we have smashed the enemy. With

ОРУЖИЕМ МЫ ДОБИЛИ ВРАГА
ТРУДОМ МЫ ДОБУДЕМ ХЛЕБ
ВСЕ ЗА РАБОТУ, ТОВАРИЩИ!

Fig. 11 Revolutionary poster by N. Kagout from 1921. The slogan reads 'By the force of arms we have smashed the enemy. With our hands we will get bread. All hard to work Comrades.'

our hands we will get bread. All hard to work Comrades', was typical of these times. It depicts two figures working an anvil against a backdrop of factories and workers. One of the two central figures is a woman, drawn in red, white and black wearing a blouse and long skirt covered with an industrial apron and her hair covered with a red scarf. The red kerchief, earnest gaze and powerful stance of the women became the new image with which Soviet women were supposed to identify. There was no place in this new world for religion, myths or, apparently, for the image of woman as mother.

Religious belief had, in fact, been suppressed at the time of the October Revolution. Churches and other religious buildings were destroyed, and religious rites were outlawed and replaced by civil ones. Christenings were abolished because of their religious character and a rite of 'entry into the ranks of the newborn' substituted. Similarly, Church weddings were replaced by civil ceremonies, with accompanying new rituals. Despite the severe penalties, including execution or internment in a labour camp, that could be meted out to religious believers, people continued in secret to celebrate births, marriages and deaths according to the forbidden customs and rituals. The split between the forbidden rites of the past and the obligatory rites of the present was especially marked in villages and among the elderly. In some rural parts of Russia the ritual of sanctifying money, harvests and new houses survived up to the 1960s. A rite called *Zaruby* ['cuts'] is performed with the participation of pregnant women and old people (that is, when the foundation of a new house is to be laid, the owner will wait until a pregnant woman or elderly person walks by). Food is prepared for the *rozhanitsas* when a child is born. Belief in sorcerers, witches, the evil eye, spells and curses is preserved even amongst the urban population.

Many natural phenomena are still explained from the perspective of myth and legend. For example, in one rural place in Central Russia, the origin of a shingle bank is explained thus:

> When they started to pull the churches down in Stalin's time, the Virgin Mary came out and went to seek shelter in that village on the far side of the lake. The shingle bank marks where she went over the water.

In view of the special place of woman as life-giver in much of Russian mythology and of the *bogomater* (mother of God) in Russian Orthodox religion, it is not surprising that the Bolshevik Party should have been reluctant to use images of mothers and families in its art and propaganda. The denial of women's role as mothers did not survive the 1930s however. With the consolidation of Stalin's power as leader, the Soviet state embarked upon a period of rapid industrialization. Women's labour power was still essential to the state but with economic expansion pressure mounted on women to produce the next generation of workers. The result was the 're-discovery' of woman's role as mother. From the period of the Second World War up to the present time the Soviet government has pursued overtly pro-natalist policies. These have included the award of the Glory of Motherhood medallions to women who bear more than ten children, the romanticization of marriage (albeit in its civil version) and comparatively generous maternity leave arrangements. Symbolic representation of women as mothers is found everywhere in the Soviet Union today from political propaganda posters to public statues commemorating political and historical events.

In practice, however, motherhood is debased and female experience of the birth process and the state of motherhood is at odds with the public imagery. Birth takes place in a closed environment in the Soviet Union with the women isolated from family members and friends. The father of the child is excluded both from labour and delivery and from the immediate post-partum period. As the majority of lower and middle rank medical workers are female, so is the rigidly regimented medical environment in which these procedures take place. Thus the reproductive processes have been shrouded in mystery and remain essentially female.

The maintenance of traditional gender roles in the Soviet Union means that women have continued to be associated with the domestic sphere even though female participation in the economy surpasses that of men. Over 90 per cent of Soviet women are either working or studying full time. Women are paid 25 to 30 per cent less than men and yet on the whole are better educated and more skilled. Women are under-represented in the highest echelons of the Soviet Union's parliamentary institutions.

The 'double burden' has been a topic of debate in the Soviet Union for some years and various solutions have been offered to ease that burden. The assumptions about the female role in society have been left largely unchallenged, however, in that that most measures introduced have aimed to help women combine work and home more easily by improving the service sector and making provision for part-time work. This concern with making life easier for women has also dominated much of the discussion among emergent women's groups. For many women the ideal is to be able to leave work to devote themselves full time to the home and to motherhood. In 1979, the first women's *samizdat* almanac, *Women and Russia*, was published illegally. The women's group which produced it became the target of police repression: many of those working on the journal were expelled from the country or arrested.

With the relaxation of censorship under Gorbachev in the 1980s, more independent feminist organizations were set up, and new journals founded. Among them the Maria group, which takes its inspiration from the *bogomater* (mother-of-god), has inserted a religious direction into the women's movement, arguing for the re-instatement of woman's 'natural' role as procreator. In reality this view of women had never more than dipped below the surface in the Russian people's consciousness during the seventy years of communist rule.

Translated by Catriona Kelly, with additional comment on the current position in the Soviet Union from Judith Pallot.

Reference and Further Reading

ON WOMEN AND MYTH IN RUSSIA:

Barker, A.M. (1986), *The Mother Syndrome in the Russian Folk Imagination* (Columbus, Ohio: Slavica Press). A psycho-analytical study of some important genres of rural folklore.

Grossman, J.D. (1980), 'Feminine Images in Old Russian literature and art' in *California Slavic Studies*, 11, pp. 33–70. Includes not only folklore but also written texts; stresses the diversity of Russian tradition.

Hubbs, J. (1988), *Mother Russia: the Feminine Myth in Russian Culture.* (Bloomington, Indiana: Indiana University Press). A determinedly upbeat survey of diverse myths, including those associated with the Virgin Mary and St Paraskeva: the existence of a matriarchy in prehistoric times is taken for granted.

GENERAL STUDIES ON MYTH AND RUSSIAN CULTURE:

Lotman, Y.M. and Uspensky, B.A. (1984), 'The role of dual models in the dynamics of Russian culture' in Ann Shukman (ed.), *The Semiotics of Russian Culture* (Ann Arbor: Yale University Press), pp. 3–35. A history of the centrality of binary oppositions in Russian thinking; itself a reflection of the dualism which it analyses.

Vernadsky, G. (1948), 'Russian paganism' in G. Vernadsky and M. Karpovich (eds), *History of Russia*, vol. 2 (New Haven, Conn.), pp. 48–56. A helpful summary of sources on the pre-Christian tradition.

WOMEN IN SOVIET SOCIETY:

Buckley, M. (1989), *Women and Ideology in the Soviet Union* (London: Harvester Wheatsheaf)

Stites, R. (1978), *The Women's Liberation Movement in Russia: Feminism, Nihilism and Bolshevism 1860-1930* (Princeton: Princeton University Press)

Waters, E. (1991), 'The Female Form in Soviet Political Iconography' in B.E. Clements, B.A. Engel and C.D. Worobec (eds), *Russia's Women: Accommodation, Resistance, Transformation* (Berkeley: University of California Press)

Bibliography by Catriona Kelly and Judith Pallot, Christ Church, Oxford.

JULIETTE WOOD

Celtic Goddesses:
Myth and Mythology

SECTION I: INTRODUCTION

Caesar, in describing the Gaulish deities, mentions only one goddess whom he calls
Minerva and who, he claims, governs arts and crafts. This *interpretatio romana* has
been given short shrift by Celtic scholars. His remarks, however, illustrate one
inescapable fact, that all speculation on Celtic gods is an *interpretatio* of a kind.
Anyone who attempts a coherent description of Celtic mythology is inevitably faced
with certain problems and, just as inevitably, has to make some suppositions to
overcome the fragmented and disparate nature of the evidence. Written sources are
either external, in the form of Greek and Roman comments about aspects of Celtic
culture which impressed them, or late vernacular texts, principally in Irish or Welsh,
produced in a Christian environment. The archaeological evidence, although
considerable, covers a wide geographical area. The bulk of it dates from the period
after Celtic societies had come into contact with the Graeco-Roman world, and,
while it can tell us much about deities and their functions, it yields very little about
the myths and rituals associated with them.

Even the use of the term 'Celtic' is in many ways a supposition implying a degree
of ethnic cohesion which is both recognizable and which could survive over time
and across geographical boundaries. The matter of terminology and sources needs
to be considered before we can begin to discuss the nature of the mythology
associated with Celtic goddesses.

The Idea of the Celt

The idea of the Celt and his specialness is so much taken for granted that it is
surprising to note how recent the use of the term is. Classical sources referred to
a number of peoples under the umbrella-term *keltoi*. It is clear from the kind of
observations these authors make, that they were referring to cultural rather than
racial similarities among a spectrum of peoples. While modern scholarship labels
these similarities quite rightly as Celtic, this does not necessarily imply any shared
consciousness among these peoples. Interestingly, a consciousness of being Celts

seems to be absent from medieval Irish pseudo-historical writing (Byrne, 1974, p. 144), and even the early Welsh prophecy *Armes Prydein*, which exhorts the Welsh to band together with various other groups to oust the English, does not imply that they have any cultural or spiritual commonality (Williams, 1955).

The use of the word in the modern sense dates only to the beginning of the eighteenth century when scholars began to study the linguistic affinities between the Celtic languages, that is Irish, Manx, Scots-Gaelic, Welsh, Breton and Cornish. Many of our ideas about heroic societies generally date to this century also, and notions about 'noble savages', such as the clean-living, independent-minded warrior Celts untrammelled by the stultifying effects of Roman bureaucracy, have clung tenaciously (compare Tacitus's approach to the Germanic tribes in the Scandinavian section of this volume, *see* p. 140). It is, however, to poets such as Matthew Arnold and W. B. Yeats that we owe the most notable features of the twilit, as opposed to the historical Celt; the notion that he possesses a natural mysticism and that cultures which speak Celtic languages might share spiritual and moral qualities.

This is not to suggest that to speak of Celtic culture is invalid. No scholar would deny the linguistic similarities or that this involves a cultural dimension, but abstractions such as Celtic consciousness, Celtic myth or even the Celtic goddess can be misleading if they are taken to imply too great a degree of unity between 'Celtic' peoples in the classical world or too great a degree of continuity between 'ancient Celts' and their descendants.

Classical and Archaeological Sources

Classical commentators refer to customs rather than to myths, and their descriptions contrast the foreignness of Celtic behaviour with the familiarity of Greek and Roman usage. Undoubtedly the Greeks and the Romans applied their cultural prejudices to the Celts and idealized peoples who lived on the periphery of the classical world, but the fact that they found aspects of Celtic society strange tells us that such elements were present, and a genuine, if distorted, view of Celtic culture underlies their observations.

Two instances which relate to women in classical report may actually reflect Celtic rituals or myths. Strabo, following an earlier work by the Greek writer Posidonius, describes an island in the Loire in France inhabited by women of the Samnite tribe. They shun male society and are possessed by a god whom Strabo calls Dionysius. During the annual re-roofing of the temple, any woman who drops her roofing material is torn apart and her dismembered body carried around the temple (Tierney, 1959/60, p. 269). The passage reflects the Roman distaste for human sacrifice, and the island account may be based on observation of some ritual or some version of a mythic story. The passage in Strabo echoes the later occurrences of all-female otherworld islands in the Irish voyage tales (*immrammas*). These later islands are places of happiness and prosperity whose inhabitants lack the maenad qualities referred to here. However, there are enough points of similarity between this and later accounts to suggest that the idea of an all-female otherworld, although not unique to them, had considerable antiquity among Celtic peoples. So, too, with another island story concerning a sleeping god, called Cronos in the classical account, guarded by nine priestesses who also have care of a magic cauldron (Rhys, 1898).

There is nothing in later vernacular tradition which corresponds with this exactly, but reflexes of this story have been seen in Merlin's captivity in Avalon, Arthur's journey to Avalon in company with Morgan and the other magical queens, virtually all the magic cauldrons in Welsh and Irish tradition, the nine witches who care for Peredur in the Welsh romance of that name, and numerous other narrative incidents. Neither beliefs about all-female societies nor bands of female priestesses are unique to Celtic tradition, but whether these are native or borrowed narrative motifs, their long currency certainly makes them an integral part of Celtic tradition.

Archaeological evidence is comparatively abundant and often accompanied by inscriptions. However, most of the relevant material dates from the period when the Celts had already made contact with the Graeco-Roman world. The iconography has clearly been affected by Mediterranean artistic trends which suggests that the belief system may have been affected as well (Lindgren, 1978). Caesar's account implies a pantheon of gods worshipped throughout the Gaulish world, while the archaeological evidence suggests that, while some figures were known over wide geographical areas, others were quite local, associated mostly with natural features such as streams and springs. On aggregate, more evidence exists for local deities, and it is possible that in regard to Celtic religion this was the more important element. As to the nature of the goddess, it may be that in dealing with Celtic deities and, in particular, goddesses, one should think of a being with a range of activities often connected with the natural world, rather than a specific function as implied by Caesar's comment on the Celtic Minerva (Sjoestedt, 1982). Recent scholarship has suggested that this goddess figure with strong affinities to nature may predate the emergence of Indo-European culture, and this of course brings us back to the problem that Celtic culture was not impervious to outside influence, and as it developed in a European context, it undoubtedly absorbed some of its influences (Gimbutas, 1982).

The linguistic similarities among the six surviving Celtic languages (five of which are native to the British Isles and one still spoken in Brittany) are undeniable. However, the relationship among these early societies is complex. Celtic societies in Britain and Ireland did not derive from a single community of continental Celts, and indeed one does not find a sustained relationship between Insular and Gaulish culture. Even among the Insular Celts, there was never a completely homogeneous culture. The Celtic languages spoken in Ireland, Scotland and on the Isle of Man form one branch of the surviving group of Celtic languages known as Goidelic, while Welsh, Cornish and Breton make up the Brittonic branch of the Celtic language family. New directions in comparative studies have set 'the Celts' within the larger context of Indo-European culture (Dumezil, 1957; Mallory, 1989), with the implication that certain features of Celtic societies are part of a wider inheritance. This has added a new dimension to our understanding of the complex nature of early societies, but it also highlights the problems of continuity, common inheritance and outside influences on cultures for which there are such fragmentary records.

Vernacular Sources

Another important consideration is the definition of *myth*. More elusive than even the Celt himself, myth is defined here as a special mode of narrative discourse which relates to basic sacred concepts (Dundes, 1986). Material relating to Celtic goddesses exists in the form of plastic representations, dedications and classical reference. Myths in any real sense do not. No literature survives from ancient Gaul (Breton is the result of a later influx). We are dependent on late sources, primarily vernacular literature, which are difficult to use as evidence for Celtic myths since as one scholar has pointed out (and most popular writers resolutely refuse to accept), 'We do not know the Celts but only the Gauls, Irish, Welsh and Bretons' (Sjoestedt, 1982, p. 3).

Even if one can resolve the difficulties inherent in the fact that the vernacular literature was produced by insular Celtic cultures, while the bulk of the archaeological and epigraphical evidence relates to continental Celts, the vernacular tales are primarily literary texts. In any case, one cannot simply peel away a veneer to see the myths and rituals of ancient Celts beneath. To use the vernacular texts in conjunction with archaeological and epigraphical evidence, as many have done as a 'source for native religious cults' (Ross, 1967, p. 25), is perilous. The archaeological record and vernacular literature can tell us much about myth and belief, but they cannot be used to validate one another without the risk of circularity.

Although mythology was an important factor in vernacular literature, so were Roman civilization, Christianity and the literary conventions of the medieval cultures of Ireland, Wales, Brittany, Scotland and, in some cases, Anglo-Norman France. Ancient structures such as myth only survive in significant ways if they continue to have relevance to the context in which they come to exist (Honko, 1989). Against the undoubted tendency of this literature to conserve what is already there, one must balance the tendency to adapt according to the norms of the prevailing society. In approaching later vernacular literature, we need to think in terms of an axis encompassing myths, the literary tales, romances and folk-tales, all drawing on the same fund of motifs and themes which are continually modified through time and in the contexts of different genres. The sources of these texts may in fact be myths which once characterized Celtic culture at an early stage and formed part of their inheritance, and many of these themes may be shared in a wider context with Indo-European culture generally. Certainly the sophisticated nature of the culture from which the literary material derives suggests a dynamism in the process of transmission. What may have been myth in origin, becomes mythic theme in later narrative material with all the changes in genre and function which this implies.

SECTION II: CELTIC GODDESSES

Introduction

The single most pervasive theme identified with Celtic goddesses is undoubtedly that of the dual-natured female figure, beautiful and hag-like by turns, in whose gift is great power. She has been variously described (in her guise as Cailleach Bhearra) as 'the most famous old lady in Irish literature' (Wagner, 1981); as 'the basic divine warrior goddess who was clearly such a fundamental and widespread concept in the religion of the pagan Celtic world' (Ross, 1973, p. 144); while a recent popular work, untrammelled by the requirement of scholarship to maintain contact with reality, suggests in relation to the apocryphal story of St Bridget and the Christ-child: 'As the goddess of the old dispensation she fosters the god of the new faith giving him a status in the otherworldly consciousness of all British and Irish believers' (Matthews, 1989, p. 268). The existence of 'the Celtic goddess' has become almost as real an assumption as the Celt himself, and in many instances even more subject to back projection of twentieth-century ideas.

Caesar does not report a particularly strong feminine element in the religious beliefs of the Gauls but numerous images of Celtic provenance depict feminine deities. Many of these are named and indicate a plurality of goddesses, although none seems to have been worshipped throughout the entire Celtic world at any period. Images of mother-goddesses are not common prior to the Romano-Celtic period, but the mother-goddess as a religious image is so pervasive that it is likely she formed part of the common heritage of all Celtic cultures and may have already been present in some of the areas they occupied. Mother-goddesses are often depicted in threes. Triplication is undoubtedly a Celtic element, while the use of the cornucopia to indicate her function as fertility bringer is almost certainly a classical artistic motif. The occurrence of classical deities with native epithets, as happens in the case of Minerva, may be a syncretic tendency attendant on contact with Rome, and may help to explain Caesar's apparent understanding of the Celtic gods in terms of a pantheon. On the whole, however, hybridization does not significantly obscure the native elements (Lindgren, 1978).

What then of the individual Celtic goddesses? They are associated with a variety of functions, and many may reflect very localized practices (Green, 1986, p. 72; Sjoestedt, 1982, p. 37; Ross, 1967, p. 265). Sometimes the name itself may indicate the goddess's function, for example, Rosmerta (The Great Provider); at other times the context in which the image is found gives an indication of her sphere of activity, as, for example, Coventina and Sequana, both of whom are connected with the power of water. Sometimes the attributes of a goddess provide a clue to her function or to the identity of her devotees. Most striking here are the horses associated with Epona and the number of Roman cavalry who sought her protection. Nothing comparable to a classical goddess of love appears in Celtic traditions, although scholars have pointed to the strong sexual characteristics of the supernatural females found in vernacular literature (Sjoestedt, 1982, p. 51).

However, this apparent lack highlights an important characteristic of Celtic cosmology. While the function of male Celtic deities falls within reasonably well-defined parameters, primarily linked to civilization, the function of particular goddesses is surprisingly elusive. While it would be a mistake to talk of a typical Celtic goddess based on this evidence (Ross, 1967, p. 291), goddesses are, depending on circumstance, associated with fertility in all its aspects, and life in all its aspects, including the converse, death.

Too little is known about the types of society and religious ideas which characterized Celtic peoples living on the continent to say with any great assurance what types of beliefs and practices clustered around the goddesses. It would be a mistake to assume that the divine world of the pagan Celts was conceived of as a direct reflection of their mundane society (Ross, 1973, p. 141). Although Welsh and Irish tradition have a strong conservative element, and the vernacular literature of both, but especially the latter, preserve some very archaic elements, scholars recognize that the lateness of the texts, their literary nature and Christian context create difficulties when they are used as sources for myth to corroborate earlier continental evidence (Jackson, 1961, p. 37). Quite extravagant claims have been made about the nature of the Celtic goddess, about how her role reflects that of women in Celtic society (see below, Section III, p. 132) and the extent to which she continues to affect the vernacular literature of other Celtic languages, Celtic Christianity and Arthurian literature. Testing the validity of our conceptions about the female principle in the mythological system which characterized the ancient Celtic peoples is of course impossible, and any consideration of Celtic goddesses has to take account of the limitations of the evidence.

However, it is possible to chart the development of certain themes in connection with female deities as they appear in archaeological, classical and vernacular contexts, and even in the later romances. These themes can be described as mythic since they reflect certain universal cultural concerns associated with life, abundance, death and the general stability of the social unit. The survival of myth in the literatures of Celtic cultures has undoubtedly been over-emphasized, and it is not just semantic quibbling to suggest that while myth has shaped many later figures, such as Rhiannon in Wales, Arthurian heroines such as Enid, numerous loathly ladies and even some later Christian saints such as Bridget, it cannot be said to have survived to any coherent extent.

Goddesses of War

Classical authors were impressed by Celtic women. Diodorus Siculus, drawing on Posidonius, says that Gaulish women were equal to their husbands in both stature and strength, but he is puzzled that Gaulish men pay so little attention to their beautiful wives (Tierney, 1959/60, p. 252). Ammianus Marcellinus describes real or reported battle frenzy on the part of Gaulish woman: tall like the men and with flashing eyes, gnashing their teeth and fighting with kicks and blows. Size and ferocity are qualities associated with the historical Celtic queens Boudica and Cartimandua, although the descriptions may owe something to Roman ideas about barbarian womanhood. Strabo, on the other hand, comments on the maternal instincts of Gaulish women (Tierney, 1959/60, p. 268), while Polybius notes their chastity (Tierney, 1959/60, p. 197). The remarks of classical authors have to be seen in the context of what they would have expected of their own women. Nevertheless, this presentation of the female as physically strong and morally forceful is quite consistent with the contrasting war-like and maternal nature attributed to a Celtic mother-goddess.

Archaeological evidence indicates cults centred around goddesses, but tells us little about myths or rituals associated with these cults, or the position of women in this worship. Lucan's famous passage in the *Pharsalia* speaks of dark groves, frightening wooden images and trees spattered with human blood (Green, 1989, quoting Lucan, p. 8) but says nothing specific about women. The maenad-like frenzy of the inhabitants of the female island echoes this, although the priestesses around Cronos's cauldron seem peaceable enough. The depiction of deities in stone was largely the result of contact with Mediterranean art forms, so very few wooden images of the kind mentioned in Lucan's text have survived. There is one clearly female figure, together with the remains of a wicker hut in which it was kept, from Ballachulish. The figure may be first century BC, but there is no hint of who she is or what kind of rites were associated with her.

The activities of the warrior queen of the Iceni, Boudica, may contain some hints about ritual. Before battle Boudica called on Andraste, presumably a titular goddess of the Iceni and clearly in this context a battle-goddess, and released a hare. Whether Boudica's action relates to her position as leader or whether its role had a priest-like function, we do not know. Interesting too is the gruesome ritual manner in which Boudica's prisoners were put to death in Andraste's grove – it was reported that women prisoners were impaled on stakes after their breasts had been cut off. This is the kind of blood bath that confirmed Roman prejudice against the barbarian Celt, and no imperialist ever presented a conquered people in a good light, but it does give us a glimpse of a Celtic battle-goddess and a possible rite associated with her.

The glimpse is all the more interesting for its comparative rarity in the context of historical sources. While a number of Irish tales contain fierce supernatural women who influence the outcome of a battle, very few of the archaeological depictions of goddesses place them clearly in a war context. Celtic goddesses sometimes appear with a raven, a chthonic bird who, presumably because of its carrion habits, was associated with death and by extension battle-death, but direct evidence for battle-goddesses is much rarer than for battle-gods among Celtic peoples. Images of goddesses are found in graves where they probably indicate protection of the dead, but clear connection with battles is more elusive. There is a Gaulish dedication to Cathubodva 'crow/raven of battle' (Ross, 1967, p. 282), an inscription at Benwell to the three Lamiae (Ross, 1967, p. 282) and Posidonius mentions the golden standards of the goddess Minerva, evidently a battle-goddess in this context (Tierney, 1959/60, p. 249), but this is hardly evidence for a pan-Celtic concept.

The supernatural women of the Irish heroic tales, whose very presence causes death, provides a possible link with mythic material attached to battle-goddesses. They do not engage in fighting themselves, which raises the possibility that a goddess who personifies the fecundity of a tribal area would also be associated with its defence. Figures who seem to have 'battle-goddess' characteristics include the Morrígan (Phantom Queen), Banbh (Crow/Raven) and Nemhain (Frenzy) and Macha. Although the figures appear separately, they also occur as a triadic grouping, sometimes as the three Morrígans. Their function relates to the outcome not the actual progress of a battle, and their effect is not invariably negative. The Dagda, a character with many of the characteristics of a father god, meets the Morrígan standing astride a river before the Battle of Magh Tuiredh, a complex episode which echoes a cosmological battle of some kind. The Dagda has intercourse with the Morrígan and ensures a favourable outcome to the battle (Cross and Slover, 1936, p. 28). However, when the same figure offers herself as a beautiful woman to Cuchulain and is rejected, she attacks him in three different animal forms during battle (O'Rahilly, 1967).

Similarities may exist between this manifestation of the Morrígan and the Washer at the Ford, a supernatural being who washes clothes before some incident or battle and whose actions foretell its outcome. A sixteenth-century Washer story is preserved in Welsh that is attached to an historical king who becomes the subject of legend. He meets a being who has been condemned to wash at the ford until she has a child by a mortal. There is a clear sexual link between the king and the supernatural being, but he does not seem to be involved in a battle (Jones, 1922). The more negative aspect of the Washer at the Ford occurs as a regular feature of ballads of the Clerk Colville type (Child, 1956). Here, she is a rejected mistress who takes revenge on her erstwhile lover. In these later examples of tale and ballad, the relationship between the male and female characters seems to have undergone a degree of personalization characteristic of later genres, such as romance, but almost wholly absent in myth and heroic literature.

The link between Romano-Celtic iconography, vernacular Irish literature and modern folk-tale is more complex than just the survival of mythic themes. It also reflects the dynamics of cultural process. The later material not only has affinities with other tales present in an international legend corpus, but the action often focuses on the personal relationships between the characters, whereas in the heroic Irish tales, and one can only assume in the mythic genre that lies behind them, personal emotion does not seem to play a very large part.

Epona

Epona is well known to Celtic scholars through her possible connections with the figure of Rhiannon in *Pedeir Keinc Y Mabinogi*. Her name is associated with the Celtic word for horse. As a goddess, images of her appear in many Celtic contexts, but there are patterns of variation and localization which caution against a too-ready tendency to think of her in pan-Celtic terms.

Epona is always accompanied by a horse, either riding (most common in northern Gaul, Germany and Burgundy) or in the midst of several horses (mostly in the Rhineland). There was a shrine dedicated to her in Burgundy (Magne and Thevenot, 1953), a region particularly rich in images of the goddess. Here, she is accompanied by a foal eating from an outstretched patera or sleeping under the feet of the goddess's mare. Her role was complex and may in part be contingent on where and when she was worshipped rather than on some overall conception of her function.

Her status as horse-goddess venerated by the Roman cavalry helped spread her cult (Linduff and Oaks in Henig, 1986, pp. 817–37), and is an example of Celtic influence on Roman civilization. Epona was the only Gaulish goddess to be officially honoured in Rome and had her own festival. Some dedications indicate that her devotees were members of cavalry units. Although male gods are associated with horses, and the cavalry was certainly a male domain, the goddess Epona presided over the health and fertility of the animal. She rides side-saddle in a ladylike manner and, to the extent that one can interpret the images in this way, her demeanour is benign. In other words, there is nothing in the imagery which would imply a war-goddess. She holds objects of fertility rather than weapons – a dish from which the foal often feeds, fruit or a cornucopia. Burgundy, the tribal homelands of the Aedui, where the goddess riding side-saddle with a foal is most common, was a centre for horse breeding. The Treveri, centred on Luxembourg, also seem to have favoured the goddess as we can assume from the number of images here. Her importance was certainly linked to that of the horse itself in Celtic society. It has been suggested that her cult, because of her association with horses, was popular among the Gaulish elite, and this in itself would help explain her popularity (Linduff and Oaks in Henig, 1986, pp. 817–37).

Equine associations are not the end of Epona's story. Many images depict her as carrying food, a cornucopia or some object of plenty consistent with her role as benefactress/guardian of horses and probably extending beyond that. Several images have been found in conjunction with therapeutic springs and in one striking instance, she appears as a water-nymph reclining on her mare. The Mediomatrici, centred on Metz, near modern Strasbourg, certainly venerated the horse-goddess, and here she may have functioned as a guardian of the dead. One image shows her on her horse seemingly leading an individual on a journey to the afterlife.

A dedication from Burgundy (Ross, 1967) links her specifically with the mother-goddesses. These may be local adaptations, but with so little evidence and with such ambiguous imagery it is impossible to be too didactic. Epona could have been a horse goddess in origin whose function later became extended to include protection of humans, healing water and guardianship of the dead. On the other hand, the cultural importance of the horse, the prestige of the Roman cavalry and their social importance could have resulted in the equine associations becoming dominant from a wider spectrum of functions. About any myths associated with her, we know nothing, and it is noteworthy that even with such a comparatively well-attested figure as Epona, firm conclusions are impossible.

Epona occurs but rarely in Britain and the best preserved image of her depicts

Fig. 12 The goddess Epona, flanked by two small horses. *Courtesy of the Trustees of the British Museum, London*

her between two little horses who feed from a dish of food (*see* fig. 12), an image popular in what is now Germany. It is possible that her appearance in Britain is linked to the presence of Roman legionary troops, but she is without doubt a Celtic deity, and we can assume, on the basis of archaeological evidence, that various Celtic tribes venerated a basically benign female deity, associated with horses and possessing, at least in some areas, mother-goddess characteristics directed to humanity. The question then arises, what later material could carry some of these associations? The most obvious is the figure of Rhiannon, the mother of Pryderi who appears in the First and Third Branches of *Pedeir Keinc Y Mabinogi*.

Y Pedeir Keinc comprise the first four tales in a collection of Welsh medieval narratives know collectively as the *Mabinogion* (Jones and Jones, 1989). These narratives appear quite late in terms of the time-scale we have been considering (Charles-Edwards, 1970), after the British Celts had been exposed to Roman, Christian and Anglo-Norman influence and had become Welsh into the bargain. Nevertheless, no one seriously questions the essentially native qualities of the tales or that they reflect to some extent older cultural codes and practices.

In the First Branch, Rhiannon appears after Pwyll seats himself on the mound known as Gorsedd Arberth, riding a horse which proceeds at a steady pace. No one can catch her, until Pwyll himself addresses her. She says she loves Pwyll but has been promised to another man. During their marriage feast, Pwyll foolishly promises her to the rejected lover, and Rhiannon advises him how to regain her and humiliate the unwanted suitor.

They return to Pwyll's kingdom, Dyfed. Rhiannon remains childless and Pwyll's advisers urge him to take another wife. When she finally has a son, he disappears mysteriously, and the waiting-women claim she destroyed the boy. She refuses to defend herself against the accusation and, although Pwyll insists she retain her position at court, she is forced to sit near the horse block and offer to carry visitors to the king's hall. Meanwhile, on May-Eve, Terynon, Lord of Gwent-ys-Coed, attacks a giant claw which attempts to steal the foal of his prize mare. Afterwards he finds a baby outside the stable. The rescued foal is given to the child and Terynon's wife raises the boy until they recognize him as Pwyll's son and re-unite him with his mother.

In the Third Branch, Pryderi, now King of Dyfed, marries his mother to Manawydan, son of Lyr. One day while they are hunting they follow a magic deer which disappears into a fortress. Pryderi enters to rescue his dogs and touches a golden bowl which holds him fast. Manawydan reports the incident to Rhiannon who follows her son. Manawydan eventually frees them both from the captor who claims to have engineered the magic in revenge for the humiliation which had befallen Rhiannon's unwanted suitor. He tells Manawydan that Rhiannon and Pryderi's punishment in the fortress had been to wear horse collars.

The above is a summary account of two complicated and artistic narratives and highlights only those elements which could possibly be related to mythology. A proper reading of the text would certainly counter Matthew Arnold's statement that the first thing that strikes one in reading the *Mabinogion* is how evidently the medieval story-teller is pillaging an antiquity of which he does not fully possess the secret (Arnold, 1891). The redactor is very much in control of his material. It is equally true that myth in the modern sense of the word would have meant nothing to him. Nevertheless, the story clearly encapsulates several mythological themes.

Rhiannon's name is derived from *Rigantona, meaning 'Great Queen' in which the ending *-ona* indicates a divine being. The equine associations are found in the punishment endured first by Rhiannon for the supposed murder of her son, in the second punishment endured by both mother and son while captive in the fortress and in the congenital pairing of child and foal on May-Eve when Terynon dispatches the thieving claw. Terynon's name is derived from *Tigernonnos, 'Great or Divine Lord', again a likely name for a deity. Manawydan vab Llyr, the name of Rhiannon's second husband, is cognate with Mannanan mac Lir of Irish tradition, but lacking the marine associations of the Irish figure, and a not uncommon instance of where Welsh and Irish tradition dramatically diverge (Mac Cana, 1970, p. 69). The close pairing of mother and son suggests a possible relationship with Maponus, the great son of the great mother, whose cult was particularly strong in northern Britain (Ross, 1968, p. 463). We know from Welsh narrative that a figure called Mabon was abducted from his mother Modron (Jones and Jones, 1989, 'Culhwch ag Olwen').

These elements are very evocative, and scholars have suggested a connection between Rhiannon and Epona. How exactly do the elements of the tale link up with what we know about Epona? The archaeological iconography does not associate the goddess with a child; it is the mare she rides who has the foal. She is occasionally associated with a male god, not specifically Maponus, and there is no indication that he was associated with a myth in which he was abducted from his mother. Many of the elements attached to Rhiannon in the two Welsh narratives are paralleled by motifs found in international folklore.[1] Rhiannon's behaviour towards Pwyll at the beginning of the tale is consistent with that of an otherworld woman who comes to the human world for a husband. This type of narrative is known outside Celtic tradition and many of the female figures are not goddesses.

The section dealing with Rhiannon and her son is even more striking for its folk narrative parallels. A widely known complex of motifs is associated with a human heroine accused of murdering her child (Wood, 1988),[2] and the idea of congenital animals is not limited to divine beings.[3] The material in the Manawydan tale is more diffuse, but even here many of the episodes have parallels in other folk narrative traditions. Even the punishment of wearing horse collars occurs in certain contexts as an actual legal punishment (Roberts, 1970).

The folk narrative affinities of the two tales do not preclude the material being mythic in origin, any more than they affect the fact that these stories are good literature. The iconography of Epona shows her in a benign association with horses, whereas the equine associations in the Welsh tales, with the exception of Pryderi's foal which is never mentioned again, occur in a negative context, as punishments. It is possible that the myth may have been 'misunderstood' in later tales, although no satisfactory reconstruction has been suggested (Gruffudd, 1953). The equine nature of the punishment is unique to the Welsh tales, but the incidents associated with Rhiannon are quite consistent with folk-tales told in many cultures.

The question arises as to whether the source for these incidents is to be found in myths which were known to earlier Celtic cultures or whether they derive from an international body of narrative which has been adapted to a Welsh context. Ultimately, we can only speculate how closely the details of Rhiannon's equine associations approximate to the concept of the horse goddess Epona, and whether she and her son, Pryderi, reflect some mother/son deity pair. Although it would be a mistake to dismiss the connections, the danger is to take the possibility for the reality and begin to read these tales as myths. The problem remains one of accurate identification of mythic elements in the absence of any mythic texts, and of adequate interpretation of these elements in the context of international folk-stories and medieval literature. The conservative nature of tradition allows us to speculate on the former and our increased understanding of the complex nature of medieval Welsh culture has greatly refined the nature of interpretation — Rhiannon on her white horse still eludes modern scholars as ever she eluded the men of Pwyll's court.

The Sovereignty Figure

The metaphor of the marriage between the king and the land persisted in Irish tradition until at least the seventeenth century, and received perhaps its most poignant modern expression in Yeats' play *Cathleen ni Houlihan*. That this metaphor may echo an important myth in which the rightful king symbolically marries the titular goddess of the land, is one of the most far-reaching suggestions yet made about the nature of Celtic goddesses and has been used to explain features of numerous Irish texts (Mac Cana, 1955/1956; O'Rahilly, 1946), Breton *lais* (Bromwich, 1960/61), Welsh prose (McKenna, 1980) and Arthurian Romance (Loomis, 1945, 1959). Unlike the horse goddess Epona, it is difficult to relate the sovereignty figure directly to anything in the earlier iconography. Deity pairs are common enough, but there is no indication that the female predominated in any way. Goddess names sometimes suggest territorial eponyms, but the bulk of the evidence comes from what is known about early kingship and from later Irish tales.

The notion of a king entering into a sacred marriage with his kingdom is not uniquely Celtic (Binchy, 1936, 1970), however some form of native kingship continued longer in Ireland and Scotland than elsewhere, and this may have been a factor in the relative strength of the tradition and explain, in part, its strong political element. The sovereignty figure, as she has come to be called, appears in many contexts. Some of the historical and pseudo-historical women in early Irish tales were euhemerized goddesses representing the sovereignty of the territory with which they were associated (Ó Máille, 1927–8, p. 129).

For example, the woman in *Baile in Scail* (*The Phantom's Frenzy*) who gives drink to each successive king of Ireland is called 'Flaith Erenn', that is, the sovereignty of Erin, although it is not clear whether this is an original feature or a later adaptation. In the Book of Invasions, the in-coming sons of Mil are confronted by three supernatural women, Ériu, Banba and Fotla, who initially oppose the invaders but, reflecting the eponymous nature of the characters, admit them on condition that their names be commemorated in the land itself (Cross and Slover, 1935, p. 14). An origin tale which validates the hegemony of the Ui Niall tells how Niall and his brothers meet a hag near a well and she asks for a kiss. Only Niall both kisses and sleeps with her, whereupon she becomes beautiful. This dual-natured figure has been seen as the forerunner of the many loathly ladies in later romance and folk-tale (Loomis, 1970).

Other examples in Irish include Queen Medb of Connaught who dominates her husbands, the comparatively late and historicized Munster figure, Mor Muman (Mac Cana, 1955, p. 114), and a number of other females preserved sometimes in quite late texts and even in contemporary folk-tales (Mac Cana, 1955, pp. 374, 412). The extent and evident importance of these narratives seems to indicate that storytellers adapted a mythological pattern concerning a goddess connected to the very land of Ireland (or one of its provinces) to historical conditions, creating a rich pattern of syncretic history in which ancient mythological themes were used to validate contemporary historical reality.

However, if we examine one of the most striking examples of the sovereign hag, the old woman (Cailleach) mentioned in the ninth-century Irish poem 'Cailleach Bhearra', *The Old Woman of Beare*, the situation may not be so clear-cut. The poem is a monologue spoken by the old woman of the poem's title in which she recalls her youth and beauty, her kingly lovers and the generous heroic world in which she lived. By contrast, she now experiences a cold and lonely old age, presumably as a solitary nun (o'Haocha, 1989). *The Old Woman of Beare*, combining pagan and Christian elements through word play on *cailleach* as nun and old woman/hag (Mac Cana, 1981, pp. 143–59), encapsulates the ambivalent cosmology of a world both pagan and Christian. Cailleach Bhearra still exists in Irish and Scots-Gaelic folklore as an extremely complex entity whose appearances cannot easily be reduced to one source, mythological or otherwise. Some aspects of the figure are undoubtedly very old. The divine principle expressed as a nurturing mother who can withhold as well as give care, is virtually universal in Indo-European societies and may even be influenced by earlier proto-European cosmology (Filip, 1977, pp. 172–9). Irish vernacular literature characterizes the figure as a titular goddess who represents the land itself and the power of kingship.

The nature of Celtic goddesses has often been described as multi-functional and indeed this helps to account for the absence of goddesses associated with one single area of concern. However, it is possible to account for the complex nature of the supernatural figures by means of a multi-layered rather than a multi-functional model which avoids the over-emphasis on the survival of myth and allows for development in later cultural contexts. The oldest level is probably the mother/fertility element which may predate specifically Celtic culture. The powerful war/death female with its strongly sexual overtones may be more specifically Celtic; while the symbolism associated with the sovereignty queen may be a later aspect of the tradition, and characteristic of the learned/literary context rather than the all-enveloping pan-Celtic goddess figure which has been suggested (Ó Crualaoich, 1988, p. 161). In the romances, the figure develops in quite another direction which comes closest to the folk-tale heroine who goes from negative to positive circumstances via such oppositions as poverty/riches, servant/queen, etc. Modern Gaelic and Irish folklore carries elements of these, but in addition characterizes her as a personification of wild nature, often inimical to human civilization, a feature which may owe something to the personification of nature prevalent in Norse tradition (Ó Crualaoich, 1988, p. 154).

While it is possible to see a thread unifying this material – a particular power associated with the female – it is also true that the figure carries quite different cultural meanings whose historical and functional relationships are obscure (Ó Crualaoich, 1988, pp. 154, 161), but who cannot simply be described as various reflexes of a 'Celtic goddess'. In learned Irish tradition, the figure seems to develop away from chthonic figures and into goddesses associated with war and death and eventually into a quasi-political role where she personifies the sovereign power of a kingdom. In later romance literature, we may still see traces of this dynastic figure, although by then the immediate source may be learned rather than mythic tradition.

SECTION III: THE IMAGE OF WOMEN
IN LAW AND SOCIETY

An extensive body of Irish and Welsh law deals with women. It provides an important index of a woman's role in society, and can often illuminate the way they are depicted in other contexts. There are numerous difficulties in handling these sources since Welsh and Irish laws are primarily jurist-made. Thus it is difficult to determine how closely they reflect actual practice, and, of course, these early codes refer to a relatively small part of the total population. Nevertheless, the law tracts provide a substantial amount of information on the position of a certain proportion of women in Ireland and Wales, and on the norms governing their behaviour.

Both Irish and Welsh society were primarily patriarchal, so a woman was defined in legal terms in relation to her male kin. This situation is reflected in the earliest Irish records dating from the sixth and seventh centuries, although women's position in relation to men changed markedly after that time. The reasons for this are not completely clear. It may have been a natural development influenced by Christianity (Binchy, 1936), although it has been suggested that the improvement in women's social status, like the prominence of women in literature, was the result of pre-Celtic influences percolating through to the legal system (MacNeil, 1935, pp. 64–7). This last point is extremely speculative, and, quite frankly, difficult to sustain given the oblique nature of early evidence, but women did enjoy a high degree of freedom in Irish law relative to the earlier period.

The change in status is most clearly observed in relation to the control of property and a woman's rights within marriage. The transfer of property is fundamental to the continuance of most societies and bulks large in any legal system. In Irish law both men and women had certain rights over their contribution to the jointly-held marriage goods. Both could own private property, although the woman was more restricted. Even in the situation in which the bulk of the marriage goods was provided by the husband, the woman had definite legal rights in matters which directly affected her position as mistress of the household and as mother, and this gave her some security within marriage.

Irish law reflected the practice of polygamy, at least in certain circumstances, and wives had different rights according to the type of marital union. On the other hand, Irish law granted women surprisingly generous grounds for divorce in comparison with other societies and with Irish society at an earlier period. Legal divorce and polygamy did not commend themselves to the Church, and even as early as the eighth century (roughly contemporary with these law tracts) Irish canon law discouraged such practices. It is difficult to judge the effect of Church law on society at large, and secular custom probably continued in tandem with canonical marriage, at least among the aristocracy, until the end of the Middle Ages (MacCurtain and Ó Corráin, 1978, p. 7).

The situation in Wales is broadly similar to that of Ireland. By the period of the Welsh texts, monogamy was the legal rule, although other types of male/female pairings are mentioned and indeed probably occurred (Jenkins and Owen 1980, pp. 15–22). It is difficult to determine how far this picture of women possessing extensive rights and a high degree of personal freedom mirrors actual practice or is just the reflection of the ideals of a learned class of jurists. Certainly the strength and power of female Celtic deities is not echoed in the legal position of women.

Even more complicated is the position of women in the arena of politics. Queen Medb, as she appears in *The Cattle Raid of Cooley*, is one of the most singular woman of literature. Strong and sexually independent, it is tempting to people Irish society with women of her character. Early references to queens refer to them only as consorts. A queen's importance increased as the power attached to the institution of kingship became consolidated, and later annals refer to the queen of a kingdom not just the consort of a king (MacCurtain and Ó Corráin, 1978, p. 10). In regard to the laws, we are undoubtedly observing social convention and not the workings of myth, but some historical and semi-historical figures were probably susceptible to a degree of standardization and, like traditional narrative, carry cultural stereotypes whose origins may be very old. In Wales, the figures of Gwenllian and Nest carry the traditional overtones of strong independent women, the one preferring death after battle rather than Anglo-Norman oppression; the other, a somewhat pale reflection of Medb in her choice of sexual partners.

SECTION IV: INTO THE TWILIGHT

In a very real sense classical writers created the first 'Celt', a barbarian who inhabited an uncivilized world full of superstition and weird practices, but had a sense of honour which somehow highlighted the shortcomings of too-complacent classical citizens. Important, too, is Geoffrey of Monmouth who created not a Celt but an idealized Briton, the scion of Arthur, defeated — treacherously, of course — by the Saxons. The Celt as noble savage emerged again in the late eighteenth century as a counter to the excesses of rationalism. James MacPherson produced a number of bogus translations of Scots-Gaelic texts which sparked off a spirited discussion about the nature of the primitive (O'Halloran, 1989).

It was the nineteenth-century emergence of the Celt as visionary which has had the greatest impact on modern scholarship. Yeats felt that Irish literature needed the input of its own tradition. He saw this tradition as essentially continuous with the past, as preserving the best and finest sentiments of the past and as necessary to the health of Irish literature (Bramsback, 1984). Yeats used native tradition, or what he perceived it to be, to create a wonderful literary world and that writers need only write good literature is a truism. He and others like him did however leave a certain legacy for which many a scholar has cursed them, namely a view of the Celt as independent minded, impatient of convention, with an affinity for the mystical over the merely logical. These twin concerns with literature and with continuity with a finer, simpler past, are the two axes around which Yeats and Arnold's theories revolved. They are also the two points on which modern folklorists, concerned with folklore as a living phenomenon manifest throughout society, are most likely to take issue. It is worth pointing out in this context, that Arnold, Yeats and Macpherson had very little acquaintance with any Celtic language, a tradition maintained by many popular writers of today.

Latterly, popular feminist ideas have added a new dimension to modern Celtic mythology, and to the noble savage and the mystic can be added a strong but loving matriarchal goddess presiding over a harmonious social and physical environment. All of this is tradition of a kind, in that it creates images and symbols relevant to a particular culture. However, the foregoing would be more adequately described as mythology about the Celts rather than Celtic mythology.

Notes

1 A motif is an element recurring in the plot of several folk-tales. These have been classified thematically in S. Thompson (1966), *Motif Index of Folk Literature* (Indiana: University of Indiana Press), from which the numbering has been taken. These motifs have been taken from J. Wood (forthcoming), *The Welsh Folk-Narrative Index* (Helsinki: Suomalainen Tiedeakatemia): T55 Girl as wooer; F302 Fairy mistress; F241.1.1.1 Fairies ride white horses; K1371.1 Lover steals bride from wedding with unwelcome suitor.
2 B311 Congenital helpful animal; T589.7 Simultaneous birth of animals and child.
3 B184.3.1 Magic boar; N774 Adventure from pursuing enchanted animal; F241.0.1 Fairy animal hunted; D1136 Magic fort; D1413.7 Basin to which one sticks; C542 Taboo: touching treasures of the otherworld; G405 Man on hunt falls into ogre's power; F171.6 Mysterious punishment in otherworld.

References and Further Reading

Binchy, D.A. (ed.) (1936), *Studies in Early Irish Law* (Dublin: Binchy)

—— (1970), *Celtic and Anglo Saxon Kingship*, The O'Donnell Lecture for 1967–8 (Oxford: Clarendon Press)

Bramsback, B. (1984), *Folklore and W.B. Yeats: The Function of Folklore Elements in Three Early Plays* (Uppsala: Uppsala University)

Bromwich, R. (1960–1), 'Celtic Dynastic Themes and the Breton Lays' in *Etudes Celtiques*, 9, pp. 439–474

Byrne, J. (1974), 'Senchas: The Nature of Gaelic Historical Tradition' in *Historical Studies*, 9, pp. 137-59

Charles-Edwards, T.M. (1970), 'The Date of the Four Branches of the Mabinogi' in *Transactions of the Cymmrodorion*, pp. 263–98

Child, F.J. (ed.) (1956), *English and Scottish Popular Ballads*, 5 vols (New York: Dover)

Cross, T.P. and Slover, C.H. (1936), *Ancient Irish Tales* (New York: Barnes and Noble)

Dumézil, G. (1952), *Les dieux des Indo-Europeans* (Paris: Presses Universitaires de France)

—— (1973), *From Myth to Fiction: the Saga of Hadingus*, trans D. Coltmann (Chicago: University of Chicago Press)

Dundes, A. (ed.) (1989), *Sacred Narrative: Reading in the Theory of Myth* (Berkeley: University of California Press)

Filip, J. (1977), *Celtic Civilization and its Heritage* (Wellingborough: Collet's; Prague: Academia Press)

Green, M. (1986), *The Gods of the Celts* (Gloucester: Alan Sutton; New York: Barnes and Noble)

—— (1989), *Symbol and Image in Celtic Religious Art* (London and New York: Routledge)

Gimbutas, M. (1982), *The Goddesses and Gods of Old Europe* (London: Thames and Hudson)

Gruffydd, W.J. (1953), *Rhiannon* (Cardiff: University of Wales Press)

Honko, L. (1989), 'Folkloristic Theories of Genre' in Anna-Leena Siikala (ed.) *Studies in Oral Narrative*, Studia Fennica, 33 (Helsinki: Finnish Literature Society)

Jackson, Kenneth (1961), *The International Popular Tale and Early Welsh Tradition* (Cardiff: University of Wales Press)

Jenkins, D. and Owen, M. (eds) (1980), *The Welsh Law of Women: Studies presented to Professor Daniel A. Binchy on his eightieth birthday* (Cardiff: University of Wales Press)

Jones, Gwenan (1922), 'The Washer at the Ford' in *Aberystwyth Studies*, 4, pp. 105–11

Jones, Gwyn and Jones, T. (1949, reprinted 1989), *The Mabinogion* (London: Dent)

Lindgren, C. (1978), *Classical Art Forms and Celtic Mutations: Figural Art in Roman Britain* (New Jersey: Noyes Press)

Linduff, F. and Oaks, L.S. (1986), 'Epona' in M. Henig and A. King (eds), *Pagan Gods and Shrines of the Roman Empire* (Oxford: Clarendon Press), pp. 817–37

Loomis, R.S. (1945), 'Morgan La Fée and the Celtic Goddesses' in *Speculum*, 20, pp. 183–203

—— (1959), 'Morgan La Fée in Oral Tradition' in *Romania*, 53, 337–67

Mac Cana, P. (1955/6), 'Aspects of the Theme of King and Goddess' in *Etudes Celtiques*, 7, pp. 76–114, 356–413; 8, pp. 59–65

—— (1970), *Celtic Mythology* (London: Hamlyn)

—— (1981), 'Mythology in Early Irish Literature' in R. O'Driscoll (ed.), *The Celtic Consciousness* (Edinburgh: Canongate; London: Dolman Press), pp. 143–55

Mac Curtain, M. and Ó Coráin, D.(1978), *Women in Irish Society: The Historical Dimension* (Westport, Conn.: Greenwood)

MacNeill, E. (1935), *Early Irish Laws and Institutions* (Dublin: Donnell), pp. 64–7

Mallory, J.P. (1989), *In Search of the Indo-Europeans: Language, Archeology and Myth* (London: Thames and Hudson)

Magne, R. and Thevenot, E. (1953), *Epona* (Bordeaux: Delms)

Matthews, C. (1989), *Arthur and the Sovereignty: King and Goddess in the Mabinogion* (London: Arkana)

McKenna, C. (1980), 'The Theme of Sovereignty of Pwyll' in *Bulletin of the Board of Celtic Studies*, 29, pp. 35–52

o'Haocha, D. (1989), 'The Lament of the Old Woman of Beare' in D. Ó Corráin, L. Breatnach and K. McCone (eds), *Sages, Saints and Storytellers: Celtic Studies in Honour of Profesor James Carney* (Maynooth: An Sagart), pp. 308–31

Ó Crualáoich, G. (1988), 'Continuity and Adaptation in Legends of Cailleach Bhearra' in *Béaloideas*, pp. 153–78

Ó Máille, T. (1927–8), 'Medb Chruachna' in *Zeitschrift fur celtische Philologie*, 17, pp. 129–46

O'Halloran, C. (1989), 'Irish Re-creation of the Gaelic Past: The Challenge of Macpherson's Ossian' in *Past and Present*, 124, 69–95

O'Rahilly, C. (ed) (1967) *Táin Bó Cuailnge from the Book of Leinster* (text and translation) (Dublin: Irish Text Society)

O'Rahilly, T.F. (1946), 'On the Origins of the Names Érainn and Ériu' in *Ériu*, 14, pp. 7–28

Roberts, B.F. (1970), 'Penyd Rhiannon' in *Bulletin of the Board of Celtic Studies*, 23, pp. 325–7

Ross, A. (1967), *Pagan Celtic Britain* (London: Cardinal)

—— (1973), 'The Divine Hag of the Pagan Celts' in V. Newell (ed.), *The Witch Figure* (London: Routledge), pp. 139–64

Rhys, J. (1898), *Legends on the Origin and Growth of Religion as Illustrated by Celtic Heathendom* (London: Williams and Norgate)

Sims-Williams, P. (1986), 'The Visionary Celt: The Construction of an Esoteric Preoccupation' in *Cambridge Medieval Celtic Studies*, 11, pp. 71–97

Sjoestedt, M.-L. (1949, reprinted 1982), *Gods and Heroes of the Celts*, trans. Myles Dillon (Berkeley: Turtle Island Foundation)

Tierney, J.J. (1959–60), 'The Celtic Ethnography of Posidonius' in *Proceedings of the Royal Irish Academy*, 60, pp. 189–275

Thompson, S. (1966), *Motif Index of Folk Literature* (Indiana: Indiana University Press)

Wagner, H. (1981), 'Origins of Pagan Irish Religion' in *Zeitschrift für celtische Philologie*, 38, pp. 1–28

Williams, I. (1955), *Armes Prydein o Lyfr Taliesin* (Cardiff: University of Wales Press)

Wood, J. (1988), 'The Calumniated Wife in Medieval Welsh Literature' in *Cambridge Medieval Celtic Studies*, 10, 25–38

Wood, J. (forthcoming), *The Welsh Folk-Narrative Index* (Helsinki: Suomalainen Tiedeakatemia)

CAROLYNE LARRINGTON

Scandinavia

SECTION I: INTRODUCTION – A SYNTHESIS

Note: Two Icelandic letters are used in what follows: 'eth' ð pronounced like *th* in 'that' and 'thorn' þ pronounced as in 'thing'.

Creation of the World

In the beginning, there was nothing, neither sand nor sea, earth nor heaven, only *Ginnungagap*, the archetypal chaos. Ice congealed in the gap, forming the cosmic giant Ymir. The only female to be involved in the creation is Auðhumla the Ur-cow, who is nourished by licking the ice – in one version she licks Ymir out of the ice also. Her milk sustains him while he asexually reproduces the next generation, begetting giants who spring up from his feet and his armpits. From these the gods are descended, on the maternal side. The gods dismember Ymir and use his body to construct the universe (*Snorra Edda: Gylfaginning*, ch. 4–8).

The gods build halls and temples for themselves, then settle down to a Golden Age existence, playing chequers with golden pieces on the field Iðavellir (Eternal Plain). After the world is built, Óðinn and two other gods are walking on the seashore and find two pieces of driftwood. From one, the ash, they form the first man, Askr; the second piece is made into a woman, Embla. Although the meaning of her name is obscure, many scholars have tried to find the meaning 'vine' or 'creeper' in it, for which there is no etymological evidence. This illustrates how the woman is first predicated as clinging, dependent, needing the support of the man, and then her name distorted to fit. These speculations are of nineteenth and twentieth-century provenance; there are no contemporary or medieval interpretations of the name (*Gylfaginning*, ch. 9).

Once the world is created, the first tribe of gods, the Æsir, become embroiled in a war with a second tribe, the Vanir. The war is apparently precipitated by the activities of Freyja, the chief female among the Vanir who is knowledgeable in a disreputable kind of magic, *seiðr*. We know that it involved tranvestism for men, and such is deplored; what female rituals were practised is unknown. Three times she is burnt as a witch, but each time rises anew. War is begun, but inconclusively, for the Vanir cannot be killed (*Poetic Edda: Völuspá*, 21–4). Finally, a truce is arranged and hostages exchanged. Njörðr of the Vanir and his children, Freyr and Freyja, come to live among the Æsir.

At the centre of the Norse cosmos stands the World-Ash of Yggdrasill, the Steed of Óðinn. Its limbs extend over all worlds, and its three roots go down into the worlds of the gods (Ásgarðr), of the frost-giants (Jötunheimar), where once Ginnungagap was, and into Niflheim, where Hel, goddess of death, has her kingdom. At the roots are sacred wells which impart wisdom. The gods meet in judgement under the tree, riding over Bifröst, the bridge of the rainbow, to their assembly-place (*Gylfaginning*, ch. 15).

The Gods and Goddesses

The Norse pantheon consists primarily of two tribes of deities, the Æsir and the Vanir, defined against the Giants, a tribe of ancient and chthonic powers, oldest inhabitants of the universe. The Æsir are the older tribe; their leader is Óðinn, the one-eyed old man, god of war, poetry and wisdom. Other prominent Æsir are þórr, killer of giants and defender of Ásgarðr, the realm of the gods; Heimdallr, the watchman; Týr, the one-handed god of justice; Ægir, the sea god; and Bragi, the god of poetry. Frigg is Óðinn's wife, chief of the Ásynjor, the female Æsir. Her child is Baldr, a god of sunlight and fertility. Gefjon is another of the Æsir, a powerful patroness of human kings. Sif is married to þórr; Iðunn possesses the apples of immortality which keep the gods young. The Vanir, the younger tribe of gods, are led by Njörðr, sea and fertility god. His children, probably by his sister, are Freyr and Freyja, also concerned with fertility. Loki is the disruptive trickster god, of giant race but allied to the Æsir, for he is Óðinn's sworn blood-brother. Loki's children, born to him by a giantess are the monstrous Miðgarðsormr, the World-serpent who lies encircling the earth in the outer sea, the wolf Fenrir, who will kill Óðinn at Ragnarök, and Hel, goddess of the dead, whose face is half corpse-blue, half healthy, human pink (*Gylfaginning*, ch. 34).

Ragnarök

The coming of Ragnarök, the end of the world, is signalled by a number of events. The first portent is the death of Baldr (*see* Section II.5, p. 149). After this catastrophe, it is only a matter of time before Ragnarök. First comes the Fimbulvetr, a terrible winter which lasts for three years with no intervening summers. Then fighting will break out among humans, and no one will be spared:

> Brothers will fight
> and kill one another,
> close relations
> commit incest.
> It is hard for men,

much wickedness is abroad;
age of axes, age of swords,
shields are riven,
a wind-age, a wolf-age,
before the world plunges headlong.

POETIC EDDA: VÖLUSPÁ, 45

Heimdallr the watchman will blow his horn, Yggdrasill will tremble and the giants begin their advance. Fenrir-wolf is loosed from his bonds, the fire-giant Muspell sails from the south with Loki at the helm of his ship, and Hrymr the frost-giant advances from the east. Óðinn falls in combat with the wolf, Freyr in fighting Surtr. Víðarr, Óðinn's son, avenges his father by tearing the wolf's jaws apart; þórr and the World-serpent destroy each other. Then one wolf will swallow the sun, and another the moon; the stars disappear from the heavens and the earth sink into the boiling sea (*Gylfaginning*, ch. 51; *Poetic Edda: Völuspá*, 41–57).

The Return

Once again earth rises from the sea; eagles fly over waterfalls hunting fish and the Æsir gather once more on the plain of Iðavellir, where they find the lost golden chequers in the grass. Baldr returns and lives together with his brother and inadvertent killer, Höðr. Hœnir, an obscure god seemingly connected with augury, cuts wooden slips to determine fate once more, and the gods occupy the hall of Gimlé, roofed with gold and brighter than the sun. Humans also survive the conflagration: Líf and Lífþrasir, Life and Life-striver, who have hidden in the world-tree, are progenitors of the next generations. A new golden age seems set to begin, but the fate-slips and the ominous dragon Níðhöggr who flies over the land, bearing corpses in his wings, suggest that evil and death are not absent from it (*Gylfaginning*, ch. 52; *Poetic Edda: Völuspá*, 59–66).

Heroic Legend

The most important cycle of legends is that connected with the hero Sigurðr, the Sîfrit of the Middle High German *Nibelungenlied*, and Siegfried of Wagner's *Ring Cycle*. The story begins with Sigurðr's father, Sigmundr, who is duped by his sister, Signý, into fathering a child on her. Signý is intent on killing her husband, who was the murderer of her father and Sigmundr's; but the quality of the children whom she has by this wretch have caused her to despair. The incestuously-born child, Sinfjötli, helps Sigmundr to kill Signý's husband, and is eventually poisoned by a wicked step-mother. Sigurðr is born posthumously to Hjördís, Sigmundr's wife. After a childhood at his step-father's court, tutored by the dwarf-smith, Reginn, his foster-father, Sigurðr avenges his father's death, kills the dragon, Fáfnir, gaining a treasure-hoard, and disposes of Reginn. Subsequently his fate becomes entangled with that of Guðrún Gjúkadóttir, his eventual wife, and the valkyrie Brynhildr, the woman he was meant to marry. After Sigurðr's death, and the suicide of Brynhildr,

Guðrún lives to see the rest of her kin destroyed, some by her own hand, some as a result of her egging them on to vengeance, some despite her best efforts (*see* Section II.7, p. 151).

Sources

What we know of Norse mythology comes from two main sources, originating in Iceland. The first is the collection known as the *Poetic Edda*, a series of poems dealing allusively with the history of the gods and the deeds of human heroes, in particular, Sigurðr Fáfnisbani (slayer of Fáfnir). The poems may date from as early as AD 800 but were not written down until c. 1270, after Scandinavia had been Christian for two and a half centuries. The second source is the *Prose* or *Snorra Edda* (c. 1225) by the Icelander Snorri Sturluson. Snorri's book shapes and rationalizes much of the mythological material; occasionally he misunderstands the poetic sources he uses. His avowed aim is to preserve the old stories so that his contemporaries can continue to understand Norse traditional poetry, which is heavily mythological in its references. Snorri makes it clear that he has no belief in the gods as such; they are represented as refugees from Troy whose sophisticated Mediterranean culture hoodwinks the northerners into worshipping them as gods. Snorri was certainly a Christian and, particularly in his account of the end of the world, we suspect that his notion of the Christian Judgement Day may have coloured his representation. The *Snorra Edda* has four sections: a *Prologue*, explaining the origin of the Æsir; *Gylfaginning*, where the bulk of the mythological information is found; *Skáldskaparmál*, which augments it; and *Háttatal* which contains very little.

The stories of Guðrún and Brynhildr are found in a number of sources. The *Poetic Edda* gives us much of Sigurðr's life-story, but, unfortunately, a missing sheaf of pages from the only manuscript contained some of the most vital poems, explaining the relationship between Sigurðr, Guðrún, Gunnarr, her brother, and Brynhildr, his bride. The *Völsunga saga*, a later prose version, gives us an account which is not always consistent with the Eddic material; the *þiðreks saga* tells another version of the story, as well as an elaborated account of Völundr the smith, while the Middle High German *Nibelungenlied* represents yet another set of traditions. In his *Prose Edda*, Snorri supplements parts of the story of Guðrún's later life.

The Latin *History of the Danish People* (Shakespeare's source for Hamlet) by the Danish historian Saxo Grammaticus (c. 1200) provides the story of Rindr. Another Latin source for information about the Germanic peoples is Tacitus's *Germania*, completed by AD 98. Scholars have made extensive and often uncritical use of this work, which was written partly as a propaganda exercise to contrast Roman decadence with Germanic nobility. Tacitus must be used with extreme caution, for the period separating him from Snorri is longer than that intervening between Snorri and us.

In the interests of simplification, I shall draw mainly on the *Poetic Edda*, augmented by Snorri, in discussion of the myths, on *Völsunga saga* and the *Poetic Edda* for the Sigurðr material, and on the Eddic *Völundarkviða* for the stories of the swan-maidens and Böðvildr, with additions from þiðreks saga and the Old English poem Deor. I use the term 'audience' throughout to denote both readers and participants in oral performances of the works.

SECTION II: MYTHS ABOUT WOMEN

1. The Goddesses — Wives and Mothers

Frigg, married to Óðinn, knows the fates of everyone, but she keeps silent about them. Although in one story she gets the better of Óðinn by tricking him into destroying his own protégé, in other contexts, Frigg is a model of wifely devotion. When Óðinn asks her whether he should venture into the hall of the giant Vafþrúðnir to contend in wisdom with him, Frigg advises him to stay at home. Having asked for advice, Óðinn proceeds to ignore it, and goes off with Frigg's blessing. We hear nothing of Frigg's reactions to Óðinn's amours; unlike the Greek Hera, she seems to be unafflicted by jealousy. Although in the Lokasenna (see II.6, p. 150) she is accused by Loki of incestuous adultery with Óðinn's brothers, the composite portrait of Frigg is of a wise, resourceful and loving wife and mother. When Óðinn falls at Ragnarök, the poet of Völuspá calls him 'Friggiar angan', the darling of Frigg, and we realize with a shock that this sinister, one-eyed old man — repulsive to the women whom he tries to seduce — is actually beloved by someone.

Freyja has some valkyrie characteristics, for she rides to battle and chooses half of the slain (Óðinn takes the other half). She drives a chariot drawn by cats, possesses a feather cloak which enables the wearer to fly and is the best goddess to invoke in matters of love, for she is very fond of erotic songs. Freyja is married to the shadowy god Óðr, of whom no other fact is known. Once, when Óðr went away on a long journey, Freyja went to search for him, weeping tears of gold — the weeping goddess paralleled in Near Eastern myth (Gylfaginning, ch. 35). Freyja is greatly desired by the giants; on one occasion the gods promise her — together with the sun and moon — to a giant builder who is to repair the walls of their citadel, Ásgarðr, if he can complete the task in one winter. The builder, who is miraculously assisted by his horse, comes perilously close to fulfilling the bargain, and had not the horse been seduced away by Loki, in the form of a mare, Freyja would have been lost (Gylfaginning, ch. 42). In the Eddic poem þrymskviða, a similar demand is made when the giant þrymr steals þórr's hammer. þórr, however, dresses up as Freyja, recovers the hammer and kills the giant.

Freyja has some animal connections. She is called a bitch in a poem by Hjalti Skeggjason, one of the first Icelandic Christians, for which he is condemned for blasphemy at the Alþingi — the Icelandic Parliament (Njáls saga, ch. 102). She is also connected with the sow — the meaning of one of her by-names, Sýr. Her cult seems to have been generally widespread in Scandinavia, judging from the evidence of placenames, and particularly concentrated in Norway.

Iðunn possesses the apples of immortality. On one occasion, Loki is captured by a giant in eagle form and only released when he promises to obtain Iðunn for him, together with her apples. Loki entices Iounn out of Ásgaror by telling her that he has found some apples similar to hers, and would like her to bring her apples to compare them. piazi the giant swoops down and carries her off. Without Iounn's rejuvenating apples the gods soon become old and grey. Loki flies to Jötunheimar, land of the giants, in Freyja's feather cloak and, finding that piazi has gone fishing, changes Iounn into a nut and flies off with her. piazi flies in pursuit but the Æsir kindle a great fire which burns up the giant's wings. He is captured and killed. The death of piazi brings Skaoi to Ásgaror (*see* II.4, p. 147) (*Skáldskaparmál*, chs 1–2, 204–14).

Freyja and Iounn represent highly desirable sexual partners for the giants. Both gods and giants seem to feel compelled to marry outside their own race, just as human tribes saw exogamic marriage as preferable to marrying within their own kin groups. While willing, and able, to take giant women like Geror, the gods will not permit exchange of their own females. Although there seems to be no implication that piazi actually covets the apples for himself – he simply wishes to deprive the gods of their benefits – it is possible the goddesses, and the attributes they possess, represent a life-giving fecundity and radiance which is alien to the bleak mountain habitats of the giants, qualities signalled by the bundling of Freyja with the sun and moon as reward for the Giant Builder.

The goddess, *Gefjon*, whose name seems to mean 'giving', is sent from the island of Fyn by Óoinn to find some land. She has four sons by a giant who are changed into oxen. In exchange for sex, King Gylfi promises her as much land as four oxen can plough in a day and a night. The four giant sons plough up a huge area – the island which is now Sjælland; the hole left behind is Lake Mälaren in Sweden which is roughly the same shape as the coastline of Sjælland (*Gylfaginning*, ch. 1).

Sigyn, Loki's wife, stands over him as he lies bound with snakes dripping venom on his face – his punishment for his role in the death of Baldr (*see* II.5, p. 149). Sigyn catches the venom in a bowl, but when she has to go to empty it the poison falling on Loki's face makes him writhe in agony – the cause of earthquakes (*Gylfaginning*, ch. 50).

2. Wooing the Reluctant Girl: Geror and Billingr's Wife

GERÐR AND THE WOOING OF SKÍRNIR

Daughter of the giant Gymir, Geror is so radiantly beautiful that 'all the sea and the air catch light from her arms'. She lives with her father in a splendid palace, surrounded by baying dogs and a wall of fire. She is seated in her hall one day when Skírnir, messenger of the god Freyr, arrives. Geror invites him in and he broaches his errand swiftly, but with a fine comedy of tact. If Geror will 'say that Freyr is not the most hateful person alive', she will be given one of the most precious treasures of the Æsir – eleven golden apples, perhaps identical with Iounn's. Geror sees through the euphemism: 'I shall never set up home with Freyr,' she retorts. Skírnir wheedles – she will have the magic ring, Draupnir, which replicates itself eight times every ninth night. 'I'm not short of gold, I own all that my father has,' responds Gerðr. Now the gloves come off: Skírnir threatens to cut off her head with the sword which Freyr has lent him. Unafraid, Gerðr says that her father will be more than a match for him, if it comes to fighting.

Since neither bribery nor physical violence avail, Skírnir tries another line of attack. He threatens Gerðr with magic, with a fate worse than death. Doomed to sit on a tussock at the end of the world as a public spectacle, consumed with sexual frustration and madness, tormented by monsters and forced to drink goat's urine, a three-headed ogre will be the only husband she can hope to get. The curse of all the gods, the Æsir and Vanir, will be called down upon her and rune-magic will cause an unslakeable nymphomania (not the metamorphosis and consequent frigidity so often the punishment of the woman who refuses the god in other traditions). Gerðr concedes defeat, brings mead to seal the bargain and names a grove where she will consent to meet Freyr. Skírnir rides home in triumph to tell Freyr that his wish will be granted (*Poetic Edda*: *Skírnismál*).

Unfortunately, we know almost nothing more of the story — Snorri (*Gylfaginning*, ch. 37) tells us that Freyr and Gerðr were married, but we cannot be certain whether this is a genuine mythological fact, or whether he has decided to regularize the relationship begun in the earlier text. Certainly, the terms in which Skírnir solicits Gerðr are not those of a marriage proposal: a rendezvous for Freyr's sexual gratification is all that seems to be required.

Various interpretations of the myth have been advanced, although few commentators face the difficulty of approving a god-hero who obtains what he wants through threats and coercion. Freyr's desirability as lover is uncompromised though, for it is Skírnir who chooses the strategies deployed in the quest, intent on getting what his master desires. The god, unimplicated in the confrontation between Gerðr and Skírnir, can still be construed as the ideal lover: in the Eddic *Lokasenna*, an important source for facts often critical of the gods, we are told that Freyr never makes any girl or married woman weep.

Early scholars interpreted Freyr as a sun god, Skírnir as his fructifying ray and Gerðr as the enclosed, fertilized field, but interpretation simply in terms of fertility myth ignores Gerðr's stubborn resistance to the wooing — why should a field not welcome the sunshine? Later scholars have seen the pattern as that of a 'sacred marriage' between the fertility god and his chosen woman, reflecting cult practices (Dronke, 1962), while others read the myth structurally in terms of social function: as a reflection of Icelandic marriage practices, or a pattern for reconciliation between feuding groups (Mitchell, 1983). This last interpretation seems improbable, since it seems to be for Gerðr herself to decide, first to have nothing to do with Freyr, and finally to submit. The father is invoked only as protector: he never appears and has no say in Gerðr's decision. Historically, women married off in such peace-settlements were not given the opportunity to dispose of themselves.

All or some of these meanings may well be present in the myth, but, crucially, we can also attempt to recuperate a meaning for women. I have told this myth from Gerðr's point of view, though in *Skírnismál*, the source of the myth, the audience is encouraged to identify with Skírnir, the messenger who must pass through all sorts of peril to reach the giant's hall, and with the moping, lovesick Freyr. Gerðr's capitulation comes as the climax to the poem, Skírnir's moment of triumph. To the women in the audience, Gerðr's apparent autonomy – her choice in saying yes or no without consulting her father – must have seemed an enviable freedom. When she married for the first time, an Icelandic woman would usually be asked to consent to the deal that her father and husband had concluded, but she was rarely in a position to reject a suitor out of hand. Yet the story demonstrates that Gerðr's choice is illusory: under patriarchy – whose coercive operation through bribery and threat is laid bare in the poem – she can answer in any way she likes as long as she says 'yes'. Unusually, the curse recognizes 'what woman wants' – sexual fulfillment and intimacy with her lover – by predicting for Gerðr the opposite condition: sexual frustration, a hideous husband, public ridicule. The curse is formulated as an antitype of romantic love, but all that a woman could, in male eyes, possibly desire: riches, sexual satisfaction and the favour of the god will be hers as soon as she decides to co-operate with the patriarchal plan (Larrington, forthcoming).

BILLINGR'S 'MÆR' OUTWITS ÓÐINN

Billingr's 'mær' (girl – either wife or daughter are possible interpretations) has no other name than that of her male relative. One day she is surprised by Óðinn, the old, one-eyed supreme god, who, infatuated with her beauty, wants to make love with her. Billingr's wife knows how dangerous it is to refuse or to thwart Óðinn in sexual matters (*see* the story of Rinda, below). Marshalling her wits she emphasizes the need for discretion, telling the importunate god to come back after dark, quoting one of his own dicta: 'in the dark a man should win himself a woman by his words'. Impatiently Óðinn waits in the reeds and at nightfall he returns, but the household is still awake. Near dawn he makes the 'journey of desire' again, but Billingr's 'mær' is absent. Instead, a bitch is tied to the bed as an insulting alternative. The god retreats, ruefully admitting that he, the god of wisdom, has been outwitted by the shrewd woman. His regret at the missed sexual encounter is tempered with powerful admiration for the woman's intelligence, a respect which reflects the Norse evaluation of women as independent and resourceful (*Poetic Edda*, *Hávamál*, 96–102).

3. Abduction and Betrayal: Rinda, Böðvildr and Gunnlöð

THE RAPE OF RINDA

Rindr, or Rinda, as she is called in Saxo, is the daughter of the Ruthenian king. Óðinn has been told that she is destined to be the mother of Baldr's avenger, and sets out to win her. Disguised, he comes to the court as a military tactician, and wins a great victory for the king. Óðinn asks for Rinda as his reward, but she persistently refuses him because of his age and unattractiveness. When he tries to kiss her, she gives him such a shove that he goes flying and bangs his chin on the floor. In revenge, Óðinn touches her with a piece of bark inscribed with spells, which drive her mad, 'a moderate sort of punishment for the continual insults he had received', comments Saxo. Finally, Óoinn disguises himself as a female physician. Rinda falls ill and turns to him for treatment. Óoinn prescribes a medicine so bitter that the patient must be tied to the bed in order to swallow it. Once Rinda is tied down Óoinn rapes her. For this dastardly act, Óoinn is sent into exile by the gods, but the son, Bø (Váli in Icelandic sources), to whom Rinda gives birth, kills Hötherus (the reflex of Höor in this version of the myth) and dies himself of wounds the next day (Saxo, p. 76ff).

A fourteenth-century record shows that when Danish women were in labour, other women would make a man of straw and dance about it 'with lascivious gestures', crying 'Canta Boui, canta Boui, quid faceret', suggesting that Bø may have been a local fertility deity (Saxo, II, p. 58).

VÖLUNDR, THE SWAN-MAIDENS AND BÖÐDVILDR

This version follows the Eddic poem *Völundarkvioa*. Völundr, prince of elves, lives in the forest, hunting and shooting with his two brothers. One day three swan-maidens appear by the lake and take off their swan-coats to spin. Each brother takes one as his wife, Völundr marrying Alvítr (All-wise). After nine years of domesticity, the women become restless; their migratory swan-natures force them to fly away. The two brothers set off to hunt for their wives, but Völundr stays at home, forging rings while waiting to see if Alvítr will come back. There he is captured by King Níoúor, who covets his treasure, and, at the behest of Níoúor's wicked queen, he is hamstrung and placed on an island where he is forced to make jewellery and ornaments for the royal household.

The king's two sons row over to see Völundr's hoard of treasures, only to be killed and made into ornaments themselves. No one knows where the princes are, so Böovildr, their sister, suspects no harm when she comes over to see Völundr with a ring, part of the booty acquired when Völundr was captured. Böovildr has broken it and flirtatiously admits to Völundr, 'I didn't dare tell anyone about it except you.' Völundr mends the ring, but he also presses beer upon her until she becomes sleepy, then rapes or seduces her (*see* fig. 13). Neither the audience, nor the befuddled Böovildr know exactly what has happened, but Völundr flies away to the court to crow his triumphant revenge at Níoúor, leaving Böovildr weeping at the departure of her 'lover'. Völundr extracts a solemn oath that the father will not kill the dishonoured daughter, to whom he now refers (ironically?) as 'the bride of Völundr', and flies away. The poem ends with a painful interview between father and daughter: 'Is what Völundr has told me true, that you and he were together on the island?' 'It is true that we were together – I did not know how to struggle against him, I could not struggle against him!' The Old English poem *Deor* depicts the aftermath for Böovildr, here called Beadohild, in a sympathetic and intuitive awareness of the woman's misery and paralysis of will when she realizes her plight:

> For Beadohild her brothers' death
> was not so painful as her own condition,
> when she clearly realized

Fig. 13 This casket, made from whalebone, dates from the eighth century. The carving seems to illustrate the story of Völundr. He is pictured at his anvil on the left; on the right are Böovildr and a companion. Völundr is handing over the intoxicating beer, while at his feet, under the anvil, the remains of Böovildr's two brothers can be seen. *Courtesy of the Trustees of the British Museum, London*

that she was pregnant; never could she
resolutely think how it would turn out:
that passed by, so may this!

DEOR, 2

All may not end so wretchedly for Böovildr. In the later thirteenth-century *þiðreks saga*, Völundr (Vélent) returns for Böovildr and marries her after executing Níoúor. Their son grows up to be a hero whose adventures occupy much of the rest of the saga.

Völundarkviða is an amalgam of two different types of story: the swan-maidens belong in fairy or folk-tale (*Märchen*), while the heroic legend of revenge is known both in Scandinavia and England. The swan-maiden episode is structurally linked to the revenge story, a link symbolized by the ring forged for the swan-maiden, which leads to Böovildr's downfall, and through the themes of captivity and flight. The swan-wife, though apparently living willingly with Völundr, comes to feel that her home is oppressive and flies south over the dark wood, leaving her husband to grieve. Völundr himself flies out of captivity, leaving his new 'bride' behind in tears. The linking ring has been analysed in Freudian terms, paired with Völundr's sword (which actually plays very little part in the story), but the ring is more easily interpreted as a symbol of marriage, ruptured when the ring is broken, then healed through the sexual union of Völundr and Böovildr (Burson, 1983; Grimstad, 1983).

GUNNLÖÐ AND THE MEAD OF POETRY

Daughter of the giant Suttungr, Gunnlöð is the keeper of the mead of poetry, which gives poetic power to whoever imbibes it. Óðinn covets the mead and adopts a cunning stratagem to get hold of it. He comes disguised on a visit to the hall of the giant, where Gunnlöo, from her golden throne, offers him a drink of the mead. Óoinn sleeps with Gunnlöo for three nights and then obtains access to the vats where the mead is kept. Gulping down the contents of all three vats, he escapes from the giant's hall, apparently with Gunnlöð's assistance, and succeeds in regaining Ásgarðr in the shape of a bird. Suttungr pursues, in eagle form, and almost catches him. The other gods see Óðinn in danger and light fires around the perimeter wall. Óðinn reaches safety, but Suttungr is burnt up in the fire.

What of Gunnlöð? Óðinn cheerfully admits that he has used her and made her weep. She has betrayed her father's trust, and has been betrayed in return. Archetype of the seduced maiden, unlike Rinda and Böðvildr, she does not even have the comfort of a child; unlike Billingr's wife, she is incapable of resisting the god (*Poetic Edda, Hávamál*, 104–10; *Skáldskaparmál*, chs 4–6).

Gunnlöð's story has recently been reworked in a novel, *Gunnlaðarsaga* by Sváva Jakobsdóttir, one of Iceland's leading feminist writers and politicians. An Icelandic girl, Dís (a significant name, *see* Section III, p. 155), visiting the National Museum in Copenhagen, is drawn back into the Bronze Age myth through a gold cup and mirror on display (*see* fig. 14 for the goddess from the Gundestrup cauldron in the Museum). Dís becomes Gunnlöð, priestess of the old religion and consecrator of kings. Óðinn, candidate for the kingship, must drink mead from the sacred cup and sleep with Gunnlöð in order to gain sovereignty over his kingdom. But Gunnlöð awakes to find Óðinn and the cup gone. Óðinn's theft represents the end of the worship of the goddess – mother, earth, giver of life and death – and the beginning of Óðinn's own cult of war, power-madness and new, unnatural technologies, the Iron Age. The cup must be recovered for women if the harmful effects of Óðinn's action, symbolized in the modern world by the effects of Chernobyl, are ever to be nullified. Dís is arrested for attempting to steal the cup from the museum. Her mother flies to Copenhagen to find out what has happened to her daughter, and as Dís unfolds the story to her, she, like the reader, is drawn into Dís's experience, cutting from the sanctuary of the goddess back to contemporary Copenhagen. A *succès fou* in Iceland, *Gunnlaðarsaga* has not yet been translated into English.

4. Marriage: Skaoi and Njöror

SKAÐI'S MARRIAGE

The giantess Skaði comes to Ásgarðr demanding reparation for the death of her

Fig. 14 A goddess from the Gundestrup cauldron, with attendants arranging her hair. *National Museum, Copenhagen*

father, Þiazi (*see* II.1, p. 142). The gods promise one of their number as a husband. Skaði readily accepts, for she hopes to gain Baldr, brightest and most handsome of the gods, as her husband. But the gods make one proviso: Skaði's potential husbands will be hidden behind a sheet and only their feet will be visible. Skaði agrees, choosing the whitest and best-shaped feet, for she is sure these must be Baldr's. However, they actually belong to Njörðr, the sea-god. Skaði is dissatisfied, and will only declare herself reconciled to the Æsir if they can make her laugh. Loki ties a goat to his testicles: the goat pulls one way and Loki the other, both shrieking loudly. Skaði finds this irresistably funny and, despite the inauspicious beginning, the marriage is contracted. Irretrievable breakdown soon occurs. Skaði's home is in the mountains, where she skis and hunts, but Njörðr cannot bear the sound of howling wolves. Nor can Skaði endure the shrieks of the gulls at Njörðr's sea-shore palace:

> I could not sleep
> in a bed by the sea
> for the din of the bird;
> he woke me
> when he came from the ocean,
> every single morning: the seagull.

The incompatibility of the couple is symbolized by their hostility to the sounds which the other loves. Finally, Skaði retreats permanently to her father's home in the mountains where she is honoured as the ski-deity (*Skáldskaparmál*, ch. 3, 212–14; *Gylfaginning*, ch. 23).

No stigma attaches to Skaði; divorce was relatively simple to obtain in Scandinavian law – a simple declaration of intent would suffice – and a woman had the right to recover her dowry from her husband. She would usually return to her father's house, from where she could easily re-marry. A divorced woman, like a widow, seems to have had more say in future matches than the woman marrying for the first time. In the *Lokasenna*, Loki claims that he has been her lover, an accusation shameful mainly because Loki was implicated in her father's death.

In *Heimskringla* (*Ynglinga saga*, ch. 8), Snorri tells us that Njörðr passed Skaði on to Óðinn, and they had lots of sons together. This is not mentioned elsewhere, but Snorri cites an obscure verse by the late tenth-century poet Eyvindr *skáldaspillir* which names Skaði as having had children with 'the friend of generous men', most plausibly Óðinn. Judith Jesch has suggested that Skaði, because of her active and warlike nature, could not be assimilated into the world of the Æsir: 'Although a minor character in Snorri's *Edda*, she is one of the most interesting, an odd woman out among the goddesses' (Jesch, 1991, p. 139). Perhaps Snorri too sensed this separateness, and tried to re-incorporate her into the Æsir's universe by marrying her off to Óðinn, a god to whom one liaison more would make little difference.

5. Motherhood

FRIGG AND THE LOSS OF BALDR

Baldr, son of Frigg and Óðinn, most handsome and kindest of the gods, reports one day that he is plagued by bad dreams and fears that his life is in danger. Óðinn's reaction is to saddle his eight-legged horse and to ride to Niflheim, the world of the dead, to the hall of Hel. He learns that the mead stands poured for Baldr in Hel's hall, that Höðr, Baldr's brother will be responsible for his death, and that Óðinn will beget Váli on Rindr in order to avenge Baldr (*see* II.3, p. 144). Meanwhile, Frigg has conceived a plan. She will go about creation, taking oaths from everything, animate and inanimate, that they will not harm him in any way: 'fire, water, iron, and every kind of metal, stones, earth, wood, sicknesses, animals, birds, poisons and snakes' all promise to do no harm. The gods invent a new game in their assembly, hurling missiles at Baldr which bounce off him, leaving him unscathed. Frigg believes her son to be safe. But Loki, the duplicitous god, goes to her in the likeness of a woman, and in the course of casual conversation, Loki flattering, Frigg complacent, Frigg mentions that the mistletoe did not swear – 'for it looked too young to give an oath.'

Frigg's visitor immediately disappears; Loki cuts a dart of the mistletoe and puts it into the hands of Höðr, the blind god who has been unable to join in the game. Loki offers to guide his throw, the mistletoe dart pierces Baldr and he falls dead. Terrible grief breaks out among the Æsir. Óðinn is the worst affected, for he knows that Baldr's death is the first sign of the coming of Ragnarök. Frigg takes charge, finding a messenger to go to Hel and find how Baldr may be recovered. Hermóðr (unknown elsewhere, unless he is identical with a figure in the Old English *Beowulf*) volunteers, returning with the news that Baldr may return if every living thing weeps for him. Once again messages are sent to every substance – and this is the reason why metals weep (i.e. are covered in condensation) when they are brought from the cold into the warm. Everything in Creation weeps for Baldr, except for an old giantess called þökk sitting in a cave – Loki in disguise. She retorts:

> þökk will weep
> with dry tears
> for Baldr's journey to the pyre;
> living or dead
> I have joy of no man's son:
> let Hel keep what she has.

Baldr cannot return until after Ragnarök, when he presages the new order (*Gylfaginning*, ch. 49).

This myth is the only depiction of motherhood in the stories of the gods. We may contrast Óðinn's mission to Hel to find out about the situation – a quest for knowledge typical of the god of wisdom – with the practical steps which Frigg takes to secure her son's safety. Complacent in her belief that he is safe, she can scarcely help bragging to the harmless old woman who comments admiringly on the success of her scheme, and the fatal omission is revealed. When Baldr is dead, Frigg's grief is played down, prominence given to Óðinn's horror as he realizes that Ragnarök is now inevitable. But Frigg promises 'all her love and favour' to the messenger who will dare the journey to Hel – again practical action. The ogress who refuses to weep is generally identified with Loki; but the terms in which she puts her refusal are worth considering. The old hag will only weep with dry tears, for her days of sexual activity are over and she contains no more moisture. Baldr is beloved by everyone; as we know, Skaði had hoped to gain him as a husband, but since she no longer has a sexual interest in Baldr, the hag consigns him to the embraces of Hel, Loki's daughter, half woman, half corpse.

6. The Goddesses Stand Accused – The Lokasenna

From the Eddic poem *Lokasenna*, perhaps translatable as 'The Ranting of Loki', we gain a great deal of – mostly discreditable – information about the Norse goddesses. The goddesses and gods have gathered at the home of Ægir, the sea god, for a feast. Þórr is absent on a giant-killing expedition in the east; Loki has been expelled from the feast because he has killed one of the servingmen, but he returns and proceeds to insult each of the guests, taunting them with their failures and peccadilloes. Predictably enough, the goddesses are accused of sexual misdemeanours: Iðunn is reproached with having slept with her brother's slayer; Gefjon has slept with a man in exchange for jewellery; Frigg has been unfaithful to her husband with his two brothers; Freyja is a witch and has been the lover of everyone present at the feast, including her brother – interrupted *in flagrante delicto* by the gods she was so embarrassed that she farted; Týr's wife – who is unnamed – has borne Loki a child; Skaði has invited Loki to her bed and he has slept with Sif, þórr's wife. Beyla, a minor goddess, probably a personification of malt used in ale-brewing, gets off lightly, accused only of being dirty. Finally, þórr returns, and with much comic blustering, silences Loki.

The goddesses stand accused, not for their sexual activity *per se*, but for sex with inappropriate people – with a brother, a brother's killer, brothers-in-law or Loki himself, the enemy of the gods. Loki also brings up past history which the goddesses might rather forget, taunting Frigg with his role in the death of her son, Baldr, and Skaði with his part in her father's killing.

Not all that we learn from the *Lokasenna* about the goddesses is to their detriment. As Loki taunts each individual, another of the guests speaks up in the victim's defence, drawing Loki's attention and providing a new target for his malice. The defenders rarely deny the truth of the accusations Loki hurls, but act rather as character witnesses. 'Don't antagonize Gefjon,' Óðinn warns, 'for she knows the fates of everyone, just as clearly as I do.' Freyja defends Frigg in the same way, 'she knows all fate, even if she does not speak out'.

Some of these accusations are certainly true. We know from Snorri that Gefjon slept with King Gylfi in order to get Zealand for herself, that Freyja introduced the alien, female form of magic *seiðr* to the gods (*see* Section I, p. 137), that Frigg slept with Óðinn's brothers Vili and Vé when he was away on a journey. Loki speaks as if the goddesses were human, and we, the audience, judge them accordingly. Thus Freyja stands accused as a promiscuous woman, even though, logically, a fertility goddess is bound to be prodigal with her favours. Incest is a human taboo, even if its practice is one of the archaic traits distinguishing the Vanir from the Æsir, for Freyja and her brother are themselves the product of a brother/sister union. We must remember however that Loki is capable of twisting the truth, obscenely glossing actions which the gods may be able to justify.

Is the *Lokasenna* simply a Christian's burlesque of the disreputable ways of the pagan pantheon? Or did the poem have a serious meaning for a pagan poet? It can be – and has been – read as an indictment, not necessarily Christian, of the gods' corruption, a demonstration of their moral bankruptcy, so that the great drama of the end of the world, the Ragnarök, functions as a cleansing and a renewal rather than as total catastrophe. Was mockery of the gods sanctioned as part of worship, as the medieval Church sanctioned the Feast of Fools? Or did their amorality finally not matter to their worshippers – their refusal to conform to human ethics demonstrating their separateness and power?

7. The Warrior Destroyed and the Heroine who Survives: Brynhildr and Guðrún Gjúkadóttir

The stories of Brynhildr and Guðrún, the most famous Germanic heroines, are found in a number of versions, ranging from the *Poetic Edda* through the thirteenth-century prose *Völsunga saga* in Norse, to the *Nibelungenlied* and, most famously, Wagner's

Ring Cycle. Brynhildr is also known as Brünhild, Guðrún appears as Kriemhilt in the German sources; in this account I shall use the Norse names, and follow the story from the *Völsunga saga*, supplemented from the *Poetic Edda*.

The hero Sigurðr has avenged the death of his father, Sigmundr, killed the dragon, Fáfnir, and his foster-father, the dwarf Reginn. Before he emerges from the fabulous world of his childhood into the historical world of the Gjúkungar court, he encounters a valkyrie, Sigrdrífa, who has been put to sleep behind a shield-rampart by Óðinn for giving victory to the wrong king in a battle. Sigrdrífa is awakened by Sigurðr to whom she gives wise counsel. At this point there is a lacuna in the *Edda* manuscript, and when the cycle of poems resumes we are deep in the tragedy of Sigurðr and Guðrún. *Völsunga saga* gives the name of the valkyrie as Brynhildr, and at the end of the wisdom monologue, Brynhildr and Sigurðr agree to marry. Sigurðr then rides off and soon appears at the home of Brynhildr's foster-father, Heimir. Brynhildr has returned and is living in a high tower; Sigurðr expresses curiosity about the tower's inhabitant and is told that Brynhildr is a fierce shield-maiden who has no interest in men. Sigurðr goes to visit and is well received, although Brynhildr prophesies that they will never marry. Inexplicably, the text suggests that they do not remember their first encounter on the mountain (*Völsunga saga*, chs 13–25).

Meanwhile, at the court of her father Gjúki, Guðrún dreams of a hawk which she treasures dearly sitting on her hand. Her women interpret the dream as signifying a splendid marriage. Sigurðr appears at Gjúki's court; Grimhildr, Guðrún's mother, gives him a drugged horn of mead causing him to lose all memory of Brynhildr, and he agrees to marry Guðrún. Grimhildr encourages Gunnarr, Guðrún's brother, to try to win Brynhildr, and with Sigurðr and his brother, Högni, he sets off to woo her. Brynhildr is in her hall surrounded by flames, and has sworn only to marry the man who can cross them. Sigurðr and Gunnarr change appearances and Sigurðr succeeds in crossing the flames. Brynhildr is suspicious, for she believes that only Sigurðr is capable of such a feat. However, she agrees to the match, and she and Sigurðr sleep together for three nights, with a drawn sword between them. At Gunnarr and Brynhildr's wedding feast, Sigurðr suddenly remembers his vows to her, but keeps silent (*Völsunga saga*, chs 26–9).

One day Brynhildr and Guðrún are bathing in the Rhine when they begin to quarrel about whose husband is superior. Guðrún reveals the true identity of the man who crossed the flames, and proves it by showing the ring, Andvaranaut, which Sigurðr took from Brynhildr while they slept together. The quarrel escalates; confronted with the truth, Gunnarr admits the deception. Brynhildr is ready to kill him, but is restrained by Gunnarr's brother, Högni. She shuts herself away in fury, taking no wine, refusing to see Gunnarr and plotting her revenge. Guðrún, now terrified at the result of her rash words, sends Sigurðr to try to mollify her. Brynhildr accuses him of treachery towards her; Sigurðr explains what has happened, and tries to persuade her to make the best of it. Brynhildr will have none of this; Sigurðr now offers to leave Guðrún and marry her, but Brynhildr refuses this too: 'I will not have two kings in the same hall,' she says, 'I don't want you or any other man.' Although

Sigurðr is so moved that his mail-coat bursts asunder, the impasse remains; Brynhildr will have nothing to do with Gunnarr, and demands that he kill Sigurðr and his son, or she will leave him. Gunnarr fears to lose her, but he and Högni are bound by oaths to Sigurðr. Their youngest brother, Guttormr, has not sworn however, and, incited by the older brothers, he kills Sigurðr in his bed. Guðrún awakes to find herself bathed in his blood. Guðrún weeps and Brynhildr laughs in triumph when she hears Guðrún's sobs. But soon she too weeps for Sigurðr: 'and no one could understand why she had asked laughing for what she grieved for with weeping'. Brynhildr stabs herself and asks to be burnt on the same pyre as Sigurðr, with the sword lying between them as it had on the three nights they had spent as man and wife (*Völsunga saga*, chs 30–3).

The *Poetic Edda* resumes in the middle of a poem in which Brynhildr incites Gunnarr to kill Sigurðr (*Brot af Sigurðarkviða*). In this version, Sigurðr is killed while out hunting, but the redactor of the manuscript observes that a number of traditions are given about Siguror's death. Certainly in later Eddic poems, in which Guðrún mourns the sorrows of her life, she recalls Sigurðr's being killed in her bed.

After Brynhildr's death, Atli, her brother, attacks the Gjúkungar, and is appeased only by gaining Guðrún as his wife. Guðrún has been inconsolable, but she is given a drink of forgetfulness and consents to the match. Later, Atli plots to gain Fáfnir's treasure, which had passed to Gunnarr and Högni at Sigurðr's death. He sends for the brothers, who, although warned by Guðrún to expect treachery, see the invitation as a challenge to their honour and arrive at Atli's court where they are overpowered and killed without revealing the location of the treasure. Guðrún avenges them by killing her two sons by Atli and preparing the flesh as titbits to accompany the ale for the Hunnish warriors and Atli himself. She reveals the horrifying origin of the food, kills Atli and burns down the hall (*Völsunga saga*, chs 34–6; *Atlakvioa*, *Atlamál*).

Guðrún then tries to drown herself in the sea, but is washed up on the shore of King Iónakr's land whom she marries and by whom she has two sons. Her daughter by Sigurðr, Svanhildr, is brought up at the court and is eventually married to King Iörmunrekkr. Iörmunrekkr's evil counsellor Bikki tells the king that the king's son Randvér is planning to marry Svanhildr himself, and in fury the king has his son hanged, and Svanhildr trampled to death by horses. Guðrún incites her two remaining sons to attack Iörmunrekkr in revenge; the sons, Hamðir and Sörli, point out that the venture is hopeless, but in fact they almost succeed in killing their erstwhile brother-in-law. Guðrún remains at home lamenting her life, her three husbands, her dead brothers, sons and daughter — 'who was a ray of sunlight in my hall'. There is no record of Guðrún's death: she remains frozen in her grief, counting over her losses as her last sons ride away to their doom (*Völsunga saga*, chs 41–44; *Poetic Edda*, *Hamoismál*).

The two figures of Brynhildr and Guðrún are central to the traditions of the Völsungs/Nibelungs, Guðrún providing the continuity between the tale of Sigurðr and his last descendant, Svanhildr. The character of Brynhildr is related to the fierce valkyrie/shield-maid, who is antipathetic to marriage. With a profound belief in her self-worth, she swears only to marry the greatest hero in the world, the man who can cross the flames around her hall. Thwarted and deceived in this she reveals her love and hate for Sigurðr in a compelling emotional climax. Sigurðr must be destroyed, for her honour is compromised by her broken oath. Quite possibly she did not commit suicide in the earliest Norse versions of the story, but lived on, triumphant over her enemies.

This tradition has been combined with a tale of high romance, in which Brynhildr becomes a victim, duped both by the forgotten engagement and by the imposture of Sigurðr. In the revelation scene, Sigurðr at first appears as a sneakingly errant husband, then as a bewildered man trying to find a compromise. But he cannot break down Brynhildr's will, which finds its final fulfilment in a *Liebestod*, burnt on the same pyre. Brynhildr has been presented as a type of the 'pre-patriarchal' woman (see Section IV, p. 157), a woman who cannot survive in the patriarchal quasi-historical world of the Gjúkungar.

Guðrún changes from a carefree girl to a sharp-tongued vixen during her brief marriage – a change which *Völsunga saga* ascribes to Sigurðr's feeding her part of Fáfnir's heart 'and then she was much grimmer than before, and wiser too' (*Völsunga saga*, ch. 28). In the *Nibelungenlied*, she metamorphoses into the monstrous, scheming Kriemhilt who uses Etzel (Atli) to entrap her brothers in revenge for Siegfried's death. The Norse text reflects a different pattern of loyalties: Guðrún will sacrifice husband and sons for her brothers' honour. Once Brynhildr is dead, Guðrún comes to dominate the story with her resolution and powers of survival. Her character gripped the imagination of Icelandic saga writers also: in *Gísla saga*, Gísli wryly notes that his sister, who is seeking to have him outlawed for the murder of her husband, has neither the temperament, nor the clan loyalty, of Guðrún Gjúkadóttir. *Laxdœla saga*'s love triangle of Guðrún Ósvifrsdóttir, Kjartan, the man she loves and whose death she encompasses, and Bolli, the man whom she marries, is clearly shaped by the *Völsunga saga* material.

SECTION III: OTHER FEMALE BEINGS

Giantess

Oldest of all beings, the giants have priority over the gods. After the universe is created from the body of Ymir, the original giant, the giants are displaced beyond the central territories of humans and gods to Jötunheimar (Land of Giants). Frost-giants live in the icy north, fire-giants in the south, from where they will advance at Ragnarök to destroy the earth. Giant-kind is regarded ambivalently: although they represent an 'Other' hated by the gods, from whom they frequently scheme to steal Freyja, they have knowledge and wisdom which the gods covet.

The giantess has contradictory aspects. She may be radiantly beautiful, desired by a god as mistress or wife, like Gerðr, or other giantesses with whom the gods have affairs. The other kind of giantess, friend of wolves and little distinguished from the ogress or troll-woman, makes her home in the mountains, as Skaði does. She is also hostile to the gods: the daughters of the giant Geirrøðr attempt to drown þórr in streams of urine and menstrual blood on his journey to their father's house (*Skáldskaparmál*, ch. 27).

OGRESS

Little distinguished from the troll-woman, the ogress may ride a wolf bridled with serpents and she rejoices at the downfall of warriors. Both ogress and troll are rather characters from folk-tale than heroic legend.

NORNS

Norns are fate figures, distinct from *fylgjur* since they are not attached to an individual or family: Urðr, the oldest of the Norns, has a well under the tree Yggdrasill. Her name is derived from the verb 'to become', cognate with Latin *vertere* – to turn. This suggests spinning, and indeed the idea of an individual's destiny as woven is prevalent in Old Norse. According to Snorri, there are two other chief Norns, Verðandi and Skuld; the names of the trio can be equated with Past, Present and Future. Other tribes of Norns are present at a child's birth, assisting the mother in labour and prophesying the child's fate (*Gylfaginning*, ch. 17).

DÍS (PL. DÍSIR)

Dísir were interpreted as female fertility spirits, or as female ancestors, to whom sacrifices were made. As spirits of the dead, they are associated both with Hel and with Freyja, who chooses half the slain – hence, perhaps the crossover into fertility cult. They are often inimical: in *Ynglingatal* (a poem found in Snorri's *Heimskringla*, a history of the early kings of Norway), a number of the kings of the Yngling line meet their deaths in suspicious circumstances connected with the dísir, for they covet the kings as their lovers. This fatal influence means that they are often conflated with ogresses, or with *fylgjur*. Freyja has the by-name Vanadís – Dís of the Vanir – and Skaði is known as öndurdís – dís of the ski.

FYLGJA (PL. FYLGJUR)

A *fylgja*, sometimes represented as an animal, sometimes a female figure, is the guardian spirit of the clan, although her appearance may mean the death of an individual member. In *Víga-Glúms saga*, Glúmr dreams of a monstrous woman whose shoulders touch the sides of the fjord. When he awakes, he knows that his Norwegian grandfather, Vígfúss, must be dead, for the *fylgja* of the kin has come to Iceland to be with him. In another saga, the paterfamilias lies dying and his *fylgja* appears, dressed in a mail-shirt, to his son, offering to accompany him. He refuses, but she is accepted by the second son, who shares his father's name.

The *fylgjur* cannot always be clearly distinguished from the dísir (*see* above); some sagas refer to supernatural women who are not classified. In *Gísla saga*, the hero is subject to dreams in which a good 'dream-woman' shows him a comfortable existence after death, feasting with his relations in a hall, and adjures him to be kind to the poor and needy. A bad 'dream-woman' torments Gísli with visions of blood and destruction. In another saga, a young man is warned not to go out one night, but he finds himself drawn into the farmyard where he is attacked by nine mounted women dressed in black. A company of nine white women come to save him, but they are too late and he dies of his injuries (*þioranda þáttr ok þórhalls*, ch. 3). It is most likely that Christian influences are responsible for the change in the *fylgja*'s character: sensing the impending Conversion and her loss of power, she becomes dangerous, symbolic of the spiritual evil of paganism. The good women who oppose her fail to avert her destructiveness – only full adherence to Christianity can overcome such powers. The good *fylgja* is later assimilated to the Christian guardian angel.

VALKYRIE

Also known in Old English, where she is equated with a witch, a raven or, more appropriately, Bellona, the Roman goddess of war. The valkyrie is literally 'chooser of the slain', but her responsibilities vary. Sometimes she must follow Óðinn's orders in choosing the bravest men to carry off to Valhöll, on other occasions she herself may choose who will be granted victory and who will die in battle. Certain valkyries choose a human hero as protégé, develop his battle skills and eventually marry him, after which they are no longer able to determine his fate. The valkyrie who is disobedient to Óðinn's commands, Sigrdrífa (Brynhildr), is put to sleep behind a ring of magic fire which can only be breached by the hero whom she must then marry. Marriage puts an end to valkyrie activities and is therefore regarded as a punishment for disobedience. One exception to this is the case of the three swan-maidens in the story of Völundr, who, after nine years of enforced domesticity, regain their freedom and fly away – this is possible because their valkyrie traits are subordinated to the swan identity (*see* II.3, p. 145).

SHIELD-MAIDENS

Sometimes conflated with the valkyrie, the shield-maiden is a female warrior, as Guðrún Gjúkadóttir is said to be in the later Eddic poem *Atlamál*, Brynhildr, or numerous women in Saxo. One such warrior is Alvild. Her father places her in a chamber protected by poisonous snakes, which Alf, her suitor, overcomes. Alvild is quite ready to marry him after this, but her mother rebukes her for being taken in by his handsome appearance without enquiring into his character and virtue. Mortified, Alvild runs off with a number of like-minded women and becomes a highly successful pirate. Eventually her fleet attacks that of Alf, Alvild is overcome, but her conqueror 'realized that they ought not be fighting with weapons but kisses'. Alf makes Alvild change back into female clothes and soon after she bears him a daughter – her seafaring days are over. Saxo goes on to explain, somewhat disapprovingly, that such warriors were formerly common in Denmark, women 'who sought the clash of arms rather than the arm's embrace, fitted to weapons hands which should have been weaving, desired not the couch but the kill, and those they could have appeased with looks they attacked with lances' (Saxo, I, 212ff).

SECTION IV: WOMEN IN HISTORY AND MYTH:
CURRENT QUESTIONS IN NORSE SCHOLARSHIP

Anne Heinrichs's structural examination of the stories of Brynhildr, Sigríðr in *stórráða* – a quasi-historical figure found in early Norwegian histories – and Guðrún Ósvífrsdóttir of *Laxdæla saga*, shows the recurrent pattern of the 'strong woman', disappointed and betrayed in the match with an equal whom she has chosen, marrying conventionally without love, and using her husband to wreak revenge on the betrayer, who now becomes the victim himself; he is killed, and the victim's wife 'psychologically destroyed'. Heinrichs argues that the story of Brynhildr and Sigurðr represents a clash of 'pre-patriarchal' and patriarchal types. Patriarchy triumphs – but a victim is provided to appease the 'gynocratic will' (Heinrichs, 1988).

Here, a caveat is necessary: although archaeological finds offer evidence for goddess worship in the Bronze Age, rock carvings indicating male warrior and hunting cults are found from the same period. That this society was in any sense matriarchal is undemonstrable; although there may have been a period of Norse prehistory before full-blown patriarchy developed, we should probably regard the Norse 'strong woman' as a literary construct, akin to the Greek Amazon who also ends up socialized or dead (Bamberger, 1974). The resistance to patriarchal authority which the strong woman shows is a historical constant, a reaction to women's oppression rather than an attempt to return to a previous matriarchal state; her dangerousness, though admired, is magnified by the male poet as a cautionary tale.

The strong woman is independent of men, though she does not command them; an independence which finds expression in 'unfeminine', militarized behaviour. This is made explicit in the contrast between Brynhildr and her sister, Bekkhildr, who prefers embroidery and other feminine skills to warfare. Brynhildr is coerced into marriage, first by Óðinn's decree that she can no longer continue as a valkyrie, secondly by her father, who decides that she must marry one of her suitors, even though Brynhildr offers to lead an army against them. She is allowed to impose conditions (only marrying the man who knows no fear and who can breach the flames around the hall), but marry she must. At her own choosing, Brynhildr sleeps with Sigurðr and has a daughter without a restrictive formal marriage contract. Although Guðrún's accusation that Sigurðr was Brynhildr's *frumverr* – her first lover – has coarse and shameful overtones, Brynhildr sees no shame in the relationship, only in the subsequent deceptions.

Essential also to the type is her isolation: although *Völsunga saga* provides Brynhildr with a family, these are late accretions, playing a negligible part in the plot. The original situation, a woman living independently, like Gerðr, in her own hall, remains clear in the tower in which Brynhildr is glimpsed by Sigurðr, and the hall protected by magic flames which the wooers must cross. When the catastrophic revelation is made, Brynhildr isolates herself in her room, significantly tearing her tapestry work, symbol of domestication, and lies in bed, apparently asleep, as if attempting to return to her state before Sigurðr first entered her life. Wisdom and prophetic powers are also attributed to Brynhildr: she educates Sigurðr and several times during the story prophesies events to come.

Another field of research which may briefly be mentioned here is the historical accuracy of the conditions and rights of women in the Family sagas, set, though probably not composed, in the tenth century. Compared with *Sturlunga saga*, a virtually eye-witness account of events in the early thirteenth century, if the picture given in the Family sagas were accurate, one would have to conclude that the introduction of Christianity had led to a lamentable decline in moral standards, with illegitimacy, wife repudiation, polygamy and concubinage widespread (Jochens, 1986a; 1986b). Since this is unlikely, it has been concluded that the Christian writers of the Family sagas were anxious to depict their ancestors as monogamous and upright individuals whose pagan ideas of sexual morality conformed to Christian ideals. A good example is the question of women's consent in marriage, for in Iceland, as throughout western Europe, the Church was engaged in a battle to make women's consent compulsory. The Family sagas show, almost without exception, that when a woman is given against her will, the marriage ends in disaster: a pattern most clearly demonstrated in the marriages of Guðrún, in *Laxdæla saga*, and Hallgerðr, in *Njáls saga*. The common saga scenes in which women are consulted about their matches are intended to show that women's consultation is 'natural', an ancient and socially sanctioned custom, a kind of propaganda for the view the Church was endeavouring to introduce (Frank, 1973; Jochens, 1986b).

Carol Clover has recently argued that the 'strong woman' figure in the Family sagas may reflect the historical situation more accurately than has previously been thought: that the widespread practice of female infanticide, combined with the 'frontier society' style of settlement pattern in the early period, brought about a shortage of marriageable women in Iceland. Thus, although they were prohibited from exercising many legal rights, women could wield a great deal of informal power (Clover, 1988).

SECTION V: POST-CLASSICAL TREATMENT OF MYTH

The rediscovery of Norse myth was pioneered by the Romantic poets of Germany and Scandinavia. Grimm's monumental four-volume *Deutsche Mythologie* began to appear in 1835, and, in parallel with the rise of the nationalist movements of the nineteenth century, translations of Norse myth and saga became available. The best known cultural manifestation is of course Wagner's *Ring Cycle*, which uses material from *Völsunga saga* and the *Nibelungenlied*, and freely adapts Snorri's *Prose Edda* for its portrayal of the gods and Valhöll. The Wagnerian treatment of the Sigurðr/Siegfried cycle provided a powerful articulation of a myth of Germanness, an epic for the emerging German nation.

In the period immediately following the First World War, a shattered Germany constructed a myth of racial identity, defined against the Judaeo-Christian tradition, using (in an uncritical and ahistorical way) ethnology and myth, from Tacitus's *Germania* through to Snorri's accounts, an ersatz alternative religion, based on nature-worship and the cult of the hero. Alfred Rosenberg's *Myth of the Twentieth Century* compounds the Germanic material with Greek and Indian myth to form a grand 'Aryan' system. Unsurprisingly, Rosenberg has little to say about women, beyond exhorting them to monogamy and asserting that no woman should be denied the opportunity to become the mother of German children (Rosenberg, 1938, pp. 592–3) – demands which, given the population imbalance after the First World War, were inherently contradictory.

Rosenberg offers an interesting gloss on the myth of Freyja and the giant-builder: Freyja, he says, is the goddess of eternal youth and beauty, Loki, the 'bastard of the gods', betrays the gods to the giant, then betrays the giant too. Óðinn is also at fault, as god of justice, since oaths are broken: 'A realisation, only today coming once more to light, lies deeply buried in this myth: the bastard thoughtlessly hands over the symbol of the race's immortality and eternal youth, and thus the noble one is also precipitated into guilt.' The future of the race lies in the hands of women, he goes on to proclaim, for if women do not maintain standards of racial purity, but instead give birth to 'a nation of black and Jewish bastards', then Germany will disappear under a 'tide of black art and Jewish pornography' (Rosenberg, 1939, pp. 510ff). Required reading in every school of the Third Reich, Rosenberg's ideas were highly influential.

Hitler professed himself bored and irritated by those, like Himmler, who wished to revive the cult of the old German gods, but the language of Rosenberg and like-minded writers helped to mould German rhetoric, providing a conceptual framework for ideas of German identity. A popular propaganda image was that of Hitler as the Hero awakening Germany, the sleeping Valkyrie, an image deriving its potency from the ancient motif of the land as bride to the king, the approaching conqueror as the husband who will sexually awaken her and make her fertile.

Other writers looked to the sagas for models of female behaviour, countertypes to the heroic model. 'Strong women', Signý, Brynhildr, Hallgerðr and Bergþóra, in *Njáls saga*, and Guðrún, in *Laxdœla*, were appropriated as mothers and wives of heroes, whose deeds they instigated. The image of the shield-maid became terrifying: in his revealing book *Male Fantasy*, exploring the psychological construction of SS men, Erik Theweleit has demonstrated how violently the Sturmabteilung (SA) and SS reacted to the 'Red' women, communists and socialists, who fought openly beside men as their comrades-in-arms. Indeed, one of the priorities of the Nazi state was to get women out of public employment and back into the home (Koonz, 1988). Deprived of active participation in the public arena, the German woman was to take on the function of saga woman as 'whetter' (Clover, 1986), urging the men to heroic deeds, reminding them always of duty and honour – a vital adjunct to Nazi propaganda. Metaphorically, the good Nazi wife and mother would, like the first-century Germanic women whom Tacitus describes, engage in 'pleading with the men, thrusting forward their bared bosoms and making them realize the imminent prospect of enslavement – a fate which the Germans fear more desperately for their women than for themselves' (*Germania*, Ch. 8). According to Theweleit, the 'white' woman (opposed to the 'red' socialist virago), most powerfully realized in mother, sister or nurse, sexless and pure, became symbolic of all that the soldier was fighting for.

The taint of Nazism has proved hard for Germanic myth to shake off. Óðinn/Wotan and Sigurðr/Siegfried remain icons of Aryan purity to white supremacists; in Oxford recently a group of 'Óðinn-worshippers' picketed a theatre in which a black singer played Wotan in Wagner's *Ring*. Revivals of Norse cult tend to be associated with extreme right-wing, masculinist and racist elements. That Óðinn certainly practised transvestism and probably homosexuality is suppressed by Wagner and Nazi writers; the image of 'the god with the spear', whom Rosenberg wished to see in the churches of the New Reich (Rosenberg, 1939, p. 617), contains contradictory elements with which modern Óðinn adherents would be distinctly ill at ease. The 'strong woman' – Valkyrie, shield-maid or Guðrún Ósvífrsdóttir, has been an empowering and positive image for Scandinavian women however. Whether reclaimed in modern literature, like Gunnlöð in Sváva Jakobsdóttir's *Gunnlaðarsaga*, or retained in different cultural manifestations – Guðrún remains the most popular girl's name in Iceland or as an unacknowledged inspiration to the women of the *Kvennalistinn*, Iceland's women's political party which holds more than 10 per cent of the seats in the *Alþingi* (Parliament) – the women of Scandinavian mythology remain a living and potent resource for their daughters today.

References and Further Reading
(in English)

PRIMARY MATERIAL:

Poetry

The Poetic Edda, with Introduction and Explanatory Notes (1962), trans. L.M. Hollander, 2nd ed. (Austin, Texas: University of Texas Press)

Prose

Deor (1966), ed. K. Malone, 4th ed. (London: Methuen)
Gísla Saga (1963), trans. George Johnston (London: Dent)
Laxdœla Saga (1969), trans. M. Magnusson and H. Pálsson (Harmondsworth: Penguin)
Njáls Saga (1960), trans. M. Magnusson and H. Pálsson (Harmondsworth: Penguin)
Víga-Glúms Saga (1987), trans. J. McKinnell (Edinburgh: Canongate)
The Saga of the Völsungs (1990), trans. J. Byock (Berkeley: California University Press)
Saxo Grammaticus (1979), *History of the Danish People*, trans. and commentary by P. Fisher and H. Ellis Davidson, 2 vols (Cambridge: Cambridge University Press)
Snorri Sturluson (1954, reprinted 1973), *Skáldskaparmál* in *The Prose Edda of Snorri Sturluson*, trans. J.I. Young (Cambridge: Cambridge University Press)
—— (1964), *Heimskringla*, trans. L.M. Hollander (Austin, Texas: University of Texas Press)
—— (1982), *The Prose Edda: Gylfaginning*, trans. A. Faulkes (Oxford: Oxford University Press)
Tacitus (1948), *Germania*, ed. H. Mattingly (Harmondsworth: Penguin)

SECONDARY WRITINGS:

Andersson, T. (1980), *The Legend of Brynhild*, Islandica 43 (New York: Cornell University Press)

Bamberger, J. (1974), 'The Myth of Matriarchy' in M.Z. Rosaldo and L. Lamphere (eds), *Women, Culture and Society* (Stanford, California: Stanford University Press), pp. 263–80

Burson, A.C. (1983), 'Swan-maidens and Smiths: A Structural Study of Völundarkviða' in *Scandinavian Studies*, 55, pp. 1–19

Clover, C. (1986), 'Hildigunnr's Lament' in J. Lindow, L. Lönnroth and G.W. Weber (eds), *Structure and Meaning in Old Norse Literature* (Odense: Odense University Press), pp. 141–83

—— [1988] (1990), 'The Politics of Scarcity', reprinted in H. Damico and A. Hennessey Olsen (eds), *New Readings on Women in Old English Literature* (Bloomington, Indiana: Indiana University Press), pp. 100–34. Originally published in *Scandinavian Studies*, 60, pp. 147–88.

Dronke, U. (1962), 'Art and Tradition in *Skírnismál*' in N. Davis and C.L. Wrenn (eds), *English and Medieval Studies Presented to J.R.R. Tolkien on the Occasion of his Seventieth Birthday* (London: Allen and Unwin), pp. 250–68

Frank, R. (1973), 'Marriage in Twelfth and Thirteenth Century Iceland' in *Viator*, 4, pp. 474–84

Grimstad, K. (1983), 'The Revenge of Völundr' in R. Glendinning and H. Bessason (eds), *Edda: a Collection of Essays*, University of Manitoba Icelandic Studies, 4 (Winnipeg: University of Manitoba Press)

Heinrichs, A. (1986), '"Annat er várt eðli". The type of the prepatriarchal woman in Old Norse literature' in J. Lindow, L. Lönnroth and G.W. Weber (eds), *Structure and Meaning in Old Norse Literature* (Odense: Odense Univeristy Press), pp. 110–40

Jesch, J. (1991), *Women in the Viking Age* (Woodbridge: Boydell Press)

Jochens, J. (1980), 'The Church and Sexuality in Medieval Iceland' in *Journal of Medieval History*, 6, pp. 377–92

—— (1986), 'Consent in Marriage: Old Norse Law, Life and Literature' in *Scandinavian Studies*, 58, pp. 142–76

—— (1986), 'The Medieval Icelandic Heroine: Fact or Fiction?' in *Viator*, 17, pp. 35–50

—— (1990), 'Old Norse Sources on Women' in J.T. Rosethal (ed.), *Medieval Women and the Sources of Medieval History* (Athens, Georgia: University of Georgia Press), pp. 155–188

Kalinke, M. (1990), *Bridal-Quest Romance in Medieval Iceland*, Islandica 46, (New York: Cornell University Press)

Koonz, C. (1987, reprinted 1988), *Mothers in the Fatherland: Women, the Family and Nazi Politics* (London: Methuen)

Kress, H. (1986), '"You will find it all rather monotonous": On literary tradition and the female experience' in F.E. Anderson and J. Weinstock (eds), *The Nordic Mind: Current Trends in Scandinavian Literary Criticism* (Lanham, Md: University Press of America)

Larrington, C.A. (forthcoming), 'What Does Woman Want? "Mær" and "munr" in *Skírnismál*' in *Alvíssmál* (Berlin), vol. 1

Mitchell, S.A. (1983), '*För Skírnis* as Mythological Model: *frið at kaupa*' in *Arkiv för nordisk filologi*, 98, pp. 108–22

Motz, L. (1980), 'Sisters in the Cave; the Stature and the Function of the Female Figures in the Eddas' in *Arkiv för nordisk filologi*, 95, 168–82

Rosenberg, A. (1939), *Der Mythos des XX. Jahrhunderts*, 156 ed. (Munich: Hoheneichen)

Sváva Jakobsdóttir (1987), *Gunnlaðarsaga* (Reykjavík: Forlagið). In Icelandic.

Theweleit, E. (1987), *Male Fantasies*, vol. I, *Women, Floods, Bodies, History*, trans. S. Conway (Minneapolis: University of Minnesota Press)

Turville-Petre, E.O.G. (1964), *Myth and Religion of the North* (Oxford: Oxford University Press)

BIRGITTE SONNE

Mythology of the Eskimos

SECTION I: THE ORDER OF THE COSMOS

The Eskimo[1] world was a tripartite one, symbolized by the interior of the feast house and its exits. In order to reach the realms of heaven the shaman would leave the level of earthly human beings, the interior of the house, either through the smoke hole in the roof or one of its corners. He/she would not proceed vertically into the air, but travel across the sea to the horizon, from where a river or the rainbow led to the heavenly abodes of certain dead humans, some species of killed land animals and birds, the stars, Moon, Sun and *Silap inua/Ellam yua*, the spirit of the air. The exit to the lower abodes started at the entrance hole in the floor, and proceeded through a subterranean tunnel, from where a lower tunnel, visible only in dreams or visions, branched off leading through the earth to the submarine abodes of other dead humans and the sea mammals. These beings, very like humans, lived in the villages according to species, the south-west Alaskan Eskimos relate. Those of north Alaska, Canada, and Greenland told stories about a female sea spirit, Sea Woman, to whose house at the bottom of the sea the life essences of the killed sea mammals would return for reincarnation. They would grow fresh bodies like foetuses and, when grown, leave the womb (the interior of Sea Woman's house) through its parturient canal (the entrance tunnel), out into the open sea.

Identical womb symbolism pertained also to the dwellings of earthly human families, whether Alaskan, Canadian or Greenlandic. They would differ regionally in their notions about the number of levels into which the upper and lower realms were subdivided, but the main division, placing the surfaces of land and sea between the upper and lower realms, held good for all of them. So too did the all-important idea about the corporeal reincarnation of the souls of dead animals, if they were permitted to return unharmed to their proper element. Crucial in that respect were game festivals, or rites on a smaller scale, and the observances of taboos separating the stages of transition in the life cycles of human beings from those of the game animals.

The Coming into Being of the Cosmic Order

How did the balance of the cosmic powers arise? Numerous differing stories were told. Any attempt at synthesizing the origin myths told by the various Eskimo societies into a single sequence of events would be a serious falsity.

First, the origin myths were told as separate stories, they were never put together into a succession of events to form an all-inclusive cultural history of development. On a smaller scale, one local group of Eskimos might combine into one sequence of events two or more stories told as separate myths by other local groups. But no attempt was made anywhere to make all of the origin myths dependent on one another in the kind of sequence of cause and effect which underlies western historical way of thought. Each origin myth would relate the origin of some phenomenon of nature, *which at the same time created some basic conditions of the earthly human way of life*. Differing myths about the origin of the same phenomenon would co-exist; differing in their accentuation of one particular aspect of this phenomenon in relation to a special cultural condition.

Second, the more important deities, who frequently arose in pairs (daughter/father, sister/brother, wife/husband) as the outcome of human creative acts, did not interact with each other. Each pair would lead a separate life in its own part of the upper or lower realms, interacting with human beings and vice versa. Consequently there was no Eskimo pantheon. The pairs of deities were not mutually related, neither by blood ties nor marriage, partnership nor ties of mutual enmity. Nor did they preside over the multitude of other human-like spirits peopling the world, be they solitary spirits or spirit races living in societies of their own. Deities and spirits could assist humans in achieving their goals; the alliance might be established through the origin of a deity or through a spirit's agreement to serve a shaman as his/her helping spirit.

Third, the Eskimos appreciated the knowledge implied in every story about the spiritual powers of the world and how to cope with them. They did not distinguish between stories that might be labelled myths (if defined as stories about deities) and stories about other spirits and human heroes by us. The only distinction made was between stories of old and those of more recent origin. Old stories went back to times immemorial, that is, to the wise ancestors while recent stories related events experienced by persons still alive or still remembered. Neither category was considered more sacred than the other and the majority of stories were public property.

Finally, the particular environmental conditions of a regional group of Eskimos would, together with its particular social organization and degree of interaction with foreigners, put a decisive stamp on the unfolding of events in their origin myths. All these factors – environment, social organization and exchange with other cultures – varied considerably within the vast area inhabited by the Eskimos: from east Greenland to north-east Siberia, from the icebound seas along the Arctic coast south to the Pacific in the west and to the Atlantic coasts of the Labrador Peninsula and south Greenland in the east.

The materials for shaping the world and for the differentiation of its beings into species were already extant at that time long, long ago, when they started to take form. Raven figured in myth as a frequent transformer and culture hero among most Alaskan Eskimos, but these Eskimos would also tell origin myths of the kind told by the Canadian and Greenlandic Inuit. In these myths, the actors *were earthly humans*, men and/or women who by adverse behaviour or extraordinary skills contributed to the creation of world order. The Eskimo way of life of hunting, fishing and gathering, originated with this order as did the life cycles of humans and game animals. These two cycles became interrelated in intricate ways that demanded the observance of numerous rites and taboos in order to sustain and not to disturb the precarious balance of cosmic powers.

The co-operation of a man with his wife was fundamental to the maintenance of this balance. He made their tools and did the hunting, she did some fishing and collecting, gave birth to their children and transformed his kill into food, clothes, boat-covers and fuel for the lamp. In ritual, the co-operative role of a wife (or a mother) was equally important.

SILA: THE COMPLEMENTARITY OF MEN AND WOMEN

Most Eskimos did not tell an origin myth for *Sila* (equivalent to *Ella* in south-west Alaska). *Sila* was considered to be a force of nature: a source of knowledge, breath and weather, which might react in a human way to the breaking of taboo with forbidding storms. In its capacity to change the sex of a newborn baby, however, *Sila* contained the distinguishing capabilities of either sex.

Mountains, stones and earth came rumbling down from heaven to form the solid mass of earth. The first human beings, baby boys and baby girls, grew out of the earth like plants and remained rooted there receiving their nourishment from the earth.

Polar Eskimos did not relate how one baby boy and girl developed into adults able to walk away from their places of birth, meet each other and get married. But once married the wife made dresses for babies, went out in search of some of them among the dwarf willows, and whenever she found one she dressed it and brought it home. In this way, human beings became numerous and now they wanted dogs. A man holding a dog harness stamped the earth yelling *hoc - hoc*. Dogs jumped out of the small hillocks.

At that time people never died. They grew old, blind, immobile and the earth became overcrowded. Nor was there a sun, moon or stars. Darkness prevailed. People had light only inside their houses, burning water in their lamps – for at that time water could burn. Then a huge flood came and drowned most of the people. An old woman among the survivors declared: 'Let us never die and thus stay in darkness.' But another old woman said: 'No, let us have both death and light.' And her words had the greater effect. The first dead human was buried under a pile of stones, but it did not know how to die properly and its ghostly figure kept wriggling up through the pile of stones, trying to return to the living. An old woman pushed it back telling it to stay there because they were leaving on a hunting trip and there was no room left for it on their small overloaded sledges. The dead person was forced to remain within its heap of stones. The light brought into the world by death allowed people to go on hunting trips and they no longer had to eat earth. When humans die they ascend to the sky and become luminous (Rasmussen, 1921–5, III).

The 'history' of this myth does not explain why the material for shaping the earth came down from heaven. The first cause is a natural event. Similarly, the later flooding of the earth was not caused or provoked by anybody, unless the overpopulation of the earth bears that meaning. But the heavenly origin of earth explains why the babies growing out of the earth are differentiated by sex and thus each possess the working capabilities of its gender at birth. The skill of a woman in sewing and that of a man in making and using tools, were considered by some Eskimos in the east to be faculties acquired by the foetus on leaving the womb. They only needed some training to become fully developed (Guemple, 1986). The air, *Sila*, from which a baby drew its first all-important breath, might even change the sex of the baby at birth according to the Greenlanders.

The knowledge of sewing received through *Sila* enabled the first married woman to take the first step towards establishing a human way of life. Nobody taught her how to make the babysuits to dress the children found in the ground and thus to raise the first family. The next step was taken by the man who made a dog harness and knew the proper words to call forth dogs from the earth. In actual life, the Polar Eskimos did not know how to make kayaks, so the dog sledge was their only means of transportation to the hunting fields.

The dog-sledge was of hardly any use in those days of eternal darkness. But a man's dog symbolized his penis and the semen ejaculated by this dog into the womb of his wife (or any female) was considered to feed the embryo in her 'house', that is, her womb. Another metaphor for semen was oil from pounded blubber, with which a woman would feed her lamp in her daily routine. The family's lamp was the source of light, heat and cooked food during the cold and dark months of winter. It was owned and tended by the wife, using dried moss for a wick.

According to mythological symbolism, her womb was also kept light and warm by a burning lamp, another inborn prerequisite of female nature. Similarly, the basic meanings of the Eskimo words for 'woman' and 'wife' are 'heat'. It inflames a man and makes him move, as does a game animal, provoking a desire to lay it/her down. The wife, *nuliaq*, 'a little woman in heat', yields to her husband, *ui*, 'the one, who rushes off', either from the house to go hunting or, figuratively, inside her vagina (Dorais, 1986). Set on fire by the heat of the womb-lamp, the sperm would burn like blubber, and turn into the blood said to be added to the foetus by its mother. The flesh of the foetus derived from that of sea mammals killed by the father and eaten both by him and his wife. However, at that time long ago, when water could burn, earth eaten by the parents and water procured by *Sila* (or the penis of the father?) was sufficient to grow foetuses.

The third most important step was taken by the old woman, who introduced death by her powerful words. Death brought starlight, permitting men at last to make full use of their dogs as transport on hunting trips. The northern Eskimos did in fact do some sealing at breathing holes in the ice during starry periods in winter – which was of course facilitated by the light of the moon if risen. But the origin of that heavenly body was related in a separate myth (*see* below, Sun and Moon: Rules of Marriage and the Division of Labour).

The first dead human nearly prevented people from leaving their first earthbound settlement. Again, an old woman's words made departure possible by ordering the dead person to remain in the burial cairn. After this, the men could use their innate capacity to hunt and bring in meat and blubber to feed humans, dogs, lamps and foetuses.

Words do have power. A Polar Eskimo explained: 'Consider a wound cut by a man in the flesh of another man. It hurts, but it will stop hurting and heal in a while. The harsh words of a sharp tongue may hurt for life' (Rasmussen, 1921–5, III). The words of people in the old days were much more effective than those uttered by recent generations. Although Eskimos made use of spells inherited from old, the power of a spell diminished with use. Still, in each generation, the words of old people carried more weight than those of younger ones. People grew wise with age, and old women, who most frequently survived their husbands, were often consulted by individuals in cases of illness or bad luck.

SUN AND MOON: RULES OF MARRIAGE AND THE DIVISION OF LABOUR

Sun and Moon used to live as ordinary humans on earth, but not as husband and wife. Sun was the younger sister of Moon, who fell in love with her and slept with her in the dark when the lamps were extinguished. Sun did not recognize him, but she smeared soot from her lamp on his face. When the lamps were relit, she saw her brother with that identifying mark and her face turned glowing red from shame. With her woman's knife, the crescent-shaped *ulu*, she cut off her breasts and offered them to her brother: 'You seem to have a taste for me, eat these as well!' Fetching a wick of lampmoss, she lit it, and going outside, started to run round in a circle. She took off from the ground and rose spirally into the air. Imitating Sun, Moon took up the pursuit, but as he stumbled in his rotation on the ground, the flame of his wick went out. It remained glowing, and thus Moon gives out light but no heat in his perpetual attempt to reach Sun along the vault of heaven. His is the cold light of winter, and whenever he disappears from the sky in winter, he travels over the icebound sea dog-sledding and hunting in order to feed the dead humans in the heavenly realm of death. Sun, however, whose lamp wick kept blazing gives out both light and heat in summer.

The farther north the storyteller of a 'Moon and Sun' variant lives, the greater she/he stresses the complete disappearance of Sun in winter and of Moon in summer. But no matter where an Eskimo variant is told it relates the origin of the interchanging of light and darkness, heat and cold with the annual cycle of changing seasons.

Among the stories about visits made to Moon by shamans or ordinary people,

Figs 15 & 16 Masks of Moon and Sun. *Courtesy of Gyldendal, Copenhagen, photographer Lennart Larsen*

those told in Canada and Greenland reveal the extent of his powers in richer detail. He is the engenderer of life on earth and in the sea by means of his dog/penis which can transform itself into a polar bear. Thus a barren woman, battered by her disappointed husband and running away from home, is invited by Moon to accompany him on his sledge to his house in the sky. During her visit she is made pregnant and eventually sent back home. The sea-tide is another effect of Moon's powers, and women's menstruation a third (it takes a man stirred by a woman to call forth the blood from her womb).

The procreative powers of Moon could hardly unfold on earth and in the sea if he were to stop being in love with Sun. In spring, when Sun reappears glowing red above the horizon, spiralling upwards day after day, the ice-cover at the sea shore breaks up in Moon's spring flood. The snow/semen, said in some myths to be sent by Moon in winter, melts/bleeds when heated by the rays of Sun to enliven the earth afresh. Wintering species of seals also bear their young in spring through Moon's powers set in motion by Sun's blazing lamp. The melting of the sea-ice brings migratory sea mammals and birds. Thus the effects of Moon perpetually chasing his fleeing sister, Sun, are likened to that of a married couple bringing forth children on earth (Sonne, 1990). Moon and Sun, however, are not a married couple, nor do they bring forth children of their own. They 'spill' their procreative forces onto the level of living beings to whom they remain tied by blood. They owe these procreative powers to the descendants of their former relatives; for in actual life a young girl had to marry a man outside the family circle of close relatives (exogamy).

Marriage was the cement of society binding one family to another and thus enlarging the circle of relatives who were obliged to co-operate with and support each other. The young couple's children would receive their names from the dead members of either family. Naming meant the final amalgamation of the two families.

Through his incestuous intercourse with Sun, Moon paid no heed to the rule of exogamous marriage. His secret intercourse with Sun is likened to cannibalism, by Sun's offering her amputated breasts as meat for Moon to eat. He had behaved no better than an unharnessed dog, who copulates indiscriminately with relatives and non-relatives and even devours relatives that happen to die. Sun and Moon are not earthly human beings. However, their continuing love affair not only brings into the world a more radiant light than that of the stars, created at the coming of death, it also powers the annual cycle of seasons during which the intermediate level of living beings passes through the cycle of diminished life, during the cold of winter and the unfolding of life in the heat of summer.

When Sun's heat increases, life becomes easy. Game abounds and summer's time is women's time, for in summer women go out of doors to do their work in the open air, *Sila*. The connection between summer and women was also made by the islanders of Nunivak in south-west Alaska. The Nunivak men would stop hunting by kayak at sea with the arrival of summer and go fishing on land in co-operation with their wives. This seasonal change in productive activities also fits in with the pan-Eskimo notion of the close relationship of women with the land (the primordial womb of human beings). Sun, summer, hunting on land and women constituted a symbolic entity.

For the Nunivakers the origin myth of Sun and Moon co-existed with that of 'Bringing the Sun':

> In a distant place two brothers grew to adulthood in almost complete darkness. Summer was darker than winter. They had a lamp, which they kept burning all the year round. They thought that they once had a mother, but they did not remember her. While growing they learned by themselves

how to hunt caribou, build kayaks and hunt seals. They became good hunters, but coming of age they began to feel that they missed both light and the company of other humans. They caught a faint glimpse of light on the horizon and travelled towards it. They were welcomed by two girls, sisters (but not of the brothers), who had anticipated their approach with aching hearts. Although they married the brothers, the sisters did not allow them to go hunting; instead they did all the hunting and hunted only caribou. Whenever they went out hunting, the younger sister opened the door to the sun and she closed it on their return. The brothers felt extremely miserable and deprived. The older brother asked the younger time and again that they should go off in search of some other inhabited place. But the younger brother, who had the visionary dreams of a shaman-to-be, had seen a greater light and wanted to stay. He decided to get hold of the sun. Guided by a voice from above he travelled across the icebound sea to the sun, tried to catch hold of it, but in vain. The voice told him to let the sun have its own way and make it rise above the horizon. He managed to push it up into the sky and into orbit. From now on the two brothers did the hunting. The journey to the sun made the younger brother a great shaman able to procure fine weather for the hunt at will.

The older brother had been reluctant to copulate with his wife, so he never begot any children. The younger brother and his wife had four children, two boys and two girls. They gave one of each sex to the older brother and his wife. The two closely interrelated families remained together in prospering co-operation.

(ABBREVIATED VERSION OF LANTIS, 1946)

Does this myth relate the dominance of women over men in a mythic past? If so, they were able to retain that dominance only at the cost of having no children and leading a lonely life, with no men to dominate. While the older brother cannot stand the irritating life with the sisters doing the hunting, it is the younger brother's innate faculty of a shaman-to-be, together with his willingness to copulate with his wife, that makes him resist his brother's wish to leave the women. It further enables him to deprive his wife of her power over the sun and to beget children.

As stated above, women were the motor of life. Their illuminating 'heat' made men move (from their dark place in this myth) in order to lie with them and beget children. As long as the lamp of the sky remained in the power of women, the men were barred from other movement – to go out of doors to go hunting. In pushing the sun into motion outside, the shaman permitted men to move about in the open as well. The cosmic order of the division of labour by sex was established. So, also, were the rules of co-operation between related families. As in actual life on Nunivak, the barren couple had the right to ask their close relatives for children in adoption. Adoption, like marriage, was a means of tying two families closely together.

This does not mean that this myth may not reflect a regret on the part of women for their lost powers to hunt themselves. In representations of married couples' faces in masks and paintings, one looks sour while the other is smiling. According to the Eskimos' own interpretation, the smiling face was that of the husband's, who typically led a more amusing and exciting life with less work to do than his wife, depicted with a sour-looking face.

Now, women did go hunting on Nunivak, and not only in that the same word was used for men's hunting and women's gathering of roots and plants. A wife would help her husband to fish for salmon in summer and to hunt caribou in winter. The communal caribou hunt in fall, however, was done exclusively by the men. The involvement of women in the winter caribou hunt explains why the mythic sun stood at the horizon – its actual position in winter at that latitude – as long as power over the sun resided with the caribou-hunting women. Consequently, the pale reflection of its light reached the dark place of the lonely brothers only in winter.

Still, would women be capable of surviving without men to do most of the hunting? Judging from the above myth this was possible in theory at the cost mentioned – of leading a lonely and childless life. Other stories imply similar ideas.

A Nunivak story about a girl, living with her grandmother in an isolated place, relates her success as a hunter. She hunts with a live muskrat, which she keeps in harness and lets loose to kill both seals and caribou. Her grandmother does all the woman's work. The muskrat shares their meals, and they are never short of food and skins for making clothes. They remain comfortably in their isolated place (Lantis, 1946).

The ability of this female hunter to catch seals makes her a genuine hunter, in contrast to the women who only hunted caribou. Sealing was an exclusively male activity on Nunivak, and a hunter's success was thought to depend ultimately on his amulets, of which one was particularly powerful: the head of an animal or a bird. Similarly, the ability of this mythic female hunter to catch seals resides with her muskrat. According to traditional Nunivak standards this female pair, where the 'hunter' owns a live amulet, is ideally complementary in the division of work by gender. The pair's resulting riches are enviable. Yet the isolated female couple begets no children and never mingles with other families.

A Greenlandic myth stresses the last point to the extreme. A widow and her adoptive daughter are left behind on an island in late fall by the families with whom they used to live. Having built a house they need food, fuel for the house-lamp and skins for clothes and bedding. The woman asks her adoptive daughter to dig a hole in the earth next to the entrance hole inside the house and fill it with water from the sea. Using a spell the older woman makes a sea scorpion emerge in the water. Then she hands her amulet, a whetstone, to the girl and asks her to catch the fish by this means. It works. The shivering women now get some bodily warmth from eating the fish. The following day a bigger and fatter fish is caught in the same way; the next day an eider duck, supplying them with a skin to use as bedding; then a small seal, providing them with blubber to feed the lamp, and also skin for making clothes. Each day a still bigger species of sea mammal emerges and is killed with the whetstone. The women suffer no distress and get busy cutting up the surplus of meat and blubber to lay up in store.

At that point a distant relative, a bachelor, arrives in his kayak. Since he belongs to the group of families that left the women behind, he is deeply surprised at finding them alive and even prospering. The women treat him splendidly. Having eaten more than his fill, he leaves them in order to fetch a boat and have the women brought back home. From now on, however, no animal, bird or fish come into the artificial pond inside the women's house – as the storyteller explains: *they were not meant to share their catches with other people.* Back home the older woman marries the bachelor. Nothing more happens that is worth a story: the three of them lead a normal family's social life, exchanging meat and blubber with other families.

So, by means of amulets and secret knowledge mythic women could make do without men. But the moral of the myth is obvious: they could not both hunt and fulfil the basic social obligation of sharing the meat and blubber of their catches with other members of society.

In apparently complete contrast to the moral of these myths, real parents might choose to bring up a daughter like a boy or a son like a girl. According to the samples taken by Saladin D'Anglure (1986), the number of children clothed and trained in the manner of the opposite sex would amount to 20 per cent among the Inuit in the area of Illulik in the central Canadian Arctic. The training did not prevent the adult girl from marrying (a man), bearing children, giving up her male activities and turning to women's work. But she might also choose to go hunting together with her husband and leave it to some close relative to look after her children.

Similarly, a 'female' boy would – as was demanded of every young man – have to kill a seal in order to get married. As a rule he would then continue hunting activities for the rest of his life. While he rarely achieved the same prolific results as men trained in sealing throughout their boyhood, he might be of valuable assistance to a wife less talented in doing housework, not because she was brought up like a boy, but simply because she was not very good at coping with her work. In other words, 'female' boys and 'male' girls were not destined to marry each other. Nor did the upbringing change their sexual orientation. 'Female' men did not marry male men, nor 'male' girls female girls. They belonged to the 'third gender', as Saladin D'Anglure labels them.

There were several reasons why parents would choose the third sex for a child: the baby's sex might be thought to have changed on its own or due to *Sila* right after birth; or a dead relative might have willed that his/her name be given to a later descendant, who at birth turned out to be of the opposite sex of the namesake.[2] Or parents, who had only boys might wish to bring up one as a girl or vice versa. This last explanation was the common one in Greenland, where several examples are on record of girls being brought up as hunters so that they would support their parents in old age. One story, claimed to be historically true, says that the shaman Aadaarutaa was so upset by the outstanding hunting abilities of one such girl that he killed her in envy, cut off her breasts and had sexual intercourse with the corpse (Vebæk, 1990). The story shows that although no taboo prevented women from doing men's work, a successful female hunter might hurt the feelings of a less successful male hunter.

Did the actual lives of 'third sex' women contradict that of the female hunters depicted in myth? No. The mythic woman who engages in hunting must either remain outside society in company with another woman, or marry a man and give up her monopoly of the hunt to her husband. An enduring marriage of a male hunter to a huntress does not figure in myth; nor does that of a huntress to a man doing exclusively the work of a woman.

To conclude: although the man's dog and the woman's lamp symbolized both their differing working roles and procreative abilities, those working roles and procreative abilities did not mean one and the same thing — the working role of one gender was not taboo to the other. However, in order to maintain the human life cycle, a woman of the 'third sex' had to marry a man and thus become part of the social network exchanging meat and blubber.

The severe taboos that were to be observed by all women until menopause, no matter what kind of work they did, indicates also the importance of gender.

SEA WOMAN: WOMEN'S TABOOS

A father gets extremely upset because his daughter, time and again, refuses to marry. Taking her out in his boat he throws her into the sea. She catches hold of the gunwale several times to be rescued, but he cuts off her finger joints, one set at a time. They become various species of sea mammals, while the fingerless girl sinks to the bottom of the sea and is transformed into the giant mistress of the species that sprang from her hands. She builds her house down there, where the life essences of dead sea mammals are re-covered in flesh in the drip-pan beneath her lamp. Her dog watches the entrance tunnel of her house.

One woman among the Netsilik Inuit in Arctic Canada introduced her variant of this origin myth, explaining:

> [In remote days] everything came out of the ground, and people themselves lived on the ground. At the time there were no animals to hunt, and they knew nothing of all the strict taboo that we have to observe now. For no dangers threatened them, but on the other hand no pleasures awaited them after a long day's toil. Then it happened ... [the origin myth of Sea Woman] ... now everything comes from her everything that people love and fear — food and clothes, hunger and bad hunting ... And for her sake people had afterwards to think out all the taboo that makes it hard to live.

(RASMUSSEN, 1929–52, VOL. VII, P. 212ff)

Most of the taboos in question came into force at menarche, after giving birth and after the death of a close relative. This last event put men under similar taboos for a shorter period of time. The taboos forbade the woman to do any work whatsoever; nor was she permitted to wash, or to comb her hair and put it up in the regional style of adult women. She could not change her clothes, move out of doors, eat meat from freshly killed animals, nor partake in the common meals of her household. She even had to use her own drinking cup. In Greenland she spent this idle period sitting on the platform facing the wall and with her back to the people moving about on the floor. In Canada and Alaska, a separate hut was made to isolate her completely.

The breaches of any such taboo would contaminate the souls of killed sea mammals and hinder their 'rebirth' from the house of Sea Woman. She too ended up in a similarly miserable state, as depicted in the myth relating the shaman's journey to Sea Woman's house in order to make sea mammals reappear in the sea:

> During a seance arranged by the female shaman 'Tuttu's Wife' to avert a threatening famine, her helping spirits, a polar bear and a walrus, appeared to her as two flames. In a kind of relay race the polar bear and the walrus threw her by her genitals far out over the ice and then suddenly disappeared. A ferocious gale broke up the ice all around her, but having climbed an iceberg for safety she was taken by another helping spirit, Twistmouth, in his kayak to the land of Sea Woman. Arriving at Sea Woman's house, Tuttu's Wife hardly dared pass by the snarling dog on the roof, but it was even worse looking into the huge entrance tunnel. A broad river filled with dirt and garbage flowing inwards left her with a path to balance on as narrow as a knife-edge. She managed to reach the steep end of the tunnel, climbed it into the house and was instantly whirled into a fight with Sea Woman. In the end Sea Woman could barely stand on her feet and had to yield to Tuttu's Wife, who started cleaning her up and combing her hair. This meant more hard work, because the breaches of taboo on earth had materialized into some sticky stuff which had matted and tangled Sea Woman's hair. Eventually, cleaned, combed, and with her hair put up the adult female way Sea Woman gratefully asked Tuttu's Wife to move her (Sea Woman's) lamp aside. In so doing Tuttu's Wife saw naked long-haired human beings jump into the entrance river that now ran outwards, clean and fresh. These men became transformed into harp seals as they swam along the entrance tunnel. Tuttu's Wife met with no obstacle on her way back home.
>
> (ABBREVIATED VERSION OF RASMUSSEN, 1921–5, VOL. II, PP. 222–7)

Obviously the depiction of Sea Woman's helpless state is modelled on the earthly woman under taboo. Like her, the fingerless Sea Woman is barred from doing any work, including cleaning herself and combing her loose matted hair. But in contrast to Sea Woman, who had to wait for a shaman to fight and help her, the woman on earth was capable of cleaning and combing herself on the day her period of taboo came to an end. Reappearing in brand new clothes, washed and with her hair put up, the woman signalled her renewed innocuous state to the hunters of the settlement. Similarly, the mythic ideal of a gentle and attractive-looking Sea Woman signified the end of a dangerous period with the sea mammals pent up in her house.

The myths about Sea Woman make explicit why the burden of taboos were much harder on women than on men. Women were by their biological nature the vehicles of human life, which passes through two main, dangerous transitional stages: birth and death. From the moment a close relative died until a child was born and made ready to receive the dead relative's name, there was a lurking danger that the life

Fig. 17 A female shaman cleans Sea Woman's hair, matted with grime caused
by human taboo violations. This allows the release of the sea-beasts.
Courtesy of the National Museum, Copenhagen, photographer Lennart Larsen

cycle of the sea mammals would become entangled with that of living humans. If
this happened, the exchange relationship between humans and sea mammals was
liable to dissolve.

THE INTERRELATED LIFE CYCLES OF HUMANS
AND GAME ANIMALS

As told in the above myth, the sea mammals left the drip-pan of Sea Woman's lamp
as humans. Jumping into the river of her 'parturient channel' they became
transformed into the individual species according to the length of their hair. The
true nature of every animal was considered to be human-like, and that of sea
mammals the more so, because they had sprung from the hands of a human girl.
Why from her hands and not some other part of her body? Because 'hands' signified
a meat-sharing relationship. People would exchange substitutes like mittens or the
front flippers of seals to confirm a deal in sharing the meat produced by either party
(Sonne, 1990). Husband and wife also made up a meat-sharing couple, co-operating
with their primary means of production – their hands. Together with their children
they formed part of a wider circle of meat-sharing, the household, consisting of two
or more families, widows and orphans interrelated by blood and marriage. Finally,
rules for meat-exchanging were also in force between the households in a winter
settlement. The meat shared and exchanged, however, was offered by the sea
mammals whose re-incarnation depended on the ritual behaviour of human beings.
They alone were responsible for keeping in motion the rebirth cycle of the sea
mammals.

We may understand the origin myth of Sea Woman in the following way: in her
refusal to marry she denied her parents the proper use of her hands. These, her

primary means of production, were also their means of extending their network of food-exchanges. Remaining unmarried, a daughter might be of some help to her mother but she would add nothing in the way of fresh meat for food. On the contrary, she would be a drain on the meat supply procured by her father, a supply which would dwindle as he grew old. A Polar Eskimo variant of the origin myth stresses this point to the extreme: by her mere refusal to marry the obstinate girl turns into a cannibal, starting to eat lumps of meat from the live bodies of both her father and mother (Kroeber, 1899).

Sea Woman became wild through her refusal to marry. She removed herself to the margin of society but remained tied to that very society due to her severed fingers, a token of a meat-sharing alliance. Human members of that society now hunt the animals into which the productive capacity of her fingers were transformed.

In Canada and Greenland, adult women were primarily responsible for maintaining both life cycles, human and animal. The latter served both as food and as the medium of social networks, based as they were on co-operation and sharing at an elementary level. Women were the mediators of this network of families most frequently interrelated by marriage. No wonder the mythic mediator between humans and animals was a woman in those parts of the Eskimo world where famine was a real threat at certain periods in the annual cycle of changing seasons.

THE MONSTER-BABY: SOME OBLIGATIONS OF A MOTHER

A mother left her baby in safety above the high tide mark of high tide in order to go fishing at the sea shore. She was too engrossed in her fishing to hear her baby screaming from hunger. It screamed all day long. In the twilight she consoled her baby and let it suck her breast. She served her family a blend of berries, meat and blubber but gave her baby no solid food.

At night when everybody were sound asleep, the mother suddenly cried out with pain. The baby had devoured her right breast. Horror-stricken, the family watched the baby wolf down the meat from a big dish; now the baby had two huge upper teeth and four lower ones. While some ran to fetch the chief and others to warn the other families, the baby crushed all the dishes with its teeth, flew at its mother and ate her up. The entire settlement took to flight, managing to cross a plank across a torrent and removing the plank before the monster-baby caught up. It screamed and ground its teeth because it could pursue them no further.

(CURTIS, 1930, PP. 259ff)

In feeding her new-born baby with some solid food (or ritually pretending to do so), the mother gave it human identity as part of the family. It became a member of the family's meat-sharing community and thus partook in its relationship with the game animals. The baby's development into a full human being was conditional on membership of this community; denied this potential, the baby would grow up wild.

A child was not born a proper human being. When offering her baby its first tiny bit of her own solid food, a Greenlandic mother would address it in the language used by spirits. This language differed from the local dialect only in vocabulary; archaic words and metaphors replaced numerous words of ordinary (earthly human) speech and had to be learned by shaman apprentices and others who wanted to communicate with the spirits.

Naming the baby after a dead relative of either the father or the mother turned it into a true member of the family. With the name it received both the personality of its namesake and the intimate social relationship within the family formerly enjoyed by its dead namesake. In relation to other living beings, the name marked off humans as an individual species with a social life distinct from that of animals. Most Eskimos did not distinguish between male and female names; a boy might get the name of his grandmother and a girl that of her grandfather. Thus, the personality embedded in the name was not gender specific.

The young mother rarely decided which name to offer her baby. This honour was usually bestowed on her mother, or her mother in-law, or an older female relative, who in some regions assisted her as midwife.

ORIGIN OF THE NARWHAL: A SELFISH MOTHER

A widow was left behind with her son and daughter. The son was blind. One day a polar bear approached the house and the mother told the boy to kill it. She helped him take aim and the bear was killed, but the mother lied to him about the kill because she wanted the meat for her own consumption. His sister secretly fed him some of the meat. He asked her to lead him to a lake, where a loon made him dive three times and thus he recovered his sight. Back home he asked her mother about the skin of the bear stretched to dry in the open. She lied once again claiming that this skin was left by one of their former housemates as a gift. Sometime later belugas [white whales] appeared near the coast. Eager to win his acceptance, the mother asked her son if she could be his partner in the hunt. They went to the shore. He attached the line to her body and harpooned a huge beluga. The wounded animal swam away carrying along the mother fastened to the line and diving with her. Every time she surfaced she cried: 'My *ulu*, my *ulu*!' – wanting her woman's knife to cut the line. Meanwhile she twisted her hair into a point. Finally she became transformed into a black he-whale with a long tusk: a narwhal.

(ABBREVIATED VERSION OF HOLTVED, 1951)

A mother was her son's female working partner as long as he remained unmarried, cutting up his catches, etc. As with her husband's catches, meat, skin, and blubber were at her disposal. She saw to it that members of their meat-sharing network received their proper portions, then she would usually serve the male members of her family with the best parts of the remaining meat. In Greenland she continued in that role even after her son had married, until his wife had given birth to a child.

To misuse her right of disposal to serve her own greedy desires was a crime. The mother of the above story committed the crime in her foolish conviction that her son would remain blind and so deserved the vengeance taken by her son.

THE TERNS: THE RITUAL ROLE OF A WIFE

An orphan girl lived in a village with her grandmother. The grandmother died and was given a proper burial by her granddaughter. The villagers lived on the fish they caught in summer. Now, one summer the fish did not come into the river and no fish were caught at all. In the winter it was very stormy and they had nothing to eat. They heard a voice in the air singing a song ending with the question: 'Are you hungry?' The spirit did not hear the people answering. He called out at every house. The orphan girl lived in the last house. People covered her up with something and the spirit heard her answer: 'Yes, we're hungry.' Then two fish dropped in through the skylight. When the people left her house the poor girl had a vision: it was a clear sunny day. She heard voices singing and saw two terns fishing on the river. They came toward her in human form and asked her to choose one of them for a husband. She chose both of them. They brought her to a fine house and went out to hunt. She called on her grandmother for help. The grandmother arrived in the shape of a young woman in her finery, bringing bead ornaments for her granddaughter. The granddaughter told one of her husbands to marry her rejuvenated grandmother. The men caught plenty of seals. The grandmother gave birth to a boy with a duck's bill in its forehead. When he grew up he caught lots of seals and fish with the beak. Next the granddaughter bore a son with one flat ear. He became a fine hunter of caribou using his ear as his hunting weapon. They stayed there and never had any trouble again.

(ABRIDGED VERSION OF LANTIS, 1946, PP. 291ff)

This orphan girl apparently became a shaman-to-be at her grandmother's death; being covered up like a shaman enabled her to answer the voice from above and go to live in the land of her vision. None of her relatives in the village missed her; moreover nobody there could marry her because she lacked the ornaments required for a wife to co-operate with her husband in ritual. On Nunivak Island, where this story was told, a daughter received her ornaments and danced wearing them in public for the first time when she was about 8 years old. The dance took place in the men's house, which also served as the cult house of the village. This dance in fact initiated the little girl into the most important ritual task in her future marriage, namely that of dancing as her husband's indispensable partner during the gift ritual. This formed part of most of the cult festivals celebrated in the men's house. A man would present gifts produced by him and his wife, while she, and their still unmarried daughters, danced in their ritual finery and he drummed and sang about how the gifts were obtained and produced. The families took turns in presenting their gifts, which were thrown into a common pile for later distribution according to individual choice. The oldest men and women were allowed to choose first, then the younger ones, each according to age but regardless of sex (Sonne, 1988).

The early initiation of a girl into her role as her future husband's dancing partner is explained by local marriage rules. A girl was married a couple of years before her first menstruation, when her much older husband would have to join her in her isolation hut. A young man was not allowed to marry until he had caught one of every kind of seal; he would usually be about 20. Both he and his mother, who had been his female working partner throughout his boyhood and adolescence, came under severe taboos after his last catch in the series of seals. After the taboo-period he was marriageable.

Returning to the poor girl of the myth, it is in the land of her vision that a proper Nunivak way of life begins. In contrast to the people living predominantly by fishing in the big rivers inland on the mainland opposite, the Nunivak islanders lived by hunting seals at sea and caribou on land. The less important summer fishing undertaken by dispersed families offered a young newly-married couple the opportunity of some privacy; each would go off alone for a honeymoon of fishing and mutual pleasure. Clearly, the myth takes a fisher village as its point of departure. The terns who offer themselves in marriage also fish, until accepted by the girl, after which they, in their true human forms, go seal-hunting as adult men. This transformation of animals into humans on the threshold of marrying a real human of the opposite sex is a recurrent theme in Nunivak mythology. Its parallel in ritual is the act performed by the young hunter concluding his period of taboo: he was to undress and run naked along the beach to signify his final transition into a true adult man; that is, a marriageable seal hunter.

Now, by calling her grandmother, the cunning girl not only receives the ornaments initiating her to marriage, but also gains a close female relative to complete the Nunivak mythic ideal of a household consisting of two related and co-operating families. The rejuvenation of the grandmother is rooted in the idea that dead relatives are reborn by name in their grandchildren. As well put by Ann Fienup-Riordan (1990, p. 47): 'The same people . . . have been on this earth from the beginning, continually cycling and recycling through life and death'.

To complete the co-operation between the two families the sons are born with an animal feature that facilitates hunting at sea and on land respectively. These features symbolize the primary amulet of a patriline without which a male member would remain a poor hunter. In combination they symbolize the annual round of activities subsumed in the hunting of seals in winter and the caribou hunt of summer (Sonne, 1988, pp. 100–8). Just as in 'Bringing the Sun' – a male shaman initiates the proper mode of co-operation between genders and families – this myth has a female shaman who sets in motion the proper Nunivak way of life.

TUTTU'S WIFE: FEMALE SHAMANS

Tuttu was said to be a lesser shaman than his wife. They quarrelled and Tuttu's wife left him for good. Tuttu worked hard to increase his shamanic powers.

One day, out sealing in his kayak, he saw a seal emerge with a rose-fish in its mouth. He started to collect tail feathers and tie them together into a long fishing line. In winter he took this line to the place on the ice where the rose-fish in the seal's mouth had indicated that the sea was extremely deep. He cut out a hole and lowered his line; though he started at sunrise the line only reached the bottom at noon. He caught a huge rose-fish. Crossing a frozen lake with the fish on his back, it caused a cracking sound that made him lose consciousness. When he came round he had gained the shaman's second sight. Continuing homeward he encountered a feathered monster. Remembering that killing such a creature would earn him the power to go down into the earth, he killed it. Eventually he was able to go to the place deep in earth, where he knew by his second sight that his wife was hiding. She willingly followed him back home.

(RASMUSSEN, 1921–5, II, PP. 221ff, ABBREVIATED)

Tuttu came apparently to equal his wife in shamanic powers. But later, when the settlement was threatened by famine and its great hunter asked Tuttu and his wife to try to save the settlement, Tuttu asked his wife to perform the task. She obeyed and, as told above, she managed very well. Her helping spirits, the polar bear and the walrus, further reveal that she had achieved one of the highest grades of a great shaman. This degree was accessible only to shamans with the sort of powers acquired by Tuttu.

This myth does not reflect the actual distribution of major and minor shamans according to gender. Male shamans were in the majority and the majority of great shamans were men. Yet the story is not impossible, since in theory nothing prevented female shamans from attaining the higher reputation of a great shaman. And a few of them did. Oosten (1986) puts forward the thesis that female shamans in some parts of Arctic Canada were not permitted to perform the tasks of great shamans of travelling to the realms of Sea Woman, below, or to Moon, above, in order to save the settlement from famine. This is contradicted by stray sources and by Saladin D'Anglure's (1986) sample of the distribution of male and female shamans according to the degree of their reputation. Yet because neither male or female shamans remained unmarried or childless, a man's working role was better suited to the training of a shaman than that of a woman. The shaman apprentice might be taught by an older shaman or receive the first helping spirit unaided in a vision, but the prolonged walks in the wilderness in search of (additional) helping spirits were to be completed by the apprentice in solitude.

Considering also the demand that the apprentice keep his/her education secret until the evening of initiation, training was much easier for a male apprentice moving freely about on hunting trips. A girl going off into the wilderness would be seen leaving and arouse suspicion, especially if she stayed away for some length of time. After marriage and the birth of children, her freedom of movement became even more restricted. In support of this, the life-stories of Greenlandic female shamans emphasize marriage as the recurrent excuse for women not accomplishing the full education of a great shaman. In addition to this obstacle, some jealousy on the part of men towards a female shaman appears to have been common. This was doubtless due to the lower standing of girls and young wives as compared to that of their brothers and husbands.

THE HIERARCHY OF AUTHORITY, OLD WOMEN AND MINOR FEMALE SHAMANS

As a rule men did the hunting. A man could not do without a woman to process his catches into food, fuel, clothes and boat-covers. Nor could a man of the 'third sex' do without a woman in order to have children. Similarly, a woman would lead a wretched life without a man (as some widows had to). But the undeniable fact that the man brought home the raw materials for the woman's productive work made most Eskimos confer authority within a family on its male members. The father was considered the head of the family in all hunting matters and he was served first together with his male housemates at meals. Older brothers had authority over younger brothers, older sisters over younger ones, and a brother over his sister whether the sister was the brother's senior or not. An Inuit husband owned his wife in certain respects. He decided on wife exchanges, a common means of strengthening a tie of an alliance between two men. He could scratch or wound her with his knife without reproach, because good manners forbade other people to interfere. He could leave her for good on the slightest occasion. But so could she, and the children went with her, never with their divorced father. The older a married woman grew and the greater the number of sons she got, the higher her standing.

Married sons bringing their wives to the household in which the mother remained the head in family affairs would take her advice or obey her orders in all matters that did not interfere with their decisions on when and where to go hunting. Such a mother retained her authority as a widow. Daughters in-law would suffer under her regime, hoping to become less dependent on her will in the future. A young widow or divorced woman with small children led an underdog life in a relative's household until she remarried. The younger and better-looking she was, and the more skilled a seamstress, the better her chances of remarrying a capable hunter. Having a son might increase her chances. Older women who were bereft of close relatives were badly off. They were frequently accused of sorcery on a par with old men of minor reputation. Yet, unless the accusation led to lynching, as might happen in times of crisis, it would confer some respect on the accused woman.

In other words, the respect paid to older people of either sex, dependent on their age and reputation for knowledge, might help a woman transcend the pattern of male authority. As pointed out by Thisted (forthcoming) in her analysis of female shamans in Greenland: minor female shamans were effective at giving advice on most sorts of illnesses and bad luck beyond the dramatic and entertaining seances of the greater shamans. Furthermore, elderly women were the main transmitters of myth in their role as babysitting grandmothers. Among adults their talent decided the reputation they enjoyed as story-tellers, irrespective of sex.

The springboard to respect for every woman was, however, constituted by her basic roles: first as mediator, binding families together by her marriage; secondly as the source of renewed life in motherhood; finally, as working partner indispensable both to husband and unmarried adolescent sons. These are the roles stressed in myth.

ACCULTURATION BRINGS ABOUT CHANGES IN MYTH

The common image of Eskimo culture as timeless and static until recent western impact eliminated its traditions, is false. Climatic changes and trading of goods, women and technical knowledge with other cultures brought about decisive change during every period of prehistory, up to the first advent of the Whites. Since the arrival of the latter is the main issue dealt with Eskimos' modern reworking of their myths, we shall limit ourselves to that subject. A report of the use made by western authors and film-makers of the same myths would make up a separate chapter (see, for instance, Fienup-Riordan, 1990).

Changes in Sea Woman Myths

In the above treatment of the myths about Sea Woman we did not take into account the diversity of variants. In some she is originally an orphan girl or a widow among strangers, that is, a girl already marginalized by society and badly treated by its proper members. Among the variants stressing her refusal to marry, several Canadian Inuit variants show her married to a fulmar and/or they identify the girl with the girl of another myth, 'Dog Husband', who married a dog and thus became the ancestress of Indians and Whites.

THE FULMAR

The fulmar seduces the obstinate girl, appearing to her as a human kayaker, and takes her as his wife to his far-away country. The following year her family go in search of her by boat, arrive at the fulmar's home and steal away with her in a hurry. When the fulmar discovers her escape he pursues them and, catching up with the boat, asks to see her hands. Denied this favour he raises a storm that almost upsets the boat. In order to save the family's life, the father throws the daughter overboard, and cuts off her fingerjoints, etc.

It is the thesis of this author (Sonne, 1990) that the inclusion of the fulmar in the myth originated among the south-east Baffin Islanders with the arrival of European whalers in Davis Strait during the seventeenth century. Wounded whales who escaped the whalers in considerable numbers would sooner or later die and be washed ashore to the benefit of the Inuit. The fulmars, the faithful companions of whaling ships, would be the first to take their share of the carcass meat out at sea, and thereby announce its arrival to the Inuit on look-out. Consistent with the idea that the severed fingers of Sea Woman signified her meat-exchange with humans, is the crediting of the fulmar with a husband's rights to these hands in myth. He deserved his share of meat as a co-operating human son-in-law would.

DOG HUSBAND

The ancestress of the Whites was once a girl who after refusing to marry was eventually married to a dog. She gave birth to a litter of dogs. Her father, who had to feed the young family, got tired of his unproductive son-in-law (Eskimo dogs do not bring in meat but are fed by their masters), and drowned him. In revenge, the daughter had her children kill their grandfather. Left without a provider she sent the dogs out in the world to fend for themselves. Various races of humans and spirits originated in this way; most usually the Native Americans of the mainland (or in otherwise uninhabited areas, a spirit people) and the Whites of a distant country across the sea. The latter were told by their mother to become rich and produce nice little gifts, implying their later return with such things to offer Inuit women.

At the date (late nineteenth century) at which the first variant is recorded relating the combination of 'Dog Husband' and the 'Origin of Sea Woman', young Inuit women would typically receive such gifts in return for their services as seamstresses, dancing partners and mistresses to white whalers on board the whaling ships. Their Inuit fathers, who served as assistants in the whaling and provided the crews with fresh meat, would earn valuable material such as iron to use for harpoon heads and other means of improving their hunting efficiency. In the men's new role of providing for both the Whites, and the mixed-blood offspring which the whalers left behind, these Inuit men were likened to the father-in-law of the mythic dog, who begot the Whites. Yet these Inuit men, who benefited from co-operation with the whalers, did not kill these dog-like Whites. These established relations incorporated the Whites into the network of exchange with sea mammals brought about by the origin of Sea Woman. Thus Sea Woman became identified with the girl who married a dog according to this author (Sonne, 1990).

Furthermore, because Sea Woman's house was close to the submarine realm of death, the earliest knowledge of the Gospel, spread among the same Inuit, produced fresh variants. According to these, Sea Woman's father descends to her territory as a devil who torments the dead on their way to the proper realm of death. The role of the Devil might also be conferred on Sea Woman herself. These transformations would explain the predominance of Sea Woman among most Canadian Inuit groups as compared to her lesser importance among, say, the Greenlanders (Sonne, 1990).

INUIT: SEA WOMAN RECREATES INUIT IDENTITY

Inuit is the title of a play composed by the first team of apprentice actors at the Tukak theatre, a dramatic school residing in Denmark. The language of the play is Greenlandic, but as the communicative effect of the play is predominantly through body language and costume, its message is also clear to an audience ignorant of Greenlandic. The more sophisticated details of meaning, however, were kindly communicated to me by Dr Kirsten Thonsgaard, who was given permission to follow the composition of *Inuit*.

Composed and staged in the mid-1970s, when the Greenlanders claimed the right to rule their own affairs independently of the Danish government, the play conveys Greenlandic ideas about their struggle to regain their ethnic identity:

A group of children engaged in a joyous singing game are visited by a
masked white spirit, who spoils the game. He forces each child to wear
a mask, symbolizing the customs introduced by the Whites in the recent
past. In their first reaction of naïve joy the masked Inuit children dance
right into the realm of fear, where souls are apt to get lost. Loss of souls
equates with loss of identity, and in distress the alienated children call out
for help. Some traditional masked spirits appear to guide one of the
children down below to the Mother of Life. This woman, who represents
a reinterpretation of Sea Woman, similarly wears a mask. As the visitors
from above enter, she tears off her clothes in a fit of rage. This act is meant
to symbolize her ascent to the level of ordinary humans. Next, in an ecstatic
shaman's song and dance she finds an outlet for her rage and thus acquires
the strength to tear off her mask. This act encourages her visitors to follow
suit, and thus everyone except the white spirit has recovered his and her
soul. But as the white spirit is still a threat to Inuit identity he is forced
into a wrestling match by one of the actors, who succeeds in tearing off
the spirit's mask. Bereft of his white identity the dead man undergoes a
serious crisis that leads to his eventual rebirth as a true human being. As
such, he is invited to join the circle of Inuit children, who resume their
joyful game. Finally he accepts the invitation.

To put the message of the play briefly: by frankly admitting their common cultural
heritage, Inuit will unite and gain the strength to fight the fatal western threat and
thus try to teach White people the Inuit way of cheerful co-existence in mutual love.

    Inuit makes use of two myths in its reinterpretation, the 'Shaman's journey to
Sea Woman' retold above, and another, relating the story of a woman who adopted
a young polar bear as her son. He became very dear to her, learned how to speak,
and played with the other children. But after a while he grew too strong and rough
and they became scared of him. Then the adults taught him how to hunt and he
became a good hunter and provider. But in the end his bear nature made him steal
from his human comrades and he was killed. This myth relates to the matrix of the
play, the singing game. In the song of this traditional 'blind man's buff' game is a
warning: 'If your baby is a small polar bear, you'd better be cautious.' The white spirit
takes up the position of the polar bear. His final transformation into a true human,
a reversal of the story's outcome, demands a reorganization of the 'Shaman's Journey'
myth as well. While in the traditional myth Sea Woman is bound to remain outside
society, dependent on earthly humans and their shamans for her well-being, the
'Mother of Life' becomes reintegrated into Inuit life on earth. In her compassion
for the scared Inuit children she takes on the role of shaman herself. She cleans
herself of the filth symbolized in her mask, deriving from the tempting goods brought
by the Whites to the Inuit. The children in the roles of masked helping spirits
similarly tear off the 'filth' hiding their true identity. Having taken the role of the
shaman, the Mother of Life ought to have been the one to fight and clean the actual
evil, the white spirit. But during the gestation of *Inuit* the female actor apprentices

strongly objected to that proposal. The Greenlandic woman, they asserted vigorously, is not an aggressive character. No, the person to fight that spirit was to be a male.

Thus Sea Woman, traditionally the reflection of the inactive woman under taboo, has in her fresh role of Mother of Life not only been transformed into a proper human being, she has become an ideal symbol of Inuit women's identity. This plea is consistent with the attempts of most peoples to understand their ethnic or national roots in the face of political threat. Looking to tradition or history for support, most of us are liable to reinvent tradition or history to make it suit our needs.

Notes

1 The label *Eskimo* refers to the interrelated languages spoken by all 'Eskimos'. *Inuit* is the term of identification preferred by the politically-conscious members of the pan-'Eskimo' organization, ICC – Inuit Circumpolar Conference. *Inuit* means human beings in the northern dialects of north-west Alaska, Canada and Greenland. The speakers of the southern dialects of south-west Alaska identify themselves as *Yupiit*, equivalent in root and meaning to *Inuit*. But *Inuit* is nevertheless repulsive to the *Yupiit* when it comes to the question of ethnic identification. Nor do the Eskimo-speaking peoples on the Pacific coast of Alaska identify themselves as *Inuit*. They consider themselves as *Aleuts*.
2. The idea of gender specific names is limited to the Illulik and a few other Canadian Inuit groups. Most Eskimos did not distinguish between male and female names before the advent of Christian missionaries.

References and Further Reading
(in English)

PRIMARY MATERIAL:

Alaska Native Language Center (1988), *King Island Tales*, (Fairbanks: University of Alaska Press), pp. 167–249

Bergsland, K. (ed./trans) (1987), *Nunamiut Stories*, Bilingual edition of stories collected by Helge Instad among Inland Eskimos of North Alaska, 1949–50 (Fairbanks: Alaska Native Language Center, College of Liberal Arts, University of Alaska; the North Slope Borough Commission on Iñupiat History, Language and Culture)

Bergsland, K. and Dirks, M.L. (eds/trans) (1990), *Aleut Tales and Narratives*, Bilingual publication of stories collected by W. Jochelson, 1909–10 (Fairbanks: Alaska Native Language Center, University of Alaska Press)

Boas, F. (1901–7), 'The Eskimo of Baffinland and Hudson Bay', I–II, in *Bulletin of the American Museum of Natural History*, 15

Boas, F. (1964), *The Central Eskimo* (1888) (Nebraska: University of Nebraska Press), pp. 175–250

Curtis, E.S. (1930, reprinted 1970), *The North American Indian*, 20 (New York and London: Johnson Reprint Cooperation).

Hall, Jr, E.S. (1975), *The Eskimo Storyteller*, (Knoxville: University of Tennessee Press)

Holtved, E. (1951), *The Polar Eskimos. Language and Folklore*, II, *Meddelelser om Grønland*, 152(2) (Copenhagen: C.A. Reitzel)

Keithan, E.L. (1976) [1974], *Alaskan Igloo Tales* (Anchorage: Alaska Northwest Publishing Company)

Kroeber, A.L. (1899), 'Tales of the Smith Sound Eskimos' in *Journal of American Folk Lore*, 12, pp. 166–82

Lantis, M. (1946), 'The Social Culture of the Nunivak Eskimo' in *Transactions of the American Philosophical Society*, N.S. 35(3) (Philadelphia: Lancaster Press), pp. 264–313

Métayer, M. (1972), *Tales from the Igloo* (Edmonton: Hurtig Publishers). Copper Inuit stories.

Nelson, E.W. (1899), *The Eskimo About the Bering Strait*, 18th Annual Report of the Bureau of American Ethnology, part 1 (Washington). Concluding section.

Ostermann, H. (ed.) (1939), 'Knud Rasmussen's Posthumous Notes on East Greenland. Legends and Myths' in *Meddelelser om Grønland*, 109(3) (Copenhagen: C. A. Reitzel)

Rasmussen, K. (1921–5), *Myter og Sagn fra Grønland*, I–III (Copenhagen: Gyldendal) (in Danish)

—— (1929–52), *Report of the 5th Thule Expedition*, vols 7(1), 8, 9, and 10 (2–3), 1921–4 (Copenhagen: Gyldendal). Arctic Canadian and north Alaskan. Some of the more important myths are dispersed in the descriptive chapters.

Rink, H.J. (1875, reprinted 1975), *Tales and Traditions of the Eskimo* (New York: AMS Press). Predominantly Greenlandic stories in English summaries.

Spencer, R.F. (1959), 'The North Alaskan Eskimo' in *Smithsonian Institution, Bureau of American Ethnology*, Bulletin, 171 (Washington: U.S. Government Printing Office), pp. 384–439

Woodbury, A.C. (1984), *Cev'armiut Qanemciit Qulirait-llu / Eskimo Narratives and Tales from Chevak, Alaska* (Fairbanks: Alaska Native Language Center, University of Alaska Press)

SECONDARY WRITINGS:

Briggs, J. (1974), 'Eskimo Women, Makers of Men' in C.J. Matthiasson (ed.), *Many Sisters, Women in Cross-Cultural Perspective* (New York: Free Press)

Dorais, J.-L. (1986), 'Agiter l'homme pour attraper la femme: la sémantique des sexes en langue Inuit' in *Études/Inuit/Studies*, 10 (1–2), pp. 171–8

Fienup-Riordan, A. (1990), *Eskimo Essays* (New Brunswick and London: Rutgers University Press), pp. 1–67, 123–45

Giffen, N.M. (1930), *The Roles of Men and Women in Eskimo Culture* (Chicago: University of Chicago Publications)

Guemple, L. (1986), 'Men and Woman, Husbands and Wives: The Role of Gender in Traditional Inuit Society' in *Études/Inuit/Studies*, 10 (1–2), pp. 9–24

Kleivan, I. (1962), 'The Swan Maiden Myth among the Eskimo' in *Acta Arctica*, Fasc. XIII, Copenhagen

Lantis, M. (1953), 'Nunivak Eskimo Personality as Revealed in Mythology' in *Anthropological Papers of the University of Alaska*, 2(1)

Oosten, J.G. (1983), 'The Incest of Sun and Moon: An Examination of the Symbolism of Time and Space in Two Iglulik Myths' in *Études/Inuit/Studies*, 7(1), pp. 143–51

—— (1986), 'Male and Female in Inuit Shamanism' in *Études/Inuit/Studies*, 10 (1-2), pp. 115–31

Saladin D'Anglure, B. (1986), 'Du foetus au chamane: la construction d'un "troisi[eme sexe" inuit' in *Études/Inuit/Studies*, 10 (1-2), pp. 25–113

Sonne, B. (1988), *Agayut. Eskimo Masks from The 5th Thule Expedition* (Copenhagen: Gyldendal)

—— (1990), 'The Acculturative Role of Sea Woman' in *Meddelelser om Grønland, Man & Society*, 13

Thisted, Kirsten (forthcoming), *Ajugassaarukkumaartutit / Intet skal være dig umuligt – Kvinder og shamanism (samt belagtet religiøs aktivitet i Grønland)* (Nuuk: Atuakkiorfik) (in Danish).

Vebæk, M. (1990), *Navaranaaq og andre. De grønlandske kvinders historie (The History of the Greenlandic Women)* (Copenhagen: Gyldendal) (in Danish)

PART 3

Asia

EMILY KEARNS

Indian Myth

I INTRODUCTION: A GENERAL VIEW

I.1 The Vedic Gods

The religious and mythological complex which has come to be called Hinduism has a textually documented history which stretches from very roughly 1200 BCE to the present day. But although there is certainly continuity in the tradition, important changes have occurred over that period in such fundamentals as styles of worship, perceived relationship of worshipper with deity, modes of theological outlook and in the actual deities most conspicuously worshipped. Thus the relationship of our oldest document, the hymns of the *Rigveda*, to contemporary Hinduism is a paradoxical one: Vedic material is still in ritual use, and to accept the authority of the Vedas is a touchstone of orthodoxy, but one would search the *Rigveda* in vain for most aspects of Hinduism which seem central today.

The purpose of the Vedas is not to narrate myth, but (in the metrical, earliest portions, for which the term *Veda* is sometimes reserved by western scholars) to supply hymns for ritual use, and (in the prose portions, the *Brāhmaṇas* and *Upanishads*) to expound what was seen as the philosophical basis of those hymns. There is thus little detailed narrative of myth, but what we can gather of the mythological picture reveals quite different emphases from those of later times. Chief of the Vedic gods is the powerful Indra, warrior-king and wielder of the thunderbolt; his power is repeatedly threatened by demons and other hostile beings, but he always retains it or is restored to his proper place. Next to him as recipient of the greatest number of hymns is Agni, god of fire and especially of the sacrificial fire which mediates between gods and their human worshippers. Varuṇa is a king like Indra, an establisher of ordinances, and particularly connected with water; Soma is the personification of the mysterious, apparently psychotropic, ritual *soma* drink; Sūrya is the Sun, and Savitṛ is also a solar deity.

Among the rest of the large pantheon, some of the figures most important in mythology as Yama, 'Controller', lord of death; the Maruts, a group of brothers associated with storms; and the Aśvins, 'horsemen', twin brothers of beneficent aspect. These gods are not forgotten in post-Vedic times, and indeed much mythological material alluded to in the Vedas is elucidated in later texts, although the later corpus tends to show a certain downgrading of these divinities. The reverse is true of two gods with a minor role in the *Rigveda*, Vishnu and Rudra (the latter identified with Śiva); these become the greatest male deities of later times (*see* I.2, p. 192).

But perhaps the most striking feature of the Vedic pantheon, when compared with that of later times, is its lack of major female figures. We might expect that Indra's wife, for instance, would be an important figure, but in fact no hymns are dedicated to her and even in mythology she remains extremely shadowy. Though she has a proper name, Śacī, she is frequently called simply by a feminine form of his name, Indrāṇī. Even the most important Vedic goddesses are clearly of a lesser rank than the top male divinities: Uṣas, the dawn, wife or sometimes mother of Sūrya, is the most conspicuous goddess, but the Vedas include hymns also to Pṛthivī, Earth (usually paired with the male Dyaus, Sky); Rātrī, the Night; Vāc, Speech; the Waters, a vague group of divine mothers; and Sarasvatī, a river-goddess who only gradually takes on some of the nature of the later goddess of that name (*see* II.1, p. 197). These deities are close to simple personifications, and their functions are mostly straightforward and well defined; if there were important myths about them, we cannot now recover them.

On the other hand, female characters do feature in some of the stories about the most prominent gods of the Vedas, though again the stories may appear in their full form only in later texts. Here we see women in a variety of roles, but usually and importantly in a close familial relation with men, as mothers, wives or sisters.

The vulnerability of motherhood is suggested in the myth of Diti, whose womb Indra enters in order to cut up the embryo which will threaten his sovereignty, yet the explicit purpose of this unpleasant story is to explain why the Maruts are several, not one. Woman is victim here; a victim discovers a strategy in a more complex narrative, that of Saraṇyū, wife of Viśvavat the Sun, who finds that she can no longer bear her husband's brilliant light; making use of the source of the problem, she creates a double from her shadow to continue her role while she herself leaves the household. This displacement of a problem from a 'real' to an 'unreal' character recurs later in some versions of the *Rāmāyaṇa* (*see* I.3, p. 195), where it is not Sītā herself, the heroine, who is abducted by the villain, but her double. We seem to have an implicit admission here that no real structural solution is found for the male-induced problems of women; the situation can only be shifted, not resolved. And, in fact, Saraṇyū's double does take on a 'real' existence when she is found to behave more affectionately to her own children than to those of Saraṇyū; the woman created to help Saraṇyū now sees her as a rival (*see* III.4, p. 209), and this leads to the discovery of the substitution.

One of the few female characters whose importance is not familial is the enigmatic Saramā, a messenger — sometimes in the form of a bitch — sent by Indra to a group of demons who have stolen his cattle. The outcome is not entirely clear:

in the hymn as it appears in the *Rigveda* (10.108), we have the impression that Saramā is coming out on top, but the later texts which expand on the myth relate that she was bribed by the demons so that Indra was forced to come in person to recover the cattle. Either way, the use of a female figure to overcome demons by indirect means (trickery or persuasion) anticipates later mythological motifs (*see* III.7, p. 217), although Saramā does not appear to use her sexuality against the demons here.

Although, in contrast to later Hinduism, the pickings from the Vedas for a mythology of women are scanty, we should bear in mind the possible limitations of the material. It must be significant that so few hymns are addressed to goddesses, but it may be that important aspects of the religious belief and practice of the time were excluded from 'official' texts. Even today it is often the case that 'village Hinduism', not to say the religion of tribal peoples, contains elements which are quite at variance with the pan-Indian tradition based on Sanskrit texts and the brahminical priesthood. A possible indication that something similar may apply to the world of the Vedas is provided by the pre-Aryan civilization of the Indus Valley. Numerous figurines and seals dating from the second millennium BCE depict female figures, and although we lack the ability to interpret the Indus Valley script so that we are handicapped in placing them in context, it seems reasonable to suppose that they have some kind of religious significance. It would undoubtedly, however, be much too simple to contrast the male deities of the Aryan invaders with the female divinities of the indigenous population. Neither can we be certain that the goddesses of later Hinduism are in any way continuous with those of the Indus Valley. The seals appear to suggest a prominent connexion between goddesses and animals, which may link with later trends, but also between goddesses and vegetative fertility, an association which is very faint in Hinduism; if there is continuity, it may have been almost totally overlaid by change.

I.2 The Gods of Later Hinduism

The gods who are most prominent in the Vedas do not disappear in the later period; Indra, Agni and the rest make frequent appearances in myths of a later date, though they are no longer the central characters. By the time of the epics, and still more the *purāṇas* (*see* I.4, p. 196), other deities have arrived, and the divine stage begins to look crowded; the Vedic estimate of thirty-three gods is expanded to 330 million in one conventional reckoning. Yet such counts are felt to be true only on one level: 'Indra, Mitra, Varuṇa, Agni . . . the real is one, the wise express it in different ways' says already a late hymn of the *Rigveda* (1.164.46), and in the later *Bṛhadāraṇyaka Upanishad* (3.9.1–9), the sage Yājñavalkya is forced by questioning to reduce the number of gods to one, effectively an impersonal concept usually called *brahman*. Thus into a system which is formally polytheistic is woven a strand which insists that polytheism is relative or apparent only; this is an element which frequently enters into the apprehension or even the actual narrative of polytheistic myth, and shifts its perceived meaning to another level.

The desire to reconcile the gods of mythology with the Upanishadic concept of brahman led not only to a new form of mythopœia but to more conscious schematizations of the pantheon. The best known of these attempts to represent the ultimate reality in mythical form is the concept of the *trimūrti* or 'triple form', in which the divine functions of creation, preservation and destruction are divided respectively between Brahmā, Vishnu and Śiva. It would be misleading to take this idea as a 'dogma' of Hinduism and to assume, for instance, that Śiva is simply the god of destruction. Those whose preferred object of worship is Śiva see him as the personal expression of a supreme deity presiding over all three functions. All the same, the scheme does give a clue to some important themes in the mythology of each god. Thus, in post-Vedic mythology Brahmā, often called 'grandfather', is always the direct agent of creation, though the manner of creation may vary (*see* I.3, p. 194). Thereafter he appears in the role of archetypal *brāhmaṇa* (brahmin) and priest, but there are few myths 'about' Brahmā, though he features frequently in the mythology of other gods. This mythological lack reflects a decreasing significance as object of worship. Having appeared on the scene later than the Vedas, Brahmā may have been important at first, as both his name (simply the masculine form of the neuter *brahman*) and his appearance in the *trimūrti* suggest, but few texts extol his greatness, and today he can claim only two major temples in the whole of India.

Vishnu's myths, too, are often appropriate to his function in the *trimūrti*. Already in the *Rigveda* (1.154.4) he supports earth and heaven, and the bulk of his mythology relates how he took animal or human form in order to save the earth – sometimes literally to support it and prevent it from sinking – at a particular moment of crisis. These forms eventually became standardized as a list of ten *avatāras*, descents or incarnations. Vishnu is above all the god who is born on this earth, whether to restore righteous order, to give his devotees an opportunity to contemplate him in approachable form or just for fun (*līlā*, II.2, p. 203).

The two avatars most conspicuous in myth and worship, the warrior-prince and exemplar of righteousness Rāma, and Krishna (also a warrior-prince, but perhaps most celebrated in the humbler exploits of his childhood and youth in a village community of cowherds) have complete narrative histories of their own, but the identification with Vishnu is fundamental to the way they are perceived. The tenth avatar, Kalkī, who is yet to come, shows a destructive aspect of Vishnu: he will bring this present, wicked age to an violent close and prepare the way for a new and perfect era.

But destruction is more prominent in the myths of Śiva. Dissolution is perhaps a better word than destruction; Śiva is closely associated with the state of non-separation, in which the perception of individual entities ceases to exist, and in this context destruction is seen as equivalent to 'liberation' or 'release' – the proper aim of every soul to escape from the cycle of birth and death, and to realize its true nature. Śiva perhaps more than Vishnu is a god of contradiction. His aniconic cult symbol, the *linga*, begins to indicate the paradoxes: clearly phallic, it speaks in some measure of sexuality and fecundity, yet in Indian iconography the erect phallus generally represents not readiness for copulation but control and retention of semen. Again, the *linga* is pillar as well as phallus, and thus links with the static, pillar form of Śiva in which he refuses to create or procreate.

Similarly, myths about Śiva present him as *both* erotic (he makes love continuously for a thousand years) *and* ascetic (he performs terrible austerities, and with the power thus accumulated shrivels up Kāma, desire personified). As husband, father and householder he also mediates the extreme poles of his nature.

The *trimūrti* is an all-male construct; it might seem that things have changed little in that respect from the Vedic picture. The earliest text to give supremacy to a female divinity is dated roughly to 500 CE, perhaps a little later (*see* I.4, p. 196), and by about the eighth century we find a different type of grouping of deities established: rather than involving a division of functions, the idea of the 'five (or six) paths' indicates that the same goal may be reached by taking any one of a group of deities as supreme. In the group of six, Brahmā has disappeared, the Vedic Sūrya has returned (his importance later declined decisively), and the remaining three places are taken by Kārttikeya, Gaṇeśa and 'the Goddess' (Devī). The first two are regarded as sons of Śiva and Pārvatī (*see* especially III.6, p. 212); Kārttikeya, also known as Skanda, is known to the epic as the general of the gods in the recurring war against the demons. In north India he has ceased to be an important object of worship, but in much of the south, where he is known as Subrahmaṇya or Murugan, his popularity is very great and he appears more prominently as a young lover, a Krishna-like figure, than as a fighter. Gaṇeśa, the elephant-headed god, is popular all over India, although only a relatively small group now regards him as their chosen manifestation of the supreme deity; rather, since he presides over the beginnings of enterprises and has the power to create or remove obstacles, he is appropriately invoked at the outset of any undertaking.

The sole female figure in the group is also the least clearly defined. Already, it seems, worship of *a* goddess is considered to be worship of *the* Goddess, and this close identification of what appear to be many cults and many mythological figures is a constant of Goddess worship from the earliest Goddess-centred text to the present day (*see* V.2, pp. 222–3). Whereas to say that Vishnu and Śiva are the same is effectively making a wider statement to the effect that the personal gods of myth are simply differing expressions of one reality, to say that Durgā, Kālī and Pārvatī are identical requires no more adjustment on the part of the listener than an affirmation of the identity of Vishnu and his avatars. Although to some extent different mythologies are attached to the different names, there are some frequently recurring characteristics which make it possible to speak of a mythological complex centring on the Goddess.

The goddesses most frequently identified with *the* Goddess, Devī, are often fierce and aggressive, or else they express a clearly marked polarity between the aggressive and the mild. Often they are solitary, but more frequently they are linked in some way with Śiva, himself an ambivalent deity. The earliest text composed solely to extol the Goddess, however, connects her more closely with Vishnu, and sometimes she is said to be Vishnu's sister (the brother-sister relation being traditionally a close one) and Śiva's wife. Vishnu's own wife Lakṣmī is less consistently identified as the Goddess, but some groups do worship Devī envisaged as the mythological Lakṣmī, as also to some extent the consort of the third member of the *trimūrti*, Brahmā's wife Sarasvatī. These modalities will be discussed more fully in Section II.2, pp. 199–203.

Of the deities of the 'six paths', only three are now widely taken as supreme deity over India as a whole: Vishnu, Śiva and the Goddess. Thus the most frequently found labels for varieties of modern Hinduism are the Vaiṣṇava, Śaiva and Śākta groups – the last being the adjective from *śakti*, 'power', conceived as female (*see* II.2, p. 200). These divisions are not watertight, especially as far as the Goddess is concerned: she may be given pride of place in what is formally termed a Śaiva temple, or some form of Vishnu's consort may be worshipped as the supreme deity in a Vaiṣṇava setting. But they give us some very rough guidelines.

I.3 Post-Vedic Mythology: Some Landmarks

Although many myths are independent stories, with only a secondary sense of belonging in a sequence of events, there is a time-scale which structures mythology – and indeed the whole world. The Indian conception of time is cyclical: millions of years are expended in the passage of a day of Brahmā, and this is followed by a night of equal length, a time of involution and non-creation. After a hundred years on this scale, Brahmā dies, and a hundred more years pass before a new Brahmā appears and the cycle begins again, *ad infinitum*. Within each day of Brahmā is repeated a thousand times a sequence of four declining ages, from the 'perfect age' following the creation to a final degraded age, the *kali yuga*. Almost all the mythological and historical events we know of are to be placed in the current sequence of four ages; we have been in *kali yuga* since 3102 BCE.

It follows that creation is a repeated event, and its importance is further diminished by the fact that it is not creation *ex nihilo;* what is is eternal, and creation is only its separation into parts, as destruction is only its coming together again as a whole. But there are, of course, creation myths of importance. The Vedas know a creator-god whose seed generates living beings when it is spilled on the earth during his intercourse with his own daughter. Later this god is named as Prajāpati ('lord of offspring'), and later still identified with Brahmā. Alternatively, a well-known, late, Vedic hymn (RV10.90) describes the creation of the world as the result of the first sacrifice, in which the gods sacrificed the Primal Person or Man (*puruṣa*) to himself; his body became the universe, in all its different parts. Purāṇic versions indicate that a proper, self-perpetuating creation must be somehow sexual in character; realizing this, Brahmā asks Śiva to produce woman from his own androgynous body, and the woman's power enables creation to proceed.

But the creation myth best known today starts from Vishnu asleep on the coils of the cosmic serpent in the middle of the ocean. A lotus stalk springs from his navel and in the flower Brahmā – now clearly subordinated – comes into being and creates the world.

Animate creation comprises not merely gods, humans and beasts, but includes other categories, such as 'sages', often differentiated from ordinary humans, and, most importantly, demons. Demons (*asuras*) are generally opposed to gods (*devas*), but the near the beginning of the present four-age cycle, when gods and demons compete for the nectar of immortality. The two sides co-operate to produce the substance by an immense churning operation on the ocean of milk, but when after several vicissitudes the nectar comes forth, Vishnu uses a trick to ensure that only the gods drink it, while the demons are deprived (*see* III.7, p. 217). Thereafter the gods' power is continually under threat from a succession of individual demons and *rākṣasas* (monsters), whose methods range from military might to supernatural power gained through the practice of rigorous austerities.

Following on the early period of the age-cycle, a further structuring of mythical time is provided by the incarnations of Vishnu. The most common sequence of ten begins with the Fish which provides a safe refuge for creatures during the flood, leading through various human incarnations of the Perfect and Second Ages, to Rāma in the Third Age, followed by Krishna at the start of the present age; the ninth incarnation is the Buddha, and the tenth, Kalkin, will come at the end of the age.

Rāma and Krishna figure prominently in the important body of connected myth which is narrated in the two great epics. Indeed, Rāma is the central subject of the *Rāmāyaṇa*, which tells the story of his struggle against the demon Rāvaṇa. Although rightfully the heir to the throne of Ayodhyā, Rāma foregoes his right through the machinations of his stepmother and willingly undergoes exile in the forest, accompanied by his wife Sītā and brother Lakṣmaṇa. Rāvaṇa abducts Sītā and takes her to his palace in Lanka, where she rejects his advances (and conveniently a curse prevents him from raping her). Backed by an army of animals raised by the monkey-general Hanumān – a popular deity – Rāma and Lakṣmaṇa cross to Lanka and eventually defeat and kill Rāvaṇa, then return with Sītā to Ayodhyā, where Rāma is crowned king (*see* III.2–4). The story-line of the *Mahābhārata* is more complex and intricate, but its core is the quarrel and war between the five Pāṇḍava brothers (sons of Paṇḍu), of whom the eldest is legitimate successor to the throne of Hastinapura, and their hundred cousins the Kauravas, led by Duryodhana. Krishna appears as the wise king of a friendly state, who eventually forms an alliance with the Pāṇḍavas; his advice to the Pāṇḍava Arjuna when the latter loses heart forms the *Bhagavadgītā*, perhaps the best-loved of all Hindu religious texts. The Pāṇḍavas win the struggle, but at the cost of the slaughter of their sons and kinsfolk, and the epic raises problematic questions about the nature of duty and right.

I.4 Sources

The hymns of the Vedas were probably transmitted in oral form for a long time before they were first written down; Indian religious texts, even of a later period, are notoriously difficult to date, and estimates of the first written versions range from 1500 to 1000 BCE. There were originally three Vedas, *Rigveda*, *Yajurveda* and *Sāmaveda*; the *Atharvaveda* was added later. Each consists of a collection of hymns or prayers, followed by the speculative treatises known as *Brāhmaṇas* and *Upanishads*, of later date; together they occupy the highest rank of religious texts, being classified as *śruti*, 'heard' or revealed literature.

The bulk of post-Vedic mythology is written down in two types of texts, the epics and the purāṇas. The 'epic period', during which the core of the epics in the form we know them was composed, is generally dated to between 300 BCE and 300 CE, although some of their material may date back much further. Each epic is traditionally attributed to a single author (Vyāsa for the *Mahābhārata*, Vālmīki for the *Rāmāyaṇa*), but it is generally acknowledged that the transmitted texts show many layers of composition, and the modern critical editions have pared down the immensely long 'vulgate' versions to produce the still bulky texts as they might have appeared about 600 CE. This is obviously a controversial procedure: in the context of Indian culture as a whole, and given that we are dealing with a partly oral tradition, we should not think of the critical edition texts as the only 'genuine' forms of the epic. It is the longer, canonical texts which have been the formative influence on a continuous tradition, and it is these which all except a handful of scholars understand by 'Vyāsa's *Mahābhārata*' and 'Vālmīki's *Rāmāyaṇa*'. The gap between the traditional and the historicizing approaches to the text can throw up some important discrepancies. It is almost certainly the case, for instance, that the earliest books of the *Rāmāyaṇa* show no awareness of Rāma's divinity, and yet the current 'meaning' of the *Rāmāyaṇa* has been formed through a continuous tradition of reading the text on the assumption that Rāma is identical with Vishnu.

Even apart from the different layers of composition in the Sanskrit texts, the protean identity of the epics is further complicated by the existence since medieval times of numerous vernacular retellings of the stories, all of which may claim to be, for instance, '*Rāmāyaṇas*', if not 'Vālmīki's *Rāmāyaṇa*'. These retellings, extending to the phenomenally popular television serials of the late 1980s, are better thought of as part of a continuous tradition of reworking epic material, often incorporating significant differences, than as a sort of 'Condensed Books' version of the original.

Both epics narrate in passing many myths which are not part of the main narrative; many more are found in the compilations known as *purāṇas* ('ancient'). As well as mythical material, these contain hymns of praise, instructions for worship, strictures on the ordering of society, and much else. Eighteen principal and many minor *purāṇas* are recognized; the bulk of this material was composed in the thousand years between 500–1500 CE (it is difficult to be more precise), and although technically the purāṇas enjoy less prestige than the Vedas, purāṇic mythology is essentially the mythology of the present day. One purāṇic text which will be frequently referred to in what follows is worth special mention, the section of the *Mārkaṇḍeya Purāṇa* known as the *Devī-Māhātmya*, or 'Glorification of the Goddess'. This is the earliest surviving text which speaks of the Goddess as supreme deity, dating perhaps from 500 CE; it narrates her victories over assorted demons, and contains praises which remain very popular at the present day.

The final major source of myths is local tradition, both written and oral. Works extolling the merits of a particular temple or pilgrimage destination, lives of local saints or groups of saints, almost always contain mythological material, and similar types of story may exist in unwritten form in local communities, priestly or lay. Some of these myths, particularly the written ones, are broadly of the type found in the Sanskrit *purāṇas*; others, springing from a village milieu, can look different. It has been usual among indologists to distinguish between a pan-Indian 'Great Tradition', associated with brahminical authority and the use of Sanskrit, and a 'Little Tradition' – or traditions – which are locally-based, associated with the vernacular and often the preserve of the lower castes. While the religious traditions of villagers and still more of tribal people are often strikingly different from the data we receive from the Sanskrit texts, and while village practice itself often seems to suggest such a polarity, there is perhaps more of a continuum than the simple schema suggests.

II GODDESS AND GODDESSES: INTERACTIONS OF MYTH AND THEOLOGY

II.1 The Goddesses of Myth

Female deities in the Vedas, we have seen, are relatively insignificant. At some date, the subordinate consorts of the male gods undergo a metamorphosis and reappear independently as a group of seven fierce goddesses most often known as the Mātṛkās. But the goddess figures who later become the most important are of a quite different type: Sarasvatī, Lakṣmī, Pārvatī, Durgā, Kālī are among the most conspicuous names of goddesses both in the *Purāṇas*, and in contemporary Hinduism, though depending on context they may be perceived in ways which differ vastly with respect both to each other and to male gods.

Sarasvatī (*see* fig. 18), more than the others, presides over a particular sphere of life – that of learning and the arts, especially music. She differs from the Vedic Sarasvatī, who is chiefly a river-goddess, and has appropriated many of the functions of Vāc, Speech, for without her there would be no language. Few myths are told about her. Sometimes she is identified with the daughter of Brahmā with whom he desires to make love – sometimes successfully – at the beginning of the cosmic aeon, but more frequently she is his non-incestuous wife. Today, however, she is more commonly worshipped than he, being the frequent recipient of worship in contexts connected with her special interests: at university ceremonies, concerts and the making of films, for instance.

Lakṣmī ('auspicious sign') is the patroness of wealth, and though her role is wider than this, it is a function which naturally gives her a wide appeal. Shopkeepers and traders dedicate their account books to her, and among many communities the popular festival of Diwali is celebrated especially in her honour: it is hoped that she will be attracted by the clean, freshly decorated house, made bright with rows of clay lamps, and be induced to stay there. Similarly, local folk-tales relate how the goddess left the house of a certain ruler, or was tricked into remaining for ever in the bazaar of a particular town. In such contexts she is little more than the personification of wealth. In common with much else that is desirable, Lakṣmī made her first appearance in this cycle of ages during the churning of the ocean (*see* I.3, p. 195), manifesting herself as a beautiful woman seated on a lotus, her most popular iconographic form today. She is also often seen with Vishnu as his consort, in the form of Lakṣmī-Nārāyaṇa. An alternative scheme, of earlier origin but still

Fig. 18 Sarasvatī – a popular
print, widely on sale in India.
This copy is from Bombay.

current, gives Vishnu two wives, Śrī (Splendour) and Bhū (Earth): Lakṣmī is often
identified with Śrī, and although Vishnu is more markedly polygamous than Śiva,
the one-wife model has generally been more popular on the level of myth. It is often
held that Lakṣmī is identical with the wives and lovers of Vishnu in his various
human manifestations, such as Sītā and Rādhā.

Pārvatī ('mountain-woman'; she is the daughter of Himālaya), Durgā ('hard of
access') and Kālī ('black') are more closely identified than the previous two
goddesses, though here too distinct stories are told about each, and each has a distinct
set of iconographic conventions. If we take the male gods as our starting-point, it is
Pārvatī (also known as Umā and Gaurī, 'white') who is most closely parallel to
Sarasvatī and Lakṣmī, since from the Śaiva point of view it is she (or alternatively,
this aspect of the Goddess) who is usually thought of as the wife of Śiva, the third of
the *trimūrti* (*see* I.2, p. 192). The mythology of Pārvatī and Śiva is rich and suggestive;
some episodes are treated in detail in the sections which follow. In general, Pārvatī is
represented as attempting, sometimes successfully, to tame her husband's wild
excesses of fury or asceticism; she stands for 'normal' values and the married state of
the householder, in opposition to behaviour which transgresses social norms.

The natures of both Durgā and Kālī are so different from this that at first it is hard to see why they should be considered in any way identical with Pārvatī. While Pārvatī is usually depicted as a docile wife next to her husband, smaller in stature than he and equipped with only two arms in contrast with his four, Durgā is rarely shown with a consort; she is seated on a lion or a tiger, and her arms are eight or even sixteen in number, each holding a weapon. The principal myth told about her, though not exclusively associated with her name, narrates her destruction of the buffalo demon, an evil being who could be killed only by a woman (*see* III.7, fig. 20). She is presented as fierce and terrifying, but in a just cause. More ambivalent is Kālī, who is often explained as an emanation of either Pārvatī or Durgā, a personification of the other goddess's anger. Her aggression is often thought of as directed not only against demons, but indiscriminately against the whole world, including humanity. She is shown as naked, emaciated, with her tongue protruding to drink blood and garlanded with human heads; but myths also relate how her fury may eventually be soothed by an appeal to her maternal instincts, and like Durgā, Kālī has often been worshipped as the Divine Mother, especially in Bengal.

II.2 '*Śakti*': Gender and Power

Since myth does not exist in a pure form, devoid of theological speculation (*see* I.2, p. 191), it is clear that mythological traditions about female deities will not only have a bearing on perceptions of their human counterparts – a largely unconscious feature of mythology – but also have often been quite consciously designed or remodelled to reflect particular ideas on sexual polarity as a metaphor in talking about the divine. Thus the changing emphasis on each partner in the relationship, for instance, of Śiva and Pārvatī/Kālī/the Goddess, is partly an unconscious reflection of deeply held views on the relationship of the sexes, but it is also the result of conscious thought on the nature of the divine. Of course, the metaphorical terms in which that thought is mythically expressed reflect perceptions of gender norms (by their negation as often as by their affirmation), but in order to approach the myths it is necessary to understand something of the various theoretical frameworks.

The clearest example will be the case of the allomorphs – personal and abstract – of Pārvatī, whose frequent identification as one aspect of the being known simply as the Goddess (Devī, *cf.* I.2, p. 193) gives some clue as to the fluid boundaries of personality and representation in this area. When named as Pārvatī, she is often a subordinate, though necessarily important, figure in Śaiva myth and thought. Śiva is self-born and undying; Pārvatī is subject to the indignities of birth and death, having previously been Satī, Śiva's first wife, and following her suicide in that incarnation being born again as the daughter of the personified Himalayan mountain. In the *Purāṇas* it is Śiva who expounds abstract theological systems and practical details of worship, while Pārvatī, the preceptor's loyal disciple, asks questions. Sometimes her attention wanders, and there are many variations on the story whereby Śiva in irritation curses her to be born on earth to atone for her lack of concentration. She shows other human weaknesses, too: fits of pique, jealousy and a desire for children, in which Śiva, the great *yogi*, has no interest. She behaves as a human female is expected to behave (*see* III.4, p. 209).

But Pārvatī is not of course a human female. One sign of this is the iconographic representation in which half of her body is joined to half of Śiva's, in the form known as *ardhanārīśvara*, the Lord who is half woman. Here too she is to some extent subordinated (hers is the left side, the less prestigious place of the wife, and there is no question of calling the form 'the Goddess who is half man'), but an essential identity is none the less affirmed. That Pārvatī and Śiva together represent the two inseparable aspects of reality is a very common line of thought, whose ramifications extend beyond the personal. Śiva is seen as undifferentiated, inactive Existence, corresponding to his mythic persona as the meditating *yogi*; Pārvatī, or rather in such abstract schemes simply the Goddess, is the principle of action, of differentiation, and as such is known as *śakti*, power (from root *śak*, to be able). 'If Śiva is joined with *śakti*, he is able (*śaktaḥ*) to create; if not, the god is not capable even of movement': these are the opening words of the *Saundaryalaharī* ('Wave of Beauty'), a hymn to the Goddess attributed to the philosopher Śankara and composed in south India between about 800 and 1400 CE.

The world as we experience it, then, is caused by *śakti*, that is by the Goddess, a contrast with the male-oriented Vedic myths of creation, although since it is essentially an explanation on a different plane it is not necessarily incompatible with them. *Śakti* being abstract while Śiva is personal (though a neuter form *śivam* is sometimes used), it may be thought of as a quality or possession of Śiva, 'his' *śakti*, and this concept is sometimes extended to the other male gods, so that each is equipped with a personal *śakti*, often identified with his consort. But the relationship may also be seen as more strictly symmetrical, so that Śiva may as well be an aspect of *śakti* as *śakti* of Śiva. In either case, it would be a mistake to suppose that the abstract and personal conceptions of *śakti* are mutually exclusive. Even when *śakti* is subdivided into various abstract types of power these subdivisions may have a personal aspect: thus the two wives of Murugan (the Tamil form of Skanda/Kārttikeya) are often explained as the *śaktis* of knowledge and of action.

The Goddess as *śakti* is closely related to the Goddess as *māyā*, a term difficult to translate, but which like *śakti* relates to the perception of the world as differentiated. *Māyā* may be that which conceals the truth that all existence is one, or that the self is not the body and mind (hence it is often rendered as 'illusion'), but depending on the philosophical standpoint adopted may also indicate actual existence in a differentiated world. Feminine connotations are not inevitable; when Krishna in the *Bhagavad-gītā* (7.14–15, 18.61) speaks of his *māyā* veiling the truth from the wicked, or causing the motion of the universe, there are no such implications. In some systems it denotes the stuff of material objects, a concept more frequently expressed by the word *prakṛti*, 'material', 'nature', a word whose full meaning emerges only in connexion with its pair and opposite, *puruṣa*. Like the historical uses of the English word 'man', *puruṣa* denotes both 'male' and 'person', and the more abstract apprehension of the *puruṣa/prakṛti* duality makes the pair roughly equivalent to spirit and matter. Inevitably, however, they also become understood as principles standing in a close relation to, perhaps metaphorically represented by, the female and male aspects of God (or Existence) and thus have some correspondence with Śiva and śakti.

Some philosophical systems hold that the two principles are ultimately one, and most accord them some sort of equality. None the less, it is clear that from standpoints which put a high value on the realization (in either sense) of the One, the principles of śakti and particularly māyā and prakṛti will carry a negative valuation as disrupters of the essential unity. They can all be seen as phenomena which disrupt or symbolically oppose spiritual progress, and to some extent their appearance as female reflects the stereotyping of women as obstacles in man's spiritual path. But we should not make too much of this. Śakti, māyā and prakṛti are after all essential in enabling us to live in this world. When a contemporary devotional song addresses the Goddess as 'primal śakti, primal māyā', it is following an old tradition of praise, and clearly intends to add to our appreciation of her greatness and beneficence.

Praises of this sort lead us through a continuum to the point where the 'female principle', or the Goddess, is recognized as supreme; where ultimate reality is in some sense apprehended as female. Such positions sometimes move the emphasis from the relationship with the male, and prefer to concentrate on the Goddess as integrating the different facets of the goddesses of myth; thus she may be called Mahā (great)-kālī, Mahālakṣmī and Mahāsarasvatī, echoing the trimūrti of male gods (see I.2, p. 192). But since the exaltation of the Goddess must lay a heavy and positive emphasis on the principle of activity, it may by contrast give a somewhat negative evaluation to the 'inert', identified as male. This idea is given iconographic expression in the common depiction of Kālī trampling the body of Śiva:

> You battle-dance on Shiva's heart,
> A garland of heads that bounce off
> Your heavy hips, chopped-off hands
> For a belt, the bodies of infants
> For earrings . . .
> . . . those feet
> Whose beauty is only deepened by blood.
>
> (RĀMPRASĀD SEN, TRANS. NATHAN AND SEELY, NO. 58)

Here the relationship of Śiva and Pārvatī has been reversed, so that now it is the female partner with four arms, indicating power and divinity, the male with two. Kālī's posture obviously indicates superiority, yet in this image she appears not as the dominant lover (though we do occasionally encounter the 'inverse' – woman on top – sexual union of Kālī and Śiva), but as the conqueror, and perhaps destroyer, for in our version the body is clearly intended to be a corpse, laid on its pyre in the cremation ground. Yet there are gentler aspects. Kālī's lower right hand, though it ends in bloody talons, makes the gesture of dispelling fear. Her feet symbolize not only conquest, but mercy and protection; her right foot rests over Śiva's heart, so that the picture could be taken to represent the complete surrender of the devotee to God and his consequent protection. This too is a reversal of the Śiva – Pārvatī

Fig. 19 Kālī on the corpse of Śiva, Kangra School, c. 1800.
In the collection of Mr and Mrs John Gilmore Ford

relationship, where it is Pārvatī who is sometimes seen as the paradigm of the worshipper. Finally, though the detail is not present in all versions, the corpse is ithyphallic. Whether this is to be interpreted in the 'natural' sense or whether, as normally with Śiva, the erect phallus indicates not arousal but the ascetic control of seed, it is clearly unexpected in a corpse. A popular saying is that *without* the Goddess, Śiva is only a corpse (*śava*), so that at first sight it seems puzzling to depict him as a corpse in her presence. The erect phallus may indicate that Kālī is to be thought of as the reviver as well as the destroyer, and this is perhaps confirmed by an unusual version which seems to show a renewed Śiva rising up from the dead body. Thus the image holds in balance horrifying and more gentle elements; what is unambiguous is that Kālī is in control.

Advocates of the Goddess's supremacy have felt the need to explain how it is that some myths seem to express a different relationship, so that beside the dominant Kālī and often identified with her we find the (more or less) submissive Pārvatī. A favoured approach to this problem invokes the concept of *līlā* – sport, play – which is prominent in other theological contexts also. God cannot be subject to necessity; therefore the phenomenal world can best be explained as a divine game. *Līlā* can also be used to explain the apparent humiliation of deities, as for instance the incarnations of Vishnu. Applied to the Goddess, then, this view holds that the supreme Devī of her own will, for the purpose of play, submits to a form of existence on a lower plane. Like Vishnu-Krishna, she takes birth from a human womb, as Satī, and from a minor divinity as Pārvatī. Like Krishna's, her childhood shows characteristics both of the Supreme Reality and of a normal, naughty child: Rāmprasād Sen imagines the infant Pārvatī in a tantrum demanding the moon, then being comforted when she is shown her own face 'shaming a million moons' in a mirror (Nathan and Seely, 1982, no. 30). And it is part of the same play when first Satī and then Pārvatī become wife, and so conventionally a lesser partner, to Śiva. The Goddess herself has, for reasons of her own, willed these events, but her ultimate supremacy remains.

A less theologically sophisticated but more truly 'mythological' explanation current at village level in many parts of south India uses a temporal sequence to account for the anomaly. In the beginning of this age was the Goddess, variously named, who laid an egg from which emerged Brahmā, Vishnu and Śiva. She desired to have sex with them but they refused on the grounds that such an act would be incestuous. Eventually Śiva agreed on condition that the Goddess would give him her third eye. She complied, and with the eye lost her power. (Compare the connexion of virginity and chastity with power, III.1–2.) This myth, with its variants, explores not only the tension between male and female deities, between male and female sexuality and power, but also that between the village goddesses, with their localized, vernacular names (Ellamman, Māriyamman, etc.) and the gods of the 'Great Tradition', those familiar from Sanskrit texts and known across all India. It equates the divine feminine with what is perceived as lesser, as lower in the hierarchy even though once supreme, at the same time as it acknowledges the inferiority of the village milieu from which it springs – for the villagers continue to worship the defeated goddess. Such an equation is of course far from universal; in many contexts, the Goddess is eminently 'respectable', even when not paired with a male god in a decent, normal marriage. It is nonetheless interesting as an indicator of the problems which occur when the Goddess is worshipped as supreme. Female supremacy runs counter to established norms: is the divine to mirror such norms, or is it to be apprehended as essentially other?

III MYTHICAL THEMES CONCERNED WITH WOMEN

III.1 Virginity and Power

Marriage and parenthood are the social norms defined for both women and men, and in ordinary life a prolongation of a girl's unmarried state would be undesirable. In divine myth, however, virginity sometimes has positive connotations: the virgin has greater power, certainly greater aggressive power, than the married woman. Frequently, mythological explorations of the theme express a tension between the desirability of this power and the fulfilment of the expected female destiny. One example is the story of the goddess Mīnākṣī, chief dedicatee of the great temple of Madurai in Tamilnadu, and often regarded as a form of Pārvatī, who is born as the daughter of the local Pāṇḍyan king. A prophecy declares that her distinctive feature, a third breast, will vanish when she meets the man who is to be her husband. Meanwhile, the virgin princess pursues a career as an invincible fighter, conquering all the enemies she encounters. But when in her northward progress she comes to the Himalayas and meets Śiva, the (unfeminine? hyperfeminine?) third breast vanishes, as does her belligerence; she is transformed into a shy and modest young girl, the epitome of the proper bride.

Here the usual values win out, though Mīnākṣī remains a powerful deity even when worshipped together with her husband; in fact, in terms of cult she seems to occupy the superior position.

The alternative possibility is exemplified by the eponymous goddess of Kanyā-kumārī (Cape Comorin, the southernmost point of India), whose name means 'virgin girl'. This goddess, as often in the most widespread myth of Devī (*see* III.7, p. 215), is expressly created in order to destroy demons. When her task is completed, she desires to marry Śiva, and he her, but the 'establishment' of gods and sages, fearful of a resurgence of demonic power, wishes to prevent the marriage so that she might retain her full powers as a virgin. The hour of the marriage is fixed for midnight, but while the bridegroom's party is still on its way, the troublesome sage Nārada imitates the cock's crow so that Śiva and his retinue assume the auspicious moment has passed, and turn back. When the goddess realizes what has happened, she curses the food prepared for the wedding banquet to become rocks and seashells – but the gods have accomplished their purpose. Reflecting the myth, Kanyākumārī, unlike Mīnākṣī, is worshipped alone in her temple (though there are traces of a connexion with the Śiva temple at nearby Sucindram), yet her image evokes neither the attack on demons nor anger at her frustrated purpose of marriage: rather, she is shown as a gentle and demure bride, perpetually waiting for the arrival of her husband.

It is often suggested that the connexion between a woman's virginity and her power is strictly analogous to the idea, well attested in myth and in practice, that male power is preserved or increased by the 'retention of seed'. But, at first sight, it seems that there is an obvious discrepancy between the two: the man does not have to be a virgin, but may begin his ascetic practice at any time, while the woman's powers, it is implied, may be extinguished once and for all by the intervention of a man. Yet, if we look more closely at the connotations of virginity, the contrast is not so stark as it first appears. Virginity in this context is a social, not a biological, phenomenon: the non-virgin is not the 'maid no more' of English folk-song, who is forever changed by one experience, but a married woman for whom sex, childbearing and caring for a husband are normal life. On one level, then, it is only the woman who rejects woman's normal experience who can be powerful, just as only the man who refuses to procreate and rejects the status of 'householder' attains power and spiritual eminence. This social perception has its physical corollary in the idea of abstention from sex.

III.2 The Chaste Wife

But the married woman is not cut off entirely from unusual powers, although she does not seem to use them for aggressive, 'masculine' purposes as does the virgin. The virgin Pārvatī wins Śiva through her austerities, but after her marriage she performs austerities once more when, affronted by her husband's joking comments on her dark complexion, she disappears in order to lead an ascetic life, and so succeeds in her aim of acquiring a fair skin. This suggests a model whereby, for women as well as men, temporary abstention from sex is only one ingredient in an ascetic programme which eventually conveys power on its practitioners, whether indirectly — in the shape of a boon from the gods — or directly. Today, outside myth, many women speak of gaining *śakti* from fasting and other austere practices.

But more often married women gain power simply through their chastity, and this power may be deployed to benefit both themselves and their husbands. When the captive Sītā is told, untruthfully, that her husband Rāma is dead, she wonders if she could have been momentarily unfaithful to him in thought, perhaps in a previous life. To be effective in this way, chastity must be unwavering, even in the mind. In Sītā's case, the point is proved when after her rescue she is put to a public test, and the power of her chastity enables her to emerge from a blazing fire unscathed. The counter-example to Sītā is Renukā, a sage's wife whose purity allows her to perform miraculous tasks such as carrying water without a pitcher; one day her thoughts stray, and she loses her powers. The consequences are dire as the sage now suspects his wife and orders their son (Paraśurāma, often reckoned as an incarnation of Vishnu) to behead her, which he does. Although in most versions Renukā is restored to life, usually through Paraśurāma's intercession, we are made aware that powers of this sort pose a potential danger to the women who possess them.

The general motif is found in a number of more local myths, of which a south Indian story may be taken as representative: Anasūyā, wife of another sage, is visited by Brahmā, Vishnu and Śiva in the guise of religious mendicants (whom it is an obligation to feed). She offers them hospitality, but they look at her lustfully and declare that they will only eat if she first takes off her clothes. As her chastity is flawless, she acquires miraculous powers when she thinks of her husband, and this gives her a way out of the dilemma: she wishes that her divine visitors should become babies, and only after this transformation complies with their request. Thus chastity is its own defence — another potentially dangerous assumption.

III.3 Choosing a Husband

A goddess who is thought of as independent may choose not to marry. Thus, in some versions, the Devī (or Durgā) refuses the amatory advances of the buffalo demon, while a village goddess declares 'I am happy without a spouse.' But this behaviour serves to highlight what is normal, and a human woman, or a goddess who has accepted some of the conditions of human existence, must submit to the constraints of society. In modern India, the 'arranged marriage' is seen as the norm, but the myths have little trace of a system whereby two sets of relatives get together and negotiate a marriage settlement. Far more prominent are story-types in which the couple themselves are able first in some way to express a personal interest in each other. The same is true of classical Sanskrit poetry, of vernacular lyrics and of modern films: none of these cases need reflect a widespread social reality.

One type of story is quite close to the familiar, 'romantic', European model. A chaste romance dawns between the couple, then the male partner asks the woman's father (formally: in practical terms, usually both parents) for his consent to the marriage. Thus, in one of the earliest episodes of the *Mahābhārata*, King Śantanu falls in love with the ferry-woman Satyavatī, and at her bidding asks her father for her hand in marriage. Problems arise at this point: the father agrees, but only on condition that her sons will succeed to Śantanu's kingdom. Since he already has a son, Bhīṣma, by a previous marriage, Śantanu is in some difficulty, until the way is eased by Bhīṣma's voluntarily taking a vow of celibacy in order to avoid any future threat to the throne from an alternative line. All of this is clearly in Satyavatī's own interest, but that interest is subsumed in the glory of her patrilineage.

One of the primary concerns of epic is precisely the establishment of genealogies – not a primary concern of divine marriages. Thus, when Pārvatī marries Śiva the bargains are struck at a purely personal level. It is true that the gods wish the union to come about so that a son born of these two may be powerful enough to dispose of a particularly troublesome demon, but Pārvatī herself is attracted to Śiva for purely romantic/devotional reasons: she loves him (from a distance) both as a woman loves a man, and as a devotee loves God. The gods' desire for the marriage contrasts with their role in the Kanyākumārī story (*see* III.1, p. 204), where it is the woman and not her son who will destroy the demons, and so does the attitude of one of the protagonists: Śiva will have nothing to do with sex after the death of his first wife Satī, Pārvatī's earlier incarnation. When Kāma, desire personified, attempts to fill him with lust for Pārvatī, Śiva burns him up, and will only deign to notice his would-be bride when she uses his own preferred methods to attract him, performing the most austere penances. He then tests her resolve in person, and finally appears to her as her future husband. The union of God and Goddess, often given a heavily symbolic value, is accomplished in potentiality without any reference to externals, but social conventions must still be carried through, if only to demonstrate how the divine transcends them. The romantic basis of the union established, parental consent is sought. Pārvatī's father, the Mountain, in consultation with her mother Menā ('Woman'), agrees to the marriage, and though many versions stress the reluctance of the parents to bestow their daughter on a person of no lineage and no apparent wealth, with a predilection for snakes and cremation-grounds, the marriage is celebrated with great pomp and with all due rites. The events leading up to Pārvatī's marriage reflect her ambiguous position as the supreme Goddess who has consented to take birth as part of a quasi-human society.

The second type of marriage story gives the woman the choice of husband not only *de facto* but by institutionalized right. Sāvitrī, famous for her wifely devotion (*see* III.4, p. 208), was sent off by her father with an escorting party to find a worthy husband. More usually, would-be husbands came *en masse* to the palace where a princess was ready to be married. Then, at a ceremony known as *svayaṃvara*, 'own choice', the princess garlanded the man she chose. Elements of a different folk-tale form of decision-making, the contest for the bride's hand, enter one of the best-known examples, the *svayaṃvara* of Draupadī in the *Mahābhārata*, and they predominate in that of Sītā in the *Rāmāyaṇa*. In both these episodes, each of crucial importance within the narrative of the epic, the hero (Arjuna and Rāma respectively) first proves his prowess by defeating the other suitors in a contest of manly skills, then takes home his bride. While from the story-telling point of view this presents no problem, since any fictional princess would obviously select the most outstanding of the competitors, there are clearly difficulties in using such episodes as evidence for real, historical procedure, where two methods of choice might well prove to be in conflict. Certainly we should be cautious about using the *svayaṃvara* as evidence of supposed 'freedom' accorded to women in early India. Although it does not appear as one of the canonical eight forms of marriage, a real custom may underlie the mythical motif, but if so it was probably confined to girls of the warrior/ruler caste, and even among this group it is easy to see how it could have been a formality, pressure being put on the girl to comply with her father's wishes.

III.4 Married Life: Goddesses and Women as Wives

'If he was a rich man, he must have had many wives' is a passing dictum of the king in Kālidāsa's play *Śakuntalā*, and though the play itself tells of the love between Śakuntalā and the king, the heroine is only one among his many wives. Polygyny is also common, though not universal, among the kings and nobles of epic. Of the kings of Hastināpura, whose story is told in the *Mahābhārata*, Śantanu takes a second wife only when his first wife Gaṅgā has left him and assumed once more her riverine shape; in the next generation, three wives are won for Vicitravīrya; in the next generation again, Pāṇḍu has two wives while his brother Dhṛtarāṣṭra has only one. In the *Rāmāyaṇa*, King Daśaratha has three wives, but his son, Rāma, has one, around whose abduction and recovery the whole epic centres. Rāma's monogamy is important, because very often Rāma (more than the polygamous Krishna, whose career is said to transcend ordinary morality) is seen as the model for a perfect life, conforming to duty in every respect. This does not affect what is expected of the woman, the ideal for whom is devotion and submission to her husband whether she is unique or one of several, but it brings her a little closer to parity.

On the divine level, too, we find models of both monogamy and polygamy, clearly influenced both by the practice of epic (and to some extent human reality), and by more abstract ideas on the relationship of male and female (*see* Section II, pp. 199–203). We have seen that Vishnu may be shown with two wives, Śrī and Bhū, or with only one (Śrī-) Lakṣmī; the latter gradually gains the upper hand, but never completely eclipses the other form. Śiva's is more clearly a monogamous marriage, at least in terms of cult representations; there is a persistent tradition, however, representing Gaṅgā, the river running from his hair, as a junior wife or lover, causing jealousy in Pārvatī. This view is of course ignored when Śiva and Pārvatī are linked with the complementarity of *puruṣa* and *prakṛti*, a link which naturally favours a monogamous marriage.

The third possibility, polyandry, is scarcely found among the gods; a goddess shows her superiority not by amassing husbands but by spurning males altogether. There is one Vedic example in the case of Sūryā, the daughter of the Sun who marries both the Aśvins. This is not so much a status indicator for her as a statement that the twin brothers are so close as to share everything, and the same is true of the well-known human case of Draupadī, wife of all five Pāṇḍava brothers. Fraternal polyandry, then, is not a real parallel to polygyny, where a measure of choice rests with the polygamous partner. It has in fact been practised among some communities in Kerala and in the foothills of the Himalayas, in neither case part of the world of the epic's originators: Draupadī's marriage enters the epic from outside the 'normal' world, and is not a usual option in the social system, though the *Mahābhārata* text knows of other examples. The abnormality is clear from the circumstances in which it comes about; Arjuna wins his bride in a competitive *svayaṃvara*, and when on the brothers' return home they tell their mother Kuntī he has 'received alms' she bids him share the gift between them all. There is horror all round, and on learning the true circumstances Kuntī attempts to retract her advice – but a mother's word is sacred. Her peculiar marriage none the less exposes Draupadī to unpleasant taunts from her husbands' enemies.

Whatever the number of partners in a marriage, the ideal for a wife is one of devotion and docility – but myths do not always present ideals. Certainly, some mythical characters appear to conform: Satī, Sāvitrī and Sītā are names often joined together and used to praise wifely devotion, or – more frequently – to disparage wifely submissiveness. But their stories are more complex than this proverbial usage would lead us to expect. Satī, Śiva's first wife, who was an earlier incarnation of his second, burns herself to death when her father insults her husband; thus although her name means simply 'good', there is a connexion with the 'satī' wife who commits, in the anglicized form, 'suttee' on her husband's death. Yet her death does not follow on that of her husband, and is in fact a consequence of her flouting Śiva's wishes, since he tries to persuade her not to attend the sacrifice from which he has been deliberately excluded. Sāvitrī, an unambiguously human woman, is celebrated for her devotion to her husband with whom she endures poverty and whom she saves from death, yet hers is the active role in the story: it is her persistence and resourcefulness in following and (sometimes) tricking Death which enables Satyavān to recover his life.

This story recalls the miraculous powers attributed to women who excel in chastity, the wife's virtue *par excellence* (*see* III.2, p. 205). Sītā is perhaps the most passive of the three, but even she places wifely devotion above wifely submission when she insists, against Rāma's wishes, on following him into exile. In the final book of the *Rāmāyaṇa* she makes what seems to be a defiant gesture when, forced to prove her chastity for a second time, she causes herself to be swallowed up by her mother Earth and to be lost to Rāma for ever. All three characters, then, although their lives are clearly centred on their husbands, exemplify chastity, loyalty and devotion, at least as much as obedience and receptivity, and at least in the case of the first two their roles are active rather than passive.

But on other occasions the behaviour of wives may be presented as much less praiseworthy; ideals and expectations generate different sets of stereotypes. In particular, it is expected that there will be jealousy and quarrelling among co-wives, divine or human. Pārvatī's reaction to Gangā has already been mentioned; similarly, popular Tamil sources recount the quarrels between Devānai (Devasenā) and Valli, the two wives of Murugan. In both cases, the jealousy is compounded by social distinctions, as the senior or legitimate wife feels her own place is being usurped by a low-caste upstart. This certainly corresponds with a not infrequent extra-mythological situation. Human co-wives also fall out; there is constant friction between Rukminī and Satyabhāmā not to mention the rest of Krishna's sixteen thousand wives. When they grow older, wives work out their rivalries through their sons; thus in the *Rāmāyaṇa*, Daśaratha's youngest wife Kaikeyī, ambitious for her son Bharata, tricks her husband and engineers the exile of her stepson, the rightful successor, Rāma. This, we are shown, is an aberration from her normal nature; in the ideal city of Ayodhyā, co-wives and their children should live together peaceably. The same, of course, would be true of relations between the wife and her husband's family, crucially important where a patrilocal joint family is the norm, but although such relations are frequently explored in localized folk-tales, 'women's problems' in general feature little in the main line of the epic, which by and large is not concerned with women's feelings except where they have repercussions on the male-dominated story-line.

However, neither relatives nor co-wives are necessary for marital disagreement: the possible presence of Gangā as a rival is by no means always invoked as a reason for the quarrels of Pārvatī and Śiva. This relationship does not deal with marriage as the concern of a group or joint family, neither does Pārvatī represent the role and status of being a wife; largely, it reflects a more personal concept of marriage as between two individuals, in which an unquestioned basic loyalty is inevitably punctuated by disagreements. It surely indicates a fundamentally male perception that it is Pārvatī who is presented as the instigator of most of these quarrels — though many would say she has ample provocation. She is jealous, rightly or wrongly, of Gangā; she takes offence when Śiva teases her for her dark complexion, and withdraws in high dudgeon; or she resents her husband's long absences practising asceticism and fails to understand his lack of interest in procreation. The ideal wife should complain at none of these things. Yet, while on one level these difficulties reflect a view of the imperfections of women's behaviour, this does not prevent Śiva and Pārvatī from being regarded as the ideal exemplar of marital love, both erotic and affective. Classical Indian aesthetic theory regards quarrels, jealousy and the like as subordinate parts of the dominating emotion ('flavour') of love, all or most of which will be contained in a complete poetic description, and temporary disharmony between lovers is widely regarded as a stimulus to greater love. In this light, the quarrels and separations of Pārvatī and Śiva should be seen not as lessening their love but increasing it and rendering it complete. Exactly the same is true of the relationship between Rādhā and Krishna, to which we now turn.

III.5 Illicit Love: Rādhā, the Gopīs and Krishna

Neither men nor women are encouraged towards extramarital sex by traditional morality, but as in many societies it is the transgressing woman who in practice is more severely condemned. If myths were simply paradigms of societal norms, then we should expect the adulterous woman to be exemplarily punished; we certainly would not expect to find her celebrated. The case of Rādhā and her fellow 'milkmaids' (*gopīs*) is perhaps unique. Krishna's youth is spent in a village, among farmers and cowherds; he is so attractive that all the women fall in love with him and desire him — sometimes attaining him, though only temporarily — for their lover. But the climax of their love is seen not as sexual union, but a dance in which Krishna replicates himself so that to each *gopī* he appears to be dancing with her alone; this is usually given a mystical significance. Among the *gopīs* is Rādhā, who after a relatively late appearance in the story rapidly becomes the best beloved and most important of the group. Not only in story, but in ritual and devotion, she is represented as Krishna's consort probably more frequently than any other woman. Yet, despite some attempts to make her Krishna's lawful wife, it is awkward for a cowherd who is really a prince to marry a milkmaid who is really a milkmaid, and the majority view has always been not only that she and Krishna were not married but that she 'belongs to another'. Krishna's behaviour is usually explained in terms of God transcending ordinary morality; Rādhā, who is more usually regarded as human than divine, becomes the paradigm for the devotee who risks everything in the quest for God as lover. The metaphor is a moving one, but it implies a model of gender relations in which the female is the lower, the natural servant of the higher male. When this is consciously realized, it tends to become less appealing, and it is scarcely surprising that in the present century Rādhā as an élite literary figure has lost much of the tremendous popularity which she once enjoyed. On the popular, devotional level she continues to be important.

Rādhā's erstwhile popularity was not of course entirely due to religious sentiment. The heroine who braves disgrace and danger to meet her lover was a favourite theme in court poetry and painting, and the ease with which in the visual arts Rādhā and Krishna merge into ordinary human lovers — even endowed with the features of the artist's patron and his current favourite — suggests that the theme had an appeal other than the metaphorical. Often, it was treated as the paradigm of the earthly love affair, and all aspects of love were described under its heading, even quarrels and misunderstandings (*see also* III.4, p. 209), since Rādhā, though devoted, is by no means totally submissive. All the same, there are clear theological elements in much of this mythical corpus. Separated from Krishna, Rādhā pines for him so intensely that she actually becomes him, and having become Krishna s/he longs for

Rādhā. The favourite episode of the exchange of clothes between the two has similar implications for some kind of identity, which is easy to relate to the perception, fundamental to many Hindu schools of philosophy, that the individual soul or self (*ātman*) is ultimately identical with the divine (*brahman*). From this point of view, the subordination of Rādhā to Krishna begins to seem less central, and a number of episodes in fact show an apparent role reversal, where it is Rādhā who is the dominant partner: the love of God for the soul is no less self-giving than that of the soul for God. Thus the lovers defy the customary hierarchy which insists that the woman serve the man, as Krishna dusts down Rādhā's feet, or even tells her to place her feet on his head. Not only conventional morality, but the basic social norms expressed in gender relations are transgressed in this all-consuming love.

EXCURSUS: WOMAN AS DEVOTEE, DEVOTEE AS WOMAN

It is worth pausing here briefly to examine one aspect of the use of mythology for devotional purposes: the devotee's self-identification with the wife or lover of the (male) deity. As the consort is to the god in myth, so the devotee aims to be to the god in daily life. But the terms can be mixed; the myths themselves, with their frequent shifts between the personal, literal level and a more metaphysical plane, sometimes suggest an equivalence between consort and devotee. When Pārvatī practises asceticism to win Śiva, is her action 'only' to gain a husband, or does she desire union with God? The consort becomes devotee, while as consort she becomes the model for the ardent worshipper of a personal God. Both women and men may imagine themselves as Rādhā, for instance, patterning their relationship with a transcendental Krishna on hers with a Krishna both human and divine. The pattern requires of a man that he shed his male pride and sense of superiority, for as in traditional society man is to woman, so is God to man and woman without distinction. The woman poet-saint Mahādeviyakka speaks of 'the haughty Master/for whom men, all men/are but women, wives' (trans. A.K. Ramanujan, *Speaking of Siva*, 1973, p. 120).

As well as using the common stock of myths for their own purposes, devotees may also create their own personal mythology. Mahādevi, for instance, refers very little to the canon of Śaiva myth, but her God is a personal figure, now lover, now husband, and their relationship undergoes vicissitudes comparable with those of Rādhā and Krishna. Devotees create mythology in another sense, as the stories of their lives are early elaborated and become part of divine mythology, the dealings of God with his worshippers. In the case of women saints, two linked motifs stand out across regional and sectarian divisions – that of a literal and perceptible merging with the (male) god at the end of their lives, and/or a subsequent identification with the god's divine consort. According to the hagiographers, Mahādevi, Aṇḍal and Mīrā, all well-known poet-saints, were severally seen to disappear when they entered the temple, came to the inner sanctum, and approached the image of the beloved deity; various temples have also their own traditions recounting how a less well-known woman disappeared in this manner. Although often marriage and merging are seen as alternatives, here they seem to be equivalent. Aṇḍal went to the temple dressed as a bride, and she is worshipped today in many Tamil temples as Vishnu's consort, identified more or less closely with Śrī-Lakṣmī or Bhūdevī.

A variant dispenses with the temple setting and the physical merging altogether, and presents the woman simply as the god's bride. Thus a devotee of Śiva significantly called Gaurī (a name of Pārvatī) is married into a Vaiṣṇava family who treat her badly because of her religious allegiance. When they go to a wedding one day, leaving her behind, Śiva appears to her in person, first as an old brahmin, next as a young man and finally – when the in-laws return – as a baby. Suspicious and indignant, the mother-in-law throws Gaurī out of the house, whereupon the baby disappears and Śiva manifests himself and takes Gaurī to his heaven. In these stories, the devotee actually becomes what she wants and aims to be – the consort of God, and in some sense one with him. With her narrative identification as the Goddess, we have come full circle; if the *Purāṇas* often represent Pārvatī as Śiva's devotee, these stories represent the devotee as Pārvatī.

III.6 Motherhood

Although 'Mother' is one of the most frequent titles of the Goddess of cult, the goddesses of mythology are not conspicuous for parenthood; neither are the gods. A detail added to the myth of the birth of Skanda/Kārttikeya/Murugan seeks to explain this apparent omission. When the gods, impatient that a son be born, interrupt the lengthy love-making of Śiva and Pārvatī, Śiva spills his seed on getting up to meet them, and Pārvatī, furious at the loss of both pleasure and progeny, curses the gods to remain without issue. Thus – with a few exceptions – children are born to the gods only when they are born as human beings.

Pārvatī herself is the only goddess to act as mother in myth. When Śiva spills his seed, she is prevented from conceiving and the seed is incubated either in the river Gaṅgā, or in the six Pleiades (*Kṛttikās*), or both, eventually producing the six-headed Kārttikeya. But on seeing the child, Pārvatī accepts him as her own, and her breasts produce milk. Gaṇeśa is usually the son of Pārvatī's own body, though he too came into being in an unconventional way: bored and lonely during one of her husband's ascetic absences, Pārvatī forms a doll to keep her company, taking its substance from the oily scrapings of her body removed in the bath, then finds that it comes to life and acknowledges her as mother. Tension and jealousy between husband and son for the woman's regard is clearly indicated in what follows: when Śiva returns, Gaṇeśa has no way of recognizing him and attempts to stop him entering Pārvatī's apartments. Furious at the sight of an unknown male in his wife's company, Śiva decapitates the stranger, but on seeing Pārvatī's grief and hearing the truth, attempts to bring the boy back to life. For one reason or another, the only head which will fit the decapitated torso is that of an elephant – this is duly attached and Gaṇeśa is revived, Śiva now becoming his father. Father-son tensions of this type occasionally recur, however, when Gaṇeśa or both sons take their mother's part when the parents quarrel.

Further oedipal problems are explored in one mythical explanation for Gaṇeśa's failure to marry: when Pārvatī asks her son what sort of bride he would like, he replies, 'Someone like you,' whereupon she, outraged at the suggestion in his words, curses him never to marry at all. Stories of quarrels between the two brothers add to the picture of familial tensions projected onto a divine plane. But, at the same time, this 'holy family' is also the ideal of the family, as Śiva and Pārvatī are the ideal of married love (*see* III.4, p. 209); there are countless depictions, élite and popular, of the family together blessing their worshippers or engaged in happy and peaceful domestic pursuits.

Although motherhood is highly valued in Indian society, human women, like goddesses, seem to be more often presented in stories as wives than as mothers. A well-known maternal figure is Kuntī, mother of the Pāṇḍava princes, an important character in the *Mahābhārata*, revered and cherished by her sons; it is her command to them to 'share what you were given' which supplies the motive for the brothers' joint-marriage with Draupadī. Kuntī is physically mother to only three of the five Pāṇḍava princes, but just as Pārvatī 'counts' as mother of Kārttikeya, so in human society also it is the social rather than the biological role which is more valued. Thus, although the princess Devakī is remembered as Krishna's natural mother, it is the village woman Yaśodā, who brings him up, who is really conspicuous and beloved in the Krishna cycle. Stories of Krishna's childhood pranks, of Yaśodā's attempts to discipline her naughty son and her soft-heartedness towards him, are extremely popular, and like Rādhā, though to a lesser extent, Yaśodā forms a model for a certain style of Krishna devotion, in which the devotee envisages Krishna as her (seldom his) son. So vivid may this relationship become that in the case of the Keralite woman saint Kururamma, who had no children of her own, it was said that Krishna in child form actually lived in her house and performed household tasks for her.

But Kuntī and Yaśodā furnish examples of being *someone's* mother – someone male – not of being a mother *per se*. Despite the strange biology involved, Pārvatī is the only character whose own experiences of motherhood are thoroughly explored, and even she is a mother of sons only – the desired sex. Mother-daughter relations are given very little attention. Pārvatī's own mother Menā is introduced into myth largely from a Śaiva standpoint, so that her reaction may demonstrate the extent of Śiva's potential to shock. So firmly opposed is she to the marriage that she beats Pārvatī and threatens to kill her, in a useless attempt to break her resolve – hardly a harmonious depiction of this relationship. A markedly different version is found in the Bengali folk-tradition, where the most important Goddess festival celebrates the periodic return of Durgā/Pārvatī to her parental home, an event mirroring everyday life and mirrored in it at the festival; here Menā longs for the arrival of her daughter and pampers her for the duration of her stay. The Bengali Durgā is also the most significant exception to the mythological rule that mothers are mothers of sons only, for here she is mother not only of Gaṇeśa and Kārttikeya, but of two daughters as well, Lakṣmī and Sarasvatī – goddesses outside the strictly Śaiva circle which elsewhere defines her family. It is surely no accident that in Bengali myth-telling, Śiva is often treated as an irresponsible buffoon, while Durgā is always taken seriously and given the utmost love and respect. The picture has thus changed from one of 'Śiva's family' to one of Durgā as mother, whose universal maternity is more clearly expressed through the existence of daughters as well as sons.

Although few goddesses are mothers in myth, maternal qualities are commonly predicated of them (rather more frequently than paternal qualities of gods). But a second conspicuous characteristic of many goddesses is fierceness. How can these two be reconciled? Even those brought up as Hindus have at times felt the difficulty:

> She looked a dreadful cursing kind of Devi, anyway. The women sometimes called her 'Mother'! Imagine, I thought, having a mother like that, with a brass head and staring, frightful brassy eyes as well. No wonder all the women were scared of displeasing her.
>
> (*THE DARK HOLDS NO TERRORS*, 1990, P. 100)

The heroine of Shashi Deshpande's novel *The Dark Holds No Terrors* is perhaps particularly sensitive, since her own mother is depicted as harsh and unloving. But mythical explorations suggest that the difficulty is not an exclusively personal or modern one. The group of seven goddesses known as *Mātṛkās* or Mothers both protect and destroy children in popular belief; the two functions are separated in the story which narrates how they are sent by Indra to kill the child Kārttikeya, but on seeing him they are overcome with tenderness and (like Pārvatī) their breasts give forth milk. Fierceness, though not directed against children, and motherliness are also opposed when Kālī kills the demon Dāruka; her fury is not quenched after his death, and only begins to ease when she is confronted with two babies to suckle. Such stories could be interpreted as 'about' motherhood, tackling the mother's ambivalent feelings of combined tenderness and aggression towards her child; from the child's point of view, however, they contain an unsettling element. The *Devīmāhātmya* combines the two motifs more harmoniously and safely: the Goddess's fierceness is directed towards manifestations of evil, and she is beseeched to let her weapons 'protect us from harm as [a mother protects her] children' (11.27). She must be aggressive precisely *because* she is a mother.

Most modern devotional attitudes tend to soften the harsher aspects of the Goddess and concentrate on her as a loving mother. 'Mother' is one of the commonest titles of individual, specialized goddesses, and to refer to 'the Mother' is more or less equivalent to saying 'the Goddess'. This may connote simply reverence, just as holy women or simply elderly women are called 'mother'. But it is also the case that devotees of the Goddess very commonly place themselves in the relation of a child to its mother. While divinity conceptualized as male may suitably be viewed as husband or lover, under normal circumstances the sexual relationship is seen as too unequal for the divine partner to take the female role. Some texts, such as the *Saundaryalaharī*, describe the beauty of the Goddess in detailed and highly erotic terms, but it is an eroticism which is held at arm's length, its fulfilment confined to her relations with Śiva. The mother–child relationship, on the other hand, is that in which every person has experienced a woman as superior. And if from time to time the mother punishes the child, this is still to be seen in the context of her love for it: 'a bad child may be born, but a bad mother does not exist' says a well-known prayer.

III.7 Women as Aggressors: Competition with the Male

We have already seen how in the myth of Mīnākṣī the warrior-princess overcomes all enemies and attempts to conquer Śiva himself, but is instead subdued by him and becomes his bride. The taming or attempted taming of the goddess by a male god or demon is a recurrent theme, often with erotic associations. A widespread version is the dance contest between Kālī and Śiva: she challenges his power, and they agree to settle the issue by a comparison of their dancing abilities, which Śiva wins either by sheer power (the universe comes close to destruction as he dances) or by a trick (she must match his movements, but is too modest to imitate his high kicks). Kālī does not usually marry Śiva in consequence of her defeat, but worships him and loses her fierceness; she may also find a place beside him in the temple, her wildness controlled and restrained. This, of course, is not the end of the matter, since unlike Mīnākṣī Kālī is not normally envisaged as rendered docile; as we have seen, in one of her most popular images she dominates Śiva, trampling his inert body underfoot. Story and image express a dissonance.

A third goddess defeated and calmed by Śiva is Gaṅgā. In one version of her story she desires to bear Śiva's son, but is judged incapable by Brahmā, whereupon in resentment she declares she will make Śiva bow his head. Only then transformed into a river, and still located in the heavenly regions, she wishes to descend to earth with such violence that Śiva's bones will be crushed and mingle in fragments with her water – a destructive eroticism. Needless to say, Śiva catches her and sustains her in his hair, whence she descends, gentle and life-giving, to earth.

As a footnote to this group of myths we may mention the pertinent observation that the pattern of male taming female is not universal: in the case of Pārvatī, it is rather she who calms and quietens Śiva, although 'tame' would be rather too strong a word for a relationship in which Pārvatī is never overtly dominant.

On the whole, then, goddesses seem to lose out against gods, but it is a different matter when the male adversary is a demon. Stories of goddess against demon follow patterns comparable with those of goddess against god, the major difference being the outcome, and related cult acts may show an ambiguity in the male partner between adversary and husband, demon and god. The best-known of these myths is that of the contest of Durgā (or simply the Goddess, Devī) with the buffalo demon, Mahiṣāsura. This demon, who is invincible except by a woman, threatens the power of the gods, but the Goddess alone takes on his army, kills his two generals, and finally himself. (She may be formed for the purpose by the male gods, or she may already be in existence, but in either case she is exalted as the supreme repository of divine power.) In some versions, Mahiṣa proposes marriage to the Goddess, and wishfully interprets her threats of violence as allusions to the battle of love. But she subdues him with violence, not he her with marriage, and the gods are restored to their proper place.

In the *Devī-māhātmya* (5–10), this episode is followed by a similar struggle in which both demons and goddesses are multiplied. At the request of the gods, the Goddess appears from Pārvatī's body as Kauśikī, in order to counter the threats of the demons Śumbha and Niśumbha. Śumbha hears of the Goddess's beauty and

Fig. 20 Durgā killing the buffalo deamon (Mahiṣāsura), Hoysala period, from Karnataka. *Courtesy of the Board of Trustees of the Victoria and Albert Museum, London, IS 77–1965*

sends a messenger to propose marriage, but she replies that she has taken a vow to marry only one who can vanquish her in battle. Her words are full of irony as she regrets the necessity of keeping the 'foolish vow'. When an emissary is sent to bring her by force, she kills him, while the lion on which she rides disposes of his army; in the next round, Kālī appears from her angry face and kills two demonic henchmen. When Śumbha himself appears at the head of a vast army, the Goddess is joined by several *śaktis* (also referred to as Mothers), corresponding in form with the male deities from whom they issue. An eighth *śakti* comes from Devī herself; her relation to the male gods is seen when she orders Śiva to act as ambassador to the enemy camp. The impressive array of goddesses wreaks havoc amongst the enemy, until Śumbha accuses Devī of acting through the agency of others. But she, proclaiming 'I am One without a second', explains that Kālī and the Mothers are only her own powers, and draws them into herself. (This contrasts with the original emanation of the seven *śaktis* from male gods, and suggests that here the text wishes to express a 'truer' view, showing that the Goddess is a unity.) Then she faces Śumbha alone and kills him.

These stories, which can be multiplied almost indefinitely in popular and localized variants (even Sītā conforms to the pattern in one Tamil source and fights Rāvaṇa) are closely related to the 'power of virginity' theme: the goddess either rejects marriage in favour of killing her suitor/adversary, or she is forced to accept marriage (or an analogous subordinate status) because of her defeat. Although she is incomparably beautiful, she does not actively use her powers of sexual attraction to subdue her enemy, relying instead on the 'masculine' method of force. There is a linked group of stories where the situation is to some extent reversed and it is the male who wishes to avoid sexual contact, while the female uses her charms and wiles to overcome his ascetic resolve; thus frequently an *apsaras* (celestial nymph) interrupts the long austerities of a sage in order to seduce him. The 'woman as temptress' seems close to the western tradition, but there is the important difference that she is not always given an entirely negative valuation; sometimes it is necessary that an end be put to vigorous austerities, since they generate such power that they may threaten the world-order. Thus the earlier career of the demons Śumbha and Niśumbha includes an episode where they perform austerities for several thousand years in order to gain power; danger is warded off this time when the gods send two *apsarases* to seduce them. Another seductive vanquisher of demons is Mohinī ('delusive'), a feminine form of Vishnu; when gods and demons compete for the nectar of immortality, Mohinī distracts the demons by her charms and gives the nectar to the gods. Her subsequent career includes several such episodes, one of which reverses the motif of the imitative dance contest in which Kālī is vanquished by Śiva. The demon Bhasma has won the boon suggested by his name, that everything he touches will turn to ash. The danger is obvious, and Mohinī is dispatched to deal with him. She successfully beguiles him and promises to yield to him if he will first dance with her, imitating every gesture that she makes. When she places her hand on her head, the demon unthinkingly follows suit – with fatal consequences.

The deliberate use of seduction in order to destroy is rare in the case of goddesses and Goddess. Seduction is a natural weapon for the *apsaras*, whose main function in other contexts as well is to be sexually attractive, and when it is attributed to a divine figure it is to a deity normally thought of as male. Vishnu is saved from the indignity implicit in the role by our knowledge that this is not his 'real' form, that s/he is 'delusive'. Playing a part associated with a seductive potential which is feared but also to some extent despised need pose no threat to one for whom it is so necessarily *only* a part. In the case of the Goddess, the role-playing would be much less obvious, and she makes little deliberate use of such conventional ploys; demons have only themselves to blame if they think of sex when they see her.

III.8 Anger and Revenge

The anger of Devī and her associates (or parts of herself) towards their various enemies is closely connected with their virginal power and rejection of sex. But just as the chaste wife accumulates a power at least partly analogous to that of the virgin, so too the married woman's anger may have a destructive power of its own – in whatever direction it is unleashed.

One story-type common throughout south India supplies a foundation-myth for literally scores of local goddess cults. An untouchable man passes himself off as a brahmin in order to marry a brahmin girl. The deception is at first successful, and sometimes children are born of the union, but eventually the woman finds out her husband's secret and, furious at her degradation and pollution, kills both him and their children. The power of her anger then transforms her into a goddess (often, though not always, called Māriyamman), who then becomes established at the place where she is still worshipped. In other versions, the outraged wife first kills herself, then in goddess form kills her husband, or commands the villagers to kill him. Often, the manner of his death gives a clear aetiology for a buffalo sacrifice performed for the Goddess – an obvious link with the classical story of Devī/Durgā, and a demonstration of the interchangeable nature of demon and husband.

But the husband is not always adversary; the woman's anger may be directed against others, *on behalf of* her husband. The classic example is Satī (*see* III.4, p. 208), who burns herself to death in her fury at her father's insult to her husband. Her vengeance is thus indirect; on hearing of her suicide, Śiva in terrible grief and anger (since anger is not exclusive to women) destroys the sacrifice from which he has been excluded, along with its sponsor and the whole company of gods and human beings assembled there.

The woman's vengeance is direct in the Tamil epic *Śilappadikāram*, whose heroine Kannagi, having been portrayed as the ideal wife who puts up with her husband's infidelity without a murmur, is eventually confronted with his unjust execution by the Pāndya king. She proves his innocence too late, then in fury tears off her left breast, casts it before her, and thus sets the whole city of Madurai on fire. Having ensured its destruction, like the Māriyamman-type she becomes a goddess through the force of her anger, and several Goddess shrines in Tamilnadu and Kerala claim a connexion with Kannagi.

In the European tradition, we are more familiar with the converse situation: the motif of male anger and violence on behalf of a threatened or abused woman. This is not unknown in India; Rāma's recovery of Sītā and killing of her abductor is an obvious example. The *Mahābhārata*'s treatment of the theme is more complex. The eventual destruction of Duryodhana, his brothers and allies by the Pāndavas springs from a conflict originally motivated by considerations of political power, but given a special intensity by the shameful treatment of the Pāndavas' wife Draupadī by their rivals. But what is remarkable about the story is that Draupadi's own anger is quite as great as that of her husbands, and in her desire for revenge she plays a significant part in spurring them on to war. In many popular retellings of the epic, the finality of Duryodhana's defeat is signalled by an action of Draupadi's: since she was humiliated by being dragged by her hair into male company at the time of her monthly period, she swears never to wash and tie up her hair (signalling the end of menstrual impurity) until she washes it in the blood of Duryodhana himself.

The theme of women's anger is a remarkable one when we consider that traditionally women are taught from an early age to suppress feelings of dissatisfaction and to comply with authority, whether parental or marital. Clearly the mythical motif expresses some sort of awareness of the explosive potential of suppressed feelings, and it has been suggested that the greater the injustices suffered by women in any particular society, the more prominent the stories of angry women and fierce goddesses become. But these myths do not, traditionally, provide models for actual behaviour; the angry women become goddesses and so escape the constraints of social norms. Recently, a few attempts have been made to harness the tradition of the angry goddess for use as an instrument of social change, and thus we find emblematic names like that of the feminist publishing house, Kali for Women. Whether such uses will go further remains to be seen – consciously, most women would still rather pattern their behaviour on the model of Sītā and other dutiful and (largely) submissive wives. But the anger of the goddess perhaps serves as a reminder of what might be.

IV MINOR FIGURES

IV.1 Individual Goddesses

In one sense, Hinduism presents thousands of goddesses aside from the 'big names'; in another sense, these goddesses are often recognized as forms of one Goddess. At an intermediate level, several names with at least regional currency stand out. Among the fierce goddesses of the south, we have already encountered *Māriyamman* (*see* III.8, p. 218), whose myths relate to themes of anger, and whose special concern is often disease, which she can both cure and inflict. Similar, and similarly widespread is the goddess *Ellamman/Yellamma*, often identified with Renukā (III.2, p. 205); local myths relate that when the decapitated Renukā, a member of a brahmin family, was restored to life, her head and body were confused with those of an untouchable woman, so that the goddess Ellamman is half brahmin, half untouchable. The theme of caste confusion is basic to Māriyamman's story, too.

In the north, *Śītalā* ('cool') offers a parallel to the role of these goddesses in presiding over disease, since her function is very clearly defined as connected with fevers and skin eruptions; she is widely worshipped. Similarly popular, especially in Bengal, is *Manasā*, goddess of snakes, cause and cure of snakebite. She is sometimes said to be the daughter of Śiva by a human woman (though this type of liaison is somewhat anomalous for a 'post-Vedic' deity, and may indicate elements of the 'little tradition'); alternatively, she is the sister of the cosmic serpent Ādiśeṣa. Her best-known myth narrates the terrible troubles she inflicts on a wealthy man and his family until he agrees to worship her.

Quite different from these is the 'new' goddess *Santosī Mā(tā)*, 'Mother Contentment', a figure scarcely known before Independence but currently one of the most popular deities among urban women of the north. She is sometimes said to be the daughter of Gaṇeśa. An articulate worshipper is quoted as saying:

> She is . . . a twentieth century incarnation of the ancient Mother Goddess. Her worship is monopolized by women, young and old, who flock to her temples across the cities of India, to pray for socially sanctioned goals rooted in contemporary anxieties. I am among those women.
>
> (ANEES JUNG, *UNVEILING INDIA*, 1987, PP. 40–1)

Also beneficent, but of more ancient pedigree, are the river goddesses, of whom by far the most prominent is *Gangā*, the Ganges. We have seen her in myth as the wife of King Śantanu (*see* III.3, p. 206), and also as the lover of Śiva (*see* III.4, p. 208; III.7, p. 215); in connection with the latter role she is sometimes said to be the sister of Pārvatī. But her most important myth is the story of her descent from heaven to earth, mediated either by the foot of Vishnu or the hair of Śiva – this important figure must somehow be incorporated in the myths of the male deities. The descent is necessary so that the earth may benefit from Gangā's purifying and life-bestowing qualities, and today Gangā is worshipped both for this-worldly benefits such as crop fertility (not in general a very prominent concern of goddesses), and for the purifying quality of her water, as well as the release from worldly existence associated with the pilgrim places on her shores, such as Hardwar, Prayāg (Allahabad) and, especially, Banaras.

IV.2 Groups of Goddesses

Other goddesses exist only or mainly in groups; thus we find the Vedis, vaguely maternal '*Waters*' (*see Apaḥ*, I.1, p. 190) and the somewhat more ambivalent *Mātrkās* (*see* III.6, p. 214). (Sometimes the latter group has a leader, Ṣaṣṭhī, but more often she is an independent, though still ambivalent, goddess concerned with children.) Such groups are often rather ill-defined; the quite widespread *Sixty-four Yoginīs* (literally female yogis, in fact attendants on Devī) are precise in number, but their functions are variously reported, though they overlap to some extent with the *Mātrkās*. Much more clearly demarcated are the *Mahāvidyās*, explicitly conceived as fearful emanations of the Goddess; they are ten in number, and though lists vary slightly, each has an individual name and iconography.

IV.3 Other Types of Being

The race of monsters known as *rākṣasas* has (rather less conspicuous than the male) female members, *rākṣasīs*, of whom the best known is Rāvaṇa's hideous sister Śuparṇakhā whose contemptuous rejection by Rāma and Lakṣmaṇa partly motivates Rāvaṇa's abduction of Sītā (*see* I.3, p. 195). Pleasanter are *yakṣīs*, depicted apparently as tree-spirits, but also corresponding to the male *yakṣas*, guardians of wealth. There are also *nāginīs* (snakes, with a human upper part) beside male *nāgas*. But mythologically the most important group of non-divine, yet superhuman, female beings is the *apsarases*, originally closely associated with water but usually thought of as nymphs or 'heavenly courtesans', whose main function is to be sexually attractive and, where appropriate, available. Their home is Indra's heaven, where they delight the gods with their dancing; they are thus fit companions for the male *gandharvas*, the celestial musicians. Frequently, however, they descend to earth in order to tempt sages and ascetics, an enterprise undertaken with varying degrees of success (*see* III.7, p. 217).

But the best-known liaison between *apsaras* and mortal man, the story of Urvaśī and Purūravas, follows a different pattern. Purūravas is not an ascetic, but a king, who on a hunting expedition rescues the *apsaras* Urvaśī ('Desire') from the clutches of a *rākṣasa*. She agrees to marry and remain with him on condition that he will never let her see him naked, but after a while some *gandharvas*, wishing for Urvaśī's return, trick Purūravas into revealing himself unclothed. Her condition broken, Urvaśī departs, but after much searching the persistent Purūravas succeeds in finding her; they are able to meet for a day each year, and children are born. Eventually he persuades the *gandharvas* to allow him to become one of them, and the couple live happily ever after. Up to the point where Urvaśī leaves Purūravas, the story is a variant on the well-known theme of the man who marries a fairy or non-human being, but the happy ending is an Indian innovation, bringing the tale in line with many others which relate the trials, separation and eventual reunion of a married couple.

V. SOME CURRENT QUESTIONS

V.1 History Versus Structure: The Case of the Goddess

A fundamental question in the study of any human phenomenon asks whether concentration on historical development or on inherent structural patterning is the more useful analytical tool. The question comes into clear focus in the study of Hinduism in general and the Goddess in particular. As we have seen (*see* I.1, p. 190), significant Goddess worship is largely lacking in the Vedas. Inspired by this anomaly, and by parallels (more apparent than real) with Greece, nineteenth and early twentieth-century scholars constructed a picture of the Aryan invaders bringing their male pantheon to an India whose indigenous inhabitants worshipped chiefly goddesses. Sometimes, this polar confrontation was heavily loaded with cultural values: the Indo-European religion was healthy and straightforward, 'primitive' in a good sense, while the indigenous forms were probably morbid and full of darkly primitive – not to say female-dominated – elements. Yet if we attempt, so far as possible, to set aside value judgements, and if we make allowance for historical simplification, the goddesses of later Hinduism do seem more likely to have developed from the non-Aryan civilizations of the Indus valley and elsewhere than from the religion of the Vedas.

But is this really the sort of question we should be asking? Obviously, the hypothesis that the Goddess of Hinduism represents a survival of pre-Aryan elements, even if provable, is insufficient as a statement of her role and significance, and approaches which implicitly give this theory as the 'answer' to a 'problem' are flawed from the outset. A major and explicit challenge to the historicizing approach towards Hindu traditions was made by the anthropologist Louis Dumont (best known for his work on caste), who argued that Indian culture could not be explained as simply a juxtaposition of Aryan and pre-Aryan, but that rather its constituent elements have a necessary and structural relation one to another; they are part of a coherent whole. In the field of mythology, this lead has been taken up most thoroughly and explicitly by Madeleine Biardeau, who in an important preface to a collection of studies on the Goddess (*Autour de la Déesse hindoue*, Paris, 1981), expounds the view that the Goddess is the essential complement who both gives meaning to and receives it from the great male gods. And this is surely what a reasonably unprejudiced reading of the myths would lead us to suppose; whatever the historical origins of goddesses or Goddess, myths about them (or her), in their current context, have things to say about both religion and society as a whole.

Those things, however, may be more fluid and various than some structural analyses would have us believe. Biardeau's view that the Goddess is a mediator between sky and earth, pure and impure, is an interesting and valid insight, but as she herself recognizes, it cannot be the final word on the subject. Such a function is no *more* valid than the consciously perceived function of the Goddess not as mediator, but as one end of the *puruṣa/prakṛti* polarity (*see* II.2, p. 200). The relation of the Goddess with individual goddesses, with male gods, with human females in their different states, with human males, with demons – all these are factors whose varying importance in any given situation will produce a different pattern. In producing the elements which make up that pattern, historical developments will have been of overarching importance, but they do not provide the key to the formation of the pattern itself.

V.2 One Goddess or Many?

The author of the only modern full-length study of the collectivity of Hindu goddesses, David Kinsley, makes a strong plea for considering these goddesses individually, rather than as different facets of one Great Goddess, Mahādevī. He feels that they should receive the same treatment as do the male gods 'whose coherent mythologies and theologies are quite unrelated to an overarching great god' (Kinsley, 1986, p. 5). But his case has met with reservations from many scholars, and rightly so. It is a useful corrective to the view which seeks to identify every goddess willy-nilly with *the* Goddess, which certainly will not suffice for analytical purposes. At the same time, we must recognize that precisely that view has been influential in forming the Goddess tradition, from the Devī-Māhātmya to the present day. From a 'pure' mythological perspective, Kinsley's view would perhaps be the more constructive, but as we have seen there is no clear line between myth and other ways of talking about the divine. What we seem to have, then, is two simultaneous patterns of apprehension, whereby goddesses both are and are not differentiated from each other. Asked whether goddesses are different, almost all Hindu respondents would answer negatively. On the other hand, patterns of behaviour often suggest that at another level a difference is perceived. The anthropologist Ann Grodzins Gold, commenting on her experience in a Rajasthani village, remarks that the same person who, when asked about the difference between Lakṣmī and the local Dasa Mātā, replied, 'It's all one illusion [māyā]', was also an expert on the elaborate and differentiating ritual and stories of Dasa Mātā herself (Ann Grodzins Gold, *Fruitful Journeys: The Ways of Rajasthani Pilgrims*, 1988, p. 30).

Similar responses — 'God is one' — are often made including male deities, but the existence of early scheme such as the 'five/six paths' (*see* I.2, p. 194), where there is one goddess and several gods, suggest that syncretism of female deities has always been easier. Goddesses appear as parts or emanations of one great Goddess from the Devī-Māhātmya onwards, and the idea of a Goddess whose local, diversely named manifestations are fragments of a whole is given full mythical expression in the tradition that when Śiva, distraught at the death of Satī, picked up her body and began a wild, universe-threatening dance, Vishnu, in order to preserve the world, cut the corpse into pieces; the place where each piece fell became an important centre of Goddess worship.

But why should it be that the divine feminine is more easily perceived as unitary than the masculine? The answer may be that from a male-dominated perspective, to be female is in itself a sufficient divergence from the norm, without considering distinctions of individuality. If Vishnu and Śiva are distinguished by a whole series of polar opposites, the distinguishing feature of the Goddess is simply to be female. On an important level, this is a negative perception, but in evaluating it we should bear in mind that the (apparently) individual and differentiated itself often receives a negative valuation (*see* II.2, p. 200). Such differentiation, paradoxically, is frequently thought of as the function of the female-connoting *śakti*; the Goddess causes multiplicity, or its illusion, while at the deepest level herself remaining one. In the Hindu context, the syncretistic tendency can be seen as an affirmation of reality.

V.3 Female Sexuality

How should women's sexual activity and desires be estimated? Many societies have seen them in an extremely negative light, and it is frequently argued that the mythical contrast between the destructive powers of goddesses who are either solitary or equipped with subordinate male partners, and the benign aspect of married goddesses is related to this viewpoint: the goddess's threatening sexuality is brought under control by her submission to male authority. The characterization of women as worthless, lustful beings, unable to control themselves, is well-documented from purāṇic discourses to tea-stall talk of the present day, and no doubt springs from causes similar to those found elsewhere among men: anxiety about paternity, the reification of women as the inevitably evil objects of men's sexual desire ('women and gold' in the Indian tradition), the gap between reality and an ideal of impossibly chaste womanhood. But is this the end of the story? And, in particular, do myths about women and goddesses really relate to this point of view?

The question has been raised by Frédérique Apffel Marglin, whose work on the temple dancers of Puri has given us new perspectives on the female and the sacred. In a recent article, she draws on her earlier work and using the pervasive Hindu polarity of the auspicious and the inauspicious, argues for a positive valuation of both female and male sexuality. While asceticism, including of course abstinence from sex, is often an approved goal in spiritually-oriented contexts, from the viewpoint of daily life it is a dangerous aberration; mythologically, severe austerities threaten the workings of the world and the power of the gods. Sexual activity, on the other hand – which is what generally tempts ascetics away from their resolve – is life-producing and affirms normal values. We are once more dealing with opposition between, on the one hand, the undifferentiated, the state of oneness and release, and on the other the world in all its parts, the everyday world – the domain of *māyā*. Whether sexuality is good depends on where you stand in this polarity.

Returning to myths about goddesses, it is apparent that a partly positive valuation of female sexuality makes better sense of the contrast in types of female deity. The unmarried goddesses are not sexually voracious, but show their independence from men by abstaining from sex, and it is not their sexuality which is brought under control by marriage but their power. There is, it is true, a partial exception to the pattern in the case of the dominant woman/goddess who kills her husband, but even this type is not a Clytemnestra-figure who kills from lust. All this shows is that married goddesses can be fierce, and that sexual activity does not always succeed in checking that sometimes beneficent, sometimes destructive power exercised more commonly by a virgin goddess. (We might argue that the virgin's very independence makes her seem sexual to males – witness the buffalo demon's amorous advances to Durgā – but, in fact, neither are married women, like Pārvatī, immune from the problem of the lecherous demon.)

Female sexuality is thus capable of a double valuation. When no demons have to be fought, and when the maintenance of the world-order takes precedence over other-worldly concerns, it is good for a woman to be sexually active – in the approved context of marriage and absolute devotion to her husband. Irregular, illicit sexual activity infringes the normal world-order as much as does sexual abstinence, but it is not a dominant concern of myth: Renukā's lapse from perfect chastity is very minor (*see* III.2, p. 205), and Rādhā's adulterous love for Krishna (*see* III.5, p. 210) belongs in a world where ordinary morality is superseded by absorption in the divine.

References and Further Reading
(in English)

SOURCES:
There is a full bibliography of major Sanskrit mythical sources in W. Doniger O'Flaherty, *Hindu Myths* (below); here I simply list a few starting-points for the non-specialist.

The Vedas
Macdonell, A.A. (1922), *Hymns From the Rigveda* (Calcutta: Association Press; Oxford: Oxford University Press)

O'Flaherty, W. Doniger (1981), *The Rig Veda* (Harmondsworth: Penguin)
Panikkar, R. (1977), *The Vedic Experience: Mantramañjari* (Berkeley and Los Angeles: University of California Press).

Purāṇas and General
Dimmit, C. and van Buitenen, J.A.B. (1978), *Classical Hindu Mythology: A Reader in the Sanskrit Purāṇas* (Philadelphia: Temple University Press)
O'Flaherty, W. Doniger (1975), *Hindu Myths* (Harmondsworth: Penguin)

The Epics
Translations of the critical editions of the two epics have been begun but not yet finished: Buitenen, J.A.B van (1973–), *Mahābhārata* (Chicago: Chicago University Press); (1984–) *Rāmāyaṇa*, by a committee of scholars under the editorship of R.P. Goldman (Princeton: Princeton University Press). There is an abridged *Rāmāyaṇa* version (1988): *The Concise Rāmāyaḍa of Valmiki*, trans. Swami Venkatesananda (Binghamton: SUNY Press).
Two of the most popular Goddess-centred texts (there are many other editions) are: (1963), *Devī-māhātmya: The Glorification of the Great Goddess*, trans. Vasudeva S. Agrawala (Varanasi: All-India Kashiraj Trust); (1987), *Saundaryalaharī*, trans. with notes by Swami Tapasyananda (Madras: Sri Ramakrishna Math).

Vernacular Texts
Sen, Rāmprasād (1982), *Grace and Mercy in Her Wild Hair: Selected Poems to the Mother Goddess*, trans. L. Nathan and C. Seely (Boulder, Colorado: Great Eastern Book Company)
Thompson, E.J. and Spencer, A.M. (eds and trans) (1923), *Bengali Religious Lyrics: Śākta* (Calcutta: Association Press)

RETELLINGS OF MYTHS:

Coomaraswamy , A.K. and Sister Nivedita (1913, reprinted 1967), *Myths of the Hindus and Buddhists* (New York: Dover Books)
Narayan, R.K. (1964), *Gods, Demons and Others* (London: Heinemann). Also American and Indian editions.
There are many retellings of the epics; among the closest to the Sanskrit texts are those of C. Rajagopalachari: (1955), *Mahābhārata*, 4th ed. (Bombay: Bharatiya Vidya Bhavan); (1958), *Rāmāyaṇa* (Bombay: Bharatiya Vidya Bhavan). Readable, and easily obtainable, are the versions by R.K. Narayan, issued in many editions in India, the UK and North America; his *Rāmāyaṇa* is based on the Tamil version by Kamban. Differing versions of the epic are discussed in P. Richman (ed.) (1991), *Many Rāmāyaṇas: The Diversity of a Narrative Tradition in South Asia* (Berkeley and Los Angeles: University of California Press); of particular interest is the contribution of V. Narayana Rao, 'A Rāmāyaṇa of Their Own: Women's Oral Tradition in Telugu', pp. 114–36.

REFERENCE WORKS:

Dowson, J. (1961, reprinted 1982), *A Classical Dictionary of Hindu Mythology and Religion*, 10th ed. (Calcutta: Rupa and Co.)
Gupta, S.M. (1973), *From Daityas to Devatas in Hindu Mythology* (Delhi and Calcutta: Somaiya Publications). Illustrated.

DISCUSSIONS OF FEMALE FIGURES IN MYTH:

The most comprehensive unified treatment is D. Kinsley (1986), *Hindu Goddesses: Visions of the Divine Feminine in the Hindu Religious Tradition* (Berkeley and Los Angeles: University of California Press). Another good starting point: Hawley, J.S. and Wulff, D.M. (eds) (1982, reissued 1986), *The Divine Consort: Rādhā and the Goddesses of India* (Boston: Beacon Press). Contains articles written from a variety of viewpoints on most of the major female figures of the Hindu pantheon, with special emphasis on Rādhā.

Also of interest:

Babb, L.A. (1970), 'Marriage and malevolence: The Uses of Sexual Opposition in the Hindu Pantheon' in *Ethnology*, 9, 2, pp. 137–48

Beck, B.E.F. (1981), 'The Goddess and the Demon: A Local South Indian Festival and its Wider Context' in M. Biardeau (ed.), *Autour de la Déesse hindoue = Puruṣārtha*, 5, pp. 83–136

Brown, C.M. (1990), *The Triumph of the Goddess: The Canonical Models and Theological Visions of the Devī-Bhāgavata Purāṇa* (Albany, NY: SUNY Press)

Brubaker, R.L. (1977), 'Lustful Woman, Chaste Wife, Ambivalent Goddess: A South Indian Myth' in *Anima*, 3, 2, pp. 59–62

Coburn, T.B. (1984), *Devī-Māhātmya: The Crystallization of the Goddess Tradition* (Delhi: Motilal Banarsidass)

Dange, S.A. (1975), 'Urvashi the Water Belle' in *Journal of the Oriental Institute* (Baroda), 25, pp. 17–46

Darian, S.G. (1978), *The Ganges in Myth and History* (Honolulu: University Press of Hawaii)

Gupta, A.S. (1962),'The Conception of Sarasvatī in the Purāṇas' in *Purāṇa*, 4, 1, pp. 55–95

Harman, W.P. (1989), *The Sacred Marriage of a Hindu Goddess* (Bloomington: Indiana University Press)

Hiltebeitel, A. (1981), 'Draupadī's Hair' in M. Biardeau (ed.), *Autour de la Déesse hindoue = Puruṣārtha*, 5, pp. 179–214

—— (1988), *The Cult of Draupadī I, Mythologies: From Gingee to Kurukṣetra* (Chicago: University of Chicago Press)

—— (1991), *The Cult of Draupadī II, On Hindu Ritual and the Goddess* (Chicago: Chicago University Press)

Kumar, P. (1974), *Śakti Cult in Ancient India* (Varanasi: Bhartiya Publishing House)

Maity, P.K. (1966), *Historical Studies in the Cult of the Goddess Manasā* (Calcutta: Punthi Pustak)

Marglin, F.A. (1985), 'Female Sexuality in the Hindu World' in C.W. Atkinson, C.H. Buchanan, M.R. Miles (eds), *Immaculate and Powerful: The Female in Sacred Image and Social Reality* (Boston: Beacon Press), pp. 39–59

Mookerjee, A. (1988), *Kali: The Feminine Force* (London: Thames and Hudson)

O'Flaherty, W. Doniger (1980), *Women, Androgynes and Other Mythical Beasts* (Chicago: University of Chicago Press)

Sivaramamurti, C. (1980), *Śrī Lakshmī in Indian Art and Thought* (New Delhi: Kanak Publications)

Shulman, D.D. (1980), *Tamil Temple Myths: Sacrifice and Divine Marriage in the South Indian Śaiva Tradition* (Princeton: Princeton University Press)

Sutherland, S.J. (1989), 'Sita and Draupadi: Aggressive Behavior and Female Role-models in the Sanskrit Epics' in *Journal of the American Oriental Society*, 109, pp. 63–79

TAO TAO LIU

Chinese Myths
and Legends

SECTION I: INTRODUCTION

At the dawn of time the universe was a black confused mass, but creatures appeared
to have moved around in it, and the one that is generally credited with the task of
reducing this chaos to the shape of the universe we know was called Pangu.[1] Pangu
was nurtured in this egg-like chaos, and slept for thousands of years. When he woke
up from this deep sleep, he started to put order into the confusion by splitting it
into half. The lighter elements floated up to become the sky and the heavier elements
sank down to become the earth. To keep them apart he pushed at the sky with his
hands and as he pushed he also grew himself, until he grew to be thousands of miles
tall, keeping the sky up until it solidified. He was like a pillar supporting the sky.
For years he did this until he grew old and died, and when he died his body
metamorphosed into all the elements of the universe: his breath became the wind,
his voice became thunder; his left eye became the sun and the right the moon; his
blood became rivers and his flesh the fields; whilst the hairs on the skin of his body
turned into trees and vegetation. So all parts of him went into creating the universe.

The most important and most powerful god was the Yellow Emperor, as he came
to be called and translated into English. The Yellow Emperor was always on the side
of the good, and for the good of mankind; so much identified was he with people
on earth – that is the people of China – that later the Chinese called themselves
'descendants of the Yellow Emperor'. The Yellow Emperor was frequently involved
in battles with other gods, such as Yandi, the Fiery God, who was supposed to have
had the same mother, but not the same father as the Yellow Emperor. Yandi, with
his children and grandchildren, all gods of fire in one form or another, ruled over
the South. In spite of his battles with the Yellow Emperor, Yandi was actually a great
benefactor to mankind; it was he who taught them agriculture and he caused the
sun to warm the crops to fruition, so that he was also called the god of agriculture'.
He also taught people about medicine, and tasted numerous herbs himself, some
of which killed him – he was supposed to have died more than seventy times in one
day. But since he was a god he always revived, and he passed on his knowledge to

mankind who did not have the benefit of immortality.

The most ferocious battle that the Yellow Emperor engaged in was with the monster Chiyou, who was thought to be a descendant of Yandi. Chiyou put fear into all who encountered him because he had the body and horns of an ox, he lived on a diet of stones, sand and metals and he made and wielded all kinds of terrifying weapons. He overcame Yandi and took his power, threatening that of the Yellow Emperor with an army of metal-clad monsters and strange beasts. The Yellow Emperor too marshalled his forces of gods and monsters, and won the final battle with the help of a drum that was made out of the skin of an animal called the Kui, which had a roar that was as loud as thunder, and a drum-stick that was made out of the biggest bone in the body of the god of thunder himself.

Most of the best-known gods in ancient Chinese myths were male, apart from Nüwa (*see* Section II, p. 233), who was credited with the creation of people. Her role was that of the nurturing mother, not only of mankind but also of their environment. There were some lesser female deities, mostly wives and daughters of other gods, whose characters and activities were not very clearly delineated, unlike in the Greek myths. But like the Greek gods, the Chinese ones were also interrelated and the mightier gods had numerous progeny.

One of the grandsons of the Yellow Emperor by the name of Zhuanxü became the god which ruled over the north, and his ability attracted the attention of the Yellow Emperor, who was weary after his titanic struggles against Chiyou. So he summoned Zhuanxü, who ruled very well but he bureaucratized many aspects of life, chiefly stopping up the paths that had led between heaven and earth, by which means gods and men had travelled freely. These paths were known as 'ladders to heaven' and lay through tall mountains and tall trees. So from his time on, the free and easy association between gods and men ceased, and they became more and more isolated from each other.

However, the gods continued to take an interest in mankind, and often helped them in times of difficulty. The two major natural problems facing the Chinese race came from drought and flood. There is a myth concerning the worst of such droughts that was the mischief of gods.

In the east there was a mighty God by the name of Dijun, whose wife Xihe lived in a sea of boiling water, where she brought up her ten sons, who were the suns of this world. They lived in a tree called the Fusang in this sea, and every morning Fuxi would take one of her sons and put him in a chariot drawn by six dragons. They would rise from the sea and drive across the sky in an appointed path, so the earth received the rays of a sun in a regular fashion, and lived by them.

This life went on for thousands of years, until the suns began to tire of it. Mischievously they decided to come out all at once. They gloried in their anarchy but it had a terrible effect upon the earth; it became scorched from the rays of not just one but ten suns. The people begged their Emperor, Yao, to intercede with the God Dijun on their behalf. Dijun could not control his unruly children, and as even the gods became affected by the activities of the suns, he ordered the heavenly archer Yi to go down to earth and shoot the suns down. He gave him a magic bow that was red and a quiverful of white arrows, hoping that the sight of the magic bow and arrows would bring his children to heel, but they were not intimidated, and Yi was obliged to shoot them down. As each fell to the ground, it turned into the shape of a black three-footed raven (such ravens have always been associated with the sun in China, and are thought by some to refer to sun spots that were observed very early on). The story of Yi the Archer does not quite end here, for he was banished to live amongst men with his wife Chang'o, and her story will be told in the next section (*see* p. 234).

Emperor Yao, the ruler on earth, had had a most unfortunate reign. First there was the drought from the suns; then there was flood – a mighty flood created by the god of water, Gonggong, whom we met earlier being defeated by the god of fire (*see* p. 227). This time it seemed as though he had a free hand as the gods appeared to have become angry with men on earth and were willing to have them punished. However, not all of the gods were so unsympathetic to men, and one of them was a god called Gun, who was a white horse in heaven, and one of the grandsons of the Yellow Emperor. He went down to earth and after some unsuccessful attempts succeeded in stopping the flood with a dam, made from some magic earth from heaven that he had stolen. When the gods found out, he was killed for daring to steal from heaven, but his body did not corrupt; instead after three years his son Yü sprang from it in the form of a dragon. It was Yü, after mighty efforts, including the subduing of gods like Gonggong and other monsters, who was able to control the flood, and mankind has been grateful to Yü ever since.

The relevance of this myth is attested in modern times by the fact that the Yellow River has always been notorious for the devastation caused by its annual flooding, and was until very recent times often known to the West as 'China's Sorrow'. It was acknowledged that if a regime failed to control the Yellow River, then it was bound to fall from power.

That Yü was born in the shape of a dragon is significant for the role of dragons in Chinese mythology. Few dragon myths survive from the ancient age, but dragons have always been associated with water and rain – unlike western fire-breathing dragons. The Chinese dragon was a powerful creature, which was not necessarily a force for either evil or good – although it often acted for good, as it brought the rains in the Spring that is so essential for planting. The Dragon Boat Festival in the south of China, which took place in spring, was probably originally a rain-making and fertility rite. The dragon-shaped boats were raced on the rivers in the hope of stimulating the dragons, who controlled the rain clouds in the sky, to emerge as well.

In China, the dragon was also the symbol for the male element, whilst the phoenix signified the female; and the dragon was the emblem of the Chinese emperor, the supreme male in ritual terms. It possibly also had associations with the 'naga', the Indian water dragons who inhabited the lower strata of the earth below men.

The myths that we have talked about so far are found in sources from mainly the BC era, but from about the second century AD Buddhism came to China from India via the Silk Route, and it had a great impact on the imagination and folklore of China. Before the arrival of Buddhism in China, the native schools of thought were in the main Confucianism and Taoism. Confucianism, based on the school of thought propounded by Confucius (551–479 BC) and his followers, was the state ideology of China for purposes of social and political organization. It called for a thoroughly practical series of relationships to be maintained between groups of people, such as between ruler and subject, between men and women and between parents and offspring, based on human values, as opposed to supernatural. It was basically a code of behaviour that was typical of a paternalistic society, where maleness and age dominated.

A woman in herself had no standing and no rights at all. She had to develop manipulative powers in order to fulfil herself, and this aspect is reflected in the myths and legends of China; often women who feature in them are seen in the roles of mother or wife.

However, because paternalistic society tended to put filial piety high as a virtue, a woman could have great powers as a parent. When her husband was alive she was subservient to him, but when he died, she could arrogate his powers, and her son was then completely subservient to her. As men often died before women and most households tended to be extended families of three generations, the widow often assumed the authority of both her husband and herself as the head of the family. Although the general supremacy of the male head of the family was undeniable, there were few households which were not ruled by a matriarchal grandmother, who held the family together and whom the entire family held in awe. This was also true in politics; as the regent dowager-empress, a woman could have total power — as many women did throughout history; sometimes they simply dispensed with the charade of regency.

Women's position in Confucian social values was low. However, simultaneously, in binary opposition to socially-minded Confucianism in the Chinese world view, Taoism had also evolved. This tried to explain the nature of all creation and the role of men within the totality. The attitude to male and female was that of complement and opposition, neither necessarily holding the upper hand, though the male, the Yang, is usually dominant. The Yin, the female element, exists side by side with the Yang in all living things, which must have a proper and healthy balance of these two elements. Whilst Taoism as a philosophy does not accommodate supernatural elements, it does accord all living and inanimate things a place of their own in creation, and acknowledges individual ways of behaviour.

Popular Taoist beliefs had a system of myths, probably pre-dating Confucianism, which contained many gods and deities; the Taoist deities might be said to be ancient and native to Chinese culture. Moreover, Taoism asserted the right of every creature, animate or inanimate, to existence in its own way, which has led it to imbue everything and every place with its particular numen. This attitude of the imagination had a tendency to develop further into a belief in spirits that inhabit everything, whether it be a particular tree or the household stove — indeed the stove god was an integral and important deity in any household.

Taoism also believed that ordinary people could become immortal through various practices, such as swallowing elixirs or meditating in uninhabited places, quite often aided by the supernatural. Men and women who became immortal in this way were known as *xian* (sometimes translated quaintly as 'fairies'), who generally had powers equal to that of deities who were born deities. But the *xian* were nearer to men and often went amongst men sometimes in disguise. Gods, immortals and their cults proliferated around the land, but as long as they did not get in the way of proper social relationships, Taoism co-existed happily with Confucianism.

The relative open-mindedness of Taoist thinking paved the way for Buddhism. As a philosophy, Buddhism offered an individual a private way to salvation, which neither of the Chinese ways of thinking had offered. The concept of Buddha both as a sage and a deity gave the Chinese a role model that had not previously existed. The Mahayana school of Buddhism which offered to all the possibility of attaining Bodhissatvahood first and then ultimately Buddhahood had a wide appeal. Though Buddhism offered salvation to all, in the pecking order of its world, women still came below men; a woman may have the desired sex change from female to male in her next incarnation, when she has perfected her religious practice – but at least she had the option.

Buddhism swept across the country as a religion, and it survives strongly even now. Many Bodhissatvas, as well as the Buddha in his different titles, were worshipped in temples in China. The most popular Bodhissatva was Guanyin (Kuan-yin), who originated as the Bodhissatva Avolokitesvara; he was introduced from India to China as a male, but changed into a goddess of compassion in China, identifying with other female goddesses of compassion that had already existed in China (*see* Section II, p. 237). Many of the other Bodhissatvas also changed their characters as they were absorbed into the Chinese culture: the Bodhissatva Maitreya, the 'Future Buddha', changed from an ascetic figure into a gross and jolly, seated 'Friar Tuck' figure with an exposed navel, known as the Mitofo, who was a symbol of luck and happiness.

The arrival of Buddhist literature also gave a strong impetus to imaginative literature. This is shown especially the example of the *Jatakamala* which were 'birth stories' of the Buddha told in an easily accessible vernacular form of prose intermingled with verse. This proved to be a source of inspiration and has given China its best fiction. The influence of Buddhism gave the narration of stories, the vehicles of myths and folklore, a new lease of life, which strengthened as it continued.

The arrival of Buddhism also stimulated more activity in Taoist circles in competition. The Taoists produced more deities whose exploits were related with gusto in the new fictional form. Later, legend and folklore drew on a wide cast list of gods and spirits from many sources. Many of these were natural phenomena deified, such as features of the landscape, mountains and rivers, which were both male and female; these often had large cult followings in certain localities, but they sometimes spread far and wide. Abstract virtues were not deified as they were in Greece, but at a more practical level Wealth was deified, and the god of wealth has many adherents, especially amongst businessmen. Even diseases could be deified, as for instance the goddess of smallpox, to whom appeals could be made at times of infection. Every guild and profession had its own god, much like patron saints in the Christian West; the scholars who had to make their way from boyhood, taking examination after examination, had their own god, Zhongkui, who in his spare time also went about exorcising devils.

In the end, all these deities existed in a highly eclectic popular religion, and gods from many traditions as well as local cults jostled and vied with each other amicably in human society. Men and women could pick and choose their faith, depending on their preference or ritual needs. It was usual for a ritual procession, such as at a funeral to contain both Buddhist and Taoist priests – to hedge your bets in the next world (when Christianity was introduced in the last century, many Chinese wanted to adopt Christianity in addition to the rituals which they already maintained – a proposal to which the missionaries could not assent). All this existed within the framework of state Confucianism which 'rendered unto Caesar all things that are Caesar's', and left the private conscience to the individual.

It is not surprising, in this medley of gods and spirits, that there should exist a strong belief in 'spirit races' who were neither human or divine. These had supernatural powers, but could not always overcome men, let alone the gods. Folklore and legends dealt extensively with the spirits of animals or inanimate objects who through great age or other means, had powers which might not necessarily be evil. These spirits often had truck with human beings, and though such associations might not be always be harmful to the human, they were usually eschewed. Into this category would fall most of the stories about fox spirits, or 'fox fairies'; the spirit of foxes who usually, though not always, took the form of nubile women and who had relationships with men. Some of the relationships were vampiristic, but some were quite benign. Many of the fox spirit stories bear the marks of male sexual fantasies.

Myths, legends and folk-tales reflect the society that produced them. The position of women was subservient to men, and their social status was in theory non-existent. But the stories show us that women did assert themselves, frequently by manipulating their menfolk. However much they were put down with laws and brutal customs – such as the post-fourteenth century practice of foot binding – they did not always give way to men. The most important arena for women's activity was the home, and as mother, especially the mother of a son, she ruled the house, economically as well as emotionally. She may not have been able to assert herself outside the home, hence the wishful thinking of tales of women like Mulan and Zhu Yingtai (*see* Section III, p. 241), who dressed up as men to fulfil themselves, but neither could the men intrude into their domain in the rear apartments of the house.

SECTION II: WOMEN IN MYTHS AND FOLKLORE

Nüwa

Nüwa was the mother goddess of ancient Chinese myths who created men. She is depicted in the earliest sources as being a woman whose lower half was in the shape

Fig. 21 Nüwa and Fuxi.

of a serpent, and she is often shown with a mate, Fuxi, similarly depicted, often with their serpent tails entwined, holding in their hands emblems such as the sun and moon, or the carpenter's square and compass. They are also in some sources alleged to be brother and sister. She created men by fashioning them out of the mud of river, and breathed life into them, so when they came to life they worshipped her as a goddess. After the effort of making individual dolls, she decided that she could speed up the process by waving a magic wand dipped in the mud, and the droplets of mud that fell from the wand turned into men and women. Having made these creatures, she also instituted marriage amongst them, so that they would procreate and have no further need for her to keep the human race going. In the days that Nüwa first created man, all creatures lived in harmony with each other, in a kind of golden age. In her delight at the life of the people, she also taught them to make a pipe of thirteen reeds for their enjoyment.

In the battle between a god of fire, Zhurong, and a god of water, Gonggong, Gonggong was defeated and in the anguish of defeat knocked down a mountain, which unfortunately happened to prop up the heavens, thereby creating a huge hole in the sky. Nüwa was much grieved by this, and took many-coloured pebbles from the bed of the river and, after working on them with her spells, succeeded in mending the hole in heaven. Yet she was unable to do anything about the damage done to the earth, which subsided under the mountain, so that the land to the east of China has always been lower than to the west, and the rivers flow downwards in an easterly direction.

Nüwa is depicted as a mother figure, well disposed towards mankind and exerting herself in a caring way to make them happy.

Chang'o

Chang'o was the wife of the archer Yi, who was sent by the God Dijun to deal with the ten suns that were scorching the earth (*see* Section I, p. 228). The God had hoped that there would be no need to kill the suns, who were his children, only to discipline them, but in the event Yi had no choice but to do that. Having executed the task, Yi received much gratitude from Yao, the Emperor of China, and all his subjects, but Dijun resented his presence in heaven, which reminded him of the death of his children, so he had him and his wife deprived of their immortality and banished from heaven.

On earth Yi had to make a living just like other men. Chang'o was most discontented with her new and inferior life, especially as she was quite blameless in the matter that had caused their banishment. Moreover Yi, in his journeys around the world, became involved with other women, such as the goddess of the River Lo, Mifei. So Chang'o felt that she had cause for complaint.

Yi decided to go seek out the Queen Mother of the West (*see* Section III, p. 242) who lived on Mount Kunlun, who was famed for her elixir of immortality made from the fruit of a tree that only flowered once every one thousand years. After braving many dangers, Yi arrived in the presence of the Queen Mother of the West, who could only give him a limited supply of the elixir, enough to give the pair of them eternal life but only enough for one person to regain immortality. Yi took the elixir home to his wife, and told her that they should share it and attain eternal life at least. Chang'o was not satisfied with only having eternal life, so whilst her husband's back was turned she swallowed the entire quantity, leaving nothing for her husband, who was now doomed to mortality.

Although Chang'o was now a goddess again she did not know where to go to enjoy her immortality. She could not go back to heaven, for the inhabitants there rejected her because of her behaviour to her husband. Instead, she chose to go to the moon, which was uninhabited by anyone except a rabbit under a cassia tree — shapes that can be made out from the earth. There she went and lived in cold splendour, and became known as the goddess of the moon.

Her husband Yi came to a sad end; he had lost the chance of regaining immortality or even eternal life, and became depressed, and was violent and bad-tempered. One of his retainers, to whom he had passed on his skills as an archer, became discontented at not being able to surpass his master, since Yi's divine origins always made him superior. This man plotted and finally succeeded in killing Yi.

In the story of Yi and Chang'o the woman's role as wife is subservient which is conducive to her becoming manipulative. Whilst Chang'o does not come out of the story very well, one is not without sympathy for her plight. Even if her efforts to improve her own life result in ostracization by her community, she does still achieve a measure of what she wanted — albeit in lone splendour as the goddess of the moon.

Weaving Girl

There lived on earth a poor orphan, the youngest of three children, who was ill-treated by his elder brothers and sisters-in-law. They decided to drive him out of the house, under the pretence of setting him up on his own, and offered him the meanest portion of the land along with just one ox. The young man laboured hard and took good care of his ox and became known as the Cowherd. One day the ox suddenly opened his mouth and spoke in the language of men, telling him that many immortal maidens would come down from the sky and would be bathing in a certain pool on earth. If he went and took the clothes of one of them, then that maiden would not be able to return to heaven and could marry him. The Cowherd did as he was told and hid the clothes of one of the women. When the others put on their clothes after their bathe and flew back to heaven, this one could not do so and she consented to live with the Cowherd and be his wife. She was called the Weaving Girl, and was the daughter of Tiandi, the god of the sky.

Years passed and the couple lived contentedly with the Cowherd tilling his land and the Weaving Girl at home looking after the house and the son and daughter that they had produced. Some versions of the story say that eventually her father and mother located her and sent guards to escort her back to heaven, and she was taken away from the Cowherd's house. Other versions of the story have it that she found the garments that had been taken from her on the day that she left heaven to bathe in the pool, and putting them on she found herself floating back to Heaven. Whatever the cause, the Cowherd saw his wife floating up into the sky, and was determined to follow her. He put his children into baskets slung from his carrying pole, and chased after his wife. Without realizing, he too was flying up in the air, and soon he looked as if he would catch up with her, but suddenly he was stopped by a fast flowing river. This was the Milky Way in the sky, or as the Chinese call it the 'Silver River'. Tiandi had created this fast flowing stream by scraping the sky with his hairpin, so that the Cowherd would not catch up with his daughter.

The Cowherd and his children tried desperately to empty the water of the river with ladles, but to no avail, and they stayed disconsolate on the bank of the Milky Way. In time they were all changed to stars, and to this day they can be seen on either side of the Milky Way. But the gods took pity on them, so on one day of the year, the seventh day of the seventh month, all the magpies fly up to the sky and form a bridge so that they are together on the same side. On that day it often drizzles with rain, and the rain is the tears shed by the Weaving Girl at seeing her husband. (In western terms, the Weaving Girl is one of the stars in the constellation of the Vega, and the Cowherd is the Aquila, with two small stars beside it, that are his children.)

The seventh day of the seventh month was a day celebrated by women as their festival in honour of the Weaving Girl, who became a kind of patron saint for skilful women. Unmarried women played games on that day to find out when they would get married, and there were competitive games to test women's skills. The identification of these particular stars with the couple has meant that they are a symbol of faith between husband and wife who are parted from each other.

Fig. 22 *The Weaving Girl with Cowherd*, from a nineteenth-century
woodblock print.

The story bears an affinity with folk-tales from other lands: the youngest son is cast out of the family and subsequently makes good; and the Weaving Girl's capture by the Cowherd is similar to the Swan Maiden theme (*see* the contribution on Scandinavia in this volume, p. 145).

Mengjiangnü

This legend is based on a historical event, the building of the Great Wall of China, which was begun by the tyrannical First Emperor of the Qin dynasty, whose reign lasted from 221 to 207 BC. The Wall was built to keep the marauding tribesmen from the north-west from invading China. Such an enormous engineering feat could not have been anything but heavy in human costs, especially as the site of the Wall is along the cold, inhospitable and mountainous lands of the north. The story is as much about the tyranny of rulers, as about loyalty of wives.

A man called Qi Liang was one of many who died in the building of the Wall. His wife, Mengjiangnü, had travelled far from their home with winter clothing and food for her husband. When she arrived and was told of the death of her husband, she was appalled to hear that no one even knew where he was buried. This meant that he could never have the proper rites said and the proper sacrifices made to ensure him a happy after-life. So she prayed to the gods to show her where he was buried and the intensity of her prayers so moved the gods that they caused the Wall to split and show her the white bones of many men who had died at the same time.

Not knowing which were the bones of her husband which she wanted to rebury properly, she prayed again for guidance. The inspiration came for her to bite her finger until it bled, and as the blood dropped on to the white bones of men, the bones which absorbed her blood, rather than let it drip off, belonged to her husband. She gathered up his bones and prepared to leave.

She was not allowed to leave by the Emperor, who demanded to see her intending to punish her. When he saw her, however, his heart was melted by her beauty, and he decided to marry her. She made it her condition that he would make a grand tomb for her husband on the other side of a great river, approached by a tall bridge, and that the Emperor himself should take part in the ritual as if he were a filial son of the dead man. He agreed, and when the burial was completed, she walked to the top of the bridge, cursed the Emperor for the tyrant that he was and threw herself to her death into the river.

Guanyin (Kuan-yin)

This name in Chinese is a shortened form of Guanshiyin which means the 'The One who Looks Down on the Utterances of the World' — that is the god who listens to pleadings from the world, a deity of compassion. As the Bodhissatva Avolokitesvara, one of the four great Bodhissatvas in the Mahayana tradition, he initially made his way into China as a male deity; some early depictions even show Guanyin with a moustache. The scholarly search for the origins of the Chinese female Avalokitesvara has been complicated and unfruitful, but it is not hard to surmise that the attributes of compassion and care that the deity was supposed to personify suit a female deity well. There were also other native Chinese goddesses, such as the Queen of Heaven, a Taoist deity, who gave special protection against dangers from the sea and had many shrines by the sea, with whom the Buddhist Bodhissatva was probably identified with. Certainly the transformation to a goddess may not have taken very long. The female representation of the Bodhisatva can be found from about the fourth century, and by the Ming dynasty the ceramic statuette of the Goddess in flowing robes, familiar to collectors in the West, was mass produced. It is an interesting transformation given the original Buddhist thinking that male is superior to female, and that a woman can make the desired sex change when her religious practice was perfected.

In China no other god held as important a place in popular worship as Guanyin, and her cult eclipsed that of the Buddha himself. The centre of the cult is at Putuo on the island of Zhoushan, off the coast of Zhejiang, in central China, and though all the evidence points to her being an imported goddess, many people believed that she was originally an ancient Chinese princess called Miaoshan.

Miaoshan was a princess who was born with Buddhist virtues such as kindliness, modesty and also vegetarianism. When her father wanted to marry her off in due course she refused, and he tried all kinds of punishments and deprivations, which she survived cheerfully as she preferred an ascetic life. In the end, her father ordered her to be killed, but the saintliness of her soul turned the underworld into a paradise, so that the gods of the underworld were obliged to send her back again – this time to Putuo where she was reunited with her body. There, through meditation, she became sublime and was able to float out of her body and help others in danger.

The king, her father, fell into a terrible sickness for which no cure could be found. Miaoshan went to him in disguise and told him that the only cure would be an eye and a hand from a living person on the island of Putuo. Attendants went there and Miaoshan offered her eye and hand, and when this only cured one half of the king, she offered the other. When the king was cured he made a pilgrimage to Putuo to give his thanks. He recognized his daughter, and in response to his grief at her mutilated body, she told him to admit his guilt and offer repentance. This he did and she was then made whole. From then on she became known as Guanyin and the protectress of all.

Madame White

This story is associated with the area around Hangzhou on the bank of the West Lake, an area of great beauty in central China. One of the most famous versions of the story is by a Ming dynasty writer, Feng Menglong (d. 1645).

A young man by the name of Xüxüan lived in Hangzhou with his sister and family. One spring, during the Festival of the Dead, he crossed the Lake to a temple on the other side; on his return, he shared the ferry with a beautiful woman dressed in white, accompanied by a maid who was dressed in blue. The journey ended with him lending her his umbrella, as it was raining, and paying the ferryman on her behalf, and he promised to visit her at her house.

The next day when Xüxüan found her, she greeted him very warmly; she told him she was in love with him and gave him fifty pieces of silver so that they could get married. Xüxüan took the silver home, but his brother-in-law found that it bore the official marks of the government treasury, which meant it had been stolen from the treasury. Xüxüan was arrested; when he told the officials where he had obtained the silver, they went to search the house but they found that it was derelict. On entering, a woman appeared dressed in white who disappeared amidst a flash of lightning, leaving a pile of silver on the ground. This was identified as the remainder of the stolen hoard, and Xüxüan was exonerated but banished.

He moved to live and work in nearby Suzhou, where he once more met Madame White, who convinced him that the episode of the silver was a mistake. So they got married and lived very contentedly. One day, Xüxüan went to a temple for a festival with his friends, much against the wishes of his wife. When he arrived the Abbot Fahai spotted him in the crowd and wanted to speak to him immediately. Fahai followed him out of the temple only to see Madame White in a boat coming up with her maid to fetch her husband. Fahai cursed the two women as demons, at which they overturned the boat and sank into the water without trace. Fahai told the frightened young man to go back to Hangzhou and to seek him out again should he be troubled.

When Xüxüan returned to his sister's house, he was horrified to find Madame

White and her maid ensconced in his house as his wife. She was angry with him and treated him sternly, refusing to let him out of her sight, and relations between them became strained. He became scared of her now that he was convinced that she was not a human being. One day he was alone in the street when Fahai appeared and gave him a bowl. He was to press the bowl down on Madame White's head as hard as he could, and Fahai would be close behind him. Xuxian did this, and saw the woman shrink smaller and smaller under the pressure of the bowl until the bowl lay on the ground, flat on its brim. Fahai came near and asked her who she was. She admitted that she was a white python who lived in the West Lake, and having fallen in love with Xüxüan on first seeing him, she had decided to take human shape. She asked pity of the monk but Fahai was adamant. He chanted spells to keep her in the bowl in the shape of a small white snake, accompanied by a blue fish which was her maid. He buried the bowl under a tall pagoda called the Leifeng Pagoda, so that she would be always imprisoned under it as long as it stood.

The story of Madame White and Xüxüan, without the supernatural elements, is that of a relationship between a man and woman that might have taken place anywhere, any time: the initial honeymoon, the interference of a third party, the souring of the relationship of the couple and the woman's growing dominance over the man, leading to their final break-up. Her non-human origins enable her to take the initiative and later excuse Xuxuan's weakness of character in leaving her. These excuses do not take anyone in, but they are admissions that in Chinese society a woman should not show her hand too openly.

In 1924 the Leifeng pagoda did fall down and the writer Lu Xun, who was in the vanguard of those battling against the traditional code of Chinese society, wrote an article on the occasion, in which he commented what a busybody the monk Fahai had been. Whatever the origins of Madame White, he wrote, she had dealt kindly with Xüxüan, and they would have been very happy together if Fahai had not come meddling. He also told the story that, after this event, Xüxüan was much blamed by many gods and men, so that he had to run away and take refuge in the shell of a crab — and the shape of a man can be seen to this day if you break open a crab and look at the shell.

SECTION III: MINOR FIGURES IN MYTHS AND FOLKLORE

Baosi

Baosi was a concubine of the last king of the Shang Dynasty (eleventh century BC), Zhou, who spent all his time at his pleasures, especially with his women, and did not rule his kingdom properly. Baosi was a beauty who seldom smiled or laughed, and Zhou spent all his time devising ways that would make her smile. Once he had all the beacons lit that warned of attacks on the capital, so that his generals raised the alarm and rushed to his aid only to find that it was a false alarm. At this trick Baosi burst into laughter. However, when the King was attacked in earnest no one came to his aid when the beacons were lit.

Baosi (*see also* Daji, below) was an example of beautiful women who could cause kingdoms to fall — a view of woman as temptress comparable to Helen of Troy.

Daji

Daji was a beautiful woman who was presented to King Yu, who ruled in the eight century BC, by his enemies. She was so captivating that the king did nothing but spend his time with her, with the result that he lost his kingdom to his enemies. She was supposed to have either killed herself or was executed when the king died.

Fox Spirits ('Fox Fairies')

Foxes were supposed to be endowed with cleverness and wisdom, who through their skills could take on the shape of women (*see* Section I, p. 232). They would often appear to men, who were alone at their studies or away from home, and offer themselves to them. These foxes did not always harm the men, and sometimes were quite beneficial to them in practical ways, as they had supernatural powers and used them to acquire possessions. Yet they were also vulnerable to forces that humans are not aware of, such as spells and magic, or even other animals. In one story, called 'Miss Ren' by Shen Jiji, dating from the eighth century, a fox woman encountered hunting dogs, changed back into her real shape and was killed by them.

The term 'fox spirit' is still used as a form of abuse for women who are perceived as sexual temptresses, a view derived from the folklore, which also embodies an unwillingness to see women as overtly sexual. As sexual creatures, not only do they then stand on the other side of the line from 'virtuous women' — wives and mothers — but they are actually thought of as being non-human.

He Xiangu (Fairy Aunt He)

He Xiangu is one of the Eight Immortals (*baxian*), the only female amongst them. They are a group of eccentric characters, who attained immortality through some magic means (*see* Section I, p. 231), and who travel around together. Her story is that she became immortal through being given a peach, the food of immortality, by another immortal. The images of the Eight Immortals were often used for pictorial motifs on artefacts. He Xiangu is always depicted with a basket of fruit. She is the token woman in this company.

The Lo River Goddess

The goddess's name was Mifei, and she was a daughter of Fuxi (*see* Section II, p. 233), who fell into the River Lo and was drowned. The gods made her the goddess of the river, and she lived there. Many men met her and fell in love with her, including Yi the archer (*see* Section II, p. 234). A poet of the second century AD, Cao Zhi, wrote a poem in her honour in which he sang the praises of the beautiful woman who he encountered once and identified as the Goddess of the River Lo.

Mencius's Mother

Mencius's Mother is not a mythical but a legendary figure; we do not even know her name, but China paid great tribute to the mothers of famous men, who were felt to have owed their beginnings to them. They were generally women of unusually strong character and embodied moral uprightness and integrity – qualities in which men often fell short, and had to be reminded of by their mothers. Mencius (372–299 AD), one of the leading philosophers in the School of Confucianism, was brought up by his widowed mother. In his boyhood she moved house three times, for she felt that she had to provide the best environment for his upbringing and live amongst neighbours who would help his moral growth. At last, she settled near a school where Mencius, as a young boy, imitated the behaviour of scholars and their pupils as they spent all their time reading and learning.

When Mencius was a student himself, he became tired of studying and wanted to give up. His mother led him to the loom where she had been weaving, and slashed the cloth. Showing him the spoilt cloth, she told him that giving up his studies was like cutting the cloth. He returned to the school.

Mencius obeyed his mother without question. As his widowed mother she had the right to expect total obedience from him, for she stood for the authority of both herself and her dead husband. As men tended to die before women, Chinese society, for all its patriarchal set-up, was dominated by matriarchs of this kind – the widowed mother and grandmother.

Mulan

Mulan was the daughter of a man who though elderly was conscripted for the army because there was no other male in the family to go in his place. Mulan offered to disguise herself and go in his stead. She put on men's clothes and equipped herself for war and rode off to answer the summons. She was successful in battle and was raised in rank to be a general. After many years when the fighting ended, she returned home, bringing with her several of her comrades-in-arms. As they were feasted by her family, she went into the women's apartments in the rear of the house and emerged wearing her women's clothes and with a female hair-do and make-up. Only then did her comrades realize that their successful general was a woman. Our earliest source for this story is a seventh-century ballad which remains very popular and is regularly re-issued in print with new illustrations. The 'wishful-thinking' element of the story – Mulan's disguise as a man – is not hard to imagine for women who have no opportunity for fulfilling themselves outside the house and home (*see also* Zhu Yingtai, p. 244).

The Old Man Under the Moon

Marriages were believed to be pre-destined, but even if one knows about the future nothing can be done. Once a man encountered an old man writing in strange characters in a book, when he asked what it was the Old Man told him that it was a book of marriages, in which all marriages were written down as soon as a person was born – it was a fate that no one could escape. Curious to know about his own life, he asked about himself; the Old Man looked it up and told him that his wife was still a baby. When pressed further, the old man told him her whereabouts; there he found a baby girl in filthy clothes on the back of a one-eyed crone at a market. He was so disgusted with her that he took out his dagger and slashed the baby, running away in the commotion.

It was many years before he was able to get married though he tried several times, at last he married the young daughter from a noble house and he was very happy. After his marriage, he noticed that his wife always wore her hair in such a way as to hide her forehead. When he asked her why, she told him it was to hide a scar because as a baby a madman had slashed her forehead. Her husband, stirred by the memory, asked after the event, and found out that his wife had been orphaned as a baby by bandits in a faraway place; she was brought back to the safety of her family after all kinds of dangers and hardships by her nurse, who had only one eye. The man realized the truth of what the Old Man Under the Moon had said, and that he had been the man who tried to kill his wife.

Queen Mother of the West

The Queen Mother of the West is a goddess from ancient Taoist mythology. *The Classic of Mountains and Seas* (*see* Section IV, p. 244) says that she had the shape of a woman, with the tail of a leopard and the teeth of a tiger, and dishevelled hair. Gradually, her appearance seemed to have assumed a more anthropomorphic shape, and in later accounts of myths she appeared as a benign middle-aged woman, as her name might suggest. She lived variously on Mount Kunlun or in the Jade Mountains, the mountainous range to the west of China, and was the guardian of the elixir of immortality, or sometimes of the peach trees whose fruit conferred immortality. Peaches have always been a symbol of long-life. She was attended by three blue birds, who brought her food. In later interpretations, these blue birds are known as her messengers, and are often referred to as messengers of love in literature.

Shamanism

China has, since ancient times, had a system of shamanism. The earliest shamans were priests and held positions of high status in society, but later, including recent times, they were the witch doctors and spirit mediums. The earliest recorded shamans were usually, though not always, men, but later more women seemed to have taken this role. The female shaman or medium operated at the lower level of popular religion and superstitious practices, and this has continued up to the present day.

The Silkworm Goddess

Once there was a man who had to leave his family to go to the wars, and his daughter, who missed him greatly, said whilst she was pasturing the horse that she would marry anyone who could bring him back home. The horse then galloped away, arrived in the presence of the father, neighing so insistently that the man got on the horse and was brought home. The family was very pleased, and the horse was treated extra well, but it would not eat and became very agitated whenever the daughter came near it. When the father found out from his daughter what she had said, he had the horse killed. It was flayed and the skin left to dry outside the house. The daughter was playing on the skin when suddenly it curled up wrapping the girl inside and flew away. Later a new creature, the silkworm, appeared, hanging on the branch of a nearby mulberry tree, eating its leaves and was assumed to be the metamorphosed girl wrapped in the horse's skin. She was later deified as the Goddess of Silkworm or Lozu.

Third Sister Liu

Third Sister Liu was a champion singer and improviser of songs in the south of the country, in the Cantonese area, who defeated all the men who sang in competition against her. The custom, still prevalent amongst minority tribes today, was that girls and boys would have singing matches that were mating festivals as well, and these sometimes lasted for days. Third Sister Liu was famed for the beauty of her songs and was known locally as the Immortal of Songs. The story is that she chose her own mate and refused to be intimidated into marrying a local grandee. She is an example of those strong-minded, independent women, who with their skills earn respect and the right to do as they pleased, especially in the matter of marriage.

The Tushan Lady

Yü, the Water Controller (*see* Section I, p. 229), was 30 years old and unmarried because he was too busy with his work. In the course of his travels he arrived at Tushan (Mount Tu) where he saw a fox with nine tails which led him to a woman whom he subsequently married. After they were married, the Tushan Lady would bring him food at work, when he called to her on a drum, but he forbade her to go to him unless he summoned her. One day he touched the drum accidentally without realizing it and when his wife approached him, she was horrified to see him in the shape of a bear, digging channels for the water. She fled, followed by her husband, and in her terror turned into stone. When Yü caught up with her and demanded his son, with whom she was pregnant, the stone split open to yield the child, who was called Qi, which means 'open'.

Wushan Goddess

Yaoji was a daughter of the god Yandi (*see* Section I, p. 227). She died and was buried on the southern slope of Wushan (Mount Wu), and was known as the Lady of Wushan. Later King Huai of Chu encountered her on the mountain, and when she left him at dawn she identified herself and told him that she manifested herself in the cloud and rain of the mountainside (a reference to cloud and rain came to be a Chinese euphemism for sexual intercourse).

Xiang River Goddesses

The first of these was named E'huang and was the daughter of the Emperor Yao (see Section I, p. 228). She married, along with her sister, Nuying, the Emperor Shun who succeeded Yao. On the death of Shun, the two women wandered in grief along the River Yangzi and the River Xiang, where they died and were buried. They became deified as the Goddesses of the River Xiang.

Zhu Yingtai

Zhu Yingtai was a talented young woman from a wealthy family from the province of Zhejiang. When it was time for her to be married, she refused to be betrothed and persuaded her family to allow her to away to study, which she did dressed as a young man. She attended school for three years during which time she fell in love with a fellow student by the name of Liang Shangbo – without ever revealing that she was a woman. At the end of her studies she returned home, after telling Liang that she would like him to marry her sister.

By the time Liang had located her home and found out who she was, she had already been betrothed to another family. He then died of a broken heart and when Zhu Yingtai passed by his grave on her way to her marriage, she wept and refused to go any further. At this point the grave mound opened up and she entered it to be swallowed up.

It was said that they took the shape of a pair of butterflies and fly around together still. (A pair of butterflies is a symbol of true-love, just like the mandarin duck, which is supposed to mate for life, and the inter-connected branch – when branches from two different trees grow into each other.)

SECTION IV: MYTHOGRAPHY

The ancient myths of China from the basin of the Yellow River, the cradle of the Chinese race, survive only in fragments, embedded in the texts of poetry and other documents that are still preserved. The nearest thing to a collection of myths that survives is a very ancient book, first mentioned in the second century BC, called the *Classic of Mountains and Seas*, which is in a very incomplete state; it started off as a book of pictures with captions, but the captions were lost in antiquity. Scholars have re-constructed the book from quotations but much remains unclear.

Poetry is a valuable source of myths, but there was no Homer to write up moving stories or construct a coherent system of the gods of ancient China. What references that are found tend to be allusions that seldom elaborate, such as in the *Classic of Songs*, sometimes known as the *Book of Odes* (eleventh to sixth century BC). The most tempting source of all is the poem 'Questioning Heaven', which is in the pre-Han collection of poems called *Songs of the South*. In it a number of questions are asked as to how heaven and earth began and which god did what, but there are no answers. Nevertheless, the fragments and allusions scattered around various texts refer to a fairly unified body of myths, with variants, that explain natural phenomena and how the world was created, in much the same way as the ancient Greek myths.

One reason that so little has survived is that the literary establishment from the time of Confucius in the sixth century BC was profoundly sceptical about the supernatural. Confucius himself rebuked a disciple for asking about gods and spirits by saying that if he did not understand enough about humans, what was he doing meddling with spirits? The answer, whilst implying the existence of the supernatural, effectively ruled it out as a proper study, let alone for onward transmission through scholarly means such as books. The Confucian emphasis on human experience also meant much attention being paid to history, even though the two may be identical in the case of early history.

Legendary and historical characters are constantly alluded to in literature, and are held up as examples of human behaviour in the same way as mythical or biblical figures are in other cultures. For example, a standard textbook for women, who were not expected to get very far if at all in reading, was the *Accounts of Outstanding Women* (Lienuzhuan), a compilation from the first century BC by the scholar Liu Xiang, who culled all the stories from surviving ancient texts, especially the Confucian Classics. The intention was that these women, virtuous in the Confucian way, would be exemplars for all women, such as Mencius's Mother (*see* Section III, p. 241). The book does contain a chapter on 'depraved women', such as Daji and Baosi (*see* Section III, p. 240), which no doubt was meant to provide negative examples. Whilst this book is not a rich source for myths, it does contain some stories, such as those about E'huang and Nuying (*see* Section III, p. 244).

Not all myths and folklore were kept out of written sources; a considerable body of fiction, especially tales of marvel, were produced from the fourth century onwards. Many of these contain themes based on myths and legends. Short stories in elegant Classical prose were written in the eighth and ninth centuries during the Tang dynasty, some of which drew on folk-tale and legend. Religious literature, in spite of Confucianism, naturally existed in China, but it tended to remain in the oral tradition, and until the advent of cheap and widespread printing in the fifteenth century, in the Ming dynasty, transmission of the popular tradition was a haphazard business. With printing, our sources of popular religion, legends and folk-tales increase dramatically. Buddhist sutras were the first to be widely propagated in print, and religious material for circulation amongst the faithful soon followed, especially stories about piety. But the most widespread sources of legends and folklore are the long novels that are based on story cycles (sometimes referred to as the 'Classical novels'), which had been circulating in the oral traditions of ballads, public story-telling and drama.

One of the best-known cycle of stories is contained in the *Journey to the West*. This tells a *Pilgrims' Progress*-like account of the monk Tripitaka, a real Buddhist theologian from the seventh century AD, who made a journey to India to collect sutras to bring back to China for the better transmission and understanding of Buddhism. Tripitaka is accompanied on this journey by three mythical figures: the Monkey, who is probably derived from the Monkey King of Indian mythology, and who also represents the spiritedness and ambition of man; the Pig, who represents the grosser appetites of man; and Sandman, a reformed ogre who possibly represents the indifference of man. The adventures they meet on the way are a mixture of exciting narrative and symbolism, culminating in their arrival in India. Many individual episodes from the story form the subject of plays and other writing. Typical of the style of derring-do of these stories, there are few women represented, and those that are often evil – appearing especially in the shape of man-eating demons.

Whilst the *Journey to the West* has a strong folklore element other story cycles are more historical. Popular concepts about the period of the Three Kingdoms (third century AD) have been entirely based on the story-cycle novel *Three Kingdoms*, which is as reliable a way of learning history, as through Shakespeare's historical plays. The *Three Kingdoms*, however, provide a range of human characters and behaviour that have been continuously alluded to ever since.

The oral tradition did not die with the advent of printing; with a population as large as China's, of which the great proportion has been illiterate, the oral tradition continued to flourish, even in the largely literate urban centres. Drama, in the form of local operas, remained particularly popular – and has done so right up to the present day – and many of their themes were based on the age-old legends and folk-tales that we know existed a thousand or more years ago. In the 1960s, the Chinese Communist Party in their drive for ideological purity denounced these local plays as archaic, decadent and feudal in concept, and banned them from being performed. After the death of Mao, most were revived and enjoyed popularity – they are often performed now on television.

The stock of such legends and folk-tales is still being continually drawn on not just for entertainment but for specific purposes, especially political. Shortly after the Communist Party took power they issued a new version of the Monkey story, called 'Havoc in Heaven', based on the episodes from the *Journey to the West* in which the Monkey acquired supernatural powers. It was interpreted as the rebellion of the humble and the weak against the powers of the establishment. Later, in 1978, after the fall from power of the much hated wife of Mao Zedong, Jiang Qing, who had acquired great influence in the latter days of her husband's rule by virtue of her marriage, one of the most popular plays performed and sold in book form was a new version of the episode from the *Journey to the West* when the Pilgrims encounter the White Boned Demon – a vampire in the guise of a woman intent on eating Tripitaka. Her annihilation was seen as a satire on the fall of Mme Mao.

Notes

1 The spelling of Chinese names in this contribution is according to the Pinyin system of transcription, and the names are pronounced more or less as the letters would suggest in English, bearing in mind that *u* is pronounced *oo* (as in *hoop*), *xi* is pronounced *shi* (as in *ship*) and *zh* is pronounced like *dr* (as in *drip*). The exception to this is the word Taoism (Daoism in the Pinyin system), which has been left in the older Wade-Giles transcription that is more familiar to English readers.

References and Further Reading

Birch, C. (1961), *Chinese Myths and Fantasies* (London: Oxford University Press)

Dudbridge, G. (1978), *Legend of Miaoshan* (London: Ithaca Press for the Board of Oriental Studies, Oxford University)

Eberhard, W. (1937), *Chinese Fairy Tales and Folktales* (London: Routledge and Kegan Paul)

Eberhard, W. (1965), *Folktales of China* (London: Routledge, Kegan and Paul)

Eberhard, W. (1970), *Studies in Chinese Folklore* (The Hague: Indiana University Research Centre for the Language Sciences)

Hawkes, D. (1967), 'The Quest of the Goddess' in *Asia Major*, 13, pp. 71–94

Jin, S. (1982), *Beijing Legends*, trans. G. Yang (Beijing: Panda Books)

Ling, M.C. and Feng, M.L. (1957), *The Courtesan's Jewel Box: Chinese Stories of the Xth–XVIIIth Centuries*, trans. G. Yang and H.Y. Yand (Peking: Foreign Languages)

Liu Sanders, T.T. (1969), *The Herdboy and the Ox* (Oxford: Oxford University Press)

Liu Sanders, T.T. and Pau, J. (1980), *Dragons, Gods and Spirits from Chinese Mythology* (London: Eurobooks)

Paul, D.Y. (1979), *Women in Buddhism* (Berkeley: Asian Humanities Press)

O'Hara, A.R. (1971), *The Position of Woman in Early China* (Taipei: Mei Ya Publications)

Qu Yuan (1985), *Songs of the South*, trans. D. Hawkes (London: Penguin Books)

Thompson, L.G. (1985), *Chinese Religion in Western Languages: A Comprehensive and Classified Bibliography of Publications in English, French and German through 1980*, Monograph of the Association for Asian Studies, 41, updated ed. of *Studies of Chinese Religion* (1976) (Tucson: University of Arizona)

Werner, E.T.C. (1932), *A Dictionary of Chinese Myths*, re-issued with new introduction 1961 (New York: The Julian Press Inc.)

Werner, E.T.C. (1922, reprinted 1986), *Myths and Legends of China* (Taipei: Caves)

Yang, H.Y. and Yang, G. (1962), *The Dragon King's Daughter: Ten T'ang Dynasty Stories* (Peking: Foreign Languages Press)

PART 4

Oceania

ISOBEL WHITE
AND HELEN PAYNE

Australian
Aboriginal Myth

Isobel White

INTRODUCTION: OUTLINE OF MYTHOLOGY

Australian Aboriginal mythology and religion cannot easily be related to those of other areas of the world because there are few shared features. The mythic beings of Australian Aboriginal belief are not like gods or goddesses elsewhere. They are human beings with supernatural powers rather than supernatural beings, and they are neither worshipped nor propitiated. There are no priests, though each community has its ritual leaders for each myth and associated ceremony. These are older men and women who have become leaders, not through inheritance but by having taken steps since their youth to gain superior knowledge. Similarly, in these egalitarian communities, the rise to secular leadership is through superior effort, knowledge and competence. In some areas, secular leadership may coincide with religious leadership since religion is a primary focus for behaviour.

The whole continent is criss-crossed with the tracks of mythical ancestral beings. At first, the earth itself was flat, dark and featureless until these travellers made it as it is today. They journeyed over the land creating mountains, rocks and rivers and other features of the landscape, as well as people, plants, trees, animals and birds, so that every natural phenomenon has its creation story and every piece of country has its associated myth. Though it might seem that these happenings were long past, the ancestral beings and their actions are also here and now, so that the living men and women are at the same time themselves and their ancestors. They must re-enact the lives of their ancestors, otherwise the land and its people will not flourish. Creation must be repeated continually. Much time therefore is devoted to ceremonies, with the actors repeating the acts of their ancestors.

When they had finished their acts of creation, some of the mythic beings went up into the sky and became stars, while others remained at their journey's end having turned themselves into rocks, hills, water holes, trees or other features of the landscape that are still visible today. In some myths, the ancestors manifest themselves as birds or animals or other creatures and behave in part like such creatures and in part like humans. Their descendants have the creature as totem or 'dreaming'.

Ownership of the myths or 'histories' (as Aborigines call them when speaking English) is passed down through the generations and includes the right and duty to organize the performance of the associated ceremony. This may be a short and simple rite performed at a particular site by a few owners of the site. There are also long ceremonial cycles that may take months or even years to complete, with a preliminary period required to make the elaborate ritual objects and to prepare the ceremonial ground. In the old days, weather and season determined when these could be held, so that in the desert areas some ceremonies could be performed only after good rains had made it possible for many of the scattered groups to come together; there would then be enough food in the vicinity to last some time. The men, who were the organizers and performers of such ceremonies, became dependent on the food collected by the women, who could therefore determine how long the ceremonies would last (Hamilton, 1980, pp. 14–15).

Rain-Making

Since so much of Australia is arid, or at best subject to prolonged drought, the Aborigines had various rites, validated by myths, performed to ensure that rain would fall in the appropriate season and to make rain when an area was suffering from drought. At an individual level men and women could be rain-makers, but the collective ceremonies were organized by men. The community I visited was in a dry area but rain normally fell in the spring – about mid-September. I was present in two successive Septembers for the annual rain-making ceremony. This is one of the many ceremonies for which men, the chief organizers and performers, require the presence and participation of women at intervals. The performance began at dusk some distance from the camp. Soon the women and children were summoned from the camp and allowed to sing and to watch the men's dancing for a time; then the women were ordered to cover themselves and the children with blankets so that they could not see the next sequence. They were then ordered peremptorily to return to the camp, only to be summoned back later. This programme continued for much of the night. The next day, in both years, rain fell (White, 1979). Undoubtedly on the occasion of the annual rain ceremony, the men of this community asserted their authority over their womenfolk but, as I discuss below, I thought the women of the Western Desert seemed to have less authority than in some other areas.

Belief in Myth

Readers might ask how far Aborigines believe in the truth of the myths recounted here. The demeanour of the tellers reveals implicit belief: the myths are 'histories', not mere 'stories' told for amusement. 'They are "living myths" . . . they were believed in by the people who told them . . . they embody "truth" purporting to depict what actually happened' (R. and C. Berndt, 1989, p. 4).

During a ceremony the performers become imbued with the power of the ancestors. While I was living in a Pitjantjatjara camp all the men left in the early morning on 'men's business'. All day the women sat in their own camps, the children

Fig. 23 Pitjantjatjara (Western Desert) women gathering for a ceremony.

stayed by their sides playing quietly, and there was no moving about or visiting. All conversation was in low tones. When a signal came that the men were returning all the women sat with their heads bowed. I was told, 'Do not look at the men, they are very powerful and very dangerous.' After some time a signal was given and normal behaviour was restored.

During the time they are dancing on the ceremonial ground the actors actually become the ancestors they represent. I was made fully aware of this belief when I was watching a secret ceremony – at which no men were allowed – performed by Pitjantjatjara women of the Western Desert. When two small snakes appeared between the feet of the two dancing women this was interpreted as the result of the two ancestral women passing the snakes in their urine to warn the gathering to stop the ceremony because some men were watching. To negate the powerful forces invoked, sand was thrown in the air, the dancers quickly rubbed out the patterns painted on their bodies and used bundles of twigs to erase their tracks in the sand (White, 1975, p. 133).

There is no doubt that there is absolute belief in the more bizarre accounts of devils and evil spirits, since the measures taken to combat them are very real. For example, among the people I live with, fires are kept alight all the time, particularly throughout the night, and many dogs are kept. *Mamu*, the dangerous evil spirits, do not come near fires; dogs can see them, though humans cannot; the loud barking of the dogs keeps them away and warns of their approach. Children are taught not to leave the circle of the firelight after dark and it takes a brave adult to do so, and then only in the company of several dogs.

It is always a surprise to one who has been brought up to regard religion as something extremely serious to find that, though the Aboriginal myths and ceremonies are treated with great respect, they are not invariably regarded as a matter for long faces and serious demeanour. Once I went camping with my friends for a few nights away from the main camp, so that they could perform their own ceremonies well away from their menfolk. One evening we were sitting round the fire while the ritual leader, a great story teller, told us the myth of Nyiru with dramatic action, until we were all quite sick with laughing. Another time of great hilarity is at the end of the first version (see later), where the actors taking the part of the newly married woman, together with a woman taking the part of a man, simulate copulation (not in the 'missionary' position) to the best of their acting skill.

A Traditionally Oriented Community

The community in which I spent some time on fieldwork was what I would call a transitional community – one that is still clinging to all practicable traditions. The older members told me that they had been 'born in the bush' and could remember seeing white people for the first time. Mission and settlement life had disrupted their economy entirely – they now ate store-bought food supplemented by hunting – but they retained many traditional practices, among them the importances of kinship in determining social relationships. Ceremonial life was still strong, though rituals at the proper sacred sites could not be performed, the people having been forcibly removed from their own country in the 1950s because of the British-Australian bomb tests.

Ceremonies for the initiation of boys into manhood were still carried out, including the rites of circumcision and subincision (the slitting open of the underside of the penis from the meatus to a point about 2.5 cm along the urethra) but the time involved was short because of the pressures of schooling and jobs, so that the long period of two or three years in the desert away from the company of women no longer occurred. The initiates were young men in the late teens or early twenties rather than boys in the first stages of adolescence. Traditionally, the circumciser promised a daughter, born or unborn, to the initiate as a future bride. Such a promise is not always honoured in recent times. Sometimes a young couple would form a liaison before the man was initiated; an attempt to observe the old formalities would be made by the young woman's father acting as circumciser of the young man.

The women's ceremonies were falling into a sad decline and some of those I saw were only revived to please me, and have not been performed since. In some of the communities of the Western and Central Deserts, the women have clung more firmly to their old ways, so that the ceremonies are regularly performed. Where the communities are in their traditional territories, the women (and the men too) can perform the appropriate rites at their own sacred sites.

Published Myths

There are few written records of Aboriginal myths from the first century of European settlement in Australia. The new arrivals struggled to reconstruct their own traditional way of life in an alien environment and showed little interest in a way of life so alien to their own. Few myths were recorded from the south-east and south-west of the continent where conquest and settlement were most complete. A few Europeans collected some fragments of myths but with little understanding that the whole continent was peopled by mythic beings. In the second half of the nineteenth century, the worldwide rise of interest in native peoples inspired a few scholars and the more educated of the settlers to write books about Australia's Aborigines, but by the standards of today they did not ask the right questions, nor were they trusted enough to be told the most sacred myths.

Since the end of the last century, and more especially in the last forty years, non-Aborigines, and some Aborigines, have begun to write down some of the great body of Aboriginal traditional myth.

Some of the early collections of myths, from the late nineteenth and early twentieth centuries, read like 'Just-so' stories and concern the reasons for the appearance and habits of animals, reptiles and birds. Such a story which appears with variations in most of the collections tells how, by guile, the plains turkey persuaded the pair of emus to cut off their wings, and in revenge the emu mother persuaded the turkey mother to reduce her brood of chicks to only two (Langloh Parker, 1896, pp. 1–5). (This tale rings untrue to anyone aware that it is the male emu who hatches and broods his chicks; this is well-known to the desert Aborigines since their sacred emu myth is about a father emu and his brood.) These 'Just-so' stories have their uses in teaching moral precepts, for they tell of those who suffered through their stupidity, pride or greed.

With the turn of the century there arose a much more serious and scholarly approach to Aboriginal mythology. In particular, A.W. Howitt (1904, pp. 779–806) wrote down the myths of the Lake Eyre people (these even included tales about the fossils of extinct giant marsupials for which that area is now famous); W.B. Spencer and F.J. Gillen told the myths of the Northern Territory peoples, mainly along the recently completed telegraph line (1899, 1904, 1914, 1927); while C. Strehlow, the pastor at the Hermannsburg Lutheran mission, collected myths from the Aranda and Loritja (1907–20). (His son, T.G.H. Strehlow, brought up speaking Aranda, continued this work a generation later.)

In the tropical north and in the inland desert areas, where European settlement is sparse, there are Aboriginal communities where the old ceremonies are still performed. In the margins of the closely settled areas, there are a few old people who can recount the myths and sing the relevant songs even if there are no longer enough of them to perform the ceremonies. During the last half century, there has been much research in these areas by anthropologists, linguists and historians — research encouraged and largely funded by the Australian Institute of Aboriginal Studies since its foundation in 1961. Noteworthy publications are *Myths of the Mungkan* by U. McConnel, published in 1957, although the myths were collected in 1930s; *Songs of Central Australia* by T.G.H. Strehlow (1971), representing a lifetime's experiences among the Aranda and Loritja; *Australian Aboriginal Mythology*, edited by L.R. Hiatt (1975); and, in 1989, a most welcome publication,

The Speaking Land, by R. and C. Berndt, containing almost 200 myths from various parts of the continent collected over the last fifty years.

SECTION II: TYPES OF MYTH

Myths can be classified into four types: those belonging to children and passed on from one generation of children to the next (not discussed here); those known to everyone, with adults telling them to children and with children present at their re-enactment; those belonging to men and kept secret from women; and those belonging to women and kept secret from men.

The majority of myths are known to men and women and are taught to the children. The whole community attends their performance – the children are of necessity there too, because they cannot be left alone in the camp while their mothers go to the ceremonial ground. All are required to know the songs and to sing them, though sometimes the men sing alone while the women beat time by hitting their thighs with cupped hands. Both men and women dance, though the more spectacular dances are performed by men in most of these ceremonies. (However, Helen Payne records that when women admit men to their ceremonies, the women are the more assertive performers.) Examples are the mortuary rites, which act the myths of the coming of death to the world; dances performed at the beginning of the cycle of ceremonies marking the initiation of boys, these dramatize the myths of the ancestors who introduced these rites; the 'increase' rites (as they are often called), though better designated as 'maintenance' rites, performed if possible at ancestral sites – some of these rites are performed by men and women alone with the other sex excluded; the rain ceremony I have already described is in this category (*see* p. 252). These public dramas are performed with reverence; they invoke the power of the ancestral beings.

Men's Myths and Secrecy

This category of myth is known to men alone, or at least women are not supposed to know them, though older women learn them in some way or other. (What matters is not so much what you know as what you are supposed to know.) These are the myths validating the secret sections of the initiation rites for boys and some parts of the 'maintenance' rites owned by men. Connected with the latter are a network of sacred places that must not be seen or visited by females and uninitiated youths. Such secrets are closely guarded by the men and secrecy has become quite sensationalized in their telling to male researchers, so that the written accounts of Aboriginal religious activities are mostly overweighted by this secrecy. The earliest serious researchers, such as Spencer and Gillen, wrote about these secrets in detail and published photographs of the performers. At that time none of those taking part could read – they hardly knew what a book was – but today such accounts are deeply offensive to living Aborigines, so that researchers take care not to reveal any secret information they have been given.

Fig. 24 Pitjantjatjara (Western Desert) woman beating time on her thigh.

It is the circumcising areas and particularly in the Central and Western Deserts that men maintain the most secrecy about some parts of their ceremonies and the associated myths. In recent times, this exaggerated secrecy has extended eastward through the movement of Western Desert people (Hercus, 1989, pp. 115–16). Thus there was considerable variation throughout the continent in the amount of women's knowledge of the men's myths and ceremonies. This was balanced to some extent by the existence of women's secret myths and ceremonies in those areas where men maintained the most secrecy.

I discuss later the ambivalent attitudes about gender relations shown in the women's myths from the desert regions. I depend on male researchers to show that men's attitudes may also be ambivalent. T.G.H. Strehlow writes that:

> . . . the female ancestors celebrated in Aranda myths are usually dignified and sometimes awe-inspiring . . . Frequently they were much more powerful beings than their male associates, and the latter sometimes lived in constant terror of their mysterious supernatural strength . . . Reverently proud of the powerful feminine characters described in their ancient legends, Aranda men look down on their own women with a certain measure of pitying contempt.
>
> (STREHLOW, 1947, P. 94)

Women's Myths and Secrecy

Thus we come to the myths and associated ceremonies known only to women. (The remarks above about older women knowing the men's secrets apply also to older men, who are allowed to know some women's secrets.) When speaking English Aborigines refer to the two realms of secrecy as 'men's business' and 'women's business' and reflect the sexual segregation of Aboriginal society, frequently described in the literature, particularly by women writers (e.g. C. Berndt, 1970; Hamilton, 1980; White, 1970). This separation is most marked in what is known as 'women's business' which includes not only the women's secret ceremonies but also all those aspects of life peculiar to women, notably childbirth and menstruation.

The myths known only to adults are of a serious nature and contain the profound secrets of a highly religious and philosophical people. These reveal something about the relations between the sexes – not so much actual relations as the fantasies and dreams of those who first announce the myths and reveal the ceremonies. (Aborigines believe that they are, and were, revealed in dreams.) Our knowledge would be better balanced if there had been more study of women, but as in the whole of anthropology, male researchers used to gain nearly all their information from men, and until quite recently they have outnumbered female researchers. Pioneers in the study of women's myth and ceremony are P. Kaberry in the 1930s, C. Berndt from the 1940s until today, and C. Ellis since the 1960s. I was fortunate to be one of the team of women that the ethnomusicologist C. Ellis led into the Western Desert in the 1960s to record on tape, film and still photography the secret ceremonies of the Andagarinja women. As a group we visited several communities and later I went alone to visit another, where I was able to witness a number of ceremonies, to learn many of the myths and to observe women's life as a participant, though I do not claim that the women revealed to me the deepest level of meaning of their myths.

Helen Payne and Françoise Dussart have recently been researching women's ceremonies, the first among Pitjantjatjara women, the second among Warlpiri women. Payne's and Dussart's work adds much to our knowledge of women's myths and ceremonies in the desert areas. Payne, an ethnomusicologist, stresses the ownership of each sacred site, associated with particular mythical ancestresses, by certain women who pass this on to her sisters, and how the ownership is validated by the songs. Dussart, an anthropologist, is concerned with the performance of the ceremonies, who has the right to perform them and how particular women can dream new ceremonies or additions to existing ones, though only within the existing mythical content.

Those of us who have been admitted to the women's ceremonies respect the promises we made not to reveal the details of the myths and ceremonies; therefore we can publish only the broad outlines. Our friends believe that ill will befall any males who see their pictures or hear the records of their singing or learn the details of their stories.

The more I think about the women's myths, those parts of the men's myths that are in the public domain, and even the more generally known stories, the more I realize how ambivalent the two sexes are in their attitudes to each other. Let me illustrate this with variations of a common pattern in the stories I have seen acted by women in the Western Desert. (I tell these stories in outline. The details and the deeper meanings are secret.)

First variation: The numbers represent acts of a play. The song words, the melody and the rhythm are different for each act.

Fig. 25 Pitjantjatjara (Western Desert) woman with a string figure illustrating a myth.

1. Two sisters journey through desert country. They find food at certain named places. (They might have created this food source, for at each place they stopped they left signs.)
2. They suffer from heat and thirst. They find water and shade. (Again they might have created these, by urinating to form a water hole and by planting their digging sticks to grow into trees.)
3. The younger sister begins her first menstruation, a sign she will soon be ready for marriage, so the elder sister instructs her in the pleasures of sex.
4. They look for a man (who may already be the elder sister's husband) and find his tracks. They have a desire for sex. This may be expressed in the euphemism 'they are looking for meat'.
5. The man is also looking for them and finds their tracks.
6. They come together and he takes both as his wives (it is proper for a man to have real or classificatory sisters as co-wives).
7. Celebratory dancing and singing.

Second variation: The first three acts are the same.

4. They find a man's tracks. They are angry with him because he has kidnapped or raped one of their 'sisters'.
5. They follow him, vowing revenge.
6. They catch him and mutilate him.
7. Celebratory dancing and singing.

A further variation is that the man may be rejected because his penis is too large and the women are frightened. He follows them, they run away and go up into the sky and become stars.

Some constellations are the end result of a major myth cycle known to both men and women in the desert. Variations of it occur in other areas of the continent. In the desert, men and women have their own secret versions, performed as separate ceremonies. Though the broad outlines of the two versions of the myth are much the same, we do not know if the sung and danced versions are similar since the male and female research workers who witnessed them have obeyed the restrictions to secrecy and have not compared their tapes and photographs.

The myth concerns Nyiru (a Don Juan figure) who finally became the constellation we know as Orion. He spends his time chasing the Kunggkarangara (or many women) who become the Pleiades or Seven Sisters (in the clear desert skies it is easy to see more than seven small stars). In the women's version, Nyiru catches and rapes one of the sisters at a time immediately after she has given birth and is therefore under a taboo. The women chase him and he is mutilated by their dogs. The women rejoice and go up into the sky and he follows them there.

This seemed to be the most significant ceremony of the women I lived with, and I saw it on a number of occasions. Though performed with extreme attention to detail, it always occasioned hilarity.

When a woman was required to take the part of a man, an older woman who had experienced her menopause was chosen. In the case of the ritual leader at our camp, who had spent the day acting the part of Nyiru, another woman told me 'she's the only man among us'. She was indeed the oldest woman there, probably the only one past menopause. This shows that in this society a woman past childbearing can be granted the status of a man in some respects. Older women have a considerable knowledge of men's secrets so this suggests that it is women's fertility that causes men to keep secrets from them. For men, it seems that it is age and infirmity that gives them access to women's secrets for I have seen two very old men (one of them blind) handling women's secret objects and reciting sections of the women's myths.

At the other end of the life cycle young girls seem to be regarded as sexless. I have seen a 9-year-old girl, whose older sister was to be promised to a young man then in segregation before initiation, being sent with food and cigarettes as gifts from his future mother-in-law. It is only while a woman is able to give birth that she is regarded as a real woman.

Myth as History

Myths may be viewed as memories of events of long ago, passed on by word of mouth through the generations. There are myths in Arnhem Land about ancestral women arriving from the sea, travelling and giving birth to many human offspring, speaking different languages in the different areas. Research suggests that human beings arrived in Arnhem Land from the north or north-west 40,000 to 60,000 years ago. The earliest arrivals must have multiplied and spread over the whole continent; thus the 'songlines' and 'histories' could possibly represent the travels of the actual human ancestors, but it is a long time for folk-memory to survive. It seems natural, moreover, for peoples who needed to travel for food, water and other necessities to have myths about mobile rather than static beings, and these myths could be about current travels, since they seem to follow trading routes throughout the continent.

R. and C. Berndt summarize and discuss certain myths from the north and from the centre which tell of women losing ritual power through giving their ritual objects to women or of men stealing these objects from the women (R. and C. Berndt, 1964, pp. 214–16). A similar myth from Cape York Peninsula told to U. McConnel relates how two girls found a bull-roarer (an object now sacred to men everywhere), but gave it to the men saying, 'It is they who will swing it. To us it will be forbidden!' These myths could be seen as evidence for a previous state of matriarchy, but only if all myths are to be taken as historical narrative. Then, logically, the following myth told to McConnel should also represent historical fact though it represents an impossibility:

> Two brothers travel together along the beach catching fish as they go. When they camp the younger brother makes a fire and fetches water, then cooks the fish. When the younger sleeps the older brother wants a woman, so he cuts off his brother's genitals and gives him a vagina and breasts. In the morning he puts the younger brother's spears with his own, makes his wife a digging stick. She makes a dilly-bag and collects shell-fish to put in it and a basket to carry her yams. When they camp she collects firewood and makes a fire.

So many myths about the origins of the land, the people and the animals are fantastic and incredible that historical explanations of myth must be discarded, including the myth of matriarchy.

The Myth of Matriarchy

In 1974 Joan Bamberger wrote the landmark paper 'The Myth of Matriarchy: Why Men Rule in Primitive Society'. At that time some contemporary feminist writers had accepted Bachhofen's theory that classical myths describing the Rule of Women in times past represented historical truth. Bamberger demonstrated the lack of any historical basis for such myths and argued that the reasons mythic women lost their power – misrule, ineptitude or sexual deviance – were used as justification of male dominance. Bamberger examined ethnographic reports of South American societies which had myths of a previous matriarchy. They shared traits found among Australian Aboriginal societies. For example, the sexes are markedly separate in secular and ritual pursuits; initiation ceremonies for boys may take months while the girls' ceremonies are brief; the loss of power by women in the myths is connected with the loss to men of certain sacred objects. There, as in Australia, a boy's initiation marks a severe and sudden separation from the rule of women to the rule of men; Bamberger suggests that it is this individual experience rather than historical truth that is represented in the myths: 'The myth of the Rule of Women in its many variants may be regarded as a replay of these crucial transitional stages in the life cycle of an individual male' (Bamberger, 1974, p. 277).

In 1988 a further significant contribution to understanding mythology and gender relations was published – *Myths of Matriarchy Reconsidered*, edited by D. Gewertz, with contributions by eminent anthropologists who had studied societies in Papua New Guinea, Indonesia, Polynesia, Vanuatu and Australia. Although some were critical of Bamberger's methods, accusing her of over-generalization, none of them had been able to find matriarchies or a history of matriarchies, though almost all were told myths of previous rule by women. F. Errington and D. Gewertz argue that 'a myth of matriarchy may be less a *charter* for an existing relationship than part of a *chart* of imaginable relationships' (p. 195, emphasis in original). In contrast, N. Thomas writes that though there were matriarchy myths in Marquesan society, 'explicit notions of male or female power, of matriarchy or patriarchy, were alien to the Marquesans: neither men nor women but chiefs were perceived to rule' (p. 177).

A. Hamilton in Gewertz's volume contributes the article on Australian Aboriginal myths and suggests that Bamberger might have selected certain episodes in South American myths in order to prove her point. While reviewing published material on Australian myths, Hamilton found that discussion here too had been based on arbitrary selection of material, with little attention to the conditions under which the myths had been collected. She writes: 'In analysing the material presented above [T.G.H. Strehlow's account of Aranda myths] it is notable that women are nowhere said to "rule". Instead we learn that women and men generally lived separately, each possessing ceremonies and scared objects' (p. 67). Elsewhere in the same article, she suggests 'the necessity of a degree of caution in making definitive statements about the relation between myth and "social structure", or the way in which "a culture" justifies and transmits its social order' (p. 61).

Myths as Explanation

All societies possess explanations of the cosmos, their own existence and their origins. In western society, scientific discoveries are replacing these (to most of us) irrational myths, but among traditionally-oriented Aborigines myths are still believed to explain the universe, nature and human beings. I have already described how the first kind of myth reported by settlers were the simple 'Just-so' stories explaining the appearance and habits of living creatures. There are also myths that explain the sun, the moon, the earth and its natural features. For example, in Tiwi mythology, Pukwi, the sun, also known as the Old Woman, made the country, the land, sea and islands; her urine made the sea salt. 'Now she travels from east to west and back along the Milky Way at night. At midday she makes camp and builds a great fire and causes great heat' (Tiwi myth related by a 9-year-old child to Goodale, 1971, pp. 3–4).

The moon is a man, Tjapara, who took Bima, the wife of a great ancestor Purukapali, off into the bush to make love, leaving her infant son alone. She stayed away too long and Purukapali found his son dead. He fought and killed Tjapara. Then he took his son in his arms and walked backward into the sea, pronouncing the fateful death decree, 'As my son has died and will never return, so shall all men.' Purukapali and his son never came back, but Tjapara the moon came back in three days (Goodale, 1971, pp. 236–7).

R. and C. Berndt (1989, pp. 372–6) tell two stories from Arnhem Land about Moon and his connection with death for human beings but rebirth for Moon. In both accounts he is with a companion; they both die but Moon comes back in three days. Constellations of stars are also connected with myths. We have already seen how Nyiru and the Kunggkarangara became Orion and the Pleiades. My friends in the Western Desert told me that the Two Men (ancestors) became Gemini and the ancestral Eagle became the Southern Cross.

While myths from northern Australia tell of female all-powerful ancestors who were responsible for creating people, in the south and in the arid central areas these are male, at least in the myths told by men to male researchers, though the Pitjantjatjara women's myths told to women stress in addition to the Two Men two important female supreme beings.

Nevertheless, it is not possible to avoid the truth that it is women who give birth and therefore are responsible for the continuance of bodily life. An important group of myths, fairly similar throughout the continent, concern explanations for conception and birth (Montagu, 1974). At special places, the totemic ancestors left spirit entities, and without the entry of one of these a woman could not give birth to a live child, though there is no doubt that women understood that intercourse was necessary first. Spirit entry probably occurred at the time of the quickening of the foetus; the woman would already suspect that she was pregnant and movement would be confirmation. Some of the totems of the child were determined by the place where the spirit entered her. This might be revealed in a dream to the father, who then took the spirit and caused it to enter his wife (for example, Bates, 1985, pp. 133–9). In other areas, the spirit would enter the woman when she walked in one of the special places and it would then be she who would announce the totem place of the infant. But in either case, men could claim the power to cause birth, because it was their ceremonies that maintained the supply of spirit children.

In many areas for which we have knowledge, particularly the desert areas, the telling of myths and the performances of the ceremonies re-enacting them are regarded as essential for maintaining the bodily and spiritual existences of societies. Women and men divide these tasks between them. Women's myths and ceremonies are about female ancestors and concern 'women's business' — the reproduction of bodily life and the maintenance of health and harmony — with men as incidental characters. Men's myths and ceremonies are about male ancestors and concern 'men's business' — the reproduction of spiritual life — with women as incidental characters (Hiatt, 1971; White, 1970).

A different explanation for the entry of spirit children was told to Luise Hercus and me by Adjamathanha men and women of the Flinders Ranges of South Australia, where the important division of society is into two matrilineal moieties. They said there were two ancestral women in the sky who held many spirit children in their arms, one holding those that would be of the Araru moiety and the other those of the Mathari moiety. These old women choose likely women on earth and send spirit children of the appropriate moiety to enter them. (The same myth is published in a paper by C.P. Mountford and A. Harvey, 1941, pp. 156–7.)

Myth as Charter

We come now to the theory that myths can be interpreted as setting a charter for behaviour, with good deeds by ancestors serving as examples and bad deeds showing how not to behave. This theory might be satisfactory if all misdeeds were punished but when we examine a number of published myths we find that this is not so: deviant behaviour may or may not be punished. There are indeed some myths that tell of exemplary behaviour but many describe dreadful deeds, trickery, cruelty, incest, rape, murder, cannibalism. The perpetrators may be male or female; many of the crimes are of a sexual nature, incest or rape by men, seduction and infidelity by women. In previous research into the myths of the desert areas, I discovered that there were frequent episodes of adulterous, incestuous or violent sexual relations, and that these misdeeds were seldom punished. These led me to the conclusion that they were in the nature of sexual fantasies (White, 1975, pp. 137–9). The exemplary ones and those where evil was punished seem to lie in the public domain, and were therefore known to children, while the bad ones are those kept secret and known only to adults. We could see an analogy here with western society, where governments may allow access to pornographic and violent films and video cassettes to adults, but not to children.

An example of proper behaviour is McConnel's myth of the two brothers told above (*see* p. 261). Another, also from McConnel, is a lengthy myth of a black snake man and his dove wife:

> They camp and move on, the husband giving instructions to the wife, which she obeys. He fishes while she collects vegetable food. She gives birth to a child and while she is in labour and resting after the birth, the husband stays in a separate camp not seeing the wife or the infant. When the lochia has ceased to flow she comes to him, shows him the child, he takes it in his arms and performs the ritual of acceptance. They continue to behave in a proper way and finally go to their own totem places and become clan totems.
>
> (SUMMARIZED FROM McCONNEL, 1957, PP. 136–41)

A myth of wrong behaviour punished was told in 1912 to D. Bates near the Great Australian Bight in South Australia:

> Some women lived by themselves and went out hunting for meat every day. The Great Snake, the upholder of the law, told them they should collect vegetable food, proper women's work and not hunt meat, for this is men's work. They continued as before so the Great Snake turned them all into tall peaked termites' nests and as these they remain to this day.
>
> (KER WILSON, 1972, P. 84)

There is a similar Walbiri myth about some women who insist on hunting with their men. They disturb the prey by being too eager; they are beaten by the men and told that 'it is a woman's task to carry burdens and not to try to hunt' (Meggitt, 1966, p. 135). The women still claim that they can hunt quite well, leave these men and hunt successfully. (While living with Aborigines I found out myself that women did not hunt with men when they were together but enjoyed going out on hunting parties with women only and were successful.)

These three myths demonstrate the proper division of labour between men and women. There are some myths showing how other institutions arose. For example, Spencer and Gillen describe how in myths told by men the ancestors gave the people such institutions as their totems, the totemic places and the totemic clans, their sacred objects, their initiation rites and the division into the four sections governing marriages (Spencer and Gillen, 1927, pp. 304–54). Meggitt was told by Walbiri men that ancestors laid down the rules for initiation and the division into subsections (Meggitt, 1962, pp. 165–7). Such myths reinforce existing and known behaviour rather than setting examples.

Here are two examples of violent and horrible deeds which *were* punished (both summarized from R. and C. Berndt, 1989):

A grandfather rapes his young granddaughter, injuring her thighs. He is killed with an axe by the girl's husband who has not yet had intercourse with her because she is still too young.

(PP. 241–4)

A father who commits incest with his young daughter is eaten by the Great Snake, who eats the girls and her older sister as well, because they also were regarded as wrong for allowing the crime.

(PP. 239–40)

What about the many myths which tell of deviant, cruel and often sadistic behaviour, where punishment does not follow? For example in the men's version of the Seven Sisters story (*see* above, p. 260), after the women have cut off Nyiru's penis it continues on its own sweet way, frightening and penetrating women, and is finally rejoined to Nyiru. This is surely not a moral tale to teach young people the rules of good behaviour. It is more credible to view it as male sexual fantasy, as I suggested in a previous paper (White, 1975, pp. 137–9).

In the myths told to McConnel the ancestors take the shape of animals, birds, lizards, snakes or insects. They behave in part like insects, in part like humans. Many of them, as in the myth above about the dove woman and her husband, the black snake man, behave according to the rules. But some do not; for example the salt-water crocodile, the 'enemy of law and order, ignoring all the strict taboos of social relationships, taking any woman who comes his way – be she mother, sister, daughter, or any other forbidden relative'. In one story, after he has performed many such incestuous acts, he goes apparently of his own will to his totem place in the salt water, but in another story, where he rapes two young girls, he is chopped to pieces by their father. In yet another myth he stole the wife of the fresh-water crocodile who fought him in revenge and drove him down to the salt water (McConnel, 1957, pp. 99–106).

Meggitt recounts at length a myth, told to him by Walbiri men:

> Two Warangari, mulga-tree, men order their wives to stay in camp while they take their sons away for circumcision. They beat their wives when these complain of being excluded from the ceremony. The wives are angered even more when the men go on their travels leaving them in charge of the boys who, they claim, should count as men now they are circumcised. In revenge they kill and eat the boys. Meantime the two men travel widely, experiencing many adventures, creating water-holes, collecting plant foods and discovering how to process them, hunting and making fire. Finally they return home, discover the terrible deeds of their wives and burn them to death in a cave. They travel once more, mourning their sons, but by a complicated series of rituals they bring their sons back to life.
>
> (SUMMARIZED FROM MEGGITT, 1966, PP. 295–300)

This myth has many interesting implications. In the first place it is women who are evil cannibals, though the writer emphasizes that cannibalism is abhorred by Walbiri today. Secondly, the myth tells of women's fury at being excluded from an important ceremony concerning their sons and at being left behind to look after them. Thirdly, the performance of women's tasks by men is interesting in contrast to the episode about women's hunting. In normal living these tasks were sex-segregated: men hunted, women collected and processed vegetable food, were responsible for fire and shelter, and for carrying burdens, and looked after children until marriage for girls and initiation for boys. The myth suggests that, if necessary, these roles could be reversed. Finally, the myth tells of men's power to create life, equally with women, when they bring the boys back to life.

SECTION III: MYTH AND GENDER RELATIONS: RECENT WORK

How far does anything we can learn from myths coincide with the reality of male/female relations in the Aboriginal societies where these myths were collected? Early reports of Aboriginal societies depicted women as mere chattels of the men and since the same reports proclaimed that Australian Aborigines were without any religion the ritual status of women did not arise. Serious study in the late nineteenth and early twentieth centuries still saw women as oppressed and subservient. Kaberry's 1939 book *Aboriginal Woman: Sacred and Profane* is regarded as a landmark in its revelation of women's importance in both religious and secular life. Considerable further study has been made of women's status, including the collection edited by F. Gale, *Woman's Role in Aboriginal Society* (1970), in which B. Hiatt (now Meehan) shows how women are vital to their community's survival since their gathering yields more food than the men's hunting (pp. 2–8). Annette Hamilton demonstrates the importance of women in marriage arrangements, Catherine Berndt stresses the segregation of the sexes in ritual and secular life, each sex in control of its own domain, with the domains interdependent and complementary. My own contribution also describes the society as sexually segregated with women serving as junior partners to the men in joint enterprises.

In 1971 another important study appeared – J. Goodale's *Tiwi Wives*; this successfully refuted a previous monograph about the Tiwi by two male writers which depicted women as mere pawns in the men's marriage games (Hart and Pilling, 1960). By living with women and studying their lives Goodale showed that in reality women played a powerful part in these games and were in many respects equal to men.

The next landmark was the appearance in 1985 of Diane Bell's *Daughters of the Dreaming*, a full-scale study of the women of a Central Australian community. From her observations (but not from the myths she was told) she claims that women are as powerful in their own domain as men are in theirs and that one should not mention inequality versus equality. She maintains that it is a subjective judgement to see women as unequal to men, conditioned by the fieldworker's upbringing in a male-dominated society. In arguments with Bell I have held to my junior partner theory, but our different conclusions may be due to the different societies we have lived with. No one would expect male/female relations to be the same all over Europe; so too there is variation in Australia. Bell studied Warlpiri and Kaytej women at Warrabri, I studied Pitjantjatjara women at Yalata. One very old Wangkangurru man from the Simpson Desert (east of the Western Desert Pitjantjatjara) once told me 'We didn't treat our women the way those Pitjantjatjara men did'. So Aborigines themselves can be critical of the way their neighbours treat women.

Most of my colleagues agree with me that women, though powerful and decisive in many matters, deferred to men in others, and that men regarded themselves as more powerful than women. The communities studied had been changed in varying degrees by alien conquest and settlement, but it was still possible to observe many traditional behaviour patterns and to learn from the older people about conditions before outside contact. It is noteworthy that we came to conclusions about women's place in Aboriginal society, about gender relations and about social structure in general from living with Aborigines and from observing the ceremonies rather than from studying the myths that these ceremonies enacted.

Conclusion

From these various methods of analysing and interpreting the myths of the Australian Aborigines, it is doubtful if any valid generalizations can be made about social structure. For example as I have already demonstrated in my 1975 article, the published myths of Central Australia show men and women travelling in separate groups and engaging in illicit sexual intercourse. In real life, most travelling was done in extended family groups, while there were extremely strict rules governing sexual intercourse with severe punishment for infringements. I do not know if the myths

I quoted were a fair sample of all myths, or only what the Aborigines chose to tell the researchers, or what the researchers chose to recount. Any generalizations must be based on a small fraction of the total mythology of one language group, let alone of the whole continent.

In the areas most closely populated now by European and other settlers, mythology has died unrecorded with the death of the former inhabitants and the destruction of their societies. In other areas much could still be collected by patient research, much is as yet unpublished, remaining in the notebooks and tapes of researchers. In her contribution to *Myths of Matriarchy Reconsidered*, Annette Hamilton (1988, p. 61) describes her current research as follows:

> I have recently been working with women's myth cycles in Central Australia which have revealed the extraordinary wealth of detail involved in proceeding via myth and song from one site to the next along the track of mythical ancestresses. Twenty separate incidents (or more) may be sung between two adjacent sites and this is only between two sites out of a possible fifty along a single track in a single linguistic zone.

In her conclusion to this article she observes that 'there seems to me to be serious dangers in extrapolating from myth to observed gender relations . . . Australian myths express a very ambivalent and ambiguous set of gender relations' (p. 69).

These quotations give some idea of the astounding number of myths that would have to be included in a total survey of Aboriginal mythology. The present account has covered only a small proportion — too small to serve as a basis for definite conclusions.

Isobel White

Helen Payne

MATRIARCHS OF MYTH

SECTION IV: INTRODUCTION

In discussing Australian Aboriginal mythology I will focus on the myths and ceremonies as practised and spoken about by women living in that area of Australia shaded on the map displayed (*see* fig. 26). In this region of Australia, Aboriginal women have a flourishing ritual life including a corpus of mythology distinct from, yet complementary to that of Aboriginal men. While the extreme separation of the sexes, so apparent in both the secular and ritual life practised by the Aborigines living in the communities situated in this region, 'has often been taken as an index of the degree to which women are second-rate citizens in Central Australian society' (Hamilton, 1979a, p. 269), the Aborigines living in these communities speak of both men's and women's 'business' (by 'business' they mean secular and ceremonial

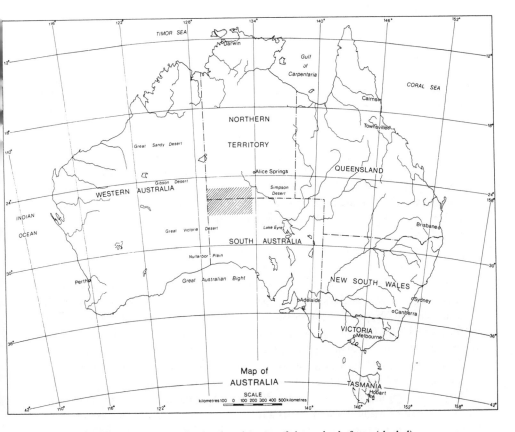

Fig. 26 Map of Australia showing the area of the author's focus (shaded).

matters governing life) and accord each an equal part in the maintenance of the 'laws' governing their lives. (By 'laws' they mean those conventions or formulae ensuring the well-being of both the members of their group and of the natural phenomena, flora and fauna on which their hunter/gatherer ancestors once depended for a livelihood.)

Women's myths are recounted both through articulations and enacted through ceremonies, the latter comprising presentations in the form of a series of what I term items, each bounded by a break in performance and lasting approximately thirty seconds, in which sung forms, danced steps and painted designs are presented by performers, with the total spectacle serving to identify particular ancestors and geographic localities for the enculturated listener/observer.

I argue that both the women's ceremonies and their myths emphasize the role and status of women as a group; independent of, but nonetheless interactive with, men.

Those myths and ceremonies on which I will focus in this paper are those that recount the life-histories or dreamings of supernatural ancestral beings. The ancestors, although now physically removed from the earth, are believed to have left their supernatural powers in the soil at those sites which they visited and/or created during their sojourn on earth. They are also believed to have created myths and ceremonies to tell others about their activities on earth and to have taught these to their human descendants before themselves departing from the earth. Since the time of the ancestors' departure from the earthly realm, the myths and ceremonies are believed to have been maintained and, via the process of oral transmission, passed from one generation to the next until finally they have reached those members of the present-day generation who hold rights to them.

Encoded within the texts of the ancestral ceremonies are the names of each of the places visited and/or created by those ancestors. On correctly naming a site, present-day performers believe that they can activate the supernatural ancestral powers stored in the soil at that site and then use these powers (as did their ancestors before them) to effect desired changes in both their own lives and the lives of others in their group.

As the ideology attributes the creation of the ancestral ceremonies and myths to the supernatural ancestral beings, the true history of their transmission from one generation to the next is obscured from public view. This obscuration has led some analysts, for example Moyle (1983, p. 92), to claim that 'in practice, as well as principle, the Dreamtime precedent is faithfully followed', and therefore to accept the ideologically-conceived dictum frequently articulated by Aborigines that form and meaning are unchanging in myths and ceremonies. On the contrary, I (Payne, 1988, pp. 217–41) have argued that the obscuration of the true history of the transmission of myths and ceremonies is crucial for the continuance of the dreaming for, as it is public approval of one's showing of items and telling of myths which assures one of being granted status and respect as a leader in one's community, it is crucial that a custodian does not receive public criticism for her performance of items and/or telling of myths. By preventing the showing of a deceased woman's ritual material for some time after her death, the ideology permits a new custodian sufficient time for the living memory of a previous custodian's renditions of items and myths to have faded prior to her telling and/or showing these (albeit inevitably in a changed format from that used by her predecessor) to others who may previously have been told or seen them enacted by her predecessor.

Thus I argue that the obscuration of the reality of the process of transmission of myths and ceremonies serves to permit individuals the right to change the myths and ceremonies of their ancestors, and that these changes will both accord with individual performance stylistic preferences and with desires for particular non-performance oriented results, to issue as a consequence of the telling of myths or performance of ceremonies. I suggest that changes in the form and meaning of myths and ceremonies are effected by individuals to make them both reflect and reinforce their individual desires for power and status in their group.

As women's rights to ritual material are publicly substantiated through their ceremonial enactments, telling of myths and unimpeded visits to the sites named in both of these forms, before I proceed to give an example of character portrayals, plots, themes, etc., presented in the myths and ceremonies themselves, I briefly outline both the ceremonial process and the mode of mythical recounting practised by women living in the shaded area on the map. However, as I am committed to both an ethical and legal agreement with those from whom I have collected information not to disclose certain details of it, I will recount details of women's myths, ceremonies, sites and indeed, of the women themselves, without disclosing their identifying features or names. In so doing, I do not believe that I will be eschewing my presentation of data in such a way as to hamper the reader's perception of it. Nonetheless, if in final consideration any of my claims appear to lack empirical support (Hamilton, 1979a, p. 238) then I, like Hamilton, must plead that this is unavoidable under the terms and conditions of both my ethical and legal agreement with those from whom I have collected the information.

Enactments of Myths: The Ceremonial Process

Ceremonial items are staged at the discretion of the woman presiding in authority over both the ancestral myth recounted in them (each item telling of one event in the ancestor's life on earth) and having authority to both show others, and herself maintain, the sites named in their texts (each item naming one site visited and/or created by that ancestor).

Ceremonial items are either enacted at the actual sites, the names of which are encoded in the item texts, or at a site removed from these. In the latter case, the site is selected by the woman assuming authority for the enactment, and usually constitutes a smooth, soft surface, such as that afforded by a sandy creek bed, over which dancers can perform their movements. If the items are not intended for presentation to both men and women, then the locality selected will furthermore be one out of earshot and sight of any male. Indeed, a woman from the performance group may be placed on the look-out for any male whose presence would result in the divulgence of women's secrets to members of the opposite sex and thus not only mar their future potency but also bring ill-effects to befall all those who had been involved in the performance. (It is believed that divulgence of secret business to members of the opposite sex may bring the wrath of ancestors to bear on those responsible for divulging it.)

Once at the selected site the woman assuming authority for the ensuing ceremonial performance will instruct others in their roles. After having first designated an area in which the main group (who I will refer to as group A – shown as A in fig. 27) should sit and built a fire (B in fig. 27) for cooking and warmth, the woman assuming authority for the activities will instruct certain members of the group to follow her away from the others. When some distance away from group A, these selected few (whom I will refer to as group E) will then be instructed to build a shelter (C in fig. 27) out of nearby foliage, behind which they can sit and prepare themselves for the dances they are about to perform for the benefit of all present at the site. Should a fire be necessary for burning bark – either to create ash for later use in painting or, indeed, for warmth – then a fire (D in fig. 27) will

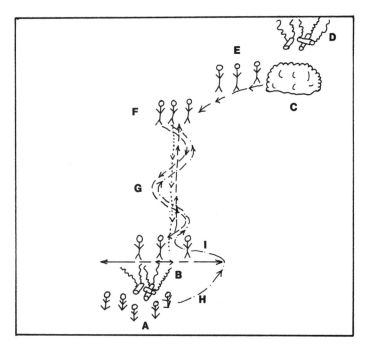

KEY

A Singers
B Singers' fire
C Bush behind which women selected to dance prepare themselves and paint for dancing
D Sometimes another fire is lit to mark the other end of the dancing ground
E Painted women enter the dancing ground
F Painted women take up their position on the dancing ground
G Painted women traverse the dancing ground in the direction of either the dotted or dashed line
H As indicated by the dashed and dotted line, one of the singers moves out onto the ritual ground to smooth over the dancers' tracks
I Painted women on reaching the singers jump in a sideways action as power is sung out of their bodies by the singers. Dirt is thrown over painted women by the singers.

Fig. 27 Diagram showing the demarcating features of a ritual ground and the relative placement of both persons and activities on it.

be lit by members of group E. Before returning to group A the woman presiding over the performance will appoint one member of group E to take charge of the preparations or else she herself will remain with group E and assume this role.

The preparations carried out by those appointed to dance (prior to their actual dancing) ensures that these women (group E) *become* the ancestors whose parts they will be taking on tile dance ground, for as Strehlow (1971, p.127) notes 'the Central Australian clansmen in their ceremonies were interested in watching not human actors, but living impersonations of supernatural beings'.

Preparation begins by the women of group E rubbing their bodies with fat. This fat acts not only as a base for later applying body paints, but is also thought to protect the women's bodies from malevolent spirits: fat being a sign of health and well-being and malevolent spirits preferring ailing or decomposing bodies. Furthermore, by making the women's bodies glisten with health, the fat is believed to attract benevolent ancestral forces (the benevolent spirits preferring the opposite to the malevolent ones, that is, healthy bodies) and to act as a lubricant, facilitating the entry of powers into the women besmeared with fat. Once supernatural powers enter women's bodies these women are considered to be those ancestors whose supernatural forces they have absorbed into themselves.

As the members of group E paint the signs of the ancestor whose power they are seeking to attract and absorb on to each other's bodies, and any objects they intend to use during their ensuing dance, they sing an item designed to lure the ancestral powers out of the soil and in to their painted designs. On being summoned by the painters, these powers are thought to be transformed from a latent state in which they are believed to have thus far been stored in the soil, to an active one, in which form they may be used by the dancers to effect desired changes in their lives.

Once the preparations for dancing have been completed by the members of group E, the woman in charge of this group will aurally signal the readiness of the members of her group to begin their enactment. On receiving an aural signal from group E, the leader of group A will instruct all members of her group to bow their heads and not to look in the direction of group E. The issuing of this command by the leader of group A ensures that the designs worn by the members of group E are not seen prior to their presentation together with the dance actions and song text intended to accompany them for, to be effective in summoning ancestral powers to change the course of events, all structures serving to identify an ancestor must be simultaneously presented by performers (see also Ellis and Tur, 1975, p. 30; Ellis et al., 1978, p. 71; Hamilton, 1979a, p. 238).

As the members of group A bow their heads, the members of group E move out from behind their screen (C in fig. 27) onto the dance ground. Once there, they take up their positions (at E in fig. 27). Remaining stationary, they then hold these positions until the leader of group A begins singing the item text intended to accompany their dancing. Once the singing has commenced the leader of group A instructs the members of her group to raise their heads and behold their ancestors who now are dancing towards them, and at the same time join in the singing of the item text.

An item concludes when the dancers reach the seated singers (following the arrows via F and G in fig. 27), that is, when group E reaches group A. At this point in the enactment, the leader of group A will commence the singing of another text to which the dancers will perform a sideways action (indicated via arrows at I in fig. 27), while swinging their outstretched arms in front of them. As they move, the dancers smear their designs and have sand thrown over their bodies by the seated singers, these actions being designed to remove the supernatural forces from their bodies and return them to a mundane state of existence. After completing these actions designed to remove all supernatural powers from their bodies, the dancers are free to rejoin group A, assured that they no longer remain possessive of any life-changing supernatural forces. As the dancers conclude their performance one of the women from group A moves out on to the dance ground (following the direction of the arrows beginning at H and proceeding via G, to F) to brush away all visible signs of the dancers' tracks (the tracks of her ancestors): either by shuffling over the dancers' tracks with her feet or by using a branch of foliage to sweep away the paths left in the sand by the dancers' feet, knees and/or bodies, etc.

At the conclusion of an entire performance session which may have lasted continuously over hours or even days and comprised many such enactments as those described above, the woman presiding over the activities will instruct *all* who have been present at the performance to take their turn at clasping a digging stick (a cylindrical stick approximately 8 cm – 3 inches – thick and 100 cm – 9 feet-long, tapered at both ends for digging in the ground and fashioned out of locally available hardwood – usually mulga (*acacia aneura*) – which she has placed vertically in the ritual ground. This they do at the same time as moving around it in a clockwise direction while singing a text designed to transport the supernatural forces activated during the performance session and absorbed into women's bodies, back through the hands of those clasping the stick, down the stick and into the soil. Once in the soil, the powers may lie dormant until next activated through a performance. This final act of a performance session ensures that no supernatural forces remain lurking in participants' bodies for, should it ever happen that women retain these supernatural forces, it is thought that great harm will befall all those who come into contact with them.

Responsibility for controlling supernatural forces is only vested in those knowledgeable older members of the female community who have undergone the necessary training in women's business to know how to call up, use and de-activate supernatural forces. Some of these knowledgeable women will be recognized by members of their community as being possessed of specialized powers, namely those to cure illness or control social relationships (*illpintji*) and those in need of using such powers will be directed to them.

Specialized Ceremonial Processes

Curative knowledge will be passed to a woman after she has learnt about other aspects of women's dreaming. It will be given to her by women who will claim to have seen positive proof of the curative events issuing from the performance of the particular items which they identify to her as curative ones. Curative items are classified according to the parts of the body for which they were known to be effective in maintaining good health, for example, stomach, head, etc. However, it always depends on the concentration of performers as to the result which issues from an item performance. For example, the performance of one item is claimed by women to ensure fertility both in young women experiencing their first menstruation, and a large and economically important site in the region. If the young menstruant is 'being sung', the concentration of those at the performance is on singing into the womb of the young menstruant, whereas if the site is being sung, it is on singing into the 'womb' of the site. In both cases, the result is the same, namely fertility, but the direction and subsequent focus of the summoned fertility power will reflect the subject/object concentrated upon by the performers.

The performance of items to maintain the health of those living around them is the province and expected duty of all women who have received adequate ritual training. This is usually the women with children, but there are certain women in the community who are recognized as *ngankari*, that is, women whose proven curative powers set them aside as especially effective executants of curative rites.

I believe it is relevant to conclude this discussion on curative items by including that which I should be able to omit, childbirth. As childbirth is so frequently considered to be a crisis in health it is necessary to validate why I do not include a discussion of items for easing pain or solving problems in childbirth.

Ellis (personal communication, 1979) reports that although she asked Andagarinja-speaking Aboriginal women to sing childbirth songs, they always refused to do so, claiming that these songs were too powerful to be sung out of context. My own repeated questioning of women on the subject of special items for easing pain, trauma or complications of childbirth always resulted in looks of amazement on the part of those questioned, and a reply going something like this: 'We don't have rites for "getting out" children, but we can sing you one!' Women, even the most senior amongst them, did not acknowledge the existence of any items for women at the time of giving birth. If complications arose at the birth, these women claimed that it was not rites but hand work, such as the turning of the child or application of pressure on the birthing abdomen, or application of hot pads of soil, etc., which was needed to help the situation. For them childbirth was no crisis, but a common occurrence.

As *illpintji* has long been cast as 'love-magic' in the literature and women's business almost exclusively seen to comprise it (Bell, 1983, p. 176), I emphasize that *illpintji* draws on the land-based affiliation of individuals to form, re-form or repair social relationships, and should not be viewed merely as singing a desired member of the opposite sex. Rather, this is but one possible function that it may assume in the hands of a specialist. Unfortunately, because of the overwhelming preponderance of the male-oriented world view that has dominated the history of anthropological and ethnological investigations into, and reports on, Australian Aboriginal culture (Bell, 1982, p. 8), this has been the function of *illpintji* most often focused upon and accorded to Aboriginal women in the literature. Moreover, this focus has occurred despite early attempts by, for example, Kaberry (1939) and Catherine Berndt (1950), to present a different view of Aboriginal women and their ritual life.

Illpintji serves as a mechanism through which women regulate social, and in particular, male-female relationships and tensions in the community (Payne, 1988, p. 87). Furthermore, as sickness is believed to have its roots not in physical disorder, but in emotional disorder, wrought of 'the intervention of supernatural forces' (Hamilton, 1971, p. 2), *illpintji* serves as an important mechanism in the maintenance of a desirable emotional balance between people.

Illpintji may be seen as a process of gaining power — often sexual — over another individual. The power gained may be negative or positive in intent. For example, widows frequently utilize *illpintji* to turn away all prospective husbands, for with no husband, a woman believes that she can work tirelessiy at increasing her ritual knowledge. As a result, young widows are both highly prized in women's business *because* of their increased skills wrought of the time they are free to devote to ritual. They are also highly feared because of their potential for rapid advancement in ritual knowledge and hence access to power-bases denied to married women burdened with children and husbands.

The young married woman constrained by child-rearing activities does not usually evince much interest in learning *illpintji*, nor would she be encouraged to learn it. It is women whose child-rearing has temporarily or permanently ceased who usually show the greatest interest in learning *illpintji*. For example, the married mother may request *illpintji* to effect a desired extra-marital affair or to 'keep' a wayward husband. On the other hand, widows or post-menopausal women are the ones who participate most freely in *illpintji* because they have nothing to fear from it.

The important aspect in all performances of *illpintji* is that it is *not* freely available to women. Rather, it must be paid for, and is only then made available after due consideration of the request by the one who holds the coveted knowledge to execute *illpintji* effectively. Women who are taught *illpintji* are held under threat *not* to perform it in the absence of their teacher lest the powers they call up get out of control. It follows therefore that a successful *illpintji* performance assures the performance director of receiving considerable status because it indicates success in a genre to which not all are given equal access.

As the gaining of power over a desired person often necessitates that the power of others over that person be first negated, and as 'those others' also have access to *illpintji*, it becomes crucial that an *illpintji* performance be effective in the first instance. The effectiveness of the performance is said to reflect both the degree of knowledge of the one being paid for the performance, and the concentration of all present on the person(s) at whom the powers are being directed during the performance.

It is always the responsibility of the woman directing *illpintji* proceedings to ensure that correct social relationships are maintained as a result of *illpintji*. For example, if a requestor is married but wishes to perform *illpintji* to 'get a lover', the woman directing the performance will ensure that both the husband of the woman making the request and the prospective lover receive the effects generated by that performance.

A woman knowledgeable in *illpintji* has the power to overturn others' relationships and restore social order when she feels that the latter is being threatened by the activities of some. *Illpintji* knowledge is thus both highly respected and highly feared amongst women and men.

I give the following brief account of the implementation of a decision to restore order through *illpintji*. (The account features substitute names for the actors.) I cite this example because it indicates a breadth of function for *illpintji* which is rarely, if ever, acknowledged in the literature:

Avril came from an area to the north of area M. She came to area M as the lover of Kunmanara whose wife was Yala. Kunmanara was the son of Ilili, who was publicly acclaimed by the women in area M as the woman knowledgeable in women's *illpintji*. On Avril's arrival in area M, she assumed residence in Kunmanara's camp. As a result of Avril's intrusion, Yala went to live in the camp of Ilili and Ilili's sister, Nyaritja. Yala was very unhappy and desired to 'fight it out' with Avril – a common means of resolving interpersonal conflict amongst women and men in area M – but Ilili and Nyaritja told her to be patient and wait. They told her that Avril would soon leave area M. Some weeks passed and Avril remained in Kunmanara's camp and moreover, looked like staying there. On conferring, Ilili and Nyaritja decided that it looked like Avril was going to stay as a co-wife to Kunmanara (not an uncommon practice in area M) so they resolved to take some action. They invited both Yala and Avril to go hunting. While on this hunting trip Ilili and Nyaritja sang *illpintji*.

The intent of their performance was known to Yala but not to Avril. The performance was intended to turn Avril away from Kunmanara, that is, to curtail her attraction to him. How did Ilili and Nyaritja achieve this? Firstly, they used items intended to turn away untoward affections. Secondly, Ilili and Nyaritja threw earth towards Avril's home country: an action believed to *redirect* Avril's affections back to her former place of residence. Thus, with *illpintji*, Ilili and Nyaritja sang Avril *into* her home country, that is, through *illpintji* they over-rode a male-female relationship with a person-place relationship. Nyaritja recounts how, as they sang, Avril's eyes welled with tears, whereupon Ilili and Nyaritja looked most surprised and enquired of Avril, 'Was she not happy with their hunting? Weren't there good rabbits here?' Avril, however, replied that she suddenly felt very homesick, an admission which Ilili and Nyaritja took as affirmation of the success of their *illpintji*. Some days after the performance, Nyaritja recounts how Avril packed her bags and bid Ilili and herself goodbye. Avril claimed that she was going because she felt the 'pull' of her own country.

At the time of Avril's departure, Kunmanara was away supervising cattle mustering. On his return, Nyaritja claims that he was at first surprised to learn of Avril's departure, but quickly the surprise turned to 'a knowing anger' as he came to realize what had caused her departure. Nyaritja recounts how he came to Ilili and Nyaritja's camp and accused them of singing away his lover. However, because he could not prove his accusation, he could take little action against them.

Nyaritja recounts how some days after Avril's departure, Kunmanara finally convinced Yala to return to his camp. Yala's subsequent compliance with Kunmanara's request restored the social order as desired by Ilili and Nyaritja. As in the literature, *illpintji* is often cast as concerning only love magic, it is significant that in the above-cited example, it was performed to maintain a person's affiliation to country, which, as a consequence, affected that person's social relationships.

Ceremonial Interpretation: A Question of Training

Interpretation of the meaning inherent in women's ceremonial enactments is governed by the level of training one has received in women's business, and this in turn is governed by one's ability to satisfy the pre-requisites for training, firstly to commence and secondly, to continue without stagnation. Not least of these pre-requisites for a woman is evidence of fertility through at least one, and preferably two, childbirths. After two births a woman is regarded as being a 'proper' woman. She is encouraged to proceed to undertake the training necessary to become a dreamer herself, that is, to become one capable of summoning life-changing supernatural forces to alter the everyday course of events.

When no longer distinguishable by one's biological processes as a woman (that is, after menopause), a woman is expected to assume full authority for ceremonial and mythical custodianship and transmission. Moreover, she will now be accorded the part of male characters in ritual enactments of myth. As it is always the enactment of the male character which represents the highlights of women's performances when staged amongst women (the role providing opportunities for ridiculing male values and attitudes), assuming the male role in performance is a privilege both requiring and providing an opportunity to 'show off' one's acting talent. (I equate the part to that offered by the cadenza in the late eighteenth and nineteenth-century concerto.) And of course the post-menopausal woman does have an act to 'show off': that of being a man. Unlike fertile younger women, she can take more risks in her performance; for, should she summon strong supernatural powers through her performance and should these later cause her to prove attractive to someone of the opposite sex, she need not fear pursuit by her admirer — she can enjoy the chase (see also White, 1975), it will not result in further child-bearing for her! Nor need she fear disclosing men's secrets, which she may have known for some time but has been forced to keep hidden lest she be discovered as knowing them. ('In this question of knowing or not knowing, it is not the actual knowledge that matters, but what one is permitted to know' [White, 1975, p. 126].) Once like a man herself, a woman is expected to know when, and in front of whom, and under what circumstances to divulge men's secrets. Indeed, she can expect to become privy to more of them: Kaberry (1939, p. 229) recording that ' "*Lubra* [Aboriginal woman] can't call 'em; *lubra* can't know, can't know" . . . "That blackfellow business. Man go away; sing him; *lubra* know. Old woman got 'em flour-bag [grey hair], that one see him" '; and Strehlow (1971, p. 653) also drawing attention to the existence of a similar situation amongst Aranda-speakers, namely 'that the Aranda women, in their advancing years, were . . . permitted to gain glimpses of that closely-guarded male realm which has been described as "sacred" '.

As women's ceremonies are interpreted by individuals according to the level of training they have received in women's business, it follows that there may be a great deal of variation between individuals' interpretation of any given ceremonial enactment. Therefore, it is difficult, if not dangerous, to view ceremonies as offering a charter for social order and behaviour; there may be as many charters as there are individual interpreters!

The Interface of Ceremonies and Myths

As ceremonial enactments present the myths in a cryptic format, permitting onlookers/listeners the opportunity to interpret the myths according to their own level of understanding of them, the woman who has authority for an enactment may either intone or articulate the details of the myth being shown by performers. She usually does this in between the enactment of items constituting the performance. This process both benefits those not skilled in decoding the condensed information being presented via item enactment, and publicly exposes an interpretation of the enactment: that of the woman having custodial rights over the items, myth and those sites named in these two forms.

SECTION V: MYTHS

The following account of myth should be understood as constituting my interpretation, as shaped by my years of training in women's business — undertaken more or less continuously since 1971 with women living in that area shaded on the map shown as fig. 26.

As in a desert environment, water is of prime concern, all sites named in women's myths comprise a landform featuring water-retention properties. In some cases, these water-retention properties will be of a permanent nature (as afforded by fissures or rockpools to be found in granitic outcrops including monoliths); in other cases they will be of a seasonal nature, with water only to be found during, and for a short time after, rainfall (as afforded by claypans or sandy creek beds). Not surprisingly, sites offering a (semi-) permanent water supply are more celebrated in women's myths and ceremonies than are those only offering a seasonal one, with the most economically important sites being 'sung into' (Bell, 1978, p. 5) from all directions as many women's myths converge at, and the paths of the ancestral beings criss-cross over, them.

As ceremonial items name important economic resources in the environment, and it is only those who publicly have gained the right to sing these sites who have the right to make use of the economic resources offered by them, it follows that ritual knowledge in a tradition-oriented society is equatable to wealth and hence, that rights to sing sites of economic worth are always open to contestation and usurpation by others desirous of securing them for themselves (Payne, 1988).

Women's myths describe the travels of female ancestors, their daily food-gathering activities, their creations of rockpools and/or water-holes, etc., and their encounters with other ancestors. In the myths which I have learnt from women living in the area shaded on the map, there only has ever been one male ancestral character and he has always been in pursuit of any female characters featured in the same myth. However, in one women's myth, rather than the male capturing one (or more) of the female ancestors of whom he was in pursuit (as happens in all of the other myths that I have learnt from women), the female ancestors set out to capture their pursuer and are successful in their exploit. I detail this myth as an example of one of the many that may be encountered in the ritual life of women living in this part of Australia.

Although in documenting the overthrowing of a male by females, this myth concerns the emergence of female independence on the one hand, on the other it both reinforces and reflects the dependency of human beings — even the most independent ones — upon the economic resources afforded by their environment. The women's overthrow of their male pursuer is synonymous with their overthrow of the guardianship of the most prized economic resource of the region — the abundant water holes and sustainable life forms offered by the monolith over which their male pursuer has hitherto exerted exclusive ownership rights by virtue of his ever-watchful presence at it.

The myth, which is named after the elder of the two sisters who feature as the central characters in it, tells how the sisters after having twice sought to reach the huge monolith (a valuable economic resource and moreover, the only one in the locality) and having twice been thwarted in their attempts by the male guardian of the monolith who on each occasion has come after them, driving them away from his 'home', decide to fashion a digging stick with which they can frighten-off their pursuer. In searching for a suitable tree out of which to fashion their stick, the sisters leave the locality of the monolith for more distant areas, only returning to it once they have fashioned their stick.

On their return, the sisters climb a granitic outcrop which affords them a clear view of both the monolith and the man. They create an item to tell of this event. As they sit on the top of this outcrop they sing this item. The myth tells how the sisters see their pursuer perched on top of the monolith and still on the lookout for them. The sisters proceed to lure their pursuer off the monolith: by painting and decorating their bodies the sisters believe that he will see how beautiful they are and, desiring them, leave the monolith to come after them. Their plan works. The man sees them and leaves the monolith, whereupon the sisters presume that he again is in pursuit of them. The myth continues to describe how the man's departure from the monolith means for the sisters that they might undertake their journey without fear of being under his constant surveillance (there being no other granitic outcrops in the locality from which he would gain such a clear view of his surroundings).

During the ensuing journey towards the monolith the sisters pause at each site which they encounter that offers them water and edible flora and/or fauna. At each of these sites the sisters create an item to tell of their journey thus far and to name the site. They then perform their newly created item while resting at the site which they have named through their performance of an item text.

The site that affords the sisters their last vantage point from which to view the monolith and separates them (via a vast stretch of plain) from the latter, is a small rocky hill, covered in witchetty bushes (*acacia kempeana*). On ascending this hill, the sisters see their pursuer on a nearby mountain range but, as he appears to be moving towards the monolith, they assume that he has given up his pursuit of them.

Once at the top of the hill the sisters rest. However, after a while the elder sister instructs her younger sister to stay hidden amongst the witchetty bushes while she travels out to the edge of the outcrop which, in lying closest to, and therefore in direct view of, the monolith, will afford her an unrestricted view of the man — their pursuer. In case their pursuer now has returned to the monolith, ascended it and is gazing out from it, on leaving the cover afforded by the witchetty bushes the elder sister edges her way across the summit of this hill by lying on her stomach. When she finally reaches the far edge she gains an unrestricted view of the monolith. She sees that there her pursuer is reclining on his back with knees bent up in the air, as if he is about to sleep. Still cautious, lest she be seen by him, the elder sister returns in the same manner as she came and reports her findings to her younger sister.

The myth then relates how on noticing the onset of nightfall, the sisters wait until darkness surrounds them before setting off on the final part of their journey to the monolith. Daybreak finds the sisters quite close to the base of the monolith, sitting concealed in the tall grass of an island located in the middle of a dried-out claypan; their pursuer still rests on top of the monolith.

On leaving their hiding place, the sisters use nearby foliage as a screen to block their view of their pursuer (and hence his of them) and move along a sandy creek bed to a large supply of edible flora. This is the sisters' first sighting of the abundance of edible plants and animals that are fed by the water 'run-off' from the monolith. The myth tells how desirous of eating some of the food that they have now come upon in their journey, the sisters pause in their mission to reach the man. However, first they must make certain that their pursuer falls into a deep sleep so that he will not awaken and see them as they eat the food. On moving a short distance away from the creek-bed onto a bare patch of earth, the sisters create and sing an item designed to send the man into a deep, dream-filled sleep. As they sing, the sisters burn their pubic hair so that on smelling it, the man will dream of having sexual intercourse with them, and therefore will enjoy his dreaming so much that he will want to continue it. While they are singing, the myth relates how a bird flies down to the sisters and encourages them in their actions. The bird moreover tells the sisters that he will place a branch on top of the monolith to signal when their singing and actions have been successful.

The bird flies back to the man and soon the sisters see his signal appear on top of the monolith. They then feel safe to stop their singing and burning and to return to feast on the abundant supply of food.

After satisfying their hunger the myth describes how the elder sister creates a dance and enacts it on the last stretch of plain that separates her from the monolith, while, seated some distance away, the younger sister sings the text which she created to accompany her sister's dancing.

There is now only the ascent and final act of capturing the man and hence gaining possession of the monolith for the sisters to undertake in order to complete their self-imposed mission. While the man continues to sleep the sisters begin their ascent but, several times during it, the man stirs so that the sisters realize that they cannot count on his dreaming of them for much longer. As they arrive at the top of the monolith the man begins to awaken but, just as he opens an eye to look at them, the elder sister who has hitherto been carrying the digging stick, raises it and brings it down on top of the reposing man's brow. The impact of her blow cracks the man's skull and sends him in to a state of unconsciousness. The sisters then bind the unconscious man and one of them places the bundle on her head. It is thus that the sisters set off on their descent of the monolith.

The sisters take it in turns to carry their heavy bundle, but it strains them and they are forced to stop and urinate down the slope of the monolith. In addition, on several occasions the sisters are forced to stop in order to re-tie their bundle. On each of these occasions they perform debilitating acts upon their captive (they dismember his body and discard the dismembered parts) so that he will never again desire or be able to pursue women.

During their descent the sisters notice a group of women travelling in the distance. They also hear their singing. They therefore become anxious to deposit their bundle and go off to join them. On reaching the plain out of which the monolith rises and noticing a nearby cave, the sisters deposit their bundle inside it, leaving only a crow, as my teachers said, 'to "eye off" the bundle as possible "tucka" '. (The word 'tucka' when used in Australian conversational practice, means food, or more specifically 'bush' food.)

My teachers informed me that the sisters on leaving the man and the monolith, victorious in their establishment of a claim to both, journey to meet the other group of women whom they had earlier sighted and heard in the distance. As the two groups of women meet, a new dreaming, that is, another myth starts — one that bears another name.

Land: Visible Verification of Myth

My teachers pointed out the features in the landscape that verified the dreaming of the two sisters for them: the sleeping man's bent knees, flowing beard and cracked skull were visible to them in the bare rock face that constituted the peak of the monolith; across the skull there was a fissure in the rock surface which they thought of as being caused by the sister's blow; next to the skull was a stunted tree, put there, they said, by the bird as a signal to the sisters that the man was in deep sleep. A large fold in the rock surface was visible running down the monolith. This my teachers thought of as the stream caused by the sisters' urine, while the three rockpools lying near to this fold they believed to be the different parts of the man's dismembered body — thrown there by the sisters.

Everywhere in the land traversed by the ancestral sisters there were signs that told my teachers of the presence and exploits of these sisters. Indeed, for those knowledgeable in the myth a sighting of the topographic features visited and/or created by the ancestral sisters instantly recalled item texts, dance steps and designs such that the one served as a mnemonic aid for the recollection of the other, and vice versa (Payne, 1984).

Creating or Recreating: Dreaming

The close association between land, myth and ceremony for the enculturated Aboriginal person is neither the simple nor static one suggested by Moyle (1983, p. 66). Instead, it is one that constitutes a kaleidoscopic picture as women create and re-create their inheritance – their dreaming – to make it accord with their present needs and secure for them certain rights, privileges and desires, the effects of which will extend into the future.

I list below brief examples of some innovations which I have observed in women's dreaming (I observed these between 1975 and the present time, while living with women in the area outlined above):

> In 1975 my teachers recounted how a single rock was the elder sister sitting, looking out in the direction of the monolith. By 1978 this rock had been worn away and was scarcely visible in the place where I had seen it in 1975. The same teachers merely omitted this section of the myth in their recounting of it to me in 1978.

> The myth of the two ancestral sisters as told by the mother of the woman who first related it to me was recorded by a colleague. She noted that it was regarded as being very secret and hence only told amongst women. When I first learnt the myth from the eldest daughter who had in turn learnt it from her late mother (the ideal is for women's myths and ceremonies to pass from mother to daughter (Hamilton, 1979b, p. 14), it was no longer secret but often related in large public ceremonial meetings.

While there are many more examples which I could cite, I refer the reader to Payne (1989, pp. 49–52) for further ones, and to Wild (1987) for further discussion as to the process of change. On each occasion when I questioned women concerning changes in their dreaming, they denied responsibility for them, saying 'this is our dreaming', by which they implied a state of immutability for dreaming.

As the ideology of the dreaming attributes all creation to supernatural ancestral beings and thus hides the identity of individual creators of dreaming, it ensures that they receive no recognition for their innovations in myth and ceremony. However, I contend that creators (or re-creators) of myth and ceremony draw their recognition from the results (measurable in terms of levels of power and status in the community) that their innovations bring for them and others in their group. Moreover, as astute politicians who recognize that their wealth and hence relative power and status in their group depends upon their winning public approval for their telling of myths, enactments of ceremonies and/or showing of sites, they recognize all those persons willing or desirous of listening to, seeing and/or being shown their dreaming as potential resources – as having political significance for their winning, losing or retaining rights to acquisitions of value in tradition-oriented society. Accordingly, the myth of the two ancestral sisters as told to me may be different when told by the same woman to another woman; this difference reflects our relative value as resources of political significance for the woman relating the myth, as well as our relative levels of training in women's business, but again, this is largely perceived by the woman relating the myth!

Dreamer's Dilemma

While ideally the recording on tape, film or video of myths and/or ceremonies should make them no less transitory than their recording in the memories of those exposed to them through the process of oral transmission, the reality is that in the minds of the practitioners of the recorded culture the tapes, films, videos, etc., which result assume the status of a permanently verifiable account of an ancestor's renditions of myths and/or ceremonies. While on the one hand, the products of the recording devices are themselves becoming used as resources of political significance to further public acceptance of women's dreaming innovations, and hence rights to assets and the power and status these bring one in tradition-oriented society, on the other hand new negotiation strategies are being developed by women to ensure that they retain their right to choose if and when they will conceal their identity as dreamers, and if and when they will reveal it (perhaps by suggestion by ' "step[ping] out" in different form [in non-human guise] for probable identification' from behind that 'shifting phantasmagoric screen' [R. Berndt, 1987, p. 188] which shields them from direct public view and hence criticism). In revealing their identity as dreamers, women can claim as theirs the power and status accorded to those beings of feminine gender who, having reached levels of seniority in the business world, stand recognized as wielders of life-changing forces in tradition-oriented society: the real matriarchs of myth!

Helen Payne

References and Further Reading

Bamberger, J. (1974), 'The Myth of Matriarchy: Why Men Rule in Primitive Society' in M.Z. Rosaldo and L. Lamphere (eds), *Woman, Culture and Society* (Stanford, Calif: Stanford University Press), pp. 263–38

Barwick, D.E. (1970), ' "And the lubras are ladies now" ' in F. Gale (ed.), *Woman's Role in Aboriginal Society* (Canberra: A.I.A.S.), pp. 31–8

Bates, D.M. (1985), *The Native Tribes of Western Australia*, I.M. White (ed.) (Canberra, National Library of Australia). Manuscript, 1912.

Bell, D. (1978), 'The Alyawarra and Kaititj Land Claim of the Central Land Council: A Statement by Diane Bell, 6 October 1978', typescript

—— (1982), 'Aboriginal Women and the Religious experience' in *The Young Australian Scholar Lecture Series*, No. 3 (Adelaide: A.A.S.R. for Charles Strong [Australian Church Memorial Trust])

—— (1983), *Daughters of the Dreaming* (Sydney: Allen & Unwin)

Berndt, C.H. (1950), 'Women's Changing Ceremonies in Northern Australia' in *L'Homme: Cahiers d'Ethnologie, de Géographie et de Linguistique* (Paris: Hermann), pp. 1–87

—— (1965), 'Women and the "Secret Life" ' in R.M. Berndt (ed.), *Aboriginal Man in Australia* (Sydney: Angus and Robertson), pp. 238–82

—— (1970), 'Digging Sticks and Spears, or the Two-sex Model' in F. Gale (ed.), *Woman's Role in Aboriginal Society* (Canberra: A.I.A.S.), pp. 39–48

—— (1983) 'Mythical Women, Past and Present' in F. Gale (ed.), *We are Bosses Ourselves: The Status and Role of Aboriginal Women Today* (Canberra: A.I.A.S.), pp. 13–21

—— (1989) 'Retrospect and Prospect: Looking Back After 50 Years' in P. Brock (ed.), *Women Rites and Sites: Aboriginal Women's Cultural Knowledge* (Sydney: Allen & Unwin), pp.1–20

Berndt, R.M. (1987) 'Other Creatures in Human Guise and Vice Versa: A Dilemma in Understanding' in M.C. Ross, T. Donaldson and S.A. Wild (eds), *Songs of Aboriginal Australia*, Oceania Monograph 32, (Sydney: Sydney University Press), pp. 68–91

Berndt, R.M. and Berndt, C.H. (1952, 1953 and 1954), 'A Selection of Children's Songs from Ooldea, Western South Australia' in *Mankind*, vol. 4, pp. 364–76, pp. 423–34 and pp. 501–8 (respectively)

—— (1964), *The World of the First Australians* (Sydney: Angus and Robertson)

—— (1989), *The Speaking Land: Myth and Story in Aboriginal Australia* (Ringwood, Vic.: Penguin)

Brock, P. (ed.), *Women: Rites and Sites Aboriginal Women's Cultural Knowledge* (Sydney: Allen & Unwin)

Coe, M. (1989), *Windradyne* (Canberra: A.I.A.S.)

Dussart, F. (1988), 'Warlpiri Women's Yawulyu Ceremonies', PhD Thesis, Australian National University

Ellis, C.J. and Barwick, L. (1989), 'Antikirinja Women's Song Knowledge 1963–72: Its Significance in Antakarinja Culture' in P. Brock (ed.), *Women's Rites and Sites: Aboriginal Women's Cultural Knowledge* (Sydney: Allen & Unwin), pp. 21–40

Ellis, C.J., Ellis, A.M., Tur, M. and McCardell, A. (1978), 'Classification of Songs in Pitjantjatjara-speaking Areas' in L.R. Hiatt (ed.), *Australian Aboriginal Concepts* (Canberra: A.I.A.S.), pp. 68–80

Ellis, C.J. and Tur, M. (1975) 'The Song is the Message' in I. Pilowsky (ed.), *Cultures in Collision* (Adelaide: Australian National Assoc. for Mental Health)

Errington, F. and Gewertz, D. (1988), 'Myths of Matriarchy Reexamined: Indigenous Images of Alternative Gender Relationships' in Gewertz (ed.), *Myths of Matriarchy Reconsidered* (Sydney: Oceania Monograph), pp. 195–211

Gaffney, E. (1989), *Somebody Now: The Autobiography of Ellie Gaffney, A Woman of Torres Strait* (Canberra: A.I.A.S.)

Gale, F. (ed.) (1970), *Woman's Role in Aboriginal Society* (Canberra: A.I.A.S.)

—— (1989), 'Roles Revisited: The Women of Southern South Australia' in P. Brock (ed.), *Women: Rights and Sites Aboriginal Women's Cultural Knowledge* (Sydney: Allen & Unwin), pp. 120–35

Gewertz, D. (ed.) (1988), *Myths of Matriarchy Reconsidered* (Sydney: Oceania Monograph)

—— (1988), 'Introduction' in Gerwertz (ed.), pp. vi–xi

Gibson, J. (1989), 'Digging Deep: Aboriginal Women in the Oodnadatta Region of South Australia in the 1980s' in P. Brock (ed.), *Women: Rites and Sites Aboriginal Women's Cultural Knowledge* (Sydney: Allen & Unwin), pp. 60–75

Goodale, J.C. (1971), *Tiwi Wives: A Study of the Women of Melville Island, North Australia* (Seattle: University of Washington Press)

Hamilton, A. (1970), 'The Role of Women in Aboriginal Marriage Arrangements' in F. Gale (ed.), *Women's Role in Aboriginal Society* (Canberra: A.I.A.S.), pp. 17–29.

—— (1971), 'Socio-Cultural Factors in Health Among the Pitjantjatjara: A Preliminary Report' (unpublished)

—— (1979a), 'Timeless Transformation: Women, Men and History in the Australian Western Desert', PhD Thesis, University of Sydney

—— (1979b), 'Women and Land' (unpublished)

—— (1980), 'Dual Social Systems' in *Oceania*, vol. 51, pp. 419

—— (1981), 'A Complex Strategical Situation: Gender and Power in Aboriginal Australia' in N. Grieve and P. Grimshaw (eds), *Australian Women: Feminist Perspectives* (Melbourne: Melbourne University Press, pp. 69–85

—— (1986), 'Daughters of the Imaginary' in *Canberra Anthropology*, 9, no. 2, pp. 1–25

—— (1988), 'Knowledge and Misrecognition: Mythology and Gender in Aboriginal Australia' in Gewertz (ed.), *Myths of Matriarchy Reconsidered* (Sydney: Oceania Monograph), pp. 57–73

Hart, C.W.M. and Pilling, A.R. (1964), *The Tiwi of North Australia* (New York: Holt, Rinehart and Winston)

Hercus, L. (1989), 'The Status of Women's Cultural Knowledge' in P. Brock (ed.), *Women: Rites and Sites of Aboriginal Women's Cultural Knowledge* (Sydney: Allen & Unwin), pp. 99–119

Hiatt, L.R., (1971), 'Secret Pseudo-procreation Rites among the Australian Aborigines' in L.R. Hiatt and C. Jayawardena (eds), *Anthropology in Oceania* (Sydney: Angus and Robertson)

—— (1975), *Australian Aboriginal Mythology* (Canberra: A.I.A.S.)

Howitt, A.W. (1904), *The Native Tribes of South-east Australia* (London: Macmillan)

Huffer, V. and Roughsey, E., et al. (1980), *The Sweetness of the Fig: Aboriginal Women in Transition* (Sydney: N.S.W. U.P.; Seattle: University of Washington Press)

Hyllus, M. and Borg, S. (1985), *Women of the Sun* (Melbourne: Penguin)

Jacobs, J.M. (1989), '"Women Talking up Big": Aboriginal Women as Cultural Custodians, a South Australian Example' in P. Brock (ed.), *Women: Rites and Sites of Aboriginal Women's Cultural Knowledge* (Sydney: Allen & Unwin), pp. 76–98

Kaberry, P. (1939), *Aboriginal Woman: Sacred and Profane* (London: Routledge)

Kennedy, M. (1985), *Born a Half-Caste* (Canberra: A.I.A.S.)

Labumore, E.R. (1984), *An Aboriginal Mother Tells of the Old and the New*, P. Memmott and R. Horsman (eds) (Melbourne: McPhee Gribble/Penguin)

Langford, R. (1988), *Don't Take Your Love to Town* (Melbourne: Penguin)

McConnel, U. (1957), *Myths of the Mungkan* (Melbourne: Melbourne University Press)

Meggitt, M.J. (1962), *Desert People: a study of the Walbiri Aborigines of Central Australia* (Sydney: Angus and Robertson)

—— (1966), 'Gadjari among the Walbiri Aborigines of Central Australia' in *Oceania*, 36, pp. 174–213 and 283–315

Montagu, A. (1937/1974), *Coming into Being Among the Australian Aborigines* (London: Routledge & Kegan Paul)

Morgan, S. (1987), *My Place* (Fremantle: Fremantle Arts Centre Press)

—— (1989), *Wananurrganya* (Melbourne: Penguin)

Mountford, C. P. and Harvey, A. (1941), 'Women of the Adnjamatana Tribe of the Northern Flinders Ranges, South Australia' in *Oceania*, 12, pp. 155–62

Moyle, R.M. (1983), 'Songs, Ceremonies and Sites: The Agharringa Case' in Peterson and Langton (eds.) *Aborigines, Land and Land Rights* (Canberra: A.I.A.S.), pp. 66–73

Mum, Shirl, with the assistance of Bobbi Sykes (1989), *Mum Shirl: An Autobiography with the Assistance of Bobbi Sykes* (Melbourne: Heinemann)

O'Brien, M. (1990), *The Legend of the Seven Sisters* (Canberra: A.I.A.S.)

Parker, K.L. (1952), *Australian Legendary Tales* (Sydney: Angus and Robertson). First published 1896–8.

Payne, H. (1984), 'Residency and Ritual Rights' in J.C. Kassler and J. Stubington (eds), *Problems and Solutions: Occasional Essays in Musicology presented to Alice M. Moyle* (Sydney: Hale and Iremonger), pp. 264–78

—— (1986), 'The Contrasting Claims of Pitjantjatjara Women's Ceremonies on Sacred and Secular Occasions' in M. Honegger and C. Meyer (eds), *La Musique et le Rite: Sacré et Profane. Actes du XIIIe Congrés de la Société Internationale de Musicologie Strasbourg, 29 août – 3 septembre 1982* (Strasbourg: University of Strasbourg), I, pp. 464–9

—— (1988), 'Singing a Sister's Sites', PhD thesis, University of Queensland

—— (1989), 'Rites for Sites or Sites for Rites? The Dynamics of Women's Cultural Life in the Musgraves', in P. Brock (ed.), *Women Rites and Sites: Aboriginal Women's Cultural Knowledge* (Sydney: Allen & Unwin), pp. 41–59

Peterson, N. and Langton, M. (1983), *Aborigines, Land and Land Rights* (Canberra: A.I.A.S.)

Rowell, M. (1983), 'Women and Land Claims in the Northern Territory' in Peterson and

Langton (eds), *Aborigines, Land and Land Rights* (Canberra: A.I.A.S.), pp. 256–67

Simon, E. (1978), *Through My Eyes* (Adelaide: Rigby)

Spencer, W.B. and F.J. Gillen (1899), *The Native Tribes of Central Australia* (London: Macmillan)

—— (1904), *The Northern Tribes of Central Australia* (London: Macmillan)

—— (1927), *The Arunta: A Study of a Stone Age People* (London: Macmillan)

Spencer, W.B. (1914), *The Native Tribes of the Northern Territory of Australia* (London: Macmillan)

Strehlow, C. and von Leonhardi, M. (1907–20), *Die Aranda-und Loritja-Stämme in Zentral Australien* (Frankfurt: Joseph Baer)

Strehlow, T.G.H. (1947), *Aranda Traditions* (Melbourne: Melbourne University Press)

—— (1971), *Songs of Central Australia* (Sydney: Angus and Robertson)

Thomas, N. (1988), 'The Contradictions of Hierarchy: Myths, Women and Power in Eastern Polynesia' in D. Gewertz (ed.), *Myths of Matriarchy Reconsidered* (Sydney: Allen & Unwin), pp. 170–84

Tucker, M. (1977) *If Everyone Cared: An Autobiography of Margaret Tucker M.B.E.* (London: Grosvenor)

Walker, D. (1989), *Me and You: The Life Story of Della Walker as Told to Tina Coutts* (Canberra: A.I.A.S.)

Ward, G. (1987), *Wandering Girl* (Broome: Magabala Books)

West, I. (1984), *Pride against Prejudice: Reminiscences of a Tasmanian Aborigine* (Canberra: A.I.A.S.)

Western Regional Aboriginal Land Council (1989), *The Story of the Falling Star* (Canberra: A.I.A.S.)

White, I.M. (1970), 'Aboriginal Women's Status: a Paradox Resolved' in F. Gale (ed.), *Women's Role in Aboriginal Society* (Canberra: A.I.A.S.), pp. 21–9

—— (1975), 'Sexual Conquest and Submission in the Myths of Central Australia' in L.R. Hiatt (ed.), *Australian Aboriginal Mythology* (Canberra: A.I.A.S.), pp. 123–42

—— (1979), 'Rain Ceremony at Yalata' in *Canberra Anthropology*, 2 no. 2, pp. 94–103

White, I.M., Barwick, D. and Meehan, B. (eds.) (1985), *Fighters and Singers: The Lives of Some Aboriginal Women* (Sydney: Allen and Unwin)

White, J.P. and Lampert, R. (1987), 'Creation and Discovery' in J.P. White and D.J. Mulvaney (eds.), *Australians to 1788*, vol.1 of *Australians: A Historical Library* (Sydney: Fairfax, Syme & Weldon), pp. 3–23

Wild, S.A. (1987), 'Recreating the *Jukurrpa*: Adaptation and Innovation of Songs and Ceremonies in Warlpiri Society' in M.C. Ross, T. Donaldson and S.A. Wild (eds.), *Songs of Aboriginal Australia*, Oceania Monograph 32 (Sydney: University of Sydney Press), pp. 97–120

Wilson, B. Ker (1972), *Tales told to Kabbarli (Daisy Bates)* (New York: Crown)

MARGARET ORBELL

Māori Mythology

SECTION I: INTRODUCTION

New Zealand (or Aotearoa, to use the Māori name) is a very isolated country, so was among the last to be settled by humans. In about 1000 AD the Māori arrived from central Polynesia, discovered forested islands full of birds but no land mammals, and in the temperate climate developed a way of life based upon fishing, food gathering, bird-hunting and, where possible, the laborious cultivation of the tropical plants, in particular the sweet potato, which they had brought with them. Although there was much concern with rank, there were not the elaborate hierarchies which existed in some other Polynesian societies. Instead, the tribal system was loosely organized and very flexible, with constantly shifting patterns of alliance between rather small tribes which traced descent from common ancestors. Chiefs had to win the agreement of their warriors rather than give orders, and oratory was a highly developed art form.

While women were considered to be much inferior to men, in many circumstances women of rank, in particular, did possess considerable influence. They did not normally take part in tribal discussions of political issues, but in other circumstances they might express their views forcefully and publicly on matters which concerned them. In marriage they were, as one might expect, generally at a disadvantage. High-ranking men usually had several wives, for these women's skills and industry in horticulture and weaving were essential for the maintenance of their status, and the lavish hospitality expected of them. Usually there was a 'main wife', and other 'little wives' some of whom might be slaves. Some women were happy to have co-wives to help with the work, but many were not.

In general, men were regarded as *tapu* or sacred, their actions restricted by social and religious usages, while women were *noa*, associated with profane, everyday concerns. A man of rank might be so *tapu* that the rules restricting his behaviour could in some respects be quite onerous, but in other ways this status was to his advantage: since such men could not carry burdens upon their sacred backs, it was the women who did most of the routine fetching and carrying (although men worked hard at other, more prestigious tasks). On the other hand, women's lack of inherent *tapu* allowed them to take the sexual initiative. Most women were able to take lovers before marriage, and it was common, perhaps customary, for them to make the first move.

Māori life and thought were to a large extent organized and structured in terms of these opposed states of *tapu* and *noa*; and it seems that these two concepts, so far-reaching in their religious, social and political applications, were sustained primarily by imagery derived from the Māori experience of male and female bodies and roles. Their social organization and their habits of thought were ultimately dependent upon ideas concerning the opposed, yet mutually interdependent, natures of men and women – ideas which find expression in their mythology.

Because of its isolation the country was among the last of the regions owned by tribal peoples to be colonized by Europeans, and this, along with other factors, led to the preservation of a great deal of the Māori heritage of myth, poetry and tradition. In 1840, when Aotearoa became a British possession, European thought had reached the point where a certain number of the colonists, recognizing similarities with Biblical and Classical literatures and 'folk' traditions, became fascinated soon after their arrival with the history and mythology of the society they had come to replace. At the same time, Māori men and women were eagerly acquiring a knowledge of reading and writing from the missionaries. By the 1850s, there were more literate Māori in the country, proportionately, than Europeans.

So in this respect the scene was set for a most unusual collaboration between the colonizers and the colonized. Many Māori authorities on oral tradition recorded in writing, or dictated to younger relatives, the myths, legends, ritual chants and songs of their tribes, mostly so that they would not be lost to their people in those fast-changing times; and European collectors of traditions (at first mainly administrators and missionaries, later the children of colonists) ensured the preservation of their writings. These manuscripts, as yet incompletely edited and translated, are now in public libraries in New Zealand, along with thousands of contemporaneous letters by Māori writers, many of them making reference to oral tradition. There are also the numerous Māori language periodicals in which, in the second half of the nineteenth century, people in different parts of the country debated politics and traditional history.

It all happened so suddenly that the myths, songs and beliefs were initially recorded before they had changed very much, if at all. The situation was quite different from that which had obtained in countries (in Europe, for example) in which the people had recorded their oral traditions some considerable time after their acquisition of literacy, when their possession of writing had become associated, in one way and another, with substantial changes in their habits of thought, beliefs and social patterns. In the early records of Māori mythology, an intricate relationship with ritual performance is clearly apparent. When the myths are read along with the ritual chants, songs and proverbs which make reference to them, their main meanings are revealed.

Many of these Māori stories are ancient in their origins. Some of the most important myths can be traced back 2,000 years to the time when the first human beings sailed from Samoa, in Western Polynesia, to explore the vast eastern ocean and colonize its tiny, scattered atolls and volcanic islands. Other Māori beliefs can be seen to have evolved in the tropical islands of this eastern region; there are quite close relationships with the traditions of peoples such as the Hawaiians and Tahitians, from whom the ancestors of the Māori parted 1,000 or more years ago. But while mythologies are in some respects astonishingly conservative, they are at the same time endlessly fluid, subject, within certain limits, to constant manipulation, embellishment and reinterpretation. Most of the important figures in Māori mythology were known throughout the country, and their main characteristics were everywhere much the same, but there was nevertheless a great deal of variation in the stories told about these people's relationships and adventures. Also, each of the main tribes possessed a body of mythology which was unique to itself and which explained the immediate origins of its founding ancestors. The tribal context is always important.

Unfortunately, nearly all of the people who recorded these myths were men. On the whole it does seem that many of the most elaborate versions of the stories and rituals had been restricted to males, taught in strict secrecy to high-ranking boys in 'schools of learning', or passed on from father to son within priestly families. Yet the intricate, rhetorical songs which make reference to myths were composed by women as well as men, if not so often, and there is plenty of other evidence that women were familiar with mythology. No doubt the European collectors of myths were largely to blame. Being male themselves, they probably gave little thought to women's experience. But the Māori men who collaborated with them would certainly have thought their own accounts the important ones, and obviously did not refer their European friends to women who could have given their own versions. These Māori men did, however, record a great deal about women in their writings; the female figures in their traditions were clearly very important to them. While the lack of accounts by women is most regrettable, and we may have lost information about mythical episodes and rituals which primarily concerned women (in particular, there may be gaps in the accounts of menstruation and childbirth), a great deal can be pieced together concerning women's roles and their experience of life.

SECTION II: MYTHS ABOUT WOMEN

These early manuscript books tell the history of the world. They begin, usually, at the beginning, with the primal parents, Rangi and Papa, who lay embraced. Rangi is both the first man and the sky; he is in fact a personification, Sky. Papa, the first woman, is the earth. She is also a personification: the word *papa* can be used of anything broad and hard, such as a flat rock or the floor of a house, and it can mean 'foundation', either literally or figuratively, so that her name is best translated as Foundation.

These first parents were so tightly embraced that everything was dark, and their children lay cramped between them; six sons are named in the best-known version of the story, though another tribal group asserts that there were three children and that one of them, Wai-nui or Great-waters, was female. Usually these children fight amongst themselves, establishing precedents and patterns of behaviour for their descendants. In particular, the warrior Tu, representing human beings, kills and devours the brothers who represent birds and edible plants. Although human beings are related to all the other living things in the world, their lives inevitably bring them into conflict with their relatives.

The children of Rangi and Papa wish to separate their parents so that there will be room to move, and light can enter the world. After a struggle, the sky and earth, despite their protests, are thrust apart by Tāne (who is another personification; the word *tāne* means male, husband, lover). Tāne is the main creator figure in Māori mythology. With this first, decisive action he creates order from chaos by separating the sky from the earth and, simultaneously, the male from the female.

Next, Tāne acquires the sun, the moon and the stars and fastens them upon his father the sky, so that there is light in the world, and the progression of day and night is established. Then he goes looking for a wife. At first he finds women who are not human, and with them he has different kinds of trees and birds, and other creatures; for example he meets Punga, who always has ugly children, and their progeny are the insects. But Tāne is not satisfied. Finally, at a place called Hawaiki, he models a human woman from soil, covers her with his garments and breathes into her mouth; she comes to life, and he makes her his wife. (Hawaiki is a paradisial homeland, the source of life and fertility. There is, by the way, no possibility here of Christian influence, despite the similarity between this story and the one in Genesis.)

Tāne's wife is usually said to be called Hine-ahu-one, or Woman-heaped-up-from-soil. She bears Tāne a daughter, Hine-titama, who grows up to be a most beautiful woman (some tribes know her as Hine-ata-uira or as Hine-i-tauira, Pattern-woman). At this point Tāne, being a fertility figure, naturally enough takes his daughter also as his wife. But presently she discovers her parentage; she is greatly shamed, and she rushes down to the night, which lies beneath the earth. There her name changes; she is known now as Hine-nui-te-pō, Great-woman-the-night. Tāne, in some versions of the story, follows her to the entrance to the underworld and begs her to return. But she refuses to do so, telling her father that his task is to go back to the world and rear their children, while she must stay below and receive them when they die.

It is this event, this separation of Tāne and Hine-nui-te-pō and their identification with their respective realms, which brings death into the world: before this time, people did not die. Later, the trickster hero Māui attempts to overcome Hine-nui-te-pō and so conquer death. He does this, in most versions of the story, by approaching her as she lies asleep and entering her body through the dangerous vagina; he is sometimes said to encounter a vulva edged with flints and flashing like lightning. But despite his great powers, Māui fails in this last undertaking; Hine-nui-te-pō wakes, and crushes him between her legs. Māui's death sets the pattern for all human beings, and Hine-nui-te-pō becomes, in this way too, responsible for the introduction of death into the world.

Before this encounter, Māui has done much for human beings, in his own nonchalant and reckless way. He is a hero who achieves his ends the 'wrong' way, by breaking the laws of *tapu*; his name, which means Left, associates him with the left side of the body, the *noa*, or profane, side. His birth is 'wrong', for he is a miscarriage which his mother throws into the sea; he survives, nurtured by spirits, and eventually returns to his family. There he quickly acquires a reputation as a troublemaker, though much that he does is of benefit to his people. Because the days are too short, he persuades his brothers to help him to snare the sun at daybreak; they administer a beating, and the sun now goes more slowly. When fire is needed, he goes seeking it from his ancestress, Mahuika, who keeps it in her fingernails; she pulls one out for him, but he is not satisfied, and he keeps extinguishing his fire and returning for more until all the fingernails are gone, and the infuriated Mahuika creates a great blaze which nearly destroys him.

On another occasion, Māui goes fishing with his brothers, despite their attempts to prevent him, and takes a magic fishhook consisting of the jawbone of an ancestress, Muri-ranga-whenua. Now, in reality, people did sometimes work human bones into fishhooks, but only when they wished especially to demean an enemy they had killed, since the association with food was most destructive of sacredness, or *tapu*. But Māui breaks the rules on a grand scale, and gets away with it. The *mana* – the power and status – of his ancestress is inherent in her jawbone, and with its aid Māui eventually pulls up the tremendous fish which becomes the island (the North Island of New Zealand) on which his descendants now live (his canoe, incidentally, is now the South Island). The only problem was that his stupid brothers ignored his instructions: Māui told them not to touch the fish until he returned from making the proper offerings to the gods, but as soon as his back was turned they started cutting it up. Unfortunately, the fish was not quite dead. It writhed and flapped, so that the land is now twisted into mountains and valleys.

Since Māui is not a *tapu* figure tales about his exploits could be freely told. They were very popular, partly no doubt because it was pleasing to think of a trickster's achieving such ends through his defiance of all the rules – until the climax of the story-cycle, when he dares to assault Hine-nui-te-pō, and comes to grief. Myths about Māui are known almost everywhere in Polynesia.

Another widely known cycle of stories concerns a very different hero, Tāwhaki, who is a paragon of the chiefly virtues, high-ranking and of splendid appearance, and therefore *tapu*, or sacred. In New Zealand, Tāwhaki is sometimes killed by jealous brothers-in-law, but comes back to life. When his father is killed, he avenges his death – in Polynesian mythology, the classic, sacred task of a warrior. His main exploit, however, is to ascend to the sky. Sometimes he does this in pursuit of his wife, Tangotango.

This woman had come down from the sky to live with Tāwhaki, having heard what a brave, handsome warrior he was, but after a quarrel she went back up to her original home. She took with her their daughter, who had been the cause of all the trouble. The problem was that Tangotango had tried to invert the usual order of things. It was normal for Māori men of rank to look after their male infants for much of the time, returning them to their mothers to be fed, while the women looked after the female babies. One early European traveller noted with apparent amazement that Māori men 'performed all the tender offices of a nurse'; he means that they did not object to changing the padding of soft plant fibres which was tucked around the babies (often, in the baskets in which they were carried). Clearly, the male pride and pleasure in male offspring was such that they were happy to cope with such practicalities; and as the boys grew bigger they were brought up largely by their fathers and other male relatives.

Perhaps because she has come from the sky, where things may have been different, Tangotango attempts to change the rules. When she becomes pregnant she tells Tāwhaki, 'If our child is a boy, I will wash him. If the child is a girl, you will do so.'

The incident which follows must have been regarded as wildly funny.[1] The child is a girl, and this dignified, high-ranking chief washes her. But after a while he cannot stand the girl's smell. He says, 'Oh, what a stink!'

Deeply offended, Tangotango snatches up the child. She stands weeping on the roof of their house, then she disappears up to the sky and does not return. So, when Tāwhaki performs this exploit of mounting up to the sky, in some tribal traditions he is looking for his wife and daughter.

In other traditions, Tāwhaki goes up to find his grandmother – a fierce woman named Whaitiri, or Thunder, who has returned to the sky after living for a time upon the earth. Usually he goes up on a vine, though sometimes a spiderweb or a kite, and he generally receives assistance from an old woman who guards the approach to this sacred realm (one name for her is Ruahine-mata-morari, Old-blind-woman). In the sky he regains his lost wife and daughter, or else discovers his grandmother, Whaitiri – who promptly presents him with one of her granddaughters as a wife.

This journey to the sky, the realm associated with light, nobility and eternal life, reveals Tāwhaki's great status and power. He is said, indeed, to have been the only man to have achieved this difficult feat (and so, in the early years of Christianity, was sometimes likened to Christ). His ascent was often referred to in poetry when a living person was honoured by being identified with him. In songs addressed to the dead, as well, the person might be told to climb up with Tāwhaki: for while it was believed that after death most souls went down to Hine-nui-te-pō, it was also thought that the souls of some high-ranking people, especially warriors, rose up to the sky, where their left eye became a star.

Tāwhaki's grandmother, Whaitiri, or Thunder, is a powerful and enigmatic figure. It is not surprising to find that Tāwhaki is related to her, since he himself is associated with thunder and lightning. Her presence in the sky provides a reason for his ascent, and she sometimes assists him, as female relatives so often do in Māori myths. But Whaitiri is also an independent figure, and a person of high status, as her celestial origin indicates. Among other things, she has control over the supply of food, especially birds and fish, which she can make plentiful or scarce. On the west coast of the North Island, where she was especially important, one authority described her as 'the first old goddess of the ages of darkness' – of the ages, that is, which occurred at the beginning of the world – and said further that it was

Whaitiri (rather than Tāne, as in the usual story) who was responsible for the separation of earth and sky — and so, the creation of the world. It is unfortunate that we have limited information about this minority tradition.

Elsewhere, in tropical Polynesia, a mythical woman named Hina, or Sina, is an archetypal figure of a wife, one who reveals aspects of the female condition and in certain respects sets the pattern for women in their daily lives. One episode reveals her as possessing a dangerous sexuality which has to be tamed: she takes an eel as a lover, and her husband Māui, with others, kills the creature and buries its head. All ends well when the head grows into the first coconut palm — the three holes on the coconut being the eyes and mouth. When the ancestors of the Māori brought this ancient myth to New Zealand, it changed somewhat. Māui chops the eel to pieces — and since the coconut palm does not grow in this country, the eel's head escapes to the rivers and becomes the source of fresh water eels, its tail flees to the ocean and turns into the first conger eel, and its blood can still be seen in the reddish wood of certain trees.

In the Māori stories of Hina and the eel, Hina is always Māui's wife. In another story, Hina is Māui's sister rather than his wife, and she is married to a man named Irawaru. When Māui turns his brother-in-law into the first dog, this is a valuable acquisition for humankind and at the same time a malicious and highly entertaining joke, especially since relationships between brothers-in-law were often uneasy. As for Hina (or Hina-uri), she is sometimes said to be so upset at her husband's transformation that she throws herself into the sea. She swims for many days, sometimes assisted by sea creatures, and she ends up finding and marrying a man named Tinirau. But this last episode more often concerns another woman, Hine-te-iwaiwa. And although Hina does in some ways represent women in general, it is Hine-te-iwaiwa rather than Hina who is the archetypal wife and mother mentioned in ritual chants.

Hine-te-iwaiwa's parentage is variously given. Sometimes she is one of Tāne's daughters. Always she is a very early ancestor. A myth tells of her long journey to find the man she has made up her mind to marry. Having heard of the handsome Tinirau, ruler of all the fish in the ocean, she swims through the sea for many days to reach his home on Motu-tapu, Sacred-island. She becomes his wife, and presently has a son. When her two jealous co-wives plot to kill her, she destroys them with a potent chant (which must certainly have been used in reality by those who had a need for such black magic). Hine-te-iwaiwa's power is such that her chant not only kills her co-wives, it turns them into greenstone, or jade, so that this treasure becomes known for the first time in the world.

In Māori society a woman's brother often had a special relationship with her sons, since they sometimes inherited rank and property from him rather than their father. This is why Hine-te-iwaiwa has a brother, Rupe, who now goes searching for her. He finds her at Motu-tapu on the very day that she has given birth to her son, Tuhuruhuru. Sometimes he carries her off, along with the boy, because Tinirau has been neglecting her. Later, though, there is a reconciliation between husband and wife.

The domestic powers and responsibilities of women were generally thought to have been established in the beginning by Hine-te-iwaiwa. Some high-ranking girls, in fact, were believed to be descended from her; when genealogists traced back an *aho tapairu*, an aristocratic female line of descent, it often ended with Hine-te-iwaiwa. Many of the important events in the lives of girls and women were marked by rituals, and the chants which were recited on these solemn occasions often made reference to Hine-te-iwaiwa. At the *tohi* ritual – a ceremony somewhat similar to baptism, which took place by running water – all infant girls were dedicated to Hine-te-iwaiwa, for their lives were to be like hers. And women in childbirth were aided by the recitation of a ritual chant which spoke of Hine-te-iwaiwa, and was said to have been recited for the first time when she was giving birth to her son. The chant's efficacy, its *mana*, was derived from this initial performance, and the woman in labour was reminded that since she was acting as Hine-te-iwaiwa had done, her ancestress had the power to help her.

Another important stage in a young woman's life was the tattooing of her lips, which took place before marriage. This was an ordeal; the tattooing implement did not merely prick the surface but chiselled the flesh. In the ritual chant recited as this was done, Hine-te-iwaiwa is named along with two more specialized ancestresses, Hine-rau-wharangi and Rukutia. Again these women are seen as the girl's predecessors: having themselves undertaken this role, they can now give the girl the strength she needs to endure it with dignity.

Hine-te-iwaiwa is said to have been the first woman to act as a *ruahine*, a woman of rank who in religious ritual removed an excess of *tapu*, or sacredness. Women, being essentially *noa*, or everyday/profane, had the power of removing *tapu* when this had become necessary, and they took part, therefore, in many rituals. One of them is still performed today. This is the ceremony which takes place at dawn to remove the excess *tapu* from a tribal meeting-house, a large house of assembly adorned with carvings of ancestors. While this house is being built and carved, it is so *tapu* that women are forbidden to approach it; the presence of the *noa* element, which women represent, would desecrate the building and threaten the success of the entire undertaking. But when the house is finished, some of this sacredness must be removed.

Formerly, this ritual sometimes involved a woman's treading the roof of the house (*see* fig. 28). Nowadays, as part of the opening ceremony, a woman of high status enters the building in the company of the *tohunga*, the priest, in order to remove the excess *tapu* and make the house safe for human habitation. In one of the ritual chants repeated at this ceremony, the woman performing this role is identified with Hine-te-iwaiwa.

Since Hine-te-iwaiwa is the generalized, archetypal figure of a wife and mother, she is associated with the women's art of weaving. At the same time, more specialized figures such as Rukutia, Niwareka and Hine-rauamoa are also held responsible for its introduction to the world.

Again, Hine-te-iwaiwa's all-purpose domestic role leads her, in one story, to mourn the dead and seek revenge. When her son Tuhuruhuru is killed in his young

Fig. 28 'Priestess performing incantations' at the ceremony to remove excess *tapu* from a new house. A sketch published by George Gray in 1853.

manhood, and vengeance must be taken, she is sent by her husband, Tinirau, to ask the assistance of a man named Whakatau – he being the specialist in this area, the archetypal figure of a warrior who exacts revenge. In calling upon her menfolk to revenge the death of a relative, Hine-te-iwaiwa establishes a pattern which women have followed ever since.

But the gaining of revenge was such a crucial issue in Māori society that the role of the mother who seeks revenge was also assigned to a specialized figure. This woman is Apakura. In some traditions, she marries Tuhuruhuru and has a son, Tuwhakararo, who is treacherously killed by another tribe. Apakura unceasingly laments his death, partly to give vent to her feelings but also to incite her tribe to vengeance. And the great avenger Whakatau – here described variously as a younger brother of Tuwhakararo, his cousin or his son – does indeed destroy the enemy. Apakura is regarded as the ancestress who taught people, especially women, how to weep for the dead, and she is often mentioned in laments for this reason.

So far we have been considering some of the main mythical figures which were known throughout the country. The accounts of these people's exploits and adventures varied considerably in different regions, but their basic significance, the archetypal roles they played, remained much the same everywhere. Because they lived in the beginning, these ancestors and ancestresses established patterns of social behaviour, providing precedents for later generations. They are not *atua*, spirits or gods, but *tāngata*, people, whose names occur on the earliest levels of the genealogies. They do not judge or evaluate human behaviour, they simply exhibit its range. Some of them are also, at the same time, natural phenomena still to be encountered in the world – as with Rangi the Sky and Papa the Earth.

Other myths are regional, dealing not with human beginnings in general but with the origins of individual tribes. While some tribes claimed descent from ancestors who had always been there – from Māui, for instance, who lived on his fish after pulling it up – most people believed that the founders of their tribes had migrated from the paradisial land of Hawaiki, which lay in the direction of the rising sun.

This mythical land, the source of life and fertility, was the setting for a number of early events (we have seen already that it is the place where Tāne made the first woman from soil). Most of the larger tribes, and many smaller ones, possess a myth telling how and why their first *tribal* ancestors left the homeland of Hawaiki for this country, the valuable possessions – plants and birds, archetypal adzes and other treasures – which they brought with them, the extraordinary obstacles which their leaders overcame, the ritual chants which they recited, the supernatural guardians which escorted their canoes, the archetypal antagonisms which occurred between rivals, the landmarks which the leaders established after making landfall, and the journeys of exploration which they then undertook, bestowing names, claiming possession and establishing boundaries.

Most of the main protagonists in these much-loved stories of tribal origins are male; less is said about the wives who accompany them. There is, however, one notable exception. In numerous traditions it is a woman who is responsible for introducing the highly prized kumara, or sweet potato. This was the main crop plant, and women played an important part in its cultivation. Generally, it is the main wife of the captain of the canoe who brings the sweet potato. One particular woman, Whakaoti-rangi, was so famous in this connection that five different tribal groups claimed her as an ancestress, and her prudence and industry were proverbial. According to one story, when her companions ate their seed tubers on the voyage, she kept hers tied up in a corner of her basket. She planted them in the new land, and they flourished greatly.

Analysis

So much for the main Māori myths, inherited stories which explained the world. Such systems of thought were universal in tribal societies, which – being small-scale, relatively isolated, with 'simple' technology and without writing – did not engage in open-ended, scientific enquiry. People in these societies have, of course, always been extremely knowledgeable about their physical environment in practical ways, highly sophisticated in the exacting disciplines which their technology and means of livelihood imposed upon them. The Māori myths offered no hindrance to such understanding. They lasted so long because they gave expression to basic preoccupations, and at the same time provided scope for endless subtlety and flexibility in their interpretation, application and elaboration. They also, among other things, made possible a great poetic tradition.

A concern with the natures and roles of males and females is, I think, the most important of all the preoccupations which find expression in Māori mythology. Our bodily experience is inescapable and, from the beginning, simultaneously physical and social. What is more, human thought – in particular, the thought of tribal peoples – is organized very largely in terms of dualities, pairs of opposites. Male and female constitute such a duality, and one with great explanatory power. In Māori thought, this male/female duality was aligned with a number of other dualities which structured the perceived world – in particular, with light/darkness, east/west, up/down, right/left, raw/cooked, *tapu/noa*, life/death. In each case, males were associated with the prestigious term (light, east, up, right, raw, *tapu*, life), and females with the non-prestigious one.

Why did women occupy this territory, associated with darkness, the setting sun, an inferior position, the (suspect) left hand, cooked food, the ordinary and profane, and death? Why, for that matter, have women been regarded in most – if not all – traditional societies as vastly inferior to men, and commonly associated with such negatively valued entities? This difficult question has been much discussed. Here, I can only touch on some aspects of Māori thinking about the sexes, as reflected in their myths. But it should be noted that while a preoccupation with questions concerning male and female is arguably the basic organizing idea in all mythologies, this may be especially apparent in the case of the Māori because the country had virtually no land mammals: only some insignificant bats, and the dogs and rats their ancestors had brought with them. Although there are plenty of birds, whales and so on in the Māori stories, animals do not play as large a part as in most mythologies. Instead, men and women confront each other in their essential natures.

We have seen that the earth is the first woman, Papa, or that – as one can equally say – the first woman is the earth. The *second* woman, Hine-ahu-one, also consists of earth, having been modelled from the soil of Hawaiki, the paradisial land which is the source of life and fertility. And when Hine-ahu-one's beautiful daughter Hine-titama, finding that her husband is also her father, rushes down to the dark realm beneath the earth (and her name is changed to Hine-nui-te-pō, Great-woman-the-night), she becomes the *third* woman to be identified with the earth – in this case with its negative aspect, its association with death. The identification of women's fertility and that of the earth is common enough in mythology, and so is the belief that women are responsible for the introduction of death into the world. Māori men claimed that if there had been no women, men would have lived forever like the stars in the sky.

Why were women, whose life-giving powers were so much valued, thought to have brought death into the world? Someone, of course, had to be blamed. One reason – though not the only one – must be that since women had started the process, they were held responsible, by an inexorable logic, for what followed. A story about a male mythical figure, Tiki, provides a parallel. It is sometimes Tiki rather than Tāne who makes the first woman, and has sex with her; or else Tāne performs this role, but Tiki is identified with Tāne's penis. Tiki's specialty is that he is the initiator of sexual intercourse, and he is mentioned for this reason in songs and proverbs. Because of this role, he is sometimes known as Tiki-rau-hanga, Tiki-who-gets-up-to-lots-of-tricks. But this elaborated name does not always refer to his role as a lover, for there are songs of mourning in which Tiki-rau-hanga is held responsible for the existence of death. In this context, his trickery is that in giving life to humans, he has also made them subject to death: this has been the final, unlooked-for outcome. Tiki can be blamed for human death, as women more usually are, for our end is in our beginning.

As well as a recognition of women's power, the myths convey a fear of women: for example, in the menacing female figures which frequently confront the heroes (sometimes they relent and turn out to be helpful grandmothers, and sometimes they do not). The reasons for this fear are certainly complex. Women's capacity to give birth and to feed their infants was of such tremendous significance that one must assume some male anxiety concerning it. As well, there seems to have been a fear of female sexuality: the episode with Hina's eel can be understood in this way, and so can Māui's death between the legs of Hine-nui-te-pō. One factor here is that women's inherently *noa* condition must have been experienced as threatening in some situations to the *tapu* men, who had to protect their sacredness from too much contact with the everyday and the profane. Men and women had to be kept properly separate − indeed, the world began when they were first separated − yet at the same time their close interaction was necessary for every kind of reason, in everyday life and in the rituals, too, in which women played an essential part. This situation must have been productive of tension. The stakes were high, and accidents were always possible. If, for instance, a woman were to step over a man's legs while he was lying down, his *tapu* would be insulted. If she did this to a boy, who was still more vulnerable, his growth would be stunted.

The women in these myths do not often set out on adventures, as the men so often do. They do, certainly, bring the sweet potato from the paradisal land of Hawaiki, and cultivate it successfully after their arrival. Apart from this, their one important journey is to find a husband: Hine-te-iwaiwa (or Hina) goes looking for Tinirau, Whaitiri comes down from the sky to marry a man named Kai-tangata, and Tangotango comes down and marries Tāwhaki. In Māori legends, too, a highborn woman sometimes sets out on a secret, difficult journey, alone or with a single servant, to find a chief whom she is determined to marry despite her family's opposition; she finally reaches him, and she does marry him. Such a concern with husbands might not seem very enterprising to a contemporary, western reader. But in choosing husbands for themselves, these women are choosing, as well, the family and the tribe within which they will live their future lives; in this setting they will not only rear children, they will exercise their skills in horticulture, weaving, food-gathering and much else. In reality, a woman's marriage, especially if she were of high rank, was very often planned by her brothers and her tribe; essentially it was a political decision. But it is known that women did sometimes get their own way against their family's opposition. We can at least conclude that the idea of a woman's asserting her independence and determining her own future was an attractive one: to women, clearly, but also, judging by the popularity of these stories, to men as well.

While most of the main protagonists in the myths are men, their success generally depends upon the assistance of women. This is remarked upon by the folklorist Katharine Luomala: 'Scarcely a Polynesian hero can be found who within five minutes of a narrator's time is not being helped in an adventure and saved from failure or restored to life by his faithful and magically-skilled sister, mother, or blind old grandmother . . . it is, of course, a tribute to the hero . . . that he can win their co-operation while other male relatives get no help' (Luomala, 1955, p. 148). Female relatives are indeed the most common helpers, kinship being such an important factor, but wives do sometimes fill this role. And women's supportive, nurturing capacity was taken so much for granted — regarded, apparently, as so inevitable, so 'natural' — that some men, when their circumstances require it, even receive protection and assistance from women previously unknown to them. When Rua-te-pupuke approaches the house of Tangaroa, who has stolen his son, we are not surprised to discover that Tangaroa is temporarily absent and that Rua-te-pupuke receives much-needed assistance from a woman he meets there. This is a common pattern, perhaps universal. It seems equally 'natural' for Jack the Giant-killer, for instance, intruding upon the giant's house in his absence, to be helped by the giant's wife.

SECTION III: SOME LESSER FIGURES

An ancient myth, surviving now in only one region, tells of a 'devouring mother' — that nightmare figure well known to mythologists. This woman, named Houmea, was married to Tangaroa. At first he did not realize she was evil. When he returned from fishing she went down in the usual way to carry up his fish, but she swallowed them instead, then pretended the sea fairies had stolen them. And one day she swallowed her two sons. The husband restored them to life with a ritual chant, then fled with his boys in his canoe. Houmea turned herself into a cormorant and pursued them across the ocean. She caught up with the canoe, her mouth gaping wide to swallow them, but they fed her hot stones and she died. These days, the storyteller adds, Houmea is still to be seen in the world in the form of a cormorant, and the name Houmea is given to evil and thievish women.

The cormorant with its extraordinary ability to swallow fish is an appropriate medium for Houmea. In traditional Māori thought there is, too, a tendency for women to be associated in various situations with water; it appears, somehow, as their natural element. We have seen that Hine-te-iwaiwa (or Hina) swims for many days to find the island where Tinirau is living. There is also Hine-poupou, who was abandoned by her husband while they were living on the shore of Raukawa (Cook Strait), the turbulent stretch of water which separates the two main islands. When her husband and his people sailed off to the other side of the strait, some fifty miles away, Hine-poupou swam after them, discovering on the way a valuable fishing rock. She forgave her husband and lived with him once more, but when he insulted her a second time she took her revenge, luring him out to sea then calling upon the taniwha, the dragons she had encountered during her long swim, to send a gale to destroy his canoe.

Fig. 29 Kurangai-tuku, a bird-headed fairy, with her pet birds and lizards. She
is carved on the door of a meeting-house opened in 1905.
Photographer, Theo Schoon

Another dangerous woman is Kurangai-tuku, a fairy who lives on her own in
the forest, hunting birds, and who herself has a bird's head, and feathers (see fig.
29). She kidnaps Hatupatu, who is wandering in the forest, and keeps him prisoner
in her cave. When he escapes, she pursues him with giant strides, stepping from hill
to hill, and he survives only because he jumps over a boiling spring, while Kurangai-
tuku, close behind, attempts to wade through it.

We have seen that specialized female figures represent different skills and
activities, such as weaving, growing sweet potatoes and weeping for the dead. In an
ancient tradition, Raukata-uri or Dark Raukata, and Raukata-mea or Red Raukata
are the sisters responsible for introducing games, music and dancing to the world;
their presence is felt now in the forest, where a narrow drooping fern is their ringlets,

and the cicada with its insistent song is Raukata-uri's voice. Two other sisters, Te Pupu and Te Hoata, are the origin and personification of the supernatural fire located in volcanoes and hot springs; when their brother Ngātoro-i-rangi climbed a mountain and nearly died from the cold, they sent fire to warm him, and it can be seen there still. Numerous other women personify natural phenomena, such as: Hine-moana, Ocean-woman; Hine-pukohu-rangi, Mist-woman; Hine-kirikiri, Gravel-woman; and Hine-tua-hōanga, Sandstone-woman.

Because sandstone was used in working the greatly prized greenstone, or jade, Hine-tuahōanga is the enemy who pursues it, in the beginning, to the valleys where it is now to be found. Sometimes as well she is the mother — or the sister — of Rata, who builds a canoe to make a voyage to avenge his father's death. When this hero needs to fell a tree for his canoe, Hine-tua-hōanga instructs him to sharpen his adze against her sandstone back; he does this, and he succeeds in his undertaking. One might not expect a warrior to have a mother with a sandstone back, but we are dealing here with ideas. Hine-tua-hōanga is a wonderful, power-bestowing presence in the world, and at the same time she is the 'female helper' through whose knowledge and powers the man can employ this presence.

SECTION IV: MYTHOGRAPHY

In the middle of the nineteenth century, when Māori myths were first recorded, they were generally regarded as historical accounts. The Māori considered the people in these stories to be their earliest ancestors. The Europeans did not believe all of the mythical figures to have been historical, but they did usually assume that Māui, Tāwhaki, Rata, Whakatau and numerous others were persons who had really existed. This is not surprising. After all, the Māori authorities were saying so. Also, there are a great many legends which tell of the activities of actual, historical ancestors from relatively recent times, and it was natural enough for the myths to be confused with these legends. The religious meanings of the myths — the archetypal significance of the protagonists, the re-enactment of their stories in ritual situations — were not understood by the first European scholars, although they were implicit in the texts they had acquired; and in fact the Māori acceptance of Christianity soon led to the abandonment of most of the traditional rituals. Although many old beliefs and practices continued for a long time, most of the myths lost much of their original significance.

In the fast-changing circumstances, the myths were reshaped and revalidated by both Māori and European thinkers. Episodes where the characters display extraordinary, 'supernatural' powers were frequently ignored or rationalized by the Europeans, and in time they tended to receive less emphasis even in Māori narratives. And both sides felt a need to reconcile differing accounts. With the tribal districts now in ready contact with each other, the storytellers and orators had to create new syntheses of the tribal myths of origin — or else, to scornfully deny the claims of other peoples. The Europeans, when they learnt of the existence of related stories from other parts of Polynesia, produced misguided attempts at elaborate historical reconstruction which in due course influenced the thinking of the Māori narrators.

The early literature on Māori tradition, in *The Journal of the Polynesian Society* and in the works of George Grey, John White, Percy Smith, Elsdon Best, Apirana Ngata, Te Rangi Hiroa, Pei Te Hurinui and many others, contains a great deal of historical and linguistic information but offers few insights as to the nature of the myths. The historical misreadings of these narratives became so convoluted and unsatisfactory that interest in them eventually lapsed, and the field was left to the European writers who endlessly produced sentimental, and generally badly written, retellings for children (thereby conveying to all concerned the message that Māori traditions were merely childish tales).

Then in the 1950s, at a time when very few scholars were concerning themselves with Māori tradition, a Danish historian of religion, J. Prytz Johansen, published two works on the mythology which for the first time brought to bear upon Māori texts a highly sophisticated understanding of myth and ritual, supported by impressive textual analyses. Johansen discusses the archetypal significance of many of the mythical figures, and examines in detail the complex relationships existing between myth and ritual. Despite the dated title of his first book, he devotes considerable attention to the female figures in these narratives. Indeed, his approach automatically establishes their far-reaching importance, whereas the previous attempts at historical interpretation led to the neglect of all mythical figures other than warriors and voyagers.

Johansen has shown that techniques commonly employed by historians of religion and literary scholars can be extremely successful when applied to the writings of tribal peoples. His pioneering work is still, unfortunately, neglected by most historians of religion and anthropologists. In New Zealand, however, it is providing a valuable precedent as scholars begin at last to undertake research on mythological texts.

The new awareness of the importance of the myths, and the desire to make accessible the many works by nineteenth-century Māori writers which remain in manuscript, is largely a consequence of the Māori cultural renaissance of recent years, along with changing attitudes among people of European descent. The retold versions of the stories are better written now, imagined more strongly, and many are by Māori authors. In a remarkable and influential work, *Wahine Toa: Women of Māori Myth*, the artist Robyn Kahukiwa and the writer Patricia Grace present interpretations of some of the 'women who have starring roles in the myth dramas'. The expression *wahine toa* means 'women of strength'. Māori women are now reclaiming their heritage, discovering the truths which the myths convey and the multiple powers and roles of which the storytellers speak.

Notes

1 We are not told this, but can safely assume it. In another incident, the handsome Tāwhaki disguises himself as an ugly old man and becomes the slave of his brothers-in-law. The collector of this account remarks that 'The European reader cannot at all enter into the witty nature of this adventure in the estimation of a Māori; the idea of a sacred chief of high rank being by mistake treated as a common slave conveys impressions to their minds of which we can inform no accurate notion' (Grey, 1961, p. 56).

References and Further Reading

Alpers, A. (1964), *Maori Myths and Tribal Legends*, later reprints (Auckland: Paul). The best collection of retold stories.

Grey, G. (1855), *Polynesian Mythology*, recent edition 1961 (Christchurch: Whitcombe and Tombs). An early collection; free translations.

Kahukiwa, R. and Grace, P. (1984), *Wahine Toa: Women of Maori Myth* (Auckland: Collins)

Luomala, K. (1955) *Voices on the Wind* (Hawaii: Bishop Museum Press). A classic introduction to Māori and other Polynesian mythologies.

Makereti (1938), *The Old-time Maori* (London: Gollancz). By a Māori woman, born in 1872, who spent her later years in Oxford with her English husband. Not very much about mythology, and some material is not first-hand, but the autobiographical sections are of great interest.

Orbell, M. (1985), *The Natural World of the Maori* (London: Thames and Hudson). Myths and folklore relating to the environment. Illustrated.

—— (1985), *Hawaiki: A New Approach to Maori Tradition* (Christchurch, NZ: University of Canterbury). Hawaiki is a paradisial land of origin.

Prytz Johansen, J. (1954), *The Maori and His Religion in its Non-ritualistic Aspects* (Copenhagen: Munksgaard)

—— (1958), *Studies in Maori Rites and Myths* (Copenhagen: Munksgaard). Highly recommended, though not easy reading. The second work is the more specialized of the two.

ELIZABETH DIAB

Hawaii

INTRODUCTION

On Monday, 30 April, 1990, the front page of the Hawaii *Tribune-Herald* carried a report on the lava flow which threatened the Star of the Sea Painted Church, the focal point of the residential district of Kalapana on the big island of Hawaii. A debate raged among members of the local community as to whether the historic church, built in 1930, should be physically moved to another location where it would be out of reach of the destructive lava, or whether it should be left to its fate along with most of the homes still standing in the area. Reporter for the *Tribune-Herald*, D. Hunter Bishop, stated:

> Some clearly wanted the church to remain, saying they would put their faith in the Lord and the Hawaiian Volcano Goddess Pele, and take their chances with the lava pouring out from Kilauea Volcano.

Many of those who attended mass at the Star of the Sea Painted Church regularly every Sunday also placed their offerings on the edge of Halema'uma'u crater, said to be the home of the goddess Pele.

The exploits of Pele first appeared in print in Hawaiian language newspapers in the 1860s, some forty years after the missionaries had landed, at a time when the old Hawaiian culture and even the language itself had seemed in danger of extinction. Prior to the coming of the missionaries in 1820, the Hawaiian child learned of the mysteries of the gods and goddesses, of the adventures of the ancestors and of the traditional ways of the Hawaiian people from respected elder family members. The Hawaiian child knew no written language but was accustomed to the rhythmic chanting by which such information was communicated, and which had been used by previous generations to preserve and pass on such knowledge. From the men and women of distant Europe and America, the Hawaiians learned another way to transmit the history of their people and in so doing made themselves vulnerable to the tides of change.

SECTION I: THE GODS

The Hawaiian word for god is *akua*, but it is a term with many applications. William Hyde Rice defines *akua* as the 'name of any supernatural being, the object of fear or worship – a god, a ghost, a demi-god, a spirit' (Rice, 1923, p. 133). It can be applied to natural phenomena, to corpses or to images made by the worshipper. The *aumakua* are deities attached to particular families or professions worshipped as guardian figures, while a *kupua* is the child of a god or goddess, born into the family of his or her worshippers as a human being, although characterized by special powers. However, these three classifications of the supernatural have no rigid boundaries: an *akua* may also be an *aumakua* to a certain group, and a *kupua* may become an *aumakua* after death if sanctified by a particular family. The relationship between a worshipper and his or her *aumakua* is a very close one, often considered to be one of kinship, with families claiming descent from their *aumakuas*. The kupua is recognized as the child of an *akua* either by the ability to adopt a form of nature associated with the *akua*, or to exert power over those forms of nature. Below the *akuas* are a vast number of lesser gods allied to particular attributes or manifestations of higher gods, and commanded in the service of those gods, while themselves commanding an infinite number of lower-ranking gods, down to the spirits, the *akua-li'i*, which occupy all forms of nature.

The four great gods, worshipped in Hawaii and much of Eastern Polynesia, and to whom the multitude of lesser gods were subordinate, are Ku, Kane, Lono and Kanaloa. These were the gods made known to the early missionaries who landed on the Hawaiian islands early in the nineteenth century. These gods are often seen as having travelled to Hawaii from some distant land, or from a mythical homeland of the gods.

Twelve such islands are said to float off the coast of Hawaii, hidden from sight except at sunrise or sunset, when they can be seen as a reddish tint on the horizon. The islands are sometimes said to be divided into three layers, or decks, the highest of all the mythical lands of the deities being known as Nuu-mea-lani (the Raised Dais of Heaven). Most commonly the gods are described as having come from the mythical homeland of Kahiki.

Beckwith quotes David Malo Kupihea, a Hawaiian elder, as saying that the great gods came to Hawaii at different times. According to Kupihea, Ku was one of the earliest gods of the Hawaiians, with Kane and Kanaloa coming later and Lono being the last to arrive (Beckwith, 1970, pp. 10–11), although it appears that Kane was the most actively worshipped at the time of the arrival of the missionaries. In the *Kumulipo*, a Hawaiian creation chant dated around 1700 and recited at the arrival of Captain Cook in 1779, the god Kane makes his appearance, along with Kanaloa the great Octopus, during the eighth period of time, the *ao* – the time of man as opposed to the preceding period of darkness called the *pa*. Neither Ku nor Lono are named in the *Kumulipo*. Unlike the *Kumulipo*, some Hawaiian creation stories bear a striking resemblance to Biblical accounts of the creation, with Ku, Kane and Lono as a triad of gods who created light out of darkness, then the heaven and the earth, with the sun, moon and stars to fill the firmament. Then man is made (often out of clay, or drawn in the earth) and given a garden in which to live, as well as a wife, sometimes created out of his right side. In some versions, the triad of gods is opposed by Kanaloa, who takes on a Lucifer role. Beckwith believes that these versions were authentically Hawaiian, and only acquired 'a colouring and an emphasis' (Beckwith, 1970 p. 46) through association with Biblical accounts of creation.

The creator god, Kane (called Tane elsewhere in Polynesia), is known in Hawaii as a great ancestral god and the god of procreation. His name is often coupled with Kanaloa, and together they are associated with the establishing and maintaining of water sources all over the islands.

There are very many subordinate Kane gods which were *aumakuas* to their devotees, and the heads of families who could claim direct descent from Kane were among the highest ranking chiefs, able to command almost god-like status and impose correspondingly rigid *kapus*, or taboos. Their presence was treated with the same degree of sacredness accorded to the gods.

The god Lono, known elsewhere in Polynesia as Rongo or Ro'o, is said to have come to Hawaii after the arrival of Kane and Kanaloa. As a god of fertility, Lono is associated with the Makahiki games, held during the rainy season, as a time of celebration when all manual labour ceased. The origin of these games was said to have come from the legend in which Lono's wife, Ka-iki-lani, was courted by a chief, and was beaten to death by Lono in a fit of jealousy, despite her protestations of innocence. Later, presumably struck by remorse, he established the games as a memorial to her. Lono then built himself a magnificent canoe and set sail alone, promising to return on a floating island (Beckwith, 1970, p. 37). During the Makahiki festival, the god is represented in wood and feathers and called Lono-Makua (Father Lono) and also as the Long-god of the Games. The image was carried ceremoniously through each district and offerings of food and clothing were made. When Captain Cook landed on the island in 1779, he was worshipped as the god Lono and his ship was seen as the floating island on which the god had promised to return.

As the god of agriculture, Lono commanded rituals which were performed in the eating house of the men, called the *mua*. It was here that the food gourd was kept, the Ipu-O-Lono, which represented the god and from which the men were required to eat ceremonially before they consumed their own meal. Women were forbidden to eat with the men as they were considered unclean during the time of their menstruation. They were also forbidden to eat certain foods used in sacrificial ritual, such as pork, the yellow coconut, most kinds of bananas and certain kinds of fish. The published findings of the Culture Committee of the Queen Lili'uokalani Children's Centre confirm that menstrual blood was considered *kapu* well into the twentieth century, although as soon as the menstrual blood had ceased and the woman had taken a purifying bath, she was highly prized by the man who wanted to father a child, this being thought to be the time of highest fertility (Pukui, Haertig and Lee, 1972, 1, p. 7).

The great god Ku, possibly the oldest of the Hawaiian gods, is worshipped as the god of fertility and prayed to for long life and well-being, for good yields from the land and the ocean, and also for success in warfare. His protection as an *aumakua* extends to those associated with the forest in any form, and those concerned with canoe building.

SECTION II: WHAT OF THE GODDESSES?

O female aumakua and ancestral chiefesses
Female aumakua at the rising and setting places of the sun,
Female (spirits) in the firmaments of the heaven and of the
clouds . . . .

To all the female aumakua
It is yours (the mana) to brush aside darkness brush aside
death, brush aside trouble.
(KAMAKAU, 1866–71, PP. 31–2)

Between the two sections of this prayer chant for acquiring a female *aumakua*, are listed twenty-four deities. The acceptance of the essential male and female duality of the universe, apparent in the natural world, is one of the central features of the Hawaiian religious chant and reflects a concept of the world in which this duality is applied to all aspects of the universe. The ancient Hawaiians worshipped pairs of rock formations resembling male and female organs as ancestral gods (*Kumulipo*, p. 56). In the *Kumulipo*, both male and female progenitors are named, amounting to some 800 pairs in all. Just as the male and female parents are placed in the natural yet opposing pairs, so natural forms are presented as allied yet opposite:

Man for the narrow stream, woman for the broad stream
Born was the hairy seaweed living in the sea
Guarded by the hairy pandanus vine living on the land
Darkness slips into light
Earth and water are the food of the plant
The god enters, man cannot enter
(KUMULIPO, P. 60)

Ku and Hina, the male and the female, the rising upright and the leaning down, are together the deities of all humankind, both those who have already been and those who are to come. Ku is associated with the upright or sharp stone, while Hina is the flat or rounded stone; Ku is the rising of the sun while Hina is the setting of the sun; Ku is the right hand while Hina is the left hand. Ku is the male generative source while Hina is female source of growth and production. They are national deities from which all can claim a common descent and to whom all can apply for succour and protection.

Hina

The goddess Hina has many forms and has attracted many story-tellers to her themes throughout Polynesia. Here are some of the tales known to the Hawaiians.

Hina, the woman of Lalo–Hana, left her home at the bottom of the sea and lived with the chief, Koni-konia. A diver was sent by the chief to retrieve Hina's belongings from the depth of the ocean. The calabash containing these belongings was opened by Hina and the moon flew out of the calabash and took its place in the sky, but leaving its reflection on the water. Guided by the reflection, Hina's brothers came looking for her in the form of *pa-o'o* fishes and were carried by the sea in the form of a great flood, which the community only escaped by climbing to the top of the highest mountain. When the waters subsided, the earth was made fertile again by the sun and the chief and his people returned (Colum, 1937). In another variation, Hina-hanai-a-ka-malama (Hina nourished on the moon) lived under the sea with her family, of whom only one other had a human form. Her brother's task was to take care of her, but he neglected his duty and retreated to the land, leaving to his sister the calabash containing the moon and the stars as food for her to live on. Having worked for the chief Koni-Konia, he returned for Hina; she married the chief and bore ten children (Beckwith, 1970, pp. 214–15).

In the *Kumulipo*, Hina-ke-ka, the bailer, gives birth to the corals, the eels and the sea–urchins as well as volcanic and black stones, and so she is called Hinahalakoa, the woman-from-whose-womb-comes-many-forms (*Kumulipo*). She is called the bailer because she floated to Wakea as a gourd used to bail water but when she is taken aboard she becomes a beautiful woman. The sea creatures are born of the union of Hina and Wakea.

As Hina-hanaia-i-ka-malama (Hina who worked on the moon) or Hina-i-kapa'i-kua (Hina the tapa beater), she is the woman who is weary of her work beating *tapa* for clothing and bed coverings, and retreats from the bad temper of her husband to the moon where she can still be seen. *Tapa* (*kapa*) is made by pounding the bark of the paper mulberry tree, and it is hard work and time-consuming. In one version, her husband tries to prevent her from leaving by hanging on to her foot, which he breaks. Thus she acquired the name Lonomoku, or Lame Lono, which has a male association through the god Lono.

Hina-a-ke-ahi (Hina of the fire) is also connected to Maui, the Polynesian hero who fished up the Polynesian islands from the bottom of the sea. Hina is said to be Maui's mother, and in a Hawaiian version of the legends, Maui slows down the sun's daily progress across the sky by lassoing it to the edge of Haleakala crater, situated on the island which bears his name, in order to give her more time to finish her *tapa* (Beckwith, 1970).

Haumea

Haumea of mysterious forms, Haumea of eightfold forms,
Haumea of four-hundred-thousand-fold forms, Haumea of
four-thousand-fold forms,
With thousands of thousands of forms.

(*KUMULIPO*, P. 114)

The goddess Haumea occupies a confusing but central position in Hawaiian myths concerning the origins and continuation of the human race. She is the patroness of childbirth, and is associated with the establishment of food supplies, and is thus regarded as a goddess of fertility. In the *Kumulipo* creation chant, three myths of the origins of the human race are blended, each involving Haumea in a different form.

In the eighth *wa* (period of time) in the *Kumulipo*, Haumea is identified as La'ila'i, the first woman born along with Ki'i the man and Kane the god, and Kanaloa the octopus. The womb of La'ila'i bears fruit in the form of the-vast-expanse-of-the-damp-forest and the first chiefs of the dim past dwelling in the cold uplands (Beckwith, 1970, p. 277). She bears offspring to both Ki'i the man and Kane the god, and the resulting dispute of succession establishes the right of the first born child of a mother to take precedence over other children.

> Kane was angry and jealous because he slept with her
> His descendants would hence belong to the younger line
> The children of the elder would be lord.
>
> (*KUMULIPO*, P. 106)

From her relation with the man Ki'i, La'ila'i produces human-kind; the *Kumulipo* lists 800 pairs, naming both men and women. It is through these two branches of La'ila'i's children that Hawaiian chiefs traced their genealogies to establish their blood rank.

Haumea is also the goddess from Nu'umealani, one of the mythical island homelands of the deities; she lived with Kanaloa and produced children through the fontanel. As this goddess, Haumea returns to mate again with her children and her children's children of successive generations. However, this abundant fertility eventually ceases as Haumea's deception is discovered after the birth of Ki'io:

> Ki'io was born, Haumea was recognized
> Haumea was seen to be shrivelled
> Cold and undesirable
> The woman was in fact gone sour
> Hard to deal with and crabbed
> Unsound, a fraud, half-blind, a woman generations old.
> Wrinkled behind, wrinkled before
> Bent and grey the breast.
>
> (*KUMULIPO*, P. 116)

As Papa, Haumea is the Earth Mother figure, wife of Wakea, the Sky-Father, who is deceived by her mate in that he sleeps with his own daughter who is their child. The desire of Wakea for his daughter is said to have resulted in the establishment of the *kapu* (taboo) on men and women sleeping together during the woman's menstrual period. In order to facilitate the coming together of himself and his daughter without arousing the suspicions of Papa, Wakea is advised by his *kahuna* (priest) to arrange days when Papa must sleep in a separate place. During the second of these nights of separations, however, Wakea fails to wake up at the chant of the *kahuna* which was meant to awaken him and he is discovered by Papa. The *Kumulipo* alludes to the story thus:

> Papa lived with Wakea; Born was the woman Ha'alolo
> Born was jealousy, anger
> Papa was deceived by Wakea
> He ordered the sun, the moon
> The night to Kane for the younger
> The night to Hilo for the first born
> Taboo was the house platform the place for sitting
> Taboo the house where Wakea lived
> Taboo was intercourse with the divine parent

(KUMULIPO, P. 125)

The dedication of *kapu* nights to the gods necessitated the establishment of a strict lunar calendar, calculations for which were kept by the priests alone and so their authority increased significantly. During the *kapu* nights women slept in a separate building called the *pe'a* and their food was cooked in a separate oven (Beckwith, 1970, p. 299).

In one version of the Papa/Wakea myth, the first child of Papa is born without arms or legs and is buried in the ground at the east corner of the house. From this spot a taro plant grows overnight and Wakea names the first child after this plant, calling it Haloa, meaning long-rootstalk. This Haloa appears to have then assumed the previously separate function of god, priest and chief. With the combination of these functions in one figurehead, the distance between the ruling chiefs and the people grew, reinforced by the imposition of religious *kapus*.

In all its variations, the Haumea myth centres around the birth of generations to come. Her essential nature is that of the fertile womb-figure, out of which life comes in all forms, resulting ultimately in the birth of the Hawaiian people through the union of Papa and Wakea. Haumea is not surprisingly then the goddess of childbirth, credited with having saved a chief's daughter on the island of Oahu from the necessity of having her child by Caesarean section, facilitating instead a natural delivery by the administration of herbs. The use of herbs in the delivery of a baby is recorded in *Look to the Source* (Pukui et al, 1972, p. 14), as is the ability of the *kahuna pale keiki* (priest-midwife) to transfer the pain of childbirth away from the woman in labour on to anyone — male or female — of their choosing. This was done after praying to Haumea.

In the *Kumulipo*, Haumea is said to have given birth through the fontanel (p. 115), but as the mother of the family of Pele, the goddess of the Volcano, Haumea delivers children from various parts of her body. One daughter, Na-maka-o-ka-hai, comes from the breasts of Haumea; of the sons, Ka-moho-ali'i is born from the top of her head while Kane-hekili (Kane of the thunder) comes from the mouth. Various other children, numbering up to forty in some versions, were born from other parts of the body (Westervelt, 1916; Beckwith, 1970).

Only Pele, known as Pele-honua-mea (Pele of sacred earth) and also as Pele-'ai-honua (Pele the eater of land), inhabiter of the still active volcano Kilauea, was born 'from the thighs' (Westervelt, 1916, p. 68).

Pele

The saga of Pele, goddess of the volcano, was translated into English by Nathaniel B. Emerson, the Hawaiian-speaking son of the Reverend John Emerson, and first published in 1915. To Emerson, the stories of the goddess and her family were a symbol for the old Hawaii so nearly annihilated by different cultural and religious influences. However, in attempting to capture the elusive essence of a dying culture, Emerson inadvertently reiterates the persistent Christian stratum in the sub-soil of Hawaiian culture — in the whole pattern of the social fabric running continuously through the history of Hawaii for the past 150 years (Pukui & Korn, 1973, p. xii). Governed inevitably by the accepted values of his time and place, Emerson's view of Pele has become the common one; she is seen as:

> a wrinkled hag asleep in a cave on a rough lava bed with banked fires and only an occasional blue flame playing about her as symbols of her power; now a creature of terror riding on a chariot of flame and carrying destruction; and now as a young woman of seductive beauty as when she sought passionate relations with the handsome prince Lohiau; but in disposition always jealous, fickle, vengeful.
>
> (EMERSON, 1915A, P. 231)

The body of myth and legend which tell the story of Pele divides into three main narrative strands, all of which are told originally in the sacred chants and dances of the *hula*.

The first concerns the migration of the fire family of Pele from their home to the island of Hawaii; the second relates the journey of Pele's youngest sister, Hi'iaka, to the island of Kaua'i to fetch the chief Lohiau as a lover for the goddess; and the third tells of the relationship of Pele and Kamapua'a, the demi-god with hog-like characteristics, around whom exists a whole separate narrative. These will be recounted below.

Much of the material as it exists in its chant form is extremely sacred, as the *hula* songs are said to come direct from the goddess Pele to the chosen *kumu-hulas* (*hula* teachers) and to those who participate in the *hula*. The lives of the *hula* dancers, both male and female, were dedicated to the service of their art. The *halau*, or hall, where the *hula* took place, was built after the observance of the strictest of *kapus*, with carefully repeated ritual prayers and sacrifices. Intercourse was forbidden to the *hula* student during periods of preparation and dedication, and the students had to maintain this chastity until after their *ailolo*, or graduation, after which time they were free from the restriction.

Laka and Kapo

The goddess Laka is invoked as the *aumakua* of the *hula*, 'a feminine symbol of sexual power and enlightenment' (Pukui and Korn, 1988, p. 186), although she has a counterpart in the figure of Kapo, a goddess also associated with the *hula* and with the arts of sorcery. Kapo and Laka are sometimes sisters, sometimes mother and daughter, while Kapo is sister to Pele, as her mother is also Haumea. However, there appears to be a sense in which Kapo and Laka are two aspects of the same deity, since Emerson's informant tells him 'Kapo and Laka were one in spirit, though their names were two' (Emerson, 1915a, p.47). In language with strong evangelical overtones, Emerson says that the dark side of Kapo is a tendency to 'commit actions that seem worthy only of a demon of lewdness' making her 'now an angel of grace and beauty, now a demon of darkness and lust'. Emerson draws a parallel between the two contrasting aspects of the goddess figure Kapo/Laka and the duality of Nature, at once benevolent and destructive. With perhaps a touch of irony, he claims that Kapo's lewdness 'was, however, only the hysteria of a moment, not the settled habit of her life' (Emerson, 1915a, p. 25). Emerson also relates an occasion on which Kapo entices the demi-god Kamapua'a away from Pele at a critical moment by an appeal to the grossness of his nature. The exact nature of the appeal is not made clear. Herb Kawainui Kane however is not so coy – he tells of Kapo's detachable vagina, used as a decoy, the imprint of which can still be seen on Koholeplepe, at Koko Head on the island of Oahu (Kane, 1987, p. 28).

SECTION III: THE PELE MYTH

Enter not the house of Pele uninvited. Come ye not without song, offering, prayer.

For Pele still lives, I swear as a fisherman, and Pele is my god!

O hovering powers, possess me help me in my telling!

(PUKUI AND KORN, 1988, P. 183)

The most complete and most often referred to translation of the Pele/Hi'iaka cycle is that told by Nathaniel Emerson's *Pele and Hi'iaka: A Myth From Hawaii* (1915), and broadly speaking, the following version is from there.

The woman Pele, known also as Pele-honua-mea (Pele of the sacred land) and as Pele-ai-honua (Pele the devourer of land), was born on the island of Kuai-he-lani in the region of Kahiki. Her mother was the goddess Haumea and her father was Kane-hoa-lani. Pele was forced to leave her homeland because of a conflict with her elder sister Na-maka-o-kaha'i, a goddess of the sea. Some say this conflict arose as a result of Pele's ambitions regarding the acquisition of fire, and others that the suspicions of Na-maka-o-ka-ha'i were aroused as to the relationship between Pele and the keeper of the fire sticks, Lono-makua, who was the elder sister's husband. Advised by her eldest brother Ka-moho-ali'i, a deity of great power, whose manifestation was the form of a great shark, Pele set sail for unknown lands in the canoe especially built for her. She takes with her many members of her family — among them her brothers Ka-moho-ali'i, Kane-apua and Kane-milo-hai, and her youngest sister, Hi'iaka. Some say this sister was born through the posterior fontanel of their mother Haumea, in the form of a clot of blood, others say she was born in the shape of an egg and carried by Pele in the warmth and safety of her armpit.

> From Kahiki came the woman Pele,
> from the land of Polapola,
> from the rising reddish mist of Kane,
> from clouds blazing in the sky, horizon clouds.
>
> Restless desire for Hawai'i seized the woman Pele.
> Ready carved was the canoe, Honua-i-Akea,
> your own canoe, O Ka-moho-ali'i,
> for sailing to distant lands.
>
> (PUKUI AND KORN, 1988, P. 54)

Pele and her entourage approach the Hawaiian archipelago from the north-west and Pele begins her search for a suitable homeland. With her *pa-oa* (a form of spade but with magic powers), she dug into the earth to reveal the fire below, but on Kaua'i, Oahu and Maui she had little success. Wherever she dug, the waters she revealed threatened to cause such explosions of steam and sand that the fires would be extinguished. Even the crater of Hale-a-ka-la on the island of Maui, which looked in all ways an impressive and promising site, proved in the end unsuitable.

Unknown to Pele, she had been trailed throughout her journey across the ocean by her eldest sister and sworn enemy, Na-maka-o-ka-ha'i, and at Hale-a-ka-la the two arch-rivals, the one symbolic of fire and the other symbolic of water, met in battle. Aided by Ha-ui, a sea *mo'o* (a form of reptilian creature, often possessed of the powers of sorcery which were common on the Hawaiian islands), Na-maka-o-ka-ha'i apparently defeated Pele, and parts of her body were washed up at Kahiki-nui where they formed Ka-iwi-o-Pele (the bones of Pele), a hill near Kauiki. Even as the family might have mourned the death of Pele, though, her spirit rose above the great summits of Mauna Kea and Mauna Loa, and Na-maka-o-kaha'i accepted that Pele was now invincible — she had become a goddess. In this spirit form, Pele moved on to the islands of Hawaii where she established herself at Kilauea, the youngest of the mountains on the island and still one of the world's most active volcanoes. Specifically, her home is now said to be the Halema'uma'u crater, which is within the boundaries of the large caldera on the summit.

Having established a home, Pele is then able to enjoy life with her sisters, the Hi'iakas (the shadow bearers). There were eight of these in all, but Pele's favourite was the youngest — the one she had carried in the form of an egg all the way from her homeland. This sister is called Hi'iaka-i-ka-poli-o-Pele (Hi'iaka in the Bosom of Pele), a beautiful girl with the temperament to match her outward appearance, and with the ability to foresee events that were still to come. It was this Hi'iaka who learned the sacred art of the *hula* from her friend Hopoe, with whom she danced in the sacred groves of the *lehua* trees.

By virtue of all these attributes, Hi'iaka was chosen by Pele to watch over her body while she slept, on the strictest instructions not to waken her till nine days and eight nights had passed. After this time Hi'iaka was to chant the spirit of Pele back from its dream-like wanderings so that it could be reunited with its sleeping body. Having left her body form of an old woman, asleep, the spirit of Pele was lured out across the ocean by the sounds of the *hula* coming from a great distance, drawing her on until she reached the northern end of the island of Kaua'i. Here the sounds came to rest and, assuming the form of a young and beautiful woman, Pele approached Haena, the house of Lohiau, a young chief of the island. Lohiau invited the handsome stranger to join the feast and to eat with him, but she persistently refused his offer of food saying she was not hungry.

For three days and for three nights Pele's passion and beauty enticed Lohiau; some say she favoured him with nothing more than kisses, others that she took him for her husband, but whatever the case, when the call came to return and she was forced to leave him, the young chief was so distraught that he hanged himself. On discovering the body, his friend Paoa promised revenge on Pele, threatening to humiliate and insult her before destroying her.

Back on Hawaii, Hi'iaka awakened Pele with the following chant:

> Awake now, awake, awake!
> Wake Goddess of multiple god-power!
> Wake Goddess of essence most godlike!
> Wake Queen of the lightening shaft,
> The piercing fourth eye of heaven!
> Awake; I pray thee awake!
>
> (EMERSON, 1915, P. 12)

The very next morning, Pele asked each of her sisters in turn if they would make the long and difficult journey to Haena to bring her lover, Lohiau, back to Hawaii. First she asked Hi'iaka-i-ka-ale (Hi'iaka of the choppy seas), telling her that she, Pele, would keep the chief for herself for five days and nights and after that he should pass to the sister as a lover. But this sister refused, as did all the other sisters. Only Hi'iaka-i-ka-poli-o-Pele, the youngest sister, agreed to go, out of love and respect for the goddess. She extracted a promise from Pele that while she was away the goddess should protect the sacred groves and her friend Hopoe – only on those conditions would she go to Kaua'i.

Hi'iaka saw that the proposed journey was to be a lonely one so she also requested a companion, and was granted Pau-o-pala'e, the woman with power over the ferns of the forest. With these concessions she would have left but was advised by members of the family that she should assert her right to the additional powers of Pele with which to face the dangers ahead. After Ka-moho-ali'i himself had interceded on her behalf, Pele granted her sister great powers associated with the elements, and having bestowed this *mana* (supernatural power coming from the gods) on Hi'iaka, she told her: 'Nothing shall avail to block your road. Yours is the power of woman; the power of man is nothing to that' (Emerson, 1915, p. 23). So Hi'iaka, wearing her *pa'u* or magic skirt, and Pau-o-pala'e, her companion, left their home in the Puna district of Hawaii.

On the way they met a woman dressed in green and bearing a pig as an offering to Pele; this woman was called Wahine-oma'o. Having seen Hi'iaka, she wanted to join her immediately, mistaking her for Pele, but she was told she must continue on her journey, make the offering to the old woman she saw lying in the pit and, if Pele agreed, she could catch up with the other two. Wahine-oma'o found the old woman, though she did not really believe that she was indeed Pele, was granted permission and so the three of them continued.

The journey of Hi'iaka across the Hawaiian archipelago to the northern most island of Kaua'i took longer than the forty days allowed by Pele, and involved the young sister in many adventures in which her courage and loyalty were tested in the extreme. While it is not possible to relate them all, here is the story of Pana-ewa, one of the most widely known and typical of her many encounters.

The *mo'o* woman Pana-ewa's territory was the forest above Hilo, now the main town on the windward side of the island of Hawaii. Pana-ewa commanded all the evil spirits which occupied the forest and brought havoc to unwary travellers in the form of swirling fog or falling trees or uneven roots underfoot. Hi'iaka determined to rid the forest of the tyranny of Pana-ewa, so she taunted the *mo'o* with memories of the lava flows which had devastated parts of the forest in the past, until Pana-ewa threatened to kill her. The *mo'o* sent down swirling fog and chilling mists, strong winds and freezing, piercing rain, all of which Hi'iaka drove back repeatedly with great sweeps of her magic skirt. Then the forest rose against her and she was trapped by the vines and struck by the falling tree branches, and she was forced to fight still harder till her arms gave way and she had to call on Pele for assistance. Pele's indifference was overcome by the appeals of Kilioe-i-ka-pua and Olu-walei-malo, who were said to be Pele's sons (acting under the guidance of Ka-moho-ali'i), and Pele unleashed the gods of war, headed by Ku-lili-ai-kaua. In the mighty battle that followed, Hi'iaka protected her companions until the worst was over and the land of Hawaii was made safe for travellers.

However, the journey across the islands is not all aggression and conflict. Hi'iaka also has opportunities to use her art both as a healer and also as a poet extolling the beauties of the lands and seas that she crosses.

On a cliff overlooking the windswept beach at Hono-lua, on the island of Maui, Hi'iaka sees the spirit of a woman who has been crippled since birth. This spirit Mana-mana-iaka-luea has no hands but she is gathering shellfish by the sea's edge and playing in the waves. Hi'iaka throws down some blossom from her wreath and the figure instantly disappears and then re-appears. Overcoming her reluctance to intervene, Hi'iaka wraps the spirit in the loin cloth of Wahine-oma'o and they continue. As they approach Wailuku the spirit becomes restless indicating that they are drawing near to the body. Hi'iaka forces the spirit to enter its body through the toe and the girl is thus restored to life. With her new hands she prepares a feast, performing her duties of preparation faultlessly, and on this occasion Hi'iaka is seen to eat a portion of the food presented to her.

Having reached Kaua'i, before going on to the house of Lohiau, Hi'iaka stops at the house of the lame fisherman, Malae-ha'a-koa, who has the reputation of being a seer. Hi'iaka appeals to heaven to help the fisherman and thus he is able to walk again. In return, the fisherman, in a long *mele* (chant), recounts the entire Pele saga, including her encounter with Kamapua'a, the pig-god.

Among the beauties of the landscape she has passed over, Hi'iaka takes time often to pause, observe and translate into chant form all that she has seen. Her observations are tinged always with the echoes of her feelings, and there is an empathy between the natural forms she encounters and her own moods, giving the literal sense of her words a deeper meaning – known in Hawaiian as the *kaona*, the hidden meaning.

After quenching her thirst from the four streams at Ka'ena, Hi'iaka searches for something she can offer in return for the benefit she has received from the land:

> With the rising of the wind I am caught by a sudden thought.
> What shall I, in my shame, give to the four bathers?
>
> My sole gift is a song.
> (PUKUI AND KORN, 1973, P. 67)

The songs of Hi'iaka are a gift celebrated in the *hula* to this day.

From the lame fisherman, Hi'iaka learns that Lohiau is dead, but she goes to see him anyway. The body had been placed in a sepulchre by his sister, but it has disappeared. Looking towards the mountains, Hi'iaka sees the dead chief's spirit hovering at the entrance to a cave and she performs an impassioned chant to entice it to stay. Hi'iaka then forces the spirit to enter the body through one of the eye sockets, pushing it down into the chest, and on through the loins into the limbs. After a period of unremitting prayer, eventually judged by Wahine-oma'o to be faultlessly performed, Lohiau is restored to full health. Using three rainbows as a ladder, Hi'iaka, Wahine-mao'a and Lohiau climb down to the village and cleansing rites are performed to remove the defilement of the contact with what had been a corpse.

To celebrate Lohiau's restoration, a great feast is held with one half of the hall screened off so that the gods may feast alone. With a sound like the beating of many wings, the gods answered Hi'iaka's call and attended the gathering. When the time came to clear the feast, it remained untouched. But in fact only the exterior remained; the inner essence had mysteriously been taken leaving the covering intact.

Persuading his friend Paoa to stay behind as deputy, Lohiau and the two women set sail to return to Hawaii. On the journey back, Hi'iaka reads the signs in the heavens and from the blood red clouds she deduces that back on the island of Hawaii the anger of Pele has been aroused and she has destroyed both the sacred groves and the beloved Hopoe. That moment's vision sees the beginning of Hi'iaka's revenge on her sister Pele, the goddess of the volcano.

Before the journey is completed, Hi'iaka visits Pele-ula, a high-ranking chieftainess patroness of the *hula* and an ex-lover of Lohiau. Pele-ula's ambition and passion compel her to bid for Lohiau's attentions in the *kilu* game. This is a game in which a disc-like object is hurled at a target which collapses if struck correctly. The successful participant could claim sexual favours from the person whose target they struck. Lohiau is increasingly torn by his feeling for Pele-ula and a new growing attraction for Hi'iaka, and he fails to shoot a true *kilu*. As a forfeit for his failure Lohiau is made to perform a dance – his execution of the dance brims over with his new found passion – but Hi'iaka is careful never to break the command of chastity which Pele has placed on her.

Eventually the travellers arrive back on Hawaii and Wahine-oma'o and Pau-o-pala'e are sent ahead to greet Pele while Hi'iaka and Lohiau stand overlooking Hilo and the land of Puna beyond. The land before them has been desolated and blackened by the fires of Pele and, as foreseen, both Hopoe and the sacred groves were destroyed in a fit of jealous rage. But the moment has come when Hi'iaka can be released from her agreement, having fulfilled her assignment faithfully, and on the brink of the caldera and in full view of the goddess Pele and her family, Hi'iaka places a *lei*, a garland, around the neck of Lohiau and clasps him to her, nose to nose. Pele tries to pass this off as a normal greeting, but then Lohiau and Hi'iaka sink to the ground in a passionate embrace, and so Pele issues the command to her sisters to swamp Lohiau with flames. The sisters, however, are reluctant and have to be sent a second time. With the help of Lono-makua, the keeper of the fire sticks, Lohiau is trapped with lava and his body consumed.

Hi'iaka is filled with a terrible surge of power at the death of Lohiau and resolves to follow him to the underworld. She tears down into the rock layers of the earth which make up the underworld. At the third level she finds the god of suicide, hanging by his neck; at the fourth level she finds Wahine-oma'o and Pau-o-pala'e, who had been killed by Pele on their return from the journey, and restores them to life. On she travels, all the way to the tenth level, her aim being to open the very floodgates and engulf the home of Pele. But she is persuaded by Wahine-oma'o, under the influence of the god Kane, that this would bring confusion to the universe, and so she ceases her journey.

Meanwhile Lohiau's spirit leads his friend Paoa from Kaua'i back to Hawaii where, standing on the edge of Halema'uma'u, he sees only four beautiful women. Pele takes the form of a withered hag, until she is enticed by the charms of Paoa and transforms herself again into a beautiful woman. Some say they then become lovers.

Hi'iaka now finds that there is not room enough on Hawaii for both herself and Pele, so she sets sail for Kaua'i, with her two loyal friends and some of her sisters. In need of restoration of spirit, she seeks the haven of the *halau* of Kou on the island of Oahu, the halau being the long-house of the *hula* school. It is the *halau* of Pele-ula, where previously Hi'iaka had protected Lohiau from the dangers of the *kilu* game. While chanting in the *halau*, she hears the echo of her own chant. It is Lohiau who has been restored to life for the second time by Kane-milo-hai, an elder brother of Pele. And so it is that Hi'iaka and Lohiau come together.

Pele and Kamapua'a

The story of Pele's contact with Kamapua'a, the demi-god whose common manifestation is that of a pig, is one of the great themes of the Pele legend. There are many versions, some emphasizing the battles fought between the opposing elements symbolized by the goddess of volcanic fire and the god whose rutting renders the earth soft and fertile, others claiming that these very oppositions came together in a union of sorts, the island of Hawaii being shaped by their agreement to lead separate lives. Whatever the variations in the telling, the meetings between Pele and Kamapua'a are undeniably sexual in nature.

Kamapua'a was born to the woman Hina, who was wife to Olapana, although it is rumoured that he was not the father of the child but was rather his uncle, the father being Kahikiula, Olapana's brother. The child was rejected by Olapana and passed eventually to his maternal grandmother. She knew at once that the child was a *kapua*, of the gods, and gave him his name — *Kama* (meaning child) and *pua'a* (meaning pig). The child grew with all the manifestations of a pig; he had a long furrowing snout and a row of hog's bristles down his back. He also grew with many powers. He had the ability to take on great size, so great he could span valleys and dam rivers with his body; at other times he could be so small that he was easily hidden in the undergrowth. However, when he was in human form he could never quite hide the bristles that still grew down his back, and so he could be identified as Kamapua'a, the hog-god.

Journeying from his home on Oahu, Kamapua'a stands on the edge of Pele's home, the crater of Halem'aum'au, and watches Pele and her sisters dancing in the fires of the pit. For a while he goes unnoticed, and then Pele's sisters see him silhouetted against the sky, a handsome figure dancing to the rhythm of a hand drum, and they desire him as a mate. Only Pele recognizes Kamapua'a for the hog that he really is, and she taunts him with all the hog-like characteristics which he cannot totally hide:

> Thou art Kamapua'a,
> The buttocks that drop without effort,
> The nose that is pierced by a cord,
> The private that joins the belly,
> The tail wags behind.

Kamapua'a replies:

> The swine-eating god has its nose corded.
> Pele is the goddess that eats swine.
> Pele grunts and groans.
> Say, Pele, keep on chiding!
> Say, Pele, keep on chiding!

(ELBERT, 1959, P. 222)

A great war of words follows, in which insult follows insult, until each side is provoked to a battle, each calling on their opposing gods for help. Pele's brothers are sent to

Fig. 30 Pele and Kampua'a. A modern woodblock print by Dietrich Varez,
an artist who lives and works in Hawaii.

overcome Kamapua'a but are enticed by his love-making god, Lono-ikiaweawealoha.
Pele commands Lono-makua, keeper of the fire-sticks, to consume the pig-god.
Kamapua'a then calls on his sister Keliiomahanaloa, who takes the form of a rain-
filled cloud and almost quenches the fires of the pit.

Only the fire-sticks are saved. Kamapua'a then changes himself into a giant hog
and swallows the whole of Halem with all its inhabitants, Pele is only saved by Lono-
ikiaweawealoha, who incites Kamapua'a to compassion, and he releases them.

Some say the stalemate was ended when Pele and Kamapua'a became as man
and wife. But they could not live amicably together so they divided the island of
Hawaii into two parts: Pele took the areas of Puna, Kau and Kona on which there
was mostly lava, and Kamapua'a took Kohala, Hamakua and Hilo where the rains
fall and the earth is moist (Fornander, 1917–19).

Others say that Pele and Kamapua'a lived together for some time and had a son
named Opelu-haa-lii, but that the tempestuous life of his mother caused his early
death and he became the fish Opelu. The union was short-lived, and after many
ferocious disagreements, Kamapua'a was driven to the sea by Pele's lava, and giving
up the battle, he leapt into the boiling sea, changing himself into the fish which grunts
like a hog and whose tough skin can withstand the hot waters. This fish is called
the *humu-humu-nuku-nuku-apua'a*. Later, Kamapua'a married a chieftainess in some
foreign land and when he returned to Hawaii Pele tried to woo him back, but he
refused her saying that their separation should stand. For this reason, the favoured
offerings to Pele are the hog or the fish (Westervelt, 1916).

Yet others say the encounter between Pele and Kamapua'a was in the form of
a sexual attack by the hog-god, which took place on a bed of the rough lava called *a'a*:

The gods were aghast at the scandal.
For once Pele found herself duped;
For once Pele shifted in bed;
For once Pele drank to the dregs —
The cup was the brew of her consort;
Her bed the spikes of *a' a*.
Stone-armored passion had slaked.
Where then was her armour of stone?
The prophets, in congress assembled,
Consult on the rape of the goddess.

(EMERSON, 1915, P. 128)

SECTION IV: OTHER LEGENDS — PELE LIVES

The *hula* master, Kahawali, had spent long weeks preparing his students for graduation, but finally the day had come when they had performed before the chief of Puna. The chief had been pleased with their performance, the master had been well praised, and then came the time of celebration. Kahawali's favourite sport was *holua* (sledging) and he took his sledge to the top of the hillside, preparing to descend with great skill and style to the waiting crowd below. His first trip down was greeted with applause and excitement from the crowd and he climbed again to his companion who was still at the top of the hill. Only now he had an old woman standing beside him. The companion told Kahawali that the woman wanted to race him and so she had borrowed the companion's sledge. Despite Kahawali's scepticism, they set off together but the old woman rolled off the sledge on a bumpy section and Kahawali overtook her without harming her. Her sledge, however, went on alone. Kahawali once again received the praise of the crowd — for the old woman they had only laughter and derision. Kahawali carried her sledge back up the hillside to where she was waiting and advised her not to try again. She insisted that it was the sledge that was at fault, and that she if she could borrow the master's she would fare better. Kahawali refused, saying that it was the skill of the rider and not the sledge which made the difference. With that he took a running start into his *holua* and hurled himself at the slope.

This time, instead of the admiration of the crowd, he heard great shouts of fear, as if some danger approached him from behind. Turning to look, Kahawali saw the old woman behind him, pursuing him on a *holua* of fiery lava. He knew then that he had refused the sledge of none other than Pele herself.

At the bottom of the hill, Kahawali ran on towards the sea, hoping to escape the torrent of lava which followed him. The crowd fled in confusion. Kahawali managed to escape in his brother's canoe, but the crowd who had laughed at the old woman were turned to stone. They can still be seen fleeing across the plains of Puna (retold from Pukui and Curtis, 1943).

Herb Kane describes how he was busy painting a mural for the history museum in Punalu'u on the southern coast of the island of Hawaii, depicting Hawaiian village life as it might have been two centuries before. While he was at work, he often had visitors, workers from the construction site and others who dropped in to 'talk story', as the Hawaiians say. As the whole project neared completion, however, security was tightened and in order to continue working, Mr Kane had to ask the security guard to unlock the door to the section of the building he was working on. About an hour after he had started, one day, he saw an elderly Hawaiian woman standing behind him, looking at the painting. Having greeted her, the painter turned back to the mural and a few minutes later she was gone, leaving him curious as to who she was, since she appeared to be pure Hawaiian. So he asked the security guard if he knew who the old woman might be. However, the security guard denied all knowledge of the woman, claiming that no one would have been able to pass by him without being seen. This occured in 1973.

In 1975 Mr Kane was on the other side of the island in Kona when the island was hit by several earthquakes, with accompanying waves which damaged some coastal areas. Being concerned about the history centre, he telephoned to find out how the area of Punalu'u had fared and, in particular, whether the mural had been destroyed. He was told that the history centre had been engulfed by a twenty foot wave which had broken all the displays, pushing them out of the back of the building and leaving a mud mark three feet up the wall.

However the mural, which extends all the way down to the floor, was completely untouched and totally dry (retold from Kane, 1987).

Much of Pele's territory now lies within the Volcanoes National Park on the big island of Hawaii, and visitors flock there in their thousands to walk across the impressive but desolate terrain between the road and the rim of the Halema'uma'u crater. Standing only a matter of feet from the edge, trying to breathe through the sulphurous gases which rise out of the ground, one experiences a feeling of extreme desolation combined with a sense of latent power which comes from knowing that somewhere close by the lava is flowing, both underground and above the surface (author's experience, 1990). There are always offerings, mostly gin bottles left by tourists and piles of stones, balanced on top of one another. The park is staffed by rangers who are always on the lookout for visitors who remove anything from within park boundaries, since it is illegal to do so. But the tourists who have already been to the park's visitors' centre know that it is not the wrath of the park ranger which lands on the hapless tourist collecting bits of lava rock or the small, smooth lava pebbles (called Pele's tears) as souvenirs or presents for their friends. The visitors' centre boasts a selection from the vast number of letters they receive from people returning their bits of rock after periods of bad luck — amounting to catastrophe in some cases:

> Five years later, ten car accidents later, two unsuccessful business ventures later and twice-broken heart later, I admit the place for the enclosed rock of lava is there where it belongs.

> (QUOTED BY KANE, 1987, P. 51)

SECTION V: TAMING THE GODDESS

We must re-evaluate all female images that have been despised by previous generations of male scholars. Behind every witch, dragoness and temptress there is a vision of female power – power that society is now ready to understand, perhaps to embrace. In comparison with the rebels, the good girls of biblical tradition have little to offer.

(GOLDENBURG, 1979, P. 74)

In Emerson's interpretation of the Pele myth, Hi'iaka-ka-poli-o-Pele is a symbol of a new order emerging from the pre-existing state of things. The old order was ruled by the supreme will of Pele, while the younger, approaching order is that of the human race which is now peopling the land that Pele made. Hi'iaka is very much this younger, more humane state, despite her familial connections with the fire goddess. The coming together of Hi'iaka and Lohiau in a traditional happy ending, as the final stage of a long journey is described as the blending together of the opposing components of male and female, while Pele symbolizes the powerful forces which had kept them apart. Emerson's closing lines are:

behold, a new spirit has leavened the whole mass, a spirit of dissent from the supreme selfishness of the Vulcan goddess, and the foremost dissident of them all is the obedient little sister who was first in her devotion to Pele, the warm-hearted little girl whom we still love to call Hi'iaka-i-ha-poli-o-Pele.

(EMERSON, 1915)

Pele's press, in general, is not flattering. The goddess is often spoken of in terms of irrationality and irresponsibility, her actions seen as destructive and prompted only by caprice. According to Westervelt, Pele was 'worshipped especially by those whose lives were filled with burning anger against their fellow-man' (Westervelt, 1916, p. 12), while the chief Lohiau is appreciative of 'the bravery, the unselfishness and the wholly lovable character of Hi'iaka' (p. 135). These general views are echoed by later commentators: 'Pele behaves as she does because she is jealous, undisciplined and violent tempered' (Luomala, 1955, p. 38). Most recently, Rita Knipe writes: 'The fire goddess desires, not loves. She passions not feels. She has no loyalty to any principle but that of her own needs, fires, jealousies and rages' (1989, p. 119).

Although pervasive these views are not universal. In a much blander, more matter-of-fact version of the Pele migration and the Hi'iaka journey, William Hyde Rice makes no generalized comments on Pele's behaviour from her actions in a particular instance. In this literal version, Pele is angered by the blatancy of her sister's actions in publicly embracing Lohiau, and thus humiliating her in front of others (Rice, 1923). Kalakaua even introduces an element of malignancy into her nature as 'in a spirit of mischief' she turns the surf boards of two fishermen to stone, thus terrifying them, while a little later she attaches a human head to the submerged hook of a fisherman, and watches him stare at it in horror – before paddling away. All this is 'to the great amusement of Hi'iaka and her companions' (Kalakaua, 1888,

p. 148). In *Myths and Legends of Our New Possessions and Protectorates*, in which the Hawaiians are somewhat condescendingly referred to as 'our new subjects – our brothers, let us rather say' (1900, p. 9), Skinner draws on Kalakaua's tone and relates the same incidents, inferring that it was unwise of Pele to send Hi'iaka as an emissary since 'the sister was not a serious creature' (p. 238).

The aim in highlighting such variations in attitudes towards the major female figures in the story is not to apportion degrees of moral culpability to either Pele or Hi'iaka, or to sort out their apologists, but to point out that such judgements, made as part of the process of storytelling as though they were moral absolutes, are in fact provisional and subject to variation.

Hi'iaka is praised for her courage and her determination, for her wisdom and her constancy, and for her chastity. Lohiau is, ultimately, her reward for these virtues. Pele is, on the other hand, labelled the 'hag':

> Alas, there's no stay to the smoke;
> I must die mid the quenchless flame
> Deed of the hag who snores in her sleep,
> Bedded on lava plate oven-hot.
>
> (EMERSON, 1915A, P. 195)

In the Hawaiian, the third line above is literally 'the woman lying snarling'; in the translation, Pele loses the strength of the snarl while acquiring a connotation that is alien to the Hawaiian view of Pele. 'Hag' is usually defined as female, often a witch or demoness, commonly repulsive and traditionally wicked, vicious and malicious (*Shorter Oxford Dictionary*, p. 912). But while Pele is, and always was, feared, she is also loved and respected. Her epithets are Pele-honua-mea, Pele of the sacred land, as well as Pele'ai-honua, Pele the eater of land. If Pele destroys land by her fits of irascibility, she also creates new land. The Hawaiian islands exist only as the result of volcanic action; in two years of volcanic activity between 1987 and 1989, over one hundred acres of new land were added to the island of Hawaii. In about ten thousand years, a new island may be added to the Hawaiian archipelago. This new volcano, named Loihi, is submerged off the coast of Kilauea, but it may ultimately rise out of the waves and take its place at the end of the existing chain. The eruptions of Hawaii's volcanoes are usually non-explosive and relatively benign, because the lava is comparatively liquid and free-flowing, posing little danger to people but remaining destructive to populated areas. Where there is high rainfall, the re-vegetation of areas buried by lava begins surprisingly quickly, sometimes in less than a year:

> Pele the earth eater gives her name to the fire that pours forth her anger and passion ('ahi'ena, pele), then blesses the recent flows with the beauty of her berry, the *ohelo*.
>
> (WIGHT, 1990)

The tendency to condemn Pele is not reflected in the affection shown towards the goddess by her own people. By modern Hawaiians Pele is often called 'Tutu Pele' (Kane, 1987, p. 7) – *tutu* being a new word that is applied to grandparents of either sex, or any relative or close friend of grandparent's generation (Pukui and Elbert, 1986, p. 177). Senior members of a Hawaiian family were accorded an important position in both family and community life. It was very common for children, especially the first-born, to be '*hanai'd*', that is given to an older relative, usually a grandparent, to raise.

The grandparent was also the person most likely to return in dreams as a guiding, supportive figure, representing the conscience that condemns or approves. Pele occupies this role most clearly, in tales of her reappearance in the recent past to warn of coming catastrophes, while in many of the traditional stories, her position has the moral authority of a respected elder. In a story told to Mary Kawena Pukui by her cousin, Pele is the kind but exacting goddess who condemns a man, Kalapana, to live and die away from his homeland because he has broken a promise to her, albeit through no fault of his own. However, Kalapana lives out his exile quite contentedly because he has seen the kind eyes of Pele (Pukui and Curtis, 1983). In this instance, Pele combines the beauty of her young persona with the maturity and command or the authoritative older figure, and with the absence of sexuality usually associated with the younger Pele.

Various definitions of the 'hag' have been highlighted by Mary Daly, who points out that the common meaning more usually associated with 'haggard', is 'worn out or emaciated', but that this is not its original meaning (Daly, 1989). The obsolete meanings listed in *Webster's Dictionary* and quoted by Daly are contradictory; a haggard is defined as 'an intractable person, especially: a woman reluctant to yield to wooing' while to be haggard is to be 'unchaste'. Daly suggests the radical re-definition of Hag can and should encompass these contradictions.

The concept of 'hag' as applied to the goddess of the volcano arises from the uncomfortable combination of the female, the sexual, the powerful and the old which uniquely combine in the popular image of Pele. This is problematic for those who cherish a post-Christian ideal of womanhood, with its emphasis on the nurturing and modest elements of femininity. To the old Hawaiian culture, such apparent contradictions presented fewer difficulties. The sexuality of both sexes was actively encouraged within certain parameters, and it is also claimed that sexual satisfaction continued into old age and that problems of impotence and frigidity were 'apparently unknown' (Pukui et al, 1979, 2, p. 84).

As well as enjoying sex as a pleasure in its own right, Hawaiians also acknowledged a more permanent relationship between men and women, although such relationships were not always monogamous. Pele proposes that Lohiau shall be a lover for both herself and Hi'iaka: often two sisters or two brothers would share the same mate, and provided these unions were by mutual consent and agreement, it is claimed they were unproblematic. However, without this permission being sought and granted, extra-marital liaisons were traumatic in their effect (Pukui et al, 2, p. 91). Pele's jealousy and anger arises from the conviction that the *kapu* she placed on Lohiau, a *kapu* which was to last only five days after they returned to Halema'uma'u, has been publicly violated. This notion of a temporary ban on sexual relations is consistent with the state of temporary chastity imposed in certain instances in Hawaiian society, which have already been mentioned.

It is in Pele's relations with Kamapua'a that her intractability is most evident, and it is tempting to see the resulting violent struggle for supremacy as a true clash of the sexes, in which Kamapua'a neatly fits the role of the ultimate chauvinist, complete with pig manifestations. The oppositional forces at work, however, are elemental as well as sexual, and the subsequent truce, by which the island of Hawaii is divided between them, is a natural outcome of the belief that nature cannot be regulated by domination. In some versions of the story, Pele is raped by Kamapua'a, while in others she temporarily engages with him sexually. Emerson combines the two, referring to 'the lustful attack made by Kamapua'a on Pele, an attack to which she gives seeming acquiescence' (1915, p. 113). By this interpretation, Pele is deprived of both her power of choice and her sexuality.

No easy link can be claimed between the power of the myth figure and the power of Hawaiian women. Such politically powerful women as existed were restricted to the *ali'i*, the aristocracy, and to the worship of Pele herself, where female *kahunas* (priests) were of the highest rank (Westervelt, 1916, p. 115). Instances of fighting women were recorded:

> for in those days and later, women not unfrequently followed their fathers, brothers to battle, generally keeping in the rear to furnish them with food and water, but sometimes in a close and desperate conflict, mingling bravely in the fight. In such cases they gave and received blows, and expected and were accorded no consideration because of their sex.
>
> (KALAKAUA, 1888, P. 299)

Women prophets were the only women to live socially as men, enjoying all the privileges of male priests, seemingly above the *kapu* of menstruation which made women less pleasing to the gods, and therefore kept them in a subordinate position (Pukui et al, 1972, 2, p. 211). Size and strength, however, were embodied in the ideal of Hawaiian beauty, and women were powerful swimmers, surfers and climbers just as the men were. Hi'iaka's feats of athleticism, exhibiting strength and stamina, would present no threat to her femininity as far as Hawaiians were concerned.

Despite these physical attributes, however, Hi'iaka remains firmly in the realms of recognizable fairy-tale. The forces of apparent evil threaten her moral purity and beauty, while she is kept apart from her charming prince until certain obstacles have been overcome. It is ironic that although it is Hi'iaka who strives for the sake of her prince, rather than the other way around, the story remains within the traditional format of the morally good and beautiful though usually passive heroine who survives the machinations of the wicked step-mother or sister, to attain bliss through union with the hero, and who then disappears thereafter from the imagination of little children everywhere. There is no mention of messy sex, painful labours or menopausal crises with which these grown-up children can later identify.

Only in the memories of the pre-contact Hawaiians, and in the echo that still exists in the written Hawaiian accessible to a small proportion of those living on the islands today, does Hi'iaka have a significant voice. Hers is the inspiration, as an observer and describer of the human conditions, for the chants and dances which make up the sacred *hula*:

Hi'iaka, because of what countless unknown poets have given to her in her name, is the greatest of all artists known in Polynesia oral literature.

(LUOMALA, 1986, P. 35)

To say that the power of the Pele myth depends on the continuing power of the erupting volcano is to state the obvious. As the personification of the force and spectacle of *Kilauea: The Newest Land on Earth* (Heliker and Weisel, 1990), Pele will continue to intrigue and captivate the imagination of the random visitor to Hawaii, a visitor to whom the exploits of Hi'iaka mean virtually nothing. In broader terms though, the story of Pele provides a more disturbing echo of a female condition, one that in its very conflicts and confusions appeals on a level that is fundamental, especially to the modern woman who attempts to exist in a world in which evaluations are still gender dictated. Hi'iaka's happy ending has a hollow ring to it, deceptive in its simplicity and tempting in its apparent fulfilment. This 'invitation to hollowness' is still constantly on offer to women and 'in so far as they succumb they cease to be female – identified and become purely feminine: adorable and deplorable, but never really horrible, never Dreadful' (Daly, 1987, p. 51). It is in daring to be sometimes old, sometimes ugly, sometimes sexual and sometimes truly horrible that Pele's appeal lies. Pele dares to be Dreadful.

References and Further Reading

Bank, O. (1986), *Faces of Feminism* (Oxford: Basil Blackwell)

Barrere, Dorothy B., Pukui, Mary K. and Kelly, Marion (1980), *Hula – Historical Perspectives* (Honolulu: Bishop Museum Press)

Beckwith, M. (1970), *Hawaiian Mythology* (Honolulu: University of Hawaii Press). Reprinted in 1989.

—— (1951), *The Kumulipo* (Honolulu: University of Hawaii Press). Reprinted in 1981.

Charlot, J. (1987), *The Kamapua'a Literature* (Hawaii: The Institute for Polynesian Studies, Brigham Young University)

Colum, P. (1937), *Legends of Hawaii* (New Haven: Yale University Press). Reprinted in 1960.

Daly, M. (1987), *Gyn/Ecology: The Metaphysics of Radical Feminism* (London: The Women's Press)

Daws, G. (1974), *Shoal of Time* (Honolulu: University of Hawaii Press)

Elbert, S.H. (ed.) (1959), *Selections from Fornander's Antiquities and Folklore* (Honolulu: University of Hawaii Press). Reprinted in 1982.

Elbert, S.H. and Mahoe, N. (1970), *Na Mele O Hawai'i Nei: 101 Hawaiian Songs* (Honolulu: University of Hawaii Press)

Emerson, N.B. (1915), *Pele and Hi'iaka: A Myth from Hawaii* (New York: AMS Press). Reprinted in 1978.

—— (1915a), *Unwritten Literature of Hawaii: The Sacred Song of the Hula* (Rutland, Vermont and Tokyo: Charles E. Tuttle). Reprinted in 1986.

Fornander, A. (1917–19), *Hawaiian Antiquities and Folklore*, vols 4 and 5 (Honolulu: Bishop Museum Press)

Goldenburg, N.R. (1979), *Changing of the Gods* (Boston: Beacon Press)

Gowen, Herbert H. (1908), *Hawaiian Idylls of Love and Death* (New York: Cochrane Publishing Co.)

Green, L. (1926), *Folk Tales from Hawaii* (New York: Vassar College)

Harding, E.M. (1973), *Women's Mysteries* (New York: Bantam Books)

Heliker, C. and Weisel, D. (1990), *Kilauea: The Newest Land on Earth* (Honolulu: Bishop Museum Press)

Johnson, R.K. (1981), *Kumulipo: The Hawaiian Hymn of Creation* (Honolulu: Topgallant)

Kalakaua, His Hawaiian Majesty David (1888), *The Legends and Myths of Hawaii* (Rutland, Vermont and Tokyo: Charles E. Tuttle). Reprinted in 1988.

Kamakau, S.M. (1866–71), *Ka Po'e Kahiko: The People of Old Hawaii* (Honolulu: Bishop Museum Press). Reprinted in 1987.

Kane, H. Kawainui (1987), *Pele: Goddess of Hawaii's Volcanoes* (Honolulu: The Kawainui Press)

Knipe, Rita (1989), *The Water of Life: A Jungian Journey Through Hawaiian Myth* (Honolulu: University of Hawaii Press)

Luomala, K. (1955), *Voices on the Wind. Polynesian Myths and Chants* (Honolulu: Bishop Museum Press). Reprinted in 1986.

Melville, L. (1969), *Children of the Rainbow* (Illinois: The Theosophical Publishing House)

Mrantz, M. (1975), *Women of Old Hawaii* (Honolulu: Aloha Publishing). Reprinted in 1987.

Pukui, M.K. and Curtis, C. (1943), *Pikoi* (Honolulu: The Kamehameha Schools Press). Reprinted in 1983.

Pukui, M.K., Haertig, E.W. and Lee, C.A. (1972), *Nana I Ke KUMU: Look to the Source*, vol. 1 and vol. 2 (Honolulu: Hui Hanai). Reprinted in 1983.

Pukui, M.K. and Korn, A.L. (1973), *The Echo of Our Song: Chants and Poems of the Hawaiians* (Honolulu: University of Hawaii Press). Reprinted in 1988.

Pukui, M.K. and Elbert, S.H. (1986), *Hawaiian Dictionary* (Honolulu: University of Hawaii Press)

Rice, W.H. (1926) *Hawaiian Legends* (New York: Kraus Reprint Co.). Reprinted in 1987.

Sahlins, M. (1987), *Islands of History* (London and New York: Tavistock Publications)

Skinner, C.M. (1900), *Myths and Legends of our New Possessions and Protectorate* (Philadelphia and London: J.B. Lippincott Co.)

Stone, M. (1976), *When God Was A Woman* (San Diego: Harcourt, Brace, Jovanovich)

Strachan, E. and G. (1985), *Freeing the Feminine* (Dunbar: Labarum Publication)

Westervelt, W.D. (1923), *Hawaiian Historical Legends* (Rutland, Vermont and Tokyo: Charles E. Tuttle). Reprinted in 1985.

—— (1915), *Hawaiian Legends of Ghosts and Ghost-gods* (Rutland, Vermont and Tokyo: Charles E. Tuttle). Reprinted in 1987.

—— (1915), *Hawaiian Legends of Old Honolulu* (Rutland, Vermont and Tokyo: Charles E. Tuttle). Reprinted in 1988.

—— (1916), *Hawaiian Legends of Volcanoes* (Rutland, Vermont and Tokyo: Charles E. Tuttle). Reprinted in 1989.

UNPUBLISHED TEXTS:

Sutton, T. (1988), 'A Bibliographic Essay on Items Concerning Pele Published since 1970' (Hawaii: School of Library and Information Studies, University of Hawaii at Manoa, Honolulu)

Wight, K., *Kilauea: In Memory and Spirit* (prepared for publication and received from the author, 1990)

Glossary of Hawaiian Terms

a' a: Rough, stony lava.

ahi: Fire, match, lightning: to destroy by fire.

'ailolo: Ceremony to mark the end of training; graduation ceremony.

akua: God, goddess, spirit, supernatural being, high-ranking deity.

akual'i: Lesser gods, numerous spirits inhabiting forms of nature.

ali'i: Chief, chieftainess, ruler, monarch, aristocracy, ruling class.

ao: Light, daylight, dawn.

aumakua: Guardian deity attached to family or profession; deified ancestor.

'ena: Raging, angry.

halau: House used for hula instruction, long house, meeting house.

holua: Sledge used on grassy slopes.

hula: Sacred dance form, often with accompanying music and song.

kahuna: Priest, priestess, minister, sorcerer, expert.

kaona: Hidden meaning, concealed reference, words with double meaning.

kapa/tapa: Paper cloth made by pounding fibrous bark.

kilu: Game with sexual forfeits; a small gourd or coconut shell used as a quoit in the game.

kumu-hula: Teacher of hula, tutor, usually a revered person.

kupua: Demi-god, local hero or deity capable of extraordinary feats, often with distinguishing characteristics from the natural world.

lei: Garland, necklace of flowers.

mana: Supernatural power, divine power.

mele: Song or chant of any kind.

mo'o: Dragon-like creature, reptile, serpent, mythological monster.

mua: Men's eating house.

'ohelo: A small native shrub of the cranberry family, sacred to Pele.

paoa: Divining rod used by Pele to test the land.

pa' u: Woman's skirt, sarong.

pe' a: Sleeping house for women during menstruation.

po: Night, darkness, time of the gods, chaos.

tapa/kapa: Paper cloth made by pounding fibrous bark.

tutu: Revered person of grandparent's generation, favourite aunt or older relative (thought to be a modern word).

wa: Period of time, era, division of time.

PART 5

America

MARTA WEIGLE

Southwest Native American Mythology

SECTION I: INTRODUCTION

The Native American Southwest, the only culture area with two books in the twenty-volume *Handbook of North American Indians* (Ortiz, 1979, 1983), encompasses a vast, diverse section of the southwestern United States (primarily Arizona and New Mexico) and northern Mexico. Its far better known northern region includes four distinct prehistoric civilizations with strong Mesoamerican ties (Hohokam, Hakataya, Anasazi, Mogollon) that began forming in the early Christian era. These are generally characterized by permanent villages in densely populated, patterned settlements, regionally differentiated architecture with specialized religious structures, cultivation mainly of corn, beans, squash, cotton and tobacco, localized raiding but little organized warfare and emphasis on ceremonial elaboration with religious, not political controls. The low desert Hohokam of southern Arizona and the Hakataya on the Lower Colorado River from the Grand Canyon south, gave rise to the Pima (probably) and Yuman peoples respectively. Presentday Pueblo Indians trace their ancestry from Western (Four Corners area of Utah, Colorado, New Mexico and Arizona) and Eastern (approximately one-third of northern New Mexico) Anasazi and Mogollon (north-central Arizona through southwestern New Mexico). Southern Athapaskans, whose descendants are now Navajos and Apaches, entered north-eastern New Mexico around the sixteenth century and moved south and west into former Anasazi and Mogollon regions (Woodbury, 1979). Basically nomadic hunters, they borrowed extensively from the agricultural Pueblos.

Because the Pueblo, Apache and Navajo peoples share so much territory, history, myth and ritual and have been so intensively studied, this article will focus only on the 'north-eastern' Native American Southwest. Spanish conquest and colonization there can be dated roughly from Francisco Vasquez de Coronado's 1540–1 expedition and Juan de Oñate's 1598 colonists who first settled among the Tewa at San Juan Pueblo, then founded a provincial capital at Santa Fe in 1610. The horse proved a more immediately significant consequence of their conquest than Christianity. Initially thought to be anthropophagous, horses and their breeding, nurture and exchange secured a central place in eastern Pueblo myth and culture almost within a decade, and shortly thereafter among western Pueblo, Apache (c. 1638) and Navajo (c. 1680) groups (Clark, 1966). Pueblo women generally received favourable comment from Spanish chroniclers for their recognizable (to Europeans) women's work of cooking, childcare, pottery making and clothing preparation. Those 'pressed into service by the conquerors incorporated Hispanic foods, livestock and tools into traditional tasks', while those 'who fled to the Navajos and Apaches to escape Spanish domination carried with them expectations of women's work roles that influenced women in Apache and Navajo societies' (Foote and Schackel, 1986, p. 18).

United States occupation began in 1846. New Mexico became a territory in 1850, a separated Arizona in 1863. Both territories gained statehood in 1912. Various United States policies about reservations and relocation drastically altered Native American societies in the Southwest and elsewhere.

Contemporary Pueblos represent four unrelated (west to east) language groups: Hopi (at Hopi), Zunian (at Zuni), Keresan (at Laguna, Acoma, Santo Domingo, San Felipe, Cochiti, Zia, Santa Ana) and Tanoan, comprising three mutually unintelligible dialects — Tewa (at San Juan, Santa Clara, San Ildefonso, Nambe, Tesuque, Pojoaque), Tiwa (northern sub-group at Taos, Picuris; southern at Sandia, Isleta) and Towa (at Jemez, formerly at Pecos). Hopi-Tewa, who speak a variety of Tewa understood with difficulty by Rio Grande Tewa, migrated from New Mexico and settled next to the Hopi on First Mesa, Arizona, in 1700. The circum-pueblo (west to east) Apachean languages and cultures include Navajo, Western Apache, Chiricahua Apache, Mescalero Apache and Jicarilla Apache.

All these Southwest peoples believe in a moderately (Apache) to highly (others) structured and bounded, layered universe and a natural world entirely imbued with supernatural meaning. All share emergence myths (historically borrowed by Athapaskans from Pueblos) that recount how the first beings emerged from the underworld(s) or womb(s) in mother earth (*see* below, p. 351), through a sacred place of emergence, and then migrated to their present residences when choices or disagreements caused various groups to take different paths. Before or during emergence and migration, monsters had to be slain and cultural rites, institutions and objects originated. Twin culture or warrior heroes often take the lead in emergence and monster-slaying. Witchcraft, for the most part equally associated with women and men, is present from the beginning and elaborately developed witchcraft belief systems are common in all the cultures. The cosmologies and emergence/origin/migration mythologies are symbolically re-enacted in most rituals.

Apache ceremonialism primarily focuses on curing, secondarily on warfare. Women and men may obtain power through dreams or visions from animals, plants and natural phenomena outside the social world. Women could become shamans and 'were common and competed on even terms with their male counterparts among the Chiricahua and Mescalero' (Opler, 1983, p. 371). During curing ceremonies, most of which emphasize removing evil, the shaman is not possessed but attracts supernaturals through song and ritual paraphernalia. Changing (White Shell)

Woman (*see* p. 337), whose variously named, monster-slaying twin sons are the main culture heroes, bestows major blessings, especially during girls' puberty rites.

Navajo cosmology, myth and ritual is much more elaborately structured. Ritual specialists, called singers, chanters or medicine men – although women infrequently can and do successfully learn these roles (Reichard, 1973, pp. xliv–v) – act as priests who learn their skills through apprenticeship, not shamanic or visionary power. Navajo chantways or sings of two, five or nine nights, sunset to sunset, are 'centered on the restoration of "pleasant conditions" for the individual ... Many chants include a bath, a sandpainting ritual, a sweat and emetic ceremony, and an all-night sing the last night. Each component ceremony is composed of ritual acts that are directed against the etiological factor (for example, bears, snakes, lightning) causing the illness' (Lamphere, 1983, p. 752). Even if the singer is a woman who supervises their creation, sandpaintings must be done by men (Witherspoon, 1977, p. 160).

Some chantways have female and male branches, distinguished not by the sex of the patient but possibly by myth protagonist. Chantway origin myths 'usually relate the misadventures of a hero or heroine [rarely; *see* Older and Younger Sisters, p. 344] who through intentional or unintentional misbehaviour gets into a series of predicaments requiring supernatural assistance for survival and causing injury or illness calling for ritual restoration, thus [acquiring] the ceremonial knowledge and power for a chantway' later taught to their people. Singers need not know the myths but 'the best' do and ideally can relate them from the very beginning (emergence) until 'the chant myth branches off from it' (Wyman, 1983, pp. 547, 556).

Deities called Holy People (*Diyin Dine'é*) live in a supernatural world paralleling the Navajos' (*Diné*, people) social one. Like the latter, it is 'not hierarchically structured ... [and] relatively undivided, ... even distinctions by age and sex, especially in the division of labor, are minimal' (Lamphere, 1983, p. 752). Nevertheless, Changing Woman (*see* p. 337), her twin sons Monster Slayer and Born for Water – who represent war power – and Sun 'form a sort of "holy family" prominent in myth and ritual'. Soon after emergence a 'first family' of First Man, First Woman (see below), First Boy, First Girl and 'their companions, Coyote (... "First Scolder"), the exponent of trickery, and *Begochídí* [transvestite son of Sun] were prominent in early events on the earth while it was being made habitable for mankind' (Wyman, 1983, p. 539).

Pueblo ceremonialism is basically agricultural, revolving around corn/maize and water/rain, although hunting and curing are also of concern. Male priests command complex rituals that must be scrupulously performed for effective control of a knowable, bounded, interconnected universe. Orientation is centripetal; there is 'a well-elaborated conception and symbolization of the middle or centre of the cosmos, represented by a *sipapu*, an earth navel, or the entire village. Usually there are many different centres because sacred space can be recreated again and again without ever exhausting the reality' (Ortiz, 1972a, pp. 142–3). *Kivas* – circular or rectangular sacred structures above, below or partially under the ground, that are setting for secret, predominantly male, religious activity – embody symbolism related to the underworlds and place of emergence, and 'although there may be numerous sacred centres, the *kiva* itself is the center of centers, or the navel of navels' (Nabokov and Easton, 1989, p. 378).

Many kinds of dualities, especially female and male, 'reverberate through Pueblo life. The sun is everywhere the father and primary fertilizing agent in the cosmos while the earth is the mother. Having separated the two long ago in myth, all the Pueblos devote endless myth cycles to bringing them back together again . . . Thus we have twin sons of the sun ascending to the upper cosmic level to visit their father or to do battle with him . . . [and] sacred clowns who are regarded as children of the sun and, wherever they constitute a permanent organization, always seem to be initiated at the equinoxes'. Sometimes culture hero or warrior twins are women, as among the Keresans (*see* p. 346). Winter ceremonial stress on medicine, war and fecundity complements summer ceremonial stress on rain and agriculture. Other dualities involve raw and cooked, ripe and unripe, hot and cold, priest and witch, the living and those who have rejoined the ancestors. All tend to be complementary and balanced symbolically in myth, ritual and belief (Ortiz, 1972a, pp. 143–5).

Kachinas, powerful and benevolent anthropomorphic spirits of the dead who bring blessings of rain, crops and healing, and *kachina* societies with all-male or inclusive memberships are found throughout the Pueblos. Public and/or private, masked or unmasked, danced impersonations of the deities/*kachinas* play an important role in belief and ritual, and are most elaborately developed at Zuni and Hopi (Griffith, 1983; Lamphere, 1983, pp. 757–8). Such impersonations and ritual dramas are generally men's province and they appear as both male and female *kachinas* (*see* Clay, p. 338; Corn, p. 339; Warrior Women, p. 347; Butterfly, p. 348; Ogres, p. 349).

SECTION II: MAJOR MYTHS ABOUT WOMEN

Ancestral Woman

Jicarilla Ancestral Woman and Man have human form but are incorporeal. Formed from clay by Black God in the underworld, Ancestral Man dreamed of a woman and awoke to find Ancestral Woman at his side. Each leans on an 'age stick' during the emergence; he emerges first of all, his wife first among women, giving him ascendancy. Apaches are descendants of this couple (Opler, 1936, p. 203; 1946, pp. 112–13).

Changing Bear Maiden

Navajo Changing Bear (Tingling) Maiden, female apotheosis of evil, is associated with lustful Coyote in opposition to her twelve good brothers and benevolent Changing Woman. At first a virgin and model housekeeper for her brothers, she is seduced by Coyote, whom she tests, then yields to and is transformed by, during sexual orgies. When Coyote is killed the enraged sister accuses her brothers and, by replacing her teeth with thorns, changes into a bear who tracks and kills eleven siblings. The youngest escapes and finally destroys his sister. Her vagina becomes porcupine or yucca fruit; her breasts, piñon nuts; tongue, cactus; entrails, snakes or herbs; and limbs, the bears of four directions. Guided by Holy People, the youngest brother then restores the eleven others (Wyman, 1970, pp. 337–8; 1973, pp. 100–1; Reichard, 1974, pp. 414–17; Haile, 1981, pp. 207–16; 1984, pp. 22–4).

Changing Woman

Apache Changing (White-Painted, White Shell) Woman ages but becomes young again and thus is thought to grant longevity. After intercourse with the Sun or other creator god, she gives birth to monster-slayers. 'Along with her sons, Changing Woman is thought of as one of the founders of Apache culture (some informants said the *only* founder) and, as such, is regarded with great fondness and admiration. Myths dealing with her teaching and exploits are still recounted, and a part of one of these myths – her sexual intercourse with the Sun – is enacted by the pubescent girl at *na ih es* [puberty rite]' (Basso, 1966, p. 151).

During the girls' puberty rite the initiand is ritually transformed into the mythological figure. 'At the request of the presiding medicine man, and "traveling on his chants", the power of Changing Woman enters the girl's body and resides there for four days [while] the girl acquires all the desirable qualities of Changing Woman herself, and is thereby prepared for a useful and rewarding life as an adult.' Her womanhood is honoured and she brings abundance and reaffirmation to her people (Basso, 1966, pp. 169–70; 1970, p. 64; Parrer, 1980). *Chiricahua* ceremony stresses 'values of love, hospitality, generosity and nonviolence' and focuses on women as 'source' of food, domestic virtue and harmony (Cole, 1988, p. 23).

Navajo Changing Woman's name suggests various etymologies: 'that she was born with the power of senescence and rejuvenation', that she is the earth and its changing seasons, or that she changes costume four times during her puberty ceremony or upon emerging from each of four rooms in her western dwelling – and hence could appear as White Shell (Bead), Turquoise, Abalone or Jet Woman (Wyman, 1970, p. 32). Also called Earth Woman, Changing Woman is 'the first mother' – 'the being who gave life to the Navajos by creating the heads of the four original clans . . . who sustains the life of her children today by producing food and other items of subsistence . . . Through rituals she bestows blessings on them and provides them with immunity from various dangerous things and protection from malevolent beings' (Witherspoon, 1977, p. 91). Her instructions for the construction, maintenance, preservation and use of *hogans* (dwellings) continue to be cited today. Changing Woman, Water Woman, Mountain Woman, Wood Woman and Sun are symbolically associated with *hogans*, which are personified in myth, song, prayer and 'ordinary conversation – they are alive; they need to be fed, cared for, spoken to, and shielded from loneliness' (Frisbie, 1980, pp. 165–6). Changing Woman is intimately associated with the important, multi-functional Blessingway rite (Wyman, 1970).

Born miraculously when the Holy People had emerged into the present world and were threatened by monsters, Changing Woman was found on a mountaintop by First Man and raised in a short time by him and First Woman. At menarche she received the prototypical puberty ceremony, *Kinaaldá*, with all Holy People in attendance at the place of emergence. She then became mother of twin monster-slayers, begat by Sun and possibly another deity. She now lives in a magnificent western dwelling.

Kinaaldá rites are patterned on Changing Woman's initiation. 'Being part of the Blessing Way complex, the *Kinaaldá* is prophylactic, rather than curative; it ushers the girl into society, invokes positive blessings on her, insures her health, prosperity and well-being, and protects her from potential misfortune' (Frisbie, 1967, p. 9). The initiand becomes Changing Woman, 'the embodiment of upward motion, growth from the earth up toward the sky . . . power she imparts to vegetation and humanity alike, as seen in two moments from the *Kinaaldá* ritual: [her] lifting of others to make them grow, and the painting of her face with an upward stroke, which is said to aid the growth of plants' (Lincoln, 1981, p. 30). Like the goddess, she benefits her people and their universe.

Clay

Many *Pueblos* tell pottery origin myths, for example *Cochiti*, where *kachinas* of Spider Woman's parents, Clay Old Woman and Clay Old Man, wear masks with white faces and red eyes: 'Old Man danced for her while she worked and when the pot was almost done he knocked it over with his foot and broke it. She snatched up his stick (a part of his regular *katcina* costume) and chased him (a pantomime which is acted out in their *katcina* appearances). Afterwards Old Man gave a bit of her clay to all the women in the village and enjoined pottery making' (Benedict, 1931, pp. 12, 208; Parsons, 1939, table 2).

Pottery is closely linked to reproduction; clay vessels are not inert but endowed with life throughout production. 'Every recorded Pueblo origin myth also describes the creation of life itself as occurring in part through the process of pottery making . . . notably so in Keresan emergence stories in which Iyatiku ("bringing to life") and her sister, Nautsiti ("more of everything in the basket"), are sent up into the light, to this earth, by Itc'tinaku (Thought Woman, Spider Woman) with baskets crammed full of seeds and clay images from which they create all forms of life.' Keresan *caciques* (religious leaders) care for their people by tending representative female and male clay images. 'As [Elsie Clews] Parsons also recorded throughout the Pueblos, small figurines, frequently unbaked and unpainted and made of cornmeal or clay, are central to rites and prayers of increase, particularly those associated with the winter solstice and Christmas. Images of domestic animals are placed on *kiva* or church altars and thereafter buried in the corral, "so that there will be more of them" . . . Similarly, a woman wanting children would make a clay "baby", take it to the altar, and then place it on a small cradleboard in a special place in her home; or, she might be given a clay or wooden baby in a miniature cradle by one of the *kachinas* which she would then care for and regard as "the heart of the child". Such clay figures are taken to be "the seed from which the real objects grow"' (Babcock and Monthan, 1986, pp. 9–10; Babcock, 1991).

Fig. 31 Cochiti Pueblo pottery Singing Mother, pre-1930, 6 inches (30 cm) high. 'This polychrome woman carrying a rather large child on her back is representative of many "singing ladies" produced at Cochiti during the early twentieth century. In modeled and painted details, she resembles both earlier and later human figures made at Cochiti' (Babcock and Monthan, 1986, p.16). *Photograph by Blair Clark, courtesy of the Museum of Indian Arts and Culture/Laboratory of Anthropology, Museum of New Mexico, Santa Fe*

Corn

Corn (maize), cornmeal and corn pollen are fundamental in *Pueblo, Apache* and *Navajo* subsistence, metaphor, myth and ritual. *Tewa* Blue Corn Woman, mother of the Summer moiety, and White Corn Maiden, mother of the Winter moiety, are 'the original mothers who were with the people before emergence, and from whom it is believed each child acquires his soul at birth'. Two midwives attend births and after four days' seclusion two naming mothers take the infant outside at dawn with two perfect ears of corn, one blue, one white, to perform the naming ceremony. Directly associated with femaleness, Blue Corn Woman rarely figures in myth; White Corn Maiden, who symbolizes 'the male principle' and who is 'fertilized magically by the Sun or some other transcendental figure', frequently appears and 'is the closest the Tewa come to the very widespread notion of a bisexual creator-god' (Ortiz, 1969, pp. 32, 89–90, 165–6).

Corn Mothers are found at *Taos, Isleta* and *Jemez. Zuni* corn maidens are growing plants with tassels as heads 'whose children are the maturing corn ears they hold in their arms'; 'in the storerooms of the houses are . . . "corn mothers", the harvested corn ears of the six directional colours' (Parsons, 1939, table 2; Tyler, 1964, pp. 145–8; Tedlock, 1979, p. 501). Seven Corn Maidens, who created the first seed 'by rubbing off bits of their own skin . . . are represented in Zuni ritual by corn ears in the colors of the six directions plus the centre. According to one Zuni legend, back at the time of the beginning, after the Corn Maidens gave the people corn seed, they rose from the earth and became the seven stars of the Big Dipper . . . The Zuni first plant corn in the spring by the light of the seven stars, which at that time rise bright overhead' (Young, 1987, p. 440).

Keresan Corn Mother Iyatiku (Laguna, Acoma), Utset (Zia) or Uretsete (Cochiti) either comes up briefly during emergence to bring corn or stays in the underworld and directs another's planting while herself receiving the dead. On earth, Utset, who had always known the name of corn, planted the first fields, declaring: 'This corn is my heart and it shall be to my people as milk from my breasts' (Parsons, 1939, table 2; Tyler, 1964, pp. 121–4). Paula Gunn Allen (1986, pp. 17–18, 22) calls Irriaku (Corn Mother) a powerful element linking humans and mother goddess Iyatiku (Corn Woman), who counsels people from the underworld and receives them back at death. As a perfect ear of corn Irriaku and thus Iyatiku is present at every ceremony. 'Without the presence of her power, no ceremony can produce the power it is designed to create and release . . . [attesting] that primary power – the power to make and to relate – belongs to the preponderantly feminine powers of the universe'.

Hopi Corn Maidens (Sa'lakwmana) appear as *kachina* dancers or dolls and puppets in various ceremonies. A *tiiponi*, the clan's mother and heart, is first to be set up when building an altar: 'It consists of a perfect ear of corn, encased in feathers and cotton twine. The base is hollow and filled with important seed and is also painted with cloud symbols. Thus it symbolizes the Hopi world: maize is the mother of all, the seeds in it are all edible vegetation . . . It is the central ritual object of every ceremonial, and also a symbol of the authority of the clan elder who preserves it. Without it, the clan and its society is destitute and weak' (Geertz and Lomatuway'ma, 1987, p. 54). Prevalent Hopi corn metaphors that 'people are corn' and 'corn plants are females' include 'young corn plants are maidens' and 'corn is our mother'. Corn and humans are symbiotic and complementary: 'Young plants are cared for as children by people; if they are properly cared for, encouraged and prayed for, they are able to mature from maidenhood to maturity. After "bearing children" and being harvested, the plants die, become corpses (*qatungwu*). Their lines of life are carried on in the ears of corn, some of which become *poshumi* [seed corn and young women capable to childbearing] for the next germination cycle. The rest become "mother" to the humans who cared for them – in the literal sense of actual nourishment, and figuratively as *tsotsmingwu*, the perfect ears of corn that are "mother" to initiates and infants' (Black, 1984, pp. 279, 282, 286).

Jicarillas treat corn pollen as one of their most important substances. Corn was 'involved in all phases of the culture and was represented in belief, medicine, and social practice. For instance, it was the custom for the mother of a newly married man to give her son's bride some corn to grind as a formal, symbolic "test" of whether she was an able homemaker . . . Ears of corn which had grown double were eaten by those who wanted many children, or were fed to horses so that they might multiply rapidly' (Opler, 1971, pp. 324–5).

Navajos use yellow cornmeal for women, white for men in blessing. Corn, which figures in almost all myth and ritual, is referred to metaphorically as a mother 'belonging to the Navaho from time immemorial': 'Corn is more than human, it is divine; it was connected with the highest ethical ideals.' Corn Beetle Girl and Corn Pollen Boy figure importantly in myth and ceremony: 'During the Navajo girl's

Fig. 32 Hopi Corn Maiden (Sa'Lakwmana) *kachina*, drawn by a Hopi man. 'The tablet represents terraced rain clouds . . . two vertical and two horizontal, one of each on each side. The object with bifid tips on each side . . . represents the squash blossom, symbolic of maidens' hair dress. Across the forehead is a symbol of an ear of corn, with two feathers attached to each end. The ring hanging over the forehead represents a fragment of Haliotis shell. There are imitation flowers made of wood in the hair. The left eye is yellow, the right blue . . . The artist has represented a garment of white feathers, over which is thrown a white ceremonial blanket with embroidered border. The two adjacent trees are pines' (Fewkes, 1903, p. 177). Plate LVI, left image, 'Hopi Calako Mana' in J.W. Fewkes (1903), *21st Report of the Bureau of American Ethnology for the Years 1899–1900. Photograph by Blair Clark, courtesy of Museum of Indian Arts and Culture / Laboratory of Anthropology, Museum of New Mexico, Santa Fe*

puberty rite, the central activity is grinding corn and preparing batter for a huge corn cake . . . to be baked in the ground during the last night of singing. [It] represents Mother Earth and, baked as a special offering to the Sun, brings special health and longevity to the girl' (Reichard, 1974, pp. 540–1; Witherspoon, 1977, pp. 92–3; Lamphere, 1983, p. 752).

Earth Mother

Navajo, Apache and *pan-Pueblo* mythologies articulate a mother earth and both literal and symbolic mothers. The Navajo 'term *shimá* has a very wide range of referents including ... one's mother by birth, the earth, the sheep herd, the corn field, and the mountain soil bundle ... If one asks Navajos if the earth is like a mother rather than actually a mother, they will respond with surprise and wonder ... [and] assert that the Earth as the outer form of Earth Woman or Changing Woman is not only an actual mother but that she is also the greatest of all mothers' (Witherspoon, 1977, p. 91).

Jicarilla Earth Mother and Black Sky 'existed alone in the beginning' and gave birth to 'parent supernatural beings [who] lived in darkness in the inner womb of the earth ... within the body of their mother ... The Earth acquired female attributes and for this reason the Jicarilla believe that people emerged from the underworld as man is born of woman today' (Tiller, 1983, pp. 444, 445).

Hopi earth/fertility deities who are not always mutually distinguished are: Hard Beings Woman's daughter, Sand Altar Woman (Tuwapongtumsi), 'the vegetation nourishing earth mother' and mother of mankind; Childbirth Water (Child Sliding-Out) Woman (Tiikuywuuti), patron of the hunt and mother of wild game; and Dawn Woman (Taalawtumsi), owner of crops and goddess of childbirth. On Third Mesa, Dawn Woman 'keeps all babies, in the form of little images, in her womb and sends these into the women of the village. Barren women may make offerings or rub their body with her image "to put a baby inside them"; continued barrenness means that the images fail to enter their body because they have a "bad heart"' (Tyler, 1964, pp. 82, 94, 133; Geertz and Lomatuway'ma, 1987, pp. 73, 128). *Zuni* Earth Mother's 'trees and bushes are her arms and hands ... and she wears a robe of yellow flowers (pollen grains) in the summer and white flowers (snowflakes) in the winter' (Tedlock, 1979, p. 499).

The complex *Tewa* word *gia*, 'mother', illustrates how all ritual, spiritual and social empowerment comes within, upon and in reciprocal relationship with Earth Mother. Biological *gias* are family mothers, some of whom become core *gias* with 'special roles in counselling and healing'. Community *gias* are both females and males who 'serve the community and assure harmony in the social/political/religious realms. Almost any older woman is called a *gia* but so is a respected male leader, or *cacique* ... Possession of desirable qualities is shown, at this level, to be more important than the discrimination or distinction of sex roles.' *Gias* also include certain female and male deities, 'the ones closest to the people [with] *gia* aspects of strength, courage, love of the people, and giving'. Ideally, 'to be alive is to be a nurturer' and earth is the traditional paradigm for living: 'The Earth is the ultimate nurturer. She is our mother or *nung be gia*. We humans move in and out of her womb as is told in the emergence myths of the Pueblos. She is constant, reliable, and always giving and forgiving. She protects and heals' (Swentzell and Naranjo, 1986, pp. 36–7).

First Woman

Navajo First Woman and Man originate in the lowest world from ears of corn or the mingling (copulation) of coloured (directional) clouds, yellow and blue for her, black and white for him. Through intellect and thought, the inner form of speech, the two create 'the inner forms of all the natural phenomena that would be prominent in the structure and operation of this world'. Their underworld incest also spawns several kinds of witchcraft (Reichard, 1974, pp. 433–8; Witherspoon, 1977, pp. 29, 39, 43, 55–7, 141).

In some versions of the separation of the sexes, for a time in the third underworld, First Woman's sexual excesses and adultery precipitate the split. Men are able to weather the separation better and women's self-abuse and excesses produce various monsters. When reunion is effected they agree that men will take the lead in sexual matters. After emergence First Woman 'decreed that women should henceforth recognize and approve of sexual relations. She made male and female genitalia so that one sex should attract the other – the penis of turquoise, the vagina of whiteshell. After treating them ritualistically, she laid them side by side and blew over them medicine (infusion), which was to cause pregnancy. She went further and determined the degree of desire – great for men, much less for women. Intercourse was to leave the penis weak, the vagina strong' (Reichard, 1974, pp. 30–1; Haile, 1981a, pp. 31–122; 1981b).

First Woman and Man in many respects mirror their foster daughter Changing Woman and Sun. When Changing Woman retires to the west they withdraw to a permanent north(east)ern home where evil and danger originate. They 'must have white corn meal sprinkled to them at night; their offerings must be remembered, not because these gods bring man good but so that they may not render futile the good that may come man's way' (Reichard, 1974, pp. 76–7, 105, 306).

Hard Beings Woman

Hopi Huru'ingwwuuti, a generatrix associated with shells, beads, turquoise and the earth's solidity, and Sun create 'living creatures from their hair, nails, body dirt, and mucus'. Complementing the eastern-rising Sun, Hard Beings Woman lives in a western ocean *kiva*, owns the moon and stars, and appears as a beautiful maiden by night, a withered hag by day. His co-equal creator, she produces Sand Altar Woman and the fertility god Muy'ingwa from parts of her cuticle rolled into a ball and hidden under a blanket (Tyler, 1964, pp. 82–5, 242; Geertz and Lomatuway'mu, 1987, p. 134).

Moon Mother

The moon is female in *Zuni*, *Keresan* (except *Zia*) and *Isleta* tradition, male in *Navajo* and at *Hopi*, *Jemez*, *Tewa* and *Taos* (Parsons, 1939, table 2; Reichard, 1974, p. 176). *Zuni* Moonlight-Giving Mother and Sun Father are wife and husband but live in perpetual separation. Both are ultimate givers of light and life, foremost among powerful supernaturals called 'The Ones Who Hold Our Roads', that is, our lives (Tedlock, 1979, p. 499).

Older and Younger Sisters

Navajo culture heroines of related Mountainway and Beautyway myths, among the very few with women protagonists, the sisters are promised as prizes to successful warriors in the Pueblo war. Won by two elders, Bear Man and Snake Man, they are seduced by magic tobacco, then flee their unwanted spouses. In separate adventures, they are rescued and taught appropriate ceremonies by the bear or snake families and other Holy People. They are reunited and return to teach the chantways before departing again to live with Holy People. (In the related *Jicarilla* Holiness Rite myth, the girls abducted by Bear and Snake do not separate, but the etiological factors and ceremonials are similar [Wyman, 1957, pp. 145–51].)

Mountain(top)way heals problems resulting from improper dealings with animals that live in the mountains, especially bears. Older Sister's journeys and adventures while being pursued by Bear Man are prominent in the female branch (Wyman, 1975, pp. 14–21).

Beautyway is closely associated with all kinds of snakes and the harm they cause. The female branch is more common; its protagonist Younger Sister resembles active chantway heroes. 'In disobedience of instructions she lights the fire at night, to find to her horror that she is surrounded by snakes; in curiosity she opens forbidden water jars letting loose a series of storms; and finally in lonesomeness she strays in forbidden directions, each time meeting disaster (captured by squash plants, shot by toad, buried in play with rock wrens).' However, both protectors' complaints about her behaviour and her own motivations are more explicit than in most (masculine) chantway myths (Spencer, 1957, pp. 150–1).

Taking as a definition of ritual an 'ongoing dialogue' – 'the means by which people, spirits, rocks, animals, and other beings enter into conversation with each other' – Patricia Clark Smith and Paula Gunn Allen (1987, pp. 177, 181) emphasize that 'the sisters are not a pair of passive princesses badgered into submissiveness by their husbands and in-laws . . . [but] strongly bonded with one another'. Younger Sister's erotic experience leaves her 'socialized but not suppressed', unlike 'most of the European folk-tale heroines who stray away from their families into the forests. Her encounters with the spirits of the land teach her what she needs to know in order to be an adult woman: to live within a family, to understand and respect the forces of nature, and maintain a ritual relationship with them.'

Salt Woman

Pan-Pueblo Salt (Old) Woman takes offence while living among people and thus moves, alone or accompanied, to a distant place, usually Zuni Salt Lake, south of the Pueblo. Properly approached, as during ritual salt pilgrimages, she is a powerful, benevolent mother, constantly giving of herself. Sometimes she is also associated with bringing rain. *Navajo* salt-gathering rites, part of Blessingway, are obsolete. Salt Woman, Changing Woman's sister who originated in the underworlds, helps the monster-slayers; salt is believed to confer strength and sometimes used as a weapon (Parsons, 1939, pp. 202, 205, table 2; Tyler, 1964, pp. 186–87, 190–1; Reichard, 1974, pp. 463, 595).

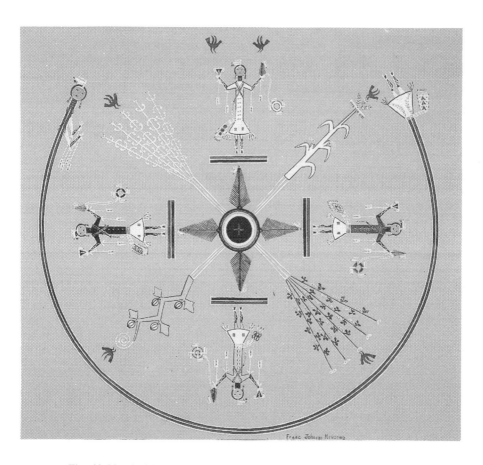

Fig. 33 Navajo Mountainway 'People of the Myth — radial' sandpainting showing 'figures of the heroine [Older Sister] of the myth of Female Mountainway, masked in weasel skin [pink] . . . around a black center with a fire [the cross] in it . . . [which] represents the corral or Dark Circle of Branches. The inner white outline "denotes where the initiates are and each successive circle denotes each type of spectator until the outer black circle which is the trees surrounding the corral. Four fir trees project from the center," and the figures carry a little fir or spruce tree in their left hands [like] the last group of dancers who enter the corral at dawn . . . [and] pass these to the body of the patient, "sanctifying him" . . . These dancers from Young Spruce Knoll commemorate the episode in the myth where White-Circle-of-Teeth-Woman saves the heroine from Bear Man by wrapping her in a spruce [fir] garment, which is "what he [Bear Man] really fears".' A rare, round-headed (not rectangular) Rainbow deity guards the image, which was painted by Woman Singer (Estsan Hatrali) of Canyon de Chelly, Arizona, and recorded by Franc Johnson Newcomb at Newcomb in 1935 (Wyman, 1975, pp. 63, 83–5). *Photograph by Barney McCulloch, courtesy of the Wheelwright Museum of the American Indian, Santa Fe, New Mexico*

Spider Woman

Keresan (Old) Spider Woman, Grandmother Spider or Thought (best translated as Creating-through-Thinking) Woman is the supreme being who creates everything by thinking, dreaming, naming and ritual singing (Tyler, 1964, pp. 82, 89–92, 116–18; Allen, 1986, pp. 98–9). *Laguna* Tse che nako is so powerful that her name is not spoken; she is called Spider Woman in ordinary discourse (Purley, 1974). *Acoma* Tsichtinako is a supreme creator and tutelary spirit, especially guiding people during emergence; *Zia* Tsityostinako is named Prophesying Woman because 'she knows (rather than deciding, or determining) what is going to happen' (Stirling, 1942, pp. 1–4; White, 1962, p. 113).

Hopi Spider Woman (Kookyangwso'wuuti) is the mother of all, helping during emergence and acting as a benevolent, stern guardian with her own shrines (Parsons, 1939, pp. 192–3). At Old Oraibi Spider Grandmother is both helpful and comically annoying for the various kinds of human beings she creates (Voth, 1905, pp. 3–4).

Jicarilla Apaches do not kill spiders, who enabled first beings to reach higher levels during the emergence, and 'the nexus . . . between the spider's web and the sunbeam is made explicit in the birth rite, where a cord of unblemished buckskin, called in the rite "spider's rope", is stretched from the umbilicus of the child towards the sun'. Old Woman Spider and other spider people help monster-slayer escape running rocks. *White Mountain* Black Spider Old Woman and naked (then clothed) Spider girls help monster-slayer survive cold in their hole by weaving cloth; the former gives him holy power for his journey to the Sun (Opler, 1938, pp. 19, 71–4; 1939, pp. 4–5).

Navajo Spider Woman and Spider Man exhale webs to hold back the waters during emergence. Spider Woman teaches weaving and cat's cradle; the discipline and thought/breath required in both the craft and the game constitutes continual, ritual re-creation of cosmic and human harmony. In monster-slayer and chantway myths, Spider Woman primarily helps but sometimes threatens culture heroes. Navajos protect spiders and rub their webs on girl babies' hands and arms so they will learn to weave without tiring (Reichard, 1974, pp. 467–9; Weigle, 1982, pp. 4–6; 1989, pp. 27–32).

Two Sisters

Keresan sisters (Uretsete or Iyatiku and Naotsete or Nautsiti) act as mediators between this and other worlds, culture heroines and mothers who create through ritual singing. They sometimes lead people out during emergence. One sister, mother of Indians, is identified with Corn Mother and acts as her earthly counterpart. The second is 'alien', portrayed as mother of whites or non-Pueblo Indians, and the two quarrel in setting up domains. Hamilton A. Tyler (1964, pp. 116–24) sees them as changed-sex twin monster-slayers or war gods, Paula Gunn Allen (1986, pp. 16, 98–9, 122–3) as sister goddesses to Spider Woman with co-equal medicine power of 'three great Witch creatrixes'.

Warrior Women

Chakwena war or enemy *kachinas* are found in several pueblos. *Hopi* Chakwena Mana, elder sister of the Chakwena *kachinas*, is portrayed as a bearded warrior with only one hair whorl completed since she was in the middle of hair-dressing when the pueblo was attacked. The men were away so half-coiffed women grabbed weapons to defend their community. Other bearded-women *kachinas* include the ogre women and Hee'e'wuuti, 'the mythical girl who espied enemies approaching the village while her mother was setting up her hair whorls ... immediately snatched a bow and arrows, and with her whorl up on one side of her head [only] – led an attack which defeated the enemy' (Fewkes, 1903, pp. 68, 82, 86; Geertz and Lomatuway'ma, 1987, p. 36).

Zuni Chakwena Woman (Tcakwena Oka) and her attendants visit in early January. They approach every door; the women inside throw out live embers, then sprinkle meal in 'house cleansing' rites thought to bring good fortune in childbirth. Chakwena Woman also participates in the *kachinas'* traditional rabbit hunt following initiations; blood from the first rabbit killed is rubbed on her legs to ensure puberty, prolific childbearing and 'so that Zuni women may have their babies easily, like rabbits'. Afterward, for four days she 'lies in for the increase of livestock and babies' on a sand bed in the *kiva*, 'tended by women who wish for her blessing in childbirth [while] men who desire her blessing on their flocks and herds bring miniature animals of clay' (Bunzel, 1932, p. 935). Called Ku'yapalitsa in myths, she is keeper of game and warrior woman leader of the Kia'nakwe army against the Zunis. She captures four Zuni gods; neither they nor game are released until Sun tells the hero that Chakwena's heart is in the rattle she carries and his arrow pierces it (Stevenson, 1904, pp. 36–38; Parsons, 1939).

Yellow Woman

Laguna, Acoma Yellow Woman (Kochinnenako) is leader of Corn Maidens, hunter, mother of twins and heroine of many tales (Tyler, 1964, pp. 166, 188–9, 213). Allen (1986, pp. 226–7) calls her 'Spirit of Woman', a 'role model' whose stories include 'abduction, meeting with happy powerful spirits, birth of twins, getting power from the spirit worlds and returning it to the people, refusing to marry, weaving, grinding corn, getting water, outsmarting witches, eluding or escaping from malintentioned spirits, and more'. She claims her name 'means Woman-Woman because among the Keres, yellow is the colour for women ... and it is the color ascribed to the Northwest. Keres women paint their faces yellow on certain ceremonial occasions and are so painted at death so that the guardian at the gate of the spirit world, Naiya Iyatiku (Mother Corn Woman), will recognize that the newly arrived person is a woman. It is also the name of a particular Irriaku, Corn Mother (sacred corn-ear bundle), and Yellow Woman stories in their original form detail rituals in which the Irriaku figures prominently'.

SECTION III: LESSER FIGURES

Bat Woman

Navajo, Apache Bat Woman is the helper who aids monster-slayer's descent from precarious heights in her burden basket. She is rewarded with feathers, which eventually change into various birds. In some Navajo myths she 'has a wing hook or a "vagina wing" by means of which she clings to rocks and makes an embarrassing noise', attempting to mislead the culture heroes (Reichard, 1974, pp. 383–4). Apaches generally associate bats and their power with horse breaking and racing; even though their wings may be used as medicine they are also disliked (Clark, 1966, pp. 70–1, 133–4, 154; Boyer, 1972).

Butterfly

Hopi Butterfly *Kachina* Maiden (Palhikwmana), associated with fertility, appears in Butterfly ('social') dances introduced from the Rio Grande Pueblos, where among the *Tewa* they connote 'spring, fertility, war and peace, and the female' (Fewkes, 1910; Sweet, 1985, p. 85; Geertz and Lomatuway'ma, 1987, pp. 61–2). *Zuni* Koyemshi, the most dangerous *kachinas*, 'carry the sacred butterfly, *lahacoma*, in their drum to make people follow them . . . anyone who follows *lahacoma* will go crazy', while in *Pueblo* lore generally women/girls are thought to 'run after butterflies' (Bunzel, 1932, p. 947; Parsons , 1939, p. 382).

    Navajo butterflies symbolize temptation and foolishness; butterfly people figure in Prostitutionway (formerly used to cast or combat 'love magic' or to deal with sexual imbalances) myths, wherein the culture hero also seduces women by changing into a butterfly (Haile, 1978). *Apache* butterflies are connected with love-making and love power. In *Jicarilla* emergence Holy Boy uses butterflies to entice out two 'foolish girls' who stayed behind in the underworld; since, 'the butterfly, symbol of the fluttering and inconstancy of women, is encised or painted on flutes which young men play to attract sweethearts' (Opler, 1938, p. 27).

Coyote Woman

Hopi-Tewa recognize both female and male coyote tricksters; the former is rarer but not considered exceptional (Parsons, 1926, pp. 285–93, 295–9). Coyote Woman is not interchangeable with Old Man Coyote; he 'seems to possess genuine "tragic flaws" . . . including excessive cleverness, inflated pride, gullibility . . . [while she] is typically depicted as treacherous and outright evil – without any hint of [his] mitigatingly pathetic qualities' (Kroskrity and Healing, 1980, p. 120).

Horned Toad

Navajos equate the horned toad with 'power, longevity, healing properties, and inner stability of the abdomen'. Frequent symbols in sandpaintings, in ordinary life they are picked up and rubbed on the body as a shield against malevolent forces. Old Lady

Horned Toad is swallowed by Coyote when he is rampaging through her cornfield. She methodically shreds his insides and emerges from his throat to admonish him against improper eating behaviour as he dies. Because she 'has come close to death and come back, her story can be alluded to in any ritual in which the chief process has to do with restoring inner health' (Toelken, 1987, pp. 393–4).

Last Remaining Monsters

Navajo Cold Woman and Old Age Woman, like males Poverty Man, Lice, Hunger Man and Death, convince monster-slayer to spare their life. Cold Woman sits naked and shivering on a mountaintop, surrounded by messenger snow buntings, and argues: 'If you kill me, the weather will always be hot; the land will dry up; the springs will cease to flow; the people will perish.' Old Age Woman walks with a cane and proclaims: 'Know that it will be the old people who will tell the young people what happened in years past. It would not be well if there were only young people on the earth' (Matthews, 1897, p. 130; O'Bryan, 1956, p. 99; Reichard, 1974, pp. 421, 454).

Mummifying Woman

Navajo chantway heroes sometimes encounter dangerous Mummifying (Thin Old, Skinny, Hunger) Woman (Woman-who-dries-you-up), a beautiful maiden who wins them in a grinding contest and takes them to her richly appointed home on a knoll. The hero awakens to discover her transformed into an ugly old woman and himself imprisoned in a structure bedecked with rags and human flesh, on a tall, barren rock. He starves until Bird Maidens first taunt, then bring food and help him down (Wyman, 1962, pp. 65–9, 111–19).

Ogres

Zuni, Hopi, Hopi-Tewa 'bogey' *kachinas* of both sexes periodically visit to terrify and discipline children and sometimes adults. Atocle (Suyuki; Hopi Atosle) *kachina*, a cannibal woman who figures prominently in Zuni mythology (*see* Vagina Women, below), threatens to eat or kidnap children (Bunzel, 1932, pp. 936–41). Ogre families living outside the Hopi and Hopi-Tewa world in caves include Grandmother (So'owuhti or Suyuku), Mother (Hahaiwuhti; So'oyok among Hopi-Tewa, who have no grandmother ogre) and Sister (mother's daughter – Soyokmana, Natas; Hopi-Tewa Siwa). They pay periodic visits, which Kealiinohomoku (1980) analyses not as punitive but as positive, very powerful medicine to help children mature and learn increasingly complex, responsible behaviour.

Vagina Women

Apache, Navajo women who kill men with their toothed vaginas are among the monsters slain or tamed by culture heroes. *Jicarilla* monster-slayer encounters four 'vagina girls,' or 'walking around' vaginas with legs and body parts who have vaginas hanging on their walls. He 'spoils' their teeth by feeding them sour berries and bargains with them to regulate menstruation, childbirth and venereal disease. He gives his mother two wall vaginas; she places them on two girls and instructs about their proper usage so 'that you may have six kinds of [female] relatives'. *White Mountain* Vulva Woman (Vulva That Kills) has all her teeth but one ('her tooth narrow') broken off by monster-slayer (Opler, 1938, pp. 66–70; 1939, pp. 21–2, 38–9, 71).

Navajo Snapping Vagina's vagina dentata produces lightning; her unnatural, adulterous cohabitations yield many lethal monsters, including Heaped (Overwhelming) Vagina, born of copulation with cactus, who 'would invite her victims to sit beside her and throw her vagina over them and kill them'. Monster-Slayer dispatches Heaped Vagina but spares her cactus, yucca and spiny-plant children. He exhausts Snapping Vagina by shooting multicolored Big Stars for her to chase around the sky, thrusts his club into her open mouth just as 'today in a fight Navajos shove their fingers into the mouth and under the lip of an opponent' and shatters her with Big Stars. Her dying whisper commands that prayersticks often be made to her (Haile, 1981a, pp. 176–7, 201–2, 204–5).

Pre-Columbian *Pueblo* vagina dentata motifs are found on Mimbres pots, which suggest *Zuni* myths recorded by Ruth Benedict in the 1930s. In some, the Ahaiyute or War Twins encounter either an evil old woman or Atocle Woman (*see* Ogres, above) who bite their necks to kill them and whom they then vanquish by scratching the inside of the women's nostrils; in others the twins break girls' toothed vaginas with false wooden penises (Carr and Gingerich, 1983). *Hopi* Jimson Weed Girls (Tsimonmamant), associated with the feared, prickly or spiny Jimson weed plant known as Sacred Datura, 'represent oversexed unmarried girls and women'. The 'term *tsimona*, imbued with connotations of narcotic powers that derange the mind and are usually fatal, is equated or coalesces with sexual aberration, which must be considered equally dangerous and devastating' (Malokti, 1983, pp. 207–8).

SECTION IV: CURRENT QUESTIONS

The Native American Southwest has been 'a mirror of American ethnology' where for over a century 'successive generations of Southwestern ethnologists' have strongly influenced 'the growth of anthropological thought' and produced 'a body of literature on the region's indigenous peoples that in terms of sheer magnitude and variety probably surpasses that of any ethnographic area in the New World' (Basso, 1979, p. 14). Although a significant number of these anthropologists were women (Babcock and Parezo, 1988), and despite studies like those on girls' puberty rites or Allen (1986), Young (1987) and Babcock (1991), it can still be said that 'the role of women in Southwestern Indian ritual drama [and mythology] is relatively unexplored' (Frisbie, 1980, p. 319). Indeed it is possible to contend that very little can be confidently asserted about Southwest Native American women in/and (mostly masculine) mythology/religion and still less about their own mythology/religion. Certainly secrecy figures in the lack of basic data, but androcentrism in fieldwork and interpretation-publication is also crucial, especially the inherent bias of patriarchal, western attitudes about the earth, creation and procreation, the artisan creator and sexuality and gender.

Using Edward B. Tylor's assertion in *Primitive Culture* (1873, 1, p. 326) that 'among the native races of America the earth-mother is one of the Great personages of mythology' and Åke Hultkrantz's 1983 essay, 'The Religion of the Goddess in North America', as end points, Sam D. Gill (1987, p. 122) contends: 'There is no possibility whatsoever of beginning with the data of North America and drawing the same conclusions . . . so commonly made . . . that Mother Earth is a major American goddess, or even more strongly put that she is the goddess of the native races of America'. Frank Hamilton Cushing's 'Outlines of Zuni Creation Myths' (1896; Weigle, 1989, pp. 205–11), which Gill (1987, p. 121) calls 'outlines of Zuni creation conceptions formulated into story form by a romantic ethnologist', are among the meagre data always cited by scholars like Mircea Éliade. The scholarly record is better viewed not as an analysis of 'the nature of culture and religion' but as 'a very powerful story . . . that makes Native Americans primitives when compared with European-Americans . . . [and] supports a range of social, economic, and political relationships, very likely oppressive, among peoples in America' (Gill, 1987, p. 128). The hegemony extends to patriarchal notions about creation and procreation.

Emergence (Wheeler-Voegelin and Moore, 1957) is basic to Pueblo, Apache and Navajo mythologies. Such myths have never been regarded as truly cosmogonic (read: 'higher' or *ex nihilo* creation by spirit, breath, dream, speech, thought as in Genesis 1, John 1 and Greek metaphysical traditions) and thus worthy of hermeneutic scrutiny, because no unordered chaos precedes the always existent, ordered worlds. Emergence myths are also considered feminine, animistic and too explicitly associated with biological gestation and parturition (read: 'lower', physical or elemental creation through accretion, excretion, parthenogenesis, copulation, division, dismemberment) generally to merit any extended attention as truly symbolic and cultural (Matthews, 1902; Callaway, 1978). Although the birth event is not a dumb, physiological circumstance, because procreation is not considered equivalent to creation, the complex language and ritual of parturient mothers, midwives and gossips (*godsibs*, attendants at and enablers of birthing) has neither informed nor privileged the study of emergence mythology in the ways that other more public and priestly, masculine, so-called spiritual mythologies have been examined and exalted (Weigle, 1989).

Paula Gunn Allen (1986, pp. 27–8) calls 'pre-Conquest' Native American women's gestation and parturition a potent ritual process of vitalization. 'When [Keresan] Thought [Spider] Woman brought to life the twin [two] sisters, she did not give birth to them in the biological sense. She sang over the medicine bundles that contained their potentials . . . [and] infused them with vitality . . . and thus they were "born" '. This is by no means the biological counterpart to the excretory, compensatory, symbolic process postulated by psychoanalytic interpreters like Alan Dundes (1962, pp. 1038, 1046), who views earth-diver myths as 'creation of the mythopoeic male'. Concentrating on the earth's creation from the small quantity of mud brought up by the diving animal, Dundes makes two assumptions: '(1) the existence of a cloacal theory of birth; and (2) the existence of pregnancy envy on the part of males.' He claims that 'whether a male creator spins material, molds clay, lays an egg, fabricates from mucus or epidermal tissue, or dives for fecal mud, the psychological motivation is much the same'. Still, women are not thought to have 'projects' in the ways men have 'babies', and the creations of the 'mythopoeic female', unless she is compensating for being 'barren', are treated as mere crafts, not artistic/intellectual conceptions and creations.

In traditional Navajo culture, 'Nilch'i, meaning Wind, Air or Atmosphere', is fundamental to creative power, according to James Kale McNeley (1981, p. 1): 'Suffusing all of nature, Holy Wind gives life, thought, speech and the power of motion to all living things and serves as the means of communication between all elements of the living world.' Thus, when Spider Woman and Man exhale webs to hold back the waters during emergence (birth), it is no less 'an effort in creative transformation' than when Navajo women weave: 'The intricate and often complex patterns created by Navajo weavers are generated in the mind and kept there through the whole process from dyeing through weaving . . . [which] requires a unique combination and coordination of conceptual and manual skills. A woven rug is a product of the mind and the body. The inner form of the rug is in the mind; the outer form of the rug is projected onto the loom,' just as all positive (cosmogonic) and negative (witchcraft) creation takes place (Witherspoon, 1977, pp. 17, 161).

A Zia Pueblo emergence myth (White, 1962, pp. 113, 115) portrays Tsityostinako (Prophesying or Spider, Thought Woman) and her two daughters (Utctsiti and Naotsiti) sitting amid clouds and fog in the Yellow World, the bottom underworld, 'like tcaiyanyi (medicinemen) in a ceremonial house' with a *manta* or blanket spread on the floor in front of them and a cane on top. 'Then, with magic and songs, they created things under the *manta*. Then they would pick up the *manta* and see what they had created. Tsityostinako could not be seen, but . . . it was she who put ideas into Utctsiti's and Naotsiti's heads. After they had created something, Tsityostinako would explain why it had been created.' There is an element of surprise in the two sisters' creations and Tsityostinako here appears as a kind of trickster.

The Native American trickster figure has received extensive attention, especially since Paul Radin's influential publication (1956) on the Winnebago trickster, later reinterpreted by Barbara Babcock Abrahams (1975) as a 'negation offering possibility', in its multivariate performance an ongoing metasocial commentary that sheds transcendent, creative light on the arbitrary order of all things. Although the trickster blurs categories of sexuality and gender, most trickster studies assume that it is 'basically' or 'first of all' male/a man. At least in presently available accounts (compare Coyote Woman, *see* p. 348), females/women simply are not accorded the variety of expression that William Bright (1987; also Haile, 1984; Toelken, 1987) catalogues for his 'natural history' of Old *Man* Coyote as wanderer, *bricoleur*, glutton, lecher, thief, cheat, outlaw, spoiler, loser, clown, pragmatist, old person and survivor. The much needed, gynocentric trickster studies in the Native American Southwest, or even elsewhere, must await sensitive, feminist performance studies of the full range of women's verbal and nonverbal humour, including their burlesquing and relationship to sacred clowns and clown societies.

By the same token, materials on sexuality and gender are inconclusive and biased. The mythic constructs, when they are even recorded at all, cannot be compared with the social ones because there is little native-centred, gynocentric data on celibacy, homosexuality, heterosexuality, bisexuality, transvestism, hermaphrodites, transsexuality and what Paula Gunn Allen (1981, p. 81; Grahn, 1984, pp. 49–72) calls 'dykes' or 'ceremonial Lesbians' who 'bond with women in order to further some Spirit and supernatural directive' and the not necessarily mutually exclusive 'Lesbians', women who are 'emotionally and physically intimate with other women'. In the case of cross-gender roles, for example, most studies centre on the cross-gender male (Whitehead, 1981); even the common designation 'berdache', which comes from the Arabic *bardaj* or boy slave kept for sexual purposes, is 'roughly defined as a person, usually male, who was anatomically normal but assumed the dress, occupations, and behavior of the other sex to effect a[n incomplete] change in gender status' (Callender and Kochems, 1983, p. 443). Inter- and intra-racial/ethnic relationships also affect these cultural constructs, and 'it is imperative to develop an analysis of variant gender roles based on the historical conditions that faced particular tribes since gender systems vary in different cultures and change as modes of production [and hegemony] change' (Blackwood, 1984, p. 42).

A truly feminist mythology is long overdue. In the Native American Southwest, as elsewhere, it would fully explicate reproductive systems and celebrate the enabling emergence rituals of childbirth, midwifery and gossip(s). Women tricksters and their creative humour(s), especially in matters of sexuality and gender, would also command focal attention for the variety of their modes of clarifying and questioning arbitrary, androcentric and Eurocentric orders. Empowering women's mythologies will require revision of existing scholarship, new fieldwork by native and non-native women and collaborative, reflexive, interpretive and expressive work by feminists from all cultures and societies.

SECTION V: MYTHOGRAPHY

The invention and commodification of the Pueblo-Navajo-Apache Southwest began in the late nineteenth century and continues in today's tourism industry and the closely linked art world. The Atchison, Topeka & Santa Fe Railway, which reached the New Mexico line in December 1878 and had established a California connection in August 1883, and its associated Fred Harvey Company, launched in 1876, were largely responsible for creating and successfully marketing 'a compelling regional identity for "The Great Southwest" of northern New Mexico and Arizona from Las Vegas [New Mexico] Hot Springs to the Grand Canyon, displaying it as a tourist attraction of sublime natural wonders, prehistoric and colonial historic significance, and colorful, tamed, native peoples, primarily Indians'. By the First World War 'Meals by Fred Harvey' had become not just 'reliably good food, service, and accommodations' but an opportunity to see 'appropriated, displayed, and marketed the cultures of the Native American and, to a lesser extent, the Spanish colonial and Anglo (primarily hunter/trapper/prospector) Southwest' (Weigle, 1989a, p. 115; McLuhan, 1985). In 1926 the Santa Fe Railway and the Fred Harvey Company inaugurated Indian Detours – chauffeured, guided car excursions 'off the beaten path' of the railroad through the Indian and Spanish Southwest 'that lies beyond the pinched horizons of your train window' (Thomas, 1978, p. 65).

The Santa Fe's founders established their railroad as a link to an envisioned but never actualized steamship line to the Orient, and Orientalism (Said, 1978) played an important role in the region's corporate and cultural image-making. 'Travelers passing the Pueblo villages of the Southwest in the eighties were invited to recall the villages of ancient Egypt and Nubia, Nineveh and Babylon, rather than to study the remains of an aboriginal life; the people were "like the descendants of Rebecca of Bible fame" ' (Pomeroy, 1957, p. 39). *Poetry* editor Harriet Monroe asked in 1920: 'Why go to Greece or China, O ye of little faith? This Southwest . . . is our own authentic wonderland – a treasure-trove of romantic myth – profoundly significant and beautiful, guarded by ancient races practicing their ancient rites' (Weigle, 1989a, p. 135). Indian Detourists were promised: 'Motorists crossing the Southwestern States are nearer to the primitive than anywhere else on the continent. They are crossing a land in which a foreign people, with foreign speech and foreign ways, offer them spectacles which can be equaled in very few Oriental lands' (Thomas, 1978, p. 196). Sylvia Rodriguez (1989, p. 93) analyses this 'mystification' process of 'symbolic objectification, omission, co-optation, and transmutation' at the so-called 'American Pyramids' of Taos Pueblo, where twentieth-century art colonists have objectified and commodified Indians 'as the mystical Other instead of as regular human beings'. By the Second World War, tourist industry personnel, artists and for that matter scholars had become culture brokers for a land like no other populated by exotic Others.

Native American women especially have been portrayed as both Other (Minh-ha, 1989) and artisans. 'If instead of regarding the other simply as an object, he [*sic*] were considered as a subject capable of producing objects which one might then possess, the chain would be extended by a link – the intermediary subject – and thereby multiply to infinity the number of objects ultimately possessed. This transformation, however, necessitates that the intermediary subject be maintained in precisely this role of subject-producer of objects and kept from becoming like ourselves' (Todorov, 1984, pp. 175–6). Southwest Indian craftswomen were primarily presented as domestic, and thus suitably contained, weavers, potters and basketmakers; they and their wares were displayed and marketed in Santa Fe/Harvey and other commercial establishments or in their own pueblos, hogans and communities.

Traditionally, crafts were associated with strict divisions of labour between women, men or transvestites (usually male) and involved ritual interactions with the raw materials and a discipline of production enacting myth and religious belief – all patterns disrupted by commodification (Parezo, Hays and Slivac, 1987). Thus, Spider Woman's weaving no longer relates to individual healing (spinning the yarn sunwise to prevent 'unravelling' in the ritual, metaphoric sense that would pose a threat to health) and cosmic harmony but to an outside marketplace: 'The Navajos explain the relationship there not in terms of the rug, the end product – which, of course, is what our culture is interested in – but in terms of the relationship with the yarn and with the sheep, and with the spinning of the yarn, which has to be done in a certain direction . . . [so] the yarn itself becomes a further symbol of man's [sic] interaction with the animal on the one hand, and with the whole cosmos on the other' (Toelken, 1976a; 1976b, p. 19).

In her association with Cochiti Pueblo, potter Helen Cordero, 'who invented the [male] Storyteller doll in 1964 . . . [and] since has reshaped Pueblo pottery, her own life, and the lives of countless other Pueblo women', Barbara A. Babcock (1987, pp. 391–2) has confronted 'the man-made Eurocentric constructions' and 'commodity fetishism that pervades not only our lives but our material culture studies with their emphasis on economics, quantification, and the products of creativity'. Asked how many Storytellers she had made, Cordero replied in exasperation, 'It's like breads, we don't count.' For her, 'the process . . . "doing it the right way, the old way," is far more important than the finished product'. This is by no means 'singular artistic [or cosmogonic] authorship and control: "I don't just get up in the morning and start making potteries. First I talk with Grandma Clay and she tells me what to do." "It's not me, it's the fire, he decides how they'll come out." "It's my grandfather, he's giving me these. He was a wise man with lots of stories and lots of grandchildrens and we're all in there, in the clay." '

Traditional Pueblo pottery making was women's domain of functional and symbolic reproduction and regeneration, with 'origin myths and legends as well as songs and drums and *kachinas* and *kivas* and all the other aspects of sacred discourse, including the ceremonial Keresan in which it is spoken . . . controlled by men' (Babcock, 1988, p. 373). For some twenty-five years Helen Cordero and numerous other Pueblo women potters, 'by creating not only *Storytellers*, but *Nightcriers*, *Drummers*, *Turtles*, and other ceremonial and mythic figures, and by exhibiting and demonstrating their art . . . have assumed the right to re-present and interpret to the outside world at least some of the aspects of the very discourse in which they are displaced . . . *At home, no womens are storytellers*, but women are potters and with the transformative power of their hands, they have contrived to tell stories about storytelling, to subvert masculine discursive control, and to profoundly disturb the distribution of power . . . They are reproducing "with a difference," and they are figuratively as well as literally playing with fire' (Babcock, 1988, p. 381). In this they become, like many other Native American women artists and writers, powerful women tricksters.

During the twentieth century, Native Americans in the Southwest and elsewhere have developed a more pan-Indian 'story' of Mother Earth in response to increasing encroachment and acculturative pressures, according to Sam D. Gill. He (1987, p. 149) claims, for example, that Navajo sandpainting depictions of sky and earth and certain designs on Navajo wedding baskets are now known 'by the English terms "Father Sky" and "Mother Earth" ' instead of the latter's earlier association with

Changing Woman and 'an aspect of the Navajo principle ... Long Life and Happiness'. Twentieth-century ecologists too have interpreted a threatened earth in feminist terms (King, 1989).

Donna Haraway (1988, pp. 593–4) calls ecofeminists 'perhaps the most insistent on some version of the world as active subject, not as resource to be mapped and appropriated in bourgeois, Marxist, or masculinist projects'. She suggests that acknowledgements of 'the agency of the world' are not simply 'appeals to a primal mother resisting her translation into resource' but include 'a sense of the world's independent sense of humor' and create 'richly evocative figures to promote feminist visualizations of the world as witty agent'. In these, 'Coyote or Trickster, as embodied in Southwest Native American accounts, suggests the situation we are in when we give up mastery but keep searching for fidelity, knowing all the while that we will be hoodwinked'. Although Haraway does not distinguish between women and men tricksters, her proposal that 'feminist objectivity makes room for surprises and ironies at the heart of all knowledge production' and her clarion 'to see feminist theory as a reinvented coyote discourse obligated to its sources in many heterogeneous accounts of the world' can serve as a call to articulate a genuine women's mythology as women coyote discourse obligated to all women's gossip about Old Woman Coyote Earth Mother.

References and Further Reading

Allen, P.G. (1981), 'Lesbians in American Indian Cultures' in *Conditions: Seven*, pp. 67–87
—— (1986), *The Sacred Hoop: Recovering the Feminine in American Indian Traditions* (Boston, Mass.: Beacon Press)
Babcock, B.A. (1987), 'Taking Liberties, Writing from the Margins, and Doing It with a Difference' in *Journal of American Folklore*, vol. 100, no. 398, pp. 390–411
—— (1988), 'At Home, No Womens Are Storytellers: Potteries, Stories, and Politics in Cochiti Pueblo' in *Journal of the Southwest*, vol. 30, no. 3, pp. 356–89
Babcock, B.A. and Monthan, G. and D. (1986), *The Pueblo Storyteller: Development of a Figurative Ceramic Tradition* (Tucson, Ariz.: University of Arizona Press)
Babcock, B.A. and Parezo, N.J. (1988), *Daughters of the Desert: Women Anthropologists and the Native American Southwest, 1880–1980* (Albuquerque, New Mexico: University of New Mexico Press)
Babcock, B.A. (ed.) (1991), *Pueblo Mothers and Children: Essays by Elsie Clews Parsons, 1915–1924* (Santa Fe, New Mexico: Ancient City Press)
Babcock-Abrahams, B. (1975), '"A Tolerated Margin of Mess": The Trickster and His Tales Reconsidered' in *Journal of the Folklore Institute*, vol. 11, no. 3, pp. 147–86
Basso, K.H. (1966), 'The Gift of Changing Woman' in *Bulletin of the Bureau of American Ethnology*, no. 196 (Washington, DC: Smithsonian Institution)
—— (1970), *The Cibecue Apache* (New York: Holt, Rinehart and Winston)
—— (1979), 'History of Ethnological Research' in A.Ortiz (ed.), *Handbook of North American Indians, Volume 9, Southwest* (Washington, DC: Smithsonian Institution), pp. 14–21
Benedict, R. (1931), 'Tales of the Cochiti Indians' in *Bulletin of the Bureau of American Ethnology*, no. 98 (Washington, DC: Government Printing Office)
Black, M.E. (1984), 'Maidens and Mothers: An Analysis of Hopi Corn Metaphors' in *Ethnology*, vol. 23, no. 4, pp. 279–88
Blackwood, E. (1984), 'Sexuality and Gender in Certain Native American Tribes: The Case

of Cross-Gender Females' in *Signs: Journal of Women and Culture*, vol. 10, no. 1, pp. 27–42

Boyer, R.M. (1972), 'A Mescalero Apache Tale: The Bat and the Flood' in *Western Folklore*, vol. 31, no. 3, pp. 189–97

Bright, W. (1987), 'The Natural History of Old Man Coyote' in B. Swann and A. Krupat (eds), *Recovering the Word: Essays on Native American Literature* (Berkeley: University of California Press), pp. 339–87

Bunzel, R.L. (1932), 'Zuni Katcinas' in *47th Annual Report of the Bureau of American Ethnology for the Years 1929–1930* (Washington, DC: Government Printing Office), pp. 837–108

Callaway, H. (1978), '"The Most Essentially Female Function of All": Giving Birth' in S. Ardener (ed.), *Defining Females: The Nature of Women in Society* (New York: John Wiley & Sons), pp. 163–85

Callender, C. and Kochems, L.M. (1983), 'The Native American Berdache' in *Current Anthropology*, vol. 24, no. 4, pp. 443–70

Carr, P. and Gingerich, W. (1983), 'The Vagina Dentata Motif in Nahuatl and Pueblo Mythic Narratives: A Comparative Study' in B. Swann (ed.), *Smoothing the Ground: Essays on Native American Oral Literature* (Berkeley: University of California Press), pp. 187–203

Clark, L.H. (1966), *They Sang for Horses: The Impact of the Horse on Navajo and Apache Folklore* (Tucson, Ariz.: University of Arizona Press)

Cole, D.C. (1988), *The Chiricahua Apache, 1846–1876: From War to Reservation* (Albuquerque, New Mexico: University of New Mexico Press)

Cushing, P.H. (1896), 'Outlines of Zuni Creation Myths' in *13th Annual Report of the Bureau of American Ethnology for the Years 1891–1892* (Washington, DC: Government Printing Office), pp. 321–447

Dundes, D. (1962), 'Earth-Diver: Creation of the Mythopoeic Male' in *American Anthropologist*, vol. 64, no. 5, pp. 1032–51

Farrer, C.R. (1980), 'Singing for Life: The Mescalero Apache Girls' Ceremony' in C.J. Frisbie (ed.), *Soutwestern Indian Ritual Drama* (Albuquerque, New Mexico: University of New Mexico Press), pp. 125–59

Fewkes, J.W. (1903), 'Hopi Katcinas Drawn by Native Artists' in *21st Annual Report of the Bureau of American Ethnology for the Years 1899-1900* (Washington, DC: Government Printing Office), pp. 13–126

—— (1910), 'The Butterfly in Hopi Myth and Ritual' in *American Anthropologist*, vol. 12, no. 4, pp. 576–94

Foote, C.J. and Schackel, S.K. (1986), 'Indian Women of New Mexico, 1535–1680' in J.M. Jensen and D.A. Miller (eds.), *New Mexico Women: Intercultural Perspectives* (Albuquerque, New Mexico: University of New Mexico Press), pp. 17–40

Frisbie, C.J. (1967), *Kinaalda: A Study of the Navaho Girls' Puberty Ceremony* (Middletown, Conn.: Wesleyan University Press)

—— (ed.) (1980), *Southwestern Indian Ritual Drama* (Albuquerque, New Mexico: University of New Mexico Press)

Geertz, A.W. and Lomatuway'ma, M. (1987), *Children of Cottonwood: Piety and Ceremonialism in Hopi Indian Puppetry*, American Tribal Religions, vol. 12 (Lincoln, Nebr.: University of Nebraska Press)

Gill, S.D. (1982), *Native American Religions: An Introduction* (Belmont, Calif.: Wadsworth)

—— (1983), *Native American Traditions: Sources and Interpretations* (Belmont, Calif.: Wadsworth)

—— (1987), *Mother Earth: An American Story* (Chicago: University of Chicago Press)

Grahn, J. (1984), *Another Mother Tongue: Gay Words. Gay Worlds* (Boston: Beacon Press)

Green, R. (1983), *Native American Women: A Contextual Bibliography* (Bloomington, Ind.: Indiana University)

Griffith, J.S. (1983), 'Kachinas and Masking' in A. Ortiz (ed.), *Handbook of North American*

Indians Volume 10, Southwest (Washington, DC: Smithsonian Institution), pp. 764–77

Haile, P.B. and Haile, O.F.M. (1978), *Love-Magic and Butterfly People: The Slim Curly Version of the Ajilee and Mothway Myths*, American Tribal Religions, vol. 2 (Flagstaff, Ariz.: Museum of Northern Arizona)

—— (1981a), *The Upward Moving and Emergence Way: The Gishin Biye' Version*, American Tribal Religions, vol. 7 (Lincoln, Nebr.: University of Nebraska)

—— (1981b), *Women versus Men: A Conflict of Navajo Emergence. The Curly Tó Aheedlíinnii Version*, American Tribal Religions, vol. 6, (Lincoln, Nebr.: University of Nebraska Press)

—— (1984), *Navajo Coyote Tales: The Curly Tó Aheedlíinnii Version*, American Tribal Religions, vol. 8 (Lincoln, Nebr.: University of Nebraska Press)

Haraway, D. (1988), 'Situated Knowledges: The Science Question in Feminism and the Privilege of Partial Ferspective' in *Feminist Studies*, vol. 14, no. 3, pp. 575–99

Hultkrantz, Å. (1983), 'The Religion of the Goddess in North America' in C. Olson (ed.), *The Book of the Goddess Past and Present: An Introduction to Her Religion* (New York: Crossroad), pp. 202–16

Kealiinohomoku, J.W. (1980), 'The Drama of the Hopi Ogres' in C.J. Frisbie (ed.), *Southwestern Indian Ritual Drama* (Albuquerque, New Mexico: University of New Mexico Press), pp. 37–69

—— (1989), 'The Ecology of Feminism and the Feminism of Ecology' in J. Pratt (ed.), *Healing the Wound: The Promise of Ecofeminism* (Philadelphia, Pa, and Santa Cruz, Calif.: New Society Publishers), pp. 18–28

Kroskrity, P.V. and Healing, D. (1980), 'Coyote-Woman and the Deer Children' in M. B. Kendall (ed.), *Coyote Stories II*, International Journal of American Linguistics Native American Texts Series, no. 6 (Chicago: University of Chicago Press), pp. 119–28

Lamphere, L. (1983), 'Southwestern Ceremonialism' in A. Ortiz, *Handbook of North American Indians Volume 10: Southwest* (Washington, DC: Smithsonian Institution), pp. 743–63

Lincoln, B. (1981), *Emerging from the Chrysalis: Studies in Rituals of Women's Initiation* (Cambridge, Mass.: Harvard University Press)

Malokti, E. (1983), 'The Story of the "Tsimonmamant" or Jimson Weed Girls: A Hopi Narrative Featuring the Motif of the Vagina Dentata' in B. Swann, *Smoothing the Ground: Essays on Native American Oral Literature* (Berkeley: University of California Press), pp. 204–20

Matthews, W. (1897), *Navaho Legends*, Memoirs of the American Folklore Society, vol. 5 (New York: American Folklore Society)

—— (1902), 'Myths of Gestation and Parturition' in *American Anthropologist*, vol. 4, no. 4, pp. 737–42

McLuhan, T.C. (1985), *Dream Tracks: The Railroad and the American Indian. 1890–1930* (New York: Harry N. Abrams)

McNeley, J.K. (1981), *Holy Wind in Navajo Philosophy* (Tucson, Ariz.: University of Arizona Press)

Minh-ha, T.T. (1989), *Woman. Native. Other: Writing Postcolonialism and Feminism* (Bloomington, Ind.: Indiana University Press)

Moon, S. (1984), *Changing Woman and Her Sisters: Feminine Aspects of Selves and Deities* (San Francisco: Guild for Psychological Studies Publishing House)

Nabokov, P. and Easton, R. (1989), *Native American Architecture* (New York: Oxford University Press)

Niethammer, C. (1977), *Daughters of the Earth: The Lives and Legends of American Indian Women* (New York: Collier Books)

Norwood, V. and Monk, J. (eds) (1987), *The Desert Is No Lady: Southwestern Landscapes in Women's Writing and Art* (New Haven, Conn.: Yale University Press)

O'Bryan, A. (1956), 'The Dîné: Origin Myths of the Navajo Indians' in *Bulletin of the Bureau of American Ethnology*, no. 163 (Washington, DC: Government Printing Office)

Opler, M.E. (1936), 'A Summary of Jicarilla Apache Culture' in *American Anthropologist*, vol. 38, no. 2, pp. 202–23

—— (1938), *Myths and Tales of the Jicarilla Apache Indians*, Memoirs of the American Folklore Society, vol. 31 (New York: G.E. Stechert)

—— (1939), *Myths and Tales of the White Mountain Apache*, Memoirs of the American Folklore Society, vol. 33 (New York: J.J. Augustin)

—— (1946), *Childhood and Youth in Jicarilla Apache Society* (Los Angeles: Southwest Museum)

—— (1971), 'Jicarilla Apache Territory, Economy, and Society in 1850' in *Southwestern Journal of Anthropology*, vol. 27, no. 4, pp. 309–29

—— (1983), 'The Apachean Culture Pattern and its Origins' in A. Ortiz (ed.), *Handbook of North American Indians Volume 10: Southwest* (Washington, DC: Smithsonian Institution), pp. 368–92

Ortiz, A., (1969), *The Tewa World: Space. Time. Being. and Becoming in a Pueblo Society* (Chicago: University of Chicago Press)

—— (ed.) (1972), *New Perspectives on the Pueblos* (Albuquerque, New Mexico: University of New Mexico Press)

—— (1972a), 'Ritual Drama and the Pueblo World View' in A. Ortiz (ed.), *New Perspectives on the Pueblos* (Washington, DC: Smithsonian Institution), pp. 135–61

—— (ed.) (1979), *Handbook of North American Indians. Volume 9: Southwest* (Washington, DC: Smithsonian Institution)

—— (ed.) (1983), *Handbook of North American Indians Volume 10: Southwest* (Washington, DC: Smithsonian Institution)

Parezo, N., Hays, K.A. and Slivac, B.P. (1987), 'The Mind's Road: Southwestern Indian Women's Art' in V. Norwood and J. Monk (eds), *The Desert is No Lady: Southwestern Landscapes in Women's Writing and Art* (New Haven, Conn.: Yale University Press), pp. 146–73

Parsons, E.C. (1926), *Tewa Tales*, Memoirs of the American Folklore Society, vol. 19 (New York: G.E. Stechert)

—— (1939), *Pueblo Indian Religion*, 2 vols (Chicago: University of Chicago Press)

Pomeroy, E. (1957), *In Search of the Golden West: The Tourist in Western America* (New York: Alfred A. Knopf)

Purley, A.P. (1974), 'Keres Pueblo Concepts of Deity' in *American Indian Culture and Research Journal*, vol. 1, no. 1, pp. 29–32

Radin, P. (1956), *The Trickster* (New York: Philosophical Library)

Reichard, G.A. (1974), *Navaho Religion: A Study of Symbolism*, 2nd edn, Bollingen Series 18 (Princeton, NJ: Princeton University Press)

Rodríguez, S. (1989), 'Art, Tourism, and Race Relations in Taos: Toward a Sociology of the Art Colony' in *Journal of Anthropological Research*, vol. 45, no. 1, pp. 77–99

Smith, P.C., with Allen, P.G. (1987), 'Earthy Relations, Carnal Knowledge: Southwestern American Indian Women Writers and Landscape' in V. Norwood and J. Monk (eds), *The Desert is No Lady: Southwestern Landscapes in Women's Writing and Art* (New Haven, Conn.: Yale University Press), pp. 174–96

Spencer, K. (1957), *Mythology and Values: An Analysis of Navaho Chantway Myths*, Memoirs of the American Folklore Society, vol. 48 (Philadelphia, Pa: American Folklore Society)

Stevenson, M.C. (1904), 'The Zuni Indians: Their Mythology, Esoteric Fraternities, and Ceremonies' in *23rd Annual Report of the Bureau of American Ethnology for the Years 1901–1902* (Washington, DC: Government Printing Office), pp. 3–634

Stirling, M.W. (1942), 'Origin Myth of Acoma and Other Records' in *Bulletin of the Bureau of American Ethnology*, no. 135 (Washington, DC: Government Printing Office)

Swann, B. (ed.) (1983), *Smoothing the Ground: Essays on Native American Oral Literature* (Berkeley: University of California Press)

Swann, B. and Krupat, A. (eds) (1987), *Recovering the Word: Essays on Native American Literature* (Berkeley: University of California Press)

Sweet, J.D. (1985), *Dances of the Tewa Pueblo Indians: Expressions of New Life* (Santa Fe, New Mexico: School of American Research Press)

Swentzell, R. and Naranjo, T. (1986), 'Nurturing: The *Gia* at Santa Clara Pueblo' in *El Palacio*, vol. 92, no. 1, pp. 35–9

Tedlock, D. (1979), 'Zuni Religion and World View' in A. Ortiz (ed.), *Handbook of North American Indians Volume 9: Southwest* (Washington, DC: Smithsonian Institution), pp. 499–508

—— (1983), *The Spoken Word and the Work of Interpretation* (Philadelphia: University of Pennsylvania Press)

Thomas, D.H. (1978), *The Southwestern Indian Detours: The Story of the Fred Harvey/Santa Fe Railway Experiment in 'Detourism'* (Phoenix, Ariz.: Hunter Publishing)

Tiller, V. (1983), 'Jicarilla Apache' in A. Ortiz (ed.), *Handbook of North American Indians Volume 10: Southwest* (Washington DC: Smithsonian Institution), pp. 440–61

Todorov, T. (1984), *The Conquest of America: The Question of the Other*, trans. R. Howard (New York: Harper and Row)

Toelken, B. (1976a), 'A Circular World: The Vision of Navajo Crafts' in *Parabola*, vol. 1, no. 1, pp. 30–7

—— (1976b), 'Seeing with a Native Eye How Many Sheep Will It Hold?' in W.H. Capps with B.P. Tonsing (eds), *Seeing with a Native Eye: Essays on American Indian Religion* (New York: Harper & Row), pp. 9–24

—— (1987), 'Life and Death in the Navajo Coyote Tales' in B. Swann and A. Krupat (eds), *Recovering the Word: Essays on Native American Literature* (Berkeley: University of California Press), pp. 388–401

Tyler, H.A. (1964), *Pueblo Gods and Myths* (Norman, Okla: University of Oklahoma Press)

Tylor, P.B. (1873), *Primitive Culture: Researches into the Development of Mythology. Philosophy. Religion. Language. Art and Custom*, 2 vols (London: John Murray)

Voth, H.R. (1905), *Traditions of the Hopi*, Field Museum of Natural History, pub. 96, Anthropological Series 8 (Chicago: Field Museum of Natural History)

Weigle, M. (1982), *Spiders & Spinsters: Women and Mythology* (Albuquerque, New Mexico: University of New Mexico Press)

—— (1989), *Creation and Procreation: Feminist Reflections on Mythologies of Cosmogony and Parturition* (Philadelphia, Pa: University of Pennsylvania)

—— (1989a), 'From Desert to Disney World: The Santa Fe Railway and the Fred Harvey Company Display the Indian Southwest' in *Journal of Anthropological Research*, vol. 45, no. 1, pp. 115–37

Wheeler-Voegelin, B. and Moore, R.W. (1957), 'The Emergence Myth in Native North America' in W. E. Richmond (ed.), *Studies in Folklore*, Indiana University Publications in Folklore, no. 9 (Bloomington, Ind.: Indiana University Press), pp. 66–91

White, L.A. (1962), 'The Pueblo of Sia, New Mexico' in *Bulletin of the Bureau of American Ethnology*, no. 184 (Washington, DC: Government Printing Office)

Whitehead, H. (1981), 'The Bow and the Burden Strap: A New Look at Institutionalized Homosexuality in Native North America' in S.B. Ortner and H. Whitehead (eds), *Sexual Meanings: The Cultural Construction of Gender and Sexuality* (Cambridge: Cambridge University Press), pp. 80–115

Wiget, A. (ed.) (1985), *Critical Essays on Native American Literature* (Boston: G.K. Hall)

Witherspoon, G. (1977), *Language and Art in the Navajo Universe* (Ann Arbor, Mich.: University of Michigan Press)

Woodbury, R.B. (1979), 'Prehistory: Introduction' in A. Ortiz (ed.), *Handbook of North American Indians Volume 9: Southwest* (Washington DC: Smithsonian Institution), pp. 22–30

Wyman, L.C. (1957), *Beautyway: A Navaho Ceremonial*, Bollingen Series 53 (New York: Pantheon Books)

—— (1962), *The Windways of the Navaho* (Colorado Springs, Colorado: The Taylor Museum of the Colorado Springs Pine Arts Center)

—— (1970), *Blessingway: With Three Versions of the Myth Recorded and Translated from the Navaho by Father Berard Haile* (Tucson, Ariz.: University of Arizona Press)

—— (1973), *The Red Antway of the Navaho*, Navajo Religion Series, vol. 5 (Santa Fe, New Mexico: Museum of Navaho Ceremonial Art)

—— (1975), *The Mountainway of the Navajo* (Tucson, Ariz.: University of Arizona Press)

—— (1983), 'Navajo Ceremonial System' in A. Ortiz (ed.), *Handbook of North American Indians Volume 9: Southwest* (Washington, DC: Smithsonian Institution), pp. 536–57

Young, M.J. (1987), 'Women, Reproduction, and Religion in Western Puebloan Society' in *Journal of American Folklore*, vol. 100, no. 398, pp. 436–45

SUSANNA ROSTAS

Mexican Mythology
Divine Androgyny But 'His' Story;
The Female in Aztec Mythology

SECTION I: INTRODUCTION

Mexico has not one but many mythologies. By the time of the Spanish Conquest in 1519, many male-centred high cultures had risen and subsequently been swept away or merged with the new. Today there are still some seventy indigenous groups who speak their own languages and have their own distinctive cultural traditions and vibrant mythologies. Mexico is thus, in many ways, even now not one nation but many.

In a historical sense, however, it is possible to speak of Mexican mythology, referring to the body of mythologies of the various Nahuatl speaking groups who lived in the Valley of Mexico in the century or so before the Spanish Conquest. These formed the basis of the mythology of the imperialist Aztecs, who consciously reconstructed history to represent themselves as the original descendants of the deities. It is largely their version of the mythologies that have come down to us today.

This chapter concentrates on the feminine in Aztec mythology, although we know little of the female figures and even less of their antecedents. I shall attempt however to point to the kinds of transformations in the goddesses that occurred as the many mythologies of the small groups, who coexisted with other rather similar neighbours, mostly on a semi-peaceful basis, were incorporated into the mythology of an expansionist empire that stretched from the Gulf of Mexico to the Pacific Ocean and as far south as Guatemala. I shall also look briefly at the changes that occurred soon after the Spanish conquest, and point to an example of one community where pre-Hispanic elements still appear in the mythology today.

I.1 'His' Story – Mythology

There were no written records until after the arrival of the Spanish and myths were thus transmitted verbally, in daily speech and through ritual and ceremony. But there are visual representations of the deities in the form of sculptures and the pictographs in the codices – unfolding screen books made from deer skin or the bark of fig trees (*amate*). The codices recorded information in a sequence of pictorial images and are primarily about the activities of leaders and deities. Often an entire myth is recorded in one image. The written sources from shortly after the Conquest are collections of poetry, ethnographic accounts of daily life and of mytho-religious practices and beliefs. But in both types of sources, it is largely only mythological characters, rather than many of their attendant myths, which make an appearance. The friars who wrote such accounts frequently had difficulty putting aside their Christian world view while their male informants often told them in part what they wanted to hear. Durán, a Franciscan, saw, for example, many parallels between Christian baptism and what appeared to be a form of it practised by the Aztecs (*see* Section II.8, Chalchiuhtlicue, p. 375). He even found a Trinity; for he claimed the Aztecs revered the Father, the Son and the Holy Ghost, calling them Tota, Topiltzin and Yolometl ('Our Father', 'Our Son' and the 'Heart of Both'). Reference was made too to Greek mythology; the goddess Chicomecóatl (*see* II.7, p. 374) being likened to Ceres, Cihuacóatl (*see* II.1, p. 370) to Venus and Chalchiuhtlicue (*see* II.8, p. 375) to Juno in Nahuatl texts recorded by Sahagún, another Franciscan friar and a first class ethnographer. But the information we have is strongly influenced not only by the fact that those who went to New Spain were men, but also by the fact that their informants were often members of the nobility. We thus have much less information about the beliefs and superstitions of the mass of the people and particularly of women.

I.2

What little we do know of female representation in mythology has to be seen in the context of a long history. The Classic Period (AD 150 to 900) saw the rise of the city of Teotihuacán in the Valley of Mexico and of the Maya in the Yucatan and Chiapas. The Teotihuacán deities were, by the middle of this period, shared by most other Mexican people: a rain god, Tláloc and his consort, Chalchiuhtlicue (*see* II.8, p. 375), the sun god, Tonatiuh and moon goddess, Metzli (*see* II.3, p. 372) and Quetzalcóatl, the Feathered Serpent. These deities were later on to form the basis of the Aztec pantheon, although the importance of Quetzalcóatl, in particular, was greatly diminished.

Teotihuacán and the later Tula, centre of Toltec culture to the west, are the two strongest cultural influences on the Aztecs. Teotihuacán flourished until c. AD 650, when the city was destroyed. Its importance as a religious centre, particularly for the god Quetzalcóatl, continued however. As he was the god of arts and learning, much emphasis was placed on these, reflected in the sophistication and artistry of the people. For Quetzalcóatl had both male and female qualities (*see* II.2, p. 371). At its height, Teotihuacán is thought to have been a city of a quarter of a million people with a well-developed pantheon of gods.

The rise of the Toltecs began in about AD 900 and at first Quetzalcóatl symbolized their culture; a man named Topiltzin-Quetzalcóatl was the great priest-ruler of Tula. But Quetzalcóatl as a god had a rival called Tezcatlipoca, a less benevolent deity, god of the night and the north, who aimed to set up a militaristic cult fed by human sacrifice. Topiltzin-Quetzalcóatl was forced to flee and, reaching the coast, was reborn as the morning star, while in a different version of the myth he leaves on a raft of serpents, journeying to the east and promising one day to return. When the Spaniards appeared, Moctezuma II, then Aztec ruler, mistook Cortés for the returning Quetzalcóatl.

After the demise of Tula (c. 1150), some Toltec traditions were kept up in the Valley of Mexico by those who had escaped. There were continuous invasions again by 'barbaric' peoples, known collectively as the Chichimeca, and a number of small, not very powerful, tribal kingdoms developed. The Chichimec wanderers who founded Tenochtitlan ('The Place of the Fruit of the Cactus'), which is today Mexico City, are said to have come from Aztlan in the north and hence became known as the Aztecs. They left the seven caves of their native land with an image of their tribal deity, Huitzilopochtli ('Hummingbird of the Left'). Their nomadic journey from Aztlan is thought to have taken two centuries and to have been fraught with difficulties. They eventually settled as defeated serfs in a place infested with snakes and vermin which they managed to make habitable. Their abilities as warriors were admired by their suzerains, one of whose princesses they requested as a wife for Huitzilopochtli; but they killed and flayed her. They were thus expelled and forced to continue their wanderings. Finally, they recognized the place where Huitzilopochtli had predicted that they were destined to settle by a sign: an eagle perched on a cactus, holding a serpent in its beak. This symbol appears today on the Mexican flag (*see* II.2, p. 371).

The Aztecs were thus descendants of nomadic peoples, belligerent in attitude and more interested in military expansion than in cultural creation. Their rise to power was rapid, but their policy of conquest outside the Valley of Mexico was to last only eighty years before being cut short by the arrival of the Spaniards. However, the city of Tenochtitlan was built mainly of stone and was greatly admired by their conquerors who compared it to Seville. The cultural heritage of the past and of the many peoples they subsequently conquered was incorporated into Aztec mythology. Huitzilopochtli, previously unknown in central Mexico, was rapidly elevated to the position of principal deity at the expense of the older deities: Tláloc and Chalchiuhtlicue, Quetzalcóatl and even the newer Tezcatlipoca.

The majority of those who lived in, or were incorporated into, this rapidly expanding empire were peasants whose way of life did not change much in material detail. It was remarkably similar to that of indigenous people in the more isolated parts of Mexico even today. Although men and women lived out their lives in rather separate spheres in a social sense, physically they were much less differentially gendered than their city counterparts would have been. Men probably had more intercourse with the wider world than women, who were largely responsible for the daily round of preparing and cooking food at home. Women also wove and made pottery. Although the family was headed by the man, women had responsibility in the house. But there was a complementarity of the sexes and their roles tended to overlap; the prime focus of daily life for both was activity in the fields. Rural people believed that their lives were controlled by the many deities representing the different forces of nature, the elements and the heavenly bodies. Spirits were divine but could also take the form of monsters. Worship of Huitzilopochtli was usually imposed on such people, but loyalty to their local indigenous deities often remained strong. Beliefs and practices among the Aztec were thus very varied.

Life in the city of Tenochtitlan was rather different. Aztec society was highly stratified and each social class and profession had its own deity; there were thirty distinct classes of priests and priestesses. The nobility (members of those families who had led Tenochtitlan to victory), were well educated. Noble women were as important as their brothers; women could hold high office, inherit property and own slaves. Both boys and girls were sent to the *Calmécac*, where they learnt by memory from priests and priestesses. Such an education was a prerequisite for a religious life. Children of the merchant classes attended another type of school, in the case of girls this was called the *Ichpocacalli*. Here they were trained in housekeeping and agriculture, and also taught the precepts of Aztec society. These were part-time boarding schools, while the *Calmécac* were full-time and both educated children until the late teens. There were also schools called the *Cuicacalli* which taught singing, dancing and the playing of musical instruments.

Women thus received an equal education with men. However, the Spaniards were informed that, in general, marriage was the best way for a woman to seek advancement. Sahagún talks about the robustness of the common woman, whom he shows not only involved in activities within the household, but also selling food, dyes, feathers and herbs in the market. He also comments on their role as curers, midwives and bonesetters (Sahagún, 1961). Citizens were taxed and men were expected to perform military service. All except slaves had access to land to grow what they needed for subsistence, either in Tenochtitlan itself or on nearby shores. Although land was considered to belong to the earth deities, each district of the city (*calpulli*) had territories which were leased out to its inhabitants.

I.3

While the mass of Aztecs accepted unquestioningly their mythology as valid cosmogonic explanation, by the time of the Spanish conquest philosophers had started to be more analytical. The Nahuas distinguished between concepts based on observation and experience and those based on superstition and magic. They had, for example, well-developed curative techniques using herbal remedies, and with their calendars could make complex astronomical calculations. They had two calendars, the 365-day solar calendar built up of eighteen named months of twenty days, plus five 'unlucky days', which was employed in conjunction with the earlier *tonalpohualli* of 260 days consisting of a series of twenty-day signs linked to thirteen numbers. This latter was a divinatory calendar used for casting horoscopes. The two together produced the fifty-two year calendar round and were more accurate than the calendar with which the Spaniards arrived; one or both are still in operation today in parts of Central America. The twenty-day signs were the names of objects, animals and plants and are often incorporated into those of the deities, while both the eighteen-months and the twenty-day signs are linked to particular deities (*see* tables 1 and 2).

Table 1 The 18 Months of 20 Days and Their Associated Deities * = Female

1	Cuahuitlehua or Atlcahualo	Tlaloque & *Chalchiuhtlicue
2	Tlacaxipehualiztli	Xipe Totec (Our Flayed Lord)
3	Tozoztontli	Tláloc & *Coatlicue
4	Hueitozozoli	Cinteotl & *Chicomecóatl
5	Toxcatl	Titlacauan & Tezcatlipoca
6	Etzalcualiztli	Tláloc
7	Tecuilhuitontli	*Huixtocíhuatl (Salt Goddess)
8	Huey Tecuilhuitl	Xilonen and *Cihuacóatl
9	Tlaxochimaco	Huitzilopochtli or Micallhuitontli
10	Xocotlhuetzi	The Otomi form of Xiuhtecuhtli (God of Fire)
11	Ochpaniztli	*Toci or *Teteoinnan
12	Teotleco	All the Gods or Pachtontli
13	Tepeilhuitl	*Xochiquetzal or Huey Patchli
14	Quecholli	Mixcóatl & Camaxtli
15	Panquetzaliztli	Huitzilopochtli
16	Atemoztli	Tláloc & *Chalchiuhtlicue
17	Tititl	Ilamatecuhtli or *Tonan
18	Izcalli	Xiuhtecuhtli (Lord of the Year)
	Nenmontemi (the 5 unlucky days)	Mountain Gods

Table 2 The 20-day Signs and Their Associated Deities

Cipactl (crocodile)	Tonancatecuhtli
Ehecatl (wind)	Quetzalcóatl
Calli (house)	Tepeyollotli
Cuetzpalin	Huehuecoyotl
Cóatl (snake)	*Chalchiuhtlicue
Miquiztli (death)	*Meztli, *Coyolxanliqui
Mazatl (deer)	Tláloc
Tochtli (rabbit)	*Mayahuel
Atl (water)	Xiuhtecuhtli
Itzcuintli (dog)	Mictlantecuhtli
Ozomahtli (monkey)	Xochipilli, Centeotl
Malinalli (prairie grass)	Patecatl
Acatl (reed)	Tezcatlipoca
Ocelotl (ocelot)	*Tlazoltéotl
Cuauhtli (eagle)	Xipe Totec, Tezcatlipoca
Cocacuauhtli (vulture)	*Itzpapalotl
Ollin (rolling movement)	Xolotl
Tecpatl (flintstone)	Tezcatlipoca
Quiahuitl	Tonatiuh
Xochitl	*Xochiquetzal

Source: Duran and Sahagún
Brundage (1979) lists *Chicomecóatl as linked to the second not to the third; Xochipilii as linked to the seventh; *Chicomecóatl as linked to the eleventh; and *Cihuacóatl as being linked with the seventeenth month. Nicholson (1971) lists *Chalchiuhtlicue as additionally linked to the third and the sixth; *Chicomecóatl as linked to the third and *Coatlicue to the fourteenth; and *Tlazoltéotl and *Atlatonan to the eleventh.

Source: Codices Borgia and Vaticanus in Van Zantwijk, 1977, p. 236

It was believed that the deities could manifest themselves as actual people. Thus Topiltzin-Quetzalcóatl in Tula was both a man and a god. His case was not unique however; various of the Aztec Emperors claimed a divine status. In oral traditions, it is often difficult to distinguish between historical fact and myth, just as in the available records it is difficult to distinguish between women who were historical figures and goddesses. As in Greek mythology, the psychic qualities or particular aspects of different types of personalities are represented by the deities, but with the few sources available to us we have little information on this, and particularly for those feminine ones. Finally, those living in Tenochtitlan, especially the nobility, were highly individuated and differentially gendered socially, physically and psychologically, rather as westerners have been until recently. The mass of the people, however, as members of largely egalitarian societies where the boundaries between the sexes were less tightly drawn up, placed less emphasis on gender differences. This is reflected in Aztec cosmology, where it is sometimes difficult to tell whether a deity is male or female (*see* fig. 34).

I.4 Cosmology – Mythology

The Aztec concept of the universe revolved around the great solar myth. In the standard version, there had already been four historical ages, known as 'Suns'. Each had in turn been destroyed and the Aztecs believed themselves to be in the fifth age, that of the 'Sun of Movement' (*Ollin Tonatiuh*) which was predicted to end also. During this 'Sun', there would be earthquakes and famines, and human beings would finally vanish forever.

The world was believed to consist of a disc surrounded by water (*Cemanahuac*), with the metaphysical or transcendental sphere of Topan (above) and Mictlan (below). The phenomenal world itself was seen to be very transitory:

> Not forever on earth, but briefly here. Even jades are shattered. Gold, broken. Ah! plumes, splintered. Not forever on earth, but briefly here.
>
> (BIERHORST, 1985A, P. 185)

For the key to the origin of the universe, the Aztecs turned their attention to Topan. Their advanced knowledge of astronomical calculation was reflected in the complex system of symbolic explanation which forms their cosmology.

Order was given to the universe by Ometéotl, universal cosmic energy and the origin of all natural forces. Ometéotl was the supreme deity, deity of duality both masculine and feminine. Ometéotl appears in various paired aspects, although masculine and feminine are not necessarily fully anthropomorphic. But Ometéotl also engendered children who are divinities in their own right and the mothers and fathers of all the other deities. 'Téotl', often translated as deity, is used also in songs to refer to stars, the sun, the moon, to birds, mammals and serpents, and to fire – in fact, to most aspects of nature. 'Téotl' thus falls short of the theistic term 'god', and is probably best conceived of as spirit (Bierhorst, 1985b).

Ometéotl lived in Omeyocan, where as Ometecuhtli and Omecíhuatl, ('Lord and

Lady of Duality'), the divine couple begot children. Ometéotl is also sometimes referred to as Tonancatecuhtli and Tonacacíhuatl ('Lord and Lady of our Maintenance or Sustenance') and more briefly as Tonan or Tonantzin, 'Our Mother', and Tota, 'Our Father'.

The heavens were believed to have thirteen layers. The earth's surface constituted the first. Through the second level travelled the moon (Metzli), likened to a rabbit, and it was also associated with Tláloc – the place rain came from and where the clouds were suspended. The third heaven, called Citlalco, was the place of the stars, of Citlalinicue ('She of the Skirt of Stars') (*see* II.13, p. 378) and Citlallatónac ('He of the Day whose Light Envelops'). The fourth heaven was that of the sun (Tonatuih). The fifth was that of the star Venus, associated with Quetzalcóatl. In the sixth heaven were the comets, 'the smoking stars'; in the seventh and eighth only colours were seen – the seventh black, the eighth blue; while the ninth was a place of storms. The tenth, eleventh and twelfth were associated with white, yellow and red were the dwelling places of the deities, while the thirteenth constituted Omeyocan. There were, in addition, nine underworlds, the ninth was the domain of Mictlan, where Ometéotl manifested as Mictlantecuhtli and Mictecacíhuatl ('Lord and Lady of the Underworld').

But although Ometéotl lived in Omeyocan and 'peopled' both the over- and underworlds, Ometéotl was also said to be at the navel of the earth, that is on its surface, at its centre and at the midpoint of the four cardinal directions. Ometéotl was in addition both day and night and as 'Lord of the Waters', Ometéotl is both Chalchiuhtlicue ('She of the Jade Skirt') (*see* II.8, p. 375) and Chalchiuhtlatonac ('He who Shines like a Sun of Jade'). Thus Ometéotl engendered not only dualities at most levels of the over- and underworld, but manifested on the earth's surface quadrupally and quintupally. Although most of the deities are referred to in the singular, they often appeared in duos or foursomes (the Tezcatlipocas) and fivesomes (*see* the Cihuateteo, II.14, p. 378).

Ometéotl, as Tonancatecuhtli and Tonacacíhuatl, engendered four sons, who were each linked to one of the cardinal directions. All were called Tezcatlipoca (shining black, or more usually, smoking mirror) although sometimes the third and fourth sons are called Quetzalcóatl and Huitzilopochtli. The first son, known as the red (or white) Tezcatlipoca, was associated with the east; the second with black and the north; the third, Quetzalcóatl, with white and the west, sometimes known as Cíhuatlampa and believed to be the land of women and the paradise to which those who had died in childbirth went. The fourth, Huitzilopochtli, was the smallest and became the principal deity of the Aztecs, associated with blue and the south, an area located to the left of the sun.

After their birth, the four sons created fire, a half sun and moon, the land of the dead, the place of the waters and the regions beyond the heavens. According to one version (*Historia de Los Mexicanos*), the sons Quetzalcóatl and Huitzilopochtli made the first man and woman: he was called Oxomoco and she Cipactónal (*see* II.15, p. 379). This couple in their turn created mankind: the Macehualtin, 'the chosen people', a term later used to refer to the common people.

Aztec thought blended ideas about cosmology with the mytho-historical. Each son had a period of ascendancy known as a 'Sun' which he won in a battle against the others, and during which there was equilibrium; the times between each change were tumultuous. Every age was linked to one of the elements; the first to earth, the second to the wind, the third to fire and the last to water. At the end of each 'Sun' or age, it was destroyed by the element that controlled it.

Although the creation myth is dominated by males in its early stages, the fourth 'Sun' was ruled by a woman, the wife of Tláloc, the goddess Chalchiuhtlicue (see II.8, p. 375). She ruled for 676 years but towards the end of her era, it rained for fifty-two years and life on earth ceased as all were swallowed up by the water and became fish.

After the disastrous end of the fourth 'Sun', a new cycle began. Quetzalcóatl voyaged to Mictlan to procure human bones to carry out the new creation. This creation took place at Teotihuacán. According to one version, all the principal deities assembled and one god sacrificed himself by throwing himself into a huge brazier to be reborn as the 'Sun'. This was the first sacrifice to Huitzilopochtli. This myth still exists today in a somewhat modified and christianized form in the community of Yaonáhuac, in the mountains of Puebla (Taggart, 1983, p. 88).

The fifth 'Sun' differed from the other four. Like the others, it was stationary to begin with, but then became a 'Sun' of movement, following a path as it rose and fell; space and time as we know them now came into existence. This is the 'Sun' of our era. The Aztecs believed that they had a cosmic struggle on their hands: the need to feed this 'Sun' to keep it moving and prevent the cataclysm that would put an end to it, too. As 'the People of the Sun', the Aztecs had to provide the sacred liquid required by the deity: blood drawn from sacrificial victims. To provide these victims, war had been instigated by Tezcatlipoca who created 400 men (possibly the 'Four Hundred Southerners') and five women, one of whom was Coatlicue (see II.2, p. 371).

Previous cultures, such as the Maya, had sacrificed the losers in a ceremonial ball game played between enemies. In the era of Aztec ascendancy, such sacrifices were either of prisoners taken during wars or the victims of the so-called *guerras floridas* (flower wars). The flower wars were ceremonial battles between neighbouring states, expressly fought to provide prisoners, which in the final years of the Empire were sacrificed in ever increasing numbers. The Maya had practised individual blood-letting as a means to achieve transcendent states of mind, and get closer to the deities. This practice was continued by the Aztecs and the eventual sacrifice of a captive who had been honoured as a god-substitute during a festival was its extreme manifestation. In the early sixteenth century, the 'Sun' was increasingly represented by the images of Cihuacóatl (see II.1, p. 370) and Huitzilopochtli.

The fifth 'Sun' almost moves out of mythological time into historical time. It is an era dominated, at least in the last two centuries before the Spanish Conquest, by increasingly militaristic tendencies. The highly chauvinistic qualities of the god Huitzilopochtli are far from the dualities of Ometéotl, the dual qualities of

Quetzalcóatl and Chalchiuhtlicue, the female ruler of the fourth 'Sun'. But Huitzilopochtli, as befitted the nature of the fifth 'Sun', although superhuman, was also 'but subject, and monarch [to the people], [yet] a fascinating, bewildering phenomenon', incarnate in the Aztecs themselves – the ideal of the warrior (quoted by Van Zantwijk, 1977, p. 129).

Thus, during the Aztec era as philosophy grew in importance, the dual metaphysical forms of Ometéotl multiplied and increased in complexity, such as Moyucoyatzin, the one who mentally conceives or creates him/herself. The educated elite were taught that all the deities were but different aspects of a single, supreme supernatural force known also as Tloque Nahuaque ('Ever Present Ever Near'). Merchants on their travels were expected to refrain from adultery having been warned that 'in every stone, in every tree the Omnipresent One (Ometéotl) is watching you'. However, for people of Tenochtitlan, the deities that they had dealings with on a daily basis were generally far removed from the non-anthropomorphic dual qualities of Ometéotl. Huitzilopochtli was almost a man, and a hunter and warrior. The goddesses, though sometimes represented as almost human, often retained more of their former characteristics of zoomorphism and androgyny, especially in the countryside. Aztec mythology was complex, the older deities of cosmology and popular expression being overlaid by the newer deities of social control. At the time of the conquest, there were some two thousand deities, accumulated from the various conquered nations that made up the Empire. Only some of these were goddesses.

SECTION II: THE GODDESSES

II.1 Cihuacóatl

'She of the Serpent Skirt', or 'Snake Woman', was the most feared and effective of the goddesses; the principal Aztec female deity. Cihuacóatl was said to be Huitzilopochtli's mother or female companion and shared a priesthood with him. It was she who incited Huitzilopochtli to war and had an enormous hunger for victims. In Tenochtitlan she was 'fed' prisoners every eight days. More victims were sacrificed to Cihuacóatl than even to Huitzilopochtli.

Cihuacóatl had been the great goddess of the Xochimilca; after their defeat she was taken over by the Aztecs and installed in Tenochtitlan. Her image was of stone and stood in her 'black house', a low shrine in the vicinity of the main plaza, where the pyramids to Tláloc and Huitzilopochtli and to Tezcatlipoca were located. The inside was dark, its entrance stopped by a plug; it thus had earthy, cave-like qualities. Unlike those of the other principal deities, her image was never moved as her priests dared not touch her. In front stood the fire god's hearth in which a perpetual fire burned. Her temple also housed the stone effigies of many other deities, which were taken out to the mountains, woods or into the caves from which they had originally been removed, either when their feast days had arrived or their help was needed. The cults of the countryside were thus subservient to Cihuacóatl, giving the Aztecs control over terrain up to 100 miles from Tenochtitlan.

Cihuacóatl was depicted with her lower face made only of bone, and her jaws wide open waiting for victims. Her hair was long and stringy and a pair of knives formed a diadem on her forehead. She was related to evil omens, was savage and brought misery to 'men'; for it was she who gave men the digging stick and the tump line. She was a night walker, screaming and weeping copiously, but she was also a warrior; on her back she carried the knife of sacrifice swaddled like a child.

Her original patronage of wild vegetation, which links her to the Chichimeca past, had largely been forgotten by the Aztecs, but as Quilaztli, she was still called upon during a difficult birth.

Cihuacóatl personified for the Aztecs the collective hunger for human victims of all the deities. There were more festivals for her than any other deity in the annual calendar. She was utilized by the state in maintaining its apparatus of government: the chief administrator of internal affairs was called the *cihuacóatl*. She was not so much a woman as the representation of the negative side of the female psyche.

II.2 Coatlicue

Coatlicue was a telluric goddess, represented by the Aztecs as part human, part zoomorphic (*see* fig. 34). She too had a thirst for blood and was hideous. Her hands are depicted as fanged serpents' heads, her feet as large claws. Her head is two coiled snakes' heads or her head may have been severed, the snakes thus possibly spurts of blood. However, her breasts are clearly visible under a necklace consisting of human hands and hearts and a pendant made of a human skull, while her skirt is a writhing mass of serpents.

'Cóatl' means snake, representing for the Mexicans the fertility of the earth and the female psyche; Cihuacóatl could change herself into a snake. But it also means 'twin', indicating reciprocity. Quetzalcóatl, one of the few gods' names in which 'cóatl' appears, was an old god who clearly represents both the masculine, the quetzal bird, and the feminine, the snake. 'Quetzalcóatl' is sometimes also glossed as the 'heavenly twins'. Coatlicue in a similar way combines the more aggressive male eagle and the female snake; the two symbols which appear on the Mexican flag.

In her myth, Coatlicue is the widowed mother of Huitzilopochtli. She already had 400 sons, the Centzon Huitznalwa ('Four Hundred Southerners') and a daughter, the goddess Coyolxanliqui (*see* II.3). While Coatlicue was sweeping one day, a tuft of feathers fell from the heavens which miraculously impregnated her. Coyolxanliqui was indignant at her mother's apparent sexual transgression, and malevolently incited her brothers to matricide. During the planned assault, on the primordial mountain, a defector amongst the half brothers warned Huitzilopochtli, then still in the womb, and he was born fully accoutred and armed. He slew some of his half-brothers, scattered the rest and decapitated Coyolxanliqui. Her body broke into many pieces and only her head remained intact.

Coatlicue was the patroness of florists. In Tenochtitlan she was worshipped as Our Mother Cóatlan, the name of one of the wards of the city.

Fig. 34 Sculpture of Coatlicue.
*Werner Forman Archive National
Museum of Anthropology, Mexico*

II.3 Coyolxanliqui

Coyolxanliqui is probably an Aztec avatar of the older moon deity, Metzli, who was often represented as male. Coyolxanliqui is depicted either as a warrior with naked breasts but helmeted head and snakes entwined around her arms and waist, or as a huge decapitated head, suggestive of the moon. The moon, so important in Teotihuacán, was of much less significance to the Aztecs, with their cult of the sun. Her half-brother Huitzilopochtli was born to combat her and her brothers, the stars. He thus rises every morning as the sun to do battle with the elements of the night.

II.4 Itzpapolotl

Itzpapolotl, 'Obsidian Knife Butterfly', was a goddess probably of Chichimec origin. The myth about her involves the Four Hundred Mimixcoa who were rather similar to the Four Hundred Southerners. They lived in the original seven caves in Aztlan and were a turbulent group, children of the earth goddess and the sun, who defied their parents. They were avenged by five additional children, one of whom became known as the god Mixcóatl (the singular form of the plural Mimixcoa). (*See* II.8, p. 375 and II.10, p. 376.)

Two of the Mimixcoa were out hunting when a pair of two-headed deer descended from the sky. The two hunters Xiuhnel ('True Turquoise') and Mimich ('Arrow Fish') pursued them but without success. Becoming tired, they desisted and set up camp for the night. The two deer then turned into women, and one of them persuaded Xiuhnel to drink some blood. He did so, copulated with her and devoured her. Then the other, Itzpapolotl, attempted to entice Mimich to eat, but instead he made a fire and threw himself into it. Itzpapolotl quickly followed him into the world of the fire, but a giant cactus had fallen from the sky which prevented her from continuing the pursuit. One of the demons dwelling in the sky saw this and tried to cast a dart at her but she escaped and wandered desolately 'combing her hair, painting her face' and lamenting the loss of Mimich. The fire gods hearing of this episode cast her once again into the fire with Mimich, whereupon she burst into five different-coloured slivers of stone. Mixcóatl picked up the white piece, which was the obsidian knife of sacrifice, wrapped it in a bundle and henceforth carried it on his back as a god in all his conquests.

Itzpapolotl was identified as an earth goddess, her spirit companion was the deer, but her offer of food to Mimich is not so much as mother nurturer but rather as a challenger. She has combative powers as does Coyolxanliqui. She is perhaps an earlier goddess of death and war, precursor of Cihuacóatl.

II.5 Tonantzin

There is a range of goddesses that represent, even more directly than Coatlicue, the power of the earth. Tonan or Tonantzin ('Our Holy Mother') was their collective name, the name given to many mountains and to the headland where, after the Spanish Conquest, the Virgin of Guadalupe (see IV.1, p. 385) is said to have appeared.

II.6 Toci or Teteoinnan

Toci, 'Our Grandmother', or Teteoinnan, 'Mother of the Gods', had female as well as chthonic qualities. Healers and physicians looked to Toci for guidance. She was the patroness of midwives, of 'those who administered sedatives at childbirth, and of those who performed abortions. Those who read the future, either by casting grains of maize or looking into water or using knotted cords consulted her.' Bath houses (temezcal), in which cleansing sweat baths were taken by men and women together, were dedicated to Teteoinnan and her image placed in front of or buried under the house.

Toci's shrine called Cihuateocalli ('House of Women') stood at the gates of the city and was a simple structure consisting of a raised platform made of wood. Here stood a white-faced but black-bodied straw image holding the paraphernalia necessary for spinning and weaving. Her principal representation, made from wood, was housed with all the other gods in the temple of Huitzilopochtli. Toci gave her name to the third feast celebrated during the month of Ochpaniztl. A slave girl, known as an ixiptla, was picked to represent her during the festival. She wove garments which, after she had been sacrificed, were draped on top of her flayed skin

Fig. 35 Chicomecóatl. *Gabriel von Max Collection, Völkerkundliche Sammlungen im Reiss-Museum der Stadt Mannheim*

and subsequently displayed prominently on the straw image on top of Toci's shrine. Toci had two divine sons, maize and its nemesis the frost (*see* II.7).

As patroness of weaving, Toci is less telluric and much more human than Coatlicue or Itzpapolotl. The next group of goddesses, who are the instigators of the three necessities of daily life, corn, water and salt, can be seen as fertility goddesses. All three Chicomecóatl, Chalchiuhtlicue and Huixtocíhuatl were companions of the Tláloque, the god of rain and his retinue.

II.7 *Chicomecóatl*

Chicomecóatl was the goddess of corn, harvested grains and fruits in general. The maize seed itself was considered to be feminine, although one of her manifestations was a son, Centéotl, interchangeable with Xilonen. Xilonen represented the young green maize, *xilotl*, described by Durán as 'she who always walked and remained fresh and tender as a young ear of corn' (1971, p. 437), while Chicomecóatl was the goddess of the ripe maize and venerated at harvest time. Her name means 'Seven Snakes'. She was sometimes represented as a snake with seven heads because of the harm she did in barren years when the seeds froze or there was a famine. But when there was abundance, she was called Chalchiuhcíhuatl meaning 'Lady Precious Stone'.

Maize, and hence its deities, has been important to all Mexican civilizations. In the Nahuat creation myth discussed earlier, the people of the first 'Sun' eat acorns, in the second maize grown in water and during the third, maize rather similar to that grown today. In the fourth 'Sun' ruled by the goddess Chalchiuhtlicue (*see* II.8), no mention of food is made but in the fifth, real corn appeared, a gift from the ant to Quetzalcóatl. This myth in modified form is still found in Nahuatl speaking areas today (Taggart, 1983, p. 89).

Chicomecóatl's festival occurred in September (the month Ochpaniztl) and was shared by two other goddesses, Atlatonan and Toci. Atlatonan was honoured first in the month. She was the deity of lepers, those who suffered from sores and physical defects. There then followed a fast after which Chicomecóatl was honoured. A slave girl was chosen as *ixiptla* to represent the goddess, dressed in fine clothes, made to dance and taken to various nobles' houses. Then, during a wake, she was placed on a litter and thanks were offered up for the fruits of the year. Subsequently, in the temple of Huitzilopochtli, she was placed in front of the image of Chicomecóatl, housed in an adjacent chamber, where the nobles paid obeisance and then broke their fast. The girl was then incensed one final time and decapitated, her blood being scattered over the image of Chicomecóatl and the corn, chilli, squash and other vegetables and seeds on which she had been standing. She was then flayed and her skin donned by a priest. The flayed skin of sacrificial victims was often likened to the leaves falling away from the ripe cob. Later, war captives and other prisoners had their hearts cut out and their bodies, with that of the girl, were then offered to the nobility for a feast.

II.8 Chalchiuhtlicue

Chalchiuhtlicue, 'She of the Jade Skirt', was, as a manifestation of Ometéotl, consort of Chalchiuhtlatonac ('He who Shines like a Sun of Jade'). Chalchiuhtlicue's skirt of jade symbolized water; in her more human form she was thus the goddess of water and wife, sister, mother or companion of Tláloc, god of rain. Both were resident in the third level of the heavens. Tláloc presided over unconstrained water and storms, while Chalchiuhtlicue is the earthly containment of water. She presided over fresh water, caring for rivers and lakes. She was respected, but also feared as she might, if ill-disposed, cause a watery death and was sometimes known as the 'foaming one' or the 'agitated one'. Often equated with the mountain that enclosed the water, she was seen as, for example, Iztaccíhuatl (White Woman), the name given to one of the large mountains that defines the Valley of Mexico. In the myth of Mixcóatl, as the 'White Chalchiuhtlicue', she gives birth to the 'Four Hundred Mimixcoa' (*see* II.4, p. 372).

Chalchiuhtlicue was an old goddess from Teotihuacán, popular and often depicted dressed as a typical Indian woman. After the birth of a baby boy, as he was being bathed, Chalchiuhtlatonac and Chalchiuhtlicue were invoked to cleanse the baby of the 'filth' which it had from both its mother and father (Sahagún, 1969).

For a girl baby, only Chalchiuhtlicue is mentioned. Babies were thus said to be 'born in water' and were washed ceremonially by special priests and priestesses for four consecutive days after birth; the babies of peasants were washed in streams and those of noble birth in a stone basin.

II.9 Huixtocihuatl

About Huixtocíhuatl, goddess of salt, very little is known other than that she had associations with water and that her consort, Opochtli, was a god connected with fishing and one of the Tláloque.

II.10 Mayahuel

Mayahuel was the personification of *maguey*, a plant used to make fibre objects and a drink called *octli*. She was represented as many-breasted because of her fecundity; as the earth goddess Mecitli (Maguey Grandmother), she suckled the five female Mimixcoa. Leaves of the *maguey* plant were likened to breasts and their ends to nipples. A story was told about her. Secluded in the recesses of the sky by her demonlike duenna Tzitzimitl, she was stolen away by Quetzalcóatl in his manifestation as the wind so that mankind might know her secret, overcome its sadness and, by drinking *octli*, learn to sing and dance. Pursued by Tzitzimitl, Quetzalcóatl in desperation changed himself and his female charge into trees but the demons tore her apart. Later, Quetzalcóatl planted the severed branches from which *maguey* grew. *Maguey* is still important today and *octli* is now known as *pulque*. Mayahuel had an entourage of the fifteen *octli* gods (the 'Four Hundred Rabbits'), who were all male and were patrons of drunkenness.

II.11 Xochiquetzal

Xochiquetzal is the goddess of love, but identified with the earth. Her name means 'Precious Flower' or, more literally, 'Flower Feather' or 'Flowery Plumage'. In one of her aspects, she is youthful beauty and exuberance and concerned with pleasure; in another she is the responsible woman; and in a third the more negative Tlazoltéotl (*see* II.12). As the youthful maiden she is concerned with sexual pleasure. For the Tlalhuica who had their capital in the town of Cuernavaca, an almost paradaisical location, her festival may have been used to introduce the young to drink and sex in a ceremonial way (Brundage, 1979, p. 160).

Various spouses are mentioned for Xochiquetzal as a matron; among them are Tláloc and Cintéotl, god of maize. Sometimes she is the female counterpart of Tonancatecuhtli, the 'Lord of Sustenance', identifying her with fertility in general, and as the mother of corn. At others, she is married to the son of the celestial couple, Cipactónal and Oxomoco. As maiden, she is the goddess of love, surrounded by a host of entertainers as she and her attendants spin and weave, but as mother, she is the source of nourishment of men and beasts.

Flowers symbolize her maidenhood and were her gift to mankind. Quetzalcóatl

Fig. 36 Xochiquetzal. *Line drawing from Codex Borgia 9*

once masturbated onto a rock from out of which a bat flew. The bat brought back a piece of Xochiquetzal's vulva. From this emanated beautiful flowers but they had no smell. The bat then flew into the underworld with yet another part of her vulva and from this came wondrously fragrant flowers.

Xochiquetzal also had connections with fruit. She lived in the 'paradise' of Tamoanchan, identified with a place called Xochicalco at the time of the Spanish Conquest, but also with Omeyocan. In Tamoanchan grew a tree covered with blooms and all sorts of fruit. The boughs were not to be broken nor the fruit plucked; but whoever picked from the tree would be fruitful in love. Succumbing to 'temptation', Xochiquetzal ate some of the fruit whereupon the tree shuddered and broke, bleeding as if wounded and revealing to all the other deities that she had broken the 'taboo' and become pregnant. The world tree grew through all the layers of the heavens, its topmost part appearing in Tamoanchan. Xochiquetzal has been described as the first female to 'sin' because she ate from the tree. Thus, as a woman, rather than a girl, her patronage was of illicit love. As Ixnextli, 'Ashes in Eyes', she is unable to look directly at the sky in daytime, just as people can never look directly at the sun. As Tláloc's wife she was seduced by Tezcatlipoca who then installed her in the underworld. In some versions, she is equated with the buried seed corn awaiting spring, but this may have been influenced by the Spaniards' knowledge of Greek mythology.

Xochiquetzal was the patron of painters, embroiderers, weavers, silversmiths and sculptors. During the feast of flowers (*Xochilhuitl*), streets and houses were adorned with floral offerings, and people decked themselves with blossoms. A maiden sat under the 'world tree' weaving. She was then sacrificed, after which a dance was held in which the various craftsmen dressed as 'monkeys, ocelots, dogs, coyotes, mountain lions and jaguars'. During this period, oblations were offered to Xochiquetzal by women, and to Chicome Xochitl by men.

Xochiquetzal is the most female of the Aztec goddesses. Her mythology has probably been the most contaminated by the European concept of womanhood –

with ideas of virginity, taboo, sin and punishment. She seems to personify the Aztec idea of the feminine and their love of flowers. Her importance is indicated by the number of different husbands attributed to her in the various versions of her myth. She was comparatively new, possibly of Toltec origin.

II.12 Tlazoltéotl

Of more importance in daily life was Tlazoltéotl, an aspect of Xochiquetzal, meaning literally 'Filth Goddess' but which can be understood as 'Sex Goddess'. On the Gulf Coast she was a mother goddess known as Tzintéotl, 'Goddess of the Rump', a name implying sex and dirt. But although 'tzintl' means anus, it also means 'base or beginning'. She was usually depicted dressed in raw cotton, with bared breasts and a coral snake around her neck, possibly symbolizing lust. She was the patroness of adultery and sexual passion but also fertility. Prostitutes and nymphomaniacs were known as 'women of Tlazoltéotl'. She could stir up passion, but also pardon it; her priests could hear confessions and cleanse those involved for she was also known as Tlaelcuani ('Filth Eater'). Tlazoltéotl personified the Aztecs obsession with filth. She was Hauxtec in origin and her male devotees in Tenochtitlan were called Hauxtecs.

II.13 Citlalinicue

Citlalinicue, 'Lady of the Skirt of Stars' or 'Star Skirt', was as an aspect of Ometéotl, consort of Citlallatónac ('He of the Day whose Light Envelops'). It was she who made the stars shine brightly at night but she had very little substance as a woman. Her story is an intellectual Aztec creation myth, an alternative version of the more standard one told earlier, but she alone is responsible for the creation. Citlallatónac is only there as a presence. In a sense then she is the great mother out of whose 'womb' came the sun, moon and all the stars, and she was the source of all wisdom. Even Quetzalcóatl and Tezcatlipoca were her sons. But for the Aztecs her powers were strictly astral; she is personified in the Milky Way and the Aztecs called it by her name. She had no cult in Tenochtitlan.

In myth, she gave birth to the obsidian knife, *tecpatl*, which fell to earth out of the sky. From it emerged the 1,600 stars or deities (four times the number of the Mimixcoa or the Huitznahua) led by Xolotl. But they were without beings to serve them and dispatched a hawk to ask the celestial mother for humans as domestics, slaves and food. She suggested they ask for the bones of former men from the Lord of the Dead. Xolotl was sent to the underworld and with difficulty successfully completed the mission. By performing autosacrifice over them, the gods created from their blood the first man and woman, whom Xolotl raised on *maguey* milk. It was with the *tecpatl* that the Aztecs performed sacrifices.

II.14 The Cihuateteo

The Cihuateteo or Cihuapipiltin were the 'Celestial Princesses' or 'Goddesses', into which the souls of the women who had died in childbirth were believed to be transformed and who dwelt in the west, the region of women (Cíhuatlampa). These women were five in number, representing the five directions, and were believed to be the female counterparts of male warriors who had been slain in battle or on the stone of sacrifice. Such men accompanied the sun on its ascent every morning, while the women helped the sun to set. They bore it down in a litter of quetzal feathers, dressed as warriors with shields in their hands given them by Cihuacóatl, and gladdening it with cries of war, before delivering it into the hands of the Micteta, the people of Mictlan, the region of the dead. It was an honour for a woman to die in childbirth and Aztec youths who were warriors would attempt to rob parts of their bodies before or after burial to give them strength in battle. During the five days between each 360-day cycle of the solar calendar, the Cihuateteo were believed to descend and haunt such places as crossroads, where shrines were usually set up to propitiate them. The spirits hoped to kidnap children, having been deprived of the opportunity to be mothers; children were thus kept away from such shrines at these times. The Cihuateteo are often represented as skull-like faces.

II.15 Cipactónal and Tlaltéotl

Cipactónal was an aged goddess, grandmother of Quetzalcóatl. Cipactónal and her husband, Oxomoco, had once belonged in the heavens but they were so antiquated that they were, by the time of the Aztecs, almost human. Sometimes they are described as the first human couple (*see* fig. 37).

The world lacked a rule or calendar by which people's lives could be regulated and the matter was referred to Cipactónal who lived in a cave. In consultation with Quetzalcóatl, the Tonalpohualli was thought up and the first day name, Cipactl decided upon after which all the rest of the 260-day calendar fell into place (*see* table 2, p. 366). Cipactl represented chaos, unstructured matter and was conceived of as a monstrous alligator inhabiting an ocean, the first of all beings. She was the earth before it had been formed, alone and bisexual. After it had formed, as the first being, the monster was known as Tlateuhctli or Tlaltéotl ('Earth Lady' or 'Earth Spirit'), 'whose every joint was filled with eyes and teeth with which she bit like a savage beast'. She was depicted also as a massive toad, slavering blood. All life was contained within her, but was not freed until her body was violated by Quetzalcóatl and Tezcatlipoca, who manifested themselves in serpent form and squeezed her in two; from one half they made the earth and the other they took back to the heavens. The deities were deeply angered by this and decided that to compensate her, all fruit of the earth indispensable to people should be born from Tlaltéotl. She sometimes cried during the night for she wanted to eat the hearts of men and would not be silenced until she had received some, nor would she bear fruit unless drenched with the blood of men.

According to another version, Tezcatlipoca and Quetzalcóatl recreated the earth after the destruction of the world by a flood and the collapse of heaven. They entered Tlaltéotl's body, one through the mouth and the other through the navel, and having met at the goddess's heart, the centre of the earth, they raised the sky again with

Fig. 37 Oxomoco and Cipactonal divining with maize kernels. *Line drawing from Codex Borbonicus 21*

the help of other deities who stood at the four corners (as trees) to support it. The stars and the night were then created, Tláloc created water and rain, Mictlantéotl the underworld and Ehécatl, human beings. In another version, she was Tlateuhctli and from her hair came the trees, flowers and grass, from her eyes the springs, from her mouth rivers and caverns, from her nose valleys and from her shoulders the mountains. The highest honour was paid to Tlateuhctli by placing a finger in the earth and then licking it, for this element was 'the Mother of the Gods and the Heart of the Earth'.

SECTION III: HER STORY

As they established themselves and increased their power, the Aztecs reconstructed mythology to suit their chauvinist and expansionist ideology. Thus the significance of the feminine was greatly reduced and debased. The backdrop of the cosmology, dominated by the supreme, androgynous presence of Ometéotl, still persisted as did the various twosomes, foursomes and fivesomes that Ometéotl engendered. But in the centuries before Aztec ascendancy, the feminine side of the essential duality had been gradually pushed into the background. The earlier Quetzalcóatl was more androgynous and numinous than Tezcatlipoca, who in turn was more divine than Huitzilopochtli; neither he nor Cihuacóatl, the principal goddess, had a place in the cosmology of Ometéotl. For the Aztecs emphasis was predominantly placed on the more negative characteristics of those goddesses most in the public eye; in Cihuacóatl, only the demonic aspects of the feminine are developed.

Yet one such goddess from the domain of Ometéotl retained her significance, Citlalinicue, who is not a woman in an earth(l)y sense and who is more important than her consort. Her myth is the only one in which a female alone is responsible for the creation and one of the few in which children are mothered, albeit in a distant, aristocratic way. She provides her high born children with servants and food while the earth(l)y Mayahuel suckles hers directly. It is clear that the overall cosmology of Ometéotl was still of significance to the educated, recorded as it is in diverse sources. Although constructed around this sophisticated ideology, Aztec mythology was in practice a popular mythology, very much part of everyday life, of the politico-religious practices dominated by the calendar and its associated festivities – in which the earth goddesses who predominated had little connection with their more astral counterparts.

Few myths have survived in any detail. It is thus difficult for us to gain a full sense of the feminine in Aztec mythology, although it clearly has a range of aspects: the mother, the maiden (for 'virgin' is very much a concept with Christian associations and there is no direct gloss for it in Nahuatl), the daughter, the whore and the malevolent woman. The goddesses on the whole are represented rather incompletely as individual personalities. Superficially, they do all have rather different roles; Mayahuel is goddess of *pulque* and drunkenness, Chicomecóatl of maize, Xochiquetzal of love. Underneath however, they are all psychically very much 'many-aspected woman'. This was less true of the male deities, who were seen more as active individuals than as representations of a collective male psyche (if such exists!).

Cihuacóatl encapsulated the traits of many earlier goddesses in the interests of social control, but none of these traits are at all well developed; there are no myths about her. As Huitzilopochtli's consort or mother, however, she was clearly seen to be of a different or lesser status than her son/husband. His temple was a high pyramid, hers a dark, telluric underground chamber, appropriate enough perhaps for an earth goddess but she is rather the goddess of death. Her 'black house' was less of a womb than a tomb, and also a tomb in a metaphorical sense for those deities taken from the surrounding countryside, who were housed there in subservience to the Aztec Empire. She was so constructed that the 'honour', or rather responsibility, for the huge number of sacrificial deaths which should have been Huitzilopochtli's, as the outgoing, conquering warrior who was almost a man, was off-loaded onto her. Thus Cihuacóatl is the deathly counterpart to Huitzilopochtli's life force, the centre of a death cult which was of the greatest importance to the Aztecs. It was represented by a number of other goddesses. Itzpapolotl as the obsidian knife of sacrifice and the Cihuateteo, the transformed souls of women who had died in childbirth. But if Itzpapolotl had been the old goddess of death, Cihuacóatl was the new. All were represented with faces that were part skeleton, and the little sugar skulls made today for the Day of the Dead (during All Souls) are a vestige of this cult.

Cihuacóatl is more of a demonic woman than a mother, a goddess who, rather than nurturing, devours men – a representation in this sense of the fear that men have of the female. Because of Cihuacóatl's links with the underworld (which should not be seen as equivalent to our hell), she wanders at night in a dishevelled state and screams and weeps copiously. Tlaltéotl manifests the same devouring tendencies; the desire for the hearts of men and for blood and is again linked to the night. In general, in this mythology, the female is linked to darkness and night, unsurprisingly to the earth and closely to the underworld as the source of life – from there came the essential element of the flowers made from Xochiquetzal's vulva, their smell. Although it is the place of the dead, the underworld is also the place where the bones are kept as the raw material from which life can be fashioned.

Cihuacóatl headed a powerful popular cult. If men are depicted as fearful of women in myth, fear and obedience were instilled in the majority of the populace by Cihuacóatl. She does not appear in any way to provide a role model for women of higher status. Myths *per se* were probably less important amongst women who were more individuated, whilst amongst poorer women and those who lived in the country, where there was much less self-determination, goddesses were rather considered to be concerned with process: the processes of birth and regeneration, which Cihuacóatl exemplified in an extreme form, blood being linked to the fecundity of the earth.

If any goddess provided a model of the feminine it was Xochiquetzal. Xochiquetzal is very much more of a woman than any other mythological figure in the sense that she had a fuller range of attributes. Flowers emanated from her vulva, which Graulich has suggested may indicate the origin of menstruation (1983, p. 134), but more probably indicates their delicacy and beauty, and shows the feminine for once completely positively.

But Xochiquetzal, we are told, also lost perfect happiness in Tamoanchan by eating the fruit – a myth that sounds very like the story of Eve. There is an ongoing debate as to whether or not the various versions of her myth have been influenced by Christianity, demonstrating the difficulties of collecting myths from subjugated oral cultures (Graulich, and responses, 1984). Another possible interpretation is that the tree symbolizes continuity, in the sense of being a perpetual support for the structure of the world in primordial timelessness. The tree occurs frequently: in the myth of Mayahuel, she becomes a tree with Quetzalcóatl; and in Tlaltéotl's myth, Quetzalcóatl and Tezcatlipoca both become trees. But the tree also implies process, the existence of time, and by eating from it, Xochiquetzal becomes pregnant. The tree breaks and bleeds, referring to fertility or, to follow Graulich's line of thought, menstruation or possibly the breaking of her hymen (but, as virginity was not important to the Aztecs, this seems unlikely). It is perhaps a symbolic protest at being brought from a state of perfection into the world of time – the initiation from maidenhood into adulthood. Perfection could only exist in Omeyocan/Tamoanchan and the theme of its loss is reiterated in many other myths, a loss for which deities of both sexes could be responsible. For all the deities existed in an intermediary state between that of Ometéotl and human beings. At times, the broken tree is rather like the bones in Mictlan from which future creations are made. In one myth, Quetzalcóatl uses them to make the fifth 'Sun', in another Xolotl, at the instigation of Citlalinicue, makes humans to serve the deities. From the broken branches of the tree planted by Quetzalcóatl in Mayahuel's myth, grew *maguey*.

Xochiquetzal undoubtedly represents female sexuality, and its socially negative side is developed in various aspects of her: as Ixnextli and more fully in Tlazoltéotl, personifying the Aztecs' obsession with filth.

There are more myths for Xochiquetzal than for any other goddess, although the myths for Mayahuel and Itzpapolotl and of Citlalinicue are more clearly pre-Aztec and the most complete ones that have survived. They are of a type familiar from other cultures where animistic thought makes no distinctions between humans and the rest of nature. They create most fully that mythic reality that can only be fully interpreted from within the culture. In these myths, women are transformed into plants or animals and objects of cultural significance. Here the body that supplies the raw material for creation is apparently female; the world being made from Tlaltéotl's torn body, her lower half forming the earth, her upper the skies and heaven. Mayahuel is the *maguey* plant whose many-breasted form is related to that of the female body, while Itzpapolotl is the transformation of a deer, becoming more of a woman as she pursues Mimich and later the origin of the obsidian knife of sacrifice.

But if Xochiquetzal was completely anthropomorphic, Coatlicue was the sort of goddess that country people would have been more familiar with. Part anthropomorphic, part zoomorphic, she was clearly female in form and yet symbolically also a representation of that duality, the masculine side being the eagle, the feminine, the snake. She was the female equivalent in many respects of Quetzalcóatl. Although her myth of giving birth to Huitzilopochtli was obviously a recent one, her form ties her into the mythic scenarios of Mayahuel and Itzpapolotl. That she still had as much importance as she did is perhaps surprising given her 'repulsive' form. Yet a goddess who was the patron of flowers, who had as close an association with flowers as Xochiquetzal, could hardly have been seen as 'repulsive' by the Aztecs. This is clearly the uncomprehending reaction of the Christians who failed to understand her symbolic qualities.

The Aztecs clearly used the strength of the feminine strategically. But can Aztec mythology tell us anything about the feminine *per se*? Coatlicue indicates further that predominantly they saw the feminine in earthy terms; Cihuacóatl is probably only somewhat more human for political reasons. The goddesses may not have been beautiful, but they were strong. Coatlicue has to fight all her children, and her daughter, Coyolxanliqui, is depicted as a helmeted warrior; both are almost androgynous.

But if blood is the symbol of fertility, it could be expected to make an appearance in relation to the earthly fertility goddesses also. We know that Chicomecóatl and Chalchiuhtlicue are, by comparison to Cihuacóatl, very human; this applies particularly to Chicomecóatl who manifests the various faces of womanhood but also a more negative aspect, as the seven-headed snake linked to the years of poor harvest. On the whole, myths are more plentiful for the older goddesses. It is thus rather surprising that they are not fuller for Chalchiuhtlicue and water. Nor, considering that Mexican culture is dependent on maize, for Chicomecóatl. It has been suggested that her myths may have been suppressed as they would remind the Aztec élite of their only too recent rural origins (Brundage, 1979, p. 79). Probably it was also because those living in Tenochtitlan had rather different concerns – agriculture and water mattered little to them, for they were more obsessed with linking astral movements to war and human sacrifice. However, that these more human goddesses were still conceived of as closely related to the more androgynous and abstract concept of Ometéotl is indicated here by the manifestation of Chalchiuhtlicue, more as spirit and less as goddess, when invoked after a birth to cleanse the new-born baby. The feminine was clearly connected with healing and for each aspect there was a representative goddess: Atlatonan, for example, was the goddess of lepers and physical defects; Teteoinnan the benefactor of sweatbaths. Myths about Chicomecóatl may well have existed in rural areas and were just never recorded, for she was a calendric deity in the Valley of Mexico and she had a highly developed cult in Tenochtitlan (with *ixiptla* representing her), where plenty of fertilizing blood was spread over the year's fruits.

It has been suggested that woman is almost totally identified with nature and the earth in this mythology. Yet there are exceptions to this in the better developed and older myths. From Itzpapolotl's body emerges the obsidian knife, central to Aztec culture and not just as the instrument of sacrifice. Citlalinicue, the only astral goddess of importance, meanwhile gives birth to the obsidian knife in the heavens from where it falls to earth. This seems to indicate that the female is involved fully in the transition of the deities from Omeyocan to the earth and with the engendering of culture. Further, Tláloc personified unconstrained water, while Chalchiuhtlicue represented contained water, albeit contained by earth. Finally, there is Cipactónal who devised the calendar with her grandson Quetzalcóatl. The difficulty here is that only sometimes is Cipactónal the female member of the primordial pair. But a clue perhaps is that Cipactl, the name given to the first sign of the calendar, is also the first of all beings and bisexual. Are we then not back to androgyny or non-differentiated spirit from which this mythology emerged and in which the Aztecs had attempted to suppress the positive aspect of the feminine? Aztec reality is, in its details, difficult for us to stomach; for the practices in which they were involved on a daily basis are so often for us the stuff of mythology.

SECTION IV: MYTHOGRAPHY

For the Aztecs, the distinction between mythology, that is the past lives of the goddesses, and the present was not a great one. The stories about them were remembered as much by their re-enactment every year during the goddess's festival as from verbal accounts. In the practice of ritual either slaves or prisoners acted as their *ixiptla*, standing in for the requisite deity. For a few hours or days, the deity lived again in the human being who was so raised up and honoured. For Xochiquetzal, her *ixiptla* sat under a tree to weave, re-enacting her myth before eventually being sacrificed.

The dividing line between humans and deities is thus a fine one. Topiltzin-

Quetzalcóatl was both god and priest-ruler in Tula. He was not however the first. Xochiquetzal is mentioned as a real woman who died in a war in Teotihuacán before the advent of the fifth 'Sun'. Several of the later Tlatoani (rulers) claimed a divine status and, some considerable time after the Conquest, there were a series of revitalization movements in which comparatively unknown men, such as Andres Mixcóatl in 1537 or Juan Cóatl in 1665, claimed a man-god status (Gruzinski, 1989).

IV.1

But the feminine as deity was to resurface again after the establishment of Christianity far more strongly than the masculine. There is no indigenous post-Conquest male equivalent of the Virgin of Guadalupe or La Malinche. In 1541, the former appeared as a brown-skinned woman to a Christianized Indian called Juan Diego. Speaking in Nahuatl the Virgin demanded that he have a church built for her on the hill of Tepeyac where Tonantzin had formerly had a shrine. From the beginning, the syncretism was thinly disguised and the cult recognized as being more for Tonantzin than the Christian Virgin. This apparition of the Virgin as a brown-skinned goddess gave back to what remained of Nahuatl culture the female part of the indissoluble duality of Ometéotl in a Christianized and hence acceptable form. For although in many ways the Virgin of Guadalupe is the mother, she is represented rather as the woman of the Apocalypse, crushing the serpent and in possession of the heavens from which she protects her chosen people.

In order to build up a following, the first friars were, on the whole, forced to fit Christian concepts to Aztec cosmology; Toci, 'Our Grandmother', was associated with St Anne, particularly in Tlaxcala, and John the Baptist with Tezcatlipoca in the valley of Puebla (Nutini, 1988, p. 109). In general, during the centuries after the Conquest, 'idols' existed behind altars especially in more isolated rural communities, enabling the pre-Christian cosmology to continue.

The church dedicated to the Virgin of Guadalupe is still of central importance to Mexican Catholicism and Tepeyac (now more generally known as La Villa) is one of the largest pilgrimage centres in Mexico. Revitalization movements are currently as active as ever. The Concheros, who perform a ritual circle dance of both men and women and who dress in Aztec-style clothing, are concerned to invoke pre-Hispanic deities rather than direct their allegiances to the Christian saints, and precisely because of this, the site of Tepeyac, home of Tonantzin, is of the greatest significance to them (Rostas, n.d.).

IV.2

On the other hand is Malintzin, a Nahuatl-speaking Indian woman who was given to Cortés during the Conquest and who became his mistress and mother of one of his children. Known as La Malinche, she acted as an interpreter and translator – a word, as Franco has pointed out, that is closely linked to the Latin root for 'treachery' (1989, p. 131). It has often been suggested that without La Malinche the conquest of Mexico by the Spaniards would have been impossible. She had iconic qualities for both the Spaniards, to whom she was the exemplary convert, and for the Indians who ascribed extraordinary powers to her (and here it should be remembered that Cortés was thought to be the returning Quetzalcóatl). Her mythological status, however, as the betrayer of Mexico has only really developed in the last two centuries or so, since Mexico gained its independence from Spain. She has come to symbolize the humiliation of the indigenous people and the need for the Mexican male to reject the feminine in himself as devalued, for La Malinche was *la chingada*, 'the fucked woman', who raped her country, who acted as the medium for conquest.

Once again a woman becomes, as did Cihuacóatl during Aztec ascendency, or Tlaltéotl in her creation myth, the territory – and literally so in the case of the latter – over which the quest for identity is fought. But the female has clearly always been of importance; for even in the male-centred cosmological creation myth, it was not a male but a female who ruled the last 'Sun' just before the earth as we now know it was created.

References and Further Reading

Mexican mythology is not easy to access. Much of the little material that exists is in still largely inaccessible primary sources and little has been published on it. Nicholson (1971) is still in many ways the standard reference, while, in his more recent book, Brundage has a chapter devoted to the goddesses (1979). Recently, Michel Graulich has looked at the mythology from a comparative and structuralist point of view, but has been criticized for using Christian concepts and failing to take account of the context in his analysis. He has published little in English (Graulich, 1983, 1981). Doris Heyden has worked in the area for some considerable time (cf. Duran, 1971) and has written on Itztpapalotl in Spanish (1976), but has published little recently, while Jacqueline De Durand-Forest publishes mainly in French (Durand-Forest, 1982).

For the section on Cosmology-Mythology, I relied on secondary sources (such as Leon-Portillo, 1963) who used such primary sources as *La Historia de Los Mexicanos por Sus Pinturas*, 1891, Nueva Colección de documentos para la historia de México, ed. J. Garcia Icazbalceta, vol. 3; and *Mexico and the Leyenda de Soles*, written down in 1558, but based on earlier documents and published in German in 1938 as *Die Geschichte de Konigreiche von Colhuacan und Mexiko*, trans. and ed. Walter Lehmann, Kohlhammer, Stuttgart, Berlin.

For the section on the Goddesses, I used Duran and Sahagún, and as a secondary source, I found Brundage invaluable.

BIBLIOGRAPHY:

Baquedano, E. (1984), *Aztec Sculpture* (London: British Museum)
Bierhorst, J. (1985a), *Cantares Mexicanos: Songs of the Aztecs* (Stanford, Ca.: Stanford University Press)
—— (1985b), *A Nahuatl-English Dictionary and Concordance to the Cantares Mexicanas* (Stanford, Ca.: Stanford University Press)
Bray, W. (1968), *Everyday Life of the Aztecs* (London: Batsford)
Brundage, B.C. (1979), *The Fifth Sun* (Austin and London: University of Texas Press)
Caso, A. (1958), *The Aztecs: People of the Sun* (Norman, Ok.: University of Oklahoma Press)
Coe, M. (1984), *Mexico* (London: Thames & Hudson)
Duran, Fray Diego (1971), *Book of the Gods and Rites & The Ancient Calendar*, ed. and trans. F. Horcasitas and D. Heydon (Norman, Ok.: University of Oklahoma Press)

Durand-Forest, J. de (1982), 'Les neuf Seigneurs de la nuit' in *Indiana: Volume en hommage à Walter Lehmann* (Berlin: Mann), pp. 103–29

Franco, J. (1989), *Plotting Women* (London: Verso)

Garibay, A.M. (1970), *La literature de los aztecas* (Mexico: Editorial Joaquin Mortiz)

Gruzinski, S. (1989), *Man-Gods in the Mexican Highlands: Indian Power and Colonial Society, 1520–1800* (Stanford, Ca.: Stanford University Press)

Graulich, M. (1981), 'The Metaphor of the Day in Ancient Mexican Myths and Ritual' in *Current Anthropology*, 22, pp. 45–60

—— (1983), 'Myths of Paradise Lost in Pre-Hispanic Central Mexico' in *Current Anthropology*, vol. 24, no. 5, pp. 575–88

—— (1984), 'On Paradise Lost in Central Mexico' in *Current Anthropology*, vol. 25, no. 1, pp. 134–5

Heyden, D. (1976), 'La diosa madre: Itzpapolotl' in *Boletin INAH*, epoca II, num. 11

Karttunen, F. (1985), *An Analytical Dictionary of Nahuatl* (Austin, Texas: University of Texas Press)

Leon-Portillo, M. (1963), *Aztec Thought and Culture: A Study of the Ancient Nahuatl Mind* (Norman, Ok.: University of Oklahoma Press)

—— (ed.) (1980), *Native MesoAmerican Spirituality* (London: SPCK)

Nicholson, H.B. (1971), 'Religion in Pre-Hispanic Central Mexico' in R. Wauchope (ed.), *Handbook of Middle American Indians*, vol. 10 (Austin, Texas: University of Texas Press), pp. 395–446

—— (1983), *The Art of Aztec Mexico* (Washington, DC: National Gallery of Art)

Nutini, H.G. (1988), *Todos Santos in Rural Tlaxcala: A Syncretic, Expressive and Symbolic Analysis of the Cult of the Dead* (Princeton: Princeton University Press)

Rostas, S.E. (n.d.), 'The Concheros of Mexico: a Search for Identity' to be published in *Dance Research*

Sahagun, Fray B. De, (1950–79), *Florentine Codex: General History of the Things of New Spain*, 13 vols, trans. A. Anderson and C. Dibble (Santa Fé: School of American Research, Santa Fé, NM and the University of Utah): 1950, *Book 1 – The Gods*; 1951, *Book 2 – The Ceremonies*; 1953, *Book 7 – The Sun, Moon, and Stars, and the Binding of the Years*; 1961, *Book 10 – The People*; 1969, *Book 6 – Rhetoric and Moral Philosophy*; 1978, *Book 3 – The Origin of the Gods*; 1979, *Book 4 – The Soothsayers, Book 5 – The Omens, Book 8 – Kings and Lords*

Soustelle, J. (1970), *The Daily Life of The Aztecs* (Stanford, Ca.: Stanford University Press)

Taggart, J. (1983), *Nahuatl Myth and Social Structure* (Austin, Texas: University of Texas Press)

Van Zantwijk, (1985), *The Aztec Arrangement* (Norman, Ok.: University of Oklahoma Press)

Virgillo, C. and Lindstrom, N. (1985), *Women as Myth and Metaphor* (St Louis, Missouri: University of Missouri Press)

PENELOPE HARVEY

South America:
The Interpretation of Myth

SECTION I: INTRODUCTION

Since the fifteenth century South America has occupied a special place in the European imagination. Despite Columbus's initial conviction that he had discovered a route to the East, it soon emerged that he had found a New World, a world so unknown that it could easily accommodate Europe's most extravagant fantasies (O'Gorman, 1961; Mason, 1990). This vast continent became associated with a utopian space, a terrestrial paradise that might contain the Garden of Eden and where the chosen races of the world could live in Christian innocence, surrounded by those legendary treasures that were later to be hidden in cities such as El Dorado. The early travellers also formulated a dark side for this New World, a side that dwelt on secrets and magical knowledge, cannibals and Amazon warriors, monstrous figures who embodied European fears of the unknown and acted out their nightmares (Bucher, 1981; Mason, 1990; Silverblatt, 1987; Taussig, 1987).

This chapter will look at narratives that the native peoples of South America have told about themselves. However, our myths about them will continue as a shadowy presence in these accounts, as we struggle to understand their words and motivations through the confusing history of stereotypes that often form the strongest links between us the readers and them the tellers.[1] It is also important to remember, especially when silently reading to oneself, that to recount a myth is not a solitary activity. Myths are told to others, in the presence of others, they are interactive events that conjoin past memories and future projects.

My interest in myth as social practice takes me on a very different course from that of the most famous exponent of South American mythology, Claude Lévi-Strauss (1964, 1966, 1968, 1971). His four volume work *Mythologiques* (*Introduction to a Science of Mythology*), which plots the structural relationships between multiple variants of many narratives, was undertaken to reveal the rationality of symbolic transformation, and ultimately to discover something about the nature of mythic thought itself. This style of analysis converts a huge variety of narrative moments into a coherent system, yet because such systems are abstracted from social practice,

Fig. 38 Andean women sit and talk while preparing straw ropes for thatching.

they inevitably tidy up and narrow down the multiple and discordant possibilities that any single tale evokes and prevent us from asking questions about the circumstances in which the tales were told, how they were recorded and remembered and how they might have been interpreted and understood by those for whom they were told.

In this respect, it is also important to consider the relationship between geographical regions and the notion of cultural continuity that is implied by the notion of a mythological system. In South American anthropology and cultural studies, the Andean region is usually separated from and contrasted with Amazonia. The Andes as a cultural space is generally taken to refer to that region colonized and politically integrated by the Inkas, and further united by the political, economic and religious institutions of the Spanish colonial regime. Through this history, practices and institutions have emerged which do indeed distinguish the two regions although the more recent experiences of migration, urbanization, centralized education, wage labour and other manifestations of the political economy of international capital link them in more ways than might initially be apparent.

However, this opposition can too easily hide the fact that the cultural practices and assumptions within each of these regions is extremely heterogeneous. If we consider the extent to which class, ethnic, gender and regional identities affect the ways in which any particular historical moment is experienced, we are led to produce a far more complex and contested image of 'culture' than that which is suggested by the very static notion of system.

In the context of this volume it is important to acknowledge the achievement of feminist scholarship in the formulation of this now somewhat commonplace critique of structuralism. Such work has explicitly sought to recover those multiple meanings, interpretations and subjectivities which globalizing discourses deny (Haraway, 1989; de Lauretis, 1987; Scott, 1988; Strathern, 1988). Their critique has been based in historicized accounts which examine the social conditions for truth and knowledge and which ultimately show how those in positions of power have attempted to impose their own notions of truth.[2] Thus, together with many other voices in the post-colonial world, they reveal how claims which are put forward as universally applicable are often only valid for men of a particular culture, class and race (Asad, 1973; Said, 1978; Clifford 1988).

In the general context of these theoretical concerns, my account of South American myth will be structured around those narrative themes that have commonly been identified in our academic and literary publications, re-presenting them not only to reveal a feminine presence, but also to emphasize the political dimension of cultural interpretation which feminist scholarship has done so much to highlight in recent years.

In the major section of this chapter I will be looking at narratives from the Andean region. I shall look first at Inka origin myths, discussing the relationship between those versions that were recorded by the early Spanish chroniclers and those that are told today. The political function of these narratives will be discussed, as will the different ways in which female agency is represented. This discussion of female agency will be continued in a section on Andean supernatural beings, particularly the Earth force (Pachamama) and the Moon. Finally, in the Andean section those narratives which concern contemporary accounts of powerful and voracious female devils will be discussed. My treatment of the vast subject of Amazonian mythology is unfortunately extremely brief and centres on a discussion of the origins of sexuality in the Alto Xingu area of central Brazil. Despite its cursory treatment, this material raises important questions concerning the relationship between myth and social relations, and forces a reconsideration of what myths about women can tell us about gender relations.

SECTION II

II.1 The Origin of the Inkas, of Ethnic Groups, of Agriculture and of Civilization
The huge and rugged terrain that extends from Colombia to Northern Chile, through Ecuador, Peru and Bolivia was once ruled by the Inkas. It was not until the mid-fifteenth century that they began to emerge as a regional power among the ethnic groups of the Central Southern Andes. Yet less than one hundred years later they had established the empire that the Spaniards were to encounter in 1532, an empire that both captured the European imagination and embodied its fantasies with its material wealth, systems of political integration and feats of civil engineering.

The empire was divided into four administrative regions and centred on the imperial capital of Cusco where the Inka, the son of the Sun, resided with his sister, Queen the Qoya, the daughter of the Moon. In this city, all the royal Inka lineages (or *ayllus*) held land and irrigation rights in a system of social organization that was expressed in the idiom of kinship. Each lineage was divided into two moieties, an upper and a lower; so too the city of Cusco, and then each province, each region and ultimately the empire itself in a system of ever-increasing inclusivity. Thus the idiom of kinship that united the ruling class was extended to their dominated populations.

The Inkas used a complex system of knotting (the *khipu*) to record historical and administrative data. The earliest written histories of the Inkas were thus translations of the *khipus*, or transcriptions of oral accounts given by those with whom the Spaniards were most able to communicate, the educated male Inka nobles who looked to Cusco as the centre of the pre-Hispanic world. These men gave their accounts of Inka origins and history in a situation of extreme political tension and often used the opportunity to exert whatever control they could over their precarious situation as they sought to establish a sense of legitimate authority in the new colonial hierarchy. Much research into the ethno-history of Peru has established that these Inka histories are primarily accounts of the political and social relationships pertaining between the different lineages and ethnic groups at the time of the Spanish conquest, and not a European-style chronology establishing the connections between the generations (Zuidema, 1964, 1982).

There are two main cycles of Inka origin myths recorded in the Spanish chronicles. One centres on their emergence from a cave at the site of Pacariqtambo (Inn of Dawn or Origin) to the south of Cusco, and tells of the adventures they experienced as they travelled northwards to found the imperial capital of Cusco (Urton, 1990). The second cycle centres on Tiwanaku and the emergence of the God Wiraqocha from Lake Titicaca, his creation of the sun, the moon, the stars and human beings (Urbano, 1981). There are even versions that link the two cycles and tell of how Manqo Qhapaq, the Inka founding ancestor, travelled underground from Lake Titicaca to Pacariqtambo before going on to found the city of Cusco (Urton, 1990, p. 3).

The Pacariqtambo myth referred to below was recorded in 1572 by Sarmiento de Gamboa. It is one of the earliest recorded versions of this myth and is important because we have some detail on the political and social contexts in which it was produced. Sarmiento drew on the testimonies of over one hundred official Inka historians, the *khipukamayoq* (knot-makers), and thus incorporated the views of an influential cross-section of the Cusco nobility. Urton (1990) gives this synopsis of the central narrative:

> At a place to the south of Cuzco called Pacariqtambo, there is a mountain called Tampu T'oqo (window house) in which there are three windows, or caves. At the beginning of time, a group of four brothers and their four sisters — the ancestors of the Inkas — emerged from the central window. The principal figure of this group was Manqo Qhapaq, the man who was destined to become the founder king of the empire. One of the first acts of the eight ancestors was to organize the people who were living around

Tampu T'oqo into ten groups, called *ayllus*. The full entourage of ancestral siblings and *ayllus* set off from Tampu T'oqo to the north in search of fertile land on which to build their imperial capital, Cuzco. Along the way, they stopped at several places to test the soil. At one of these stops, Manqo Qhapaq and one of his sisters, Mama Oqllu, conceived a child whom they named Sinchi Ruq'a. After a period of wanderings filled with marvelous events the entourage arrived at a hill overlooking the valley of Cuzco. Recognizing by miraculous signs that this was their long-sought-after home, the Inkas descended from the mountain and took possession of the valley.[3]

(URTON, 1990, PP. 13–14)

Urton argues that in the telling of this myth, the Inka nobility are making a series of statements about their social and political identity and are thus establishing a framework for the interpretation of Inka social organization. The relationships between the eight ancestors, the four brother/sister or husband/wife pairs, are expressed in terms of the hierarchical moiety system that organized the Inka empire using the same images of hierarchy and difference – age, gender and affinity. The ancestors, as a group, are also set in a hierarchical opposition to the two outsiders who emerge from the side windows or caves. Finally, the eight original ancestors organize the local population into ten ethnic groups, also divided into two moieties. Thus the myth posits three related yet hierarchically ranked social units: (i) the royal lineages, directly descended from the original Inka ancestor couples; (ii) the non-royal lineages descended from the ethnic groups that the ancestors created; and (iii) the outsiders descended from the beings that emerged from the lateral caves/windows.

The references to specific spatial locations are also of great symbolic importance in this account and further mark out the relationship between the centre of the empire and its conquered territories.

On the journey that the ancestors make from Pacariqtambo to the place where they found the city of Cusco a series of dramatic events take place. The myth tells how after they set off, one of the male ancestors, Ayar Kachi (salt ancestor), is making trouble and disturbing the others. To get rid of him they trick him by sending him back to the cave to collect some forgotten items and once inside a huge boulder is rolled across the entrance. The journey continues and as they climb to the top of the hill that overlooks the valley of Cusco, a second ancestor, Ayar Uchu (hotpepper ancestor), turns to stone. Finally, they arrive at the point that is to become the centre of the city and Ayar Awka (enemy ancestor) is also transformed into a stone pillar. Thus it is Manqo Qhapaq, his four sisters and his son who go on to found and build the city of Cusco.

The story thus provides an account of the concrete and visible links between Cusco, the centre of empire, and Pacariqtambo, a place outside the centre that can represent the conquered periphery.

The myth claims a permanent connection between the royal lineages and the local ethnic groups objectified in the person of the first ancestor who remains at the place of origin. The point where the second ancestor turned to stone marks the border between the two regions of the lower moiety of the empire and provides a concrete, visible and sacred connection between the centre and the periphery. Finally, at the centre of Cusco itself, the presence of the third ancestor marks a further sacred and physical link between the two moieties of Cusco and the four quarters of the Empire.

Following Urton, I have emphasized the ways in which this imperial origin myth serves a series of ideological purposes. It provides an account of the origin of the hierarchical links between the royal lineages and the conquered ethnic groups, and also relates these links to concrete features of the landscape itself. However, these meanings are in many ways specific to that period in the sixteenth century when Sarmiento de Gamboa constructed his account.

The Pacariqtambo myth is told today by people with a different history and different preoccupations from those of the disenfranchised nobles of the sixteenth century. Urton himself recorded the following version in Pacariqtambo:

> Now we are going to talk. In Pacariqtambo there appeared near this town all together the three Inka brothers, the 'Hermanos Ayares'; this place is called Tampu T'oqo. From the ancient time of the appearance of the Hermanos Ayares from Pacariqtambo, the Inkas lived in the ruins built there in Maukallaqta and Pumaurqu. There, there are beautiful ruins, made by the Inkas, of stone that was brought to that place from Murunpampawayqo (valley of the spotted plain); from that quarry they carried stones to Maukallaqta and they made beautiful buildings. In that time, how lovely was the hill of Pumaurqu near Mollebamba; how beautiful was that great hill. There, the Inkas slept in the later afternoon in the entrance (guarded by) ... the beautiful little pumas; the beautiful, labyrinthine little things lying at the bottom of the valley. In that opening was the entrance to the Inka's house. There, we have finished speaking.[4]

(URTON 1990, P. 128)

The narrator of this version is concerned to establish his connection to the events of which he tells and thus we find, as is common in local rather than central versions of these myths, extremely detailed references to local places. Details of the journey, so important to the Inka nobles, are here subordinated to the establishment of where exactly the Inkas came from, and the subsequent linking of particular contemporary people to these prestigious ancestors.

It is also significant that the female ancestors have disappeared from this contemporary version of Inka origins, an absence which relates to their symbolic importance in the original version. The imperial myth, which sought to mark political and kinship hierarchy, used gender as a metaphor of rank. While the Inka lineages were founded by both male and female ancestors, each of the emergent lineages was associated with either a male or female ancestor and ranked accordingly, the female status depending on the male with whom she was associated.

Silverblatt's study of Inka gender ideologies (1987) stresses that gender parallelism was an important principle of Inka social organization. Thus, the Qoya, the daughter of the moon, was in charge of all feminine aspects of empire, including cults to female deities. However, while some women held considerable power in the Inka state, the ultimate authority was the male Inka. Thus gender parallelism implied but did not entail gender equality. As the empire consolidated, gender parallelism was increasingly used to denote hierarchy as the dominated ethnic groups were feminized in relationship to the dominant, conceptually male, Inka lineages. This gendered idiom was powerful as it used an image of complementarity and interdependence to mark a hierarchical relationship.

Gender parallelism is more strongly marked in the Tiwanaku myths that tell of the origin of the major sacred crops of the Andes, and of the introduction of civilization by the Inka ancestors:

> While peopling the city, our Inca taught the male Indians the tasks that were to be theirs, such as selecting seeds and tilling the soil. He taught them how to make hoes, how to irrigate their fields by means of canals that connected natural streams, and even to make these same shoes that we still wear today. The queen, meanwhile, was teaching the women how to spin and weave wool and cotton, how to make clothing, as well as other domestic tasks. In short, our sovereigns, the Inca king, who was master of the men, and Queen Coya, who was mistress of the women, taught their subjects everything that had to do with human living.
>
> (GARCILASO DE LA VEGA, 1976 [1609], VOL. I, 42–4)

The attribution of the origins of cultural production to the Inka ancestors characterizes the imperial legends, and differentiates them from those of the conquered ethnic groups. The deities and ancestors of the dominated peoples of the Andes were subordinated and disempowered by the Inkas, who integrated them into their cosmology, subtly changing their functions and status to undermine their creative autonomy. In this realignment of divine power, the supreme male deity was the Sun, and the supreme female deity the Moon and it was to the cults of the Moon that all women of the empire owned their ultimate allegiance (Silverblatt, 1987, pp. 47–50). However, colonial documents show that while Inka cosmology was forcefully asserted it was not universally accepted.

Thus we find in the following narrative that *coca*, a sacred Andean plant, was acquired by local people thanks to the guile of their gods and the beauty of the Indian woman who protects them from the Inka's wrath. The creative agents in this story are both male and female, acting together in a relationship of hierarchical complementarity:

> They also tell how in ancient times only the sun ate *coca* . . . and that the *huacas* [local deities/founding ancestors] were very envious of this and tried to steal the seeds of the bushes away from the sun and so they waited for an occasion when he was drunk, and sent a message with a llama, Urau,

to the moon, wife of the sun, in which they asked for the bag in which he kept those leaves. The moon refused to give it on the first and second until on the third they took it from her by a trick. When the sun awoke he knew what had happened and determined to kill Urau and would have done so had it not been for the intercession of a beautiful indian woman and even though he did not want to do it, while she was entreating him, Urau fled and came to Canta, a place three days away from Lima where the indians received him with great applause and began to adore him as a God.

(DUVIOLS, 1973)

II.2 Supernatural Beings – Female Forces of Regeneration

In the campaigns for the extirpation of idolatry that were carried out in the Viceroyalty of Peru in the sixteenth and seventeenth centuries, the ecclesiastical authorities recorded copious accounts of continuing allegiances to local reproductive deities, and to more generalized creative forces such as the Pachamama (Earth force), the Mamaqocha (Sea force) and the Saramama (Maize force) (Arriaga [1621], 1968; Duviols, 1971; Sallnow, 1987; Silverblatt, 1987):

> It was a common thing among the Indians to adore the fertile earth ... which they called Pachamama, offering her *chicha* [maize beer] by spilling it on the ground, as well as *coca* and other things so that she would provide for them; to make this, they placed a long stone in the midst of their fields in order to invoke the virtues of the earth from that point, so that she would protect their fields; and at harvest time, if Indians saw potatoes that had a different form from the rest, or ears of maize or other crops with a different shape from the others, they had the custom of adoring them and making many ceremonies to venerate them, drinking and dancing, viewing these as signs of good fortune ... [A]nd thus, for the same effect, when it was time to plow, turn over the earth, sow and harvest corn, potatoes, *quinoa*, and other vegetables and fruits of the earth, they would offer her, in similar fashion, fat, *coca*, *cuy* [guinea pig], and other things, and all the time drinking and dancing.[5]

(SILVERBLATT, 1987, PP. 24–5 FROM MURUA 1946, P. 278)

The Pachamama is a supernatural figure that continues to have considerable importance in the lives of contemporary Andean peoples:

> At the creation of the world the Pachamama said: 'I am the *Santa Tierra*. I am the one who creates and nurtures. For me you will *soplar la coca* [blow the coca]:[6]
>
> Ever since the creation she has been respected. She lives here below the *Santa Tierra*, inside the earth. The earth lives. All of us are living in her with all the Christians. All of Peru hails her. We live by working on top of her. Like our mother she is creating and nurturing us. But our

mother is mortal whereas the earth never dies. When we die we disappear into the earth: she is absorbing us. From her hair grows. This is the pasture and the wool for the animals. The animals feed themselves on this pasture.

She looks after us: all the animals and all of mankind. She looks after us like our mother. She has created all her children, including the Incas. She cares for the *apus* [the hill spirits], for everyone.

People make an offering to the *Pachamama* for their crops and their animals so that the animals do not sicken and that we have good harvests.

'For the welfare of the animals you will make me an offering in Carnival and the fiesta of St James. For a good harvest you will make an offering on the fiesta of Our Lady of Purification and on *Jueves de Comadres* [Thursday before Ash Wednesday]. On these days you will treat me.'

(GOW, 1976, P. 209)

Despite the association between Pachamama and the figure of the 'Earth Mother' that this account invokes, the relationship between Pachamama and the earth, motherhood and even femininity itself often challenges our notions of the benign, nurturing Earth Mother.

The term Pachamama combines two complex semantic elements. While 'mama' can mean mother, it also carries the more general connotation of a source of fertility:

In pre-Spanish cult, *mama* had a precise meaning, denoting unusually-shaped maize cobs or tubers, or images of them fashioned from stone, gold or silver and called 'mamasara' 'mamapapa' etc. (mama maize, mama potato). Similarly the most exquisite lumps of raw metal were also called *mamas* of the mines. Mama in this sense could have a masculine as well as a feminine meaning. In any event the term refers more to a source of fertility than to a biological mother.

(HARRIS, 1988, P. 67)

These male and female aspects of the deity or *mama* are illustrated in the following testimony concerning the worship of Mamayuta, Corn Mother:

Catalina Marmita had told . . . how in the heights of this village she guarded and cared for some earthen jars which were named Mamayutas, that one had breasts and the other was a man, and she kept them inside a uah, and for this purpose she had placed inside [the trough] coca, plumes of birds, and ears of corn and balls of colored wool; and these Mamayutas were kept there in that trough as the Mother of the corn of their fields and of other things which they take to be in the [Mamayutas'] name . . . and in like fashion, next to this trough they have another, and inside of it women place their newly born children who had died, whom they take there to offer to the Mayutas in order that they consume them; dead guinea pigs wrapped up in bits of cloth are also in the trough, all as offerings to the Mamayutas.[7]

(SILVERBLATT, 1987, PP. 34–5 CITING BIBLIOTECA NACIONAL DEL PERU, B1715, F.21V)

Just as the term 'mama' denotes far more than our term 'mother', so 'Pacha' extends beyond the concept of 'earth'. It refers to particular areas of time or space, to delimited periods, mythological ages and specific territories (Harris, 1988). It is thus not surprising to find that Pachamama is a supernatural force that embraces far more than agricultural production. The Pachamama is rooted in local geography, as are the predominantly male sprits of the mountains, and is invoked for all manner of indigenous production including mining, animal rearing, weaving and pottery (Bastien, 1978; Isbell, 1978; Mariscotti de Gorlitz, 1978; Nash, 1979; Silverblatt, 1987; Sallnow, 1987; Allen, 1988; Harris, 1988). Even wage labourers call on Pachamama, the life force of the major roads along which they have to travel to reach their places of work (Harvey, 1987).

The Pachamama is frequently presented as the wife or partner of sources of male fertility — particularly the rain and thunder gods, or alternatively the mountain spirits, thus embodying the generative force of gender parallelism referred to above. These depictions of the Pachamama emphasize that her importance as a female deity lies not in a feminine essence but in the dialectical opposition between male and female forces upon which supernatural agency is predicated.

The Pachamama shares the dangerous, even capricious nature of all Andean supernatural powers. One important feature common to these forces is that their relationship with the human community is characterized as one of mutual consumption. Human subsistence involves the extraction of the substance of these spirits, which must be replaced with offerings. These offerings take many forms, small burnt packages of mainly vegetable substances (*despacho*), animals, even human life itself. Thus since humans continually take from the earth, and the wider environment in which they dwell, they must replenish these sources of reproduction. This replenishment is done on a daily basis, with small offerings of coca or libations of alcohol. However, when the extractive process is intense or not fully reciprocated, these earth forces take on their most dangerous aspect as manifested in the male and female devils of the tin mines of Bolivia. Here the owners of the mine, the *Tio* or *Supay* (uncle or devil) and his partner the *China Supay* (female devil), dwell below the ground. They are the source of the mine's riches, but their diabolic nature is stressed and the miners have to make continual offerings to them in an attempt to ensure a degree of safety. These figures are thus distinguished from the protective, nurturing manifestations of the earth force whose more gentle attributes are, in this instance, transferred to the Virgin of the Mineshaft (Nash, 1979). Thus the Christian figure embodies the benign while the pagan figures embody malign power, in accordance with the Christian dichotomization of good and evil.

Since the introduction of Catholicism in the sixteenth century, the benign aspects of Pachamama have been associated with the Virgin Mary. Shrines to the virgin appeared in sites that had previously been dedicated to Pachamama (Sallnow, 1987) and Andean people often address the Pachamama as if addressing a Christian saint, calling her Santa Tierra Pachamama (Saint Earth Pachamama). However, despite this identification, the Pachamama's fullest force and character is quite distinct from and at times even opposed to that of the Catholic virgin mother.

Thus while the Pachamama has frequently been depicted by indigenist writers, national governments and romantic travellers as an essential female deity, as a generous, nurturing, providing mother, indigenous peoples stress both creative fertility and danger. She is capable of malicious attacks and voracious hunger as well as ensuring fertility, productivity and safety. The complex nature of *Pachamama* is expressed very clearly in Gose's account of how the people of Huaquirca, a small town in the South Andean Department of Apurimac, responded to his questions about *Pachamama*:

> The only time I heard the *pachamamas* discussed in any detail in Huaquirca was during the *t'inkas* [libations].[8] When I asked a woman what a *pachamama* is during one of these rites, she responded by holding up a pinch of soil between her thumb and forefinger, and saying 'this'. A similar identification with the soil has been reported elsewhere (Platt, 1980, p. 153), but this does not exhaust the specificity of the gesture. While travelling in the *puna* above Huaquirca, I was twice warned about sleeping outdoors in corrals with 'altars', for the *pachamamas* are likely to appear in dreams, trying to seduce the unwary. I was told to resist at all costs since 'they always take something' (i.e. castrate or rip out heart and lungs). Should I be forced to sleep in such a corral, my instructions were to cross myself, invoke the holy trinity, and eat a tiny pinch of earth from the floor of the house connected to the corral, but above all, to pour libations for the *pachamama* without fail every time and place I drink. Elsewhere, the kissing of dirt from the floor of the house has been reported as a means of appeasing a dwelling spirit known as the *condor mamani* (Buechler, 1980, p. 56), and ingestion of a pinch of soil has been cited as a means of avoiding supernatural attack (Manya, 1969, p. 137; Oblitas Poblete, 1978, pp. 38, 95). Here I would argue, then, that the pinch of soil does not represent the earth in general, but the spirit of a particular habitation or grazing territory.
>
> (GOSE, 1986A, P. 286)

Just as the Pachamama has a totally benign manifestation in the figure of the Virgin, so too there are Andean powers who embody dangerous, malign forces. These are usually gendered, and frequently female, displaying in exaggerated form the voraciousness and sexuality which characterizes one aspect of the Pachamama.

SECTION III

III.1 *Condemned Spirits and Flying Heads*

These supernatural figures appear to have emerged in the region as a response to colonial insistence on manifestations of evil in the Andean universe, and their determined association between indigenous deities and the European devil (Silverblatt, 1987; Taussig, 1987). The presence of such 'devils' is now ubiquitous and thus the narratives which refer to them are often cast in terms of contemporary experience rather than with reference to mythic time.

One of the most common of such spirits is the *condenado*, the condemned soul, who wanders the Andean landscape. These souls have been refused entry into heaven, or the land of the dead, because of heinous sins, such as incest and murder, committed during their lifetimes. Their Sisyphean punishment is continually to strive to climb the icy glaciers, always to fall before their aims is achieved.

Both the Pachamama and the hill spirits are dangerous Andean powers, but the *condenados* embody their negative aspects as the antithesis of productive force. They take both male and female form, but it is particularly the female *condenado* who tricks men into sexual relations with fatal results. Many of the stories follow a similar narrative sequence in which one partner goes away on a journey and seemingly returns before the appointed time. What has really happened is that the returned traveller is the *condenado* in the guise of a spouse or loved one. The disguises are always perfect, even the voice. The unsuspecting partner eats and sleeps with the *condenado*, and only realizes their mistake on the following day when the real traveller returns. The consequences are frequently fatal. Alternatively, the man who travels alone might come across a *condenado* on his journey, again in the guise of a beautiful woman. If he weakens and eats and sleeps with her he too will die.

Unlike the reciprocal relations between humans and the hill spirits, and the Pachamama, on which earthly fertility depends, humans gain nothing from the *condenados*. The sharing of food and bodily substance is extractive, the *condenados* greedily consume human energy in what are often explicitly cannibalistic acts:

The owner of a large herd of alpacas lived high up on Mount Ausangate. He had one single child. Once he went off to the village to buy some things and his wife stayed behind with the baby. It was only 2 years old. Watching and watching for her husband the woman said: 'He'll come soon, he'll come soon, he will arrive any minute.' She went on looking but her husband didn't appear. The sun was about to set behind the hill, it was already turning yellow. Then a woman wearing a white jacket came from the direction of Chiliq. She was in a hurry, running along the slope. So the woman called out to her: 'Come over here, mama,' she said. She beckoned to her with her hand. Then the other woman stopped. She didn't want to do what she said, but she went on calling her, 'Come, mama.' And so, that woman in the white jacket, came back down to the house. 'Let's sleep together. My husband has gone to the village but he hasn't appeared. We can sleep here together.' She took her to the house and began to cook. She put fuel on the fire. The baby began to cry. When it cried the woman in the white jacket said: 'Bring it to me. I will hold your baby.' 'Hold him for me, mama,' said the woman handing it over. The fire wouldn't light. The child was screaming. Since it went on screaming and because she still couldn't light the fire, the woman turned round and said: 'Give him to me, mama. I will put him on the breast.' But he would not suck. 'Leave it, mama. I'll hold him for you,' said the woman in the white jacket. The baby's voice was fading away. 'Is he sleeping, mama?' his mother asked. When she turned round the woman's mouth was covered in blood. The baby was eaten right down to the waist. That woman was a *condenado*. 'I'm just going to tie up the cattle,' the woman said and left the house. When she had left she hid among the cows. The cows were tied up already. At that moment, coming in under the cows, the woman in the white jacket called her. 'Mama, come, come!' But she didn't come out from under the cows. Then the *condenado* got annoyed. 'I couldn't get out,' the woman said. The *condenado* came up to her. When she came up the cattle just said 'huuuj'. It scared her. As it was already dark she wasn't a woman any more but had changed into a *condenado*. They stayed up together, until dawn, eating the baby. At dawn that woman left. When she was far away she took on the form of a woman. (That condemned woman, why had she come?) She had a brother. That woman and the man, her brother, had sexual relations. Afterwards the man died. The woman also died. Because of this the Lord sent her to the heights of Mt Ausangate. The man was sent to another place. Then God allowed her to eat the people in this area. So she began to eat the people, although she still hadn't eaten very many.

(RECORDED IN OCONGATE IN 1985)

The flying heads (*uma/cabezas voladoras*) share many of the characteristics of the *condenados*:

Once a young man had got involved with a young woman. But the young woman said to the young man that he should not visit her on Fridays and Tuesdays because she had engagements, but as the months went by he began to wonder: 'Why doesn't she want me to visit her on Fridays and Tuesdays?' The young man got more and more impatient, and decided to visit her one Tuesday. Tuesday arrived, and finally the young man set off for the house of his loved one, who was a witch, and on those days she took her head off, and began to wander through the streets, while her body remained prostrate on the bed letting out horrible shrieks (qar-qar-qar). The young man saw, through one of the holes in the door, and realized what was happening, he went into the room screwing up his courage, at the neck of the girl he put a large pile of ash, and then crawled under the bed, waiting for her to arrive, and finally the head came into the room wanting to get back to its normal state, but couldn't fix itself on, because the neck had ash on it, and the young man couldn't contain himself and began to laugh and the witch as she couldn't get her head back on her body, immediately threw herself onto the young man's shoulder, sticking to it. Frightened, the young man began to run into the country where there were many prickly pears growing. The young man said to her: 'I want to eat prickly pears, I'm going to pick a few so that you can eat.' But the witch didn't want to. Finally after a lot of insisting, the witch said that he could pick prickly pears, the young man spread out his poncho so that she could wait for him while he was picking, the young man took his chance and began to run, terrified, not knowing where he was going. A deer passed by where the witch was, the witch threw herself onto the back of the animal, who began to run through the plants, the prickly pears, where there were a lot of spines, the hair of the witch was caught in the prickly pears and she died. The deer went on running through the plants, frightened.

(ANSION, 1987, PP. 146–7)

While there have been claims that the flying heads are precolumbian figures, it also seems likely that their identification with women, with witchcraft and with voracious female sexuality is a feature of the European imaginative interpretation of Andean beliefs that have been re-incorporated into Andean 'tradition'. The association of her transformation into a flying head on Fridays and Tuesdays reinforces this position, since these were inauspicious days in the folk calendars of medieval Europe. In many ways these witches with flying heads are similar to the *condenados* in that they take possession of human beings in a parasitic relationship which drains people of their life-force.

Such parasitic figures are not exclusively female. The *naqaq*, the Andean slaughterer who mesmerizes his victims, slits their throats and drains their bodies of the grease which ensures human vitality, is one of the more vivid male manifestations of such figures (Gose, 1986b). Women can also be deceived by male *condenados*, and still-born children are believed to be offspring of sexual relations with hill spirits. The evil of these spirits is thus not focused on their femininity but appears to centre on the denial of reciprocity which their relationships with human beings entail, they eat (and eating is a common metaphor for sexual relations in the Andean region) but they do not feed.

Throughout this section on Andean myths and narratives it has been possible to see the presence of European notions of a Manichaen split between good and evil co-existing with indigenous depictions of supernatural power as intrinsically ambiguous. Ideal social relations, whether these be between humans and supernatural powers or between men and women, are essentially complementary, reciprocal and regenerative. Such reciprocity can imply hierarchy, as between gods and humans, rulers and ruled, men and women, without implying the destructive negativity manifest in relations with the devil spirits. In the following and final section, the relationship between spirit and human relations will be discussed in more detail.

SECTION IV

IV.1 Amazonia: Sexuality and Violence

This final example and all too brief reference to Amazonian mythology has been chosen to stress the dangers of seeing myths as representations of, or charters for, real social relations. Myths similar to the one summarized below are found in many areas of lowland South America. They are narratives that tell how men, who have been subordinated by women, manage to steal the source of women's power. The following is a Mehinaku story, concerning monstrous women spirits known as the Yamurikuma. It describes the origins of certain contemporary Mehinaku practices, namely the secret male cults, the sacred flutes and the threat of death or gang-rape, which prevents women from seeing these magical objects:

> In ancient times the men lived alone far away, they lived badly, naked, with no proper possessions, no weapons, no fire, no hammocks. They were forced to masturbate instead of having proper sex. The women on the other hand lived in a proper village with a female chief. They owned everything that is needed for a civilized life, such as houses, cotton, feather headdresses and the Kauka flutes which they had made. They wore male ornaments and body paint. They had a house for the Kauka flutes. The men saw the women playing the flutes there. They said 'This is bad, the women have stolen our lives' and they decided to take action. They made bullroarers. They thought they could have sex with their wives very soon. Running into the village whirring the bullroarers they managed to catch all the women and rip off their male decorations. They lectured them, telling them that they should wear female ornaments alone and leave the flute-playing to the men. The women ran to hide in their houses. At night the men came in the dark and raped the women. In the morning the men went fishing. After that the women could not go into the flute's house.

> (McCALLUM, 1992, AFTER GREGOR, 1985, P. 112)

Anthropologists have previously assumed that myths such as these can help us to interpret gender relations in the groups among whom they are told. Bamberger (1974) argued that these 'myths of matriarchy' explain and legitimate contemporary male dominance, and establish 'the proper set of behaviours expected between the sexes' (Bamberger, 1974, p. 274). More recently, Gregor (1985) has argued that male/female relations among the Mehinaku, native people of the Alto Xingu of central Brazil, are structured around aggression and male feelings of insecurity concerning the sexual and reproductive powers of women, again taking the myth as a symbolic representation of actual gender relations among the Mehinaku.

McCallum (1992) challenges this way of reading the myth — as a charter or model for social relations. She points out that while there are groups in Amazonia where male/female relations are very confrontational, the Mehinaku are not one of these. Indeed, their social relations centre on the importance of kinship, and on the complementarity of male and female agency in the production of these positive, moral, social relations. While sexual difference is marked, it is not the case that men's activities are valued more than women's. How then should we interpret the myth?

McCallum isolates two key problems with Gregor's interpretation. In the first place, he treats the narrative as a representation of real human gender relations, ignoring the fact that the characters in the myth are not humans but spirits living in mythic time. The second problem is that his treatment of the myth isolates it from the general social context to which it refers. Mehinaku hear and understand this myth in terms of their knowledge of kinship, of spirits and of ritual. This knowledge cannot be read off the myth itself but must be found in the wider context of Mehinaku social practice.

Gregor treats myths as if they are dreams showing the subconscious fears and desires of Mehinaku men, vehicles exploring the basic hostility between men and women. He treats associated rituals in a similar vein. The central section of his book is an analysis of the Pequi fruit rituals which he sees as expressions of pure sexual antagonism and indeed he labels them 'Gender Wars'. Whilst he argues that men are the victors in this 'war', it seems more likely that the central concern of the rituals is not sexual hegemony at all, but rather the creative interaction between male and female. The Pequi rituals consist of a series of games pitting male wit, ingenuity and strength against female, and vice versa. They are concerned with human sexuality, and in particular with fertility and productivity. In contrast, the flute and Yamurikuma ritual cycles are concerned with the original creation of sexuality, not with sexuality *per se* (McCallum, 1992).

Thus the flute ritual, with its violent sanctions of gang rape, is enacted in conjunction with the Pequi rituals, in which perfect sexual relations are depicted and in which appropriate male and female sexualities are brought together in games that are exciting, funny, and reciprocal. Men and women engage in these games as equal complementary partners. The flute ritual, by contrast, is about the origins of sexuality, about the creation of difference between men and women. In the enactment of these rituals, the female spirits of the flutes inhabit the men's bodies, and thus endow them with a crazy spirit sexuality that is both male and female. This sexuality goes nowhere, it is not productive, and is thus opposed to the appropriate and desirable sexuality of the Pequi rituals. Indeed, it is precisely because the spirit sexuality is crazy that it can act to harm women. The gang-rape of a woman who sees the flutes is not thought of as a punishment for transgression but as the agency of the spirit's uncontrolled, anti-social, angry sexual desire. Thus, far from representing actual human gender relations, this myth together with the rituals to which it refers, enables the Mehinaku to enact pre-human sexuality, and to distinguish it from the appropriate, gendered sexuality celebrated in the Pequi rituals.

IV.2 Conclusions

The material presented above has raised several questions concerning the relationship between feminist scholarship and the study of mythology. An important characteristic of mythic narratives, and one that distinguishes them from other accounts of human experience, is that they focus on places, epochs and characters that are in some sense beyond the realm of normal human social relations. The relationship between the gender relations of myth and those of everyday life is thus a complex one, and I would argue, one that we can only begin to access with considerably more cultural knowledge than the myths themselves provide. Thus Inka myths of complementary agency tell us little of the imperial use of such narratives in the struggle to establish and maintain political hierarchy, while the Mehinaku myths that might appear to denote the establishment of male dominance are told by people who value and enact egalitarian gender relations.

My understanding of feminism, in its broadest sense, is of a political project, predicated on (various) western notions of gender hierarchy, which seeks to undermine this hierarchy or at least to reveal the contingency, and historical specificity, of the gender differences on which it is based. Feminism is thus inscribed within particular notions of gender, personhood, power and value which poses problems when we attempt a feminist analysis of the social practices of non-western peoples (Strathern, 1988). Can we step outside our own notions of gender and still maintain a political voice that speaks to the feminist project? And if, as I have argued, myths cannot be assumed to reveal the nature of the gender relations of those who tell them, do we simply use them as a mirror to tell ourselves about our own ways of understanding gender difference?

A careful consideration of any mythological corpus will undoubtedly reveal many powerful female figures and modes of female agency, and the project of unveiling these might appear to provide information with which to challenge essentialist notions of feminine passivity. However, the presence of clearly gendered agents does not necessarily imply that the myth can be read as a representation of gender relations. The narratives concerning the voracious sexuality of female Andean devils are most centrally concerned with the consequences of a breakdown of reciprocity and not any particular feature or understanding of femininity, just as the Mehinaku men who threaten to gang-rape women essentially refer to the origins of sexuality and the process of human relations, which has allowed them to escape the awful spectre of endemic sexual antagonism.

It is thus in this sense that while recovering female figures for our history of mythology, we need to consider as far as possible the conditions in which particular narratives are produced and the many ways in which they are understood. When we ask what myths mean, what they are about, we have to remember that meanings are established in social relationships, and thus also ask for whom myths mean and how such meanings are perpetuated. The answers to these questions will take us beyond the myths themselves and beyond the scope of this short chapter. The relativism of anthropology makes it hard to isolate and universalize the category 'woman'. However, the political commitment of the feminist project, with its emphasis on absence and difference, can encourage us to recognize those voices in these texts, which are all too often silenced by their abstraction into the written form and by our power as readers to remove them from the social relations in which they were produced.

Notes

1 A brief consideration of how native Latin American has been represented in recent films illustrates this point. *The Mission* shows an innocent people subjected to the barbarity of European 'civilization'. The native peoples shown in *Emerald Forest* starkly represent the contrast between the noble and the brutish savage, as does the recently acclaimed *Dances with Wolves* – in this case with reference to native peoples of North America. More recently

the television appearances of the Kayapo and the BBC film on the Kogi of Colombia reformulate our moral salvation through Native Americans in terms of contemporary ecological concerns.

2 The links between this field of feminist scholarship and postmodern critique of structure is very clearly discussed in L. Nicholson (ed.) (1990), *Feminism/Postmodernism* (London: Routledge).

3 Reprinted by permission of University of Texas Press.

4 Reprinted by permission of University of Texas Press.

5 Reprinted by permission of University of Princeton Press.

6 People chew coca to acquire energy and propitious productive conditions. Those who chew coca continually blow on the carefully selective leaves before they put them into their mouth and thus maintain the links between themselves and the Pachamama and/or the hillspirits.

7 Reprinted by permission of Princeton University Press.

8 These offerings may be of alchohol, coca, burnt offerings or even blood sacrifice. They are known by various names in the Andean region of *herranza* (branding), *despacho* (dispatching), *haywarisqa* (handing over) and *ch'alla* (libation) (P. Gose [1986a], *Work, Class, Culture in Huaquirca: A Village in the Southern Peruvian Andes*, Ph.D. dissertation (London: London School of Economics).

References and Further Reading

Allen, C. (1988), *The Hold Life Has: Coca and Cultural Identity in an Andean Community* (Washington DC: Smithsonian Institution Press)

Ansion, J. (1987), *Desde el Rincon de los Muertos: El Pensamiento Mitico en Ayacucho* (Lima: Gredes)

Arriaga, P.J. de (1968) [1621], *The Extirpation of Idolatry in Peru*, trans. L. Clark Keating (Lexington: University Press of Kentucky)

Asad, T. (ed.) (1973), *Anthropology and the Colonial Encounter* (London: Ithaca Press)

Bamberger, J. (1974), 'The Myth of Matriarchy: Why Men Rule in Primitive Society' in M. Rosaldo and L. Lamphere (eds), *Women Culture and Society* (Stanford: Stanford University Press), pp. 263–80

Bastien, J. (1978), *Mountain of the Condor: Metaphor and Ritual in an Andean Ayllu* (St Paul, Minnesota: West Publishing Co.)

Bucher, B. (1981) *Icon and Conquest: A Structural Analysis of the Illustrations of de Bry's Great Voyaqes*, trans. Basia Miller Gulati (Chicago: University of Chicago Press)

Buechler, H.C. (1980), *The Masked Media: Aymara Fiestas and Social Interaction in the Bolivian Highlands* (The Hague: Mouton)

Clifford, J. (1988), *The Predicament of Culture: Twentieth-Century Ethnography Literature and Art* (London: Harvard University Press)

Duviols, P. (1971), *La Lutte contre les Religions Autochtones dans le Perou Colonial* (Paris and Lima: Institut Français d'Etudes Andines)

—— (1973) [1619], 'Un Mythe de L'origine de la coca (Cajatambo)' in *Bulletin del Institut Francais d'Etudes Andines*, vol. II:i

Garcilaso de la Vega (1976) [1609], *The Incas: The Royal Commentaries of the Inca*, trans. M. Jolas, ed. A. Gheerbrant (New York: Avon Books)

Gose, P. (1986a), *Work, Class and Culture in Huaquirca: A Village in the Southern Peruvian Andes*, Ph.D. dissertation (London: London School of Economics)

—— (1986b), 'Sacrifice and the Commodity Form in the Andes' in *Man*, vol. 21, no.2, pp. 296–310

Gow, D. (1976), *The Gods and Social Change in the High Andes*, Ph.D. dissertation (Madison: University of Wisconsin)

Gregor, T. (1985), *Anxious Pleasures: The Sexual Lives of an Amazonian People* (Chicago: University of Chicago Press)

Haraway, D. (1989), *Primate Visions: Gender, Race and Nature in the World of Modern Science* (London: Routledge)

Harris, O. (1988), 'La Pachamama: Significados de la Madre en el Discurso Boliviano' in *Mujeres Latinoamericanas: Diez Ensayos y Una Historia Colectiva* (Lima: Flora Tristan), pp. 57–79

Harvey, P. (1987), *Language and the Power of History: The Discourse of Bilinquals in Oconqate (Southern Peru)*, Ph.D. dissertation (London: London School of Economics)

Isbell, B.J. (1978), *To Defend Ourselves: Ecology and Ritual in an Andean Villaqe* (Austin: University of Texas)

de Lauretis, T. (1987), *Technologies of Gender: Essays on Theory, Film and Fiction* (Bloomington: Indiana University Press)

Lévi-Strauss, C. (1964), *Le Cru et le Cuit* (Paris: Plon)

—— (1966), *Du Miel aux Cendres* (Paris: Plon)

—— (1968), *L'Oriqine de Manieres de Table* (Paris: Plon)

—— (1971), *L'Homme Nu* (Paris: Plon)

Mariscotti de Gorlitz, A.-M. (1978), *Pachamama Santa Tierra: Contribucion al estudio de la religion autoctona en los Andes centro-meridionales* (Berlin: Gebr. Mann Verlag)

Mason, P. (1990), *Deconstructing America: Representations of the Other* (London: Routledge)

Manya, J. (1969), 'Temible Nakaq?' in *Allpanchis* 1 (Cusco: Instituto de Pastoral Andino), pp. 135–8

McCallum, C. (1993), 'Ritual and the Origin of Sexuality in the Alto Xingu' in P. Gow and P. Harvey (eds), *Violence, Sexuality and Cultural Difference* (London: Routledge)

Murua, M. de (1946) [1590], *Historia del origen y geneologia real de los Incas*, ed. C. Bayle (Madrid: Consejo Superior de Investigaciones Cientificas, Instituto Santo Toribio de Mogrovejo)

Nash, J. (1979), *We Eat the Mines and the Mines Eat Us: Dependency and Exploitation in Bolivian Tin Mines* (New York: Columbia University Press)

Nicholson, L. (ed.) (1990), *Feminism/Postmodernism* (London: Routledge)

Oblitas Poblete, E. (1978), *Cultura Callawaya* (La Paz: Ediciones Populares Camalinghi)

O'Gorman, E. (1961), *The Invention of America: An Inquiry into the Historical Nature of the New World and the Meaning of its History* (Bloomington: University of Indiana Press)

Platt, T. (1980), 'Espejos y Maiz: El Concepto de Yanantin entre los Machas de Bolivia' in E. Mayer and R. Bolton (ed.), *Parentesco y Matrimonio en los Andes* (Lima: Pontificia Universidad Catolica del Peru, Fondo Editorial)

Said, E. (1978), *Orientalism* (London: Routledge & Kegan Paul)

Sallnow, M. (1987), *Pilgrims of the Andes: Regional Cults in Cusco* (Washington DC: Smithsonian Institution Press)

Sarmiento de Gamboa, P. (1942) [1572], *Historia de los Incas* (Buenos Aires: Emece Editores)

Scott, J.W. (1988), *Gender and the Politics of History* (New York: Columbia University Press)

Silverblatt, I. (1987), *Moon, Sun and Witches: Gender Ideologies and Class in Inca and Colonial Peru* (Princeton: Princeton University Press)

Strathern, M. (1988), *The Gender of the Gift: Problems with Women and Problems with Society in Melanesia* (Berkeley: University of California Press)

Taussig, M. (1987), *Shamanism, Colonialism and the Wild Man: A Study in Terror and Healing* (Chicago: The University of Chicago Press)

Urbano, H.O. (1981), *Wiracocha y Ayar: Heroes y Funciones en las Sociedades Andinas* (Cusco: CERA Bartolome de las Casas)

Urton, G. (1990), *The History of a Myth: Pacariqtambo and the Origin of the Inkas* (Austin: University of Texas Press)

Zuidema, R.T. (1964), *The Ceque System of Cuzco: The Social Organization of the Empire of the Inca* (Leiden: E.J. Brill)
—— (1982), 'Myth and History in Ancient Peru' in I. Rossi (ed.), *The Logic of Culture* (South Hadley, Mass.: Bergin & Garvey), pp. 150–75

OTHER SUGGESTED READING:

Basso, E. (1985), *A Musical View of the Universe: Kalapalo Myth and Ritual Performances* (Philadelphia: University of Pennsylvania Press)
Brown, M. (1985), *Tsewa's Gift: Magic and Meaning in an Amazonian Society* (Washington DC: Smithsonian Institution Press)
Gow, P. (1991), *Of Mixed Blood: Kinship and History in Peruvian Amazonia* (Oxford: Clarendon Press)
Guss, D. (1989), *To Weave and Sing: Art, Symbol and Narrative in the South American Rain Forest* (Berkeley: University of California Press)
Harrison, R. (1989), *Sings, Songs and Memory in the Andes: Translating Quechua Language and Culture* (Austin: University of Texas Press)
Hill, J.D. (ed.) (1988), *Rethinking History and Myth: Indigenous South American Perspectives on the Past* (Urbana: University of Illinois Press)
Howard-Malverde, R. (1990), *The Speaking of History: 'Willapaakushayki' or Quechua Ways of Telling the Past* (London: Institute of Latin American Studies)
Hugh-Jones, C. (1979), *From the Milk River: Spatial and Temporal Processes in Northwest Amazonia* (Cambridge: Cambridge University Press)
Hugh-Jones, S. (1979), *The Palm and the Pleiades: Initiation and Cosmology in Northwest Amazonia* (Cambridge: Cambridge University Press)
Lizot, J. (1985), *Tales of the Yanomami: Daily Life in the Venezuelan Forest* (Cambridge: Cambridge University Press)
Overing Kaplan, J. (1975), *The Piaroa: a People of the Orinoco Basin: A Study in Kinship and Marriage* (Oxford: Clarendon Press)
Perrin, M. (1987), *The Way of the Dead Indians: Guajiro Myths and Symbols*, trans. M. Fineberg (Austin: University of Texas Press)
Rappaport, J. (1988), *The Politics of Memory: Native Historical Interpretation in the Colombian Andes* (Cambridge: Cambridge University Press)
Rasnake, R. (1988), *Domination and Cultural Resistance: Authority and Power among an Andean People* (Durham, NC: Duke University Press)
Urton, G. (ed.) (1985), *Animal Myths and Metaphors in South America* (Salt Lake City: University of Utah Press)
Salomon, F. and Urioste, G. (1991), *The Huarochiri Manscript* (Austin: University of Texas Press)
Steward, J.H. (ed.) (1946–50), *Handbook of South American Indians* (Washington DC: Smithsonian Institution Press)
Steward, J.H. and Faron, L.C. (1959), *Native Peoples of South America* (New York: McGraw-Hill)
Wachtel, N. (1977), *The Vision of the Vanquished: The Spanish Conquest through Indian Eyes 1530–1570* (New York: Barnes & Noble)

Also, articles in *Journal of Latin American Lore* and *Latin American Indian Literatures*

Glossary of Quechua (Qu.) and Spanish (Sp.) Terms

Ayllu (Qu.): Local community or kin group.
Chicha (Sp.): Fermented maize beer.

Condenado (Sp.): Condemned spirit.

Condor mamani (Qu.): Dwelling spirit.

Cuy (Qu.): Guinea pig.

Despacho (Sp.): Dispatch, offering to nature spirits.

Huaca/waq'a (Qu.): Local sacred place or ancestor.

Khipu (Qu.): Knotted cord abacus used by the Inkas.

Khipukamayoq (Qu.): The keeper and reader of the Khipu.

Naqaq (Qu.): Slaughterer.

Puna (Qu.): High plateau zone of the Andes, above tree level.

Quinoa (Qu.): Native Andean grain.

T'inka (Qu.): Libation.

Uma (Qu.)/*Cabeza Voladora* (Sp.): Head/Flying head.

PART 6

Goddesses in the Twentieth Century

ROSEMARY
ELLEN GUILEY

Witchcraft as Goddess Worship

From historical and anthropological perspectives, witchcraft is a form of sorcery, the use of magical power to effect change. As such, witchcraft exists universally, and probably has been used since humankind first banded together in groups. Neolithic cave paintings, such as the famous sorcerer of Trois Frères in France, show that primitive people had at least a grasp of magic: that by performing a rite to contact the supernatural, ordinary mortals could ensure a successful hunt for themselves.

Witchcraft as sorcery continues to be practised around the world; witches have always been amongst us, casting their spells. Almost universally, witchcraft is associated with evil, though some witches in western culture claim to be 'white', or good. Within the last few decades in the West, Witchcraft (with a capital 'W') has been reformulated into a religion concerned with benevolent magic. Witchcraft – or *Wicca*, the *Craft* or the *Old Religion*, as it is also called – combines magic with pagan religions and mythologies. It recognizes a bipolar Divine, God and Goddess, and gives emphasis to the latter.[1] All followers are priests and priestesses. Women generally have the ultimate authority, and in covens, or groups, of Witches led by a partnership of high priestess and high priest, the high priestess is considered supreme.

How this religion came to be is not entirely clear. Witches prefer to cloak their practice in secrecy and mystery, a necessity, they say, born of centuries of harassment and persecution. Claims are made that the religion has a past stretching back hundreds of years, at least, if not into antiquity. However, there is no historical evidence to prove such claims, nor is any evidence forthcoming from Witches themselves. Claims that 'witchcraft' has been practised in one's family for generations do not constitute proof of a *religion* of Witchcraft. Such witchcraft probably has been little more than magical rites with a pagan flavour. From the writings that have been made public, Witchcraft as a religion appears to be a post-World War II phenomenon that has invented itself as it has grown, drawing its strength from a popular interest in the occult and mythology, a disaffection from mainstream religion and the rise of feminism.

The religion as it is currently practised has a patchwork mythology borrowed from other religions. It has a creed and philosophy, but no liturgy beyond a few fundamental rituals. There is very little dogma and no central authority. There is a great deal of diversity and invention. Before discussing these elements, it is helpful to consider the roots of, and early influences on, the development of Witchcraft as a religion.

BACKGROUND AND STRUCTURE

The man credited with bringing Witchcraft the religion to public awareness is Gerald B. Gardner (1884–1964), an English civil servant who had a lifelong interest in the occult and archaeology, and who was a nudist. From 1924 to 1936, Gardner worked in the Far East, including Malaysia, where he became acquainted with Oriental magical and mystical practices. After his return to England, he became involved with an occult group, the Fellowship of the Crotona, which had Theosophist, Co-Masonic and Rosicrucian underpinnings. There he met a coven of Witches who initiated him into their group in 1939. They claimed to be 'Hereditary Witches' who practised 'the Old Religion' passed down through centuries.

Gardner, who had already written two novels, wanted to write a book about Witchcraft but was forbidden by coven secrecy rules and was discouraged by the fact that England still had an ancient law against witchcraft in force. Gardner was permitted by his high priestess to cloak his knowledge in a novel, *High Magic's Aid*, written under the pseudonym 'Scire' (his magical name) and published in 1949. There is no mention of Goddess in that book, only worship of the 'old gods' who were referred to solely as 'Janicot', possibly a term of Basque origin (*Jainco*, meaning 'God'), and probably borrowed from the writings of Pierre de Lancre, a witch judge who prosecuted accused witches in the Basque region in the early seventeenth century.

In 1951, after the witchcraft law was repealed and Gardner's high priestess was dead, Gardner went public about Witchcraft. He formed his own coven, drawing on fellow members of a nudist club to which he belonged, and self-professed Witches. In 1953, he initiated Doreen Valiente into the coven; Valiente, who became his high priestess, was to prove a significant influence in the development of a Goddess-oriented Craft.

The Witchcraft Gardner had learned from his first coven was written down by him in a 'Book of Shadows', a term still used by Witches for their personal diary of Craft philosophy, rituals and spells. The term 'Book of Shadows' was not of ancient Witchcraft origin, as Gardner intimated, but probably was borrowed by him from a contemporary magazine article about an old Sanskrit manuscript. As his followers were to find out, Gardner – who falsely passed himself off as holding a doctorate of philosophy – was not honest about many things concerning Witchcraft.

If Witchcraft was indeed a centuries-old organized religion, Gardner inherited precious little in the way of formal material. The Book of Shadows that Gardner gave to Valiente showed borrowings from other sources, most notably Aleister

Crowley (1875–1947), the *enfant terrible* of ceremonial magic. Gardner had met Crowley in 1946 and had been given by him a charter to operate a lodge of the Ordo Templi Orientis (O.T.O.), an occult order devoted to Tantric sex magic. Gardner acknowledged his appropriation of material only when confronted with it by Valiente. He justified his reliance on Crowley by his entitlement, as a charter-holder of the O.T.O., and because the rituals from his old coven were so fragmentary that they could not be made workable without supplement. He admired the pagan flavour of Crowley's writings and thought they served his purpose.

Valiente objected to the Crowley material because of Crowley's tainted reputation, so Gardner allowed her to revise the 'Book of Shadows'. She disposed of much of the Crowley material. Together, she and Gardner were the primary force in formalizing the essential rites and philosophy of the Craft. The pre-eminence of Goddess was yet to come. While Valiente has maintained that a Goddess element has always been part of the Craft, many Witches believe she is primarily responsible for the prominence now given to Goddess, as well as to women, in the Craft. As for Gardner, he insisted that God should have dominance, and that women in the Craft should be subservient to men.

Gardner wrote two non-fiction books on Witchcraft which caught the public's fancy: *Witchcraft Today* (1954) and *The Meaning of Witchcraft* (1959), in which he presented a vague but romantic picture of modern-day Witchcraft as a true survival of an ancient religion. He was greatly influenced – as probably was his first coven – by the controversial 'witch-cult' theory of anthropologist Margaret A. Murray. Murray (1921) maintained that the witchcraft that was persecuted by the Church during the Middle Ages and Reformation was not a product of imagination, but was an organized pagan religion, the cult of Diana, that had survived unbroken from Paleolithic times. She said that witchcraft was more widespread and organized during the Inquisition than most historians believed.

Murray's theory was later proved to be without merit. While it is evident that pockets of paganism survived long into the dominance of Christianity, this does not make all pagans 'witches', nor does it demonstrate that a religion called Witchcraft existed. During the Inquisition, the term 'witch' was applied freely, a convenient heresy catch-all for anyone who wished to bring the Church down upon an enemy. The so-called 'confessions' of accused witches as recorded in trials are suspect due to the unspeakable tortures used to extract them. The alleged sabbats, at which witches were said to feast on babies and fornicate with the Devil, are most likely distorted accounts based upon pagan rites. The Church viewed all pagan rites as Devil worship, and all pagan gods as devils or the Devil.

While some accused witches undoubtedly were witches in the magical sense – the village wise woman or cunning man who cast spells for pay – that also is no evidence for a religion of witchcraft.

It was inevitable that once Witchcraft was out in the open in Britain that sensationalist media coverage should follow, especially since Gardner's brand of Witchcraft featured rituals in the nude. Fearful of a possible backlash, some members of Gardner's coven, primarily a man named 'Ned', drafted a set of proposed Craft

Fig. 39 Witch riding on the Devil's he-goat to the *Walpurgisnacht*, goaded on by playful Amoretti, by Albrecht Dürer.

rules for conduct in order to protect secrecy. Gardner then announced the existence of allegedly ancient 'Craft laws', but even his own coveners were skeptical. Valiente was angered to find that the 'laws' required the high priestess to acknowledge God as the ultimate power, and that her office should always be filled by a young woman because youth was 'necessary' in the representation of Goddess. In 1957 Gardner's coven broke up, with Valiente and others going their own ways. Meanwhile, Gardner's Witchcraft took hold in Canada and the United States in the 1960s, and found fertile ground in the anti-establishment youth movement and the budding feminist movement. Most new members of the Craft accepted the pseudo-history of an unbroken religious tradition extending to ancient times. Copies of the 'Craft laws' were circulated and passed off as ancient in origin. New members found further reinforcement and inspiration from Robert Graves's *The White Goddess* (1946), which contends that the original supreme deity in Europe and the Mediterranean was a goddess, not a god, and that a return of Goddess worship is the only hope for the spiritual salvation of western civilization. Graves also accepted Murray's witch-cult. (*See* Diane Purkiss's observations about Graves in this volume, p. 443.)

When Murray's theory was shattered and some of the fallacies about Gardner's 'ancient, unbroken religion' were exposed, Witchcraft the religion was forced to look for a past. It grafted itself more firmly onto a revival of paganism and Goddess worship. While some Witches still support the witch-cult theory (Crowley, 1989) and look for scraps to connect modern practices to the past, many acknowledge that their religion is an ongoing reconstruction of pagan fertility, mystery and ecstasy rites – minus blood sacrifices – combined with elements of folk magic and ceremonial magic. Thus, the Craft can be said to maintain an air of antiquity. As its philosophy has developed, Witchcraft has been interpreted by its followers as a mystical path, and has been compared to the individuation process described in the psychology of Carl Jung.

In practice, Witchcraft is divided into numerous traditions. The Gardnerian tradition, based on Gardner's material, is dominant. The second largest tradition is Alexandrian, named after Alexander Sanders (1926–88), an English Witch who copied a good deal of Gardner's material. In the United States, the Dianic tradition, a feminist expression of the Craft, has a large following. There are countless smaller traditions, each with its own interpretation of the Craft. Essentially, anyone can start a tradition and set whatever practices she or he chooses.

While the Supreme Being in Witchcraft is bipolar, emphasis is given to Goddess over God. This emphasis is largely a product of the feminist movement. Even Murray (1931), in positing the existence of an unbroken witch cult through the ages, emphasized that worship centred on a Horned God under the aegis of, usually, a male leader. The emphasis on Goddess is a deliberate effort to address what Witches perceive as a grievous imbalance preached in the patriarchal religions of Christianity, Judaism and Islam. Catholic Christianity may have its cult of Mary, but the Queen of Heaven, as the mother of Jesus is called, is neither mortal nor goddess but frozen in between. In the West, there is no religion that recognizes the Divine Feminine save for Witchcraft (and other Neo-Pagan revivals), and it is this feature above all others that attracts new followers. Both men and women join to find both the transcendant Goddess as co-creator of the universe and the immanent Goddess force within – the highest expression of anima or the Great Mother archetype residing deep in the unconscious. Some Witches combine religion and politics and pursue a feminist agenda. Others are politically 'green'. Others wish only to focus on a spiritual quest.

The role of magic varies from group to group and Witch to Witch. Some adherents do join the Craft because they want to become magicians. Some of these individuals may drop out and pursue paths with groups devoted strictly to ritual magic. Within the Craft, magical powers are considered part of one's spiritual development; they are acquired and developed along the way, and are used to serve Goddess. As her representatives on earth, Witches must use magic for the greater good of humanity. The use of magic to harm is proscribed. The *Wiccan Rede*, a Witch's version of the Golden Rule, states, 'An' it harm none, do what ye will.' (Gardner attempted to give this an ancient origin, but it seems to be yet another borrowing from Crowley in his famous Law of Thelema, 'Do what thou wilt shall be the whole of the law . . .'.) The 'Threefold Law of Return', which appears to be a post-Gardner borrowing from *Aradia* (*see* p. 419), states that magic, good or bad, rebounds upon the originator magnified three times; the Witch foolish enough to cast evil magic will receive a boomerang effect three times over. This outlawing of so-called black magic seems to have been done for the primary purpose of making Witchcraft more palatable to a skeptical and antagonistic public. It is a peculiarly Christian view on the morality of magic that sets Witchcraft as religion apart from witchcraft as sorcery. In any society where sorcery is part of daily life and politics, a witch who declines to curse an enemy because it isn't 'right' (one is tempted to say because it isn't 'Christian') is worthless in her or his office. Nonetheless, the Craft laws have become established in the religion, and most Witches seek to abide by them. Many see themselves as Goddess's instruments of healing.

As a religion, Witchcraft has only the barest skeleton of organization. Many Witches practice as 'solitaries', alone and in private, while others collect in covens that follow a tradition. Some high priestesses have some authority over several covens – those which have 'hived off' from a mother coven – but no one reports to a central authority. Typically, a coven numbers from three to thirteen individuals, male and female (some feminist and gay Witches band together in all-female or all-male covens). In the dominant traditions, there are established forms for rituals, raising magical powers, initiations and observing the sabbats, seasonal celebrations based on pagan agrarian festivals. Individualism and eclecticism are prized among Witches, who feel free to develop and change their rituals to suit their own ever-changing needs. Song, dance, poetry, chanting and live drama are integral to religious expression.

The philosophy and rituals of Witchcraft are derived in a large part from the occult philosophies and ritual magic ceremonies of Freemasonry and the Hermetic Order of the Golden Dawn, which in turn were drawn upon the Greco-Egyptian mysteries, the *Corpus Hermeticum* and the Western Kabbalah, a magical philosophy based upon the mysticism of the Jewish Kabbalah and Tree of Life. Other original influences are *The Key of Solomon*, a *grimoire*, or textbook, of magical incantations attributed to the Biblical King Solomon (an important text in the Hermetic Order of the Golden Dawn) and the Tuscan legend of Aradia (Herodias), daughter of Diana and her brother, Lucifer, god of light. In addition to borrowing ritual material from Aleister Crowley, a one-time member of the Golden Dawn, Gardner borrowed poetry from Rudyard Kipling and injected elements of eastern magic and mysticism, probably stemming from his time in Malaysia.

Other Witches have also drawn from the occult novels of Dion Fortune (1892–1946) and from Apuleius's *The Golden Ass*, which provides a blueprint for the mysteries of Isis. Crowley is still used, especially his 'Hymn to Pan'.

According to Gardner, his old coven recognized a Moon Goddess, whom they called 'Airdia' and 'Areda' (probably corruptions of Aradia), but, as has been noted, the Goddess aspect of the Craft was one-dimensional pending the contributions of Valiente and those who have been inspired by her.

CENTRAL BELIEFS, MYTHS AND RITES

The Supreme Being is recognized as bipolar, male and female, in God and Goddess. Both God and Goddess are in turn personified by various pagan deities. The Craft draws primarily upon the mythologies of the Egyptians, Greeks, Celts, Babylonians and Sumerians. Some covens give emphasis to Teutonic mythology.

Goddess is 'She of A Thousand Names' who can be worshipped and petitioned in any of her numberless guises. Some covens, ever eclectic, draw upon Native American mythologies, and even upon the religions of Hinduism and Buddhism in recognizing names and aspects of Goddess. Witches study the mythologies of interest and construct rites around them. Frequently, Witches take the name of a goddess or god as their magical Craft name.

Above all, Goddess is seen as the Triple Goddess with the three aspects of virgin, mother and crone. These aspects, the three phases of womanhood, are in turn related to phases of the moon, with which Goddess is identified. The virgin, or new moon, is Artemis/Diana, the huntress, the wild and free young woman who belongs to no man. The mother, or full moon, is the matron, the nuturer at her peak of fecundity and sexuality; she is Selene, Demeter, Ishtar, Isis, Queen Maeve. The crone, or waning and dark moon, is the old woman past menopause, the hag, the Wise Woman, the keeper of the mysteries of death, the destroyer to whom all life must return in death. In this aspect, she is frequently represented as Hecate, a triple goddess in herself, and sometimes as Kali.

God is usually called the Horned God (even 'Old Hornie') after pagan deities such as Pan and Cernunnos. He is lord of nature, the fertilizer of life, the Sun to Goddess's Moon, the sacrificial king of pagan rites whose blood and dismembered body are scattered upon the fields to ensure the continuing fecundity of the land. While God is considered co-equal to Goddess, he is given far less attention in rituals and writings.

The personified gods and goddesses also are seen as archetypes, primal urges and forces residing deep within the collective conscious of humankind. Connecting with these archetypes and bringing them into consciousness is part of the spiritual development pursued by many Witches.

The central myth of Witchcraft is the myth of rebirth. Gardner (1954) called it 'The Myth of the Goddess'; it is also called 'The Legend of the Descent of the Goddess into the Underworld' (Farrar, 1971). Gardner opined that the story was Celtic in origin and that it was constructed to explain Witchcraft beliefs and rituals. It is a variation on the descent myths such as of Demeter and Kore/Persephone, Inanna and Dumuzi and Ishtar and Tammuz, and probably was adapted by Gardner to justify some of his practices. The text of the Myth of the Goddess varies slightly from author to author; Witches are fond of changing and embellishing texts to give stories a different or personal flavour. The version given here is that of Gardner:

> Now G. [Goddess] had never loved, but she would solve all the mysteries, even the mystery of Death, and so she journeyed to the nether lands. The guardians of the portals challenged her. 'Strip off thy garments, lay aside thy jewels, for nought may ye bring with you into this our land.' So she laid down her garments and her jewels and was bound as are all who enter the realms of Death, the mighty one.
>
> Such was her beauty that Death himself knelt and kissed her feet, saying: 'Blessed be thy feet that have brought thee in these ways. Abide with me, but let me place my cold hand on thy heart.' And she replied: 'I love thee not. Why doest thou cause all things that I love and take delight in to fade and die?' 'Lady,' replied Death, "tis age and fate, against which I am helpless. Age causes all things to wither; but when men die at the end of time, I give them rest and peace and strength so that they may return. But you, you are lovely. Return not; abide with me.' But she answered: 'I love thee not.' Then said Death: 'As you receive not my hand on your heart, you must receive Death's scourge.' 'It is fate, better so,' she said, and she knelt. Death scourged her and she cried: 'I know the pangs of love.' And Death said, 'Blessed be,' and gave her the fivefold kiss, saying: 'Thus only may you attain to joy and knowledge.' And he taught her all the mysteries, and they loved and were one; and he taught her all the magics. For there are three great events in the life of man — love, death and resurrection in the new body — and magic controls them all. To fulfill love you must return again at the same time and place as the loved ones, and you must remember and love her or him again. But to be reborn you must die and be ready for a new body; to die you must be born; without love you may not be born, and this is all the magic.
>
> *(WITCHCRAFT TODAY)*

(Compare Iris Furlong's account of 'The Descent of Inanna to the Netherworld' in this volume, p. 17.)

The myth is reflected in current practice. Witches believe in reincarnation in some form. Most rites are performed in the nude ('skyclad') when possible. Gardner insisted on nudity and this was probably his invention. (Some self-professed 'Hereditary Witches' in the UK say they have always worshipped robed.) Binding with cords and scourging also are part of traditional Witch ritual, and probably are Gardner's contributions, perhaps from his exposure to eastern occultism. Binding parts of the body to reduce blood flow, as well as scourging, are ancient practices used by adepts and mystics to attain altered states of consciousness. Francis King (1970) goes so far as to say that Gardner introduced these practices into Witchcraft because he had a penchant for voyeurism and sado-masochism. However, Valiente (1989) cites a classical precedent in the frescoes of the Villa of Mysteries at Pompeii, which depict a young woman, perhaps undergoing initiation, who begins clothed, is flagellated and at the end dances in the nude. Also, Witches point to the legend of *Aradia,* in which Diana sends Aradia to earth to instruct witches in their magical ways and how to destroy their oppressors. The legend was recorded by an American folklorist, Charles Godfrey Leland (1889), who claimed to receive it as oral lore from a Tuscan witch named 'Maddalena'. According to the legend, when Aradia has finished instructing witches, she is recalled to heaven by Diana. Aradia's parting instructions to her witches are:

> Whenever ye have need of anything,
> Once in the month, and when the moon is full,
> Ye shall assemble in some desert place,
> Or in a forest all together join
> To adore the potent spirit of your queen,
> My mother, great Diana . . .
> And as the sign that ye are truly free,
> Ye shall be naked in your rites, both men
> And women also: this shall last until
> The last of your oppressors shall be dead; . . .

Regardless of the origin of their ritual nudity, most Witches accept it as Craft practice and espouse its benefits. Starhawk, a leading feminist American Witch, contends that nudity establishes a closeness and honesty among coveners and 'is a sign that a Witch's loyalty is to the truth before any ideology or any comforting illusions' (Starhawk, 1979, p. 83).

'Blessed be,' as Death says in the 'Myth of the Goddess', is a Witch salutation. The 'fivefold kiss' which Death gives Goddess also is part of the Craft, given in various rituals and especially upon initiation. The Witch is kissed upon five parts of the body: the feet, the knees, above the pubic hair, the breasts and the lips. The kisses are accompanied by this blessing:

> Blessed be thy feet that have brought thee in thy ways.
> Blessed be thy knees that shall kneel at the sacred altar.
> Blessed be thy phallus/womb without which we would not be.
> Blessed be thy breasts formed in beauty and in strength.
> Blessed be thy lips that shall utter sacred names.

The fivefold kiss is done with the intent of recognizing the body as the temple of Goddess or God. As a fertility religion, Witchcraft believes the sensual and sexual should be honoured and celebrated.

Finally, the sexual act between Goddess and Death is observed in the Craft ritual called the 'Great Rite', seen as a *hieros gamos* or union with the godhead. The Witches become God and Goddess, participating in the creative force of the universe, part of the eternal cycle of birth, death and rebirth. The Great Rite may be performed either 'in truth' or 'in token', that is, as an actual sexual act or as a symbolic act in which an *athame*, a ritual knife, is thrust into a chalice full of wine.

The central 'Myth of the Goddess' plays a role in all initiations. Like Masonry, most traditions have three degrees. The first-degree initiate undergoes a spiritual death of the old self and is reborn a Witch, a child of Goddess. He or she enters the magical circle cast for the rite, and symbolically enters the Craft, 'in perfect love and perfect trust', a phrase borrowed from Crowley. Initiation into the second degree involves a re-enactment of the 'Myth of the Goddess', in which the initiate 'meets death'. By so doing, he or she loses the self and thus gains control over it, and also over the transformations of life and death. Initiation into the third degree, at which point the priest and priestess become high priest and high priestess and are qualified to run their own coven, involves the 'Great Rite'. In the early public days of the Craft, stories abounded of the 'Great Rite' being performed 'in truth' before covens, whose members either watched or discreetly turned their backs. According to Valiente (1989), many of these stories were unfounded. Today's Craft members usually opt for 'in token' when the rite is done before a coven, although Witches who so desire may perform the rite 'in truth' in private beforehand. In addition to third-degree initiations, the 'Great Rite' is performed at certain sabbats, at 'handfastings' (a Witch marriage ceremony) and in certain magical rites as one of the means of raising magical power set forth by Gardner.

Witches also celebrate the Myth of the Goddess in rites and dramas that act out their concepts of the Eleusinian Mysteries and the mysteries of Isis, Ishtar and Inanna.

Another central rite of Witchcraft is 'Drawing Down the Moon', in which the high priestess invokes the Goddess force into her and becomes a channel for that divine energy. The rite derives its name from its alleged source, the witches of ancient Thessaly, who were said to be renowned and feared for their magic. According to legend, the Thessalian witches were magically empowered by the moon, which they controlled and 'drew down' from the sky.

'Drawing Down the Moon' is one of the most solemn and holy of Craft rites. The high priest invokes Goddess, residing in the moon, to come down to earth through the high priestess and speak to the Witches present. Seen from another perspective, the high priest assists the high priestess in evoking from within her the divine aspect of her own Higher Self. Goddess is petitioned by whatever names and personifications suit the coven, the individuals or the moment.

Once Goddess is invoked, the high priestess traditionally delivers the 'Charge of the Goddess'. If the high priestess is truly entranced and becomes a medium for a higher force, her delivery sparkles. Divinely inspired, she extemporizes. At the least, her recitation of the 'Charge', even if by rote, reaffirms Goddess as the Alpha and Omega of all life, immanent and transcendent.

The 'Charge of the Goddess' is the closest thing to liturgy in the Craft; it is certainly the Witches' Creed. It exists in various forms in virtually all traditions. As late as 1979 (Starhawk), the Charge was being passed off as possibly of ancient origin and unknown authorship. Gardner presented a version in his initial 'Book of Shadows', attributing it to Roman times and the 'ancient mysteries.' However, it was obviously drawn from *Aradia* and Crowley's *Liber Legis*, and owed a debt to the 'Charge' read to Masonic initiates. Valiente rewrote the 'Charge', retaining much of the language from *Aradia* but ejecting the Crowley material. Her initial version of the 'Charge' was in verse; she then rewrote it in prose, providing scripts for both high priestess and high priest. Valiente's version has been much copied. The following is an abbreviated form offered by Starhawk (1979):

> Listen to the words of the Great Mother, who of old was called Artemis, Astarte, Dione, Melusine, Aphrodite, Ceridwen, Diana, Arionrhod, Brigid and by many other names:
>
> 'Whenever you have need of anything, once in the month, and better it be when the moon is full, you shall assemble in some secret place and adore the spirit of Me who is Queen of all the Wise. You shall be free from slavery, and as a sign that you be free you shall be naked in your rites. Sing, feast, dance, make music and love, all in My presence, for Mine is the ecstasy of the spirit and Mine also is joy on the earth. For My law is love unto all beings. Mine is the secret that opens upon the door of youth, and Mine is the cup of wine of life that is the Cauldron of Ceridwen that is the holy grail of immortality. I give the knowledge of the spirit eternal and beyond death I give peace and freedom and reunion with those that have gone before. Nor do I demand aught of sacrifice, for behold, I am the mother of all things and My love is poured out upon the earth.' Hear the words of the Star Goddess, the dust of whose feet are the hosts of heaven, whose body encircles the universe:
>
> 'I who am the beauty of the green earth and the white moon among the stars and the mysteries of the waters, I call upon your soul to arise and come unto me. For I am the soul of nature that gives life to the universe. From Me all things proceed and unto Me they must return. Let My worship be in the heart that rejoices, for behold — all acts of love and pleasure are My rituals. Let there be beauty and strength, power and compassion, honor and humility, mirth and reverence within you. And you who seek to know Me, know that your seeking and yearning will avail you not, unless you know the Mystery: for if that which you seek, you find noth within yourself, you will never find it without. For behold, I have been with you from the beginning, and I am that which is attained at the end of desire.'
>
> *(THE CHARGE OF THE GODDESS)*

RELIGIOUS HOLIDAYS

The sabbats are the religious holidays of the Craft and are based on pagan agrarian and seasonal festivals. There are four major sabbats and four minor ones. Major, or 'greater', sabbats are *Imbolc* (also *Imbolg* or *Oimelc*) on 2 February; *Beltane* on 30 April; *Lughnasadh* (also *Lammas*) on 1 August; and *Samhain* on 31 October. Minor, or 'lesser', sabbats are the equinoxes and solstices that mark the change of seasons: 21 March (called *Ostara*), 21 June (Midsummer), 21 September (*Mabon*) and 21 December (Yule). Rituals vary according to tradition, coven and even individual, but the majority reflect the Witches' 'Wheel of the Year', as the seasons are called. Goddess presides and presents the different aspects of her triple nature: she brings forth life, nutures it to fruition and destroys it. God, however, goes through an annual cycle of birth, death and rebirth. He is born at the winter solstice, marries Goddess at Beltane, is at his peak as the Sun King at the summer solstice and sacrifices himself at Lughnasadh harvests. Folklore traditions also are observed, such as candle-lighting on Imbolc (Christianized as Candlemas), Morris dancing at Beltane and Midsummer, and the making of corn dollies at Lughnasadh.

GODDESS IN MAGIC

In the art of magic, or the casting of spells, Witches look to Goddess for power and blessing. They derive their magical powers from Goddess in her lunar aspect. Magical powers wax and wane in accordance with the phases of the moon; thus, certain spells must be done at certain times in the lunar cycle. (This practice is widespread in folk magic.) The new moon is considered the best time for beginnings. Spells aimed at increase and boon are best done during the waxing moon; the night of the full moon is the height of benevolent magical power. Spells aimed at decrease and banishing the unwanted are best done during the waning moon. At each phase, an appropriate aspect of the Triple Goddess is invoked for the spell. Witches also may invoke a personification of Goddess suited to the nature of the spell. For example, Aphrodite may be petitioned for a love spell, or Panacea for a healing spell.

SUMMARY

As presently practised, Witchcraft as a religion seeks to rediscover the transcendant Divine Feminine, and to affirm the divine feminine within both women and men. It reconstructs pagan fertility rites and mysteries which followers see as affirmations of the sacredness of the body, the connection of humankind to nature and the eternal cycle of life, death and rebirth. That Witchcraft has no ancient history or mythology of its own is not reason to invalidate it as a religious movement. In a day when mainstream religion is moribund, Witchcraft offers, at least to some, a spiritual path of vitality and creativity. Both Jung and mythologist Joseph Campbell attested to the tremendous power of myth in the collective unconscious of humanity; without myth, we are cut off from our spiritual roots. Campbell lamented the absence of myth in modern Western culture and advocated the study of comparative mythology, which he said would lead to an understanding of the experience and meaning of life. Witchcraft's resurrection of ancient pagan myths, and of archetypes in the form of pagan deities, most notably the Great Goddess herself, is a response to spiritual barrenness.

One must ask why this religious movement is called 'Witchcraft', however, when it presents itself as the antithesis of witchcraft as sorcery. (There are other forms of pagan revivals known as Neo-Paganism in general.) Witchcraft the religion fights constant and formidable battles against deeply ingrained negative perceptions of witches and witchcraft. The public often fails to appreciate the distinction between Witchcraft the pagan revival religion and witchcraft the evil sorcery (and therefore a form of Satanism).

Some Witches vow to fight to 'reclaim' the word 'witch' as a term of female power. In fact, there is nothing to reclaim. Witches have always been perceived, almost universally, as malevolent beings. Other Witches further muddy the waters by disowning the past, insisting that they have nothing to do with historical witchcraft.

Witchcraft came to call itself a religion largely because of Murray's witch-cult theory and Gardner's dressed-up rites. His original coven cannot be said to have practised a religion, which is an organized system of faith and worship. A religion with no workable rituals, as he said of his coven, is no religion at all.

However, Murray, Gardner and Graves were among the forces that helped open the door to a revival of paganism and Goddess worship. But the acceptance into the mainstream of Witchcraft as a religion undoubtedly will continue to be hampered by the misnomer of 'Witchcraft'.

Notes

1 I refer to Goddess without the article throughout, since we do not refer to God as 'the God'. 'The Goddess' turns her into an object and diminishes her status – she must be given equal due with her masculine counterpart who has dominated our psyches for too long.

References and Further Reading:

Adler, M. (1986), *Drawing Down the Moon*, revised ed. (Boston: Beacon Press)

Buckland, R. (1986), *Buckland's Complete Book of Witchcraft* (St Paul: Llewellyn Publications)

Crowley, V. (1989), *Wicca: The Old Religion in the New Age* (London: The Aquarian Press)

Farrar, J. and S. (1984), *The Witches' Way* (London: Robert Hale)

Farrar, S. (1983), *What Witches Do: A Modern Coven Revealed*, revised ed. (Custer, Wash.: Phoenix Publishing Co.)

Gardner, G.B. (1954), *Witchcraft Today* (New York: Magickal Childe Publishing)

—— (1982), *The Meaning of Witchcraft* (New York: Magickal Childe). First published 1959.

Graves, R. (1966), *The White Goddess* (New York: Farrar, Straus and Giroux). Amended and enlarged edition.

Guiley, R.E. (1989), *The Encyclopedia of Witches and Witchcraft* (New York and Oxford: Facts On File)

—— (1991), *Harper's Encyclopedia of Mystical and Paranormal Experience* (San Francisco: HarperSanFrancisco)

King, F. (1970), *Ritual Magic in England* (London: Spearman)

Leland, C.G. (1889, 1990), *Aradia, the Gospel of the Witches* (Custer, Wash.: Phoenix Publishing)

Luhrmann, T.M. (1989), *Persuasions of the Witch's Craft: Ritual Magic in Contemporary England* (Cambridge, Mass.: Harvard University Press)

Monaghan, P. (1981, 1990), *The Book of Goddesses & Heroines* (St Paul: Llewellyn Publications)

Murray, M.A. (1921), *The Witch-Cult in Western Europe* (London: Oxford University Press)

—— (1931), *The God of the Witches* (London: Sampson Low, Marston and Co.)

Neumann, E. (1963), *The Great Mother: An Analysis of the Archetype*, 2nd ed. (Princeton: Princeton University Press)

Russell, J.B. (1980), *A History of Witchcraft* (London: Thames and Hudson)

Starhawk (1979), *The Spiral Dance: A Rebirth of the Ancient Religion of the Great Goddess* (San Francisco: Harper & Row)

Stone, M. (1976), *When God Was A Woman* (San Diego: Harcourt Brace Jovanovich)

—— (1979, 1984), *Ancient Mirrors of Womanhood* (Boston: Beacon Press)

Thomas, K. (1971), *Religion and the Decline of Magic* (New York: Charles Scribner's Sons)

Valiente, D. (1973), *An ABC of Witchcraft Past and Present* (Custer, Wash.: Phoenix Publishing)

—— (1989), *The Rebirth of Witchcraft* (London: Robert Hale)

JANE CAPUTI

On Psychic Activism: Feminist Mythmaking

Gyn/Ecology . . . involves the dis-spelling of the mind/spirit/body pollution that is produced out of man-made myths . . . it also . . . involves speaking forth the New Words.

MARY DALY (1978, P. 315)

I hold to the traditional Indian views on language, that words have power, that words become entities. When I write I keep in mind that it is a form of power and salvation that is for the planet. If it is good and enters the world, perhaps it will counteract the destruction that seems to be getting so close to us. I think of language and poems, even fictions, as prayers and small ceremonies.

LINDA HOGAN (1982, P. 352)

By creating a new mythos — that is, a change in the way we perceive reality, the way we see ourselves, and the ways we behave — *la mestiza* creates a new consciousness.

GLORIA ANZALDÚA (1987, P. 80)

In *Sexual Politics* (1969, 1970, pp. 64–5), Kate Millett wrote that 'under patriarchy the female did not herself develop the symbols by which she is described'. Mary Daly, in *Beyond God the Father* (1973, p. 8), declared that 'women have had the power of naming stolen from us'. One of the most significant developments to emerge out of the contemporary feminist movement is the quest to reclaim that symbolizing/naming power, to refigure the female self from a gynocentric perspective, to discover, revitalize and create a female oral and visual mythic tradition and use it, ultimately, to change the world.

Throughout this century, feminist thinkers have continued to expose the patriarchal bias of mythographers (past and present) and the ways that these entrenched mythic symbols and paradigms construct and maintain phallocentric reality (e.g., Daly, 1978, 1984). Simultaneously, as the existence of this volume indicates, feminist thinkers actively reinterpret ancient myth, focusing attention on female divinities, supernaturals and powers that have been repressed and silenced. And this is no mere academic pursuit. Rather, feminist use of myth stems from an understanding of myth to be a 'language construct that contains the power to transform something (or someone) from one state or condition to another . . . it is at base a vehicle, a means of transmitting paranormal power' (Allen, 1986, p. 103). Thus, with varying degrees of self-consciousness, women as 'witches' call mythic themes and personae into present time as a way to 'cast spells . . . to promote changes of consciousness . . . To respell the world means to redefine the root of our being. It means to redefine us and therefore change us . . .' (Sjöö and Mor, 1987, p. 425).

Carol P. Christ (1979) writes that one of the most basic feminist symbols – the Goddess – positively values female *will*: 'In ritual magic, the energy raised is directed by willpower. Women who celebrate in Goddess circles believe they can achieve their wills in the world' (p. 284). Such rituals need not be overtly sacred ceremonies to a Goddess, but can take the forms of writings, demonstrations, speeches, informal gatherings. Whenever feminists engage in energy-raising mythic/symbolic thought and image-making, capable of reconceptualizing reality and changing the world, this is what I call *psychic activism*.

In the gynocentric tradition of the Keres people (Pueblo Indians of what is now New Mexico), the creatrix is Ts'its'tsi'nako, Thought-Woman, also known as Thinking Woman or Spider Grandmother (*see* Marta Weigle's contribution to this volume, p. 346). Pueblo writer Leslie Marmon Silko (1977, p. 1) narrates their creation myth:

> Ts'its'tsi'nako, Thought-Woman,
> is sitting in her room
> and whatever she thinks about
> appears.
>
> She thought of her sisters,
> Nau'ts'ity'i and I'tcts'ity'i,
> and together they created the Universe
> this world
> and the four worlds below.
>
> Thought-Women, the spider,
> named things and
> as she named them.
> they appeared.

Thought-Woman creates the world by thinking and speaking it into being, by telling its story. As another Pueblo Indian writer, Paula Gunn Allen (1986, p. 122), observes: 'The thought for which Grandmother Spider is known is the kind that results in physical manifestation of phenomena: mountains, lakes, creatures, or philosophical – sociological systems.' Phallocentric thought/myth results in the physical manifestation of phenomena such as social inequality, toxic waste, nuclear weapons, genocide, gynocide. When women refuse and refute these thoughts/myths and instead foray into the realm traditionally forbidden to our sex – the realm of the sacred storytellers, symbol and myth-makers – we participate in the creative powers of Thought Woman, employing thinking, naming and willing as forms of power exercised consciously and/or intuitively in the creation of the world(s) we inhabit.

In this essay, I will discuss representative forms of psychic activism, based in a multiplicity of mythic traditions and evidenced in writings and actions by United States feminists. This is not to claim that this is a purely U.S. phenomenon; I use these examples because this is the culture I best know.

DREAMING IN FEMALE

I came into the movement [Black Power], trying to be the perfect African woman. In the process I find out there used to be cult of women in Africa who were warriors . . . who cut a man's penis and stuck it in his mouth as a mark that they had done this . . . I learn that the lightning bolt originally belonged to a female deity. I started learning things that whisper of very strong women . . . I had to confront, finally, the 'men's room' . . . I mean a room in this collective spiritual household where women were not allowed to go, because according to the males we would be struck by lightning if we went in there. So one day I just on my own decided I'm going to walk in there and . . . *smash a myth*.

(LUISAH TEISH IN ANZALDÚA, 1981, 1983, P. 231)

I am an old woman with a deck of cards
A witch, an Amazon, a Gorgon
A seer, a clairvoyant, a poet.
I have visions of becoming and
I dream in female.

(BARBARA STARRETT, 1974, P. 26)

The journey engaged in by many contemporary feminists is twofold: one involving both patriarchal myth-smashing and woman-identified myth-making. Beginning in the late 1960s, innumerable feminists began to reject patriarchal myth and to dream openly in female, conjuring up diversely named Goddesses, Amazons, Warriors, Witches, Two-Headed Women (psychics or mediums in African-American traditions) (Teish, 1983, 340–2; Walker, 1988, pp. 1–2), Mermaids, Gorgons, Sibyls and Crones as metaphors of cosmic/female power. A lesbian-feminist journal, *Amazon Quarterly*, appeared; the Artemis Café opened in San Francisco; a lesbian-feminist collective in Washington DC named itself 'The Furies'; and a New York radical feminist group dubbed itself W.I.T.C.H. (Women's International Conspiracy from Hell).

These namings are rarely arbitrary; they deliberately recall a specific mythic power from the past into the present. For example, a radical feminist nurses group named itself *Cassandra*, because 'We are all too actively aware of the fact that nursing's voice is not heard, and more basically that women's voices are not heard in the world. But we know that although myths are very powerful, we do re-create myths' (quoted in Culpepper, 1983, p. 343). This re-creation of myth is what Emily Culpepper (1983, p. 192), in her superb study of the use of symbols in the women's movement, calls 'gynergetic symbolization'. As she observes: 'Breaking out of the bondage of being Woman/The Other/Symbol, women become Self-conscious subjects, primary symbolizers who weave our own view of the Self and cosmos' (p. 161).

The drive to become a psychic activist, to smash phallocentric myth while creating woman-identified words, symbols and myths is a major force behind the extensive philosophical writings of Mary Daly. In *Beyond God the Father (1973)*, *Gyn/Ecology* (1978), *Pure Lust* (1984) and *Websters' First New Intergalactic Wickedary of the English Language* (Daly with Caputi, 1987), this self-described 'Revolting Hag' critiques patriarchal myth while inventing an astonishing variety of mythic identities for women and names for female power. *Muses, Fates, Gorgons, Furies, Harpies, Amazons* and *Dragons* are some of the more familiar personae she presents as preferred female role models. Simultaneously, she takes words such as *Spinsters, Witches, Hags, Crones, Nags, Scolds, Witches, Prudes* and *Shrews* – all with negative associations in phallocentric contexts – and redefines them as shimmering metaphors for female strengths. For example, 'spinning' in Daly's view is a mythic activity reflecting the Fates and Mother Goddesses who characteristically spin and weave the cosmos into being. Thus, a *Spinster* is one who 'participates in the whirling movement of creation' as well as one 'who has chosen her Self, who defines her Self, by choice, neither in relation to children nor to men, who is Self-identified' (1978, p. 3).

Psychic activism is at the root of Daly's philosophy. In *Pure Lust* (1984) she writes: 'Symbols . . . participate in that to which they point. They open up levels of reality otherwise closed to us and they unlock dimensions and elements of our souls which correspond to these hidden dimensions and elements of reality' (p. 25). Most frequently, Daly refers to her new words and images as *metaphors*, because metaphor, while it includes the power of symbols, also evokes 'action, movement . . . Metaphors function to Name change, and therefore they elicit change . . . [metaphor] is associated with transforming action' (p. 25). Such metaphors work to change not only the self, but also the world. Daly continues, 'the word *reality* is nothing less than an Ontological Battleground. The risks are ultimate' (p. 394). She calls upon women to fight fire with Fire, to become metapatterning, metapatriarchal 'Artists' – shape-shifting and spinning gynocentric metaphors to Name and hence elicit transmutations, both personal and social, to move out of patriarchal reality and into what she calls 'Metamorphospheres' (p. 408).

Daly has been one of the most prolific generators of gynergetic symbolization; her new words and symbols have been widely welcomed and extremely influential. Yet, *Gyn/Ecology* has been subjected to some criticism for ethnocentrism. In 1979, poet Audre Lorde (1981, 1983) wrote a personal letter to Daly, asking why the Goddess images Daly used in *Gyn/Ecology* were 'only white, western-european, judeo-christian? Where was Afrekete, Yemanje, Oyo and Mawulisa? . . . because so little material on non-white female power and symbol exists in white women's words from a radical feminist perspective, to exclude this aspect of connection from even comment in your work is to deny the fountain of non-european female strength and power that nurtures each of our visions' (pp. 94–5). Daly originally replied to Lorde in a face to face meeting in 1979, explaining her positions and concerns. In a new Introduction (1990) to *Gyn/Ecology* she notes that 'Apparently Lorde was not satisfied [by this meeting], although she did not indicate this at the time. She later published and republished slightly altered versions of her originally personal letter to me' (p. xxx). Daly has not published an extensive written reply to this now open letter for, as she further states in the introduction, 'It continues to be my judgement that public response in kind would not be a fruitful direction.' She, does, however, suggest that *Gyn/Ecology* is not a 'compendium of goddesses. Rather, it focuses primarily on myths and symbols that were direct sources of christian myth,' and continues 'I regret any pain that unintended omissions may have caused others, particularly women of colour, as well as myself. The writing of *Gyn/Ecology* was for me an act of bonding with women of all races and classes, under the varying oppressions of patriarchy' (p. xxx).

In *The Black Unicorn* (1978), Lorde herself provides a valuable glossary of African Goddesses and traditions. Understanding as well that individual names have been lost, in a later poem, 'Call', Lorde (1983, pp. 73–5) cries out to 'Aido Hwedo: The Rainbow Serpent; also a representation of all ancient divinities who must be worshipped but whose names and faces have been lost in time'. Lorde commingles evocations of Aido Hwedo with names of African Goddesses as well as historical and contemporary women: Rosa Parks, Fannie Lou Hamer, Assata Shakur, Yaa Asantewa. Ancestor reverence is intrinsic to African religions (Teish, 1985), and it remains so to much of contemporary African-American feminist symbolizations. Luisah Teish (1983, p. 333) declares: 'The veneration of our foremothers is essential to our self respect.'

This importance of the connection to ancestors is one of the central themes in Alice Walker's (1983) extraordinary tribute to the lost and unrecognized genius of African-American foremothers in her essay, 'In Search of Our Mothers' Gardens', and recurs in the works of scores of novelists and poets, including Toni Morrison, Sonia Sanchez, Toni Cade Bambara and Paule Marshall. The ancestors invoked include not only historical figures such as Sojourner Truth (Walker, 1988, pp. 97–8), but also individual grandmothers (Chandler, 1990), and 'the poets in the kitchen' (Marshall, 1983, p. 12) – common women, denied public voice because of racist and sexist oppression, who nonetheless spoke daily and powerfully in what Paule Marshall calls the 'wordshop of the kitchen'. Significantly, a publishing house founded by and for women of colour is named 'Kitchen Table Press'.

Clearly, not only mythic personae change among different cultures, but also mythic sources and emphases. Paula Gunn Allen (1989, pp. 23–4) writes: 'The [American] Indian collective unconscious ... encompasses much more than goddesses, gods, and geometric symbols. More important than its characters are narrative strands, historical trauma, and other sorts of information that lend significance and pattern to individual and communal life.' Luisah Teish (1985) invokes the tradition of European witchcraft, but reminds us that feminists also must reclaim the two-headed woman, the root worker (herbalist) and the matrifocal tradition of *Voudou*. Poet and essayist Marilou Awiakta (1988) uses Amazons as a metaphor in her essay on the power of her Cherokee ancestresses, but rejects the image presented in Greek mythology. Moreover, she ties the story of her own menstrual coming of age among the elders at the menstrual lodge with the story of Nanyehi, the last 'Beloved Woman' (head of the Women's Council of the Cherokee Nation) and the events leading up to the historical trauma of the Cherokee removal:

> These women are not the Amazons of the Greek fable. While they are independent and self-defined, they do not hate men and use them only at random for procreation . . . But did the Greek patriarchs tell the truth? . . . I'm wary of the Greeks bearing fables. Although there is little proof that they described the Amazons accurately, ample evidence suggests that they encountered – and resented – strong women like my Grandmothers and characterized them as heinous in order to justify destroying them (a strategy modern patriarchs still use) . . . why should I bother with distant Greeks and their nebulous fables when I have the spirits of the Grandmothers, whose roots are struck deep in my native soil and whose strength is as tangible and tenacious as the amber-pitched pine at my back. (pp. 129–30)

Like Awiakta's Amazons/Grandmothers, radical, feminist evocations of Goddesses must be just so tangible, tenacious and rooted in the world. Women, as Christ (1979, p. 277) argued, certainly do need the Goddess in order to acknowledge 'the legitimacy of female power as a beneficent and independent power'. But that Goddess cannot be imagined as always white, heterosexual, maternal or ethereal, for, as Sjöö and Mor (1987, pp. 417–18) remind us:

> . . . the Goddess [does not] 'live' solely in elite separatist retreats, dancing naked in the piney woods under a white and well-fed moon. The Goddess at this moment is starving to death in refugee camps, with a skeletal child clutched to her dry nipples . . . The Goddess is on welfare, raising her children in a ghetto next to a freeway interchange that fills their blood cells and neurons with lead. The Goddess is an eight-year-old girl being used for the special sexual thrills of visiting businessmen in a Brazilian brothel. The Goddess is patrolling with a rifle . . . trying to save a revolution in Nicaragua. The Goddess is Winnie Mandela in South Africa, saying 'Don't push me.' I.e., the Goddess IS the world – the Goddess is *in* the world. And *nobody* can escape the world.

Along with the widespread resurgence of Goddess imagery, radical feminist psychic activists conjure specific powers and symbols in response to particular social crises. Next I will turn to several examples of this: the Gorgon as a force inspiring resistance to sexual violence and the multifarious symbolizations wrought by the anti-nuclear and ecofeminist movements.

REPULSIVE TO MEN

Since the early 1970s, the Medusa, the Greek Gorgon with hair of snakes who was able to turn men to stone merely by gazing upon them, has been a power symbol for feminists. Like much of Greek myth, the story of the Medusa is rooted in African, gynocentric elements (Sjöö and Mor, 1987, p. 209; Walker, 1983, p. 629).

In a stirring article, Culpepper (1986) analyses not only the significance of the Gorgon face as a symbol of contemporary women's rage, but also the ways that 'feminists are *living* the knowledge gained from tapping deep and ancient symbolic/mythic power to change our lives' (p. 23). She relates an incident which occurred one night in 1980 as she sat alone in her house working. Someone knocked at the door and, after looking out and thinking it was someone she knew, she opened the door. A stranger came in and immediately attacked her. Culpepper, at first off guard, gathered herself and fought back, throwing out the would-be attacker. She includes a selection from her journal recalling the incident: 'I am staring him out, pushing with my eyes too. My face is bursting, contorting with terrible teeth, flaming breath, erupting into ridges and contortions of rage, hair hissing. It is over in a flash. I can still see his eyes, stunned, wide and staring, almost as if *I* am acting strange, as if *I* were acting wrong!' (p. 24). Afterwards, she realized that she 'needed to look at the terrible face that had erupted and sprung forth from within' during her fight:

> As I felt my face twist again into the fighting frenzy, I turned to the mirror and looked. What I saw in the mirror is a Gorgon, a Medusa, if *ever* there was one. This face was my own and yet I knew I had seen it before and I knew the name to utter. 'Gorgon! Gorgon!' reverberated in my mind. I knew then why the attacker had become so suddenly petrified. (p. 24)

In this world where men daily perpetrate outrages upon women, as Culpepper notes, it is imperative that women 'learn how to manifest a visage that will repel men when necessary . . . The Gorgon has much vital, literally life-saving information to teach women about anger, rage, power and the release of the determined aggressiveness sometimes needed for survival' (p. 24).

Gorgons do not live only in the imaginary/past world of myth and story. Rather, they/we live today. Robin Morgan (1977, p. 142) writes, 'We are the myths. We are the Amazons, the Furies, the Witches. We have never not been here, this exact sliver of time, this precise place.' Deeply realizing this truth, as Culpepper demonstrates, can be literally life-saving.

SPINNING AT THE GATE

On 20 March, 1980, The Spinsters, 'an affinity group of women-identified women', performed a myth-based protest at a nuclear power plant in Vermont USA, by weaving intricate designs of coloured yarn between the trees of the entrance to the plant. Their accompanying leaflet read in part: 'We, as life-givers, will not support

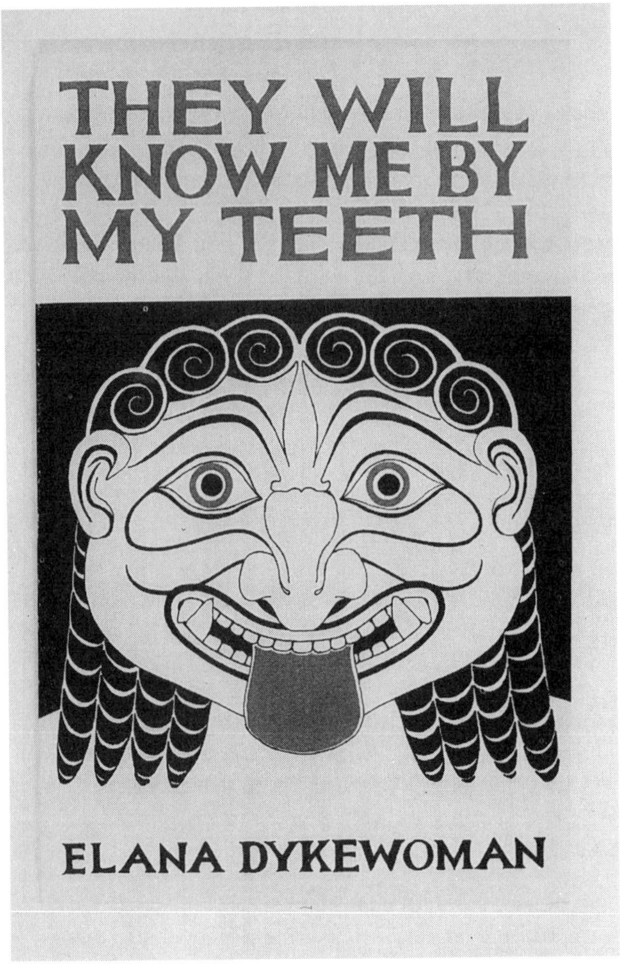

Fig. 40 From the cover of Elana Dykewoman's book of poetry, *They Will Know Me By My Teeth: Stories and Poems of Lesbian Struggle and Survival* (Northampton, Mass.: Megaera Press), which figures the Gorgon as a power symbol of lesbian-feminism and lesbian separatism. *Reproduced courtesy of Laura Kaye and Megaera Press*

any life-threatening force. Nuclear madness imminently endangers our children, their future and the earth. On Monday, March 31, women will be reweaving the web of life into the site of Vermont Yankee' (Reid, 1982, p. 290). This practice, repeated in countless feminist anti-nuclear demonstrations, deliberately invokes the metaphoric web of Spider Woman; indeed, the web symbol (pointing to the interconnection and interdependency of all life) has become primary to the language and philosophic underpinnings of the ecofeminist movement.

Other symbols also are evoked in anti-nuclear theory and activism. Since both phallo-sexual and nuclear violations are rooted in the same ethic of masculinist domination (Caputi, 1987), it makes sense that the Gorgon also intuitively would be invoked as an anti-nuclear symbol. From Freud on, the Medusa has signified castration and the Gorgon does signify women's capacity to emasculate what Diana Russell (1989) calls 'nuclear phallacies'. In another vein, Barbara Deming (1982, p. 43) writes:

This is a song for gorgons—
Whose dreaded glances in fact can bless.
The men who would be gods we turn
Not to stone but to mortal flesh and blood and bone.
If we could stare them into accepting this,
The world could live at peace.

Moreover, as Daly and I suggest in *The Wickedary*, the Gorgon is she whose '*face can stop a clock*'. Since 1947, the *Bulletin of the Atomic Scientists* has published a 'doomsday clock' which depicts how many minutes there are to 'midnight', that is, how close the world is to nuclear holocaust:

> Spinsters Spinning about-face face the fact that clockocracy's clocks are elementary moons . . . Lusty women, in tune with the Moon, pose the poignant Question: Is the Moon's Face the Face that can stop the doomsday clock?
>   . . . women as Gorgons look toward the madmen and turn them to stone – the doomsday men with their doomsday clocks . . .
>
> (DALY WITH CAPUTI, 1987, PP. 281–2)

Another mythic figure of female power, that of the ancient woman, the ancestor or Crone, also manifests as an anti-nuclear metaphor. As feminist mythographer Barbara Walker (1986) relates, the Crone is the general designation of the third of the Triple Goddess's aspects (embodied in figures such as Hecate and Kali) and one associated with old age, death, the waning moon, winter and rebirth. As a harbinger of rebirth, the Crone's appearance signals a call to profound transformation and healing. Nor Hall (1980, p. 197) writes that the function of the old wise woman 'is to be of assistance in times of difficult passage. As midwife to the psyche she is constellated in "emergency" situations where a spirit, a song, an alternative, a new being is emerging.'

In the face of a global ecological emergency, Barbara Walker (1986, pp. 175–8) calls for the reinstitution of the Crone, not as some 'deity actually existing "out there"', but as a chosen metaphor:

> Most of all the Crone can represent precisely the kind of power women so desperately need today, and do not have: the power to force men to do what is right, for the benefit of future generations and of the earth itself . . . Metaphors like these take on practical meaning in women's capacity to see through men's pretenses and to reject men's self-serving images. Men feared the judgmental eye of the wisewoman even when she was socially powerless. This, then, is the chink in the armor of patriarchal establishments. When many women together say no and mean it, the whole structure can collapse . . . She had better do it soon, for he is already counting down to doomsday.

ECOFEMINISM

The planet, our mother, Grandmother Earth, is physical and therefore a
spiritual, mental, and emotional being. Planets are alive, as are all their
by-products or expressions, such as animals, vegetables, minerals, climactic
and meteorological phenomena. Believing that our mother, the beloved
Earth, is inert matter is destructive to yourself.

(PAULA GUNN ALLEN, 1990, P. 52)

The area of feminist activism that most overtly politicizes symbolization and
spirituality is the ecofeminist movement. Caroline Merchant (1981, 1990) has
demonstrated that in western thought women and nature consistently have been
associated and jointly devalued, and that the modern metaphor of the Earth as
machine has been used to further patriarchal domination. To counter these toxic
beliefs and metaphors, 'Radical feminism . . . celebrates the relationship between
women and nature through the revival of ancient rituals centered on Goddess
worship, the moon, animals, and the female reproductive system . . . Spirituality is
seen as a source of both personal and social change. Goddess worship and rituals
. . . lectures, concerts, art exhibitions, street and theater products, and direct political
action . . . all are examples of the re-visioning of nature and women as powerful
forces' (Merchant, 1990, p. 101).

Merchant cautions, however, that ecofeminism runs 'the risk of perpetuating the
very hierarchies it seeks to overthrow' (p. 102) by stressing biological femaleness and
the identification of women with nature. 'Any analysis that makes women's essence
and qualities special ties them to a biological destiny that thwarts the possibility of
liberation' (p. 102). I agree that ecofeminists must beware adopting a dualistic
worldview. Yet when we acknowledge such aspects of 'biological destiny' as the
capacity to give birth, menstruation, menopause, aging and death, and place positive
valuations on these, this actually is a profoundly revolutionary act in a
woman/body/earth hating society, dedicated to denying these bodies/destinies.
Merchant continues: 'A politics grounded in women's culture, experience, and values
can be seen as reactionary' (p. 102); here she alludes to a widespread critique
(proffered mainly by socialist and postmodern feminists) deriding as 'essentialist'
(based in a belief in differing female and male natures) and 'totalizing' (ignoring vast
historical and cultural differences) those philosophical approaches that celebrate
women's culture or experiences. For example, Mary Lydon (1988, p. 138) writes: 'To
claim essential womanhood, to assert oneself as subject, to demand the freedom to
write "like a woman," to reclaim women's history, to speak their sexuality is a
powerful temptation. Yet it must be resisted, I would argue, taking a leaf from
Foucault's book.'

To my mind, however, this postmodern approach is seriously flawed and
functions, as Susan Bordo (1990, p. 136) maintains, 'to harness and tame the visionary
and creative energy of feminism as a movement of cultural resistance and
transformation'. Essentially, it profoundly disempowers women by submitting to

masculinist authority and forbidding feminist bonding, mythmaking and the invocation of what, at least at this historical moment, many of us conceptualize as gynocentric values. Imagining an open-ended gynocentric culture does not require the erasure of women's diversity or the worship of a fixed female essence – quite the opposite. Of course, as many thinkers have observed (e.g. Omolade, 1980), if what is promoted as 'women's culture' is actually middle-class, Euro-American women's culture, this would be genuinely reactionary. Still, female bonding and myth-making can occur based not on some illusory all-embracing female culture, but on women's common 'Otherness' to patriarchy (Daly 1984, p. 394–5).

Elinor Gadon (1989) and Gloria Orenstein (1990) have explored in their works on feminist sacred art, the ways that ecofeminist beliefs can assume visual forms as artists root their works in archaic (Earth) Goddess imagery. Gadon (1989, p. 256) calls such artists 'the visionaries, the seers of our time' and avers that those artists 'who are reclaiming the sacred iconography of the Goddess are creating a new social reality'. Artists who incorporate Earth-based spirituality and Goddess imagery in their works include Ana Mendieta, Judith Anderson, Betty LaDuke, Betsy Damon, Helene Aylon and Vijali.

A central part of ecofeminist spirituality is the concept, rooted in the African, Native American and pre-industrial European traditions, that the Earth (understood as female) and everything on it is alive, that 'everything', as Alice Walker (1988, p. 139) declares, 'is a human being'. Carol Lee Sanchez (1989), a Laguna Pueblo (New Mexico) thinker, poet and artist, extends this concept to include even inanimate objects. Pointing to 'an ever-widening gulf between "daily life" and "spirituality"' in technological culture, she avers: 'I believe Euro-Americans waste the resources and destroy the environment in the Americas because they are not spiritually connected to this land base, because they have no ancient mythos or legendary origins rooted to this land' (p. 345). She deplores the modern western schism between the sacred and the profane and contrasts it to the Tribal tradition that recognizes 'all things in the known universe to be equally sacred'. Sanchez believes that not only must all non-Tribal Americans acknowledge and become thoroughly familiar with the indigenous spiritual frameworks of this hemisphere, but that we must rethink our culture's social and technological processes and philosophies and compare them with Tribal principles, philosophies and social structures, working ultimately toward the creation of 'a non-Indian Tribal community'. Such a community formally acknowledges the sacredness of everyday life through songs and ceremonies. It also would reverence the realities of the modern world, for:

> I believe it is time to create new songs of acknowledgement as well as ceremonies that include metals, petrochemicals, and fossil fuels, electricity, modern solar power systems, and water power systems. I also believe it is very important to make sacred, to acknowledge the new ways and elements in our lives – from nuclear power . . . to plastics to computers. It is time now, again, for the entire world to honour these Spirits, these new molecular forms in order to restore harmony and balance to our out-of-control systems and in particular, to our modern technologies. (pp. 352–3)

Sanchez is *not* proposing that non-Indians somehow become Indians. Rather, she is suggesting that non-Indians learn from and synthesize Tribal philosophies and practices into daily practice and technological realities, thus becoming members of a never-before-seen new world Tribal community.

NEW MYTHIC IDENTITIES

Thus far, I have examined a number of mythic models and metaphors cast into being by feminist thinkers. In this last section, I briefly will examine three others to show further the range of contemporary imaginings: the griot-historian, the *mestiza* and the cyborg.

Barbara Omolade (1990a) invokes and reshapes a multiplicity of symbols in her conception of the Black feminist scholar as a 'griot historian', including the 'griot' (an African court personage, usually a man, whose function was to praise royal lineage) and the African *orisha*,[1] Oshun (goddess of love and rivers):

> A 'griot historian' is a scholar in any discipline who connects, uses, and understands the methods and insights of both Western and African world-views and historical perspectives to further develop a synthesis – an African American woman's social science with a unique methodology, sensibility, and language . . . She carves out new lands of the mind while reaching back to her spiritual and cultural sources, the major one of course being African, with its rivers and memories. One river named for the African orisha, Oshun, a symbol of female power and sensuality, is a guiding power for the griot-historian's quest.

Omolade invokes the ancestor and enacts the pattern of both myth-smashing and myth-making:

> The griot-historian must 'break de chains' of Western thought . . . be baptised by some force outside the tradition of Western civilization and become submerged in the waters of Black women's pain, power, and potential . . . the griot-historian . . . must overcome her fear of the stigma of being the daughter of Aunt Jemima, the granddaughter of 'negra wenches' . . . the great granddaughter of Africans called 'primitive and animal-like.' Seeing the woman beyond the shame affirms the use of historical truths to sing praise songs which resurrect the lives and experiences of the orisha, the warrior, and the 'drylongso' Black woman. (p. 285)[2]

Chicana thinker and poet Gloria Anzaldúa (1987) proposes yet another identity grounded in her unique position as a woman who has grown up 'between two cultures, the Mexican (with a heavy Indian influence) and the Anglo (as a member of a colonized people in our own territory)' (preface, unpaged). A *mestiza*, of course, is a woman who borders races, but in Anzaldúa's conception, includes one who straddles psychological, sexual and spiritual boundaries. Thus accustomed to transcending dividing lines:

... she can't hold concepts or ideas in rigid boundaries ... by remaining
flexible [she is] ... able to stretch the psyche horizontally and vertically
... The new *mestiza* copes by developing a tolerance for contradictions,
a tolerance for ambiguity ... She learns to juggle cultures. She has a plural
personality ... The work of *mestiza* consciousness is to break down the
subject-object duality that keeps her a prisoner and to show ... how
duality is transcended. The answer to the problem between the white race
and the colored, between males and females, lies in healing the split that
originates in the very foundation of our lives, our culture, our languages,
our thoughts. A massive uprooting of dualistic thinking in the individual
and collective consciousness is the beginning of a long struggle, but one
that could ... bring us to the end of rape, of violence, of war. (pp. 79–80)

Omolade and Anzaldúa's mythic identities spring from a racial and, in Anzaldúa's
case, a sexual (Lesbian) background. Another feminist identity, that of Donna
Haraway's (1985) 'cyborg', is located in what many other feminists would consider
to be prime patriarchal reality – science and technology.

In Haraway's view, 'the boundary between science fiction and social reality is an
optical illusion' (p. 66). The cyborg is a fictional creature, 'a hybrid of machine and
organism', but, as Haraway argues, in social reality we now *are* cyborgs, living in ways
that break down the borders between animal, human and machine. In her schema,
the cyborg betokens a 'world without gender, which is perhaps a world without
genesis, but maybe also a world without end' (pp. 66–7). Haraway refuses the
worldviews of such feminists as Susan Griffin, Audre Lorde and Adrienne Rich who
'insist on the organic, opposing it to the technological' (p. 92). Taking a
postmodernist stance, she aims to deconstruct those premises which she deems to
have contributed so heavily to the structure of the 'Western self', distinctions ordered
in the Adam and Eve myth which presupposes a state of 'original unity ... with
nature' (p. 67) and innocence. 'Cyborg writing is about the power to survive, not on
the basis of original innocence, but on the basis of seizing the tools to mark the world
that marked them as other' (pp. 93–4). Haraway urges that feminists see technology
and science not only as agents of 'complex dominations', but as 'possible means of
great human satisfaction' (p. 100). She concludes: 'Though both are bound in the
spiral dance, I would rather be a cyborg than a goddess' (p. 101).

Intriguingly, all three of these rousingly imaginative identities are based upon
synthesis; all seek ways to break from western paradigms and to transcend dualism.
While Omolade and Anzaldúa imagine identities formed as a result of and in
opposition to colonialism, Haraway's cyborg results from technology; it remains to
be seen if Haraway's cyborg is truly oppositional or if 'seizing tools to mark the world'
merely continues a long-established pattern of phallo-technological domination/
manipulation. Moreover, is innocence a thoroughly bankrupt concept? Can't we point
to some states which signify if not 'innocence' then integrity, e.g. the body of the
girl before incest, Native American societies before colonization and genocide?
While feminist symbolizers must suspect those old patriarchal images, we, equally,

must be wary of the shiny new ones. As Haraway herself acknowledges, the cyborg is the 'offspring of militarism and patriarchal capitalism' (p. 68). She simultaneously deems it an 'illegitimate offspring', thus possessing radical potential; still, the cyborg's complicity in constructing the patriarchal present (and future) must continue to be explored (Caputi, 1988).

Whether by naming ourselves Cyborgs or Goddesses, Two-Headed Women, *Mestizas* or Crones, it is clear that feminists, as Mary Daly prophesied in the early 1970s, are laying claim to the power of Naming and hence realizing (making real) ourselves and the world we invoke. This multifaceted and gynergetic foray into language, myth, symbol and image is one of the most elemental feminist strategies in our quest to change – and then change again – the world.

Notes

1 Barbara Omolade (1990b) defines the 'orisha' as 'a formal name given to the pantheon of deities within the Yoruba (West Africa subjected nationality) from which many new world Africans are descended. The orisha are daily represented in the ritual, oracles and prayers of Yoruba practitioners. The orisha are mediators, protectors and consolers of humans, hence insulating the supreme being from the mundane foibles of everyday human life. Each practitioner has a personal orisha, which visits them during possession and trance work.

2 Omolade (1990b) defines 'drylongso' as a term developed by members of the African-American community to convey a sense of the everyday and the ordinary. John Langston Gwaltney's description of the term in his book, *Drylongso: Self-Portraits of Black Americans*, reflects on the normative aspect of Black life and a sense of the core values of Black culture 'that ordinary African Americans express and reflect on ... these ordinary African Americans make up the majority of African Americans, not the junkies or geniuses so often portrayed in the popular and intellectual cultures of American Society'.

References and Further Reading

Allen, P.G. (1986), *The Sacred Hoop: Recovering the Feminine in American Indian Traditions* (Boston, Mass.: Beacon Press)

—— (ed.) (1989), *Spider Woman's Granddaughters: Traditional Tales and Contemporary Writing by Native American Women* (New York: Fawcett Columbine)

—— (1990), 'The Woman I Love Is a Planet; The Planet I Love Is a Tree' in I. Diamond and G.F. Orenstein (eds), *Reweaving the World: The Emergence of Ecofeminism* (San Francisco: Sierra Club Books), pp. 52–7

Anzaldúa, G. (1981, 1983), 'O.K. Momma, Who the Hell Am I?: An Interview with Luisah Teish' in C. Moraga and G. Anzaldúa (eds), *This Bridge Called My Back: Writings by Radical Women of Color* (New York: Kitchen Table: Women of Color Press), pp. 221–31

Anzaldúa, G. (1987), *Borderlands/La Frontera: The New Mestiza* (San Francisco: Spinsters/Aunt Lute Book Company)

Awiakta, M. (1988, 1984), 'Amazons in Appalachia' in B. Brant (ed.), *A Gathering of Spirit: A Collection by North American Indian Women* (Ithaca, NY: Firebrand Books), pp. 125–30

Bordo, S. (1990), 'Feminism, Postmodernism, and Gender-Scepticism' in L.J. Nicholson (ed.), *Feminism/Postmodernism* (New York and London: Routledge), pp. 133–56

Caputi, J. (1987), *The Age of Sex Crime* (Bowling Green, Ohio: Bowling Green State University Popular Press, 1987; London: The Women's Press, 1987)

—— (1988), 'Seeing Elephants: The Myths of Phallotechnology' in *Feminist Studies*, vol. 14, no. 3, pp. 486–524

Chandler, Z. (1990), 'Voices Beyond the Veil: An Interview of Toni Cade Bambara and Sonia Sanchez' in J.M. Braxton and A.N. McLaughlin (eds), *Wild Women in the Whirlwind: Afra-American Culture and the Contemporary Literary Renaissance* (New Brunswick, NJ: Rutgers University Press), pp. 342–62

Christ, C.P. (1979), 'Why Women Need the Goddess' in C. Christ and J. Plaskow (eds), *Womanspirit Rising: A Feminist Reader in Religion* (San Francisco: Harper & Row), pp. 273–87

Culpepper, E. (1983), 'Philosophia in a New Key: The Revolt of the Symbols', PhD Thesis, Harvard University

—— (1986), 'Gorgons: A Face for Contemporary Women's Rage' in *Woman of Power*, issue 3, Winter/Spring, pp. 22–5, 40

Daly, M. (1973), *Beyond God the Father: Toward a Philosophy of Women's Liberation* (Boston: Beacon Press)

—— (1978), *Gyn/Ecology: The Metaethics of Radical Feminism* (Boston: Beacon Press)

—— (1984), *Pure Lust: Elemental Feminist Philosophy* (Boston: Beacon Press)

—— (1990), *'New Intergalactic Introduction' to Gyn/Ecology: The Metaethics of Radical Feminism* (Boston: Beacon Press)

Daly, M. with Caputi, J. (1987), *Websters' First New Intergalactic Wickedary of the English Language* (Boston: Beacon Press)

Deming, B. (1982), 'A Song for Gorgons' in P. McAllister (ed.), *Reweaving the Web of Life: Feminism and Nonviolence* (Philadelphia, Pa: New Society Publishers), pp. 43–4

Gadon, E. (1989). *The Once & Future Goddess: A Symbol for Our Time* (San Francisco: Harper & Row)

Gwaltney, J.L. (1980), *Drylongso: Self-Portraits of Black Americans* (New York: Random House)

Hall, N. (1980), *The Moon and the Virgin: Reflections on the Archetypal Feminine* (New York: Harper & Row)

Haraway, D. (1985), 'A Manifesto for Cyborgs' in *Socialist Review*, no. 80, March-April, pp. 65–107

Hogan, L. (1982), 'Daughters, I Love You' in P. McAllister (ed.), *Reweaving the Web of Life: Feminism and Nonviolence* (Philadelphia: New Society Publishers), pp. 352–3

Lorde, A. (1978), *The Black Unicorn* (New York: W.W. Norton)

—— (1981, 1983), 'An Open Letter to Mary Daly' in C. Moraga and G. Anzaldúa (eds), *This Bridge Called My Back: Writings by Radical Women of Color* (New York: Kitchen Table: Women of Color Press), pp. 94–7

—— (1986), *Our Dead Behind Us* (New York: W.W. Norton)

Lydon, M. (1988), 'Foucault and Feminism: A Romance of Many Dimensions' in I. Diamond and L. Quinby (eds), *Feminism & Foucault: Reflections on Resistance* (Boston: Northeastern University Press), pp. 135–47

Marshall, P. (1983), 'The Poets in the Kitchen' in *Reena and Other Stories* (Old Westbury, NY: The Feminist Press), pp. 3–12

Merchant, C. (1981), *The Death of Nature: Women, Ecology, and the Scientific Revolution* (San Francisco: Harper & Row)

—— (1990), 'Ecofeminism and Feminist Theory' in I. Diamond and G.F. Orenstein, *Reweaving the World: The Emergence of Ecofeminism* (San Francisco: Sierra Club Books), pp. 100–5

Moraga, C. and Anzaldúa, G. (eds), *This Bridge Called My Back: Writings by Radical Women of Color* (New York: Kitchen Table: Women of Color Press)

Morgan, R. (1977), *Going Too Far: The Personal Chronicle of a Feminist* (New York: Random House)

Omolade, B. (1980), 'Black Women and Feminism' in H. Eisenstein and A. Jardine (eds), *The Future of Difference* (New Brunswick: Rutgers University Press), pp. 247–57)

—— (1990a), 'The Silence and the Song: Toward a Black Woman's History through a

Language of Her Own' in J.M. Braxton and A.N. McLaughlin (eds), *Wild Women in the Whirlwind: Afra-American Culture and the Contemporary Literary Renaissance* (New Brunswick, N.J.: Rutgers University Press), pp. 282–98

—— (1990b), Personal letter

Orenstein, G.F. (1990), *The Reflowering of the Goddess* (New York: Pergamon, The Athene Series)

Reid, C. (1982), 'Reweaving the Web of Life' in P. McAllister, *Reweaving the Web of Life: Feminism and Nonviolence* (Philadelphia, Pa: New Society Publishers), pp. 289–94

Russell, D.E.H. (ed.) (1989), *Exposing Nuclear Phallacies* (New York: Pergamon Press, The Athene Series)

Sanchez, C.L. (1989), 'New World Tribal Communities: An Alternative Approach for Recreating Egalitarian Societies' in J. Plaskow and C.P. Christ (eds), *Weaving the Visions: New Patterns in Feminist Spirituality* (San Francisco: Harper and Row), pp. 344–56

Sjöö, M. and Mor, B. (1987), *The Great Cosmic Mother: Rediscovering the Religion of the Earth* (San Francisco: Harper & Row)

Silko, L. (1977), *Ceremony* (New York: Signet Books, New American Library)

Starrett, B. (1974), 'I Dream in Female: The Metaphors of Evolution' in *Amazon Quarterly*, vol. 3, no. 1, pp. 13–27

Teish, L. (1983), 'Woman's Spirituality: A Household Act' in B. Smith (ed.), *Home Girls: A Black Feminist Anthology* (New York: Kitchen Table: Women of Color Press), pp. 331–5

—— (1985), *Jambalaya: The Natural Woman's Book* (San Francisco: Harper & Row)

Walker, A. (1983), 'In Search of Our Mothers' Gardens' in *In Search of Our Mothers' Gardens: Womanist Prose by Alice Walker* (San Diego, Calif.: Harcourt Brace Jovanovich), pp. 231–43

—— (1988), *Living by the Word* (San Diego, Calif.: Harcourt Brace Jovanovich)

Walker, B.G. (1983), *The Woman's Encyclopedia of Myths and Secrets* (San Francisco: Harper & Row)

—— (1986), *The Crone: Woman of Age, Wisdom and Power* (San Francisco: Harper & Row)

DIANE PURKISS

Women's Rewriting of Myth

I have cast my lot with those
who, age after age, perversely,
with no extraordinary power,
reconstitute the world.

(ADRIENNE RICH, 'NATURAL RESOURCES', 1978)

Ever since myths came into existence, women have been involved in writing and rewriting them.[1] In many cultures, women are story-tellers; it is misleading to speak solely of women's 'rewriting' of myth, since the term implies that man was its prime maker. In this essay, however, I focus particularly on an area of myth production in which women have been outsiders and latecomers: the place of classical myth and mythography in western literature in the twentieth century, and some women writers' interventions in this particular discursive field.[2]

A myth is not a single entity, but a diversity of stories told differently in different times and places (see Barthes, 1972). Myths are often caught up in contemporaneity, just as they were for their inventors. As part of that history, myths have been part of literary and academic self-definitions. Classical myths are, in Alicia Ostriker's phrase, handed *down*; they belong to high culture, and are largely transmitted by educational and cultural authorities (Ostriker, 1981). Consequently, classical myth is not merely authoritative and high in itself; it also confers prestige on texts which display their author's knowledge of it. Classical myth became a way for literary communities to constitute themselves and exclude others. Since few women had access to the classical education required, their participation was particularly difficult (Anderson and Zinsser, 1990, pp. 332–52; Ostriker, 1981, pp. 316–17).

For feminists, the rewriting of myths denotes participation in these historical processes and the struggle to alter gender asymmetries agreed upon for centuries by myth's disseminators. When feminists envisage that struggle, they often think of the rewriting or reinterpretation of individual stories: for example, by changing the focus of the narrative from a male character to a female character, or by shifting the terms of the myth so that what was a 'negative' female role-model becomes a positive one. Christine de Pisan provides a charming example: she argues that Medea and Circe were female scientific pioneers rather than witches (de Pisan, 1405, pp. 69–70). This approach reproduces 'images of women' feminism, demanding that literary texts both reflect reality or experience and also provide positive role-models. There are many problems with this critical strategy: its insistence that 'positive' images of women are somehow timeless, its refusal to recognize the literariness of literature. Most importantly, attempts to produce positive role models and tell feminist stories will repeatedly founder if we assume that stories can be excised from text, culture and institution, that their meanings are not circumscribed by their histories. I shall illustrate this by looking at the generation of a myth especially popular with recent feminists, arguing that the feminist revival of the goddess does not come straight to us from prehistoric women, but was invented by men earlier this century for reasons which had nothing to do with empowering women.

The influential ideas of Rousseau, in which civilization characteristically acts to corrupt or obscure the instinctual verities of primitive societies, rediscovered in the person of the Noble Savage, led indirectly to a reinterpretation of classical myth (Rousseau, 1762). Certain mythic stories came to seem significant not solely as marks of participation in 'high' civilization, but as pointers to prehistory, markers of civilization's secret or buried identity. As such, they appeared to promise the truth of that which is beyond history and beyond culture, not subject to the vicissitudes of time and change. An exegetical and literary tradition grew up which saw myth as the disregarded but fundamental truth of human nature, or a set of ideals about human nature which needed to be restored to the degenerate consciousness of a corrupt civilization. Ironically, this view found its finest and most sophisticated expression in the psychoanalytic theories of Sigmund Freud, though Freud's texts can also be read as a critical engagement with some of its more egregious sentimentalities. Freud used mythic narratives to describe the truths submerged in the unconscious. Like the unconscious, myths are for Freud the buried letters of civilization; like dreams and riddles, they are signposts to what cannot be acknowledged in rational and civilized discourse.

This set of assumptions was developed – though differently – by Freud's one-time disciple Jung. For Jung, myths constituted a universal cultural unconscious, called by him the collective unconscious, which manifested itself in a series of cultural archetypes, such as the Maiden, Mother and Crone and the Great Mother (see Samuels, 1985). Like Freud, Jung read mythic stories as containing universal truths, of value because they escaped the specificity of culture. For both, a complex interpretative process was necessary in order to recover the truths lodged in myths previously treated as 'mere' stories. Unabashed by the example of Mr Casaubon's never-to-be-finished Key to All Mythologies, numerous early twentieth-century writers set out to try to discover the truths which lay 'behind' the myths.

Writers like Erich Neumann, Robert Graves, Arthur Evans and Sir James George Frazer shared a belief in the power of a certain single archetype, and the influence of a particular narrative of creation and loss (see Neumann, 1963). Like Freud in *Moses and Monotheism*, all these thinkers believed in an originary matriarchy, signified by the worship of a deity called variously the Great Goddess or the Great Mother (Freud, 1939). This narrative was in turn based on the contract theories of Rousseau and others, who accounted for women's subordination with reference to the marriage contract by producing a myth of the origins of patriarchy in the prehistorical world (Pateman, 1989a, 1989b). Such narratives are always difficult to equate with any feminist political purpose, and as Adrienne Rich points out, Neumann and others were not interested in liberating real women but in releasing men from their psychological problems (Rich, 1972).

My point here is not to dislodge the historical narrative itself but to point to the specificities determining its emergence. As is widely known, Homeric hero stories were an important part of the discourse of patriotism and militarism during the First World War (Parker, 1987; Jenkyns, 1980). At the same time, they had become awkwardly and embarrassingly associated with the homoeroticism of *fin-de-siecle* culture, and with fears of homosexuality among the troops (Dijkstra, 1986). These joint pressures can be clearly seen in Graves's *The White Goddess*, one of the most influential of the works valorizing a primeval matriarchy and Great Goddess. Graves writes on the relations of women writers to the Goddess and of her importance to male poets:

> He [Ben Jonson] knew the risk run by sentimental Apollonians when they try to be wholly independent of women: they fall into sentimental homosexuality . . . However, woman is not a poet: she is either a muse or she is nothing . . . A woman who concerns herself with poetry should, I believe, either be a silent Muse and inspire the poets by her womanly presence, or she should be the Muse in a complete sense; she should be in turn Arianhrod, Blodeuwedd, and the Old Sow . . . who eats her farrow.
>
> (GRAVES, 1948, PP. 446–7)

The Goddess is important here chiefly because she prevents the dreaded onset of sentimental homosexuality. Her function, rapidly equated with the function of woman-in-poetry, is to stand between men and other men, inspiring healthily heterosexual songs. What is most noteworthy is that under no circumstances can woman be a *poet*. She can be a silent or active/complete muse, but in either case her role remains ancillary; she exists chiefly to regulate male poetic output and prevent it from taking any 'wrong' turns.

For Graves, woman therefore occupies the position of symbol rather than subject, bearer rather than creator of meaning. Graves makes it apparent that this symbolic role is *for men*; the Muse exists to regulate men's relations with each other, not in her own right. It also becomes clear that the truth-claims of myths as the hidden secret repressed by civilization, are written by Graves as truths *about* femininity *for* men. A discourse of mythography which valorizes the truth of a central female figure as a bearer of power and meaning functions to block women from any kind of cultural engagement other than ancillary ones. Graves's Muse may write and may eat her children, but she is still a figure in a poetic discourse which assumes the poet to be male.

This discourse of mythography defined the Great Mother as a figure in male writing by insisting that such female figures were the dark, repressed underside of civilization. While this was the basis of their claim to ahistorical and universal validity, civilization was thus repeatedly constructed as a business for men. Men had lost their connection with the 'dark continent' of myth, so that dark continent was 'naturally' gendered female; since women were excluded from civilization they could become the bearers of this unknown knowledge. But this set of tropes also worked to *reinforce* women's exclusion from civilization and from poetic practice, since they came to signify a space above or beyond those activities which could make an appearance only in the work of male poets.

Given these constraints, it's surprising at first to discover that twentieth-century women writers and artists constantly strive to engage with and re-figure women's representation in classical myth, and that a particular group of them have found inspiration in Graves and Neumann for their efforts (Sjöö, 1990; Orenstein, 1982; Stein, 1989; Walker, 1985, 1986; Daly, 1978; *see* Jane Caputi's contribution to this volume, p. 425). Since the 1970s, a number of popular feminist fantasy novels have also sought to represent a goddess-worshipping or originary matriarchy (Bradley, 1987; Cranny-Francis, 1989; see also Renault, 1958, 1962): these novels develop the narrative of what Rita Felski terms Romantic feminism, in which woman's instinctual relationship with nature is stressed (Felski, 1989).[3] Some of these women are articulators of a more general movement to 'restore' the worship of the Great Goddess and to valorize women's 'special' links with the earth and with nature. If the projects of Graves and Neumann are in thrall to a masculinist representation of woman, why have so many women appropriated their theories? Perhaps certain feminists 'misread' or re-read these texts productively to formulate a position from which to write and speak, by taking the Jungians' essentialist propositions for truths about the repression of woman's nature by patriarchy. They could cast themselves as the bearers of secret feminine knowledge actually unavailable to male writers.

However, this means that radical feminist claims of utter separatism are invalid, since their theories are predicated not on stories produced thousands of years ago by women, but on a masculine discourse of myth. In Donna Haraway's influential terms, these women may wish to be goddesses, but they are cyborgs all the same (Haraway, 1989). Their engagement depends on accepting some of the terms of what they engage with, even as they lay claim to an originary innocence or separatist integrity. The problem is that the terms accepted depend heavily on an essentialist notion of a bodily femininity assumed to be reflected in – rather than produced by – the myths they elaborate. Moreover, radical feminists often appear to believe that role-models can be reworked without changing the discourses from which they derive their meaning. By rewriting the myth – changing the narrative, changing the position of the speaker, changing the spaces available for identification – you are held to be at once making a dramatic break with the myths as told by the fathers, and also to be recovering the dark, secret, always unconscious truths which the fathers have struggled to repress. These moves are analogous to Mary Daly's problematic theory of language. As Meaghan Morris argues, Daly assumes that it's possible to change the meaning of particular words without altering the discourses in which they are spoken and through which their meanings are constituted (Morris, 1982). I shall show in what follows that the rewriting of myth cannot be limited to the rewriting of particular favoured or disliked figures. It can extend to complex engagements with the very place of myth in literature, the place of the woman writer in relation to those discourses, and the displacement of myth as a buried truth of culture.

Because the narratives of Greek and Roman myth are rich in female figures, women poets have used the stories as a point of engagement with the literary tradition. The most common strategy used by twentieth-century women poets is an identification of the female speaking voice with that of a woman character in myth who remains silent, objectified or inaudible in previous narrations of the story. The fairy-tale and mythological retellings of Anne Sexton offer many instances of this strategy. In her poem on the Apollo/Daphne story, Sexton reorders both the scene of the myth and the central character in it. Whereas Ovid and others end the story with Daphne's metamorphosis, this is Sexton's starting-point:

> Too late
> To wish I had not run from you, Apollo,
> blood moves still in my bark-bound veins.
>
> (SEXTON, 1981, P. 17)

This shift in point of view allows Sexton subtly to reinterpret the myth. Rather than celebrating Daphne's chastity and her fortunate escape, Sexton figures her metamorphosis as sign and cause of acute sexual frustration. The equation of Daphne's voice with the poem itself, achieved by making her its sole narrator, draws attention to the way Apollo uses her metamorphosis to reward male poets while it signifies her own exclusion from agency and creativity:

> I build the air with the crown of honor: it keys
> my out of time and luckless appetite.
> You gave me honor too soon, Apollo.

However, Sexton does not quite elude the masculinist terms on which the myth rests. Though the poem rewrites Ovid by insisting that Daphne has a vocal if frustrated sexuality, that sexuality is also represented as a result of victimage. Indeed, for Sexton Daphne's desire seems actually to be constituted by her stasis, her bound passivity. What cannot be envisaged in the terms of the myth as told by Sexton is a female sexuality associated with agency rather than disempowerment. The poem laments this, but cannot imagine an alternative.

A different kind of voicing is used by Liz Lochhead in her poem 'The Ariadne Version'. This is the only retelling of a classical myth in her volume *The Grimm Sisters*, which as its title suggests is primarily a rewriting of fairy- and folk-tales from a perspective clearly influenced by feminism. Unlike Sexton, who despite her colloquialisms and self-conscious roughness also writes in the mainstream of lyric poetry, Lochhead writes almost exclusively in a kind of postmodern demotic which makes extensive and ironic use of popular culture, cliché and the slogans of commerce. This mixture of high and low is a crucial part of her strategy in retelling Ariadne's story. Again unlike Sexton, Lochhead does not merge the voice of female character and the voice of the poem itself:

> Of course Ariadne was in it,
> right up to here,
> the family labyrinth – lush
> palatial and stained with sacrifice,
> maybe money grew on trees
> for Minos in summer Crete but
> Ariadne imagine it
> sizzling on the beach all day . . .
>
> Ariadne decided
> she'd be off like a shot with the first man
> who looked halfways likely.
> So she'd better
> kill off her own brute bit
> her best friend, her brother:
>
> (LOCHHEAD, 1984, PP. 97–8)

The poem's title suggests a translation or edition, often called versions. But this is not a scholar's reconstruction: it is Ariadne's untold story. Her ordinariness, represented by the language of eighties' youth, is sharply contrasted with the traditional association of the classics with high culture and inaccessible scholarship. Lochhead also radically rewrites the story: in this version, it is Ariadne who kills the Minotaur, 'her own brute bit' who 'burst inside her recently/like a bull in a china shop'. This killing allows her to 'go ultra feminine' and to escape with Theseus, but Lochhead does not allow the reader to forget that the sacrifice of sexuality to femininity will only involve Ariadne in a repetition of her disempowerment within the family.

Like Sexton, Lochhead makes an appeal to women's experience here. Whereas in Sexton this appeal is based on a moderately colloquial modernism representing the speaking voice, in Lochhead it is based on her juxtaposition of myth with twentieth-century popular culture. While this vocabulary unsettles the discourse of myth by breaking down the link between the classics and high culture, it does so at the expense of partially affirming the timelessness of myth. By presenting the rewritten story of Ariadne in language which invites the reader to identify her with contemporary young women, Lochhead suggests the continuing relevance of the story as a political parable – its power to make visible the truths of women's lives.

A less complex appeal to female experience is evident in Judith Kazantzis's 'Clytemnestra'. Kazantzis's poem begins with a comic recapitulation of what is 'known' about Clytemnestra: 'queen of the grand absurd name/Clytie in her nightie' (Kazantzis, 1980). This knowing is subordinated to and displaced by the plangent lyricism of Clytemnestra's narration of her own story in her own voice:

Iphigenia my daughter sits upon my lap
in the evening, talking.
I brush her black hair, and kiss her shoulders,
she wriggles and smiles, don't do that
kisses me with a soft mouth . . .

I saw you, graveless
your ashes fed to Poseidon
small handful of my daughter
plump and twelve years old
whose body they burned.

(KAZANTZIS, 1980)

Jokes about femininity in a nightie are made to seem obscene beside the tender evocation of Clytemnestra's motherhood and her sensuously-evoked daughter's body. But this apparently simple poem, lavishly praised by Jan Montefiore (1987) for its suppression of analysis in favour of dramatic narrative, conceals the crucial analysis on which its meaning depends. The violence implicit in the dismissive jokes is linked with the violence of war and the family violence symbolized by Iphigenia's death. These violences are gendered male by Kazantzis, and are set over against the gentleness and nurturativeness of the mother–daughter relationship. The meaning of the myth for women thus emerges clearly from the poem, even though there is little overt analysis. Indeed, the 'truth' of Clytemnestra's tenderness is partially established by the apparently simple language in which her maternity is described. Like all simple language, it purports to a transparency which goes beyond textuality: it solicits identification with Clytemnestra not as an individual but as a representational mother and tender woman. The stress on Clytemnestra's bodily relationship with Iphigenia helps to generate this notion of transhistorical maternity. The body often appears as a realm of truth and experience which goes beyond culture.

Appealing as Kazantzis's poem is, it illustrates a real problem for women writers' adoption of a politics of identification with female figures in myths and legends. It is Kazantzis's ability to generate an identification of all women readers with Clytemnestra which gives her work its purchase on the rewriting of Clytemnestra's story, and also much of its power as poetry. But to do this, Kazantzis has to postulate a real, shared and timeless female nature, one based on the body and on the experience of maternity. This is problematic because it necessarily excludes many women while purporting to be universal. Moreover, such valorizations of a feminine maternal body and personality which is and has always been nurturative and non-violent, have much in common with the ideology of gender which feminism sets out to oppose, an ideology in which the subordination of women was predicated on biological determinism, the centrality of motherhood and woman's supposed lack of aggressive feelings, often equated with her weakness (Segal, 1988). Of course, there are significant differences between this view and that of Kazantzis, but at the same time there are similarities which underline the difficulty of writing our way out of patriarchy through myth. Rather, there seems to be a danger of writing our way deeper and deeper into it.

This problem arises from Kazantzis's appropriation of the role created for myth by nineteenth and early twentieth-century mythography, an appropriation also made by Lochhead and Sexton. For though she denies the truth of male stories and knowings about Clytemnestra, Kazantzis replaces these with her own truth-claims. Her story is the true story, the final version, the recovery of a lost or buried voice. These figurations of the female 'side' of the story as that which has been lost or forgotten is what helps to establish their plausibility in the light of a literary discourse which positions myth itself as the space of the lost or forgotten truth. Kazantzis thus rewrites the myth of Clytemnestra as an individual narrative, but to do this she has to leave the discourse of myth where it is.

So how might women writers rewrite the discourses of myth while rewriting individual myths? I now want to examine some women's writings which intervene in individual myths in ways which problematize not just the truth-claims of an individual story or version of a story, but also the truth-claims of the mythic corpus itself. I shall begin by analysing some works which make use of what became the psychoanalytic model of mythic signification.

Since Freud and Jung alike represented myths as part of the masculine cultural unconscious, femininity was constructed as the unconscious of the unconscious, the dark continent of the dark continent (Irigaray, 1985; Grosz, 1990). In psychoanalysis, a crucial notion is that the return of what has been repressed or silenced has the power to undo the stable constructions of identity and culture built on its repression (see Mitchell, 1974). French feminists have made extensive use of this notion in relation to the repressed place of femininity. The return of the feminine has the power to shake male culture by undoing its central logic. However, in referring to 'femininity', Irigaray and Kristeva do not speak of a transhistorical essence located in, for example, maternity or reproductive capacity. Rather, they refer to a femininity which is itself a product of the culture and language which represses it. Femininity is, precisely, that which is excluded from patriarchal representations and can only be glimpsed in their gaps and silences. For it to return, and to unsettle that which repressed it, a special process is required, because what is returning is *not* something always present in every individual woman. For Irigaray, this takes the form of a problematic mimicry of the position of the hysteric, who articulates publicly in her body postures the history forgotten by her society, including the history of 'low' culture (Cixous and Clement, 1986). As Clair Wills has pointed out, also writing on this theory in relation to women's lyric poetry, the problem lies in differentiating a hysteria recuperable by patriarchy from one which is always already recuperable *as* hysteria (Wills, 1989). I want to try to suggest some ways in which certain women's writings on the terrain of myth play with the notion of an Irigarayan hysteria.

H.D.'s poem 'Eurydice' looks at first sight like a mere reversal of gendered speaking-positions.[4] In the writings of male poets, Orpheus usually represents the poetic mastery of the male writer, and his journey into the underworld illustrates the origins of this mastery in male knowledge of the dark continent of death and sexuality. This interpretive telling reduces Eurydice to a figure who merely symbolizes an aspect of Orpheus's artistic mastery. Woman is the *bearer* of meaning, but man is its *maker* or *controller.* In inverting the relationship between who speaks and who is spoken to by voicing the poem through Eurydice, H.D. therefore does more that merely give a voice to one silenced. She calls into question the logic of representation and creation on which the Orpheus narrative is based. And in doing this, she unsettles the kinds of truth–claims associated with the masculine discourse of myth as its own dark continent of repressed but recoverable verity. The poem is cast as a lament. Eurydice reproaches Orpheus for his failure:

> So you have swept me back,
> I who would have walked with the live souls
> above the earth,
> I who could have slept among the live flowers
> at last;
> so for your arrogance
> and your ruthlessness
> I am swept back
> where dead lichens drip
> dead cinders upon moss of ash;
>
> (H.D., 1983, P. 51)

Here Eurydice identifies a lack in Orpheus, but she identifies it as arrogance and ruthlessness, not as a failure of nerve. This is explained in the second section:

> What was it you saw in my face?
> the light of your own face,
> the fire of your own presence?
> What had my face to offer
> But reflex of the earth?
>
> (H.D., 1983, P. 52)

Orpheus looks at Eurydice because he is narcissistic; he wants and needs to catch a glimpse of his own reflection. H.D. makes visible not just male self-centredness, but the narcissistic base of male poetic mastery. Male poetry is a search for self-replication which ends not in the acquisition of knowledge of the underworld, but in loss caused by the male desire to capture knowledge with a look. What is lost is the illusion of masculine self-mastery (from Orpheus's point of view), but from Eurydice's point of view her voice – her life – is not only lost but silenced in this struggle for masculine poetry. Eurydice's being is seen as autonomous in relation to Orpheus's reflective presence ('I have the fervour of myself for a presence/and my own spirit for light') which suggests that she can discover a selfhood which goes beyond his, but only at the cost of suffering.

It is instructive to compare this rewriting with that of Elaine Feinstein. Like H.D., Feinstein is elliptical and riddling; she refuses a femininity which would identify itself with the simple in order to explore the fragmentation of the female subject within patriarchy. But Feinstein's verse is closed where H.D.'s is open. If H.D. represents hell as an enclosed female space which can open like a rose through its own agency, she represents Eurydice's voice as a series of breaches and fissures in syntactical structure. For Feinstein, the voice of the dead Eurydice is closed by the tight ellipsis of verse. Feinstein's use of this tight structure is closed in another sense as well; it suggests the riddle, which contains spaces which must be filled in by readers' interpretations (see Wills, 1989). The formal features of the poem thus reflect (upon) Eurydice's place as a mere metaphor within Orpheus's song; Eurydice is limited, enclosed by that place:

> The dead are strong,
> That winter as you wandered
> The cold continued, still
> The brightness cut
> my shape into the snow:
> I would have let you go!
>
> Your mother blew
> my dust into your lips
> a powder white as cocaine,
> my name, runs to your nerves
> and now I move again in your song,
> You will not let me go.
>
> The dead are strong.
> Although in darkness I was lost
> and had forgotten all pain
> long ago: in your song
> my lit face remains
> and so we go.

(FEINSTEIN, 1980, P. 24)

Eurydice is figured here both as the voice which speaks the poem, and as a series of representations created by Orpheus. As in H.D.'s poem, the disjunction between the two is emphasized; Feinstein figures Eurydice for Orpheus as a shadow, a name, and a face in a song, tropes which recall H.D.'s figure of Eurydice as mirror. But for Feinstein these figures of Eurydice are magically connected to her. The shadow and the name are part of the tradition of sympathetic magic; by exerting power over these representations of a person the magician exerts power over the person. Orpheus's status as magician is especially evident in the second stanza, where his power to summon Eurydice in song is directly linked to his inhalation of her dust, figured as a stimulant drug (a modern form of shamanistic inspiration). Orpheus's power over Eurydice is figured as an absorption of her energy which turns her into a mere figure in his poetry. What Feinstein shows clearly is the repercussions of this poetic practice for the woman herself. Unlike H.D., Feinstein insists that Eurydice does not desire rescue. Male desire for her power to 'inspire' verse excludes her from the nirvana of forgetfulness into which she has pleasurably sunk. The reiteration of the phrase 'let me go' has the force of a plea, and also signifies Eurydice's death as a release from Orpheus, or from masculine poetic power: a pleasurable letting-go.

Both Feinstein and H.D. explore a linkage between femininity as the grounds of male inspiration and femininity's association with death and loss. If female figures in myth are characteristically the site of a male knowledge set over against their control by the male poet, in H.D. and Feinstein Eurydice becomes the creator of a knowingness lost in the moment when it is subjected to male control, signified as the gaze (theoria) and the process of creation (poesis). They challenge and change the discourse of myth in literary culture by asking who can know the truths of myth and who can articulate them, and by asking if the very process of knowing valorized by male creativity is self-defeating.

The exploration of the nexus of femininity, death, creation and renunciation or forgetting is continued by Jenny Joseph in her extraordinary work, *Persephone*. The Demeter-Persephone story is central for feminists who valorize the Jungian archetype of the Great Goddess and its concomitant dependence on the role of the mother. As I have argued, this particular feminist strategy can lapse into a problematic bodily or psychological essentialism. In selecting this myth as the structure of her work, does Joseph succeed in evading these problems?

Persephone is a remarkable mixture of genres and formats. The mythic narrative is told in an expansive set of translations of and variations upon the Homeric *Hymn to Demeter*, but this narrative is constantly broken off by the irruption of illustrative stories in a variety of modes from both high and popular culture. There are 'art' photos as well as a photo-story from true confession magazines, a fragment of an academic conference paper and a women's magazine 'problem page', a one-act play, short stories in realist and magic-realist modes, lyric poems and fragmentary epistolary narratives. These stories expand on aspects of the main mythic narrative. Like Lochhead, Joseph uses popular idiom and form to question the division between a permanent high culture based on the classics, a middle-class culture based on the realist narrative, and an intrinsically ephemeral and formulaic popular culture. All three cultural modes are rewritten by Joseph; *Persephone* cannot be read as an attempt to sanctify or clean up popular culture through high culture. The rewriting of Homeric hymns as photostories questions the elevation of the classics, and the irruption of lyric, epic and sacred narrative into secular realism calls notions of reality into question.

The subject-matter of the stories and other illustrative materials also unsettles the significance routinely attached to classical myths by high culture. Rather than locating myth as a mark of elevated civilization or as its repressed underside, Joseph tries to show how the personal – a realm gendered feminine in criticism on lyric poetry – can be 'read' in terms of mythic narratives. This might seem a dubious strategy, prone to replicating the problems of realist writing itself. But in the case of classical myth, such domestications can be read as powerfully strategic disruptions rather than as moves towards a premature authentication through traditional modes. By translating classical myth into personal story, Joseph deconstructs the assumed linkage between myths and the masculine world of war, sport, politics and education. She also dilutes the other-worldly high sentiment of both mystical and Christian privileging of classical myth. Her use of the popular and the 'ordinary' also operates to disrupt essentialist reading and writing of the Demeter-Persephone myth. The identification of the myth with the average and the ordinary prevents it from being represented as the dark continent of a male civilization or a signifier of a buried aspect of the male psyche. Joseph also avoids an essentialist assertion of a female monopoly on feelings of loss, bereavement and maternity. Though most of the stories which illustrate Demeter's grief at Persephone's disappearance are narratives of female/maternal loss and pain, one is a brief realist narrative of a café-owner whose business is about to fail, and who finally breaks down in grief at the realization (Joseph, 1986, pp. 58–60).

This account implies that Joseph reduces the Demeter-Persephone story to a few essential themes – grief, loss, recovery, change. In fact, the interplay between the myth and the illustrative stories is extremely complex. The café-owner, for example, does not merely lose his business. As a dispenser of food, he is acting out a maternal role, giving nourishment to the hungry and especially to children. One child robs him and abandons him, so that what is figured is the loss of a maternal role and also a maternal failure to control the world and the child. This is both an acute and subtle rewriting of the Demeter-Persephone myth and a representation of maternity which goes beyond biologism.

In implying that the griefs of maternity are not confined to women, Joseph suggests that they may be general aspects of human experience in a manner which may appear to rule out gender altogether. However, she is attentive elsewhere to the social construction of women's experience of their bodies as sites of conflict and violent intervention. Many of the realist narratives represent women's experience of birth, pregnancy and rape, and these indicate vividly that sexuality and maternity are not necessarily instinctual, but may be socially mediated or forced upon women. Another story writing the loss of Persephone tells of a woman who seeks an abortion after a miscarriage has already threatened: there is a powerful and disturbing description of the doctor's violence in performing the operation, which makes it evident that the willed loss of a child is turned into a rape by medicine:

> The doctor tugged and a sound shot out of her mouth. She had never in her life, not even while giving birth, never, felt anything like that. She thought he had pulled away her whole inside, that her flesh was being peeled away inside from her bone cage as you take the skin off coley.
>
> (JOSEPH, 1986, PP. 79–80)

In her extremity, the woman curses the man she has desired without fruition for years: 'because I wanted you and you dragged my innards toward you but you never did a thing to help'. Her desire for the man and his control over her body are revisioned as the doctor's violence, then as rape: 'And then she was left and the man had gone and it was finished' (p. 80). This woman combines the stories of Demeter and Persephone as told by Joseph; loss of a child and desire for a man coalesce.

At the same time, it must be noted that what Joseph herself terms the 'fatalistic' aspect of the myth and her retelling of it causes problems. Fatalism never seems a useful political strategy, and Joseph's equation of women's specific difficulties with a *necessary* process of grief and loss must ring alarm bells. It presents the danger of representing women as victims too: Demeter's 'revenge' on the earth is not fictionalized as the anger or rebellion of female subjects, but as a set of natural forces (storms, bad weather) and as a failure to attend to private duties (to do the housework, for instance).

I want to close by looking at a text which breaks with some of the strategies I have been describing. Many of the poems discussed so far involve female identification with a single mythic figure, or in the case of Joseph, with a single figure of three chronological aspects. From Kazantzis's assertion of the tender truth behind the Clytemnestra story of female violence to Joseph's sympathetic evocations of Demeter's grief, all these women posit single female figures as metaphors of themselves. I want therefore to look at a poem which refuses an unproblematic identification of a single female figure, exploring instead the irreconcilable dualities of a femininity fractured in culture and in the individual subject.

Of all the women poets of the post-war era, Sylvia Plath exemplifies most clearly the identification of the woman writer with the woman of violence. In 'Edge', one of her most compelling and unsettling lyrics, two female figures of the classical world are simultaneously evoked: the suicidal Cleopatra, and the murderous Medea:

> The woman is perfected.
> Her dead
>
> Body wears the smile of accomplishment
> The illusion of a Greek necessity
>
> Flows in the scrolls of her toga
> Her bare
>
> Feet seem to be saying:
> We have come so far, it is over.
>
> Each dead child coiled, a white serpent,
> One at each little
>
> Pitcher of milk, now empty.
> She has folded
>
> Them back into her body as petals
> Of a rose close when the garden
>
> Stiffens and odours bleed
> From the sweet, deep throats of the night flower.
>
> (PLATH, 1981, PP. 272–3)

Plath evokes first Cleopatra, whose serpents in Shakespeare are babies suckling her breast, and then Medea, whose 'illusion of a Greek necessity' is revenge on Jason, her unfaithful husband. Medea's revenge takes the form of child-murder. The woman in the poem hovers undecidably between the two figures, one whose 'children' killed her, one who killed her children, one whose violence turns towards her own flesh through her 'children', one whose violence turns outwards through her children. The woman's necessity is Greek, but she wears a Roman toga. This is an undecidability which will not allow the truth of woman to be located in an individual myth, or the truth of myth in an individual woman. But both deaths complete the woman; they fold her children back into her body, but do her children eat her or does she eat them? Perfection or completion is possible to the woman only because she contains both kinds of female violence: the female internalization of violence against women, and the female agent who externalizes that violence. Similarly, the children are both outside her body, suckling her empty breasts ('pitchers of milk') and inside the body, folded in like the petals of a flower. As often in Plath (Montefiore, 1987), the image of the flower evokes female sexuality and the troubling openness of the female body. Here, however, that body is not unequivocally open; as a dead body it is monumental, impenetrable and completed by its internalization of what was once messily extruded (children). The final image of Artemis-Diana reinforces the closure of death:

> The moon has nothing to be sad about,
> Staring from her hood of bone.
> She is used to this sort of thing.
> Her blacks crackle and drag.
>
> (PLATH, P. 275)

The moon is detached, perfected like the body of the woman, pared down to the bare bone of death with no troublingly open flesh, and no rebellion of the body against its own product. She accepts the violence on display here as commonplace: 'she is used to this sort of thing'. Which is more than we are.

Alan Sinfield has described Plath's position in her late poetry as that of an hysteric. Female hysteria both accepts and refuses the organization of female sexuality under patriarchy, allowing women simultaneously to act out and refuse femininity (Sinfield, 1988; Mitchell, 1974; Cixous and Clement, 1983). That radical split is enacted here: Plath identifies, rather than identifying with, a set of opposing stories about women's violence in relation to their bodies and their children. But she makes no gesture towards recuperating these stories for a socially sanctioned femininity. Rather the poem speaks from the position(s) of femininities driven out of society to be its violent other. More importantly, it refuses to take up a single position: the woman is not unequivocally either aggressor or victim, but neither and both. Plath speaks from the extreme and opposed positions they represent, the position designated as the limit, the absolute 'Edge'. The poem itself does a kind of violence to our ideas of what is appropriate, what can be said and who can say it.

Perhaps Plath's hysteria retains its genuine power to unsettle because it is displayed by *her* as a controlled loss of control, a structured deconstruction, rather than by a male expert who is authoritatively placed to unravel its secrets. The efforts of many of those disturbed by Plath's work seem bent on occupying precisely the space of Charcot or Freud, the position of the male expert who 'explains' and thus recuperates the woman's display so that her opening is not a disturbing explosion but the result of theory and male speculation (Russo, 1986; for examples of Plath criticism of this kind, see Sinfield's astringent review).

Any strategy which adopts an extreme tactic runs the risk of dismissal *as* extremism. But it is important not to overstate the power of such recuperations. In Plath's case they have failed to make the reading I have outlined unthinkable or unsayable. In the case of the other poets I have been discussing, I may seem to have told a story of failure and difficulty and doubt. However, I want to close by suggesting that *no* possible strategy of rewriting myth (or anything else) can really constitute the kind of absolute, clean and revolutionary break with discourse and order sought in the days of feminism and poststructuralism's greatest confidence. This does not imply that judgement must be suspended; it's more important to be wary and even ironic about the strategies available when none are foolproof. A bit of political *nous* is useful too; it's self-evident that there are occasions when one story will be more helpful than another. Women must continue to struggle to tell the stories otherwise. The possibilities are endless.

Notes

1 For an early instance, see John J. Winkler (1990), *The Constraints of Desire: The Anthropology of Sex and Gender in Ancient Greece* (London and New York: Routledge), on Sappho.

2 I write about the problems of a particular mythic corpus in a particular social configuration; I do not mean to count for the very different situations of women of other countries, period and races.

3 For an ironic and highly subversive use of similar strategies, see Monique Wittig and Sande Zeig (1979), *Lesbian Peoples: Materials for a Dictionary* (New York: Avon).

4 This poem is relatively early in H.D.'s *oeuvre*; I do not mean my analysis of it to hold good for her much more complex and lengthy treatment of classical myth in her later works *Trilogy*, *Helen in Egypt* and her Sappho poems. For an analysis of these poems, see Rachel Blau du Plessis (1986), *H.D.: The Career of that Struggle* (Brighton: Harvester).

References and Further Reading

PRIMARY SOURCES:

D., H. [Hilda Doolittle] (1983), *H.D.: Collected Poems*, ed. Louis L. Martz (New York: New Directions)

de Pisan, Christine (1405, reprinted 1983), *The Book of the City of Ladies*, trans. Earl Jeffery Richards (London: Picador)

Feinstein, Elaine (1980), *The Feast of Eurydice* (London: Next Editions)

Freud, Sigmund (1939, reprinted 1985), 'Moses and Monotheism: Three Essays' in *The Origins of Religion*, trans. James Strachey, vol. 13 of *The Pelican Freud Library* (Harmondsworth: Penguin)

Joseph, Jenny (1986), *Persephone* (Newcastle-Upon-Tyne: Bloodaxe)

Kazantzis, Judith (1980), *The Wicked Queen* (London: Sidgwick and Jackson)

Lochhead, Liz (1984), *Dreaming Frankenstein and Collected Poems* (Edinburgh: Polygon)

Plath, Sylvia (1981), *Collected Poems*, ed. and intro. Ted Hughes (London: Faber)

Rousseau, Jean-Jacques (1762, 1968), *The Social Contract*, trans. Maurice Cranston (Harmondsworth: Penguin)

Sexton, Anne (1981), *Anne Sexton: The Complete Poems* (Boston: Houghton Mifflin). Foreword by Maxine Kumin.

SECONDARY SOURCES:

Anderson, Bonnie S. and Zinsser, Judith P. (1990), *A History of their Own*, 2 vols (Harmondsworth: Penguin)

Barthes, Roland (1972), *Mythologies*, trans. Annette Lavers (London: Paladin). First published in French in 1957.

Bradley, Marion Zimmer (1985), *The Mists of Avalon* (London: Macmillan)

Cixous, Hélène and Clement, Catherine (1986), *The Newly-Born Woman*, trans. Betsy Wing, Theory and History of Literature Series, vol. 24 (Manchester: Manchester University Press)

Cranny-Francis, Anne (1990), *Feminist Fictions* (London: Routledge)

Daly, Mary (1979), *Gyn/Ecology* (London: Women's Press)

Dijkstra, Bram (1986), *Idols of Perversity: Fantasies of Feminine Evil in Fin-De-Siecle Culture* (Oxford: Oxford University Press)

Du Plessis, Rachel Blau (1986), *H.D.: The Career of that Struggle* (Brighton: Harvester)

Felski, Rita (1989), *Beyond Feminist Aesthetics* (London: Hutchinson Radius)

Graves, Robert (1948, reprinted 1961), *The White Goddess: A Historical Grammar of Poetic Myth* (London: Faber)

Grosz, Elizabeth (1990), *Sexual Subversions* (London and Sydney: Unwin Hyman)

Gubar, Susan (1981, reprinted 1986), '"The Blank Page" and the Issues of Female Creativity' in Elaine Showalter (ed.), *The New Feminist Criticism: Essays on Women, Literature and Theory* (London: Virago), pp. 292–313

—— (1985, first published 1982), 'Sapphistries' in Estelle B. Freedman et al. (eds), *The Lesbian Issue: Essays from Signs* (Chicago and London: The University of Chicago Press)

Haraway, Donna (1989), 'A Manifesto for Cyborgs: Science, Technology, and Socialist Feminism in the 1980s' in Elizabeth Weed (ed.), *Coming to Terms: Feminism, Theory, Politics* (New York: Routledge), pp. 173–204

Irigaray, Luce (1985), *Speculum of the Other Woman*, trans. Catherine Porter (Ithaca: Cornell University Press)

Jenkyns, Richard (1980), *The Victorians and Ancient Greece* (Oxford: Blackwell)

Mitchell, Juliet (1974), *Psychoanalysis and Feminism* (Harmondsworth; Penguin)

Montefiore, Jan (1987), *Feminism and Poetry: Language, Experience, Identity in Women's Writing* (London: Pandora)

Morris, Meaghan (1982, reprinted 1988), 'A-mazing Grace: Notes on Mary Daly's Poetics' in *The Pirate's Fiancée: Feminism, Reading, Postmodernism* (London: Verso)

Neumann, Erich (1963), *The Great Mother: An Analysis of the Archetype*, trans. Ralph Manheim, Bollingen series 47 (Princeton: Princeton University Press)

Orenstein, Gloria Feman (1982, reprinted 1990), 'The Reemergence of the Archetype of the Great Goddess in Art by Contemporary Women' in Hilary Robinson (ed.), *Visibly Female: Feminism and Art: An Anthology* (London: Camden)

Ostriker, Alicia (1981, reprinted 1986), 'The Thieves of Language: Women Poets and Revisionist Mythmaking' in Elaine Showalter (ed.), *The New Feminist Criticism: Essays on Women, Literature and Theory* (London: Virago), pp. 314–38

Parker, Peter (1987), *The Old Lie: The Great War and the Public School Ethos* (London: Constable)

Pateman, Carole (1989a), *The Sexual Contract* (Cambridge: Polity)

—— (1989b), *The Disorder of Woman* (Cambridge; Polity)

Renault, Mary (1958), *The King Must Die* (London: Sceptre)
—— (1962), *The Bull From the Sea* (Harmondsworth: Penguin).
Rich, Adrienne (1972, reprinted 1980), 'The Antifeminist Woman' in *On Lies, Secrets and Silence: Selected Prose, 1966–1978* (London: Virago)
—— (1978), *The Dream of A Common Language* (New York: Norton)
Russo, Mary (1986), 'Female Grotesques: Carnival and Theory' in Teresa de Lauretis (ed.), *Feminist Studies/Critical Studies* (London and New York: Macmillan), pp. 213–29
Samuels, A. (1985), *Jung and the Post-Jungians* (London: Macmillan)
Segal, Lynne (1987), *Is the Future Female? Troubled Thoughts on Contemporary Feminism* (London: Virago)
Sinfield, Alan (1988), *Literature, Politics and Culture in Postwar Britain* (Oxford: Blackwell)
Sjöö, Monica (1990), 'Interview' by Moira Vincenteli in Hilary Robinson (ed.), *Visibly Female: Women and Art: An Anthology* (London: Camden)
Stein, Diane (1989), *Stroking the Python: Women's Psychic Lives* (St Paul, Minn.: Llewellyn Publications)
Walker, Barbara G. (1985), *The Woman's Encyclopedia of Myths and Secrets* (New York: Harper and Row)
—— (1986), *The I Ching of the Goddess* (New York: Harper and Row)
Wills, Clair (1989), 'Upsetting the Public: Carnival, Hysteria and Women's Texts' in K. Hirschkop and D. Shepherd (eds), *Bakhtin and Cultural Theory* (Manchester: Manchester University Press)
Winkler, John J. (1990), *The Constraints of Desire: The Anthropology of Sex and Gender in Ancient Greece* (London and New York: Routledge)
Wittig, Monique and Zeig, Sande (1979), *Lesbian Peoples: Material for a Dictionary* (New York: Avon)

Notes on the
Contributors

Athalya Brenner took her BA at the University of Haifa, her MA at the Hebrew University in Jerusalem, and her Ph.D. at the University of Manchester. She is a Lecturer in Bible Studies at Oranim College of Education, Israel, and in General Studies (Gender Relations) at the Technion – Israel Institute of Technology. Among her books are: *Colour Terms of the Old Testament* (Journal for the Study of the Old Testament Press, 1982), *The Israelite Woman* (1985), *The Song of Songs* (in the Old Testament Guides Series, Sheffield Academic Press, 1989) and with Y.T. Radday (eds.), *On Humour and the Comic in the Hebrew Bible* (Almond Press, 1990).

Jane Caputi is an Associate Professor of American Studies at the University of New Mexico, Albuquerque. She is the author of *The Age of Sex Crime*, a feminist analysis of the atrocity of sexual murder, and collaborated with Mary Daly on *Websters' First New Intergalactic Wickedary of the English Language*.

Elizabeth Diab was born in Bombay and moved to England in her early teens. Trained initially as an actress, she has since moved into broadcasting and writing. She has worked for a time as an arts administrator, and has a degree from the Open University. Her fascination with Hawai'ian mythology began with an extended trip to the Islands a few years ago.

Iris Furlong has been a freelance journalist and television producer. After studying at the Institute of Archaeology at the University of London, she took a doctorate from the University of Birmingham, Department of Ancient History and Archaeology. Her doctoral thesis, *Divine Headdresses of the early Dynastic Period* (BAR International, Oxford), appeared in 1987.

Rosemary Ellen Guiley is an author who writes about the paranormal and alternate realities. A journalist by background, she holds a bachelor's degree in communications from the University of Washington in Seattle, Washington. Her most recent books include *The Encyclopedia of Witches and Witchcraft* (1989) and *Harper's Encyclopedia of Mystical and Paranormal Experience* (1991). She lives in the suburbs near New York City.

Penelope Harvey is Lecturer in Social Anthropology at the University of Manchester. She has a Ph.D. in Social Anthropology (London School of Economics,

1987) and has done fieldwork in the Southern Peruvian Andes (1983–5; 1987; 1988). Her research interests include: language, power and the politics of identity; knowledge and cultural representation; and gender and sexuality. She has recently published D. Cameron, E. Frazer, P. Harvey, B. Rampton and K. Richardson (eds), *Researching Language: Issues of Power and Method in Social Science* (Routledge, 1992); P. Gow & P. Harvey (eds), *Sexuality Violence and Cultural Difference* (Routledge, 1992); 'Gender, Power and Bilingualism' in P. Wilkins (ed.), *Women and Second Language Use* (Berg, 1992); and 'Gender, Community and Confrontation: The Structuring of Power Relations in Drunkenness' in M. McDonald (ed.), *Gender and Addiction* (Berg, 1991).

Emily Kearns is a lecturer at St Hilda's College, Oxford. Although her publications to date have been mainly in the field of ancient Mediterranean religion, she has travelled widely in India and is interested in the comparative aspects of Indo-European and other mythologies.

Catriona Kelly is British Academy Fellow in Russian, Christ Church, Oxford. Her publications in the field of Russian modernism and popular culture include *Petrushka, the Russian Carnival Puppet Theatre* (Cambridge University Press, 1990), and articles on representations of women in urban popular culture in L. Edmondson (ed.), *Russian Women and Society* (Cambridge University Press, 1991) and J. Costlow, S. Sandler and J. Vowles (eds.), *Sexuality and the Body in Russian Culture* (Stanford University Press, 1991)

Carolyne Larrington read Medieval English Language and Literature at St Catherine's College, Oxford. After teaching English in Japan, she returned to Oxford where she wrote a D.Phil thesis on wisdom poetry in Old Icelandic and Old English, forthcoming as *A Store of Common Sense* from Oxford University Press. She is currently Supernumerary Fellow in Medieval English at St John's College, Oxford.

Tao Tao Liu (a.k.a. Tao Tao Liu Sanders) was born in China, and educated in London and at Lady Margaret Hall, Oxford, where she read English, followed by a doctorate in Chinese Literature. She has translated Chinese poetry and written on Chinese poetry and fiction, especially of the twentieth century. She is University Lecturer in Modern Chinese at Oxford and Fellow of Wadham College.

Margaret Orbell is the Reader in Māori at the University of Canterbury, Christchurch, New Zealand. She specializes in the study of the mythology and traditional poetry of New Zealand Māori and other Polynesian peoples. Among her publications are several volumes of translations and *The Natural World of the Māori* (Thames and Hudson, 1985). Her Ph.D. thesis was on 'Themes and Images in Māori Love Poetry' – poetry composed exclusively by women.

Helen Payne is an ethnomusicologist whose study of the ritual life of Western Desert Australian Aboriginal women has been ongoing since 1971. She has lectured in both Australian Aboriginal Studies and ethnomusicology programmes at the various South Australian institutions of higher education. Her research findings have appeared in both international and national publications and broadcasts. In addition, but complementary to her research role, she holds office and is active in international and national organizations aimed at promoting the interests of women.

Diane Purkiss is Lecturer in English at the University of East Anglia. She has published articles on women prophets and on the seventeenth-century 'woman debate' and has also edited a collection of essays entitled *Women, Texts and Histories*, with Clare Brant, to be published by Routledge. She is now working on a book on gender and politics in Milton and seventeenth-century women's writing.

Susanna Rostas has a Ph.D. in Social Anthropology for which she worked in an indigenous community in Southern Mexico. She has since returned to Mexico to research religious conversion to protestant sects. Most recently she has begun a project in Mexico City on the Concheros, who perform a sacred circle dance. She currently teaches Anthropology at Goldsmith's College, London, lives in Cambridge and paints in her spare time.

Veronica Seton-Williams took her BA at the University of Melbourne, a Post-Graduate Diploma in Archaeology at University College, London, and her Ph.D. from the Institute of Archaeology, London. A field Egyptologist and archaeologist, she specializes in excavating city sites. She is an Honorary Research Fellow of University College, London. Among the works she has published are: *A Short History of Egypt, Blue Guide to Egypt, Egyptian Legends and Stories, Greek Legends and Stories* (in preparation).

Birgitte Sonne took a Ph.D. in the Sociology of Religion at the University of Copenhagen in 1973 and has held various University and Research Council Scholarships. She has taught at the Institute of the Sociology of Religion, Copenhagen University, Department of Greenlandic, Aarhus University, and Institute of Eskimology, Copenhagen University, and has been an editor for the interactive video project, *Siulleq*, about Greenland, with Danish Radio. She has written numerous papers and some books on traditional and acculturated Eskimo religion.

Barbara Smith gained a First in Classical Civilization at North London Polytechnic in 1986, after which she has spent four years researching a social anthropology thesis at Goldsmith's College, University of London, on the relationship between ancient Greek myth and ritual. She is better known, though, for her lesbian erotic fiction, most recently in *Serious Pleasure* and *More Serious Pleasure*, published by Sheba.

Julia Vytkovskaya trained as a psychiatrist and now produces gramophone records of readings from folk-tales for children. She lives in Moscow.

Marta Weigle received a doctorate in Folklore and Folklife from the University of Pennsylvania and is now University Regent's Professor in American Studies and Anthropology, and Chair of the Department of American Studies at the University of New Mexico. Her research interests include narrative, women and oral tradition, and Southwest (US) studies. Among her numerous publications are *Brothers of Light, Brothers of Blood: The Penitentes of the Southwest* (1976), *Spiders and Spinsters: Women and Mythology* (1982), with Peter White *The Lore of New Mexico* (1988), and *Creation and Procreation: Feminist Reflections on Mythologies of Cosmogony and Parturition* (1989).

Isobel White took her BA and MA at Girton College, Cambridge, and pursued graduate work in Canada and the USA. She was Senior Tutor and Lecturer in Anthropology at Monash University, Victoria, Australia from 1964–77. She has specialized in the study of Australian Aboriginal women, in particular their secret ceremonies. She has lived in Australia since 1953 and is now engaged in writing and editing.

Juliette Wood took her first degree in philosophy, and then studied folklore at the University of Pennsylvania where she wrote a doctoral thesis on the medieval narrative tradition. She has also taken graduate degrees in Celtic from University College of Wales, Aberystwyth and Oxford University. As University of Wales Fellow from 1986–8, she completed a comprehensive type and motif index of Welsh folk-tales to be published by Folkore Fellows Communications. She is currently Honorary Lecturer in the Department of Welsh at University of Wales College, Cardiff.

INDEX OF NAMES

INDEX OF THEMES